"NO USE A-MOANIN' AN' A-GROANIN'- NO USE A-SOBBIN' AN' A-THROBBIN'!! YO' HAS ACTED **VURRY PEEKOOLYAR** T' ME LATELY, DAISY MAE, SO AH IS PUNISHIN' YO' BY REFOOZIN' T' REZOOM FRIENDLY RELAYSHUNS"
MOO!!
4-8
861

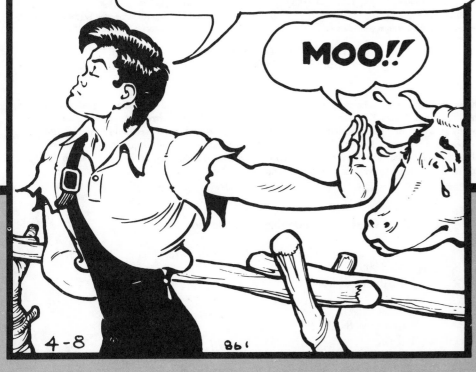

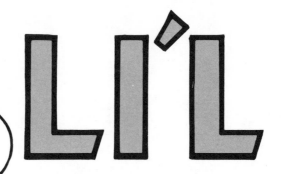

LI'L ABNER

Dailies

Volume Eight: 1942

Al Capp

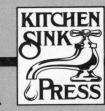

KITCHEN SINK PRESS

Princeton Wisconsin

ISBN 0-87816-068-X (hardcover)
ISBN 0-87816-069-8 (softcover)

This is the eighth volume of the complete *Al Capp's Li'l Abner*, reprinting the 1942 daily strip. The series is published by Kitchen Sink Press, **Denis Kitchen**, publisher. The series editor is **Dave Schreiner**. The cover was designed and colored by art director **Ray Fehrenbach**, who, with **Christi Scholl**, retouched and assembled the strips for publication. Final proofreading was done by **Doreen Riley**. We wish to thank members of the Capp estate for their cooperation in publishing this series, **Maurice Horn** for his introduction, and **Bill Blackbeard** of the San Francisco Academy of Comic Art for supplying us with the few missing strips we needed to complete this volume.

Library of Congress Cataloging-in-Publication Data

Capp, Al, 1909-
   Li'l Abner : dailies.

   Includes index.
   Contents: v. 8. 1942
   I. Title.
PN6728.L5C29   1988   741.5'973   88-12831
ISBN 0-87816-068-X (v. 8)
ISBN 0-87816-069-8 (pbk. : v. 8)

Li'l Abner in wartime: the mystery of the dog that didn't bark in the night

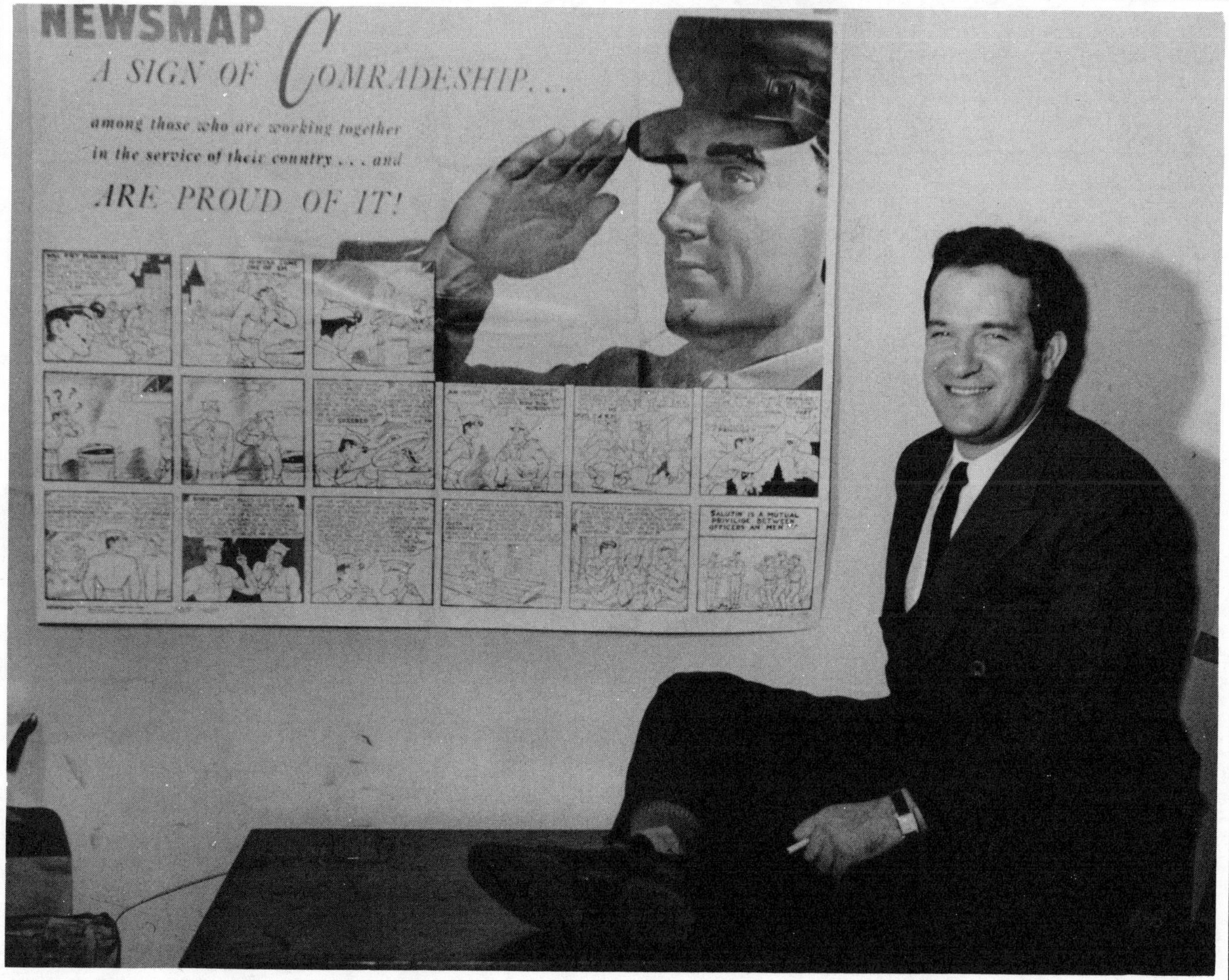
NEWSMAP
A SIGN OF COMRADESHIP...
among those who are working together
in the service of their country . . . and
ARE PROUD OF IT!

Al Capp poses with his lesson on saluting, 1943.

by Maurice Horn

Commentators agree that the 1940s constitute the period in which Al Capp's *Li'l Abner* hit its stride and assumed the classic form we remember today. In the previous decade, the strip had hewed close to the familiar lines of parodic adventure, albeit with telling forays into social criticism and satire, trends that became more and more pronounced as the 1930s wore on. This emergence in a few short years from a hillbilly strip into the status of a major literary feature was paralleled by *Li'l Abner's* growing popular success (one of the few instances in comic strip history when popular and literary tastes conjoined). This was evidenced by the number of comic book reprints of the strip beginning in 1939, as well the 1940 adaptation of *Li'l Abner* to the movie screen. Therefore, as this volume unfolds, Capp could be expected to perform at the top of his imaginative and narrative powers—and he does.

The daily strip that opens this volume carries a highly symbolic date—December 9, 1941, two days after the bombing of Pearl Harbor and one day after the U.S. declaration of war on Japan. Two days after that, on December 11, Germany would declare war on the United States, which would reciprocate within 24 hours. As it turns out, this run of *Li'l Abner* almost exactly covers America's first full year of wartime, from its entry into the lists to the North African landings and the Battle of Stalingrad; from the clash at Midway Island to the struggle for Guadalcanal.

Since newspaper strips are delivered to the syndicates weeks in advance of actual publication dates, one can't expect to find an echo of the momentous happenings that were splattered all over the front and inside pages of newspapers at that time, but it is an indication of Capp's interest in topical matters (and his life-long love of the movies) that the first Abner adventure in this volume is an affectionate take-off on *Citizen Kane*.

There is poetic justice in the fact, since *Citizen Kane's* relative failure at the box office, coming as it did after a meteoric start, is blamed by

---

Maurice Horn is editor of The World Encyclopedia of Comics.

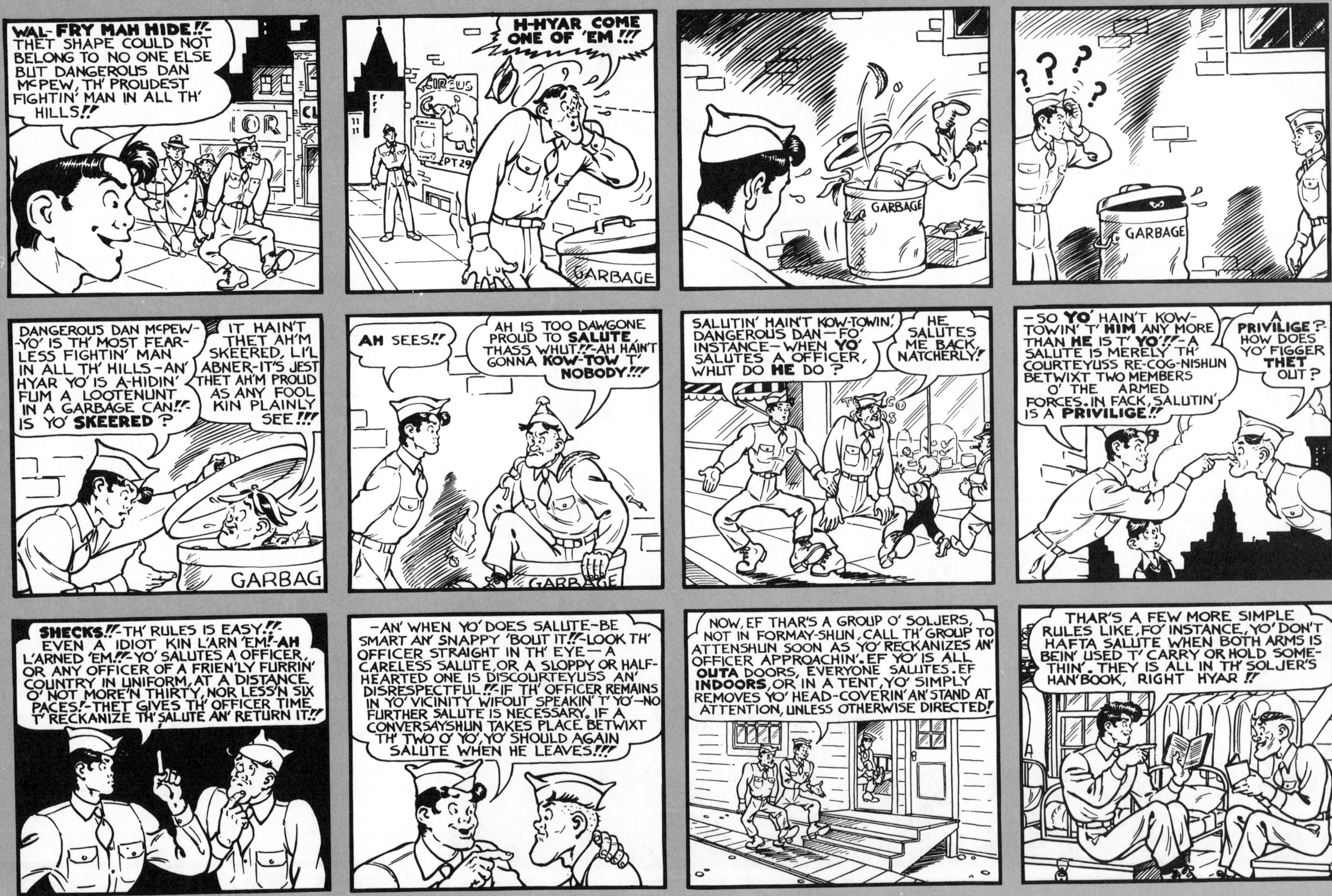
WAL-FRY MAH HIDE!!- THET SHAPE COULD NOT BELONG TO NO ONE ELSE BUT DANGEROUS DAN McPEW, TH' PROUDEST FIGHTIN' MAN IN ALL TH' HILLS!!
H-HYAR COME ONE OF 'EM!!!
GARBAGE
GARBAGE
? ? ? ?
GARBAGE
DANGEROUS DAN McPEW--YO' IS TH' MOST FEARLESS FIGHTIN' MAN IN ALL TH' HILLS-AN' HYAR YO' IS A-HIDIN' FUM A LOOTENUNT IN A GARBAGE CAN!!- IS YO' SKEERED?
IT HAIN'T THET AH'M SKEERED, LI'L ABNER-IT'S JEST THET AH'M PROUD AS ANY FOOL KIN PLAINLY SEE!!!
GARBAG
AH SEES!!
AH IS TOO DAWGONE PROUD TO SALUTE, THASS WHUT!!-AH HAIN'T GONNA KOW-TOW T' NOBODY!!!
SALUTIN' HAIN'T KOW-TOWIN', DANGEROUS DAN—FO' INSTANCE—WHEN YO' SALUTES A OFFICER, WHUT DO HE DO?
HE SALUTES ME BACK, NATCHERLY!
—SO YO' HAIN'T KOW-TOWIN' T' HIM ANY MORE THAN HE IS T' YO'!!—A SALUTE IS MERELY TH' COURTEYUSS RE-COG-NISHUN BETWIXT TWO MEMBERS O' THE ARMED FORCES. IN FACK, SALUTIN' IS A PRIVILIGE!!
A PRIVILIGE?- HOW DOES YO' FIGGER THET OUT?
SHECKS!!-TH' RULES IS EASY!!- EVEN A IDIOT KIN L'ARN 'EM!!-AH L'ARNED 'EM!!-YO' SALUTES A OFFICER, OR ANY OFFICER OF A FRIEN'LY FURRIN' COUNTRY IN UNIFORM, AT A DISTANCE O' NOT MORE'N THIRTY, NOR LESS'N SIX PACES!-THET GIVES TH' OFFICER TIME T' RECKANIZE TH' SALUTE AN' RETURN IT!!
—AN' WHEN YO' DOES SALUTE—BE SMART AN' SNAPPY 'BOUT IT!!—LOOK TH' OFFICER STRAIGHT IN TH' EYE—A CARELESS SALUTE, OR A SLOPPY OR HALF-HEARTED ONE IS DISCOURTEYUSS AN' DISRESPECTFUL!!-IF TH' OFFICER REMAINS IN YO' VICINITY WIFOUT SPEAKIN' T' YO'—NO FURTHER SALUTE IS NECESSARY. IF A CONVERSAYSHUN TAKES PLACE BETWIXT TH' TWO O' YO', YO' SHOULD AGAIN SALUTE WHEN HE LEAVES!!!
NOW, EF THAR'S A GROUP O' SOLJERS, NOT IN FORMAY-SHUN, CALL TH' GROUP TO ATTENSHUN SOON AS YO' RECKANIZES AN' OFFICER APPROACHIN'. EF YO' IS ALL OUTA DOORS, EVERYONE SALUTES. EF INDOORS, OR IN A TENT, YO' SIMPLY REMOVES YO' HEAD-COVERIN' AN' STAND AT ATTENTION, UNLESS OTHERWISE DIRECTED!
THAR'S A FEW MORE SIMPLE RULES LIKE, FO' INSTANCE, YO' DON'T HAFTA SALUTE WHEN BOTH ARMS IS BEIN' USED T' CARRY OR HOLD SOMETHIN'. THEY IS ALL IN TH' SOLJER'S HAN'BOOK, RIGHT HYAR!!

GARBA
SALUTIN' IS A PRIVILIGE INJOYED BY MEMBERS O' TH' ARMED FORCES IN GOOD STANDIN'!-PRISONERS AN' OTHER VARMINTS DON'T HAVE TH' RIGHT T' SALUTE!!!
CUSS ME EF YO' HAIN'T RIGHT! BUT THAR'S SO MANY RULES 'BOUT SALUTIN'- IT'S ALL SO CONFOOZIN'!
SALUTIN' IS A MUTUAL PRIVILIGE BETWEEN OFFICERS AN' MEN!!!

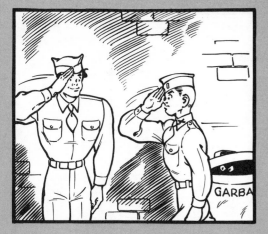

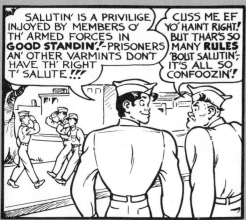

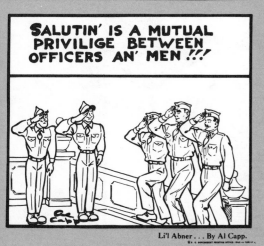

Li'l Abner . . . By Al Capp.

most film critics on the outbreak of hostilities, along with William Randolph Hearst's unholy wrath. Abner's search for "Cherry Blossom" is a clear reference to the search for Kane's "Rosebud" in the movie, and it comes as a further wink on Capp's part that Abner's secret, like Kane's, is buried deep within the folds of childhood memories. As though these clues weren't enough, the artist further tips his hand by having Orson Welles himself appear in a featured part, as Orville Wolf, the latest in a long list of would-be Daisy Mae seducers. Perhaps Capp was repaying a debt to *Citizen Kane's* studio, RKO, which had also produced the *Li'l Abner* movie the preceding year; more likely he was repaying a debt to Welles who, on a previous occasion, had said a few kind words about Capp's creation. However that may be, the sequence shows how closely attuned to its times *Li'l Abner* could be.

As 1942 inexorably unfolds (and after that, all the other agonizingly slow years of wartime) the reader might be forgiven for expecting to see the *Abner* strip reflect the vicissitudes, agonies and triumphs of the war—especially at a time when most newspaper strips, like Milton Caniff's *Terry and the Pirates*, were rushing headlong into the fray. There are a few echoes of the struggle to be found in the Sunday page, particularly in the *Abner* topper, *Advice fo' Chillun*. Even in the daily strips reprinted here there are a few hints now and then. "Support the USO" stamps can be found with increasing frequency plastered on walls and car doors, and allusions to contemporary events are occasionally mouthed by one character or another. Joe Btfsplk, the world's worst jinx, announces in his very first daily appearance: "Home agin! Wal—ah spent a very injoyable winter wif Hitler in Russia!" In the strip for Christmas Day, Mammy untypically extends the love of her boy to all other boys: "In other words, we gotta treat 'em like we want other folks t'treat *our* boys!! *All* of 'em is *somebody's* boys—all of 'em is fine boys!!"

Yet, compared to the sentiments expressed in other newspaper strips of the period, this is paltry stuff. It is as though Capp didn't want to look down all the dark implications of the war in his comic strip. It is therefore legitimate to ask the question: why?

Abner appeared in uniform only in posters done for the U.S. Army's morale divison. Here, Abner teaches Dangerous Dan McPew to salute. (See page 5 for the full poster.)

In her introduction to Volume 5 of this series, Julie Capp Cairol explains that her father "wanted Dogpatch to be a kind of refuge both from and for the world—a reminder of peace." And indeed, the July 4, 1942, strip makes this explicit. Al Capp was a complex individual, however, and there must have been more complex reasons for his deliberate avoidance in *Li'l Abner* of the central event of the 20th century: World War II. That he couldn't let Li'l Abner enlist in the Army, as so many other comic strip heroes were busily doing, seems natural enough. Abner in uniform would have been a greater comfort to the Axis than to the Allies. There also must have been the realization that, next to the Gestapo and the SS, Black Rufe and the murderous Scraggs were pikers, and that, compared to the Thousand Year Reich and German-occupied Europe, Dogpatch was a positive Eden. History, in all its hideousness, was striking at the very rationale of the *Abner* universe; yet Capp was artist enough to be able to transcend the strip's premises. He chose not to do so, however.

It is quite possible that the contrary-minded Capp didn't want to be seen following the mob of cartoonists who had jumped with both feet on the opportunity the war gave them for refreshing their tired plots or adopting a new outlook. Capp was no camp follower, and he might have been afraid that, had he joined the crowd, *Li'l Abner* would have become just another propagandizing, morale-boosting strip. In addition, the exigencies of war are restricting for the true creator: patriotism and natural empathy would no doubt have severely curtailed the strip's outrageous satire; and Capp must have been alert to the dangers that too great an identification with his characters would further undermine the strip's esthetic purposes.

There is also the matter of Ham Fisher and *Joe Palooka*. During his years of penuriousness, Capp had spent some time ghosting the strip for Fisher, and it is there that he claimed to have created the hillbilly characters of Big Leviticus and his cohorts. Fisher vehemently denied the claim. In the years intervening, Capp and Fisher had gone their separate and successful ways. Fisher had been one of the very first cartoonists to support the administration's war-preparedness program. In 1940, he had Palooka enlist in the Army and follow the stages of basic training, all of which were depicted in tones of unbridled enthusiasm, with the result that both Palooka and Fisher had been commended by President Roosevelt and Secretary for War Henry Stimson. Capp must

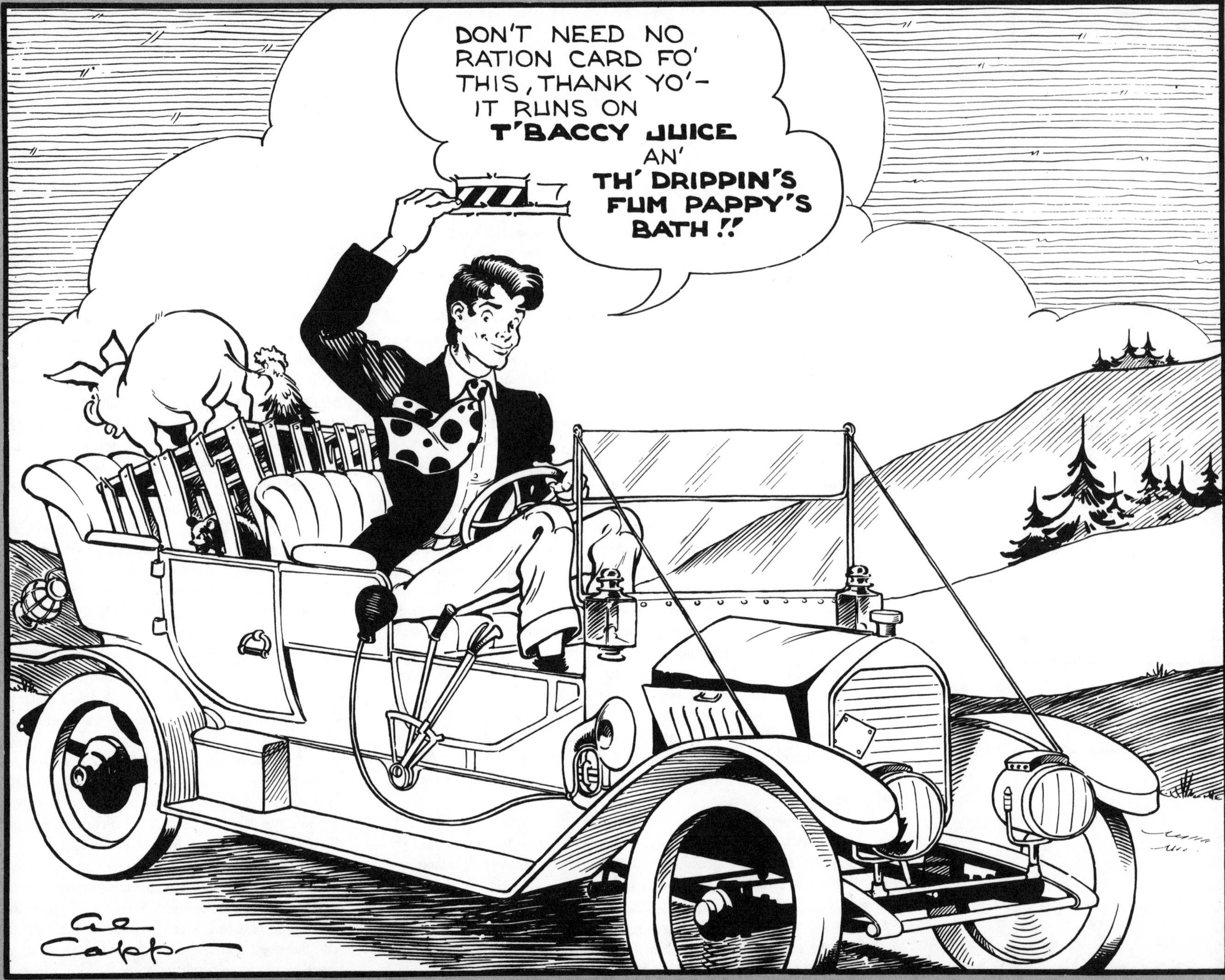
DON'T NEED NO RATION CARD FO' THIS, THANK YO'- IT RUNS ON T'BACCY JUICE AN' TH' DRIPPIN'S FUM PAPPY'S BATH!!
Al Capp

From the collection of Jon-Peter F. Smith

have been understandably reluctant to take on this superpatriotic friend of presidents and war secretaries on his own ground. As late as 1942, he found it within himself to praise his erstwhile employer in the piece he contributed to Martin Sheridan's *Comics and Their Creators*: "I worked with Fisher for several months and owe most of my success to him, for I learned many tricks of the trade while working alongside of him." For his part, Fisher never neglected an opportunity to take pot-shots at his former employee. In the same Sheridan book he averred that "many comics are based on hillbillies since I first used Big Leviticus in my strip." To top it off, in 1942 Fisher brought Leviticus back into *Joe Palooka* to have him take part in the North African campaign. Capp may have decided *not* to send his hillbillies into battle so as to avoid any unwelcome comparisons.

The brutalizing effects of the war couldn't be ignored, however, and their impact on Capp and his strip can be discerned in oblique but revealing ways. A mounting savagery courses through many of the wartime adventures, starting with the episode in this volume in which the Scraggs are hired by the physically and morally repulsive J. P. Fangsby, "America's number one sportsman hog-breeder," to kidnap the Yokums' pet pig Salomey as a mate for his prize porker, Boar Scarloff. In carrying out their assignment, the Scraggs display a callousness and wanton disregard for human life that is unprecedented, even for them. At one point, after they have nabbed the hapless Gus Goosegrease by mistake, they kick him over a precipice, and to Fangsby's horrified protestations Romeo Scragg replies: "So what? Yo' said he were absolutely worthless." After having finally captured Salomey and received their thousand dollar reward, the same Romeo modestly acknowledges Fangsby's congratulations in these words: "Shecks! 'Twarn't nuthin'!! We didn't hafta kill more'n nine or ten folks!" The episode concludes with Fangsby being barbecued by the Scraggs—although by mistake—and served as the main dish at the banquet he had prepared for his fellow hog breeders.

Even more disturbing, because the villains of the piece are not caricatural Dogpatch outlaws, is the last episode to appear in this volume: to revive the sagging career of senile movie star Lorna Goon, her manager conspires to set up Li'l Abner in such a way that the youth would seem to have committed suicide for the love of the aging Lorna, by substituting real bullets for the blanks Abner thinks are in the gun.

At left, Abner promotes gas rationing, which began in 1942.

In these and other *Abner* narratives, Capp can be seen veering sharply away from satirical farce to black comedy. In this respect he is not far removed from film director Ernst Lubitsch, who was then traveling much the same road in such movies as *To Be Or Not to Be*. (It must be noted that Lubitsch chose to confront evil head-on by setting his comedy smack in the middle of Nazi-occupied Warsaw.) If, as Alan Gowans has suggested in *The Unchanging Arts*, Al Capp's *Li'l Abner* "was a comment and allegory on the historic American dream and what was happening to it in the mid-20th century" (and this is the generally accepted view of the strip), then at least every other story from the period 1942-45 is a comment and allegory (however oblique) on the war's impact on American society.

It would be wrong to assume that the war was Capp's only preoccupation at the time. He was then at the height of his creative powers and took advantage of his increasing creativity not only to spin topical allegories, but also to further elaborate the Dogpatch mythos and enlarge his already sizeable cast of characters. Some of the new faces of 1942 are, in addition to Joe Btfsplk, the aptly-named Barney Barnsmell and his even more malodorous cousin Big Barnsmell ("th' *inside* man at th' skonk works"), not forgetting such colorful bit players as a telegram-singing hillbilly, a psychoanalyst named Dr. Jekyll, a prizefighter called Battlin' Cherry Blossom, "Beer Barrel" Polkis the Polish sport, and an organ grinder and pet billed as "Adolfo and his monkey Benito" (ah, the war again). Numerous enough to field a small team are the variably-gifted scions of the Jones clan: the jack-of-all trades Available ("Ah is *allus* available to mah friends—fo' a *price*, natcherly!"), and his cousins Disgustin' ("Yo' *is* disgustin', Disgustin'!"), Embraceable (whose charms no male—except Li'l Abner—is able to resist), Unbearable (whose presence even Abner can't bear), and Unmentionable (whose aspect is so horrifying Capp only dares to show his hairy arms and legs).

In addition to his fanciful flights of topicality, Capp also had recourse to more conventional forms of humor, firmly setting himself in the American traditon of Mark Twain, Finley Peter Dunne ("Mr. Dooley"), and even Will Rogers, at those not infrequent times when he turns sentimental. Some examples will suffice. After Abner bumps heads with the bull known as "Black Death" and is laid out as dead, the Mexican attendants return and discover he's disappeared. "We laid the dad Americano out here—an' covered hees face weeth an Americano newspaper!! Now—both are gone," muses one. "Ah well—the Americano was of no use since he was dad—but that newspaper had Americano fonnies een eet!!", bewails the other. To Nosey McBlabber who unexpectedly shows up at his own murder trial to deny he has been killed despite the issuance of an official death certificate, the presiding judge indignantly retorts: "It says hyar, plain as day—*Yo' is daid!!* It got a official gov'munt stamp on it!! Ah hopes yo' won't try to insinooate th' gov'munt is a *liar!!*", and then goes on: "Dogpatch is a modern, intellygunt *un*sooperstishus commoonity—an' we don't believe in ghosts—so—*ah gives yo' ten minutes t'git outa this commoonity, ghost!!*"

And finally, a very American bit of self-deprecating humor. After having given up his fruitless search for Cherry Blossom, Abner resigns himself to the fate Dr. Jekyll had forecast for him in case of failure, with these words: "R-reckon ah better g-go back t'Dogpatch an' lose mah mind—(gulp)—thar's no *better* place t'lose it!!"

While 1942 is a pivotal year, questions about the road not taken still nag the mind. With the hounds of war unleashed all over the globe, why are only a few feeble yelps heard in *Li'l Abner*? Granted that Capp for multiple reasons couldn't send his protagonists to the front lines, he could have let the war come to them, as Chester Gould did with *Dick Tracy*. One can easily imagine how spies, saboteurs, fifth columnists, German-American bund members, and other "Axis rats" would have become fodder for Capp's savage wit and relentless satire. Capp's poison pen would have worked wonders on such live targets, and these would have provided sources of black humor in ways the fictional Scraggs could never achieve. Barring that, Capp could have used the war as a background, the way such strips as *Dixie Dugan* or *Freckles and His Friends* did, and comment on the issues by indirection.

Yet Capp chose to do none of these things. In spite of speculation, the mystery, like Sherlock Holmes' dog that didn't bark in the night, may never be solved.

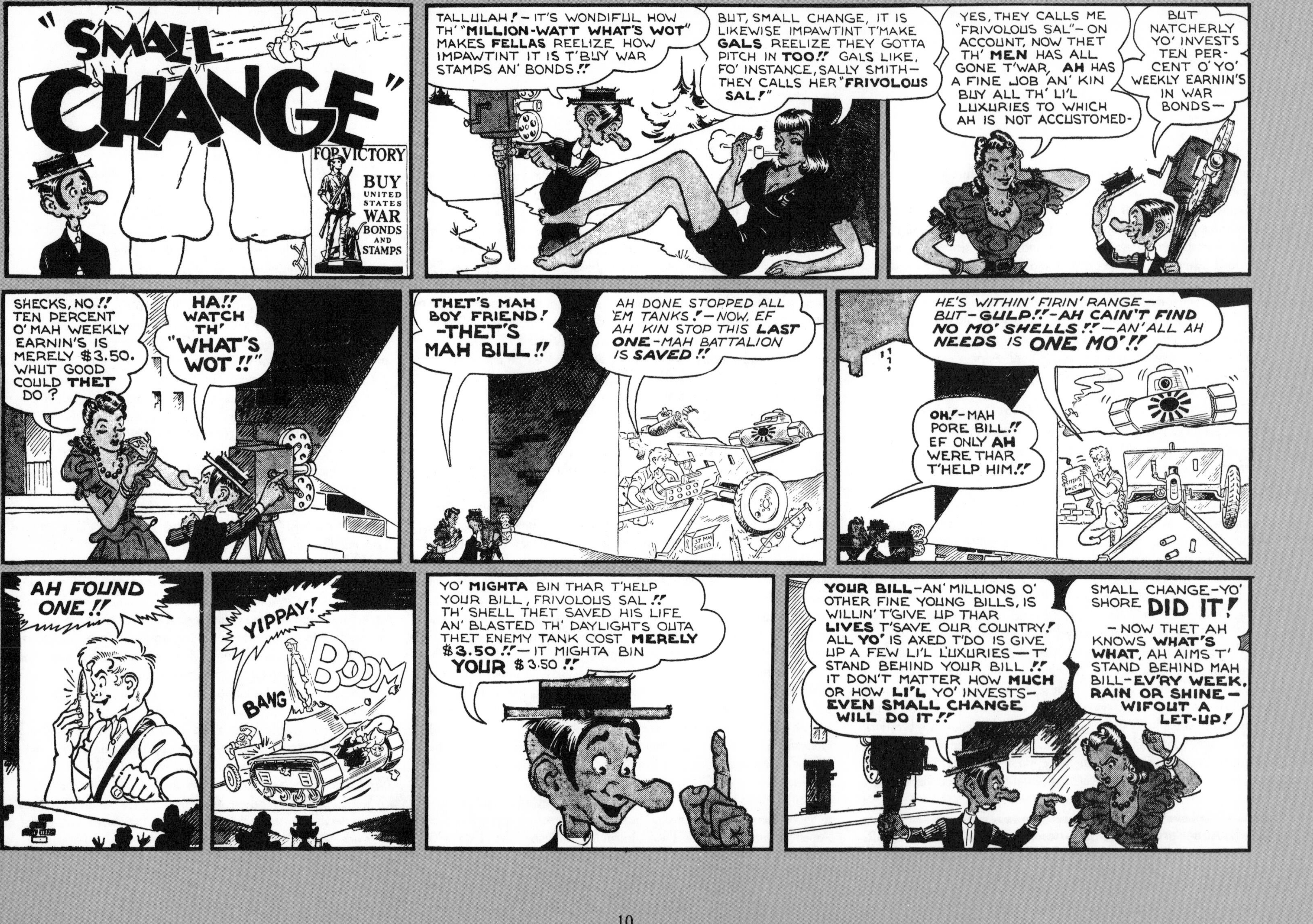
"SMALL CHANGE"
FOR VICTORY
BUY UNITED STATES WAR BONDS AND STAMPS
TALLULAH! – IT'S WONDIFUL HOW TH' "MILLION-WATT WHAT'S WOT" MAKES FELLAS REELIZE HOW IMPAWTINT IT IS T'BUY WAR STAMPS AN' BONDS!!
BUT, SMALL CHANGE, IT IS LIKEWISE IMPAWTINT T'MAKE GALS REELIZE THEY GOTTA PITCH IN TOO!! GALS LIKE, FO' INSTANCE, SALLY SMITH– THEY CALLS HER "FRIVOLOUS SAL!"
YES, THEY CALLS ME "FRIVOLOUS SAL"– ON ACCOUNT, NOW THET TH' MEN HAS ALL GONE T'WAR, AH HAS A FINE JOB AN' KIN BUY ALL TH' LI'L LUXURIES TO WHICH AH IS NOT ACCUSTOMED-
BUT NATCHERLY YO' INVESTS TEN PER-CENT O' YO' WEEKLY EARNIN'S IN WAR BONDS–
SHECKS, NO!! TEN PERCENT O' MAH WEEKLY EARNIN'S IS MERELY $3.50. WHUT GOOD COULD THET DO?
HA!! WATCH TH' "WHAT'S WOT!!"
THET'S MAH BOY FRIEND! -THET'S MAH BILL!!
AH DONE STOPPED ALL 'EM TANKS! – NOW, EF AH KIN STOP THIS LAST ONE-MAH BATTALION IS SAVED!!
37 MM SHELLS
HE'S WITHIN' FIRIN' RANGE– BUT–GULP!!–AH CAIN'T FIND NO MO' SHELLS!!–AN' ALL AH NEEDS IS ONE MO'!!
OH!–MAH PORE BILL!! EF ONLY AH WERE THAR T'HELP HIM!!
AH FOUND ONE!!
YIPPAY!
BOOM
BANG
YO' MIGHTA BIN THAR T'HELP YOUR BILL, FRIVOLOUS SAL!! TH' SHELL THET SAVED HIS LIFE AN' BLASTED TH' DAYLIGHTS OUTA THET ENEMY TANK COST MERELY $3.50!!– IT MIGHTA BIN YOUR $3.50!!
YOUR BILL–AN' MILLIONS O' OTHER FINE YOUNG BILLS, IS WILLIN' T'GIVE UP THAR LIVES T'SAVE OUR COUNTRY! ALL YO' IS AXED T'DO IS GIVE UP A FEW LI'L LUXURIES – T' STAND BEHIND YOUR BILL!! IT DON'T MATTER HOW MUCH OR HOW LI'L YO' INVESTS– EVEN SMALL CHANGE WILL DO IT!!
SMALL CHANGE–YO' SHORE DID IT!
– NOW THET AH KNOWS WHAT'S WHAT, AH AIMS T' STAND BEHIND MAH BILL–EV'RY WEEK, RAIN OR SHINE– WIFOUT A LET-UP!

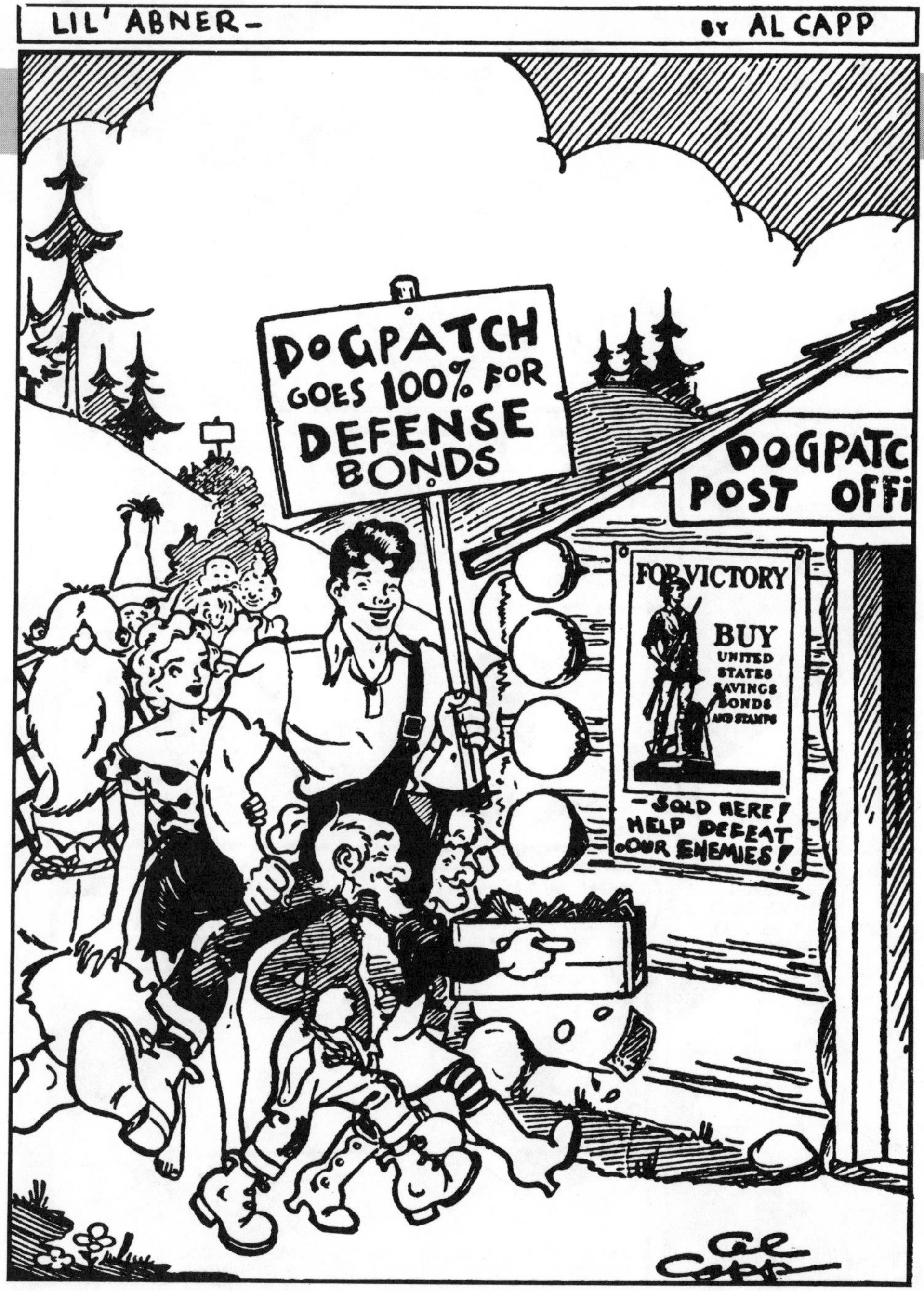
LIL' ABNER-
BY AL CAPP
DOGPATCH GOES 100% FOR DEFENSE BONDS
DOGPATC
POST OFFI
FOR VICTORY
BUY
UNITED STATES SAVINGS BONDS
-SOLD HERE! HELP DEFEAT OUR ENEMIES!
Al Capp

1942: War Work

by Dave Schreiner

In late 1941, the United States entered the European and Asian war, making it worldwide. As stated in Maurice Horn's introduction, Al Capp did not directly invite the war into *Li'l Abner*. He devoted several strips in successive years to explain why. The first appeared on July 4, 1942, and it set the tone for those that showed up in 1943 and 1944.

> *Dear Friends:*
>
> *This seems the right day to answer a question many of you have asked me—"When is Li'l Abner going into the Army?"*
>
> *Li'l Abner isn't going into the Army. And this is why—*
>
> *Perhaps Li'l Abner and his friends, living through these terrible days in a peaceful, happy, free world, will do their part—by thus reminding us that* this is *what we are fighting for*—to have that world again. *A world where a fella can do pretty much as he pleases as long as he doesn't bother his neighbors—a world where a fella can worship God in his own way—and where the next fella's got the same right—a world where a fella and his gal can look up at the moon just for the foolishness of it—and not because there may be planes up there coming to blast 'em both off the earth—a world where a fella is free to be as wise or foolish as he pleases—but, mainly,—an earth where a fella is free!!*
>
> *That world has disappeared—until we win this war. Perhaps this small section of our daily newspaper can do its part best by helping us to remember that a free world once did exist*—and will again!!
>
> *—Al Capp*

So the war stayed out of *Li'l Abner*, although gas rationing, blackouts and other manifestations of homefront inconveniences showed up when Capp needed them for plot. Perhaps he felt that bringing the war into the strip trivialized what was going on across the oceans. It's quite possible that he felt contempt for those strips that were facilely patriotic; that jumped on the bandwagon for little other purpose than to stop questions about why a character wasn't in uniform. Perhaps he wanted to guard his characters from embarrassing fits of unrealistic flagwaving. Perhaps he knew that as the war went on, mindless morale-boosting patriotism would come face to face with reality, and would crumble into cynicism. Contrary to propaganda, the GIs actually fighting the war weren't fighting for apple pie and baseball, they were struggling to stay alive, and perhaps Capp felt that any easy patriotism on his part would in the long run make the strip look foolish.

And maybe he just couldn't see a good way to make room for the war in his increasingly satirical humorous plotline, and he sincerely wanted to make the strip a little oasis away from the content of the rest of the newspaper. Capp was not a booster in the *Li'l Abner* of 1941-2, he was becoming a commentator. However, he was extremely active in contributing his considerable artistic talents to the war effort outside the strip itself.

On this page, a Post Office poster promoting Savings Bonds. At left, opposite page, Capp's SMALL CHANGE was syndicated free to newspapers by the Treasury Department.

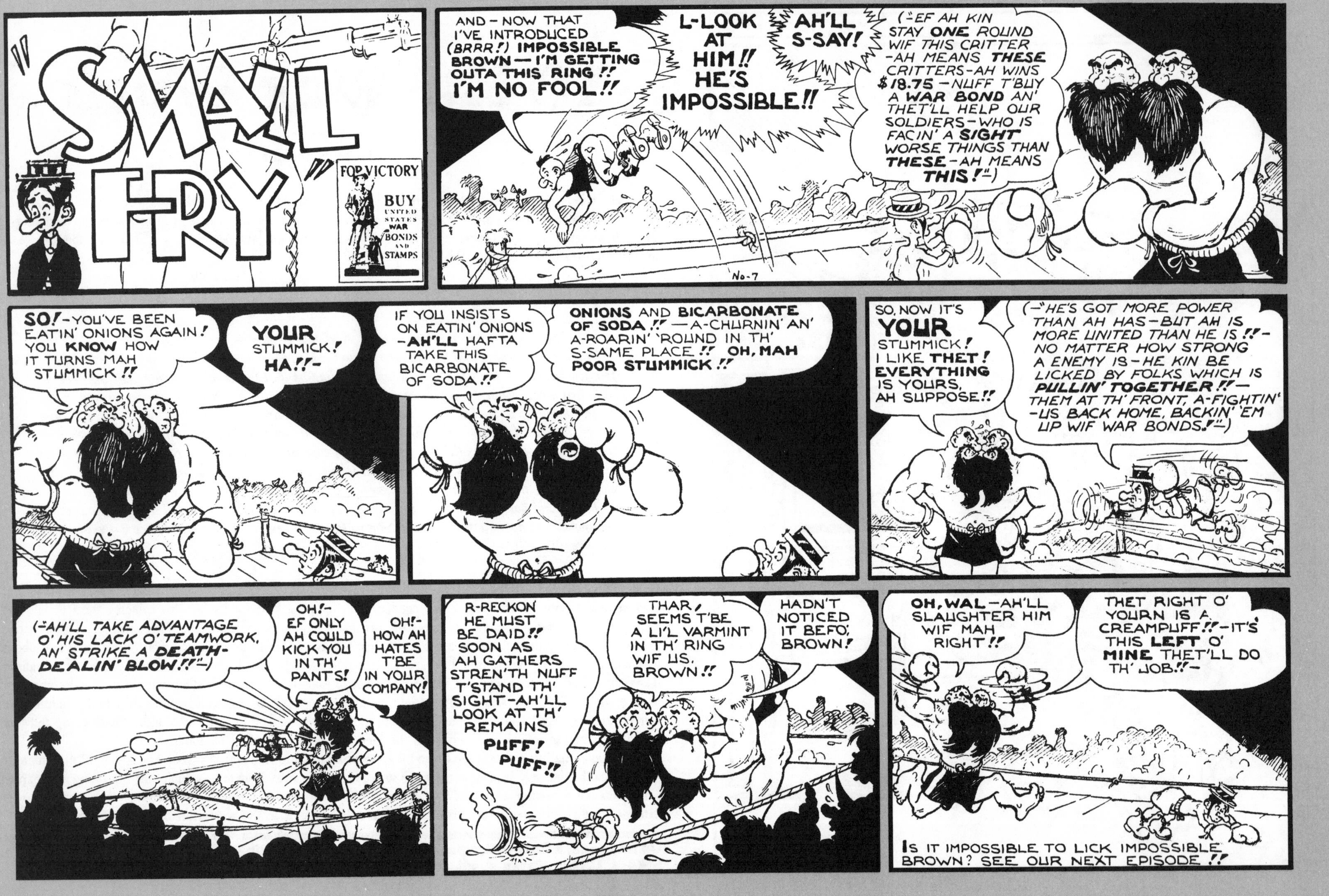
"SMALL FRY"
FOR VICTORY
BUY UNITED STATES WAR BONDS AND STAMPS
AND – NOW THAT I'VE INTRODUCED (BRRR!) IMPOSSIBLE BROWN — I'M GETTING OUTA THIS RING!! I'M NO FOOL!!
L-LOOK AT HIM!! HE'S IMPOSSIBLE!!
AH'LL S-SAY!
("EF AH KIN STAY ONE ROUND WIF THIS CRITTER -AH MEANS THESE CRITTERS-AH WINS $18.75 —NUFF T'BUY A WAR BOND AN' THET'LL HELP OUR SOLDIERS—WHO IS FACIN' A SIGHT WORSE THINGS THAN THESE-AH MEANS THIS!")
No-7
SO!-YOU'VE BEEN EATIN' ONIONS AGAIN! YOU KNOW HOW IT TURNS MAH STUMMICK!!
YOUR STUMMICK! HA!!-
IF YOU INSISTS ON EATIN' ONIONS -AH'LL HAFTA TAKE THIS BICARBONATE OF SODA!!
ONIONS AND BICARBONATE OF SODA!! —A-CHURNIN' AN' A-ROARIN' 'ROUND IN TH' S-SAME PLACE!! OH, MAH POOR STUMMICK!!
SO, NOW IT'S YOUR STUMMICK! I LIKE THET! EVERYTHING IS YOURS, AH SUPPOSE!!
("HE'S GOT MORE POWER THAN AH HAS-BUT AH IS MORE UNITED THAN HE IS!!- NO MATTER HOW STRONG A ENEMY IS-HE KIN BE LICKED BY FOLKS WHICH IS PULLIN' TOGETHER!!— THEM AT TH' FRONT, A-FIGHTIN' -US BACK HOME, BACKIN' 'EM UP WIF WAR BONDS!")
("AH'LL TAKE ADVANTAGE O' HIS LACK O' TEAMWORK, AN' STRIKE A DEATH-DEALIN' BLOW!!")
OH!- EF ONLY AH COULD KICK YOU IN TH' PANTS!
OH!- HOW AH HATES T'BE IN YOUR COMPANY!
R-RECKON HE MUST BE DAID!! SOON AS AH GATHERS STREN'TH NUFF T'STAND TH' SIGHT-AH'LL LOOK AT TH' REMAINS
PUFF! PUFF!!
THAR, SEEMS T'BE A LI'L VARMINT IN TH' RING WIF US, BROWN!!
HADN'T NOTICED IT BEFO', BROWN!
OH, WAL-AH'LL SLAUGHTER HIM WIF MAH RIGHT!!
THET RIGHT O' YOURN IS A CREAMPUFF!!-IT'S THIS LEFT O' MINE THET'LL DO TH' JOB!!-
IS IT IMPOSSIBLE TO LICK IMPOSSIBLE BROWN? SEE OUR NEXT EPISODE!!

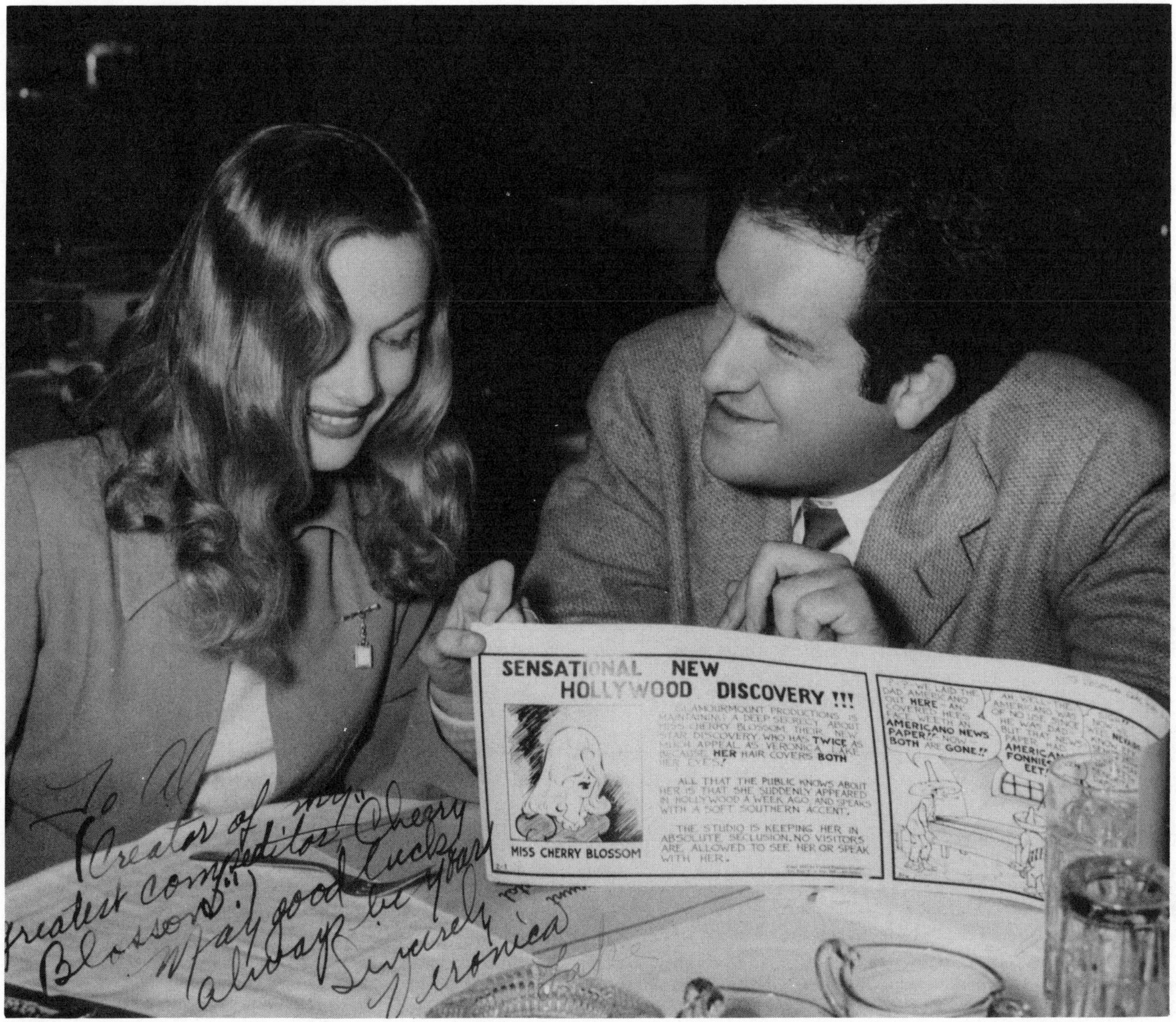
SENSATIONAL NEW HOLLYWOOD DISCOVERY !!!
ALL THAT THE PUBLIC KNOWS ABOUT HER IS THAT SHE SUDDENLY APPEARED IN HOLLYWOOD A WEEK AGO AND SPEAKS WITH A SOFT SOUTHERN ACCENT.
THE STUDIO IS KEEPING HER IN ABSOLUTE SECLUSION. NO VISITORS ARE ALLOWED TO SEE HER OR SPEAK WITH HER.
MISS CHERRY BLOSSOM

He saved his war work for special jobs, for the military, the Red Cross, and the War Bond Division of the Treasury Department. For the latter he created *Small Change*, initially called *Small Fry* until the more propitious title presented itself. It was the first strip ever syndicated by the U.S. government. A Sunday page, it concerned the efforts of the title character to promote enough pocket change to buy war bonds at $18.75 a pop. Rejected by the military as physically unfit, Small Change will do anything honest to make money for bonds, and he lectures various slackers he meets along the way to buy bonds, too. At least 75 of these pages exist. Capp was paid a dollar per year for the strip, which was the rate of wartime pay for certain high-powered consultants and executives who made their real money elsewhere. Capp later told E. J. Kahn, Jr., in a *New Yorker* profile, that he once tried to claim $8,000 expenses one year for producing the strip, and it was denied. The Internal Revenue Service allegedly told him that "a man with a dollar-a-year job ought to have better sense than to shell out eight thousand times that amount on incidental expenses."

For the military, he did a series of posters addressing such matters as saluting and venereal disease. The VD poster was rejected, as was one done by Milton Caniff. As Caniff told it later, "They turned down my poster because my bad girls were too good looking. They turned down Al's because he overplayed it a bit. They knew he had the audience and they were anxious to get him involved, but he couldn't quite find the handle they wanted. They wanted to be specific about condoms, but not *too* specific. They could get drawings done by somebody who wasn't well known, and that could illustrate the little book the chaplain or medic gave you. If they had a cartoonist like Al, the poster he did would almost defeat itself. The men would be looking at Li'l Abner and what he said about it, ha ha ha, instead of the message."

Capp told Kahn that he had problems with the VD strip well before it was rejected. The chaste, woman-fearing Abner was the star of these educational posters; they were all labeled "Private Li'l Abner."

"I couldn't very well point up the horrors of venereal diseases without having somebody catch one," Capp said. "But I was damned if I'd

Al Capp meets Veronica Lake, inspiration of "Cherry Blossom." The inscription reads: "To Al, creator of my greatest competitor, Cherry Blossom. May good luck always be yours. Sincerely, Veronica Lake." Lake's trademark "peekaboo" hairstyle was a prewar fashion hit. On page 12, SMALL CHANGE began life as SMALL FRY.

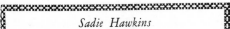

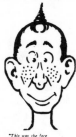

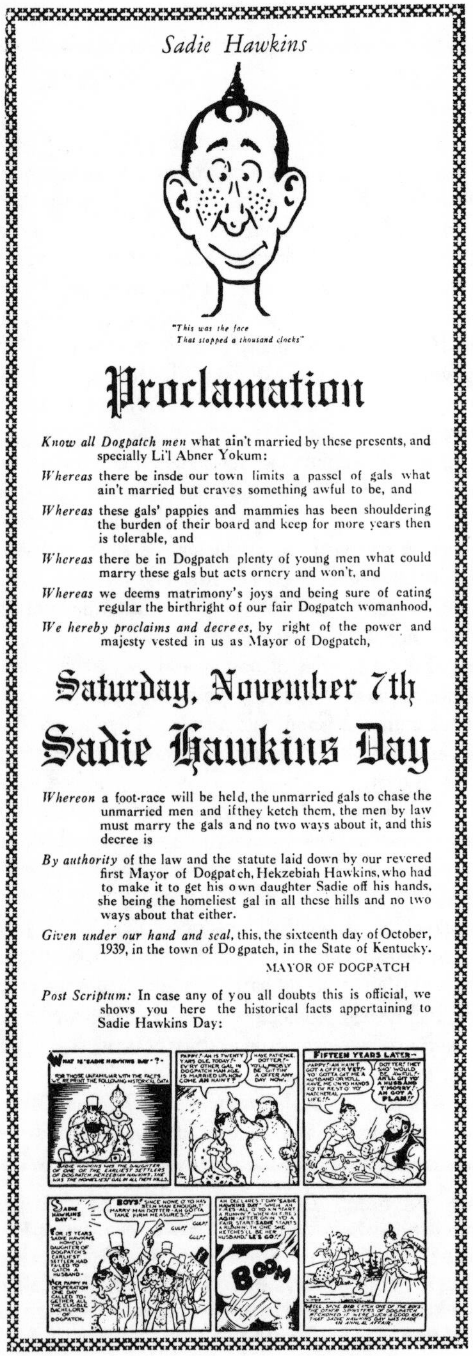

Sadie Hawkins

"This was the face That stopped a thousand clocks"

Proclamation

Know all Dogpatch men what ain't married by these presents, and specially Li'l Abner Yokum:

Whereas there be insde our town limits a passel of gals what ain't married but craves something awful to be, and

Whereas these gals' pappies and mammies has been shouldering the burden of their board and keep for more years then is tolerable, and

Whereas there be in Dogpatch plenty of young men what could marry these gals but acts ornery and won't, and

Whereas we deems matrimony's joys and being sure of eating regular the birthright of our fair Dogpatch womanhood,

We hereby proclaims and decrees, by right of the power and majesty vested in us as Mayor of Dogpatch,

Saturday, November 7th
Sadie Hawkins Day

Whereon a foot-race will be held, the unmarried gals to chase the unmarried men and ifthey ketch them, the men by law must marry the gals and no two ways about it, and this decree is

By authority of the law and the statute laid down by our revered first Mayor of Dogpatch, Hekzebiah Hawkins, who had to make it to get his own daughter Sadie off his hands, she being the homeliest gal in all these hills and no two ways about that either.

Given under our hand and seal, this, the sixteenth day of October, 1939, in the town of Dogpatch, in the State of Kentucky.

MAYOR OF DOGPATCH

Post Scriptum: In case any of you all doubts this is official, we shows you here the historical facts appertaining to Sadie Hawkins Day:

WHAT IS "SADIE HAWKINS DAY"?—
FOR THOSE UNFAMILIAR WITH THE FACTS WE REPRINT THE FOLLOWING HISTORICAL DATA
PAPPY!–AH IS TWENTY YARS OLE TODAY!– EV'RY OTHER GAL IN DOGPATCH MAH AGE IS MARRIED UP. HOW COME AH HAIN'T?
HAVE PATIENCE, DOTTER!– YO'LL PROB'LY BE GITTIN' A OFFER ANY DAY NOW.
FIFTEEN YEARS LATER—
PAPPY!–AH HAIN'T GOT A OFFER YET!– YO' GOTTA GIT ME A HUSBAND OR YO'LL HAVE ME ON YO HANDS FO' TH' REST O' YO' NATCHERAL LIFE!!
DOTTER! THET SHO' WOULD BE AWFUL!– AH'LL GIT YO' A HUSBAND T'MORRY!– AH GOT A PLAN!!
BOOM

destroy the technical perfection of my boy even for my country." One of Abner's friends was elected, as also happened in the How to Salute poster reprinted elsewhere in this volume. The VD poster passed through some channels of the military unscathed, but was finally rejected by the Chief of Chaplains.

Late in the war, Capp wrote and drew *Al Capp by Li'l Abner*, a booklet for servicemen-amputees distributed by the Red Cross. In it, Abner, in his inimitable way, recounts how Capp lost his left leg in an accident at age nine, and how he adjusted to the trauma. From touring military hospitals and personal experience, Capp knew the biggest problem amputees faced was acceptance. They were depressed, they resented pity, and they feared their sex lives were over. His comic book addressed these feelings. He acknowledged the problems he had learning to use a prosthetic device. He admitted feeling self-conscious around even old friends after the accident. A major portion of the book dealt with Capp's courtship of Catherine Cameron and their marriage. The book had a sunny outlook, emphasizing a stiff-upper-lip approach appropriate to the context, and it didn't fully reflect the difficulties Capp had had in learning to walk with a wooden leg.

Elliott Caplin, Capp's younger brother, recalls that when Al volunteered to tour hospitals, doctors initially banned him from the wards. If the amputees thought they would walk as badly as Capp, the doctors said, "they'd blow their brains out." Capp had to learn from an expert how to walk correctly. It was so painful that after the war, he went back to his old way. The Caplin family had been too poor to afford the different legs young Al needed to keep pace with his growth. Instead of progressing through eight legs from the age of nine until he reached his full growth, Elliott estimates he had two. Extending an existing device to compensate for growth didn't work. Somehow, Capp fashioned his own way of walking, which apparently was utilitarian but not pretty. During his war tours, though, he painfully walked in a morale-boosting way.

• • •

The 1942 run of *Li'l Abner* introduced two characters that stand out in a stellar year of humor and tall tales. One was a long-nosed little hustler named Available Jones. His motto: "I can be had—for a price!" If he wasn't so amiably dumb, and honest by his own standards, and didn't have such an endless family, Available could pass for Sammy Glick in *What Makes Sammy Run?* However, Capp didn't view Available in the same indignant light author Budd Schulberg viewed Sammy. It's obvious that Capp liked Available, as was right, since the character was so instantly...available...for any sort of plot twist. Every variety of human (and inhuman) animal funneled through Available's office in the years following 1942, and all of them somehow brought misery to Abner. Available started a lot of stories that Abner had to finish.

The other character was Joe Btfsplk, world's worst jinx. He became one of Capp's most famous creations, even if nobody could pronounce his name. For starting, and then twisting, and then rescuing plots, Joe and Available were hard to beat.

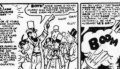

At left, newspapers let their readers know when Sadie Hawkins Day occurred in 1942.

• • •

While Capp was having a banner year with his strip, construction of a huge military complex began on 59,000 acres in an isolated and primitive area along the Clinch River in eastern Tennessee. The top secret complex was in the Appalachian foothills and it was being built to isolate and enrich a radioactive isotope to be used in a new and powerful weapon under intense planning near Los Alamos, New Mexico. The fenced reservation was called the Clinton Engineer Works. The rough town being built within the fence was named Oak Ridge. The workers and the residents, who were to live within the fence for the next two years, called the whole mess "Dogpatch."

Caniff, Milton, "The Two Minute Furlough," *The Complete Male Call*, Kitchen Sink Press, Princeton, Wis., 1985.

Caplin, Elliott, "We Called Him Alfred...," *Cartoonist ProFiles*, 1979

Fussell, Paul, *Wartime: Understanding and Behavior in the Second World War*, Oxford University Press, New York, 1989.

Grun, Bernard, *The Timetables of History: A Horizontal Linkage of People and Events*, Simon & Schuster, New York, 1975.

Kahn, E. J., Jr. "OOFF!!! (SOB!!) EEP!!! (GULP!!) ZOWIE!!!!—II, *The New Yorker*, 1947.

Manchester, William, *The Glory and the Dream, A Narrative History of America, 1932-1972*, Little, Brown and Co., Boston, 1973.

Rhodes, Richard, *The Making of the Atomic Bomb*, Simon & Schuster, New York, 1986.

The Two Lorna Goons

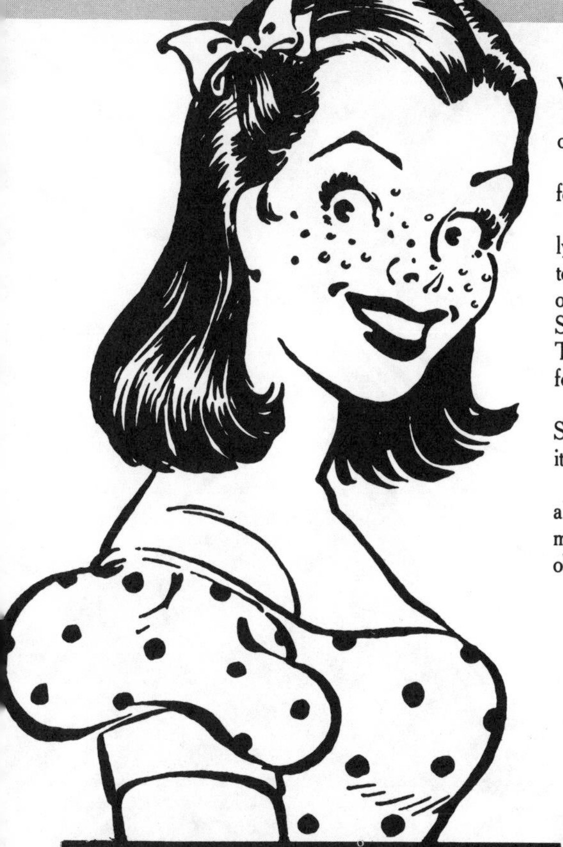

On November 25, 1942, the aging Hollywood actress Lorna Goon made her debut in *Li'l Abner*. Vain, arrogant, ghoulish in appearance, the name was a perfect fit.

Trouble is, in September of 1941, another Lorna Goon had appeared, this one the plain-Jane fiance of Barney Barnsmell, pictured at left.

Granted, the first Lorna was a bit player, and would not appear again, and the name was too good for Al Capp not to reuse.

But Lorna Goon appeared a second time because of an emergency. The second Lorna was originally named Scarlett O' Horror, as any fool who looks at the panel on the right can plainly see. In October of 1942, Capp had begun his aborted parody of Margaret Mitchell's *Gone With the Wind* on the Sunday page [see volume five's introductory material]. The first page in the projected four-Sunday strip sequence met with an immediate negative reaction from Mitchell and her lawyer husband. They started a suit charging copyright infringement, and Capp and United Features Syndicate were forced to apologize in a Sunday page of December, 1942.

Before the storm from Atlanta broke over his head, Capp had begun producing the daily strip featuring Scarlett O'Horror. He was forced to go back and hastily paste over the offending name and reletter it Lorna Goon before it was published.

Judging from the space left over in balloons, the pasteovers continued for a number of weeks. While all this mechanical work was a nuisance, Capp's narrative did not suffer, and he covered the change most admirably in the strip of December 16, when Abner sends his love poem to the actress. It is obvious the last two lines of the poem originally read:

Ah'd druther jump in the lake tomorror
Than not get no letter from Scarlett O'Horror.

He revised it to:

Ah'd druther jump in the lake tomorror noon
Than not get no letter from Lorna Goon.

The revision doesn't quite scan, but then Abner doesn't quite scan, either.

—D.S.

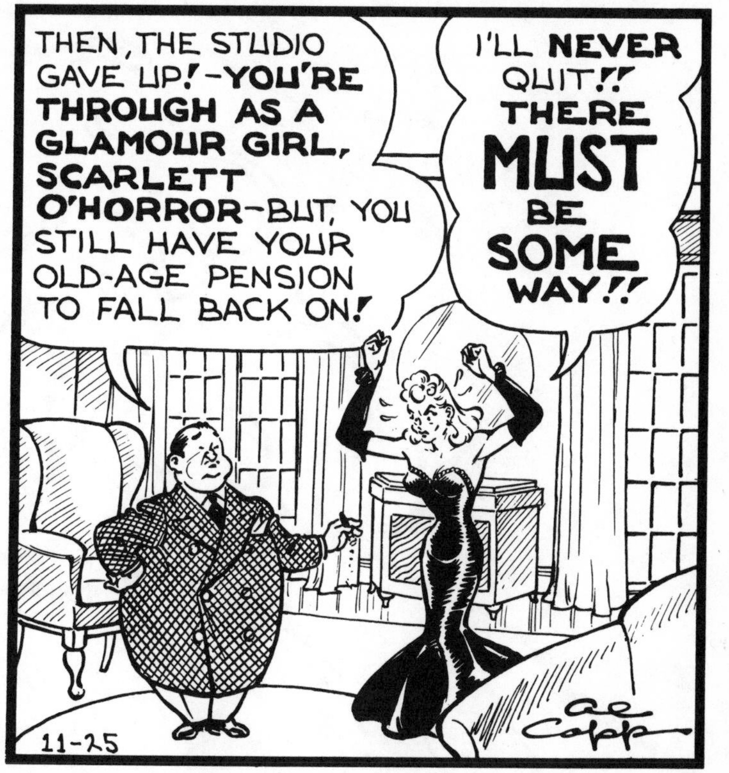

THEN, THE STUDIO GAVE UP! -YOU'RE THROUGH AS A GLAMOUR GIRL, SCARLETT O'HORROR-BUT, YOU STILL HAVE YOUR OLD-AGE PENSION TO FALL BACK ON!
I'LL NEVER QUIT!! THERE MUST BE SOME WAY!!
11-25
Al Capp

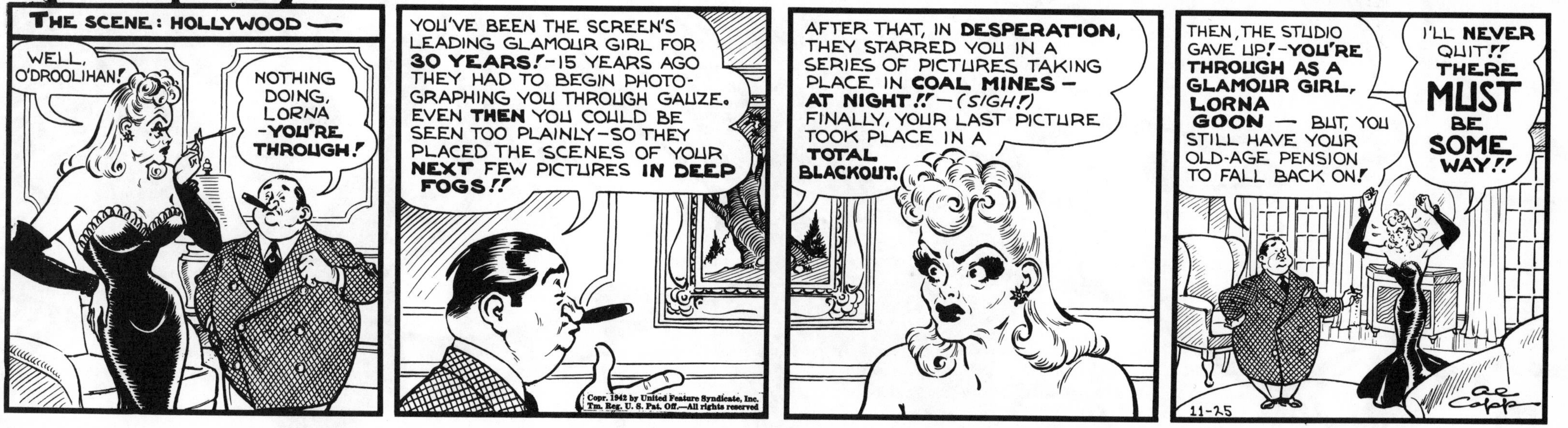

THE SCENE: HOLLYWOOD —
WELL, O'DROOLIHAN!
NOTHING DOING, LORNA -YOU'RE THROUGH!
YOU'VE BEEN THE SCREEN'S LEADING GLAMOUR GIRL FOR 30 YEARS!-15 YEARS AGO THEY HAD TO BEGIN PHOTOGRAPHING YOU THROUGH GAUZE. EVEN THEN YOU COULD BE SEEN TOO PLAINLY-SO THEY PLACED THE SCENES OF YOUR NEXT FEW PICTURES IN DEEP FOGS!!
Copr. 1942 by United Feature Syndicate, Inc. Tm. Reg. U. S. Pat. Off.—All rights reserved
AFTER THAT, IN DESPERATION, THEY STARRED YOU IN A SERIES OF PICTURES TAKING PLACE IN COAL MINES - AT NIGHT!!-(SIGH!) FINALLY, YOUR LAST PICTURE TOOK PLACE IN A TOTAL BLACKOUT.
THEN, THE STUDIO GAVE UP! -YOU'RE THROUGH AS A GLAMOUR GIRL, LORNA GOON — BUT, YOU STILL HAVE YOUR OLD-AGE PENSION TO FALL BACK ON!
I'LL NEVER QUIT!! THERE MUST BE SOME WAY!!
11-25
Al Capp

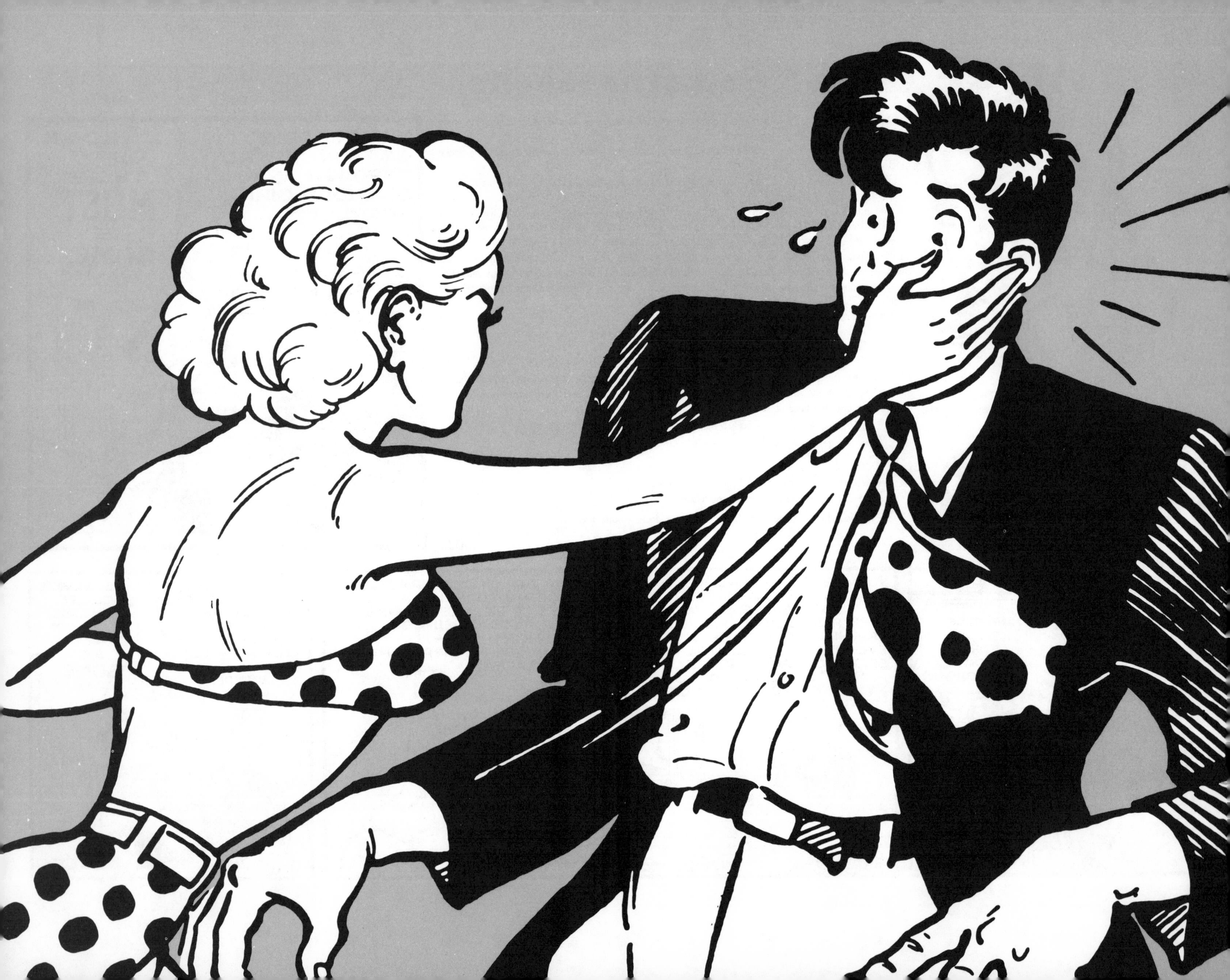

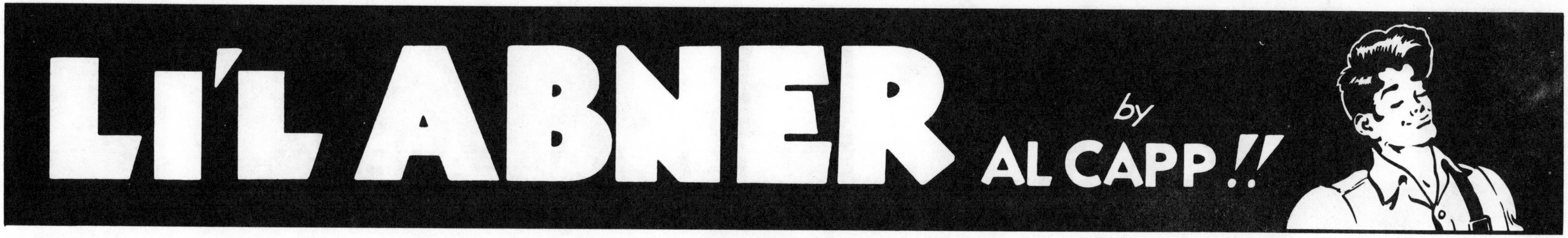
LI'L ABNER
by
AL CAPP !!

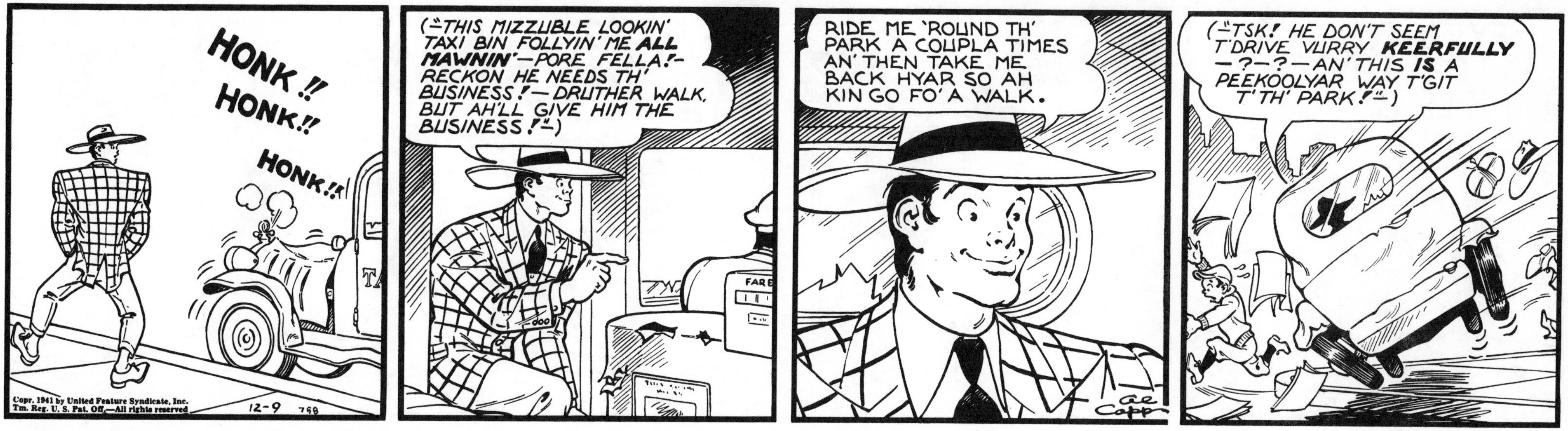
HONK !!
HONK !!
HONK !!
Copr. 1941 by United Feature Syndicate, Inc.
Tm. Reg. U. S. Pat. Off.—All rights reserved
12-9 798
(–THIS MIZZUBLE LOOKIN' TAXI BIN FOLLYIN' ME ALL MAWNIN'–PORE FELLA!– RECKON HE NEEDS TH' BUSINESS!–DRUTHER WALK, BUT AH'LL GIVE HIM THE BUSINESS!–)
FARE
RIDE ME 'ROUND TH' PARK A COUPLA TIMES AN' THEN TAKE ME BACK HYAR SO AH KIN GO FO' A WALK.
Al Capp
(–TSK! HE DON'T SEEM T'DRIVE VURRY KEERFULLY –?–?–AN' THIS IS A PEEKOOLYAR WAY T'GIT T'TH' PARK!–)

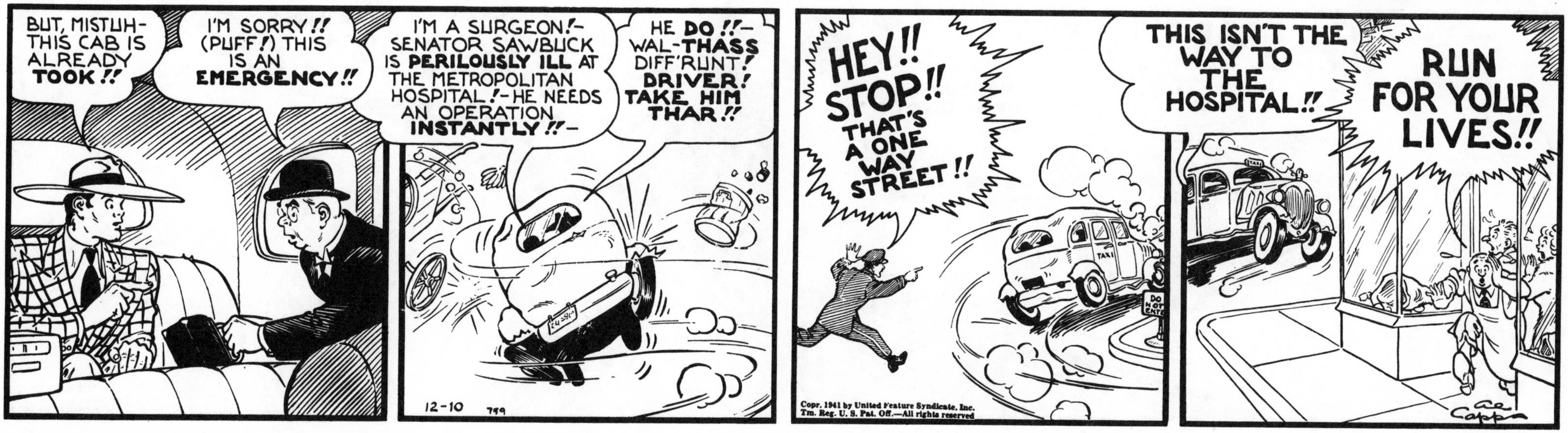
BUT, MISTUH– THIS CAB IS ALREADY TOOK !!
I'M SORRY !! (PUFF!) THIS IS AN EMERGENCY !!
I'M A SURGEON!– SENATOR SAWBUCK IS PERILOUSLY ILL AT THE METROPOLITAN HOSPITAL!–HE NEEDS AN OPERATION INSTANTLY !!–
HE DO !!– WAL–THASS DIFF'RUNT! DRIVER! TAKE HIM THAR !!
12-10 799
HEY !! STOP !! THAT'S A ONE WAY STREET !!
TAXI
Copr. 1941 by United Feature Syndicate, Inc.
Tm. Reg. U. S. Pat. Off.—All rights reserved
THIS ISN'T THE WAY TO THE HOSPITAL !!
RUN FOR YOUR LIVES !!
Al Capp

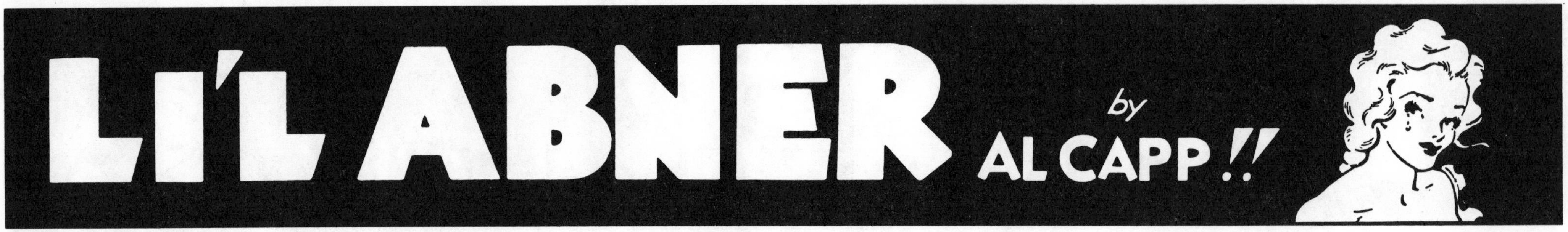
LI'L ABNER
by
AL CAPP!!

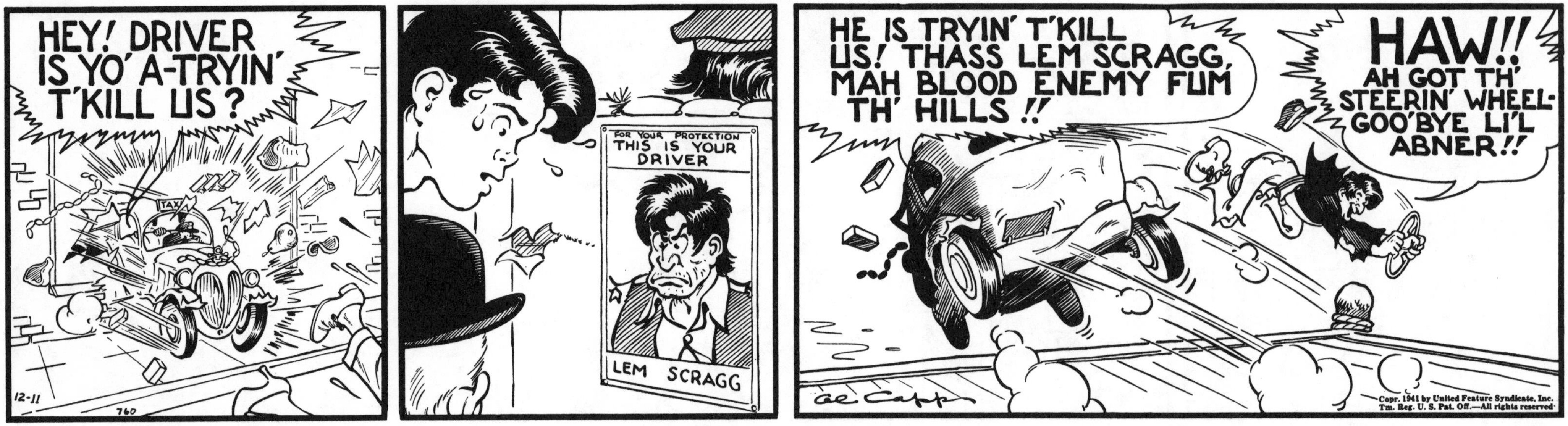
HEY! DRIVER IS YO' A-TRYIN' T'KILL US?
TAXI
12-11
760
FOR YOUR PROTECTION THIS IS YOUR DRIVER
LEM SCRAGG
HE IS TRYIN' T'KILL US! THASS LEM SCRAGG, MAH BLOOD ENEMY FUM TH' HILLS!!
HAW!! AH GOT TH' STEERIN' WHEEL- GOO'BYE LI'L ABNER!!
Al Capp
Copr. 1941 by United Feature Syndicate, Inc.
Tm. Reg. U. S. Pat. Off.—All rights reserved

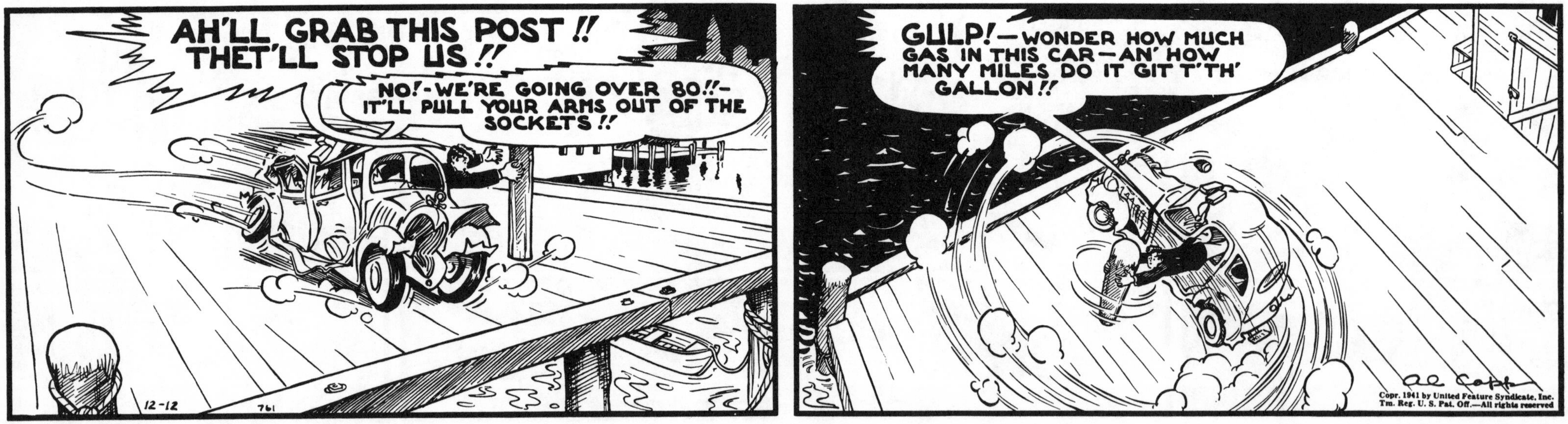
AH'LL GRAB THIS POST!! THET'LL STOP US!!
NO!-WE'RE GOING OVER 80!!- IT'LL PULL YOUR ARMS OUT OF THE SOCKETS!!
12-12
761
GULP!—WONDER HOW MUCH GAS IN THIS CAR—AN' HOW MANY MILES DO IT GIT T'TH' GALLON!!
Al Capp
Copr. 1941 by United Feature Syndicate, Inc.
Tm. Reg. U. S. Pat. Off.—All rights reserved

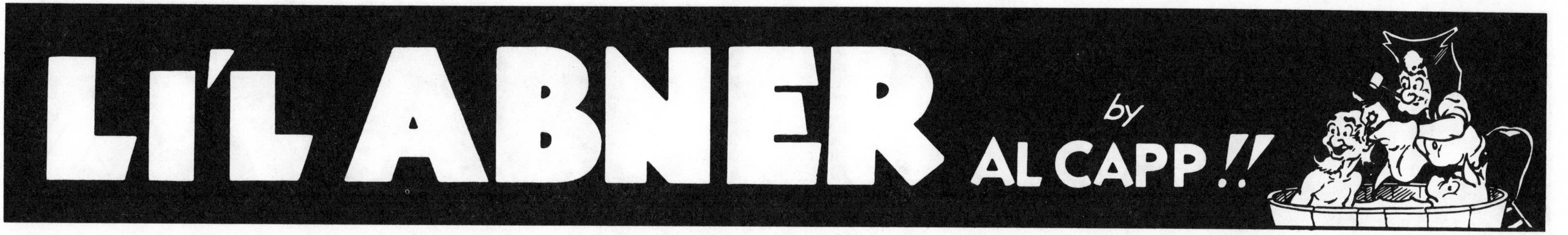
LI'L ABNER
by
AL CAPP!!

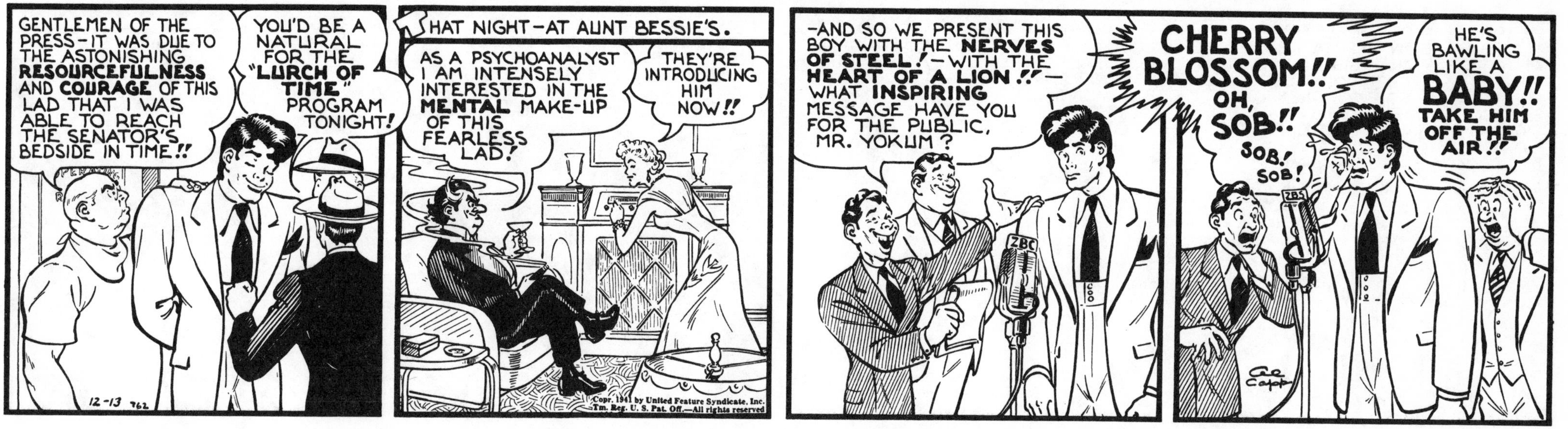
GENTLEMEN OF THE PRESS—IT WAS DUE TO THE ASTONISHING RESOURCEFULNESS AND COURAGE OF THIS LAD THAT I WAS ABLE TO REACH THE SENATOR'S BEDSIDE IN TIME!!
YOU'D BE A NATURAL FOR THE "LURCH OF TIME" PROGRAM TONIGHT!
12-13
THAT NIGHT—AT AUNT BESSIE'S.
AS A PSYCHOANALYST I AM INTENSELY INTERESTED IN THE MENTAL MAKE-UP OF THIS FEARLESS LAD!
THEY'RE INTRODUCING HIM NOW!!
Copr. 1941 by United Feature Syndicate, Inc. Tm. Reg. U. S. Pat. Off.—All rights reserved
—AND SO WE PRESENT THIS BOY WITH THE NERVES OF STEEL!—WITH THE HEART OF A LION!!—WHAT INSPIRING MESSAGE HAVE YOU FOR THE PUBLIC, MR. YOKUM?
ZBC
CHERRY BLOSSOM!! OH, SOB!!
SOB! SOB!
HE'S BAWLING LIKE A BABY!! TAKE HIM OFF THE AIR!!

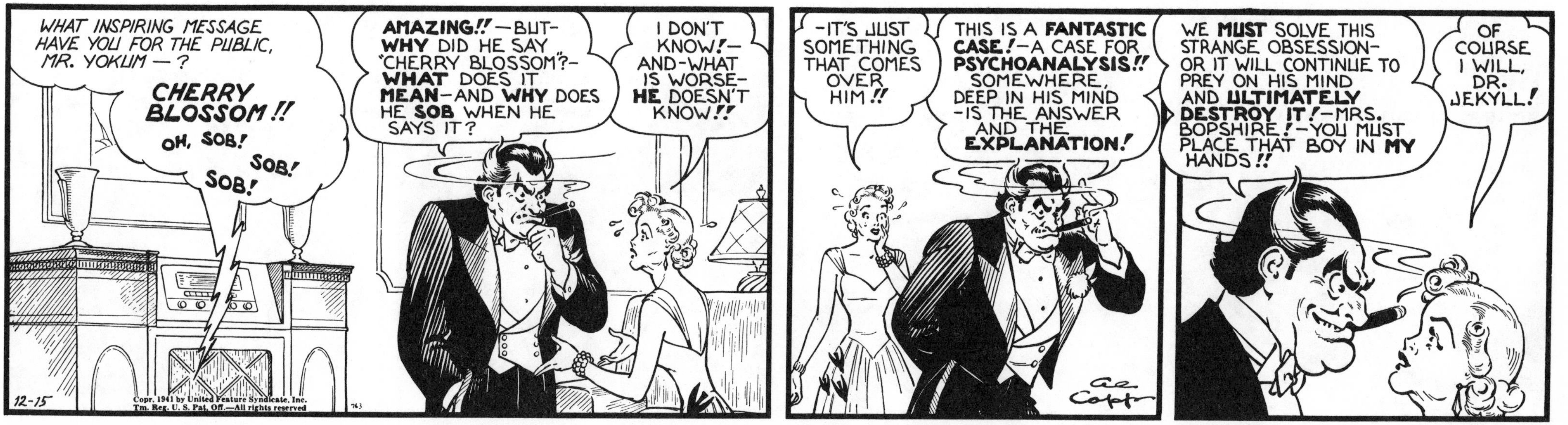
WHAT INSPIRING MESSAGE HAVE YOU FOR THE PUBLIC, MR. YOKUM—?
CHERRY BLOSSOM!! OH, SOB! SOB! SOB!
AMAZING!!—BUT—WHY DID HE SAY "CHERRY BLOSSOM"?—WHAT DOES IT MEAN—AND WHY DOES HE SOB WHEN HE SAYS IT?
I DON'T KNOW!—AND—WHAT IS WORSE—HE DOESN'T KNOW!!
12-15
Copr. 1941 by United Feature Syndicate, Inc. Tm. Reg. U. S. Pat. Off.—All rights reserved
—IT'S JUST SOMETHING THAT COMES OVER HIM!!
THIS IS A FANTASTIC CASE!—A CASE FOR PSYCHOANALYSIS!! SOMEWHERE, DEEP IN HIS MIND—IS THE ANSWER AND THE EXPLANATION!
WE MUST SOLVE THIS STRANGE OBSESSION—OR IT WILL CONTINUE TO PREY ON HIS MIND AND ULTIMATELY DESTROY IT!—MRS. BOPSHIRE!—YOU MUST PLACE THAT BOY IN MY HANDS!!
OF COURSE I WILL, DR. JEKYLL!

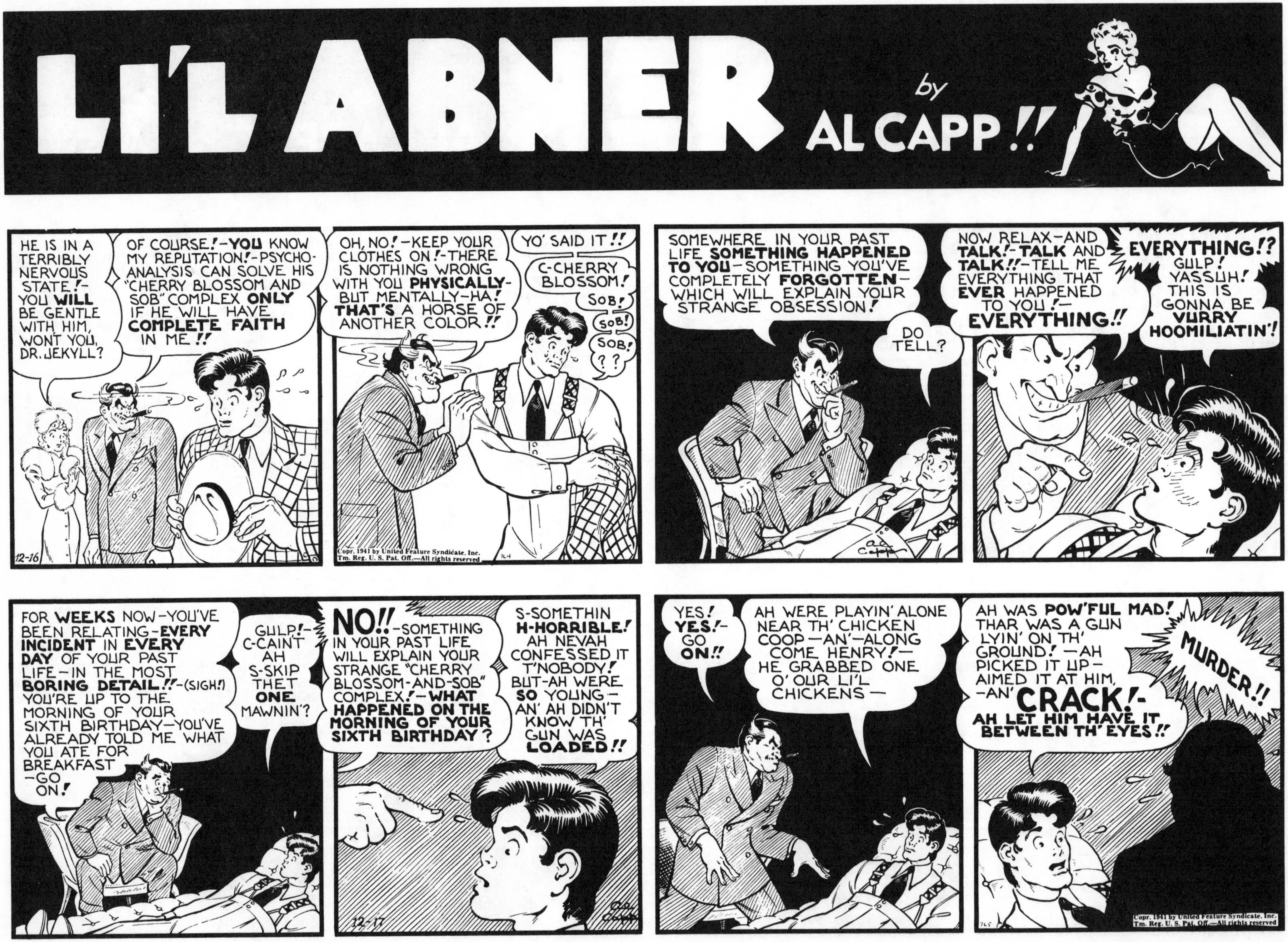
LI'L ABNER
by AL CAPP!!
12-16
HE IS IN A TERRIBLY NERVOUS STATE!- YOU WILL BE GENTLE WITH HIM, WONT YOU, DR. JEKYLL?
OF COURSE!-YOU KNOW MY REPUTATION!-PSYCHO-ANALYSIS CAN SOLVE HIS "CHERRY BLOSSOM AND SOB" COMPLEX ONLY IF HE WILL HAVE COMPLETE FAITH IN ME!!
OH, NO!-KEEP YOUR CLOTHES ON!-THERE IS NOTHING WRONG WITH YOU PHYSICALLY-BUT MENTALLY-HA! THAT'S A HORSE OF ANOTHER COLOR!!
YO' SAID IT!!
C-CHERRY BLOSSOM!
SOB!
SOB!
SOB!
??
Copr. 1941 by United Feature Syndicate, Inc. Tm. Reg. U. S. Pat. Off.—All rights reserved
SOMEWHERE IN YOUR PAST LIFE SOMETHING HAPPENED TO YOU-SOMETHING YOU'VE COMPLETELY FORGOTTEN-WHICH WILL EXPLAIN YOUR STRANGE OBSESSION!
DO TELL?
NOW RELAX-AND TALK!-TALK AND TALK!!-TELL ME EVERYTHING THAT EVER HAPPENED TO YOU!-EVERYTHING!!
EVERYTHING!? GULP! YASSUH! THIS IS GONNA BE VURRY HOOMILIATIN'!
FOR WEEKS NOW-YOU'VE BEEN RELATING-EVERY INCIDENT IN EVERY DAY OF YOUR PAST LIFE-IN THE MOST BORING DETAIL!!-(SIGH!) YOU'RE UP TO THE MORNING OF YOUR SIXTH BIRTHDAY-YOU'VE ALREADY TOLD ME WHAT YOU ATE FOR BREAKFAST-GO ON!
GULP!-C-CAINT AH S-SKIP THET ONE MAWNIN'?
NO!!-SOMETHING IN YOUR PAST LIFE WILL EXPLAIN YOUR STRANGE "CHERRY BLOSSOM-AND-SOB" COMPLEX!-WHAT HAPPENED ON THE MORNING OF YOUR SIXTH BIRTHDAY?
S-SOMETHIN H-HORRIBLE! AH NEVAH CONFESSED IT T'NOBODY! BUT-AH WERE SO YOUNG-AN' AH DIDN'T KNOW TH' GUN WAS LOADED!!
12-17
YES! YES!-GO ON!!
AH WERE PLAYIN' ALONE NEAR TH' CHICKEN COOP-AN'-ALONG COME HENRY!-HE GRABBED ONE O' OUR LI'L CHICKENS-
AH WAS POW'FUL MAD! THAR WAS A GUN LYIN' ON TH' GROUND!-AH PICKED IT UP-AIMED IT AT HIM, -AN' CRACK!-AH LET HIM HAVE IT BETWEEN TH' EYES!!
MURDER!!
Copr. 1941 by United Feature Syndicate, Inc. Tm. Reg. U. S. Pat. Off.—All rights reserved

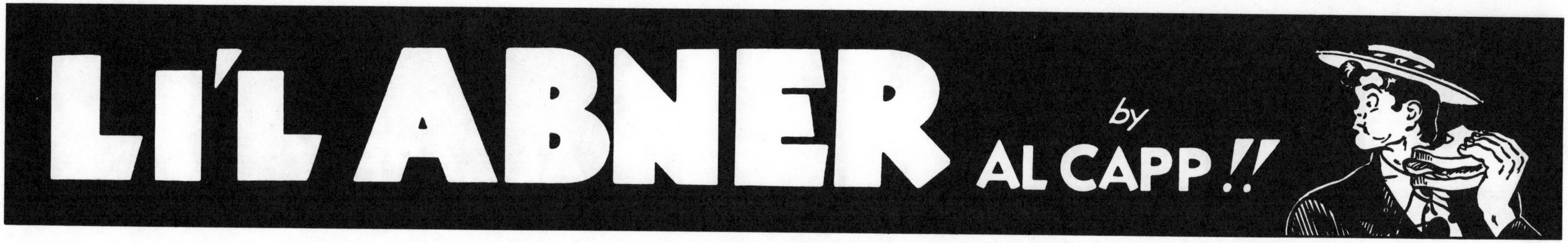

LI'L ABNER
by AL CAPP!!

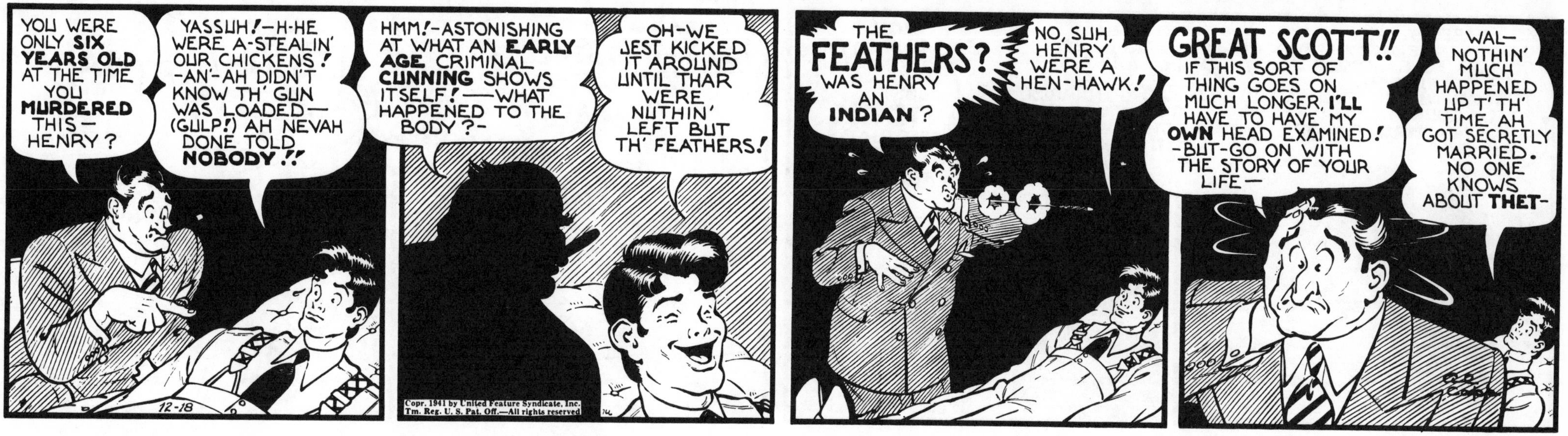

YOU WERE ONLY SIX YEARS OLD AT THE TIME YOU MURDERED THIS—HENRY?
YASSUH!—H-HE WERE A-STEALIN' OUR CHICKENS!-AN'-AH DIDN'T KNOW TH' GUN WAS LOADED—(GULP!) AH NEVAH DONE TOLD NOBODY!!
12-18
HMM!-ASTONISHING AT WHAT AN EARLY AGE CRIMINAL CUNNING SHOWS ITSELF!—WHAT HAPPENED TO THE BODY?-
OH-WE JEST KICKED IT AROUND UNTIL THAR WERE NUTHIN' LEFT BUT TH' FEATHERS!
Copr. 1941 by United Feature Syndicate, Inc. Tm. Reg. U. S. Pat. Off.—All rights reserved
THE FEATHERS? WAS HENRY AN INDIAN?
NO, SUH, HENRY WERE A HEN-HAWK!
GREAT SCOTT!! IF THIS SORT OF THING GOES ON MUCH LONGER, I'LL HAVE TO HAVE MY OWN HEAD EXAMINED! -BUT-GO ON WITH THE STORY OF YOUR LIFE—
WAL—NOTHIN' MUCH HAPPENED UP T' TH' TIME AH GOT SECRETLY MARRIED. NO ONE KNOWS ABOUT THET-

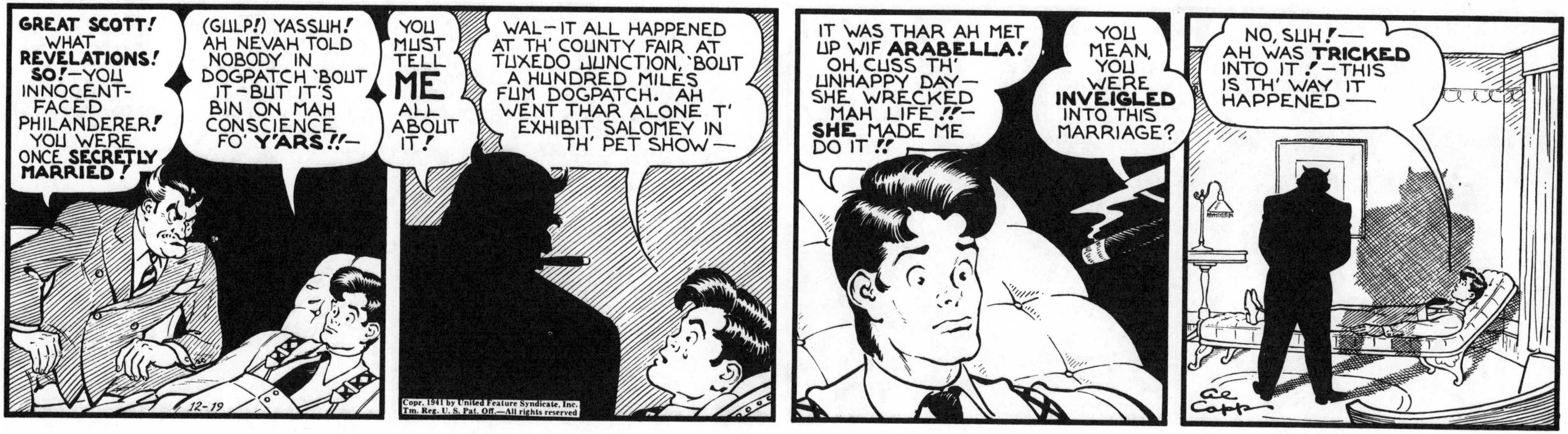

GREAT SCOTT! WHAT REVELATIONS! SO!—YOU INNOCENT-FACED PHILANDERER! YOU WERE ONCE SECRETLY MARRIED!
(GULP!) YASSUH! AH NEVAH TOLD NOBODY IN DOGPATCH 'BOUT IT—BUT IT'S BIN ON MAH CONSCIENCE FO' Y'ARS!!—
12-19
YOU MUST TELL ME ALL ABOUT IT!
WAL—IT ALL HAPPENED AT TH' COUNTY FAIR AT TUXEDO JUNCTION, 'BOUT A HUNDRED MILES FUM DOGPATCH. AH WENT THAR ALONE T' EXHIBIT SALOMEY IN TH' PET SHOW—
Copr. 1941 by United Feature Syndicate, Inc. Tm. Reg. U. S. Pat. Off.—All rights reserved
IT WAS THAR AH MET UP WIF ARABELLA! OH, CUSS TH' UNHAPPY DAY—SHE WRECKED MAH LIFE!!—SHE MADE ME DO IT!!
YOU MEAN, YOU WERE INVEIGLED INTO THIS MARRIAGE?
NO, SUH!—AH WAS TRICKED INTO IT!—THIS IS TH' WAY IT HAPPENED—

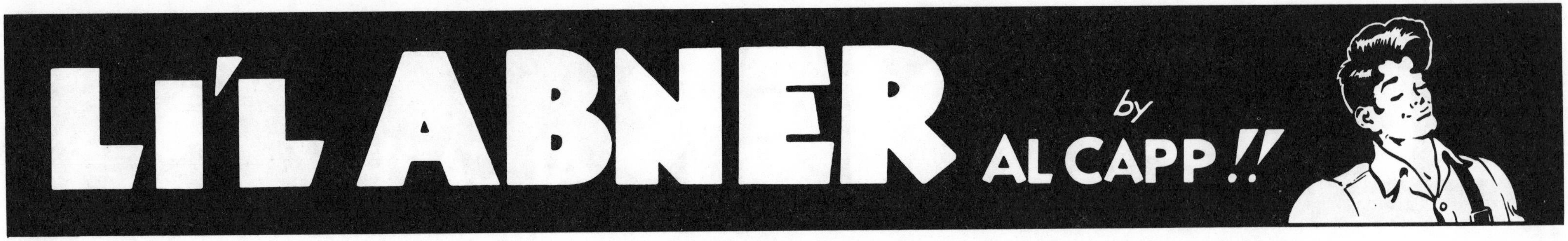
LI'L ABNER
by
AL CAPP!!

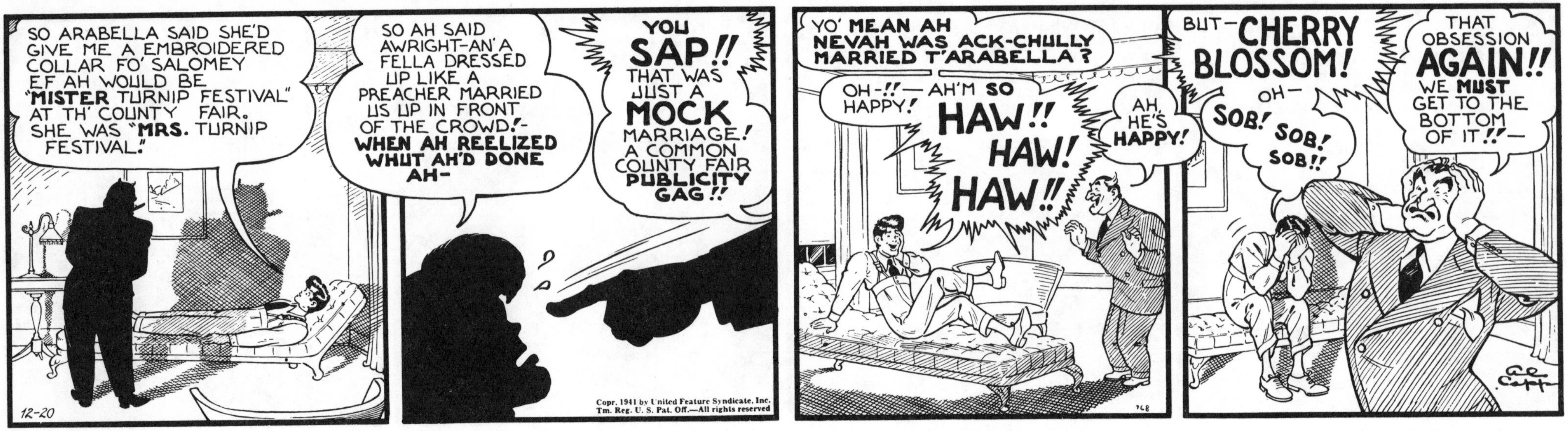
SO ARABELLA SAID SHE'D GIVE ME A EMBROIDERED COLLAR FO' SALOMEY EF AH WOULD BE "MISTER TURNIP FESTIVAL" AT TH' COUNTY FAIR. SHE WAS "MRS. TURNIP FESTIVAL."
12-20
SO AH SAID AWRIGHT-AN' A FELLA DRESSED UP LIKE A PREACHER MARRIED US UP IN FRONT OF THE CROWD!- WHEN AH REELIZED WHUT AH'D DONE AH-
YOU SAP!! THAT WAS JUST A MOCK MARRIAGE! A COMMON COUNTY FAIR PUBLICITY GAG!!
Copr. 1941 by United Feature Syndicate, Inc. Tm. Reg. U. S. Pat. Off.—All rights reserved
YO' MEAN AH NEVAH WAS ACK-CHULLY MARRIED T'ARABELLA?
OH-!!— AH'M SO HAPPY!
HAW!! HAW! HAW!!
AH, HE'S HAPPY!
BUT-CHERRY BLOSSOM!
OH-
SOB! SOB! SOB!!
THAT OBSESSION AGAIN!! WE MUST GET TO THE BOTTOM OF IT!!—

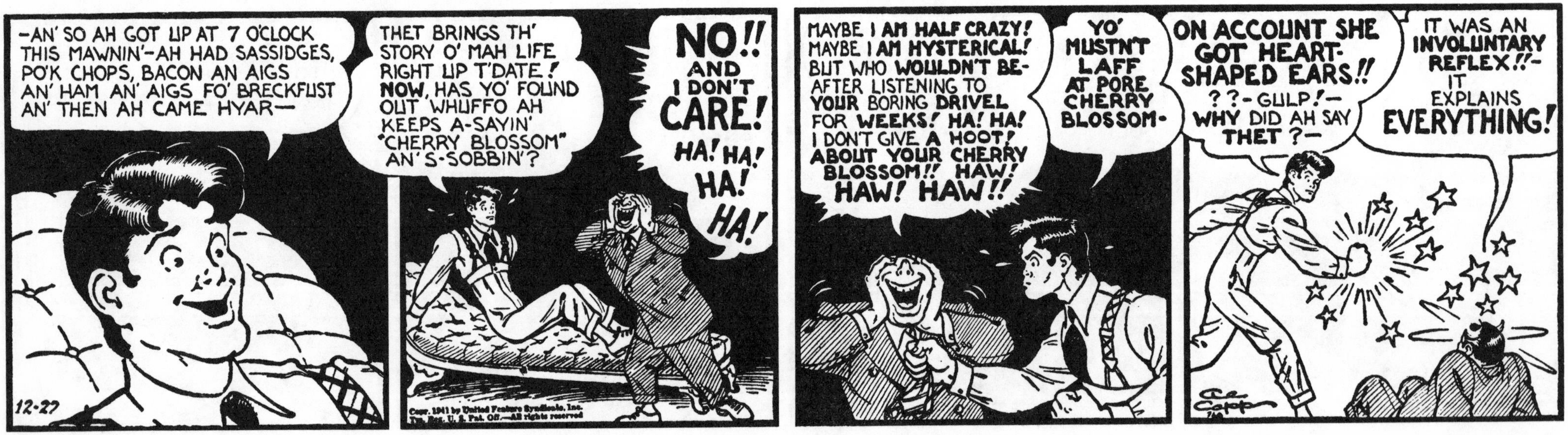
-AN' SO AH GOT UP AT 7 O'CLOCK THIS MAWNIN'-AH HAD SASSIDGES, PO'K CHOPS, BACON AN AIGS AN' HAM AN' AIGS FO' BRECKFUST AN' THEN AH CAME HYAR—
12-27
THET BRINGS TH' STORY O' MAH LIFE RIGHT UP T'DATE! NOW, HAS YO' FOUND OUT WHUFFO AH KEEPS A-SAYIN' "CHERRY BLOSSOM" AN' S-SOBBIN'?
NO!! AND I DON'T CARE!
HA! HA! HA! HA!
MAYBE I AM HALF CRAZY! MAYBE I AM HYSTERICAL! BUT WHO WOULDN'T BE-AFTER LISTENING TO YOUR BORING DRIVEL FOR WEEKS! HA! HA! I DON'T GIVE A HOOT! ABOUT YOUR CHERRY BLOSSOM!! HAW! HAW! HAW!!
YO' MUSTN'T LAFF AT PORE CHERRY BLOSSOM-
ON ACCOUNT SHE GOT HEART-SHAPED EARS!! ??-GULP!- WHY DID AH SAY THET?-
IT WAS AN INVOLUNTARY REFLEX!!- IT EXPLAINS EVERYTHING!

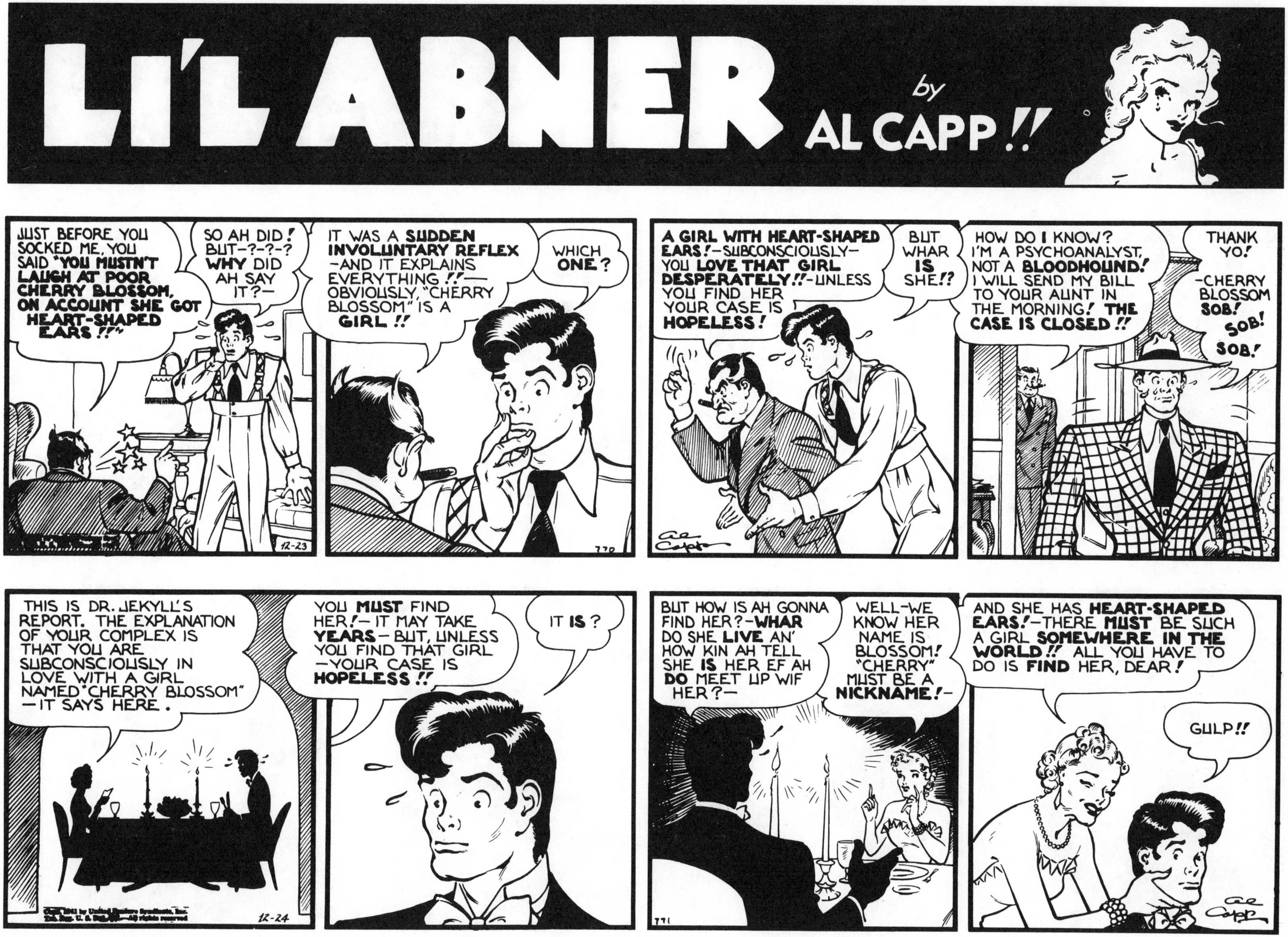
LI'L ABNER
by AL CAPP!!
JUST BEFORE YOU SOCKED ME, YOU SAID "YOU MUSTN'T LAUGH AT POOR CHERRY BLOSSOM, ON ACCOUNT SHE GOT HEART-SHAPED EARS!!"
SO AH DID! BUT-?-?-? WHY DID AH SAY IT?-
12-23
IT WAS A SUDDEN INVOLUNTARY REFLEX -AND IT EXPLAINS EVERYTHING!!— OBVIOUSLY, "CHERRY BLOSSOM" IS A GIRL!!
WHICH ONE?
A GIRL WITH HEART-SHAPED EARS!-SUBCONSCIOUSLY- YOU LOVE THAT GIRL DESPERATELY!!-UNLESS YOU FIND HER YOUR CASE IS HOPELESS!
BUT WHAR IS SHE!?
HOW DO I KNOW? I'M A PSYCHOANALYST, NOT A BLOODHOUND! I WILL SEND MY BILL TO YOUR AUNT IN THE MORNING! THE CASE IS CLOSED!!
THANK YO!
-CHERRY BLOSSOM SOB!
SOB!
SOB!
THIS IS DR. JEKYLL'S REPORT. THE EXPLANATION OF YOUR COMPLEX IS THAT YOU ARE SUBCONSCIOUSLY IN LOVE WITH A GIRL NAMED "CHERRY BLOSSOM" —IT SAYS HERE.
12-24
YOU MUST FIND HER!— IT MAY TAKE YEARS— BUT, UNLESS YOU FIND THAT GIRL —YOUR CASE IS HOPELESS!!
IT IS?
BUT HOW IS AH GONNA FIND HER?-WHAR DO SHE LIVE AN' HOW KIN AH TELL SHE IS HER EF AH DO MEET UP WIF HER?-
WELL-WE KNOW HER NAME IS BLOSSOM! "CHERRY" MUST BE A NICKNAME!-
AND SHE HAS HEART-SHAPED EARS!—THERE MUST BE SUCH A GIRL SOMEWHERE IN THE WORLD!! ALL YOU HAVE TO DO IS FIND HER, DEAR!
GULP!!

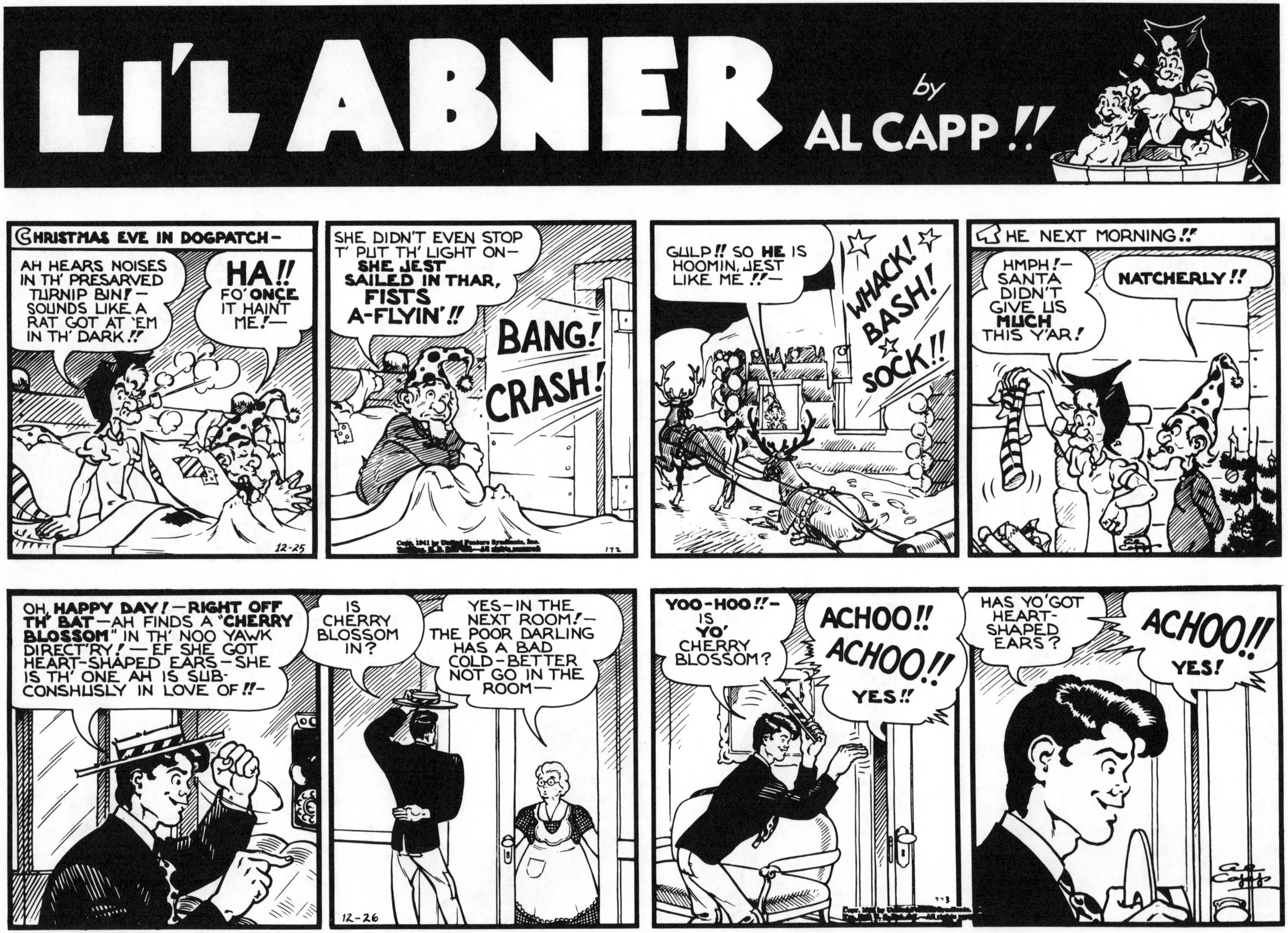
LI'L ABNER
by
AL CAPP!!
CHRISTMAS EVE IN DOGPATCH–
AH HEARS NOISES IN TH' PRESARVED TURNIP BIN!– SOUNDS LIKE A RAT GOT AT 'EM IN TH' DARK!!
HA!! FO' ONCE IT HAINT ME!–
12-25
SHE DIDN'T EVEN STOP T' PUT TH' LIGHT ON– SHE JEST SAILED IN THAR, FISTS A-FLYIN'!!
BANG!
CRASH!
GULP!! SO HE IS HOOMIN, JEST LIKE ME!!–
WHACK!
BASH!
SOCK!!
THE NEXT MORNING!!
HMPH!– SANTA DIDN'T GIVE US MUCH THIS Y'AR!
NATCHERLY!!
OH, HAPPY DAY!–RIGHT OFF TH' BAT–AH FINDS A "CHERRY BLOSSOM" IN TH' NOO YAWK DIRECT'RY!–EF SHE GOT HEART-SHAPED EARS–SHE IS TH' ONE AH IS SUB-CONSHUSLY IN LOVE OF!!–
IS CHERRY BLOSSOM IN?
YES–IN THE NEXT ROOM!–THE POOR DARLING HAS A BAD COLD–BETTER NOT GO IN THE ROOM–
12-26
YOO-HOO!!– IS YO' CHERRY BLOSSOM?
ACHOO!! ACHOO!! YES!!
HAS YO' GOT HEART-SHAPED EARS?
ACHOO!! YES!

LI'L ABNER

by AL CAPP!!

SO YO' IS CHERRY BLOSSOM WIF TH' HEART-SHAPED EARS!!

ACHOO! YES!!

MAH SEARCH HAS ENDED!! —OH, CHERRY BLOSSOM —AH LOVES YO'!— IN A SUB-CONSHUS WAY, OF COURSE!!

12-27

YEAH?

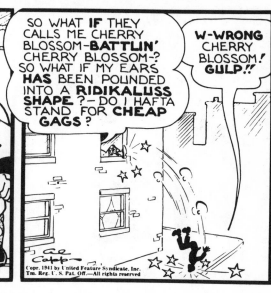

SO WHAT IF THEY CALLS ME CHERRY BLOSSOM—**BATTLIN'** CHERRY BLOSSOM—? SO WHAT IF MY EARS **HAS** BEEN POUNDED INTO A **RIDIKALUSS SHAPE**?—DO I HAFTA STAND FOR **CHEAP GAGS**?

W-WRONG CHERRY BLOSSOM! GULP!!

in person! ALL THIS WEEK!! "CHERRY BLOSSOM" in her AMAZING *hula dance*

AT LAST! AH HAS **FOUND** HER!

DIVOLI THEATRE

12-29

AT THE THEATRE-AFTER THE MATINEE— GLAD I CAUGHT YOU BEFORE YOU LEFT, CHERRY! MAGNIFICENT PICTURES IS SENDING A **TALENT SCOUT** HERE TO LOOK YOU OVER, THIS WIRE SAYS!—

A PICTURE **TALENT SCOUT**! I HAVE A DATE —BUT THAT CAN WAIT!!

AH WANTS T'SEE MISS CHERRY BLOSSOM!—D-DO THET SIGN **REALLY** MEAN ME?

STAGE DOOR KEEP OUT THIS MEANS YOU!

(-"UNUSUAL SENSE O' HUMOR FOR A HOLLYWOOD **BIGSHOT**!"-) IT MEANS EVERY-BODY **BUT** YOU! **STEP IN**, PAL!

(-"GULP!-SHE'S WEARIN' HER HAIR OVER HER EARS!"-) —IT'S-UH-HARD T'TELL 'EF YO' IS TH' TYPE-DRESSED TH' WAY YO' IS!

I'LL GET INTO A BATHING SUIT!—

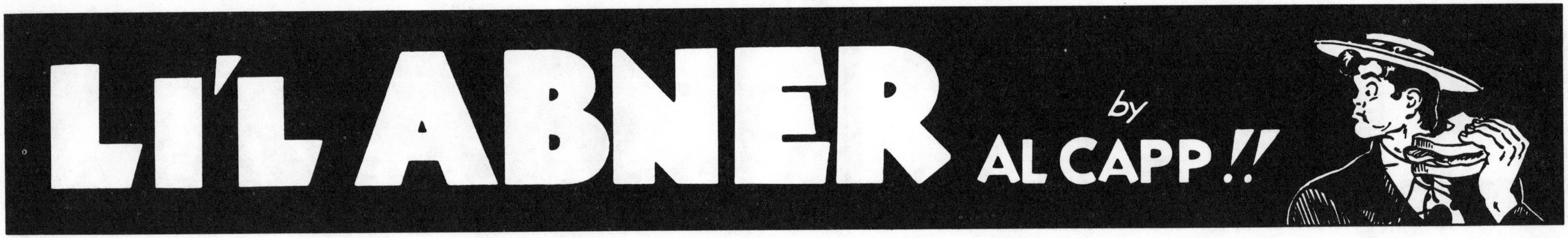
LI'L ABNER
by
AL CAPP!!

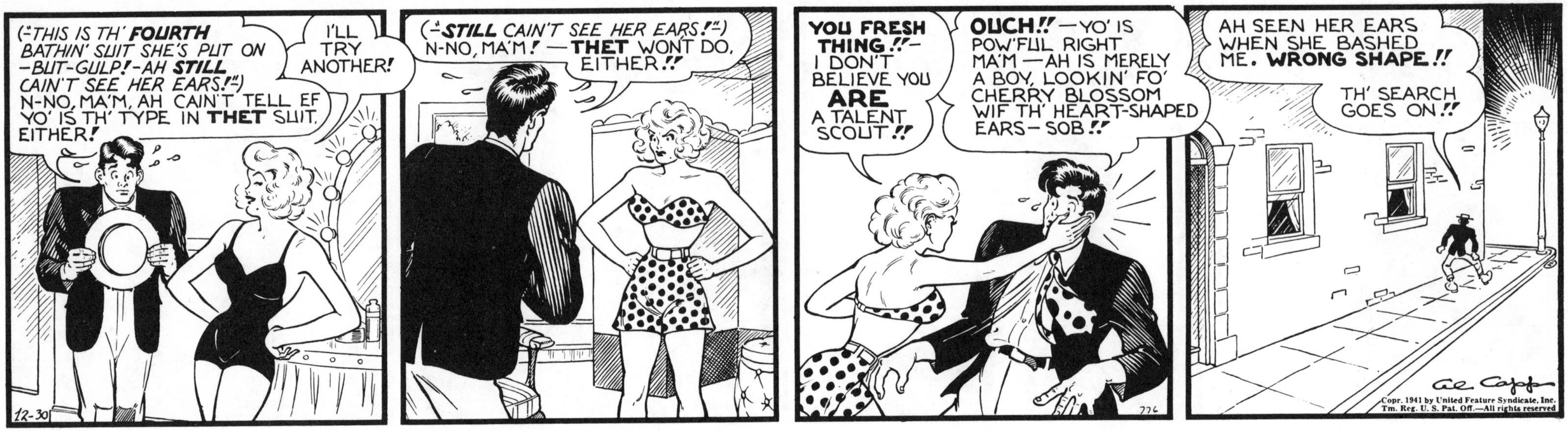
(-THIS IS TH' FOURTH BATHIN' SUIT SHE'S PUT ON -BUT-GULP!-AH STILL CAIN'T SEE HER EARS!-) N-NO, MA'M, AH CAIN'T TELL EF YO' IS TH' TYPE IN THET SUIT, EITHER!
I'LL TRY ANOTHER!
12-30
(-STILL CAIN'T SEE HER EARS!-) N-NO, MA'M! —THET WON'T DO, EITHER!!
YOU FRESH THING!!- I DON'T BELIEVE YOU ARE A TALENT SCOUT!!
OUCH!! —YO' IS POW'FUL RIGHT MA'M —AH IS MERELY A BOY, LOOKIN' FO' CHERRY BLOSSOM WIF TH' HEART-SHAPED EARS— SOB!!
776
AH SEEN HER EARS WHEN SHE BASHED ME. WRONG SHAPE!!
TH' SEARCH GOES ON!!
Al Capp
Copr. 1941 by United Feature Syndicate, Inc. Tm. Reg. U. S. Pat. Off.—All rights reserved

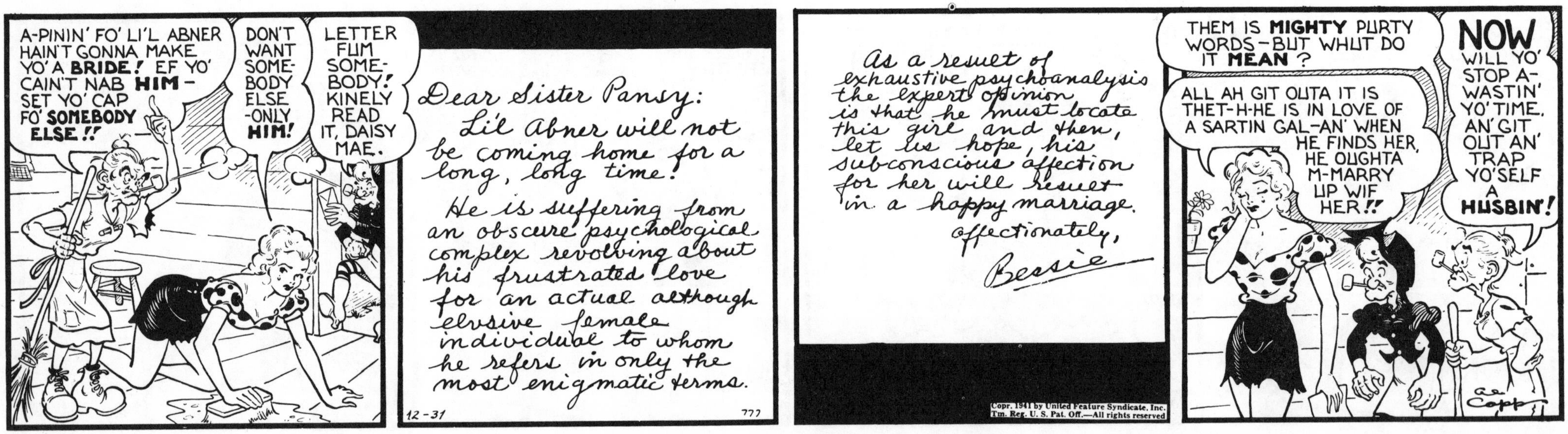
A-PININ' FO' LI'L ABNER HAIN'T GONNA MAKE YO' A BRIDE! EF YO' CAIN'T NAB HIM - SET YO' CAP FO' SOMEBODY ELSE!!
DON'T WANT SOME-BODY ELSE -ONLY HIM!
LETTER FUM SOME-BODY! KINELY READ IT, DAISY MAE.
Dear Sister Pansy:
Lil Abner will not be coming home for a long, long time!
He is suffering from an obscure psychological complex revolving about his frustrated love for an actual although elusive female individual to whom he refers in only the most enigmatic terms.
12-31
777
As a result of exhaustive psychoanalysis the expert opinion is that he must locate this girl and then, let us hope, his subconscious affection for her will result in a happy marriage.
affectionately,
Bessie
Copr. 1941 by United Feature Syndicate, Inc. Tm. Reg. U. S. Pat. Off.—All rights reserved
THEM IS MIGHTY PURTY WORDS-BUT WHUT DO IT MEAN ?
ALL AH GIT OUTA IT IS THET-H-HE IS IN LOVE OF A SARTIN GAL-AN' WHEN HE FINDS HER, HE OUGHTA M-MARRY UP WIF HER!!
NOW WILL YO' STOP A-WASTIN' YO' TIME, AN' GIT OUT AN' TRAP YO'SELF A HUSBIN'!
Al Capp

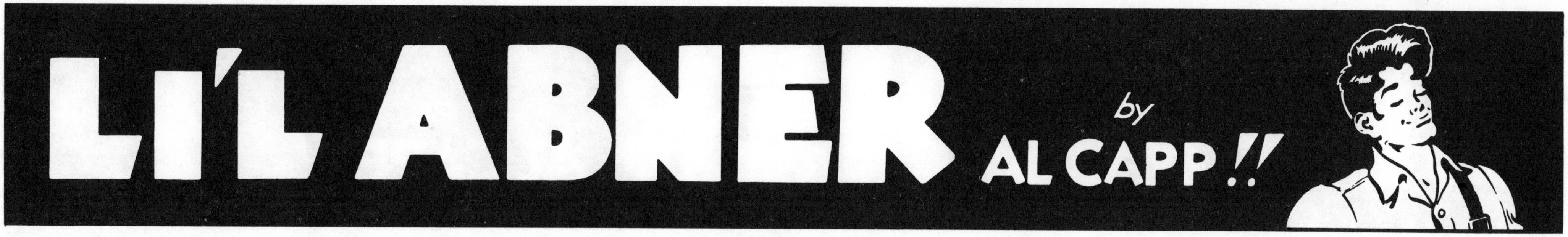
LI'L ABNER
by
AL CAPP!!

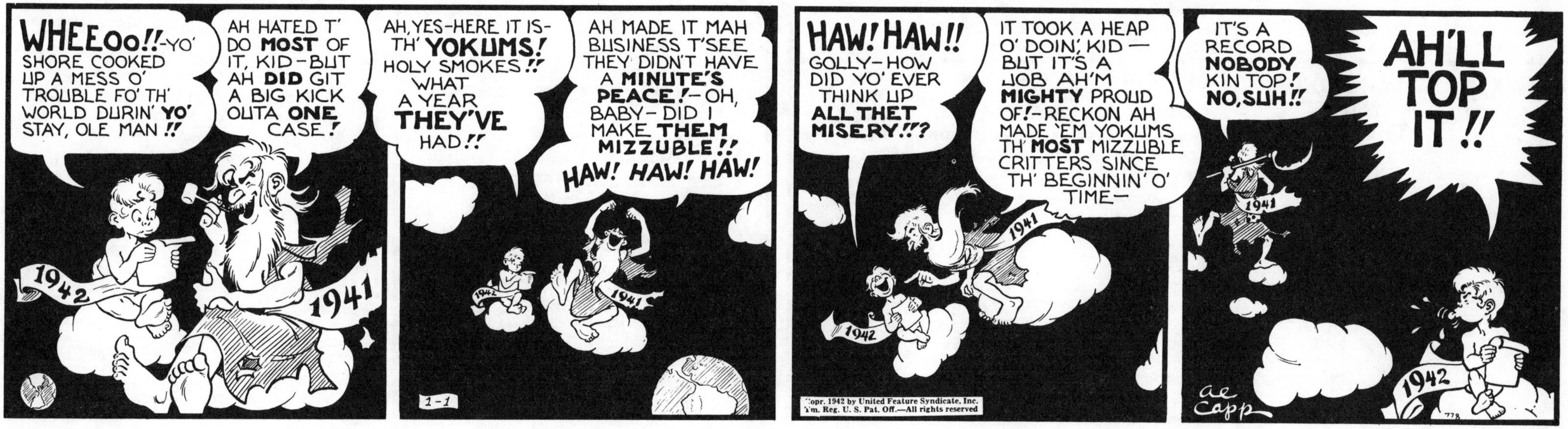
WHEEoo!!-YO' SHORE COOKED UP A MESS O' TROUBLE FO' TH' WORLD DURIN' YO' STAY, OLE MAN!!
AH HATED T' DO MOST OF IT, KID-BUT AH DID GIT A BIG KICK OUTA ONE CASE!
1942
1941
AH, YES-HERE IT IS-TH' YOKUMS! HOLY SMOKES!! WHAT A YEAR THEY'VE HAD!!
AH MADE IT MAH BUSINESS T'SEE THEY DIDN'T HAVE A MINUTE'S PEACE!-OH, BABY-DID I MAKE THEM MIZZUBLE!!
HAW! HAW! HAW!
1-1
HAW! HAW!! GOLLY-HOW DID YO' EVER THINK UP ALL THET MISERY!!?
IT TOOK A HEAP O' DOIN', KID-BUT IT'S A JOB AH'M MIGHTY PROUD OF!-RECKON AH MADE 'EM YOKUMS TH' MOST MIZZUBLE CRITTERS SINCE TH' BEGINNIN' O' TIME-
Copr. 1942 by United Feature Syndicate, Inc. Tm. Reg. U. S. Pat. Off.—All rights reserved
IT'S A RECORD NOBODY KIN TOP! NO, SUH!!
AH'LL TOP IT!!
al capp

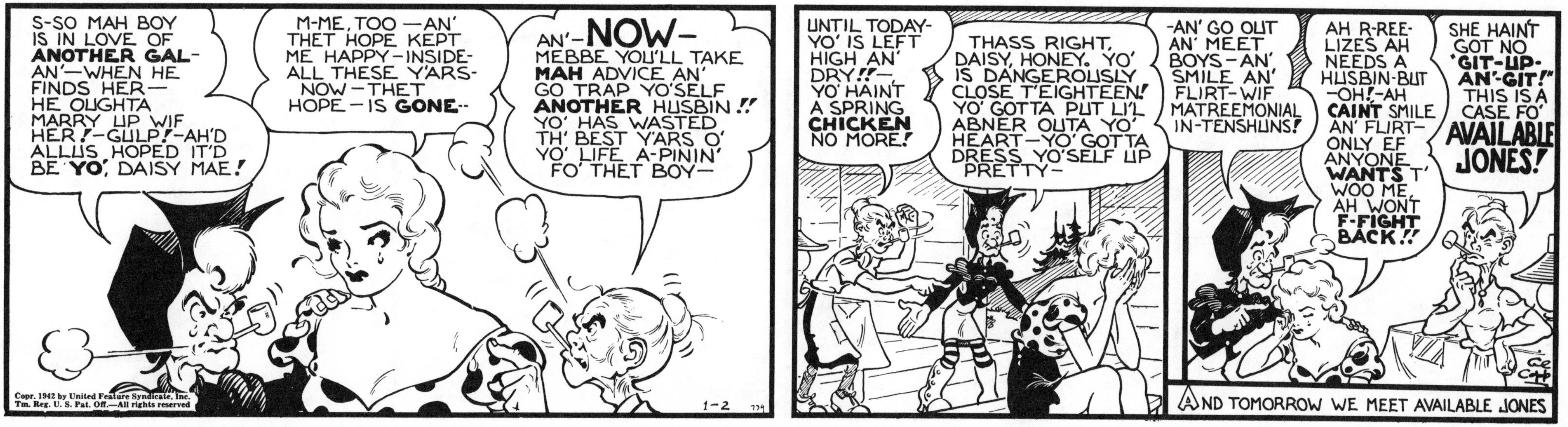
S-SO MAH BOY IS IN LOVE OF ANOTHER GAL-AN'-WHEN HE FINDS HER-HE OUGHTA MARRY UP WIF HER!-GULP!-AH'D ALLUS HOPED IT'D BE YO', DAISY MAE!
M-ME, TOO-AN' THET HOPE KEPT ME HAPPY-INSIDE-ALL THESE Y'ARS-NOW-THET HOPE-IS GONE--
AN'-NOW-MEBBE YOU'LL TAKE MAH ADVICE AN' GO TRAP YO'SELF ANOTHER HUSBIN!! YO' HAS WASTED TH' BEST Y'ARS O' YO' LIFE A-PININ' FO' THET BOY-
Copr. 1942 by United Feature Syndicate, Inc. Tm. Reg. U. S. Pat. Off.—All rights reserved
1-2
UNTIL TODAY-YO' IS LEFT HIGH AN' DRY!!-YO' HAIN'T A SPRING CHICKEN NO MORE!
THASS RIGHT, DAISY, HONEY. YO' IS DANGEROUSLY CLOSE T'EIGHTEEN! YO' GOTTA PUT LI'L ABNER OUTA YO' HEART-YO' GOTTA DRESS YO'SELF UP PRETTY-
-AN' GO OUT AN' MEET BOYS-AN' SMILE AN' FLIRT-WIF MATREEMONIAL IN-TENSHUNS!
AH R-REE-LIZES AH NEEDS A HUSBIN-BUT-OH!-AH CAIN'T SMILE AN' FLIRT-ONLY EF ANYONE WANTS T' WOO ME, AH WON'T F-FIGHT BACK!!
SHE HAIN'T GOT NO "GIT-UP-AN'-GIT!" THIS IS A CASE FO' AVAILABLE JONES!
al capp
AND TOMORROW WE MEET AVAILABLE JONES

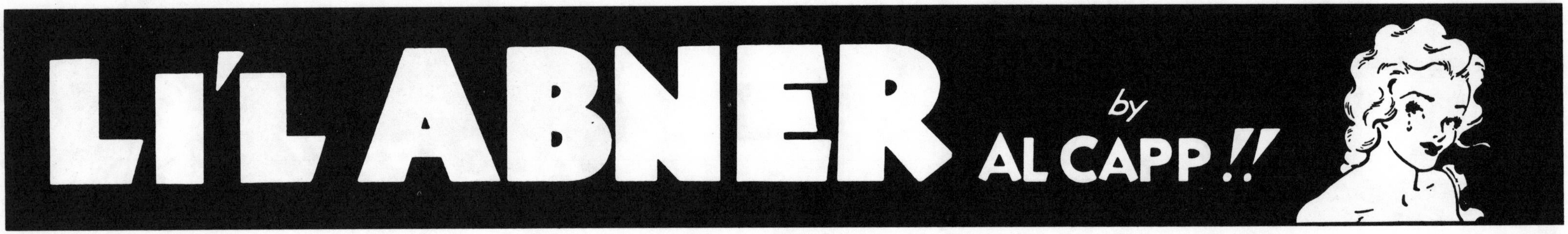

LI'L ABNER
by
AL CAPP !!

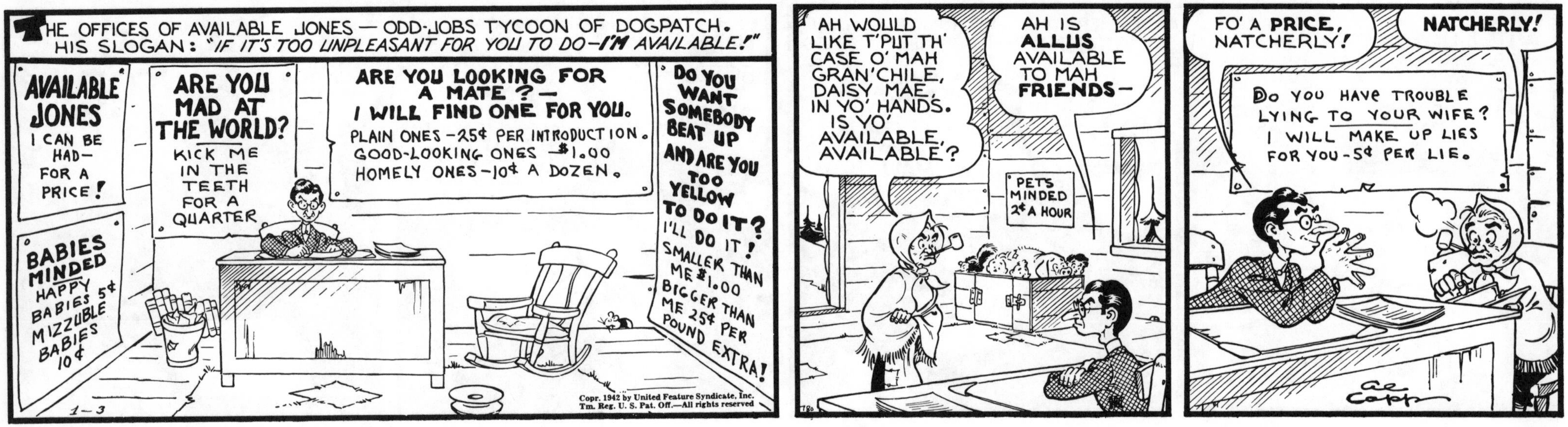

THE OFFICES OF AVAILABLE JONES — ODD-JOBS TYCOON OF DOGPATCH. HIS SLOGAN: "IF IT'S TOO UNPLEASANT FOR YOU TO DO—I'M AVAILABLE!"
AVAILABLE JONES I CAN BE HAD— FOR A PRICE!
ARE YOU MAD AT THE WORLD? KICK ME IN THE TEETH FOR A QUARTER
ARE YOU LOOKING FOR A MATE?— I WILL FIND ONE FOR YOU. PLAIN ONES-25¢ PER INTRODUCTION. GOOD-LOOKING ONES-$1.00 HOMELY ONES-10¢ A DOZEN.
DO YOU WANT SOMEBODY BEAT UP AND ARE YOU TOO YELLOW TO DO IT? I'LL DO IT! SMALLER THAN ME $1.00 BIGGER THAN ME 25¢ PER POUND EXTRA!
BABIES MINDED HAPPY BABIES 5¢ MIZZUBLE BABIES 10¢
1-3
Copr. 1942 by United Feature Syndicate, Inc. Tm. Reg. U. S. Pat. Off.—All rights reserved
AH WOULD LIKE T'PUT TH' CASE O' MAH GRAN'CHILE, DAISY MAE, IN YO' HANDS. IS YO' AVAILABLE, AVAILABLE?
AH IS ALLUS AVAILABLE TO MAH FRIENDS—
PETS MINDED 2¢ A HOUR
780
FO' A PRICE, NATCHERLY!
NATCHERLY!
DO YOU HAVE TROUBLE LYING TO YOUR WIFE? I WILL MAKE UP LIES FOR YOU-5¢ PER LIE.
Al Capp

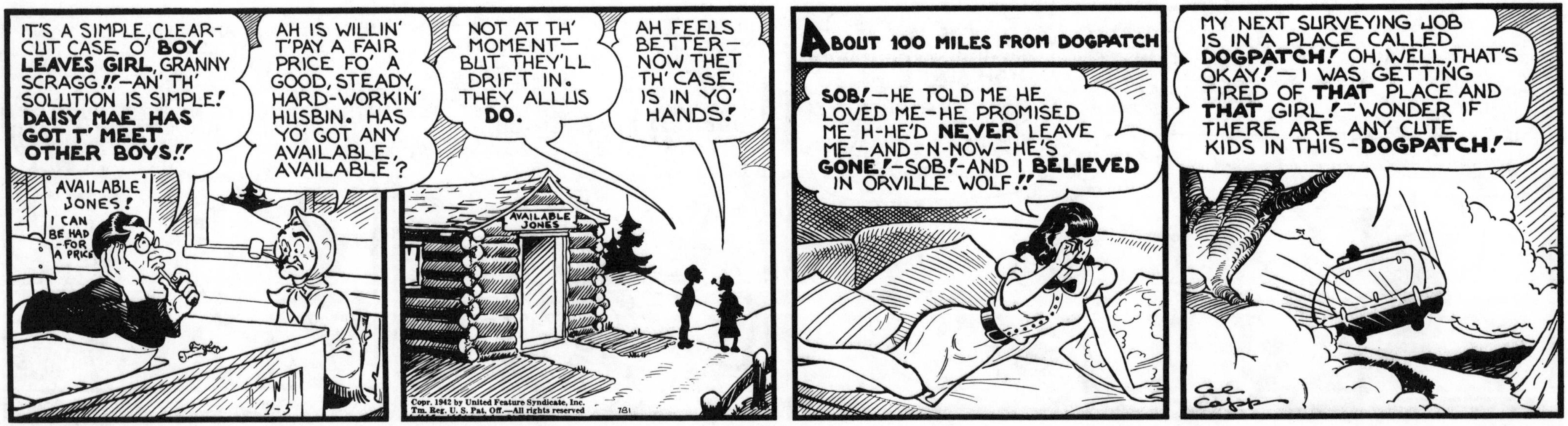

IT'S A SIMPLE, CLEAR-CUT CASE O' BOY LEAVES GIRL, GRANNY SCRAGG!!—AN' TH' SOLUTION IS SIMPLE! DAISY MAE HAS GOT T' MEET OTHER BOYS!!
AH IS WILLIN' T'PAY A FAIR PRICE FO' A GOOD, STEADY, HARD-WORKIN' HUSBIN. HAS YO' GOT ANY AVAILABLE, AVAILABLE?
AVAILABLE JONES! I CAN BE HAD -FOR A PRICE
1-5
NOT AT TH' MOMENT— BUT THEY'LL DRIFT IN. THEY ALLUS DO.
AH FEELS BETTER— NOW THET TH' CASE IS IN YO' HANDS!
AVAILABLE JONES
Copr. 1942 by United Feature Syndicate, Inc. Tm. Reg. U. S. Pat. Off.—All rights reserved
781
ABOUT 100 MILES FROM DOGPATCH
SOB!—HE TOLD ME HE LOVED ME-HE PROMISED ME H-HE'D NEVER LEAVE ME-AND-N-NOW-HE'S GONE!-SOB!-AND I BELIEVED IN ORVILLE WOLF!!—
MY NEXT SURVEYING JOB IS IN A PLACE CALLED DOGPATCH! OH, WELL, THAT'S OKAY!—I WAS GETTING TIRED OF THAT PLACE AND THAT GIRL!—WONDER IF THERE ARE ANY CUTE KIDS IN THIS-DOGPATCH!—
Al Capp

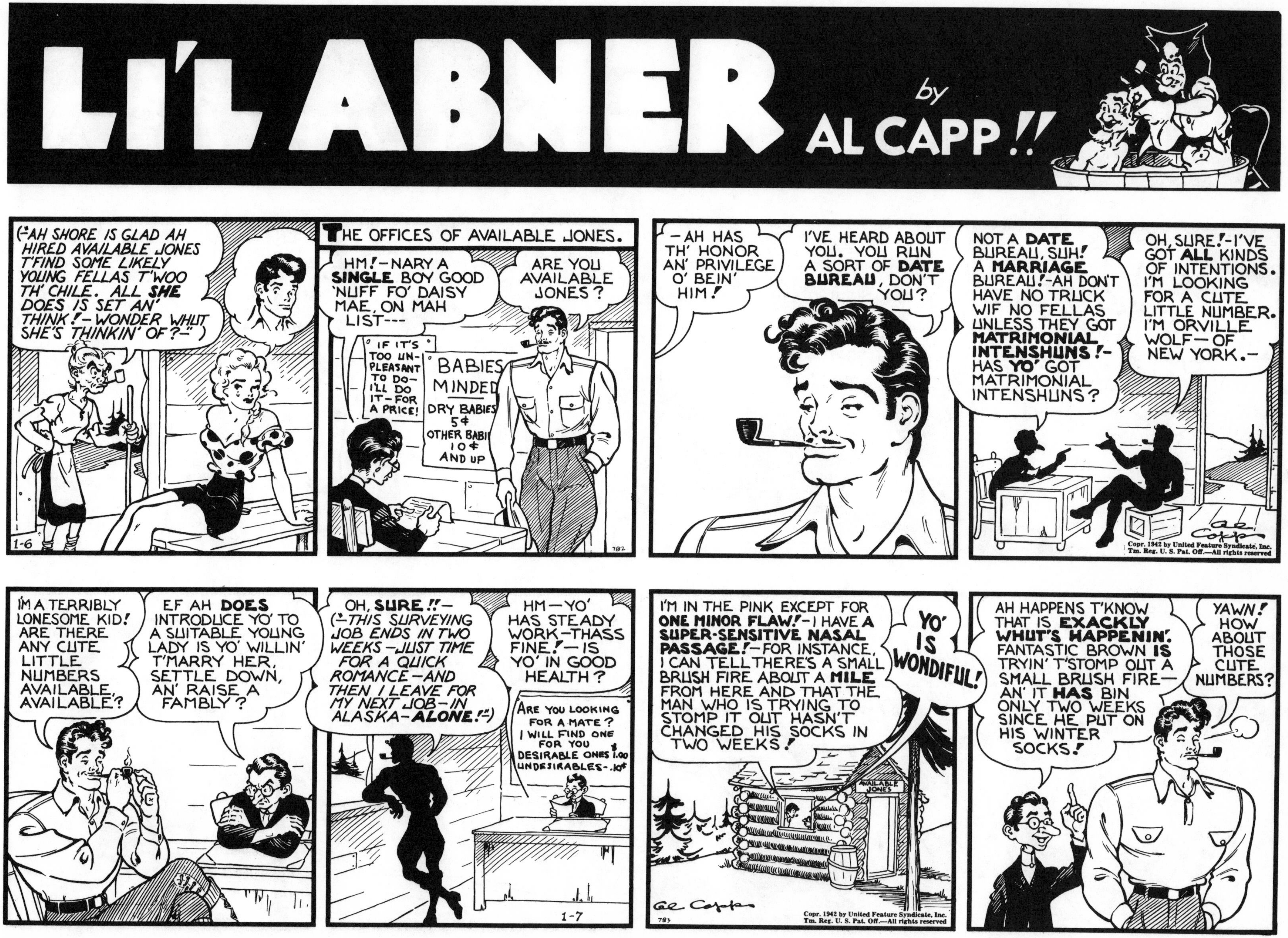
LI'L ABNER
by AL CAPP!!
("AH SHORE IS GLAD AH HIRED AVAILABLE JONES T'FIND SOME LIKELY YOUNG FELLAS T'WOO TH' CHILE. ALL SHE DOES IS SET AN' THINK!–WONDER WHUT SHE'S THINKIN' OF?–")
1-6
THE OFFICES OF AVAILABLE JONES.
HM!–NARY A SINGLE BOY GOOD 'NUFF FO' DAISY MAE, ON MAH LIST---
ARE YOU AVAILABLE JONES?
IF IT'S TOO UN-PLEASANT TO DO–I'LL DO IT–FOR A PRICE!
BABIES MINDED
DRY BABIES 5¢
OTHER BABI 10¢ AND UP
782
–AH HAS TH' HONOR AN' PRIVILEGE O' BEIN' HIM!
I'VE HEARD ABOUT YOU. YOU RUN A SORT OF DATE BUREAU, DON'T YOU?
NOT A DATE BUREAU, SUH! A MARRIAGE BUREAU!–AH DON'T HAVE NO TRUCK WIF NO FELLAS UNLESS THEY GOT MATRIMONIAL INTENSHUNS!–HAS YO' GOT MATRIMONIAL INTENSHUNS?
OH, SURE!–I'VE GOT ALL KINDS OF INTENTIONS. I'M LOOKING FOR A CUTE LITTLE NUMBER. I'M ORVILLE WOLF–OF NEW YORK.–
Al Capp
Copr. 1942 by United Feature Syndicate, Inc. Tm. Reg. U. S. Pat. Off.—All rights reserved
I'M A TERRIBLY LONESOME KID! ARE THERE ANY CUTE LITTLE NUMBERS AVAILABLE, AVAILABLE?
EF AH DOES INTRODUCE YO' TO A SUITABLE YOUNG LADY IS YO' WILLIN' T'MARRY HER, SETTLE DOWN, AN' RAISE A FAMBLY?
OH, SURE!!–("THIS SURVEYING JOB ENDS IN TWO WEEKS–JUST TIME FOR A QUICK ROMANCE–AND THEN I LEAVE FOR MY NEXT JOB–IN ALASKA–ALONE!")
HM–YO' HAS STEADY WORK–THASS FINE!–IS YO' IN GOOD HEALTH?
ARE YOU LOOKING FOR A MATE? I WILL FIND ONE FOR YOU DESIRABLE ONES $1.00 UNDESIRABLES–.10¢
1-7
I'M IN THE PINK EXCEPT FOR ONE MINOR FLAW!–I HAVE A SUPER-SENSITIVE NASAL PASSAGE!–FOR INSTANCE, I CAN TELL THERE'S A SMALL BRUSH FIRE ABOUT A MILE FROM HERE AND THAT THE MAN WHO IS TRYING TO STOMP IT OUT HASN'T CHANGED HIS SOCKS IN TWO WEEKS!
YO' IS WONDIFUL!
AVAILABLE JONES
Al Capp
783
Copr. 1942 by United Feature Syndicate, Inc. Tm. Reg. U. S. Pat. Off.—All rights reserved
AH HAPPENS T'KNOW THAT IS EXACKLY WHUT'S HAPPENIN'. FANTASTIC BROWN IS TRYIN' T'STOMP OUT A SMALL BRUSH FIRE–AN' IT HAS BIN ONLY TWO WEEKS SINCE HE PUT ON HIS WINTER SOCKS!
YAWN! HOW ABOUT THOSE CUTE NUMBERS?

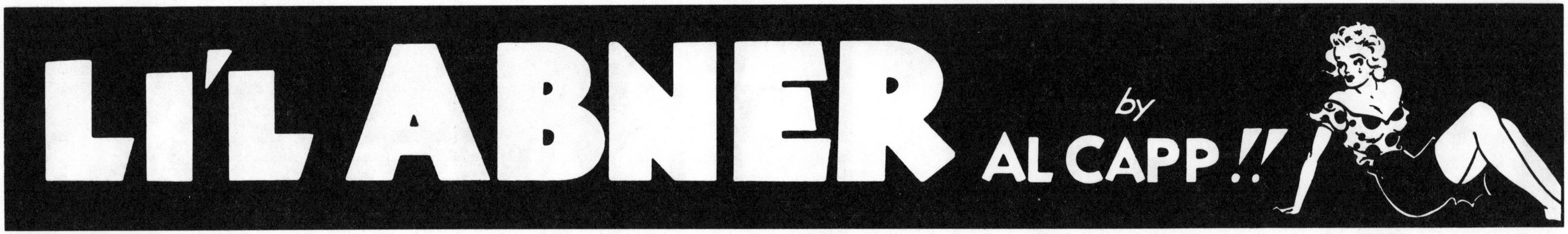
LI'L ABNER
by
AL CAPP!!

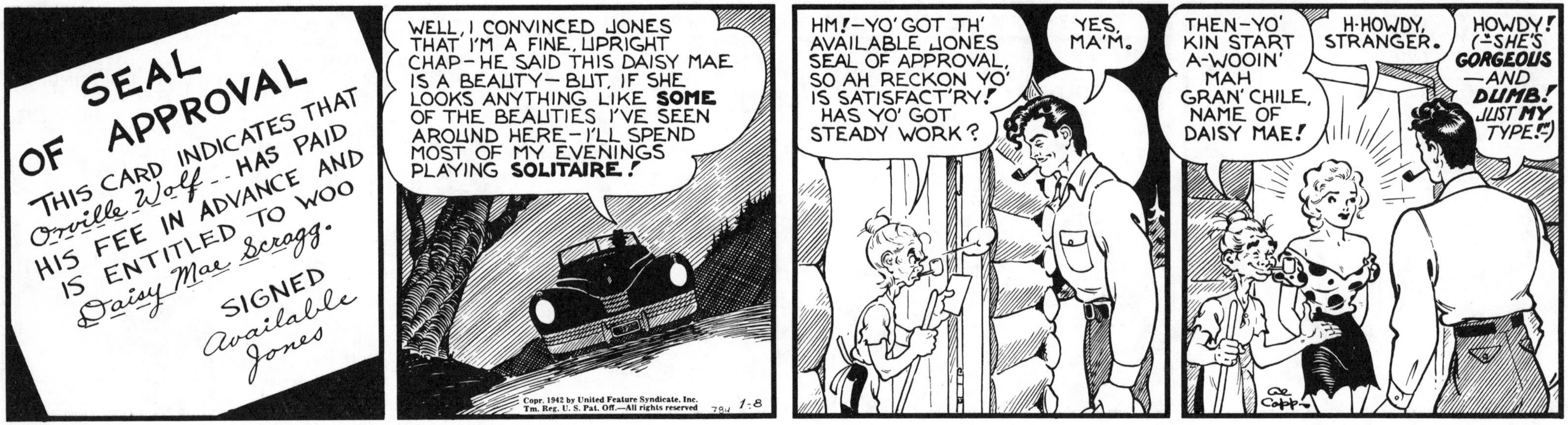
SEAL OF APPROVAL
THIS CARD INDICATES THAT Orville Wolf -- HAS PAID HIS FEE IN ADVANCE AND IS ENTITLED TO WOO Daisy Mae Scragg.
SIGNED Available Jones
WELL, I CONVINCED JONES THAT I'M A FINE, UPRIGHT CHAP - HE SAID THIS DAISY MAE IS A BEAUTY - BUT, IF SHE LOOKS ANYTHING LIKE SOME OF THE BEAUTIES I'VE SEEN AROUND HERE - I'LL SPEND MOST OF MY EVENINGS PLAYING SOLITAIRE!
Copr. 1942 by United Feature Syndicate, Inc.
Tm. Reg. U. S. Pat. Off.—All rights reserved
1-8
HM! - YO' GOT TH' AVAILABLE JONES SEAL OF APPROVAL, SO AH RECKON YO' IS SATISFACT'RY! HAS YO' GOT STEADY WORK?
YES, MA'M.
THEN - YO' KIN START A-WOOIN' MAH GRAN' CHILE, NAME OF DAISY MAE!
H-HOWDY, STRANGER.
HOWDY! (-SHE'S GORGEOUS - AND DUMB! JUST MY TYPE!-)
Al Capp

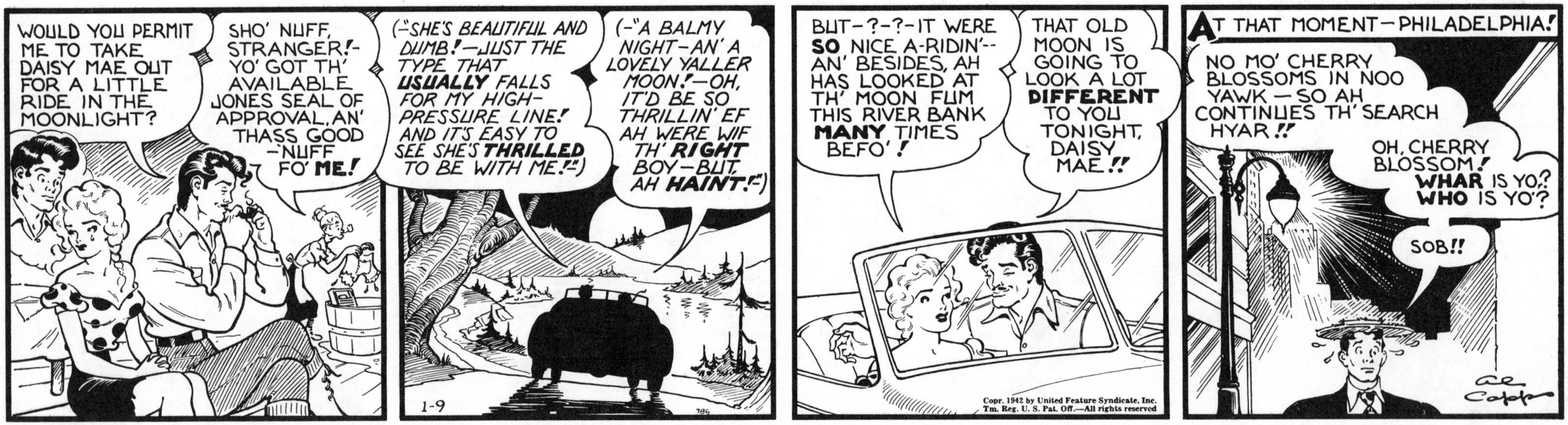
WOULD YOU PERMIT ME TO TAKE DAISY MAE OUT FOR A LITTLE RIDE IN THE MOONLIGHT?
SHO' NUFF, STRANGER! - YO' GOT TH' AVAILABLE JONES SEAL OF APPROVAL, AN' THASS GOOD -NUFF FO' ME!
(-"SHE'S BEAUTIFUL AND DUMB! - JUST THE TYPE THAT USUALLY FALLS FOR MY HIGH-PRESSURE LINE! AND IT'S EASY TO SEE SHE'S THRILLED TO BE WITH ME!"-)
(-"A BALMY NIGHT - AN' A LOVELY YALLER MOON! - OH, IT'D BE SO THRILLIN' EF AH WERE WIF TH' RIGHT BOY - BUT, AH HAINT!"-)
1-9
BUT-?-?-IT WERE SO NICE A-RIDIN'-- AN' BESIDES, AH HAS LOOKED AT TH' MOON FUM THIS RIVER BANK MANY TIMES BEFO'!
THAT OLD MOON IS GOING TO LOOK A LOT DIFFERENT TO YOU TONIGHT, DAISY MAE!!
Copr. 1942 by United Feature Syndicate, Inc.
Tm. Reg. U. S. Pat. Off.—All rights reserved
AT THAT MOMENT - PHILADELPHIA!
NO MO' CHERRY BLOSSOMS IN NOO YAWK - SO AH CONTINUES TH' SEARCH HYAR!!
OH, CHERRY BLOSSOM! WHAR IS YO'? WHO IS YO'?
SOB!!
Al Capp

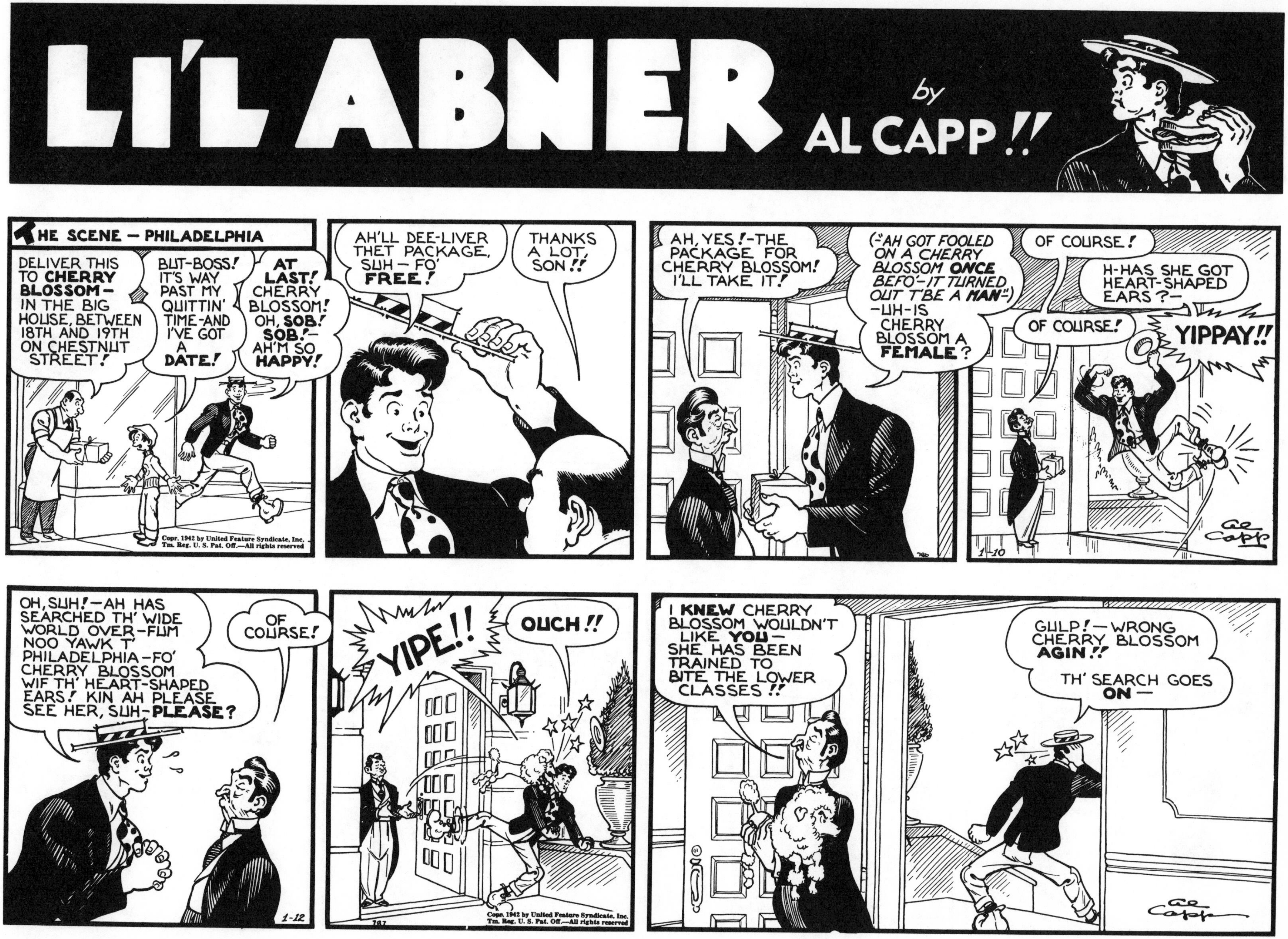
LI'L ABNER
by
AL CAPP!!
THE SCENE – PHILADELPHIA
DELIVER THIS TO CHERRY BLOSSOM – IN THE BIG HOUSE, BETWEEN 18TH AND 19TH ON CHESTNUT STREET!
BUT-BOSS! IT'S WAY PAST MY QUITTIN' TIME-AND I'VE GOT A DATE!
AT LAST! CHERRY BLOSSOM! OH, SOB! SOB!– AH'M SO HAPPY!
Copr. 1942 by United Feature Syndicate, Inc. Tm. Reg. U. S. Pat. Off.—All rights reserved
AH'LL DEE-LIVER THET PACKAGE, SUH – FO' FREE!
THANKS A LOT, SON!!
AH, YES!-THE PACKAGE FOR CHERRY BLOSSOM! I'LL TAKE IT!
("AH GOT FOOLED ON A CHERRY BLOSSOM ONCE BEFO'- IT TURNED OUT T'BE A MAN!") -UH-IS CHERRY BLOSSOM A FEMALE?
OF COURSE!
H-HAS SHE GOT HEART-SHAPED EARS?–
OF COURSE!
YIPPAY!!
1-10
Al Capp
OH, SUH!–AH HAS SEARCHED TH' WIDE WORLD OVER–FUM NOO YAWK T' PHILADELPHIA–FO' CHERRY BLOSSOM WIF TH' HEART-SHAPED EARS! KIN AH PLEASE SEE HER, SUH-PLEASE?
OF COURSE!
1-12
YIPE!!
OUCH!!
Copr. 1942 by United Feature Syndicate, Inc. Tm. Reg. U. S. Pat. Off.—All rights reserved
I KNEW CHERRY BLOSSOM WOULDN'T LIKE YOU– SHE HAS BEEN TRAINED TO BITE THE LOWER CLASSES!!
GULP!–WRONG CHERRY BLOSSOM AGIN!!
TH' SEARCH GOES ON–
Al Capp

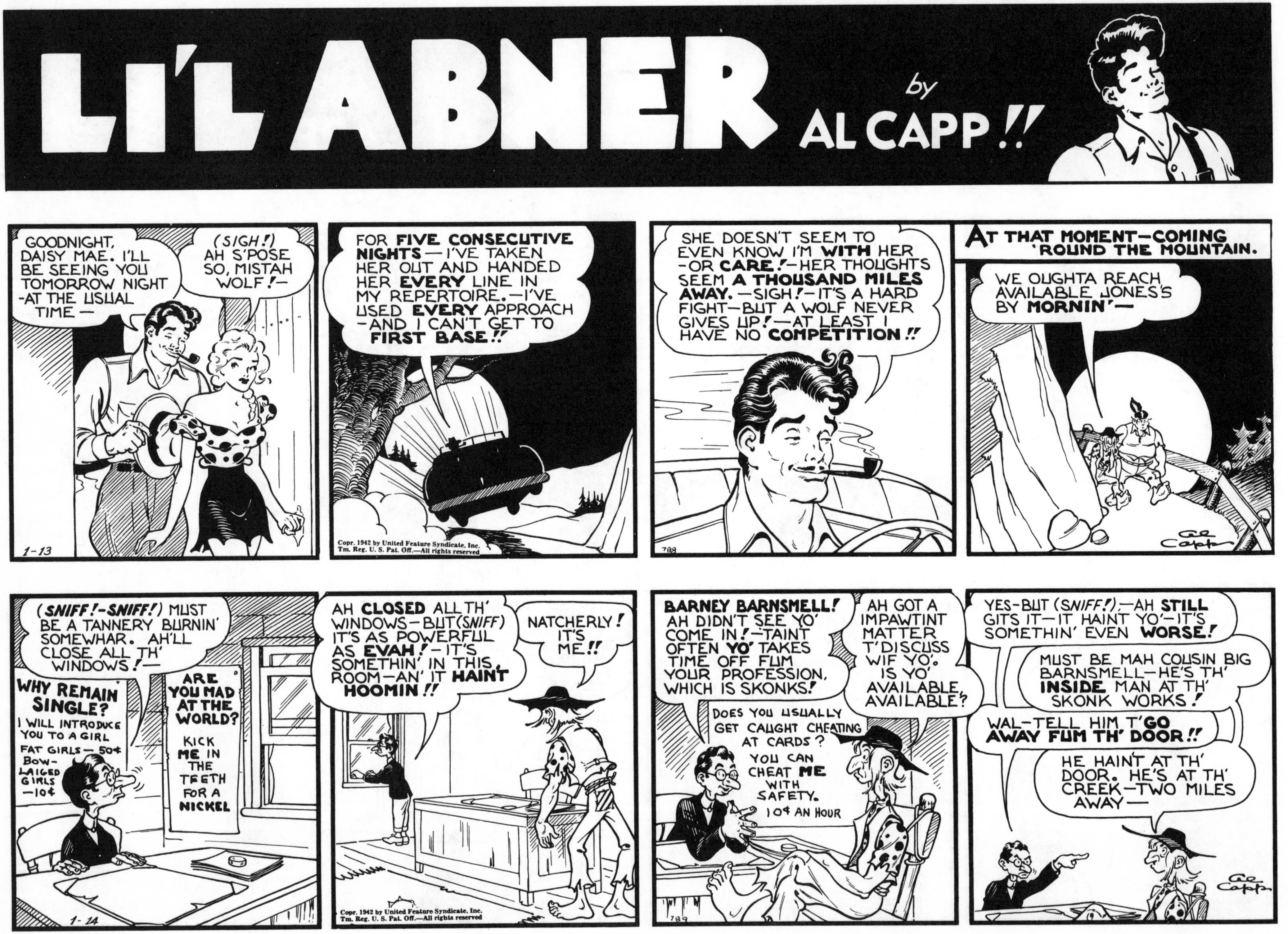
LI'L ABNER
by AL CAPP!!
GOODNIGHT, DAISY MAE. I'LL BE SEEING YOU TOMORROW NIGHT -AT THE USUAL TIME—
(SIGH!) AH S'POSE SO, MISTAH WOLF!—
1-13
FOR FIVE CONSECUTIVE NIGHTS—I'VE TAKEN HER OUT AND HANDED HER EVERY LINE IN MY REPERTOIRE.—I'VE USED EVERY APPROACH -AND I CAN'T GET TO FIRST BASE!!
Copr. 1942 by United Feature Syndicate, Inc. Tm. Reg. U. S. Pat. Off.—All rights reserved
SHE DOESN'T SEEM TO EVEN KNOW I'M WITH HER -OR CARE!—HER THOUGHTS SEEM A THOUSAND MILES AWAY.—SIGH!—IT'S A HARD FIGHT—BUT A WOLF NEVER GIVES UP!—AT LEAST I HAVE NO COMPETITION!!
788
AT THAT MOMENT—COMING 'ROUND THE MOUNTAIN.
WE OUGHTA REACH AVAILABLE JONES'S BY MORNIN'—
Al Capp
(SNIFF!-SNIFF!) MUST BE A TANNERY BURNIN' SOMEWHAR. AH'LL CLOSE ALL TH' WINDOWS!—
WHY REMAIN SINGLE? I WILL INTRODUCE YOU TO A GIRL FAT GIRLS—50¢ BOW-LAIGED GIRLS—10¢
ARE YOU MAD AT THE WORLD? KICK ME IN THE TEETH FOR A NICKEL
1-14
AH CLOSED ALL TH' WINDOWS—BUT (SNIFF) IT'S AS POWERFUL AS EVAH!—IT'S SOMETHIN' IN THIS ROOM—AN' IT HAINT HOOMIN!!
NATCHERLY! IT'S ME!!
Copr. 1942 by United Feature Syndicate, Inc. Tm. Reg. U. S. Pat. Off.—All rights reserved
BARNEY BARNSMELL! AH DIDN'T SEE YO' COME IN!—TAINT OFTEN YO' TAKES TIME OFF FUM YOUR PROFESSION, WHICH IS SKONKS!
AH GOT A IMPAWTINT MATTER T'DISCUSS WIF YO'. IS YO' AVAILABLE, AVAILABLE?
DOES YOU USUALLY GET CAUGHT CHEATING AT CARDS? YOU CAN CHEAT ME WITH SAFETY. 10¢ AN HOUR
789
YES-BUT (SNIFF!)—AH STILL GITS IT—IT HAINT YO'—IT'S SOMETHIN' EVEN WORSE!
MUST BE MAH COUSIN BIG BARNSMELL—HE'S TH' INSIDE MAN AT TH' SKONK WORKS!
WAL-TELL HIM T'GO AWAY FUM TH' DOOR!!
HE HAINT AT TH' DOOR. HE'S AT TH' CREEK—TWO MILES AWAY—
Al Capp

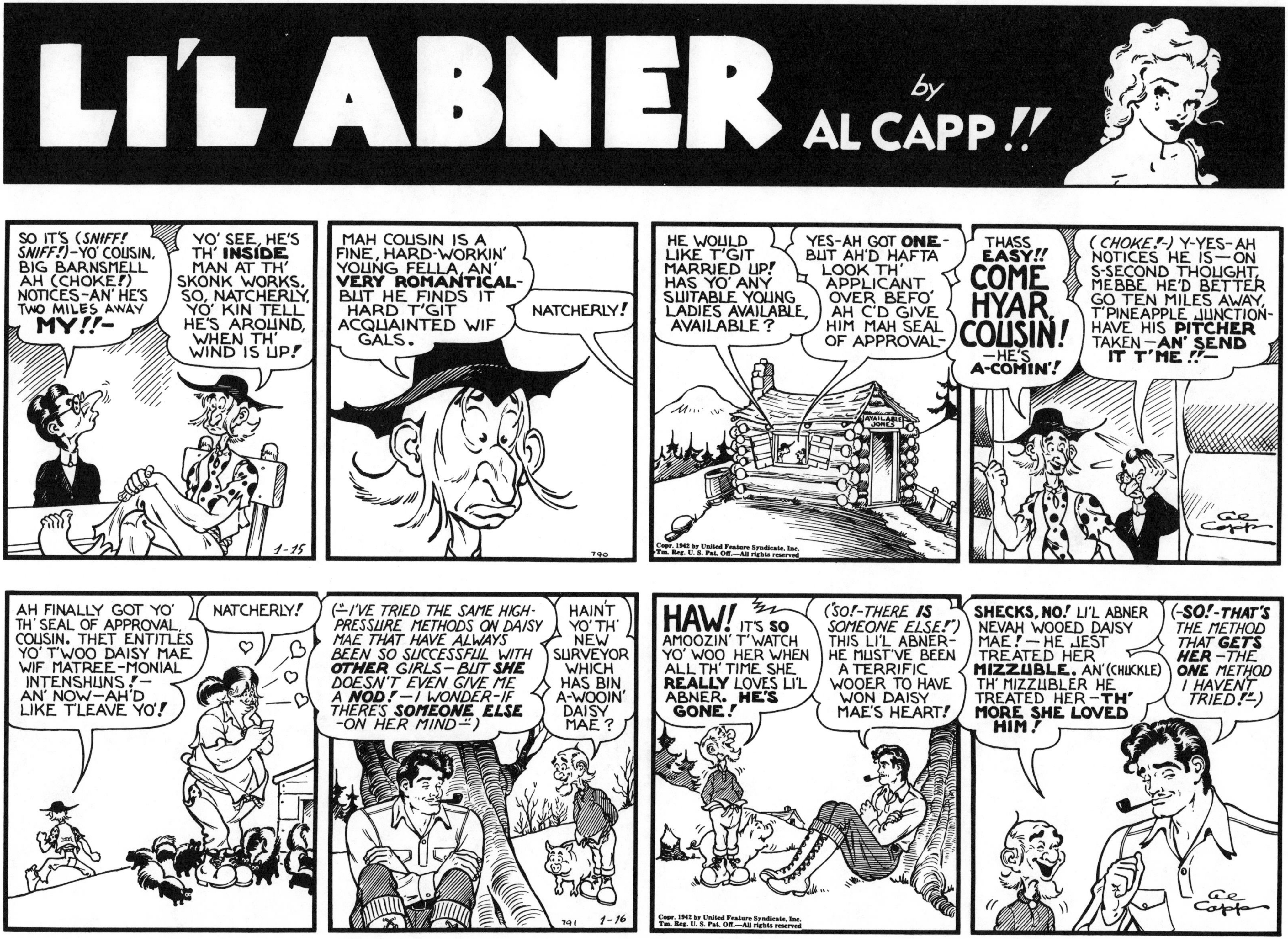
LI'L ABNER
by AL CAPP!!
SO IT'S (SNIFF! SNIFF!)–YO' COUSIN, BIG BARNSMELL AH (CHOKE!) NOTICES–AN' HE'S TWO MILES AWAY MY!!–
YO' SEE, HE'S TH' INSIDE MAN AT TH' SKONK WORKS. SO, NATCHERLY, YO' KIN TELL HE'S AROUND, WHEN TH' WIND IS UP!
1-15
MAH COUSIN IS A FINE, HARD-WORKIN' YOUNG FELLA, AN' VERY ROMANTICAL– BUT HE FINDS IT HARD T'GIT ACQUAINTED WIF GALS.
NATCHERLY!
790
HE WOULD LIKE T'GIT MARRIED UP! HAS YO' ANY SUITABLE YOUNG LADIES AVAILABLE, AVAILABLE?
YES–AH GOT ONE– BUT AH'D HAFTA LOOK TH' APPLICANT OVER BEFO' AH C'D GIVE HIM MAH SEAL OF APPROVAL–
AVAILABLE JONES
Copr. 1942 by United Feature Syndicate, Inc. Tm. Reg. U. S. Pat. Off.—All rights reserved
THASS EASY!! COME HYAR, COUSIN! –HE'S A-COMIN'!
(CHOKE!–) Y-YES–AH NOTICES HE IS—ON S-SECOND THOUGHT, MEBBE HE'D BETTER GO TEN MILES AWAY, T'PINEAPPLE JUNCTION– HAVE HIS PITCHER TAKEN—AN' SEND IT T'ME!!–
AL CAPP
AH FINALLY GOT YO' TH' SEAL OF APPROVAL, COUSIN. THET ENTITLES YO' T'WOO DAISY MAE WIF MATREE-MONIAL INTENSHUNS!— AN' NOW—AH'D LIKE T'LEAVE YO'!
NATCHERLY!
(–I'VE TRIED THE SAME HIGH-PRESSURE METHODS ON DAISY MAE THAT HAVE ALWAYS BEEN SO SUCCESSFUL WITH OTHER GIRLS—BUT SHE DOESN'T EVEN GIVE ME A NOD!—I WONDER–IF THERE'S SOMEONE ELSE –ON HER MIND–)
HAIN'T YO' TH' NEW SURVEYOR WHICH HAS BIN A-WOOIN' DAISY MAE?
791 1-16
HAW! IT'S SO AMOOZIN' T'WATCH YO' WOO HER WHEN ALL TH' TIME SHE REALLY LOVES LI'L ABNER. HE'S GONE!
("SO!–THERE IS SOMEONE ELSE!") THIS LI'L ABNER– HE MUST'VE BEEN A TERRIFIC WOOER TO HAVE WON DAISY MAE'S HEART!
Copr. 1942 by United Feature Syndicate, Inc. Tm. Reg. U. S. Pat. Off.—All rights reserved
SHECKS, NO! LI'L ABNER NEVAH WOOED DAISY MAE!—HE JEST TREATED HER MIZZUBLE. AN' (CHUCKLE) TH' MIZZUBLER HE TREATED HER—TH' MORE SHE LOVED HIM!
(–SO!–THAT'S THE METHOD THAT GETS HER—THE ONE METHOD I HAVENT TRIED!–)
AL CAPP

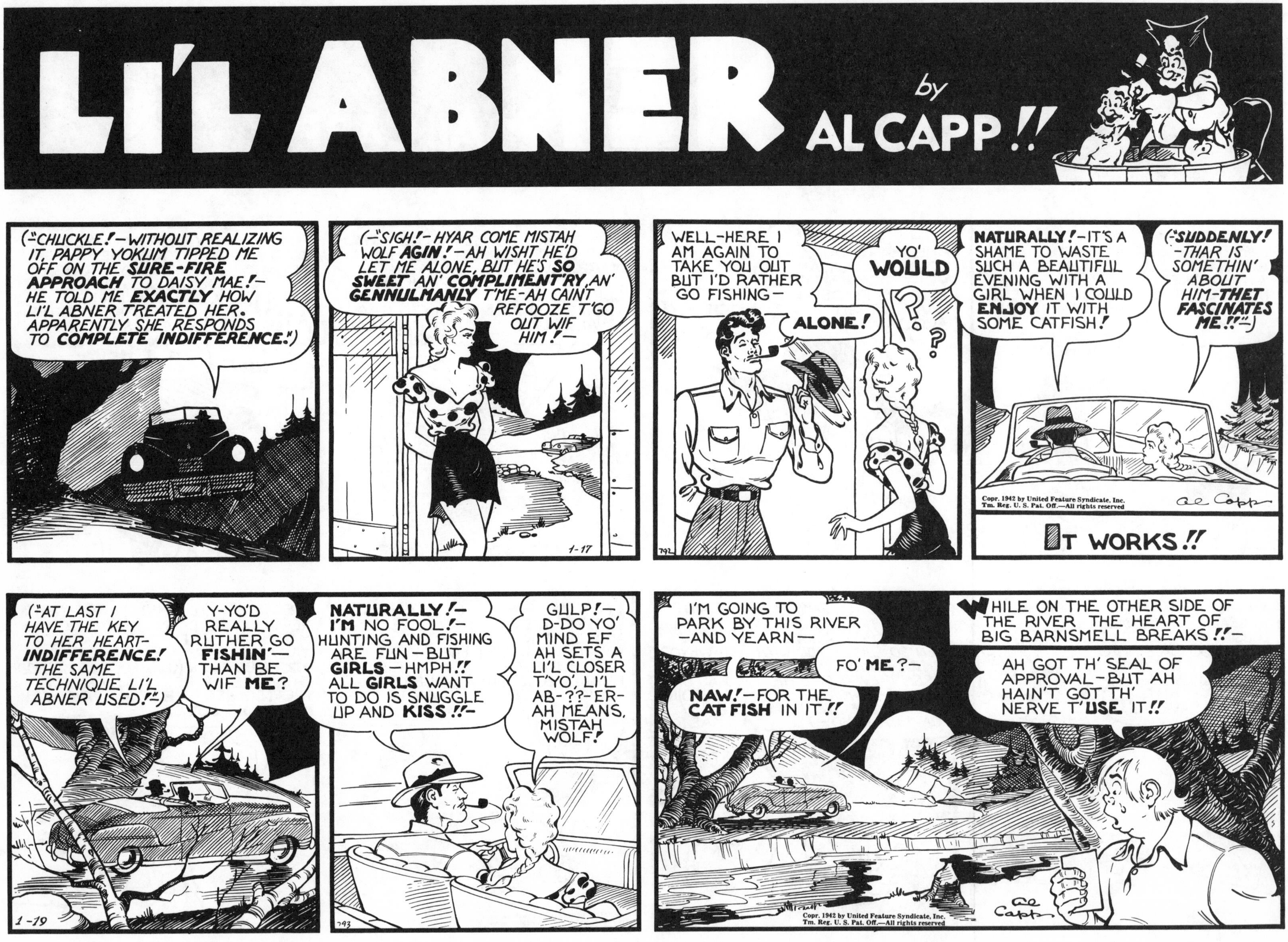
LI'L ABNER
by AL CAPP!!
("CHUCKLE!"—WITHOUT REALIZING IT, PAPPY YOKUM TIPPED ME OFF ON THE SURE-FIRE APPROACH TO DAISY MAE!—HE TOLD ME EXACTLY HOW LI'L ABNER TREATED HER. APPARENTLY SHE RESPONDS TO COMPLETE INDIFFERENCE.")
(—"SIGH!—HYAR COME MISTAH WOLF AGIN!—AH WISHT HE'D LET ME ALONE, BUT HE'S SO SWEET AN' COMPLIMENT'RY, AN' GENNULMANLY T'ME-AH CAINT REFOOZE T'GO OUT WIF HIM!"—
1-17
WELL-HERE I AM AGAIN TO TAKE YOU OUT BUT I'D RATHER GO FISHING—
ALONE!
YO' WOULD
? ?
792
NATURALLY!—IT'S A SHAME TO WASTE SUCH A BEAUTIFUL EVENING WITH A GIRL WHEN I COULD ENJOY IT WITH SOME CATFISH!
("SUDDENLY!—THAR IS SOMETHIN' ABOUT HIM—THET FASCINATES ME!!"—)
Copr. 1942 by United Feature Syndicate, Inc. Tm. Reg. U. S. Pat. Off.—All rights reserved
Al Capp
IT WORKS!!
("AT LAST I HAVE THE KEY TO HER HEART-INDIFFERENCE! THE SAME TECHNIQUE LI'L ABNER USED!")
Y-YO'D REALLY RUTHER GO FISHIN'—THAN BE WIF ME?
1-19
NATURALLY!—I'M NO FOOL!—HUNTING AND FISHING ARE FUN—BUT GIRLS—HMPH!! ALL GIRLS WANT TO DO IS SNUGGLE UP AND KISS!!—
GULP!—D-DO YO' MIND EF AH SETS A LI'L CLOSER T'YO', LI'L AB-??-ER-AH MEANS, MISTAH WOLF!
793
I'M GOING TO PARK BY THIS RIVER—AND YEARN—
FO' ME?—
NAW!—FOR THE CAT FISH IN IT!!
WHILE ON THE OTHER SIDE OF THE RIVER THE HEART OF BIG BARNSMELL BREAKS!!—
AH GOT TH' SEAL OF APPROVAL—BUT AH HAIN'T GOT TH' NERVE T'USE IT!!
Al Capp
Copr. 1942 by United Feature Syndicate, Inc. Tm. Reg. U. S. Pat. Off.—All rights reserved

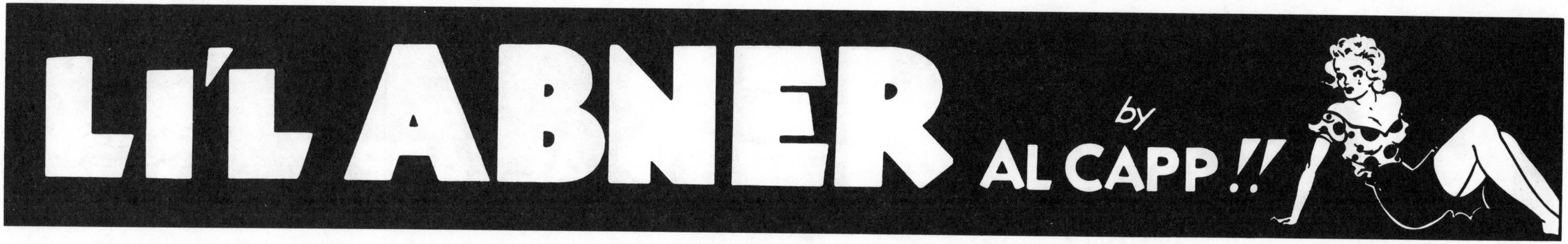
LI'L ABNER
by
AL CAPP!!

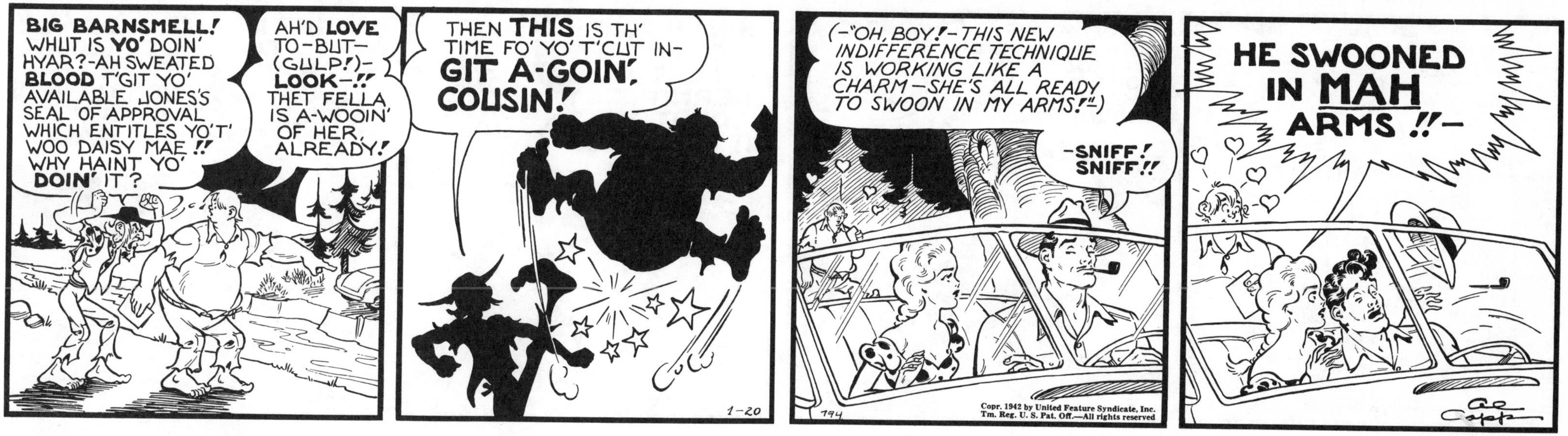
BIG BARNSMELL! WHUT IS YO' DOIN' HYAR?-AH SWEATED BLOOD T'GIT YO' AVAILABLE JONES'S SEAL OF APPROVAL WHICH ENTITLES YO'T' WOO DAISY MAE!! WHY HAINT YO' DOIN' IT?
AH'D LOVE TO-BUT-(GULP!)-LOOK-!! THET FELLA IS A-WOOIN' OF HER, ALREADY!
THEN THIS IS TH' TIME FO' YO' T'CUT IN-GIT A-GOIN', COUSIN!
1-20
(-"OH, BOY!-THIS NEW INDIFFERENCE TECHNIQUE IS WORKING LIKE A CHARM-SHE'S ALL READY TO SWOON IN MY ARMS!"-)
-SNIFF! SNIFF!!
794
Copr. 1942 by United Feature Syndicate, Inc. Tm. Reg. U. S. Pat. Off.—All rights reserved
HE SWOONED IN MAH ARMS!!-
Al Capp

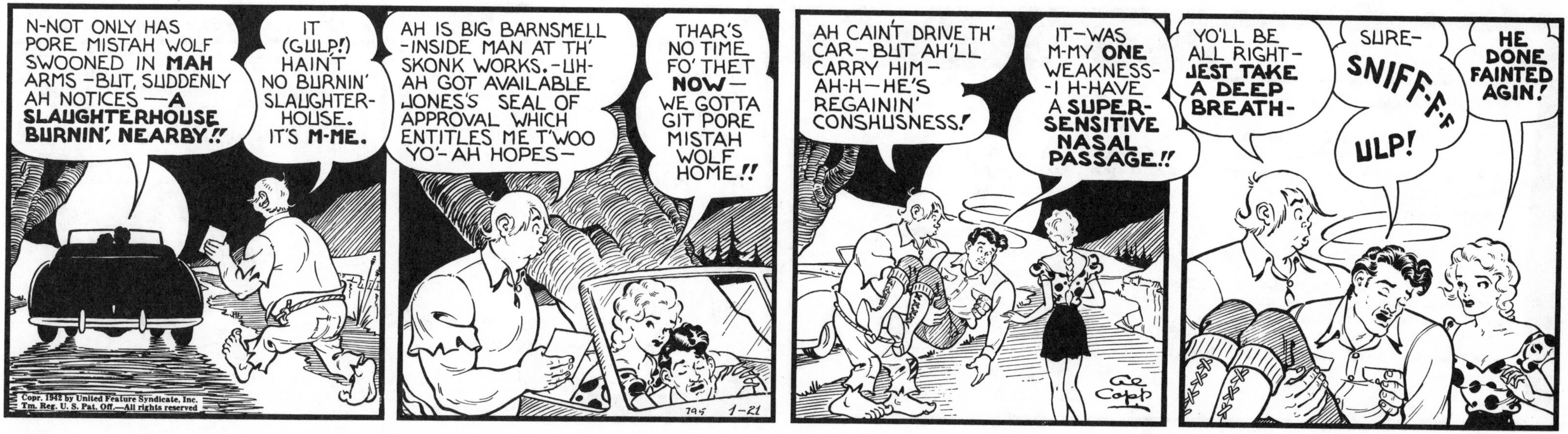
N-NOT ONLY HAS PORE MISTAH WOLF SWOONED IN MAH ARMS-BUT, SUDDENLY AH NOTICES-A SLAUGHTERHOUSE BURNIN', NEARBY!!
IT (GULP!) HAIN'T NO BURNIN' SLAUGHTER-HOUSE. IT'S M-ME.
Copr. 1942 by United Feature Syndicate, Inc. Tm. Reg. U. S. Pat. Off.—All rights reserved
AH IS BIG BARNSMELL-INSIDE MAN AT TH' SKONK WORKS.-UH-AH GOT AVAILABLE JONES'S SEAL OF APPROVAL WHICH ENTITLES ME T'WOO YO'-AH HOPES-
THAR'S NO TIME FO' THET NOW-WE GOTTA GIT PORE MISTAH WOLF HOME!!
795 1-21
AH CAIN'T DRIVE TH' CAR-BUT AH'LL CARRY HIM-AH-H-HE'S REGAININ' CONSHUSNESS!
IT-WAS M-MY ONE WEAKNESS-I H-HAVE A SUPER-SENSITIVE NASAL PASSAGE!!
Al Capp
YO'LL BE ALL RIGHT-JEST TAKE A DEEP BREATH-
SURE-
SNIFF-F-F
ULP!
HE DONE FAINTED AGIN!

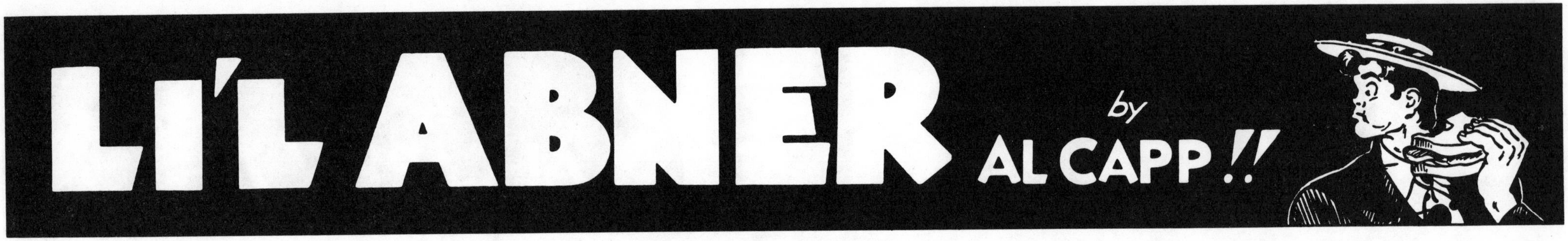
LI'L ABNER
by
AL CAPP!!

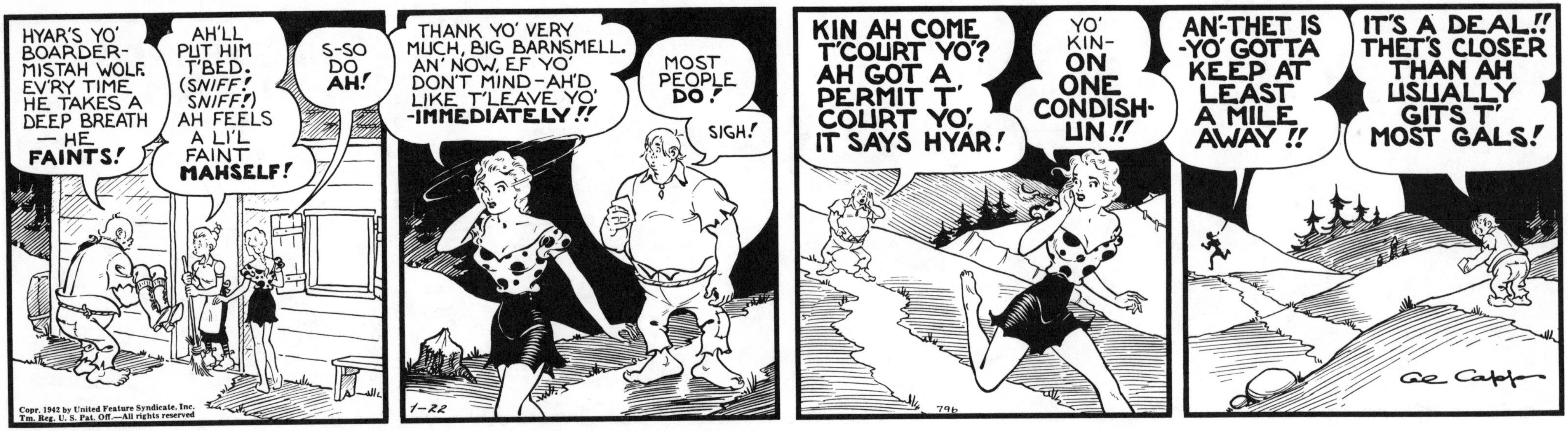
HYAR'S YO' BOARDER- MISTAH WOLF. EV'RY TIME HE TAKES A DEEP BREATH — HE FAINTS!
AH'LL PUT HIM T'BED. (SNIFF! SNIFF!) AH FEELS A LI'L FAINT MAHSELF!
S-SO DO AH!
Copr. 1942 by United Feature Syndicate, Inc. Tm. Reg. U. S. Pat. Off.—All rights reserved
THANK YO' VERY MUCH, BIG BARNSMELL. AN' NOW, EF YO' DON'T MIND - AH'D LIKE T'LEAVE YO' - IMMEDIATELY!!
MOST PEOPLE DO!
SIGH!
1-22
KIN AH COME T'COURT YO'? AH GOT A PERMIT T' COURT YO', IT SAYS HYAR!
YO' KIN - ON ONE CONDISH-UN!!
796
AN'-THET IS -YO' GOTTA KEEP AT LEAST A MILE AWAY!!
IT'S A DEAL!! THET'S CLOSER THAN AH USUALLY GITS T' MOST GALS!
Al Capp

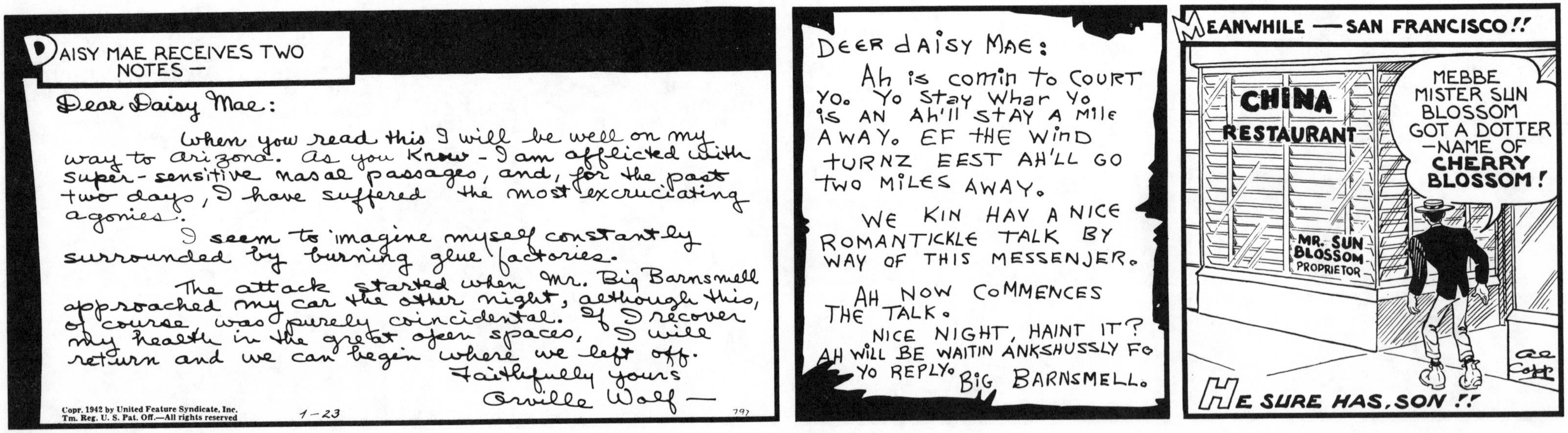
DAISY MAE RECEIVES TWO NOTES —
Dear Daisy Mae:
When you read this I will be well on my way to Arizona. As you know - I am afflicted with super-sensitive nasal passages, and, for the past two days, I have suffered the most excruciating agonies.
I seem to imagine myself constantly surrounded by burning glue factories.
The attack started when Mr. Big Barnsmell approached my car the other night, although this, of course, was purely coincidental. If I recover my health in the great open spaces, I will return and we can begin where we left off.
Faithfully yours
Orville Wolf —
Copr. 1942 by United Feature Syndicate, Inc. Tm. Reg. U. S. Pat. Off.—All rights reserved
1-23
797
DEER DAISY MAE:
Ah is comin to COURT YO. YO Stay Whar YO is AN AH'LL STAY A MILE AWAY. EF THE WIND TURNZ EEST AH'LL GO TWO MILES AWAY.
WE KIN HAV A NICE ROMANTICKLE TALK BY WAY OF THIS MESSENJER.
AH NOW COMMENCES THE TALK.
NICE NIGHT, HAINT IT?
AH WILL BE WAITIN ANKSHUSSLY FO YO REPLY. BIG BARNSMELL.
MEANWHILE — SAN FRANCISCO!!
CHINA RESTAURANT
MEBBE MISTER SUN BLOSSOM GOT A DOTTER - NAME OF CHERRY BLOSSOM!
MR. SUN BLOSSOM PROPRIETOR
Al Capp
HE SURE HAS, SON!!

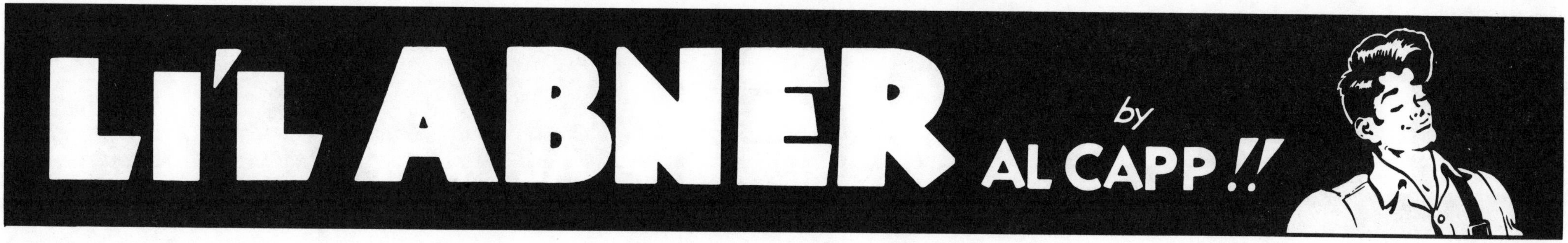
LI'L ABNER
by
AL CAPP!!

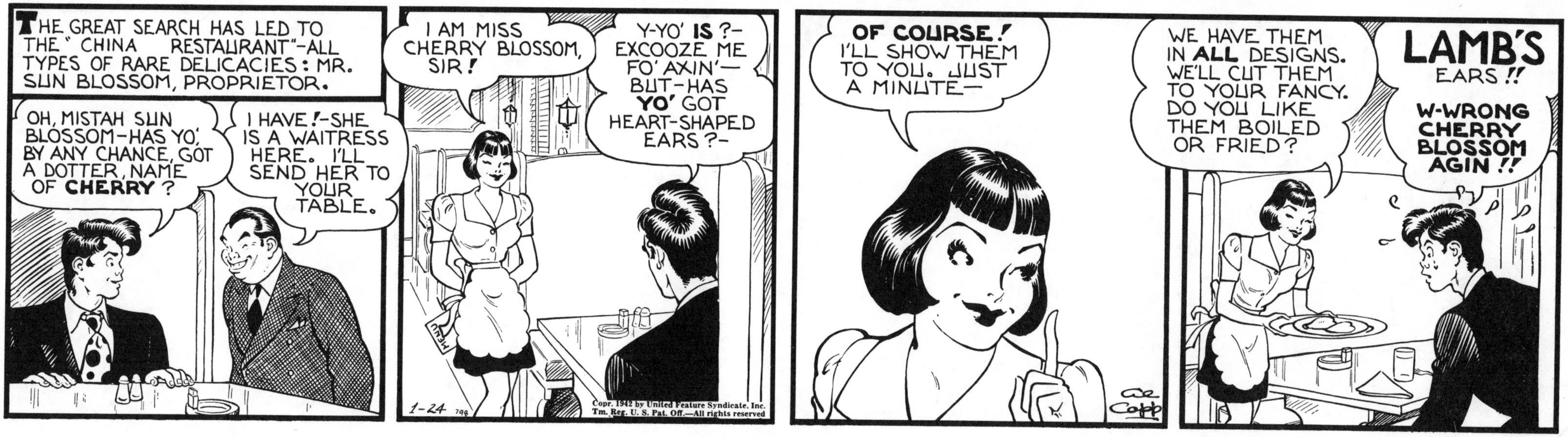
THE GREAT SEARCH HAS LED TO THE "CHINA RESTAURANT"-ALL TYPES OF RARE DELICACIES: MR. SUN BLOSSOM, PROPRIETOR.
OH, MISTAH SUN BLOSSOM-HAS YO', BY ANY CHANCE, GOT A DOTTER, NAME OF CHERRY?
I HAVE!-SHE IS A WAITRESS HERE. I'LL SEND HER TO YOUR TABLE.
I AM MISS CHERRY BLOSSOM, SIR!
Y-YO' IS?-EXCOOZE ME FO' AXIN'-BUT-HAS YO' GOT HEART-SHAPED EARS?-
MENU
1-24
Copr. 1942 by United Feature Syndicate, Inc. Tm. Reg. U. S. Pat. Off.—All rights reserved
OF COURSE! I'LL SHOW THEM TO YOU. JUST A MINUTE—
Al Capp
WE HAVE THEM IN ALL DESIGNS. WE'LL CUT THEM TO YOUR FANCY. DO YOU LIKE THEM BOILED OR FRIED?
LAMB'S EARS!!
W-WRONG CHERRY BLOSSOM AGIN!!

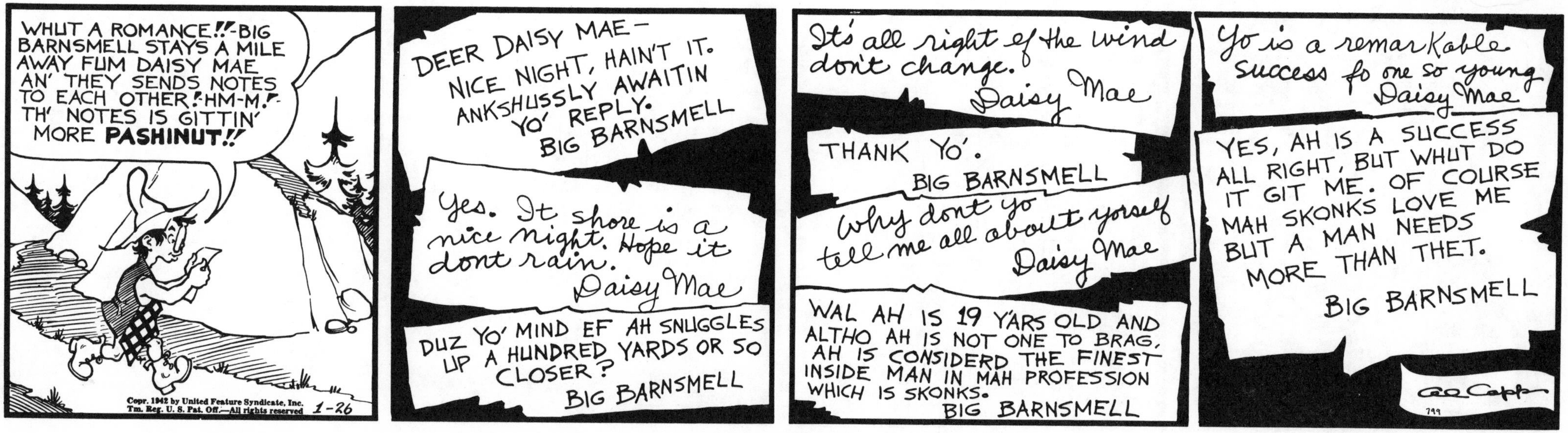
WHUT A ROMANCE!!-BIG BARNSMELL STAYS A MILE AWAY FUM DAISY MAE AN' THEY SENDS NOTES TO EACH OTHER!-HM-M!-TH' NOTES IS GITTIN' MORE PASHINUT!!
Copr. 1942 by United Feature Syndicate, Inc. Tm. Reg. U. S. Pat. Off.—All rights reserved
1-26
DEER DAISY MAE—NICE NIGHT, HAIN'T IT. ANKSHUSSLY AWAITIN YO' REPLY. BIG BARNSMELL
Yes. It shore is a nice night. Hope it dont rain. Daisy Mae
DUZ YO' MIND EF AH SNUGGLES UP A HUNDRED YARDS OR SO CLOSER? BIG BARNSMELL
It's all right ef the wind don't change. Daisy Mae
THANK YO'. BIG BARNSMELL
Why dont yo tell me all about yorself Daisy Mae
WAL AH IS 19 YARS OLD AND ALTHO AH IS NOT ONE TO BRAG, AH IS CONSIDERD THE FINEST INSIDE MAN IN MAH PROFESSION WHICH IS SKONKS. BIG BARNSMELL
Yo is a remarkable success fo one so young Daisy Mae
YES, AH IS A SUCCESS ALL RIGHT, BUT WHUT DO IT GIT ME. OF COURSE MAH SKONKS LOVE ME BUT A MAN NEEDS MORE THAN THET. BIG BARNSMELL
Al Capp

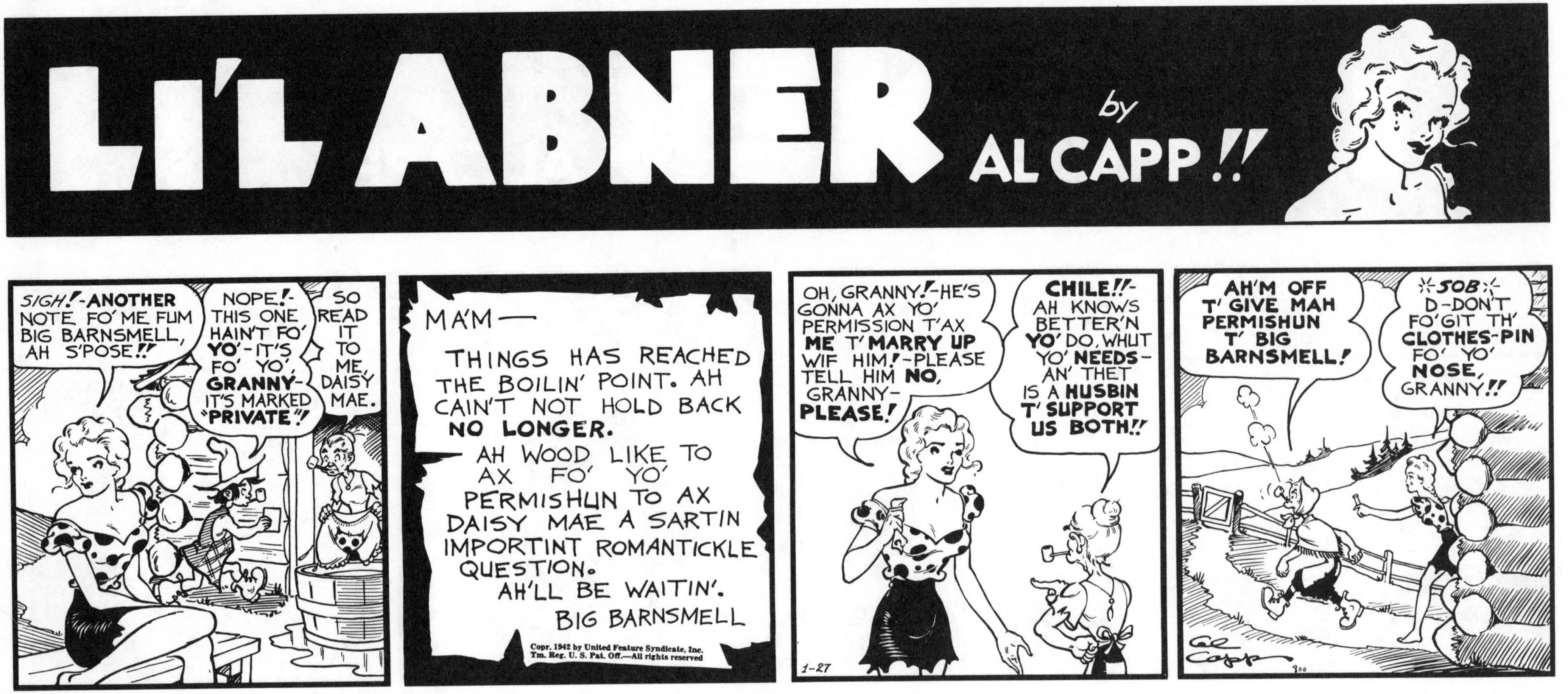

LI'L ABNER
by AL CAPP!!
SIGH!-ANOTHER NOTE FO' ME FUM BIG BARNSMELL, AH S'POSE!!
NOPE!-THIS ONE HAIN'T FO' YO'-IT'S FO' YO' GRANNY-IT'S MARKED "PRIVATE"!!
SO READ IT TO ME, DAISY MAE.
MA'M—
THINGS HAS REACHED THE BOILIN' POINT. AH CAIN'T NOT HOLD BACK NO LONGER.
AH WOOD LIKE TO AX FO' YO' PERMISHUN TO AX DAISY MAE A SARTIN IMPORTINT ROMANTICKLE QUESTION.
AH'LL BE WAITIN'.
BIG BARNSMELL
Copr. 1942 by United Feature Syndicate, Inc. Tm. Reg. U. S. Pat. Off.—All rights reserved
OH, GRANNY!-HE'S GONNA AX YO' PERMISSION T'AX ME T'MARRY UP WIF HIM!-PLEASE TELL HIM NO, GRANNY-PLEASE!
CHILE!!-AH KNOWS BETTER'N YO' DO, WHUT YO' NEEDS-AN' THET IS A HUSBIN T' SUPPORT US BOTH!!
1-27
AH'M OFF T' GIVE MAH PERMISHUN T' BIG BARNSMELL!
SOB D-DON'T FO'GIT TH' CLOTHES-PIN FO' YO' NOSE, GRANNY!!
Al Capp

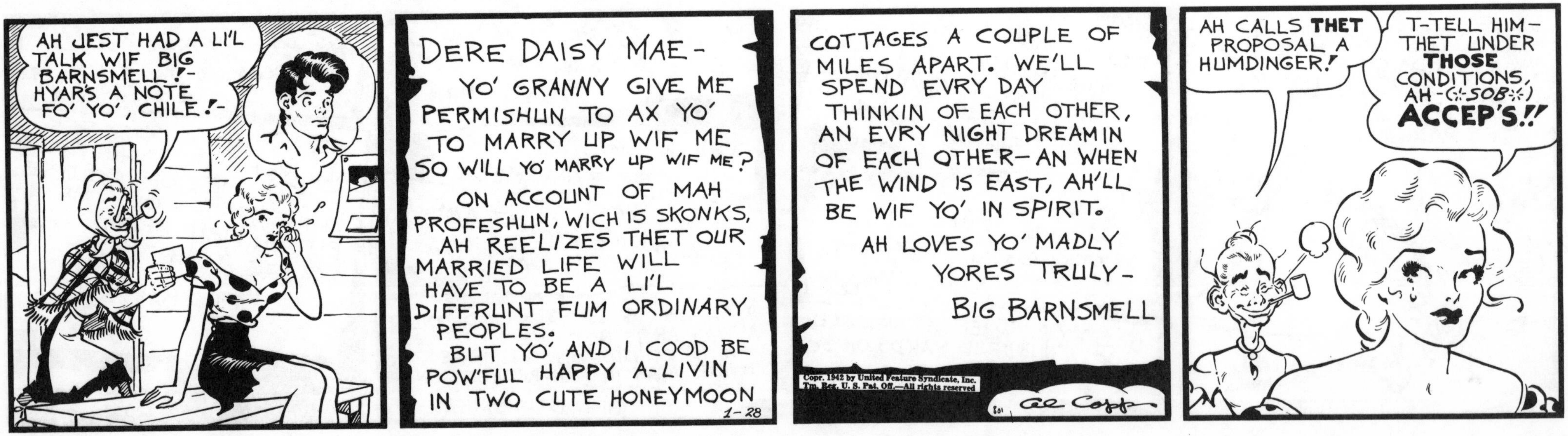

AH JEST HAD A LI'L TALK WIF BIG BARNSMELL!-HYAR'S A NOTE FO' YO', CHILE!-
DERE DAISY MAE-
YO' GRANNY GIVE ME PERMISHUN TO AX YO' TO MARRY UP WIF ME SO WILL YO' MARRY UP WIF ME?
ON ACCOUNT OF MAH PROFESHUN, WICH IS SKONKS, AH REELIZES THET OUR MARRIED LIFE WILL HAVE TO BE A LI'L DIFFRUNT FUM ORDINARY PEOPLES.
BUT YO' AND I COOD BE POW'FUL HAPPY A-LIVIN IN TWO CUTE HONEYMOON
1-28
COTTAGES A COUPLE OF MILES APART. WE'LL SPEND EVRY DAY THINKIN OF EACH OTHER, AN EVRY NIGHT DREAMIN OF EACH OTHER-AN WHEN THE WIND IS EAST, AH'LL BE WIF YO' IN SPIRIT.
AH LOVES YO' MADLY
YORES TRULY-
BIG BARNSMELL
Copr. 1942 by United Feature Syndicate, Inc. Tm. Reg. U. S. Pat. Off.—All rights reserved
Al Capp
AH CALLS THET PROPOSAL A HUMDINGER!
T-TELL HIM-THET UNDER THOSE CONDITIONS, AH-(SOB) ACCEP'S!!

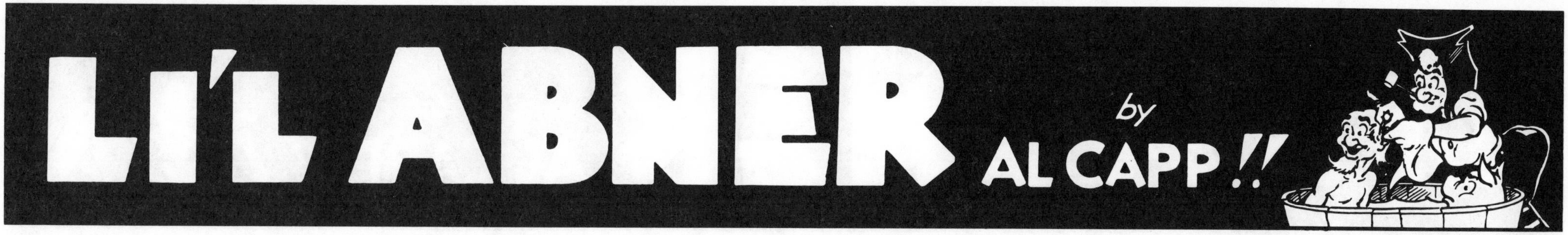

LI'L ABNER
by
AL CAPP!!

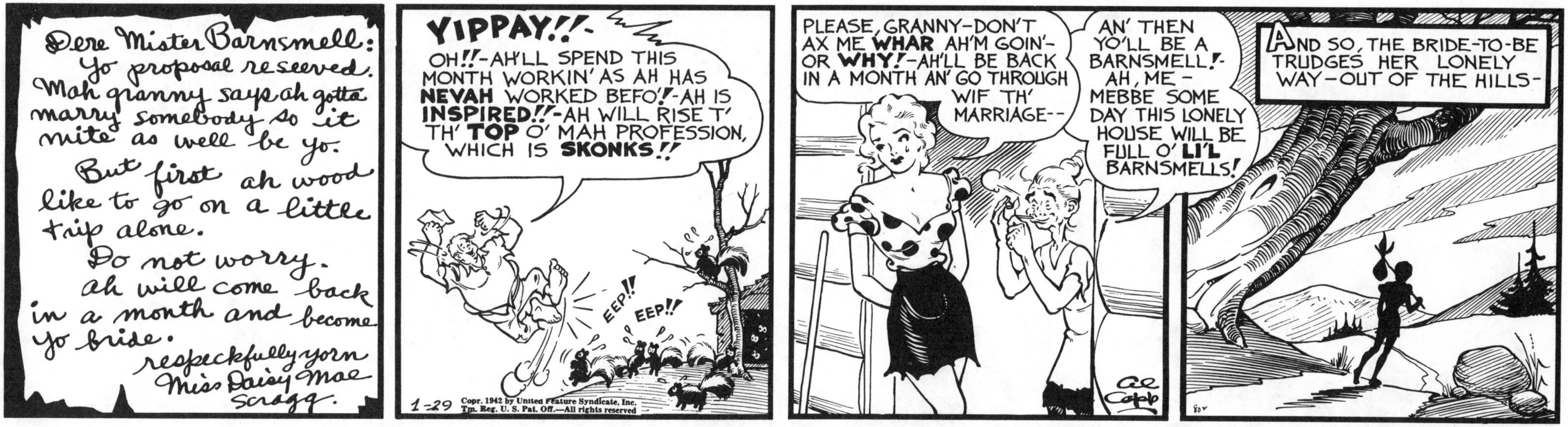

Dere Mister Barnsmell: Yo proposal reseeved. Mah granny says ah gotta marry somebody so it mite as well be yo. But first ah wood like to go on a little trip alone. Do not worry. ah will come back in a month and become yo bride. respeckfully yorn Miss Daisy Mae Scragg.
YIPPAY!!-
OH!!-AH'LL SPEND THIS MONTH WORKIN' AS AH HAS **NEVAH** WORKED BEFO'!-AH IS **INSPIRED!!**-AH WILL RISE T' TH' **TOP** O' MAH PROFESSION, WHICH IS **SKONKS!!**
EEP!!
EEP!!
1-29
Copr. 1942 by United Feature Syndicate, Inc. Tm. Reg. U. S. Pat. Off.—All rights reserved
PLEASE, GRANNY-DON'T AX ME **WHAR** AH'M GOIN'-OR **WHY!**-AH'LL BE BACK IN A MONTH AN' GO THROUGH WIF TH' MARRIAGE--
AN' THEN YO'LL BE A BARNSMELL!-AH, ME-MEBBE SOME DAY THIS LONELY HOUSE WILL BE FULL O' **LI'L** BARNSMELLS!
Al Capp
AND SO, THE BRIDE-TO-BE TRUDGES HER LONELY WAY-OUT OF THE HILLS-

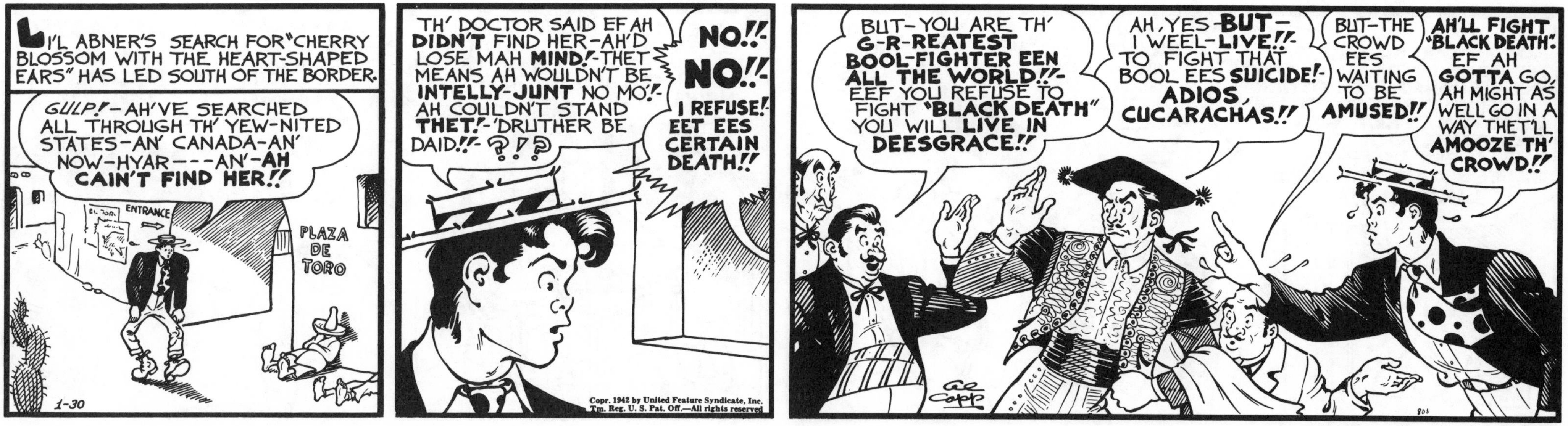

LI'L ABNER'S SEARCH FOR "CHERRY BLOSSOM WITH THE HEART-SHAPED EARS" HAS LED SOUTH OF THE BORDER.
GULP!-AH'VE SEARCHED ALL THROUGH TH' YEW-NITED STATES-AN' CANADA-AN' NOW-HYAR---AN'-**AH CAIN'T FIND HER!!**
ENTRANCE
PLAZA DE TORO
1-30
TH' DOCTOR SAID EF AH **DIDN'T** FIND HER-AH'D LOSE MAH **MIND!**-THET MEANS AH WOULDN'T BE **INTELLY-JUNT** NO MO'!-AH COULDN'T STAND **THET!**-'DRUTHER BE DAID!!-?!?
NO!!-
NO!!-
I REFUSE!-EET EES CERTAIN DEATH!!
Copr. 1942 by United Feature Syndicate, Inc. Tm. Reg. U. S. Pat. Off.—All rights reserved
BUT-YOU ARE TH' **G-R-REATEST BOOL-FIGHTER EEN ALL THE WORLD!!**-EEF YOU REFUSE TO FIGHT **"BLACK DEATH"** YOU WILL **LIVE IN DEESGRACE!!**
AH, YES-**BUT**-I WEEL-**LIVE!!**-TO FIGHT THAT BOOL EES **SUICIDE!**-**ADIOS, CUCARACHAS!!**
BUT-THE CROWD EES WAITING TO BE **AMUSED!!**
AH'LL FIGHT "BLACK DEATH"! EF AH **GOTTA** GO, AH MIGHT AS WELL GO IN A WAY THET'LL **AMOOZE TH' CROWD!!**
Al Capp

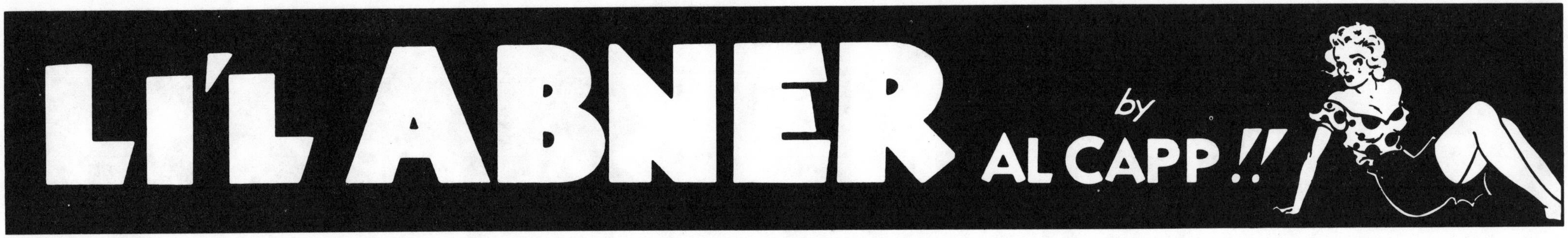
LI'L ABNER
by
AL CAPP !!

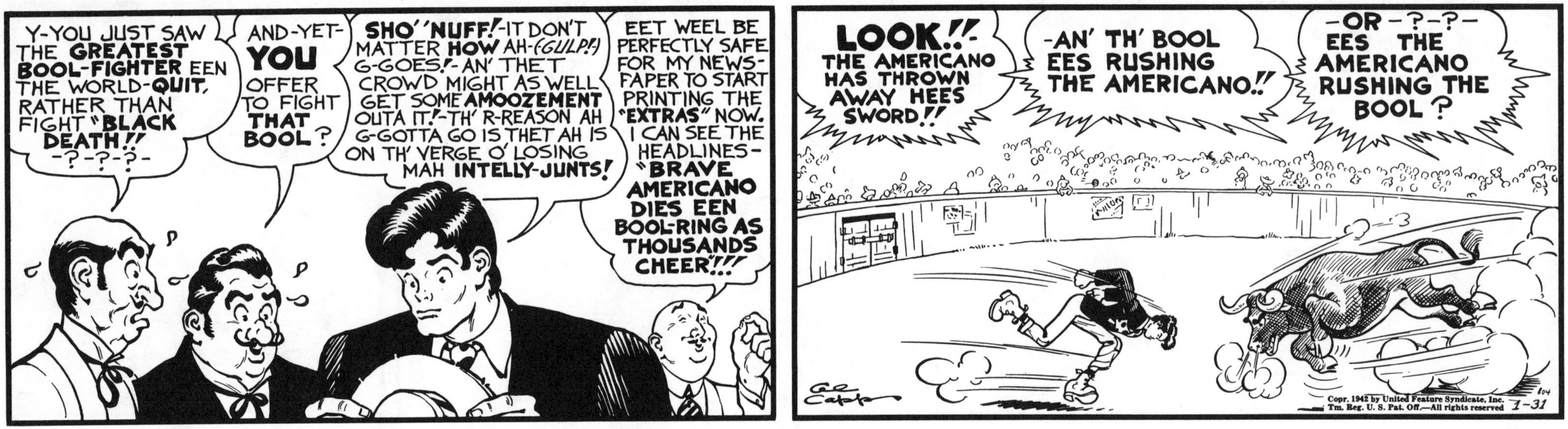
Y-YOU JUST SAW THE GREATEST BOOL-FIGHTER EEN THE WORLD-QUIT, RATHER THAN FIGHT "BLACK DEATH!!" -?-?-?-
AND-YET- YOU OFFER TO FIGHT THAT BOOL?
SHO' 'NUFF!-IT DON'T MATTER HOW AH-(GULP!) G-GOES!-AN' THET CROWD MIGHT AS WELL GET SOME AMOOZEMENT OUTA IT!-TH' R-REASON AH G-GOTTA GO IS THET AH IS ON TH' VERGE O' LOSING MAH INTELLY-JUNTS!
EET WEEL BE PERFECTLY SAFE FOR MY NEWS-PAPER TO START PRINTING THE "EXTRAS" NOW. I CAN SEE THE HEADLINES- "BRAVE AMERICANO DIES EEN BOOL-RING AS THOUSANDS CHEER"!!!
LOOK!!- THE AMERICANO HAS THROWN AWAY HEES SWORD!!
-AN' TH' BOOL EES RUSHING THE AMERICANO!!
-OR-?-?- EES THE AMERICANO RUSHING THE BOOL?
Copr. 1942 by United Feature Syndicate, Inc. Tm. Reg. U. S. Pat. Off.—All rights reserved
804
1-31

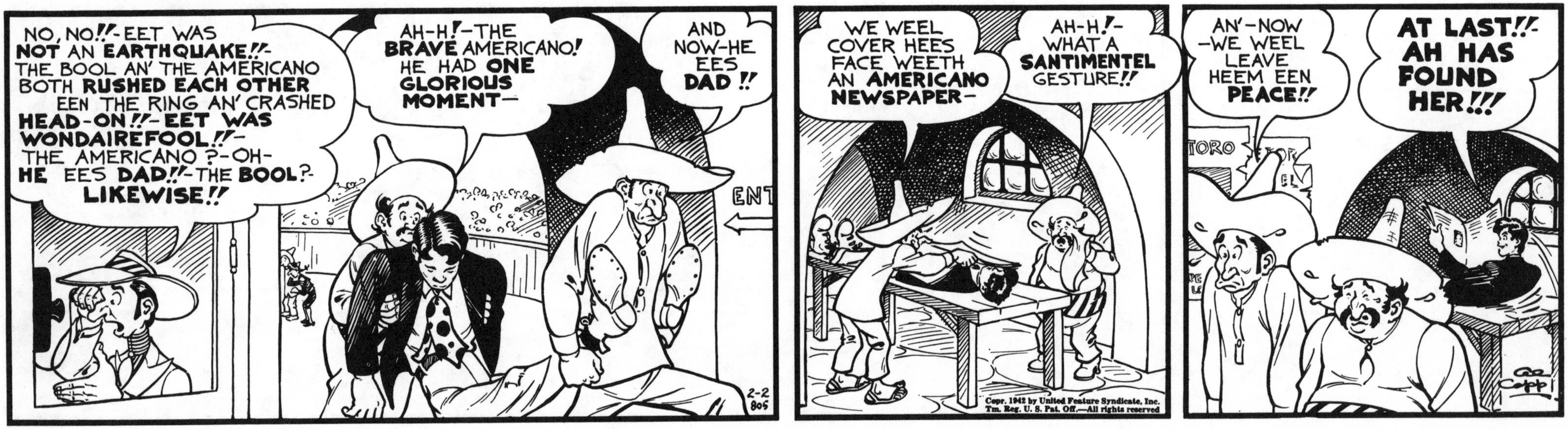
NO, NO!!-EET WAS NOT AN EARTHQUAKE!!- THE BOOL AN' THE AMERICANO BOTH RUSHED EACH OTHER EEN THE RING AN' CRASHED HEAD-ON!!-EET WAS WONDAIREFOOL!!- THE AMERICANO?-OH- HE EES DAD!!-THE BOOL?- LIKEWISE!!
AH-H!-THE BRAVE AMERICANO! HE HAD ONE GLORIOUS MOMENT-
AND NOW-HE EES DAD!!
ENT
2-2
805
WE WEEL COVER HEES FACE WEETH AN AMERICANO NEWSPAPER-
AH-H!- WHAT A SANTIMENTEL GESTURE!!
Copr. 1942 by United Feature Syndicate, Inc. Tm. Reg. U. S. Pat. Off.—All rights reserved
AN'-NOW -WE WEEL LEAVE HEEM EEN PEACE!!
AT LAST!!- AH HAS FOUND HER!!!
TORO

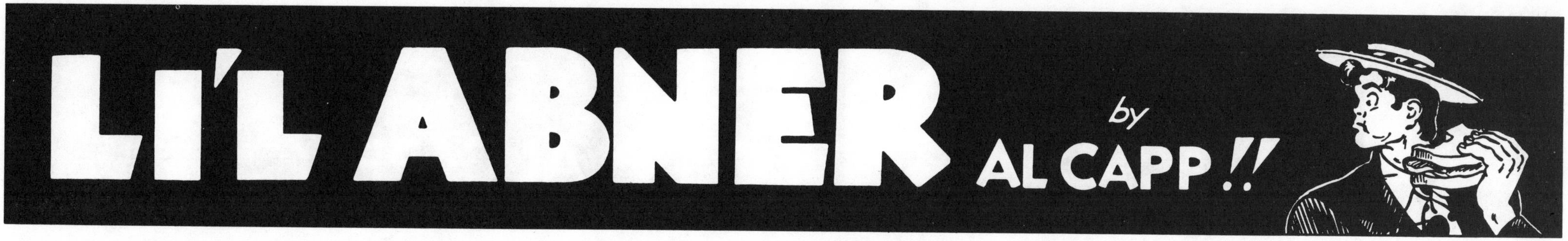
LI'L ABNER
by
AL CAPP !!

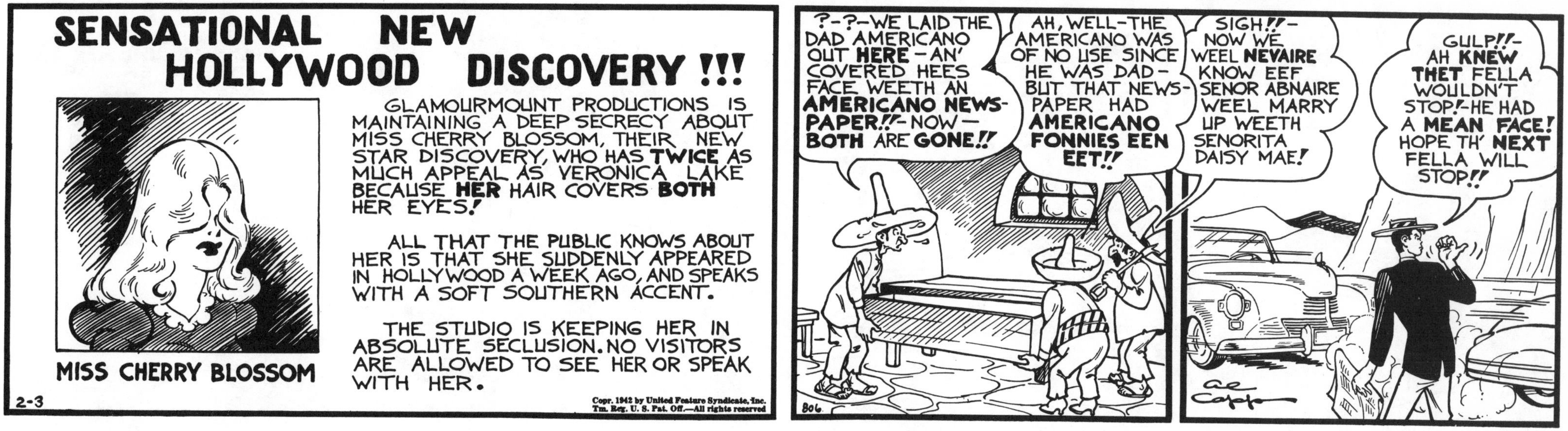
SENSATIONAL NEW HOLLYWOOD DISCOVERY !!!
GLAMOURMOUNT PRODUCTIONS IS MAINTAINING A DEEP SECRECY ABOUT MISS CHERRY BLOSSOM, THEIR NEW STAR DISCOVERY, WHO HAS TWICE AS MUCH APPEAL AS VERONICA LAKE BECAUSE HER HAIR COVERS BOTH HER EYES!
ALL THAT THE PUBLIC KNOWS ABOUT HER IS THAT SHE SUDDENLY APPEARED IN HOLLYWOOD A WEEK AGO, AND SPEAKS WITH A SOFT SOUTHERN ACCENT.
THE STUDIO IS KEEPING HER IN ABSOLUTE SECLUSION. NO VISITORS ARE ALLOWED TO SEE HER OR SPEAK WITH HER.
MISS CHERRY BLOSSOM
2-3
Copr. 1942 by United Feature Syndicate, Inc. Tm. Reg. U. S. Pat. Off.—All rights reserved
?-?-WE LAID THE DAD AMERICANO OUT HERE—AN' COVERED HEES FACE WEETH AN AMERICANO NEWS-PAPER!!-NOW—BOTH ARE GONE!!
AH, WELL-THE AMERICANO WAS OF NO USE SINCE HE WAS DAD-BUT THAT NEWS-PAPER HAD AMERICANO FONNIES EEN EET!!
806
SIGH!!-NOW WE WEEL NEVAIRE KNOW EEF SENOR ABNAIRE WEEL MARRY UP WEETH SENORITA DAISY MAE!
GULP!!-AH KNEW THET FELLA WOULDN'T STOP!-HE HAD A MEAN FACE! HOPE TH' NEXT FELLA WILL STOP!!
AL CAPP

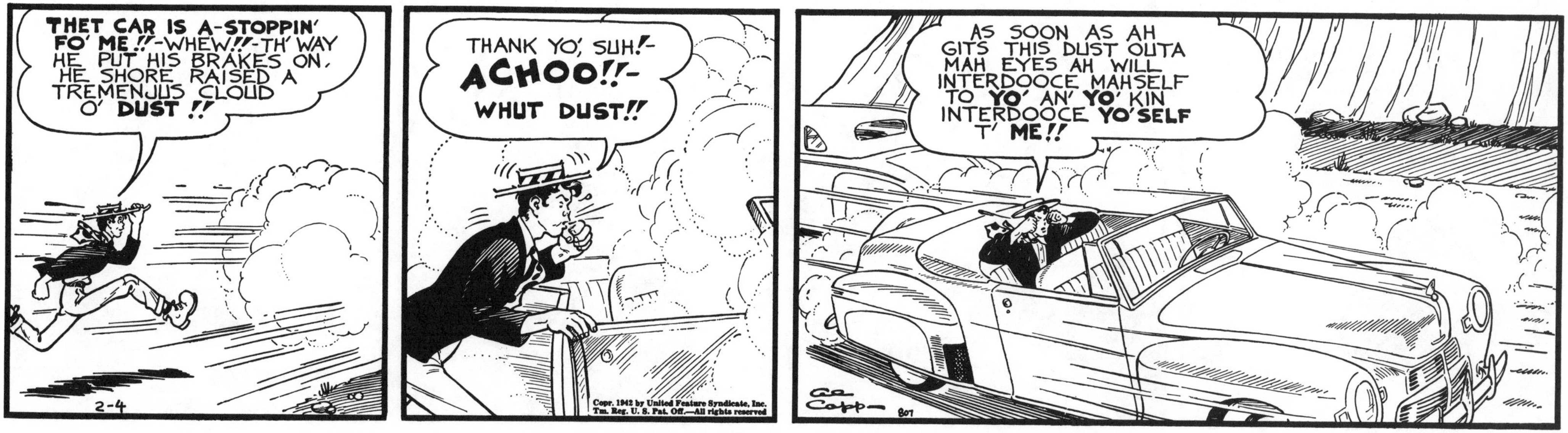
THET CAR IS A-STOPPIN' FO' ME!!-WHEW!!-TH' WAY HE PUT HIS BRAKES ON, HE SHORE RAISED A TREMENJUS CLOUD O' DUST!!
2-4
THANK YO', SUH!-ACHOO!!-WHUT DUST!!
Copr. 1942 by United Feature Syndicate, Inc. Tm. Reg. U. S. Pat. Off.—All rights reserved
AS SOON AS AH GITS THIS DUST OUTA MAH EYES AH WILL INTERDOOCE MAHSELF TO YO' AN' YO' KIN INTERDOOCE YO'SELF T' ME!!
AL CAPP
807

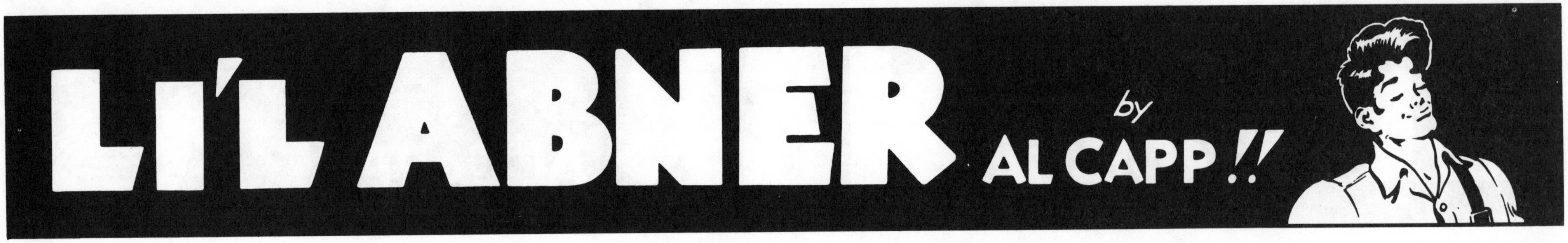
LI'L ABNER
by
AL CAPP!!

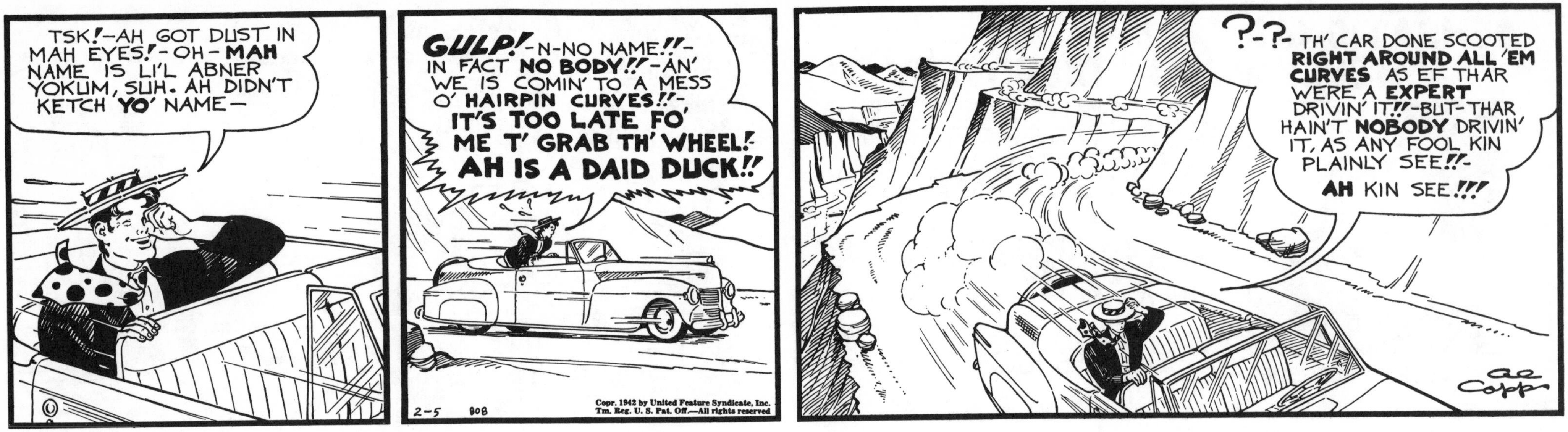
TSK!-AH GOT DUST IN MAH EYES!-OH-MAH NAME IS LI'L ABNER YOKUM, SUH. AH DIDN'T KETCH 'YO' NAME—
GULP!-N-NO NAME!!-IN FACT NO BODY!!-AN' WE IS COMIN' TO A MESS O' HAIRPIN CURVES!!-
IT'S TOO LATE FO' ME T' GRAB TH' WHEEL!-AH IS A DAID DUCK!!
2-5
808
Copr. 1942 by United Feature Syndicate, Inc. Tm. Reg. U. S. Pat. Off.—All rights reserved
?-?-TH' CAR DONE SCOOTED RIGHT AROUND ALL 'EM CURVES AS EF THAR WERE A EXPERT DRIVIN' IT!!-BUT-THAR HAIN'T NOBODY DRIVIN' IT, AS ANY FOOL KIN PLAINLY SEE!!-
AH KIN SEE!!!
Al Capp

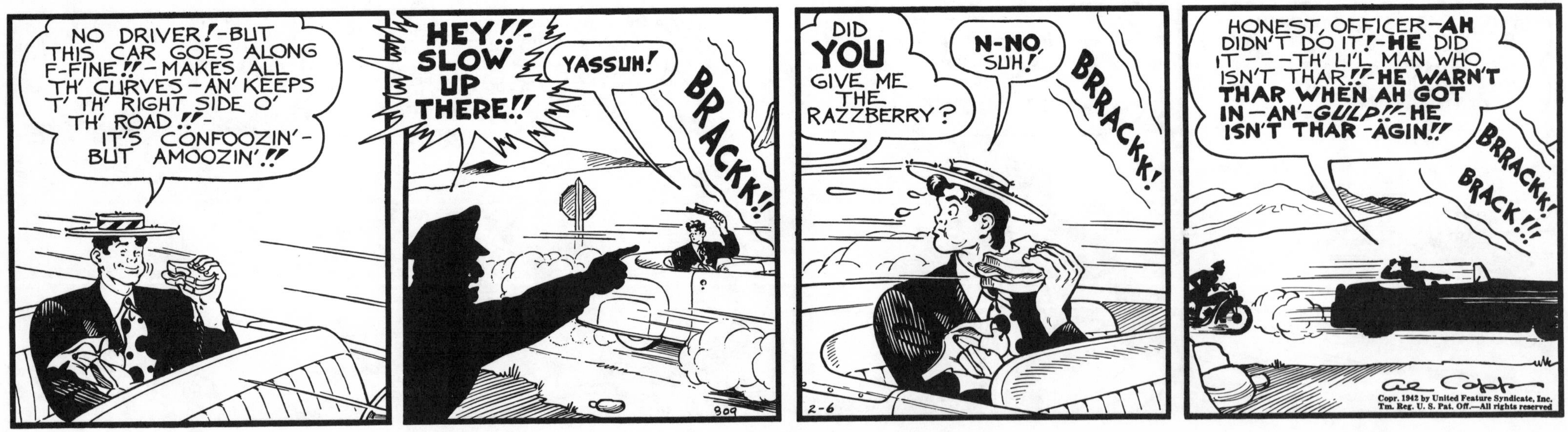
NO DRIVER!-BUT THIS CAR GOES ALONG F-FINE!!-MAKES ALL TH' CURVES-AN' KEEPS T' TH' RIGHT SIDE O' TH' ROAD!!-IT'S CONFOOZIN'-BUT AMOOZIN'!!
HEY!!-SLOW UP THERE!!
YASSUH!
BRACKK!!
809
DID YOU GIVE ME THE RAZZBERRY?
N-NO SUH!
BRRACKK!
2-6
HONEST, OFFICER-AH DIDN'T DO IT!-HE DID IT---TH' LI'L MAN WHO ISN'T THAR!!-HE WARN'T THAR WHEN AH GOT IN-AN'-GULP!!-HE ISN'T THAR-AGIN!!
BRRACKK!
BRACK!!!
Al Capp
Copr. 1942 by United Feature Syndicate, Inc. Tm. Reg. U. S. Pat. Off.—All rights reserved

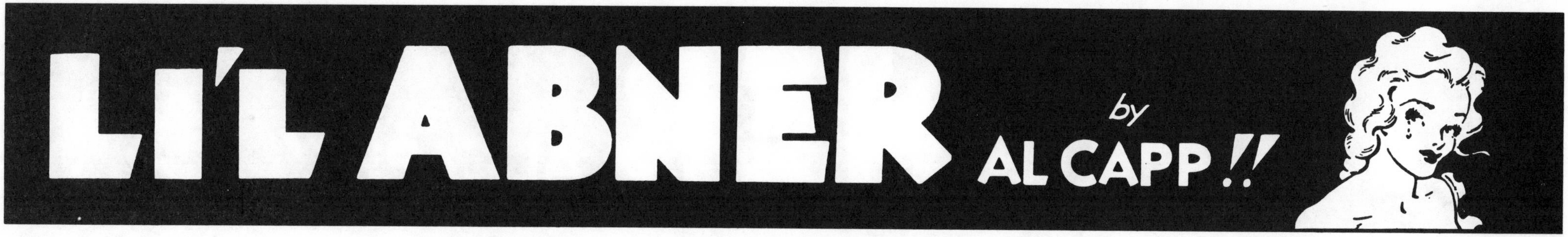
LI'L ABNER
by
AL CAPP!!

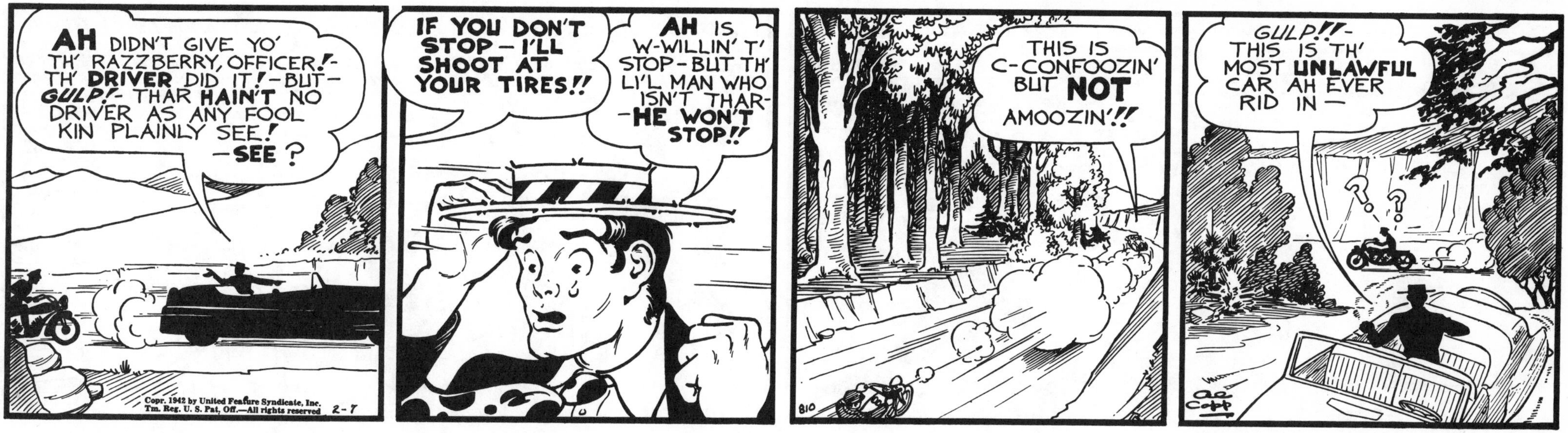
AH DIDN'T GIVE YO' TH' RAZZBERRY, OFFICER!- TH' DRIVER DID IT!- BUT- GULP!- THAR HAIN'T NO DRIVER AS ANY FOOL KIN PLAINLY SEE! -SEE ?
Copr. 1942 by United Feature Syndicate, Inc. Tm. Reg. U. S. Pat. Off.—All rights reserved 2-7
IF YOU DON'T STOP – I'LL SHOOT AT YOUR TIRES!!
AH IS W-WILLIN' T' STOP- BUT TH' LI'L MAN WHO ISN'T THAR- -HE WON'T STOP!!
THIS IS C-CONFOOZIN' BUT NOT AMOOZIN'!!
GULP!!- THIS IS TH' MOST UNLAWFUL CAR AH EVER RID IN –

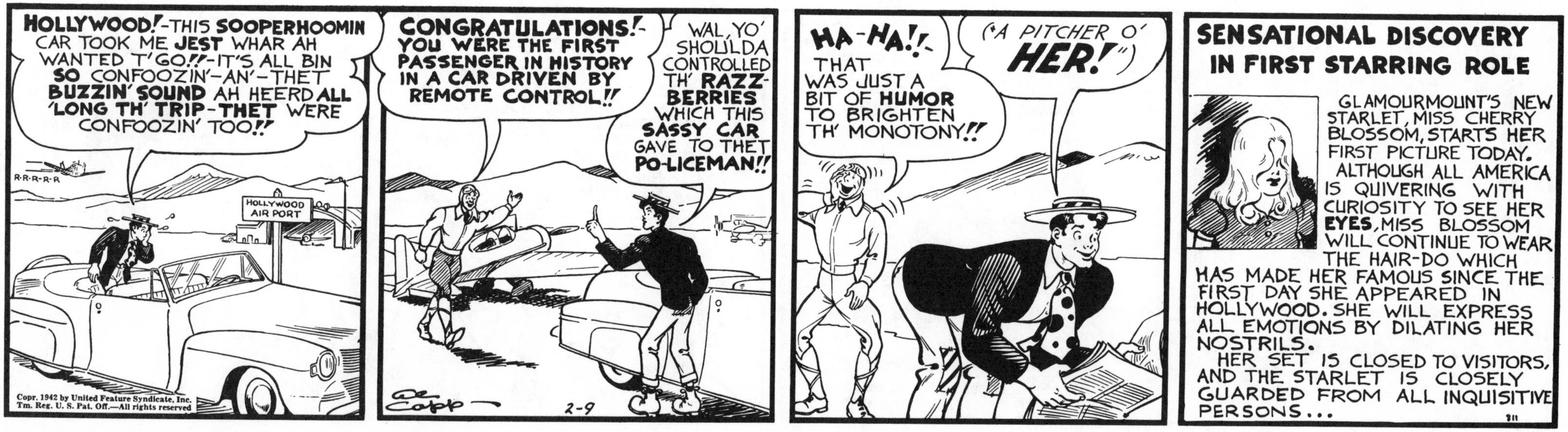
HOLLYWOOD!-THIS SOOPERHOOMIN CAR TOOK ME JEST WHAR AH WANTED T'GO!!-IT'S ALL BIN SO CONFOOZIN'-AN'-THET BUZZIN' SOUND AH HEERD ALL 'LONG TH' TRIP-THET WERE CONFOOZIN' TOO!!
R-R-R-R-R
HOLLYWOOD AIR PORT
Copr. 1942 by United Feature Syndicate, Inc. Tm. Reg. U. S. Pat. Off.—All rights reserved
CONGRATULATIONS!- YOU WERE THE FIRST PASSENGER IN HISTORY IN A CAR DRIVEN BY REMOTE CONTROL!!
WAL, YO' SHOULDA CONTROLLED TH' RAZZ-BERRIES WHICH THIS SASSY CAR GAVE TO THET PO-LICEMAN!!
2-9
HA-HA!!- THAT WAS JUST A BIT OF HUMOR TO BRIGHTEN TH' MONOTONY!!
("A PITCHER O' HER!")
SENSATIONAL DISCOVERY IN FIRST STARRING ROLE
GLAMOURMOUNT'S NEW STARLET, MISS CHERRY BLOSSOM, STARTS HER FIRST PICTURE TODAY.
ALTHOUGH ALL AMERICA IS QUIVERING WITH CURIOSITY TO SEE HER EYES, MISS BLOSSOM WILL CONTINUE TO WEAR THE HAIR-DO WHICH HAS MADE HER FAMOUS SINCE THE FIRST DAY SHE APPEARED IN HOLLYWOOD. SHE WILL EXPRESS ALL EMOTIONS BY DILATING HER NOSTRILS.
HER SET IS CLOSED TO VISITORS, AND THE STARLET IS CLOSELY GUARDED FROM ALL INQUISITIVE PERSONS...

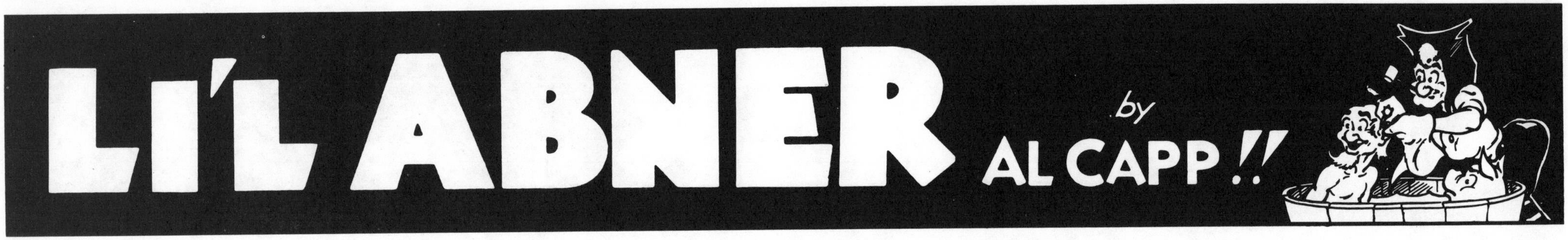

LI'L ABNER
by AL CAPP!!

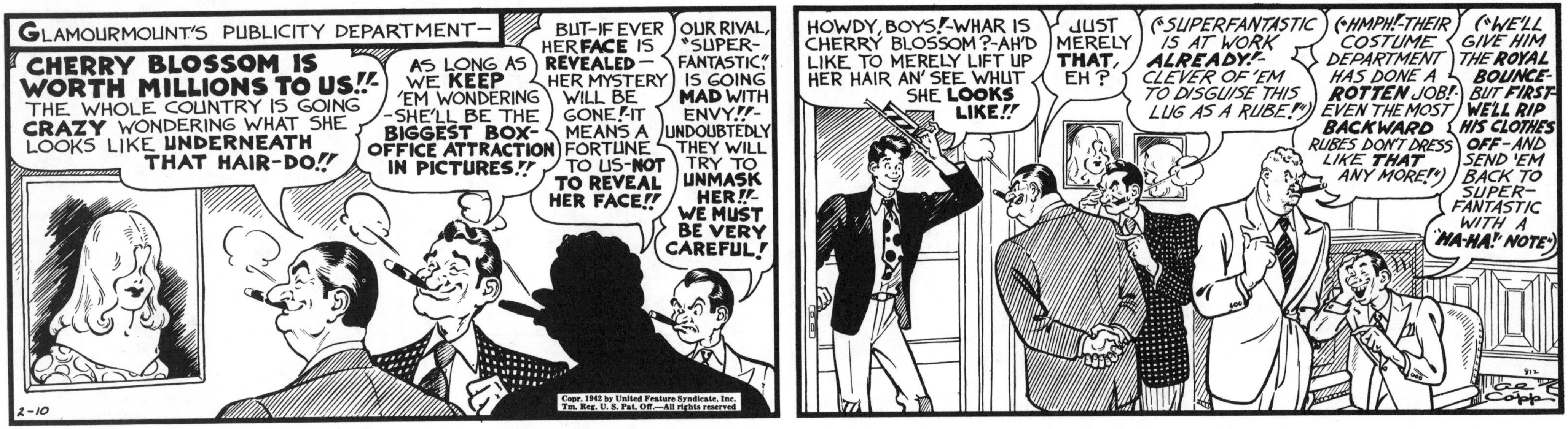

GLAMOURMOUNT'S PUBLICITY DEPARTMENT–
CHERRY BLOSSOM IS WORTH MILLIONS TO US!!-THE WHOLE COUNTRY IS GOING CRAZY WONDERING WHAT SHE LOOKS LIKE UNDERNEATH THAT HAIR-DO!!
AS LONG AS WE KEEP 'EM WONDERING -SHE'LL BE THE BIGGEST BOX-OFFICE ATTRACTION IN PICTURES!!
BUT-IF EVER HER FACE IS REVEALED – HER MYSTERY WILL BE GONE!-IT MEANS A FORTUNE TO US-NOT TO REVEAL HER FACE!!
OUR RIVAL, "SUPER-FANTASTIC," IS GOING MAD WITH ENVY!!-UNDOUBTEDLY THEY WILL TRY TO UNMASK HER!!-WE MUST BE VERY CAREFUL!
2-10
Copr. 1942 by United Feature Syndicate, Inc.
Tm. Reg. U. S. Pat. Off.—All rights reserved
HOWDY, BOYS!-WHAR IS CHERRY BLOSSOM?-AH'D LIKE TO MERELY LIFT UP HER HAIR AN' SEE WHUT SHE LOOKS LIKE!!
JUST MERELY THAT, EH?
("SUPERFANTASTIC IS AT WORK ALREADY!-CLEVER OF 'EM TO DISGUISE THIS LUG AS A RUBE!")
("HMPH!-THEIR COSTUME DEPARTMENT HAS DONE A ROTTEN JOB!-EVEN THE MOST BACKWARD RUBES DON'T DRESS LIKE THAT ANY MORE!")
("WE'LL GIVE HIM THE ROYAL BOUNCE-BUT FIRST-WE'LL RIP HIS CLOTHES OFF-AND SEND 'EM BACK TO SUPER-FANTASTIC WITH A "HA-HA!" NOTE")
AL CAPP

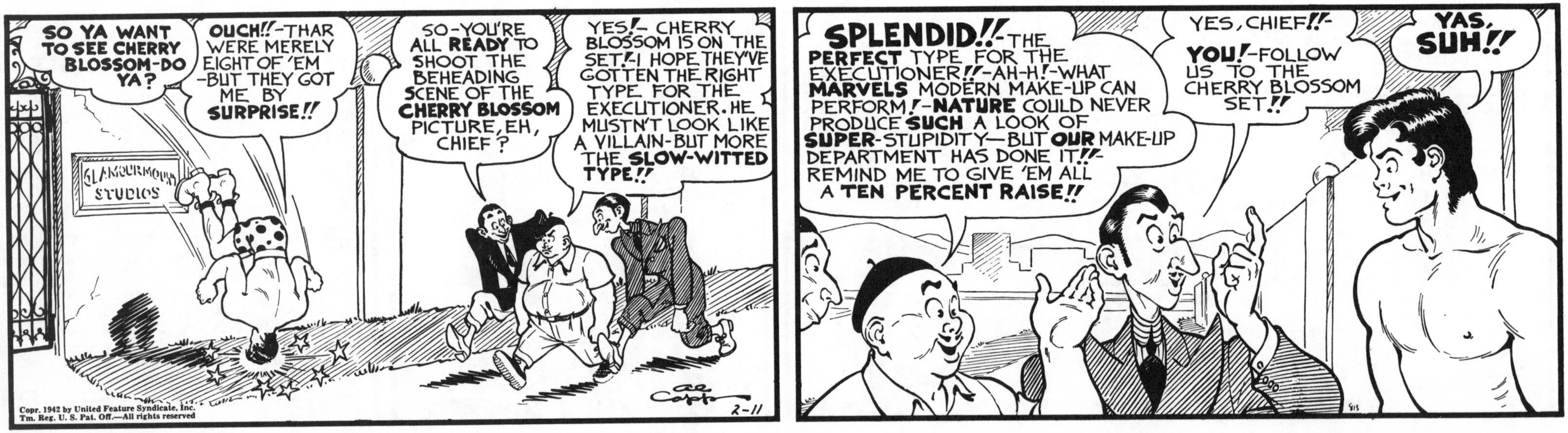

SO YA WANT TO SEE CHERRY BLOSSOM-DO YA?
OUCH!!-THAR WERE MERELY EIGHT OF 'EM -BUT THEY GOT ME BY SURPRISE!!
GLAMOURMOUNT STUDIOS
SO-YOU'RE ALL READY TO SHOOT THE BEHEADING SCENE OF THE CHERRY BLOSSOM PICTURE, EH, CHIEF?
YES!-CHERRY BLOSSOM IS ON THE SET!-I HOPE THEY'VE GOTTEN THE RIGHT TYPE FOR THE EXECUTIONER. HE MUSTN'T LOOK LIKE A VILLAIN-BUT MORE THE SLOW-WITTED TYPE!!
AL CAPP
2-11
Copr. 1942 by United Feature Syndicate, Inc.
Tm. Reg. U. S. Pat. Off.—All rights reserved
SPLENDID!!-THE PERFECT TYPE FOR THE EXECUTIONER!!-AH-H!-WHAT MARVELS MODERN MAKE-UP CAN PERFORM!-NATURE COULD NEVER PRODUCE SUCH A LOOK OF SUPER-STUPIDITY—BUT OUR MAKE-UP DEPARTMENT HAS DONE IT!!-REMIND ME TO GIVE 'EM ALL A TEN PERCENT RAISE!!
YES, CHIEF!!-
YOU!-FOLLOW US TO THE CHERRY BLOSSOM SET!!
YAS, SUH!!

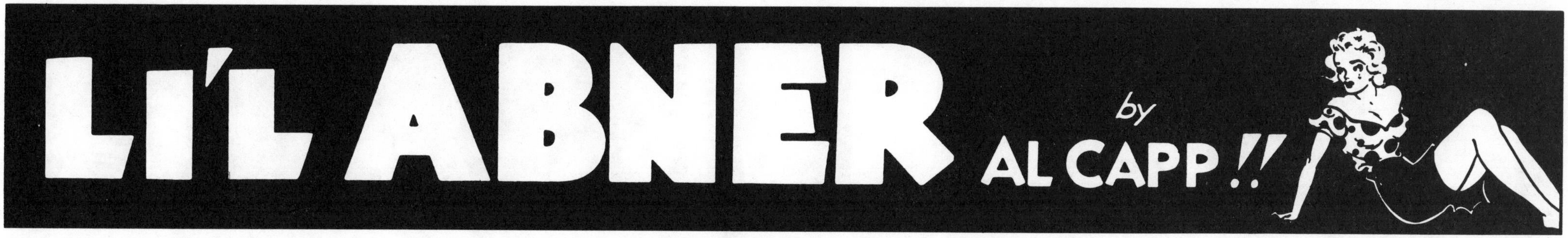

LI'L ABNER
by
AL CAPP!!

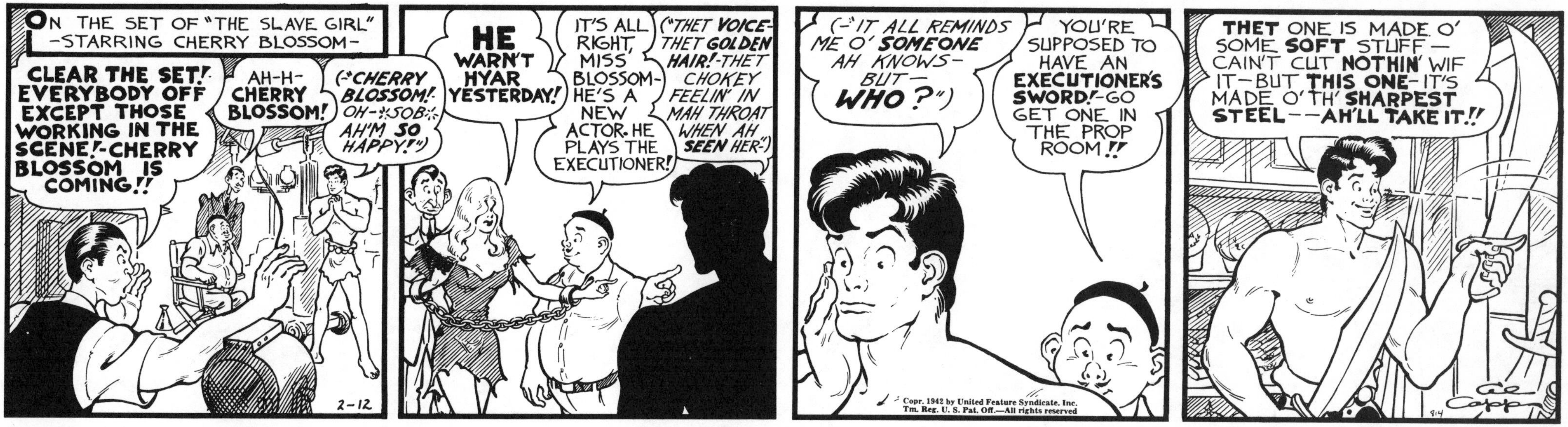

ON THE SET OF "THE SLAVE GIRL" -STARRING CHERRY BLOSSOM-
CLEAR THE SET!-EVERYBODY OFF EXCEPT THOSE WORKING IN THE SCENE!-CHERRY BLOSSOM IS COMING!!
AH-H- CHERRY BLOSSOM!
("CHERRY BLOSSOM!-OH-*SOB*-AH'M SO HAPPY!")
2-12
HE WARN'T HYAR YESTERDAY!
IT'S ALL RIGHT, MISS BLOSSOM-HE'S A NEW ACTOR.HE PLAYS THE EXECUTIONER!
("THET VOICE-THET GOLDEN HAIR!-THET CHOKEY FEELIN' IN MAH THROAT WHEN AH SEEN HER-")
("-IT ALL REMINDS ME O' SOMEONE AH KNOWS-BUT-WHO?")
YOU'RE SUPPOSED TO HAVE AN EXECUTIONER'S SWORD!-GO GET ONE IN THE PROP ROOM!!
Copr. 1942 by United Feature Syndicate, Inc. Tm. Reg. U. S. Pat. Off.—All rights reserved
THET ONE IS MADE O' SOME SOFT STUFF-CAIN'T CUT NOTHIN' WIF IT-BUT THIS ONE-IT'S MADE O' TH' SHARPEST STEEL--AH'LL TAKE IT!!
Al Capp

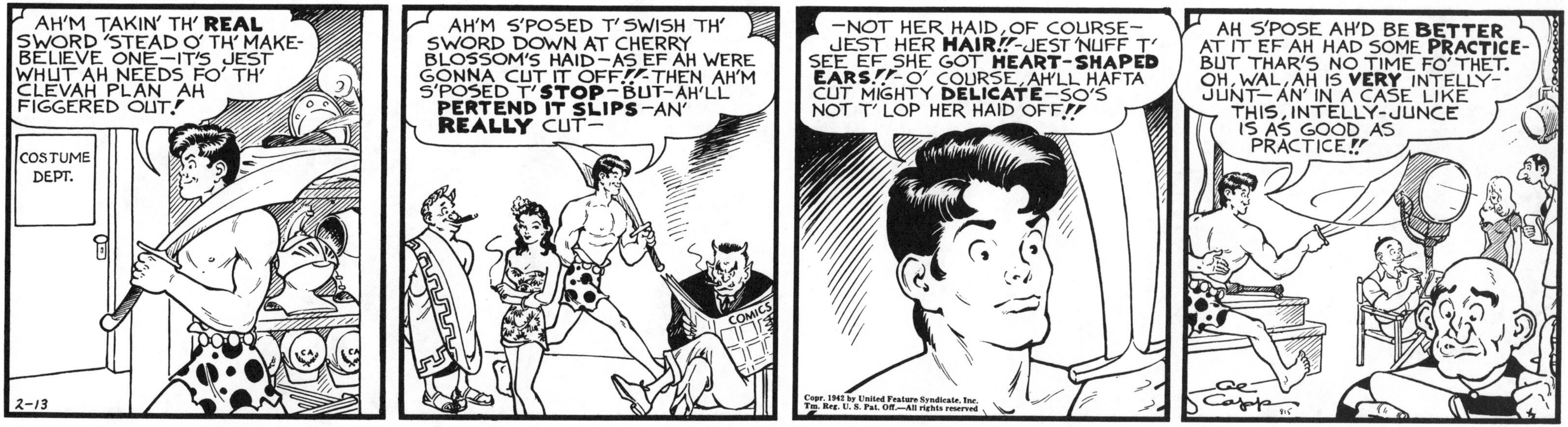

AH'M TAKIN' TH' REAL SWORD 'STEAD O' TH' MAKE-BELIEVE ONE-IT'S JEST WHUT AH NEEDS FO' TH' CLEVAH PLAN AH FIGGERED OUT!
COSTUME DEPT.
2-13
AH'M S'POSED T' SWISH TH' SWORD DOWN AT CHERRY BLOSSOM'S HAID-AS EF AH WERE GONNA CUT IT OFF!!-THEN AH'M S'POSED T' STOP-BUT-AH'LL PERTEND IT SLIPS-AN' REALLY CUT-
COMICS
-NOT HER HAID, OF COURSE-JEST HER HAIR!!-JEST 'NUFF T' SEE EF SHE GOT HEART-SHAPED EARS!!-O' COURSE, AH'LL HAFTA CUT MIGHTY DELICATE-SO'S NOT T' LOP HER HAID OFF!!
Copr. 1942 by United Feature Syndicate, Inc. Tm. Reg. U. S. Pat. Off.—All rights reserved
AH S'POSE AH'D BE BETTER AT IT EF AH HAD SOME PRACTICE-BUT THAR'S NO TIME FO' THET. OH, WAL, AH IS VERY INTELLY-JUNT-AN' IN A CASE LIKE THIS, INTELLY-JUNCE IS AS GOOD AS PRACTICE!!
Al Capp

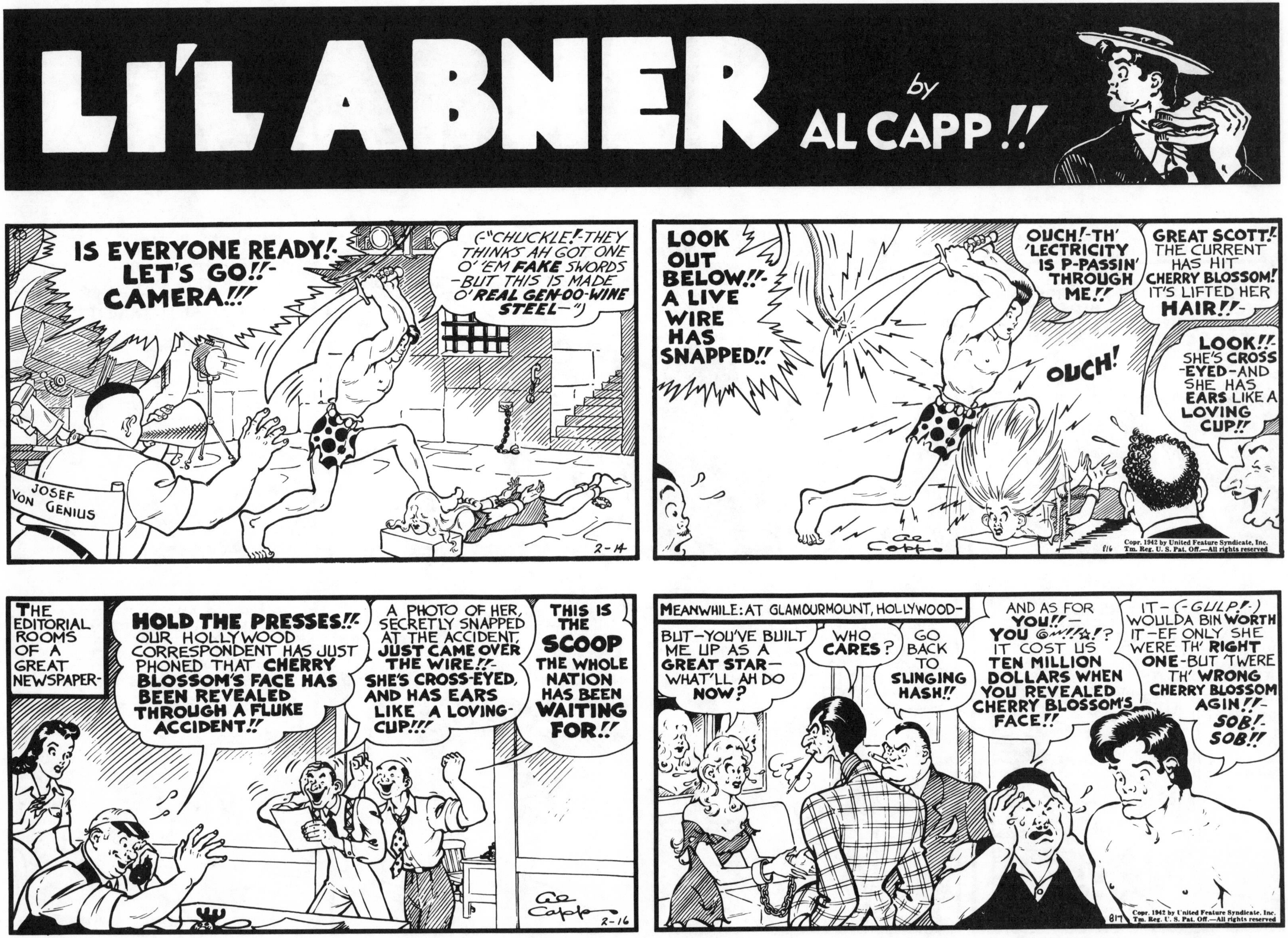
LI'L ABNER
by
AL CAPP!!
IS EVERYONE READY!- LET'S GO!!- CAMERA!!!
(-"CHUCKLE!"-THEY THINKS AH GOT ONE O' 'EM FAKE SWORDS -BUT THIS IS MADE O' REAL GEN-OO-WINE STEEL-")
JOSEF VON GENIUS
2-14
LOOK OUT BELOW!!- A LIVE WIRE HAS SNAPPED!!
OUCH!-TH' 'LECTRICITY IS P-PASSIN' THROUGH ME!!
GREAT SCOTT!- THE CURRENT HAS HIT CHERRY BLOSSOM! IT'S LIFTED HER HAIR!!-
OUCH!
LOOK!!- SHE'S CROSS-EYED-AND SHE HAS EARS LIKE A LOVING CUP!!
Copr. 1942 by United Feature Syndicate, Inc. Tm. Reg. U. S. Pat. Off.—All rights reserved
THE EDITORIAL ROOMS OF A GREAT NEWSPAPER-
HOLD THE PRESSES!!- OUR HOLLYWOOD CORRESPONDENT HAS JUST PHONED THAT CHERRY BLOSSOM'S FACE HAS BEEN REVEALED THROUGH A FLUKE ACCIDENT!!
A PHOTO OF HER, SECRETLY SNAPPED AT THE ACCIDENT, JUST CAME OVER THE WIRE!!- SHE'S CROSS-EYED, AND HAS EARS LIKE A LOVING-CUP!!!
THIS IS THE SCOOP THE WHOLE NATION HAS BEEN WAITING FOR!!
2-16
MEANWHILE: AT GLAMOURMOUNT, HOLLYWOOD-
BUT-YOU'VE BUILT ME UP AS A GREAT STAR-WHAT'LL AH DO NOW?
WHO CARES?
GO BACK TO SLINGING HASH!!
AND AS FOR YOU!!- YOU @!!!☆!? IT COST US TEN MILLION DOLLARS WHEN YOU REVEALED CHERRY BLOSSOM'S FACE!!
IT-(-GULP!-) WOULDA BIN WORTH IT-EF ONLY SHE WERE TH' RIGHT ONE-BUT 'TWERE TH' WRONG CHERRY BLOSSOM AGIN!!- SOB!- SOB!!
Copr. 1942 by United Feature Syndicate, Inc. Tm. Reg. U. S. Pat. Off.—All rights reserved

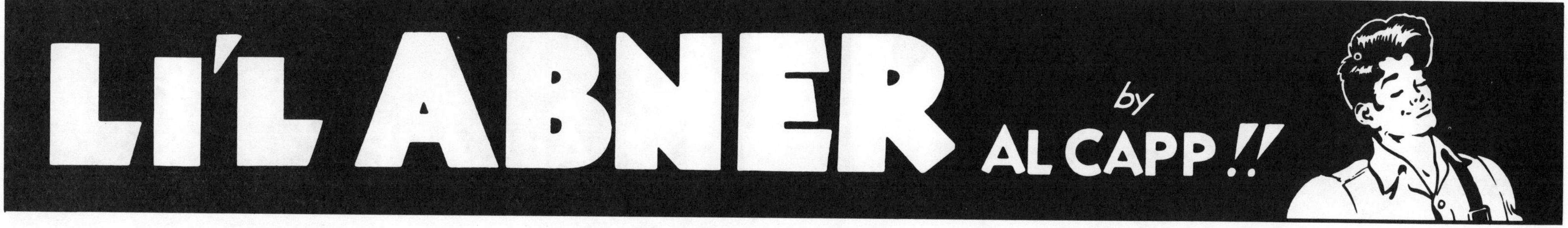
LI'L ABNER
by AL CAPP!!

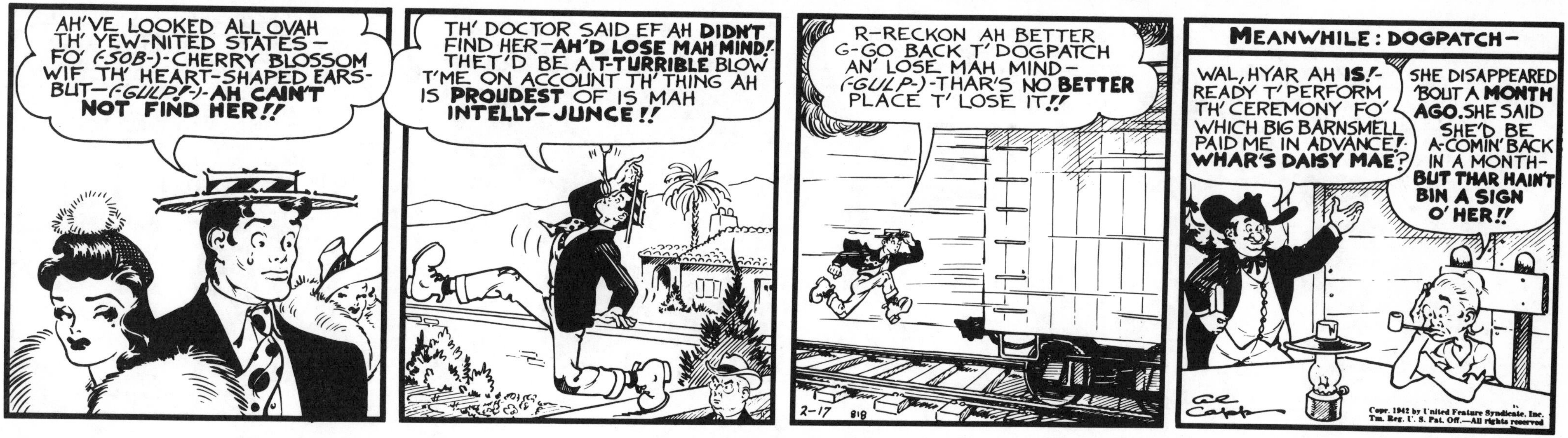
AH'VE LOOKED ALL OVAH TH' YEW-NITED STATES – FO' (-SOB-) – CHERRY BLOSSOM WIF TH' HEART-SHAPED EARS – BUT – (-GULP!-) – AH CAIN'T NOT FIND HER!!
TH' DOCTOR SAID EF AH DIDN'T FIND HER – AH'D LOSE MAH MIND! THET'D BE A T-TURRIBLE BLOW T'ME ON ACCOUNT TH' THING AH IS PROUDEST OF IS MAH INTELLY-JUNCE!!
R-RECKON AH BETTER G-GO BACK T' DOGPATCH AN' LOSE MAH MIND – (-GULP-) – THAR'S NO BETTER PLACE T' LOSE IT!!
2-17
818
MEANWHILE: DOGPATCH –
WAL, HYAR AH IS! – READY T' PERFORM TH' CEREMONY FO' WHICH BIG BARNSMELL PAID ME IN ADVANCE! – WHAR'S DAISY MAE?
SHE DISAPPEARED 'BOUT A MONTH AGO. SHE SAID SHE'D BE A-COMIN' BACK IN A MONTH – BUT THAR HAIN'T BIN A SIGN O' HER!!
Al Capp
Copr. 1942 by United Feature Syndicate, Inc.
Tm. Reg. U. S. Pat. Off.—All rights reserved

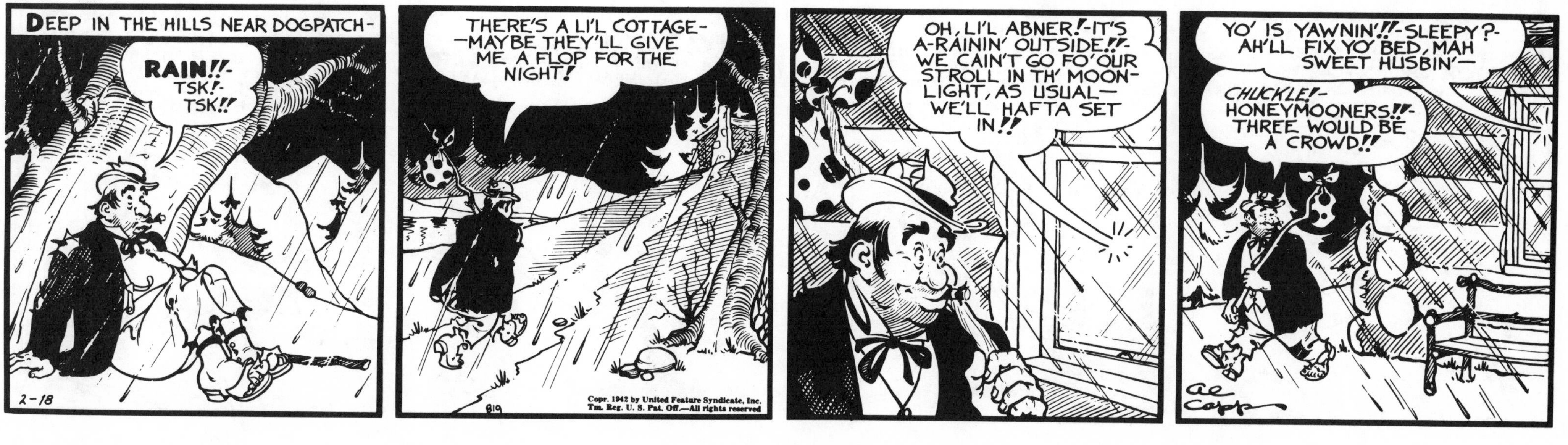
DEEP IN THE HILLS NEAR DOGPATCH –
RAIN!! – TSK! – TSK!!
2-18
THERE'S A LI'L COTTAGE – MAYBE THEY'LL GIVE ME A FLOP FOR THE NIGHT!
819
Copr. 1942 by United Feature Syndicate, Inc.
Tm. Reg. U. S. Pat. Off.—All rights reserved
OH, LI'L ABNER! – IT'S A-RAININ' OUTSIDE!! – WE CAIN'T GO FO' OUR STROLL IN TH' MOONLIGHT, AS USUAL – WE'LL HAFTA SET IN!!
YO' IS YAWNIN'!! – SLEEPY? – AH'LL FIX YO' BED, MAH SWEET HUSBIN' –
CHUCKLE! – HONEYMOONERS!! – THREE WOULD BE A CROWD!!
Al Capp

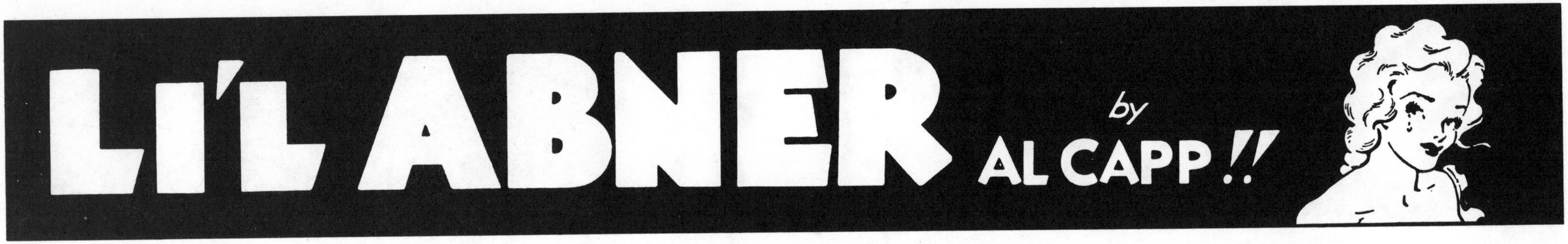

LI'L ABNER
by
AL CAPP!!

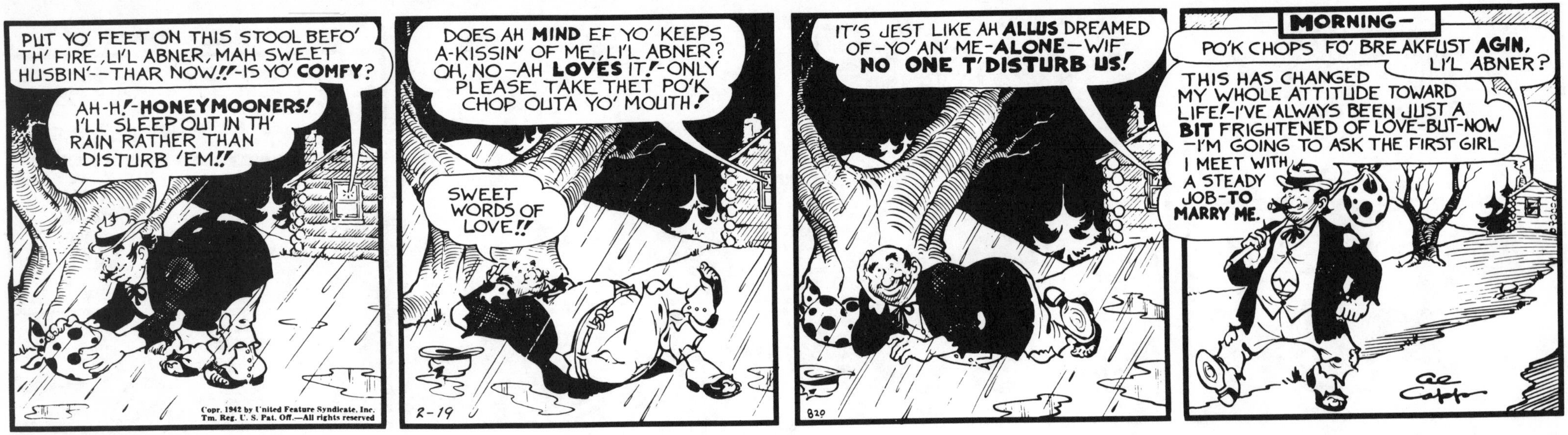

PUT YO' FEET ON THIS STOOL BEFO' TH' FIRE, LI'L ABNER, MAH SWEET HUSBIN'--THAR NOW!!-IS YO' **COMFY**?
AH-H!-**HONEYMOONERS!** I'LL SLEEP OUT IN TH' RAIN RATHER THAN DISTURB 'EM!!
Copr. 1942 by United Feature Syndicate, Inc. Tm. Reg. U. S. Pat. Off.—All rights reserved
DOES AH **MIND** EF YO' KEEPS A-KISSIN' OF ME, LI'L ABNER? OH, NO-AH **LOVES** IT!-ONLY PLEASE TAKE THET PO'K CHOP OUTA YO' MOUTH!
SWEET WORDS OF LOVE!!
2-19
IT'S JEST LIKE AH **ALLUS** DREAMED OF-YO' AN' ME-**ALONE**-WIF **NO ONE T'DISTURB US!**
MORNING-
PO'K CHOPS FO' BREAKFUST **AGIN**, LI'L ABNER?
THIS HAS CHANGED MY WHOLE ATTITUDE TOWARD LIFE!-I'VE ALWAYS BEEN JUST A **BIT** FRIGHTENED OF LOVE-BUT-NOW-I'M GOING TO ASK THE FIRST GIRL I MEET WITH A STEADY JOB-**TO MARRY ME.**
AL CAPP

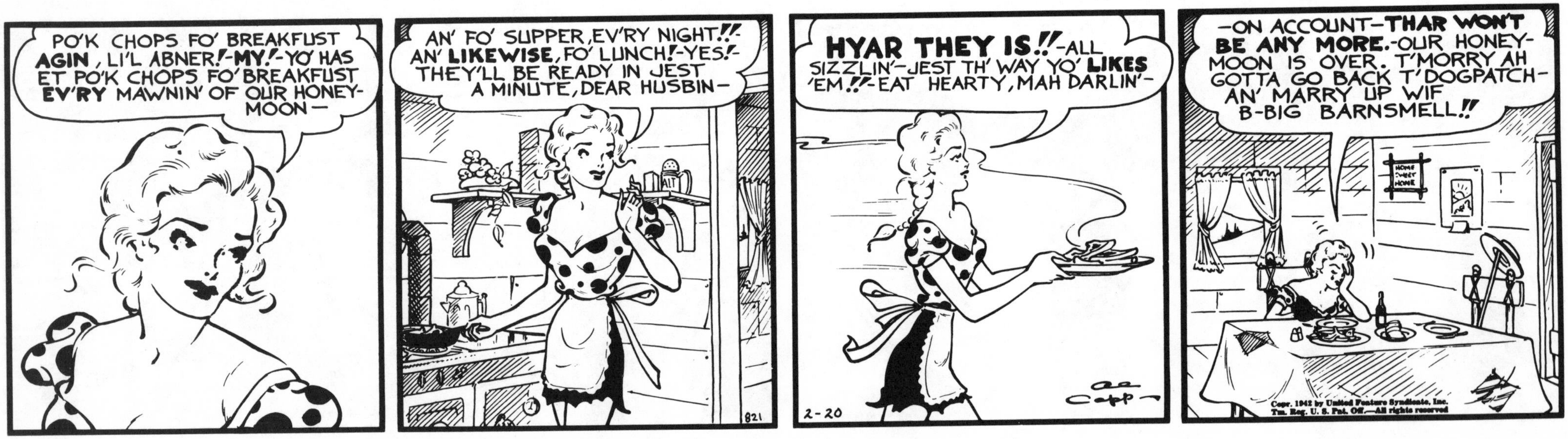

PO'K CHOPS FO' BREAKFUST **AGIN**, LI'L ABNER!-**MY!**-YO' HAS ET PO'K CHOPS FO' BREAKFUST **EV'RY** MAWNIN' OF OUR HONEY-MOON-
AN' FO' SUPPER, EV'RY NIGHT!!-AN' **LIKEWISE**, FO' LUNCH!-YES!-THEY'LL BE READY IN JEST A MINUTE, DEAR HUSBIN-
HYAR THEY IS!!-ALL SIZZLIN'-JEST TH' WAY YO' **LIKES** 'EM!!-EAT HEARTY, MAH DARLIN'-
2-20
AL CAPP
-ON ACCOUNT-**THAR WON'T BE ANY MORE.**-OUR HONEY-MOON IS OVER. T'MORRY AH GOTTA GO BACK T'DOGPATCH-AN' MARRY UP WIF B-BIG BARNSMELL!!
HOME SWEET HOME
Copr. 1942 by United Feature Syndicate, Inc. Tm. Reg. U. S. Pat. Off.—All rights reserved

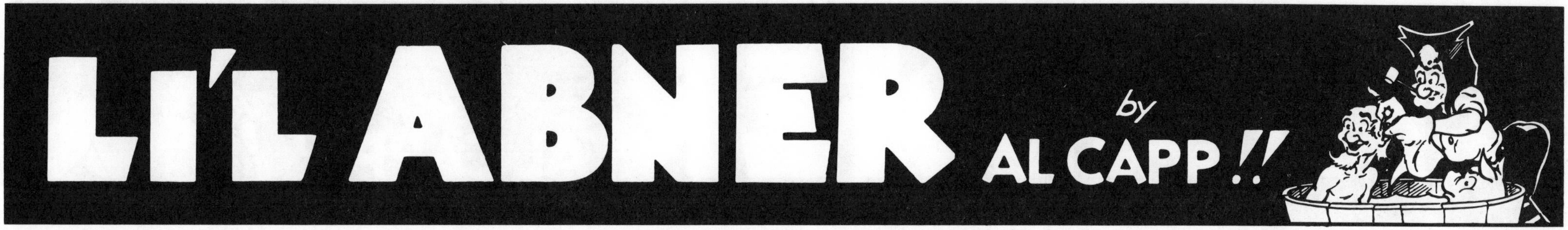
LI'L ABNER
by
AL CAPP!!

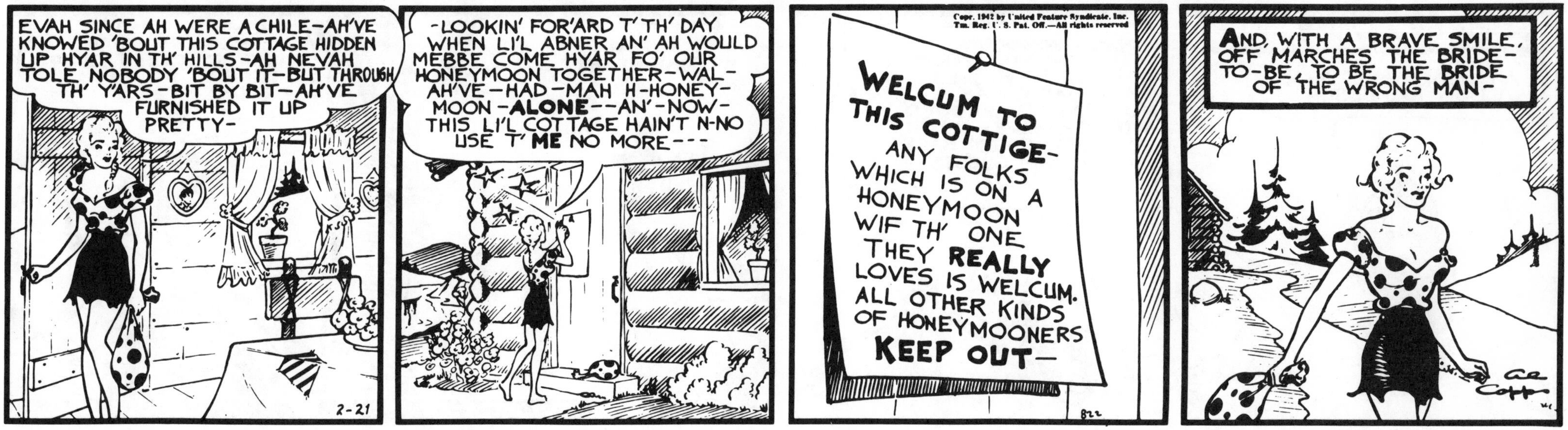
EVAH SINCE AH WERE A CHILE—AH'VE KNOWED 'BOUT THIS COTTAGE HIDDEN UP HYAR IN TH' HILLS—AH NEVAH TOLE NOBODY 'BOUT IT—BUT THROUGH TH' YARS—BIT BY BIT—AH'VE FURNISHED IT UP PRETTY—
2-21
—LOOKIN' FOR'ARD T' TH' DAY WHEN LI'L ABNER AN' AH WOULD MEBBE COME HYAR FO' OUR HONEYMOON TOGETHER—WAL—AH'VE—HAD—MAH H-HONEY-MOON—**ALONE**——AN'—NOW—THIS LI'L COTTAGE HAIN'T N-NO USE T' **ME** NO MORE———
Copr. 1942 by United Feature Syndicate, Inc. Tm. Reg. U. S. Pat. Off.—All rights reserved
WELCUM TO THIS COTTIGE— ANY FOLKS WHICH IS ON A HONEYMOON WIF TH' ONE THEY **REALLY** LOVES IS WELCUM. ALL OTHER KINDS OF HONEYMOONERS **KEEP OUT**—
AND, WITH A BRAVE SMILE, OFF MARCHES THE BRIDE-TO-BE, TO BE THE BRIDE OF THE WRONG MAN—
AL CAPP

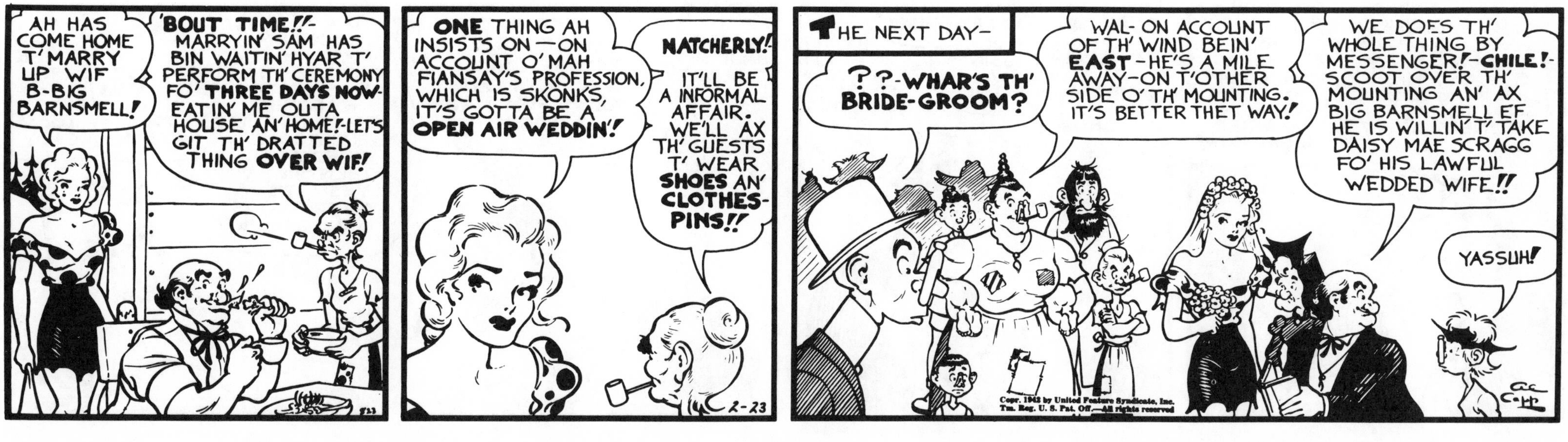
AH HAS COME HOME T' MARRY UP WIF B-BIG BARNSMELL!
'BOUT TIME!!— MARRYIN' SAM HAS BIN WAITIN' HYAR T' PERFORM TH' CEREMONY FO' **THREE DAYS NOW**—EATIN' ME OUTA HOUSE AN' HOME!—LET'S GIT TH' DRATTED THING **OVER WIF!**
ONE THING AH INSISTS ON—ON ACCOUNT O' MAH FIANSAY'S PROFESSION, WHICH IS SKONKS, IT'S GOTTA BE A **OPEN AIR WEDDIN'!**
NATCHERLY!! IT'LL BE A INFORMAL AFFAIR. WE'LL AX TH' GUESTS T' WEAR **SHOES** AN' **CLOTHES-PINS!!**
2-23
THE NEXT DAY—
??—**WHAR'S TH' BRIDE-GROOM?**
WAL—ON ACCOUNT OF TH' WIND BEIN' **EAST**—HE'S A MILE AWAY—ON T'OTHER SIDE O' TH' MOUNTING. IT'S BETTER THET WAY!
WE DOES TH' WHOLE THING BY MESSENGER!—**CHILE!**—SCOOT OVER TH' MOUNTING AN' AX BIG BARNSMELL EF HE IS WILLIN' T' TAKE DAISY MAE SCRAGG FO' HIS LAWFUL WEDDED WIFE!!
YASSUH!
AL CAPP
Copr. 1942 by United Feature Syndicate, Inc. Tm. Reg. U. S. Pat. Off.—All rights reserved

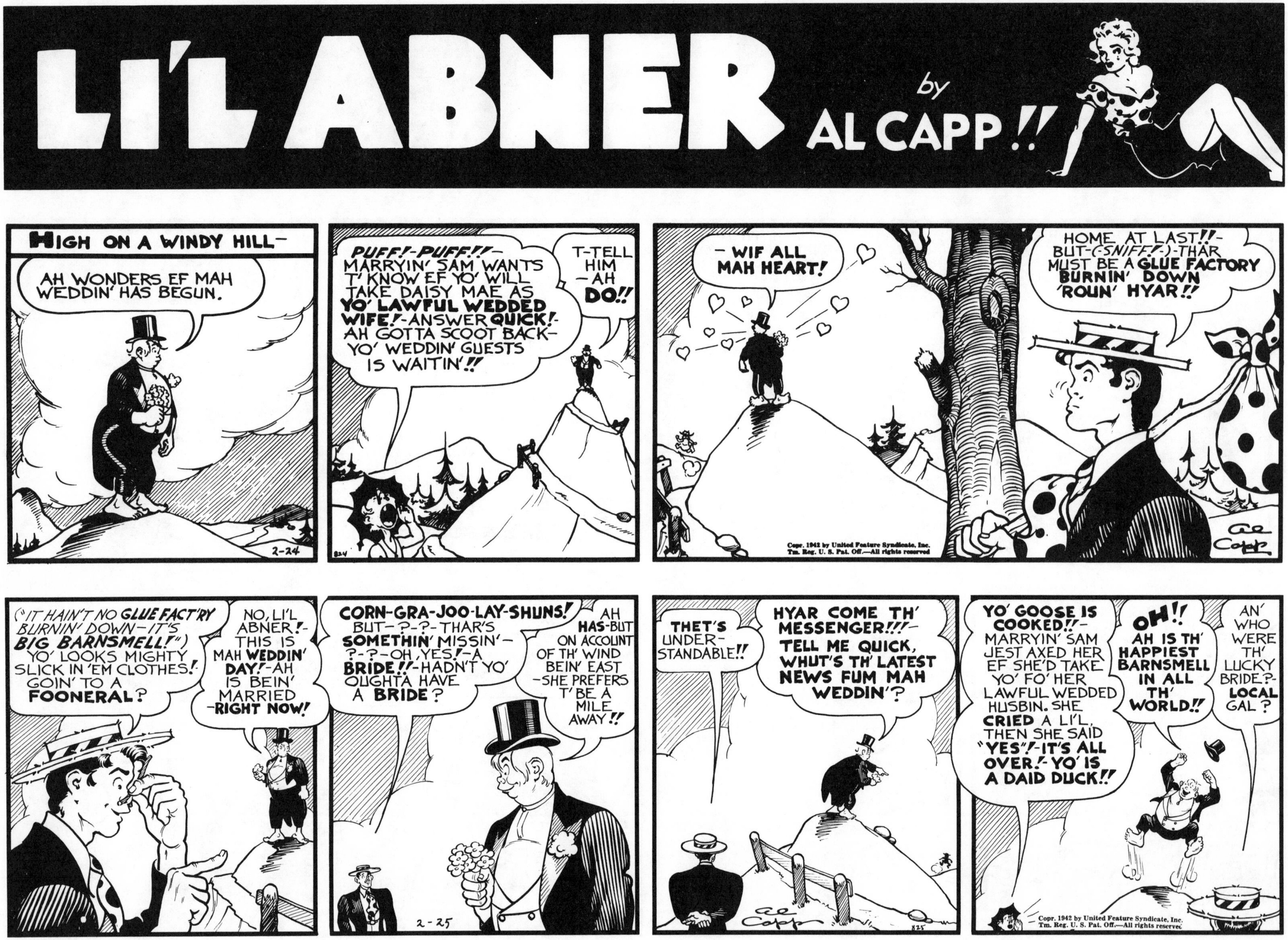

LI'L ABNER
by
AL CAPP!!
HIGH ON A WINDY HILL–
AH WONDERS EF MAH WEDDIN' HAS BEGUN.
2-24
PUFF!-PUFF!!– MARRYIN' SAM WANTS T' KNOW EF YO' WILL TAKE DAISY MAE AS YO' LAWFUL WEDDED WIFE!-ANSWER QUICK!- AH GOTTA SCOOT BACK- YO' WEDDIN' GUESTS IS WAITIN'!!
T-TELL HIM –AH DO!!
– WIF ALL MAH HEART!
Copr. 1942 by United Feature Syndicate, Inc. Tm. Reg. U. S. Pat. Off.—All rights reserved
HOME AT LAST!!- BUT-(-SNIFF!-)-THAR MUST BE A GLUE FACTORY BURNIN' DOWN 'ROUN' HYAR!!
Al Capp
("IT HAIN'T NO GLUE FACT'RY BURNIN' DOWN-IT'S BIG BARNSMELL!") YO' LOOKS MIGHTY SLICK IN 'EM CLOTHES!- GOIN' TO A FOONERAL?
NO, LI'L ABNER!- THIS IS MAH WEDDIN' DAY!-AH IS BEIN' MARRIED –RIGHT NOW!
CORN-GRA-JOO-LAY-SHUNS! BUT–?-?-THAR'S SOMETHIN' MISSIN'– ?-?-OH, YES!-A BRIDE!!-HADN'T YO' OUGHTA HAVE A BRIDE?
AH HAS-BUT ON ACCOUNT OF TH' WIND BEIN' EAST –SHE PREFERS T' BE A MILE AWAY!!
2-25
THET'S UNDER-STANDABLE!!
HYAR COME TH' MESSENGER!!!– TELL ME QUICK, WHUT'S TH' LATEST NEWS FUM MAH WEDDIN'?
Al Capp
YO' GOOSE IS COOKED!!– MARRYIN' SAM JEST AXED HER EF SHE'D TAKE YO' FO' HER LAWFUL WEDDED HUSBIN. SHE CRIED A LI'L, THEN SHE SAID "YES"!-IT'S ALL OVER!-YO' IS A DAID DUCK!!
OH!! AH IS TH' HAPPIEST BARNSMELL IN ALL TH' WORLD!!
AN' WHO WERE TH' LUCKY BRIDE?- LOCAL GAL?
Copr. 1942 by United Feature Syndicate, Inc. Tm. Reg. U. S. Pat. Off.—All rights reserved

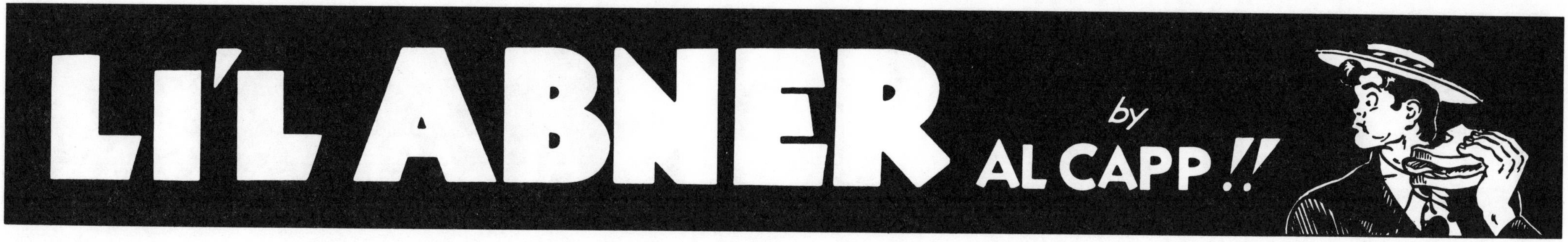
LI'L ABNER
by
AL CAPP!!

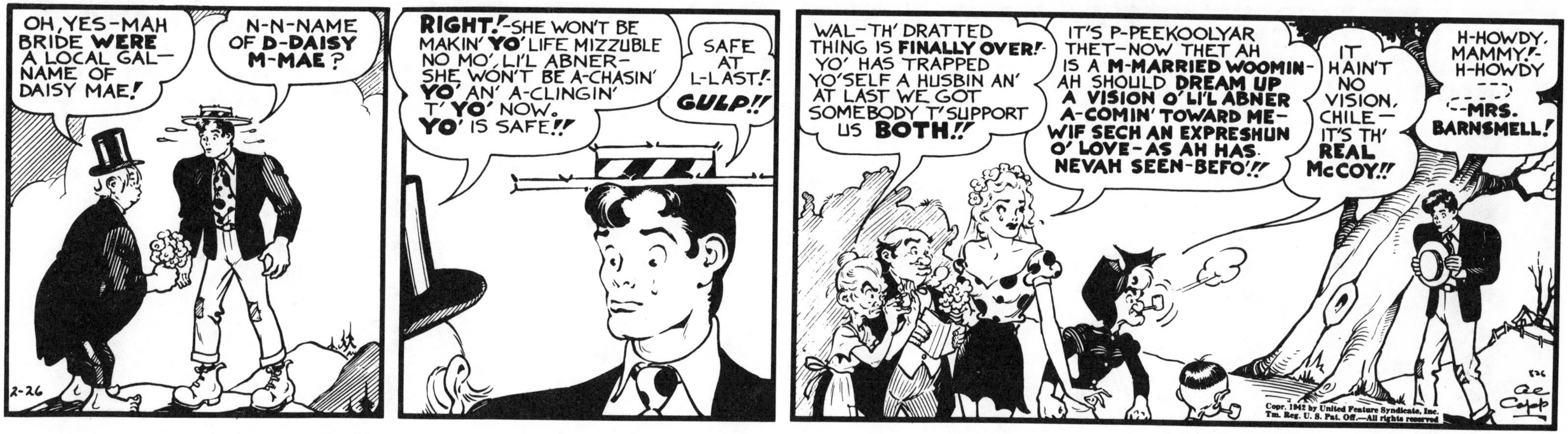
OH, YES-MAH BRIDE WERE A LOCAL GAL-NAME OF DAISY MAE!
N-N-NAME OF D-DAISY M-MAE?
2-26
RIGHT!-SHE WON'T BE MAKIN' YO' LIFE MIZZUBLE NO MO', LI'L ABNER-SHE WON'T BE A-CHASIN' YO' AN' A-CLINGIN' T' YO' NOW. YO' IS SAFE!!
SAFE AT L-LAST!-GULP!!
WAL-TH' DRATTED THING IS FINALLY OVER!-YO' HAS TRAPPED YO'SELF A HUSBIN AN' AT LAST WE GOT SOMEBODY T'SUPPORT US BOTH!!
IT'S P-PEEKOOLYAR THET-NOW THET AH IS A M-MARRIED WOOMIN-AH SHOULD DREAM UP A VISION O' LI'L ABNER A-COMIN' TOWARD ME-WIF SECH AN EXPRESHUN O' LOVE-AS AH HAS NEVAH SEEN-BEFO'!!
IT HAIN'T NO VISION, CHILE-IT'S TH' REAL McCOY!!
H-HOWDY, MAMMY!-H-HOWDY --MRS. BARNSMELL!
Copr. 1942 by United Feature Syndicate, Inc. Tm. Reg. U. S. Pat. Off.—All rights reserved
Al Capp

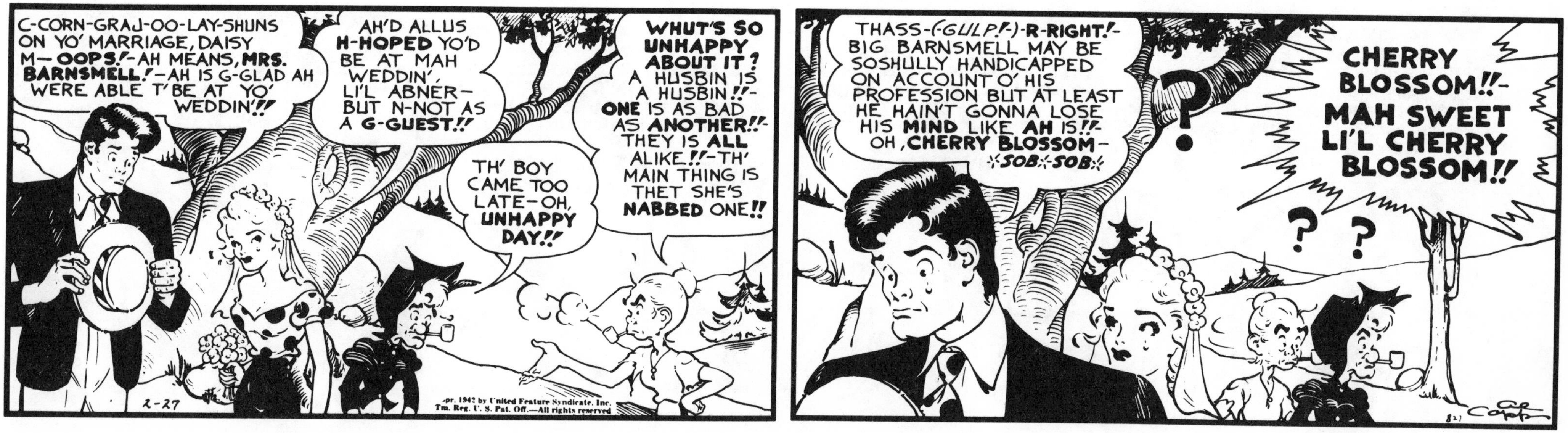
C-CORN-GRAJ-OO-LAY-SHUNS ON YO' MARRIAGE, DAISY M-OOPS!-AH MEANS, MRS. BARNSMELL!-AH IS G-GLAD AH WERE ABLE T'BE AT YO' WEDDIN'!!
AH'D ALLUS H-HOPED YO'D BE AT MAH WEDDIN', LI'L ABNER-BUT N-NOT AS A G-GUEST!!
TH' BOY CAME TOO LATE-OH, UNHAPPY DAY!!
WHUT'S SO UNHAPPY ABOUT IT? A HUSBIN IS A HUSBIN!!-ONE IS AS BAD AS ANOTHER!!-THEY IS ALL ALIKE!!-TH' MAIN THING IS THET SHE'S NABBED ONE!!
2-27
Tm. Reg. U. S. Pat. Off.—All rights reserved
THASS-(-GULP!-)-R-RIGHT!-BIG BARNSMELL MAY BE SOSHULLY HANDICAPPED ON ACCOUNT O' HIS PROFESSION BUT AT LEAST HE HAIN'T GONNA LOSE HIS MIND LIKE AH IS!!-OH, CHERRY BLOSSOM-SOB-SOB
?
CHERRY BLOSSOM!!-MAH SWEET LI'L CHERRY BLOSSOM!!
? ?
Al Capp

LI'L ABNER by AL CAPP!!

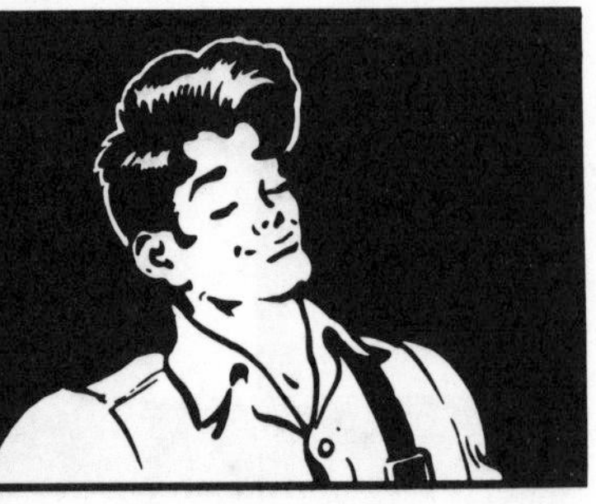

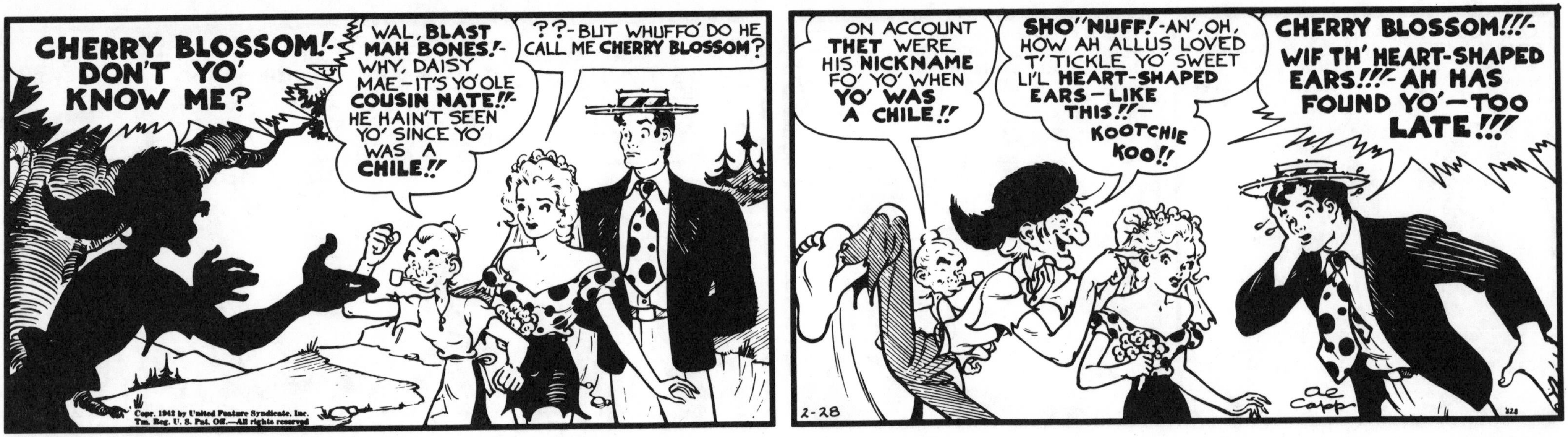

CHERRY BLOSSOM!- DON'T YO' KNOW ME?
WAL, BLAST MAH BONES!- WHY, DAISY MAE—IT'S YO'OLE COUSIN NATE!!- HE HAIN'T SEEN YO' SINCE YO' WAS A CHILE!!
??-BUT WHUFFO' DO HE CALL ME CHERRY BLOSSOM?
Copr. 1942 by United Feature Syndicate, Inc. Tm. Reg. U. S. Pat. Off.—All rights reserved
ON ACCOUNT THET WERE HIS NICKNAME FO' YO' WHEN YO' WAS A CHILE!!
SHO' 'NUFF!-AN', OH, HOW AH ALLUS LOVED T' TICKLE YO' SWEET LI'L HEART-SHAPED EARS—LIKE THIS!!— KOOTCHIE KOO!!
CHERRY BLOSSOM!!!- WIF TH' HEART-SHAPED EARS!!!- AH HAS FOUND YO'—TOO LATE!!!
2-28

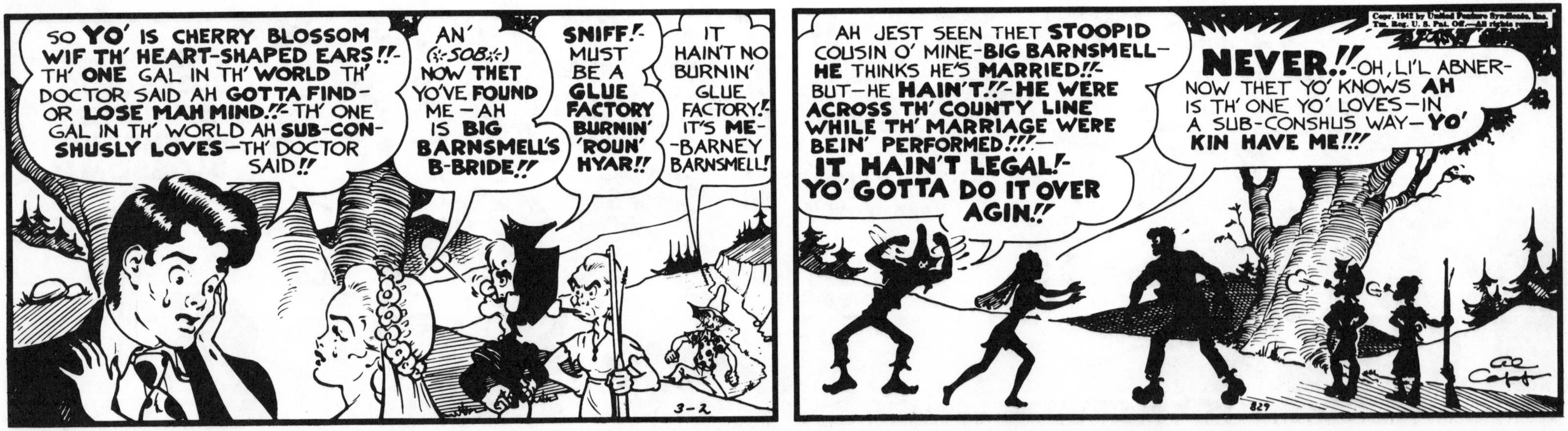

SO YO' IS CHERRY BLOSSOM WIF TH' HEART-SHAPED EARS!!- TH' ONE GAL IN TH' WORLD TH' DOCTOR SAID AH GOTTA FIND—OR LOSE MAH MIND!!- TH' ONE GAL IN TH' WORLD AH SUB-CONSHUSLY LOVES—TH' DOCTOR SAID!!
AN' (-SOB-) NOW THET YO'VE FOUND ME—AH IS BIG BARNSMELL'S B-BRIDE!!
SNIFF!- MUST BE A GLUE FACTORY BURNIN' 'ROUN' HYAR!!
IT HAIN'T NO BURNIN' GLUE FACTORY!- IT'S ME- -BARNEY BARNSMELL!
3-2
AH JEST SEEN THET STOOPID COUSIN O' MINE-BIG BARNSMELL—HE THINKS HE'S MARRIED!!- BUT—HE HAIN'T!!- HE WERE ACROSS TH' COUNTY LINE WHILE TH' MARRIAGE WERE BEIN' PERFORMED!!!— IT HAIN'T LEGAL!- YO' GOTTA DO IT OVER AGIN!!
NEVER!!-OH, LI'L ABNER—NOW THET YO' KNOWS AH IS TH' ONE YO' LOVES—IN A SUB-CONSHUS WAY—YO' KIN HAVE ME!!!
Copr. 1942 by United Feature Syndicate, Inc. Tm. Reg. U. S. Pat. Off.—All rights reserved

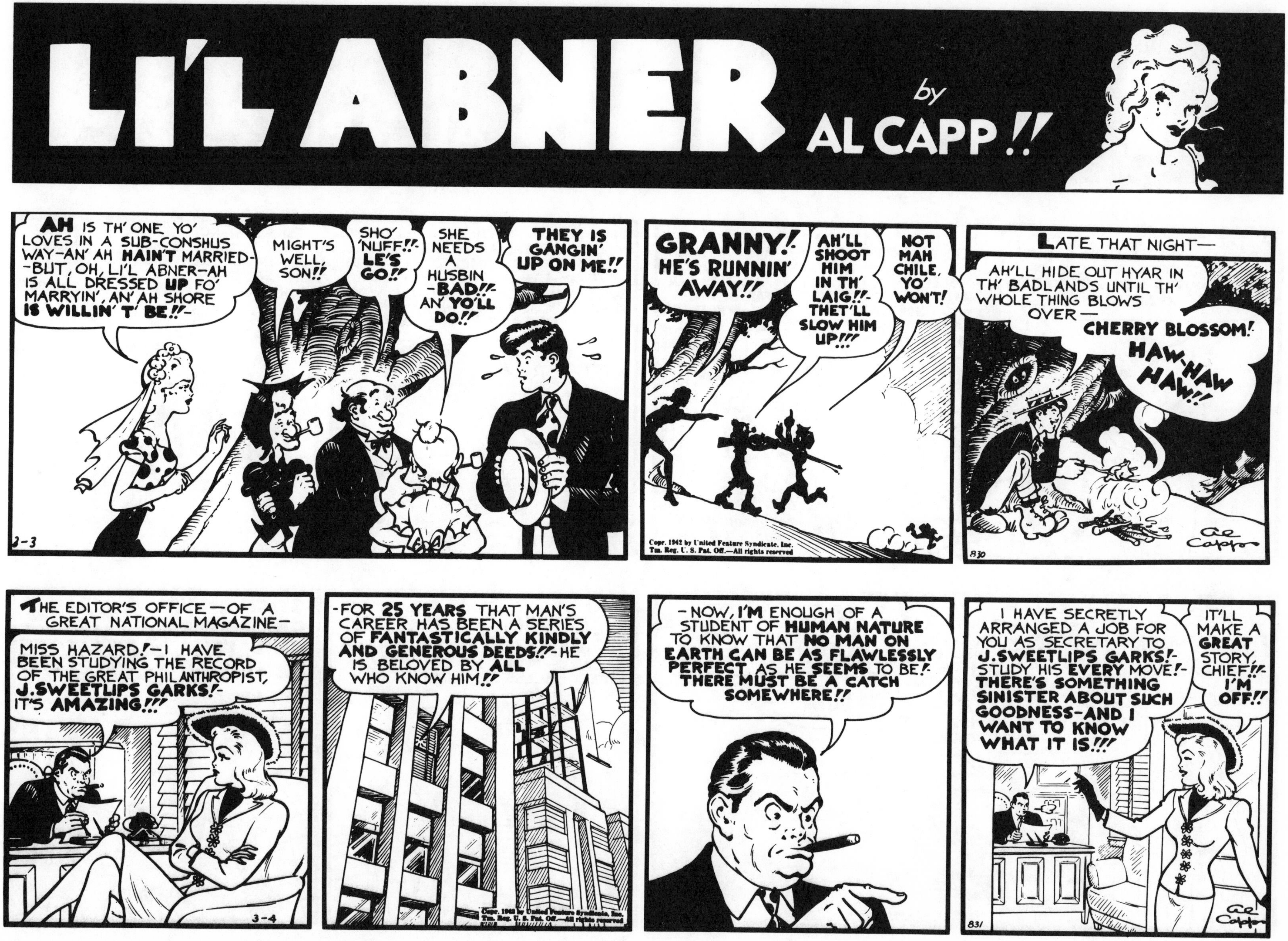

LI'L ABNER
by AL CAPP!!
AH IS TH' ONE YO' LOVES IN A SUB-CONSHUS WAY-AN' AH HAIN'T MARRIED--BUT, OH, LI'L ABNER-AH IS ALL DRESSED UP FO' MARRYIN', AN' AH SHORE IS WILLIN' T' BE!!-
MIGHT'S WELL, SON!!
SHO' 'NUFF!!- LE'S GO!!
SHE NEEDS A HUSBIN -BAD!!- AN' YO'LL DO!!
THEY IS GANGIN' UP ON ME!!
3-3
GRANNY! HE'S RUNNIN' AWAY!!
AH'LL SHOOT HIM IN TH' LAIG!!- THET'LL SLOW HIM UP!!!
NOT MAH CHILE, YO' WON'T!
Copr. 1942 by United Feature Syndicate, Inc. Tm. Reg. U. S. Pat. Off.—All rights reserved
LATE THAT NIGHT—
AH'LL HIDE OUT HYAR IN TH' BADLANDS UNTIL TH' WHOLE THING BLOWS OVER — CHERRY BLOSSOM!
HAW-HAW HAW!!
830
THE EDITOR'S OFFICE—OF A GREAT NATIONAL MAGAZINE—
MISS HAZARD!—I HAVE BEEN STUDYING THE RECORD OF THE GREAT PHILANTHROPIST, J. SWEETLIPS GARKS!- IT'S AMAZING!!!
3-4
-FOR 25 YEARS THAT MAN'S CAREER HAS BEEN A SERIES OF FANTASTICALLY KINDLY AND GENEROUS DEEDS!!-HE IS BELOVED BY ALL WHO KNOW HIM!!
-NOW, I'M ENOUGH OF A STUDENT OF HUMAN NATURE TO KNOW THAT NO MAN ON EARTH CAN BE AS FLAWLESSLY PERFECT AS HE SEEMS TO BE!- THERE MUST BE A CATCH SOMEWHERE!!
I HAVE SECRETLY ARRANGED A JOB FOR YOU AS SECRETARY TO J. SWEETLIPS GARKS!- STUDY HIS EVERY MOVE!- THERE'S SOMETHING SINISTER ABOUT SUCH GOODNESS-AND I WANT TO KNOW WHAT IT IS!!!
IT'LL MAKE A GREAT STORY, CHIEF!!- I'M OFF!!
831

LI'L ABNER by AL CAPP!!

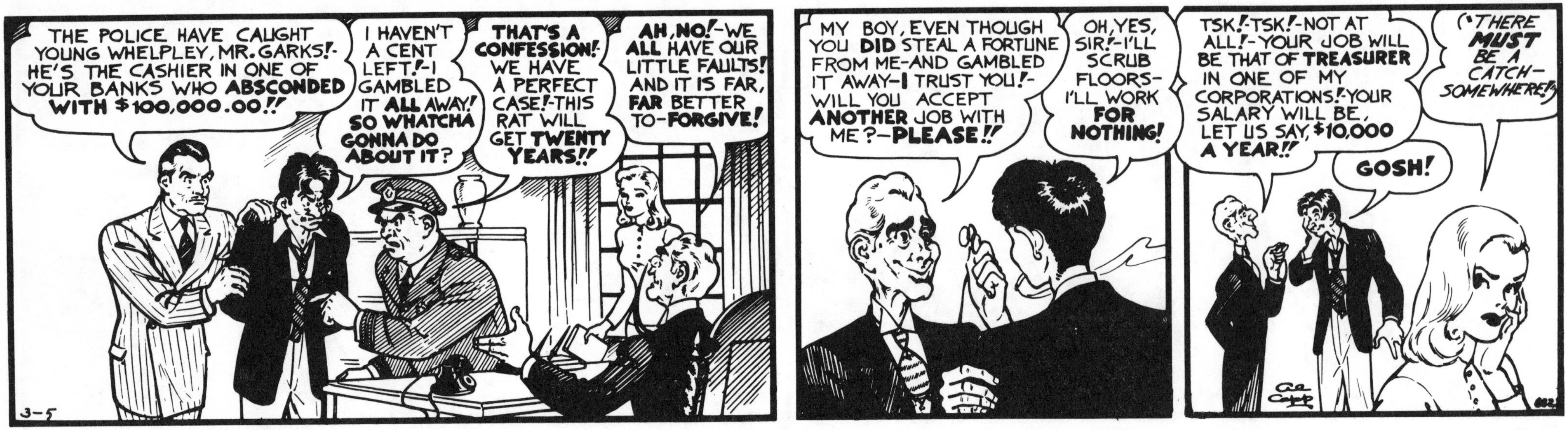

THE POLICE HAVE CAUGHT YOUNG WHELPLEY, MR. GARKS!- HE'S THE CASHIER IN ONE OF YOUR BANKS WHO ABSCONDED WITH $100,000.00!!
I HAVEN'T A CENT LEFT!-I GAMBLED IT ALL AWAY! SO WHATCHA GONNA DO ABOUT IT?
THAT'S A CONFESSION!- WE HAVE A PERFECT CASE!-THIS RAT WILL GET TWENTY YEARS!!
AH, NO!-WE ALL HAVE OUR LITTLE FAULTS! AND IT IS FAR, FAR BETTER TO-FORGIVE!
3-5
MY BOY, EVEN THOUGH YOU DID STEAL A FORTUNE FROM ME-AND GAMBLED IT AWAY-I TRUST YOU!- WILL YOU ACCEPT ANOTHER JOB WITH ME?-PLEASE!!
OH, YES, SIR!-I'LL SCRUB FLOORS- I'LL WORK FOR NOTHING!
TSK!-TSK!-NOT AT ALL!-YOUR JOB WILL BE THAT OF TREASURER IN ONE OF MY CORPORATIONS!-YOUR SALARY WILL BE, LET US SAY, $10,000 A YEAR!!
GOSH!
("THERE MUST BE A CATCH- SOMEWHERE!")

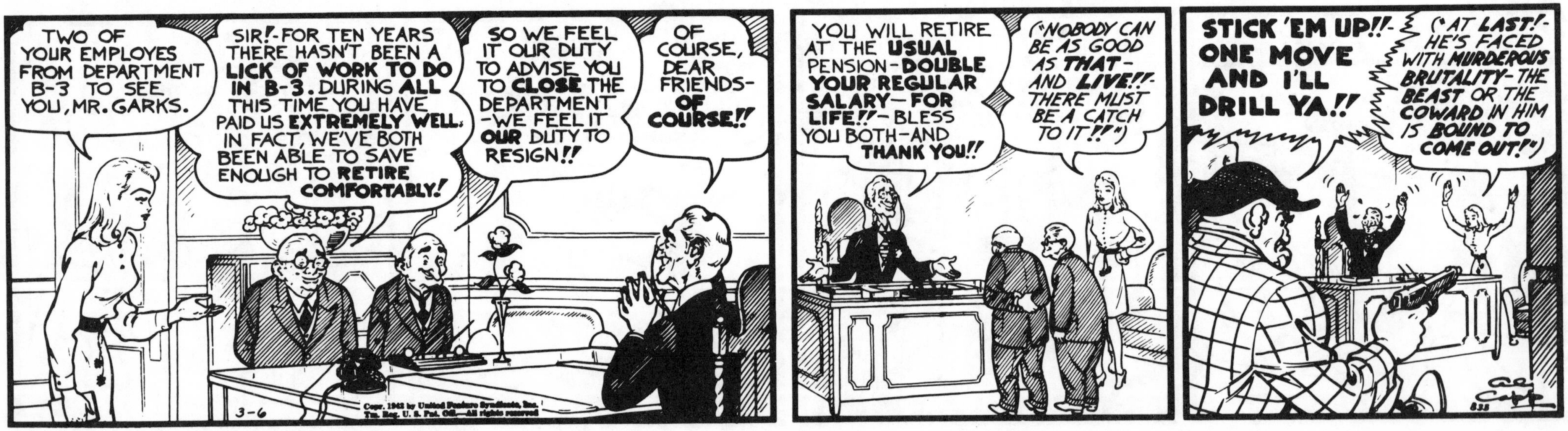

TWO OF YOUR EMPLOYES FROM DEPARTMENT B-3 TO SEE YOU, MR. GARKS.
SIR!-FOR TEN YEARS THERE HASN'T BEEN A LICK OF WORK TO DO IN B-3. DURING ALL THIS TIME YOU HAVE PAID US EXTREMELY WELL. IN FACT, WE'VE BOTH BEEN ABLE TO SAVE ENOUGH TO RETIRE COMFORTABLY!
SO WE FEEL IT OUR DUTY TO ADVISE YOU TO CLOSE THE DEPARTMENT -WE FEEL IT OUR DUTY TO RESIGN!!
OF COURSE, DEAR FRIENDS- OF COURSE!!
3-6
Copr. 1942 by United Feature Syndicate, Inc. Tm. Reg. U. S. Pat. Off.—All rights reserved
YOU WILL RETIRE AT THE USUAL PENSION-DOUBLE YOUR REGULAR SALARY-FOR LIFE!!-BLESS YOU BOTH-AND THANK YOU!!
("NOBODY CAN BE AS GOOD AS THAT- AND LIVE!!-THERE MUST BE A CATCH TO IT!!")
STICK 'EM UP!!- ONE MOVE AND I'LL DRILL YA!!
("AT LAST!- HE'S FACED WITH MURDEROUS BRUTALITY-THE BEAST OR THE COWARD IN HIM IS BOUND TO COME OUT!")

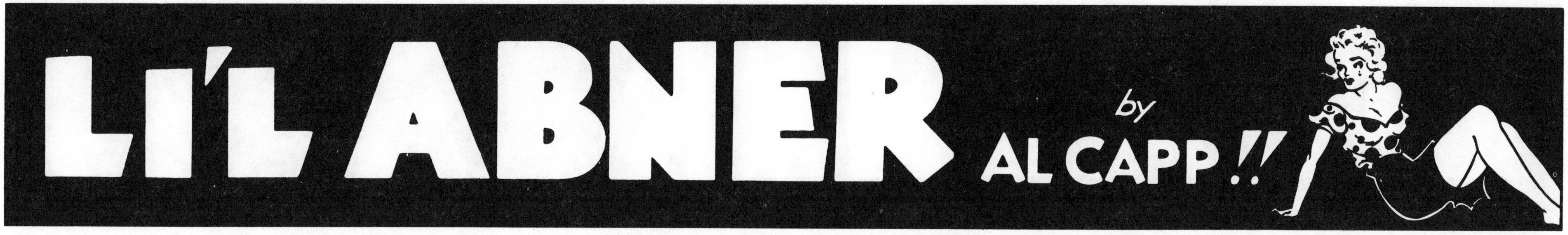
LI'L ABNER
by
AL CAPP!!

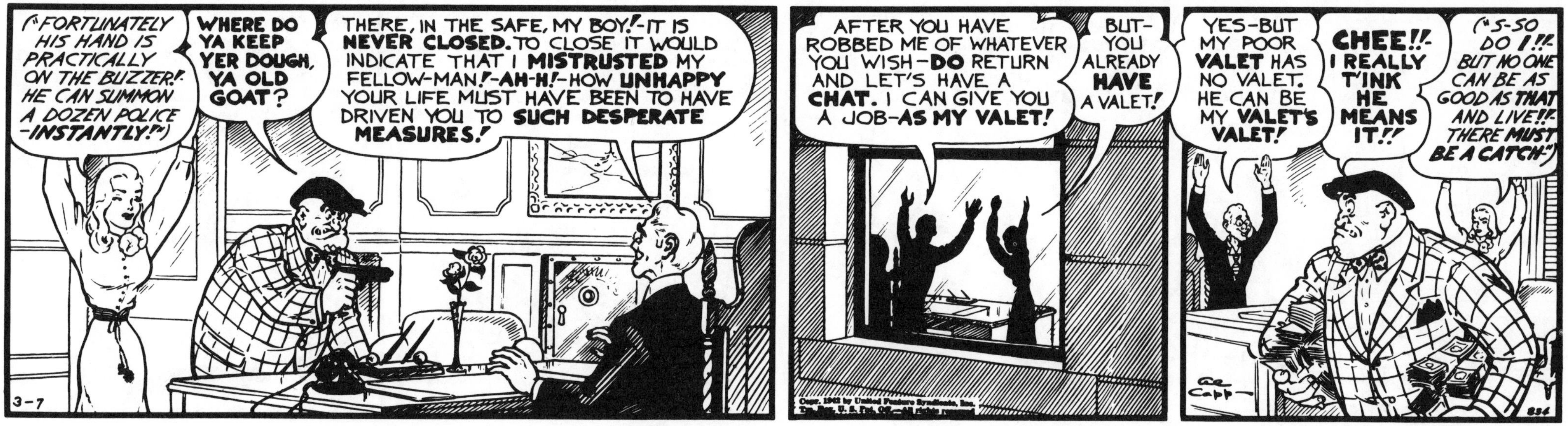
("FORTUNATELY HIS HAND IS PRACTICALLY ON THE BUZZER!- HE CAN SUMMON A DOZEN POLICE -INSTANTLY!")
WHERE DO YA KEEP YER DOUGH, YA OLD GOAT?
THERE, IN THE SAFE, MY BOY!- IT IS NEVER CLOSED. TO CLOSE IT WOULD INDICATE THAT I MISTRUSTED MY FELLOW-MAN!- AH-H!- HOW UNHAPPY YOUR LIFE MUST HAVE BEEN TO HAVE DRIVEN YOU TO SUCH DESPERATE MEASURES!
3-7
AFTER YOU HAVE ROBBED ME OF WHATEVER YOU WISH- DO RETURN AND LET'S HAVE A CHAT. I CAN GIVE YOU A JOB- AS MY VALET!
BUT- YOU ALREADY HAVE A VALET!
YES- BUT MY POOR VALET HAS NO VALET. HE CAN BE MY VALET'S VALET!
CHEE!!- I REALLY T'INK HE MEANS IT!!
("S-SO DO I!!- BUT NO ONE CAN BE AS GOOD AS THAT AND LIVE!!- THERE MUST BE A CATCH")
Al Capp
834

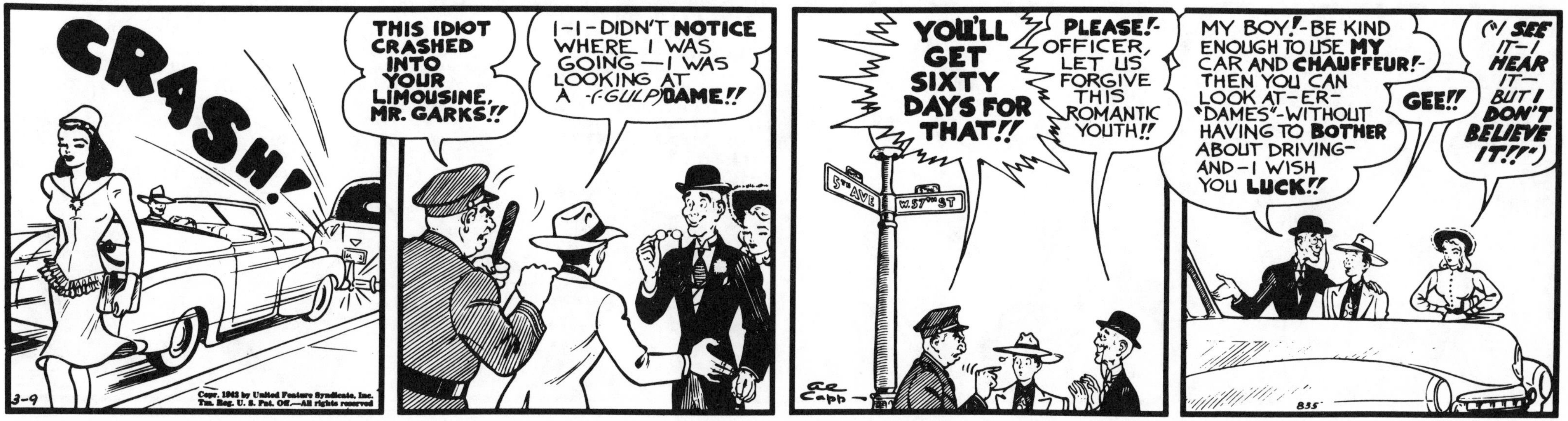
CRASH!
3-9
Copr. 1942 by United Feature Syndicate, Inc.
Tm. Reg. U. S. Pat. Off.—All rights reserved
THIS IDIOT CRASHED INTO YOUR LIMOUSINE, MR. GARKS!!
I-I- DIDN'T NOTICE WHERE I WAS GOING — I WAS LOOKING AT A -(-GULP) DAME!!
YOU'LL GET SIXTY DAYS FOR THAT!!
PLEASE!- OFFICER, LET US FORGIVE THIS ROMANTIC YOUTH!!
5TH AVE
W. 57TH ST
Al Capp
MY BOY!- BE KIND ENOUGH TO USE MY CAR AND CHAUFFEUR!- THEN YOU CAN LOOK AT- ER- "DAMES"- WITHOUT HAVING TO BOTHER ABOUT DRIVING- AND- I WISH YOU LUCK!!
GEE!!
("I SEE IT- I HEAR IT- BUT I DON'T BELIEVE IT!!")
835

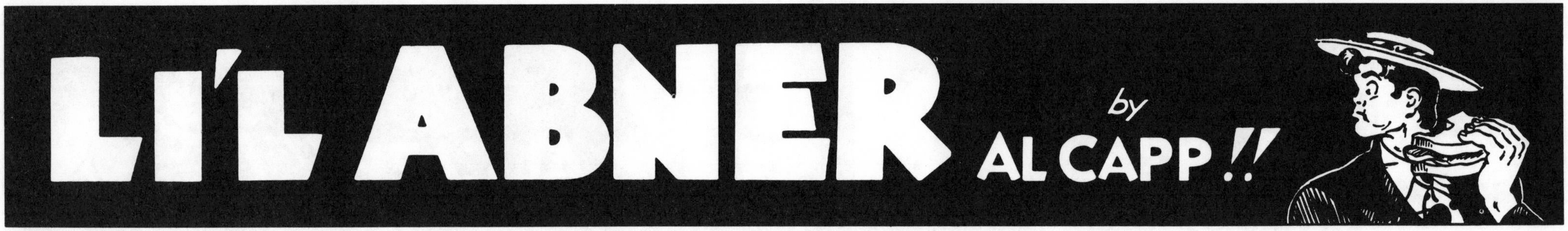
LI'L ABNER
by
AL CAPP!!

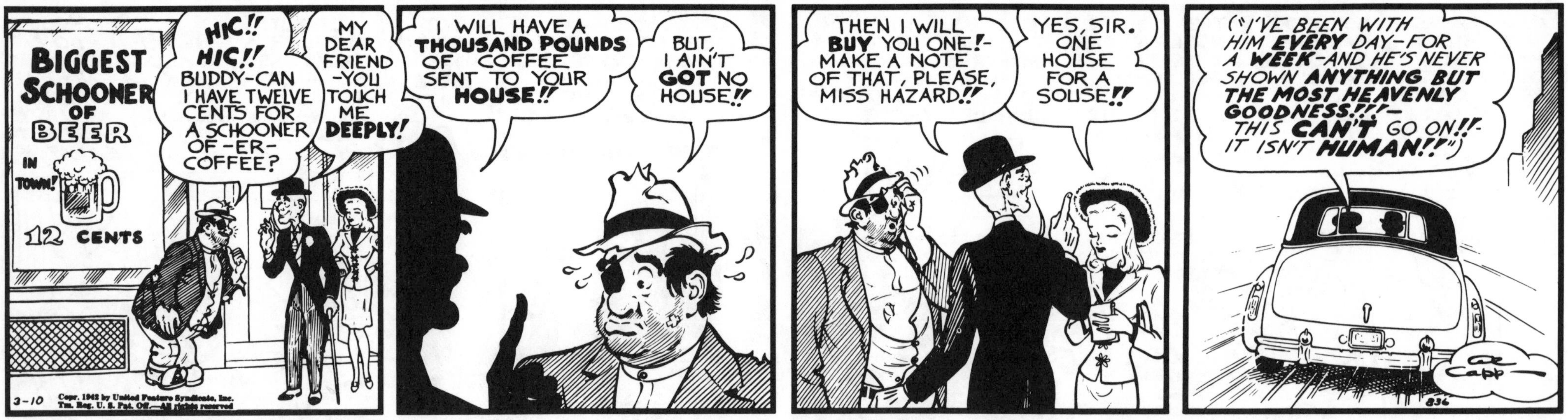
BIGGEST SCHOONER OF BEER IN TOWN! 12 CENTS
HIC!! HIC!! BUDDY-CAN I HAVE TWELVE CENTS FOR A SCHOONER OF-ER-COFFEE?
MY DEAR FRIEND-YOU TOUCH ME DEEPLY!
3-10
Copr. 1942 by United Feature Syndicate, Inc. Tm. Reg. U. S. Pat. Off.—All rights reserved
I WILL HAVE A THOUSAND POUNDS OF COFFEE SENT TO YOUR HOUSE!!
BUT, I AIN'T GOT NO HOUSE!!
THEN I WILL BUY YOU ONE!-MAKE A NOTE OF THAT, PLEASE, MISS HAZARD!!
YES, SIR. ONE HOUSE FOR A SOUSE!!
("I'VE BEEN WITH HIM EVERY DAY-FOR A WEEK-AND HE'S NEVER SHOWN ANYTHING BUT THE MOST HEAVENLY GOODNESS!!!-THIS CAN'T GO ON!!-IT ISN'T HUMAN!!")
Al Capp
836

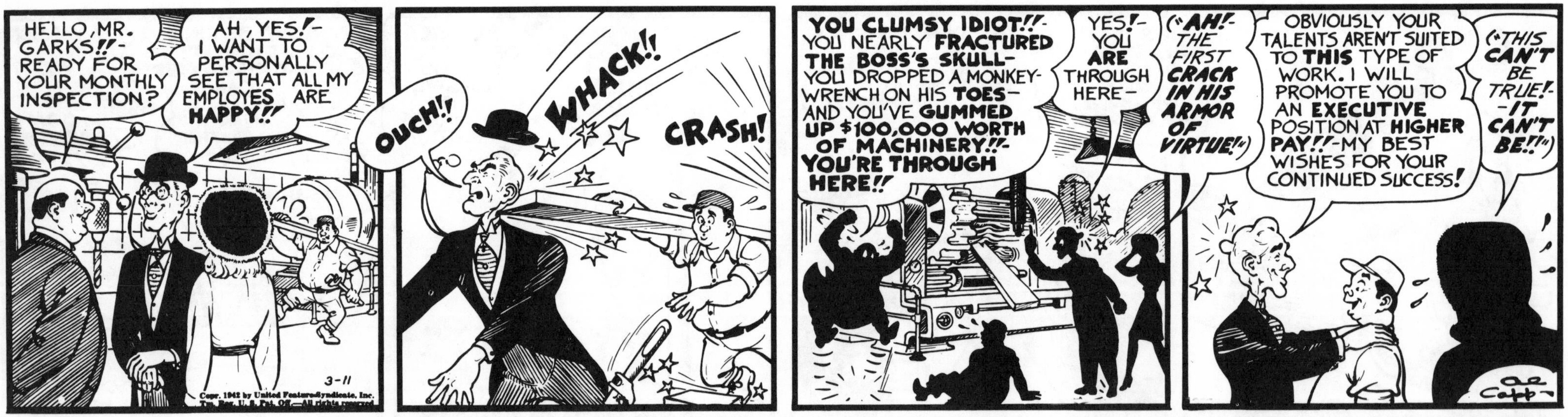
HELLO, MR. GARKS!!-READY FOR YOUR MONTHLY INSPECTION?
AH, YES!-I WANT TO PERSONALLY SEE THAT ALL MY EMPLOYES ARE HAPPY!!
3-11
Copr. 1942 by United Feature Syndicate, Inc. Tm. Reg. U. S. Pat. Off.—All rights reserved
OUCH!!
WHACK!!
CRASH!
YOU CLUMSY IDIOT!!-YOU NEARLY FRACTURED THE BOSS'S SKULL-YOU DROPPED A MONKEY-WRENCH ON HIS TOES-AND YOU'VE GUMMED UP $100,000 WORTH OF MACHINERY!!-YOU'RE THROUGH HERE!!
YES!-YOU ARE THROUGH HERE-
("AH!-THE FIRST CRACK IN HIS ARMOR OF VIRTUE!")
OBVIOUSLY YOUR TALENTS AREN'T SUITED TO THIS TYPE OF WORK. I WILL PROMOTE YOU TO AN EXECUTIVE POSITION AT HIGHER PAY!!-MY BEST WISHES FOR YOUR CONTINUED SUCCESS!
("THIS CAN'T BE TRUE!-IT CAN'T BE!!")
Al Capp

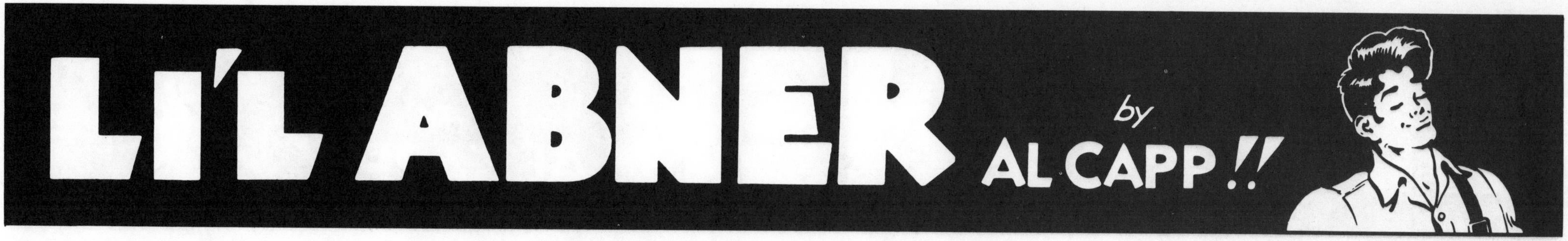
LI'L ABNER
by
AL CAPP!!

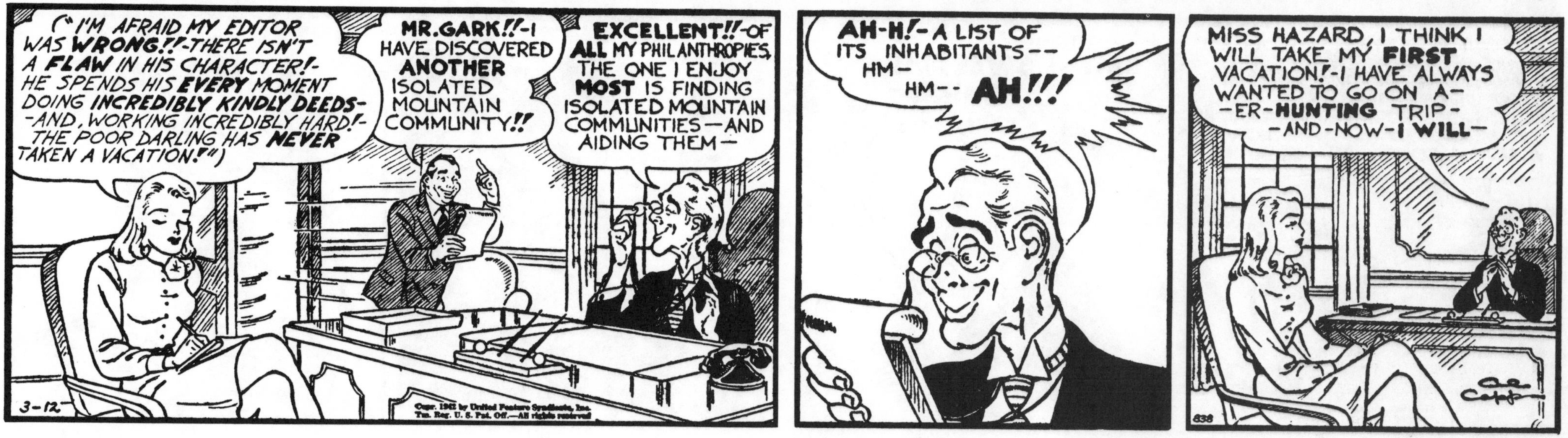
("I'M AFRAID MY EDITOR WAS WRONG!!-THERE ISN'T A FLAW IN HIS CHARACTER!-HE SPENDS HIS EVERY MOMENT DOING INCREDIBLY KINDLY DEEDS--AND, WORKING INCREDIBLY HARD!-THE POOR DARLING HAS NEVER TAKEN A VACATION!")
MR. GARK!!-I HAVE DISCOVERED ANOTHER ISOLATED MOUNTAIN COMMUNITY!!
EXCELLENT!!-OF ALL MY PHILANTHROPIES, THE ONE I ENJOY MOST IS FINDING ISOLATED MOUNTAIN COMMUNITIES—AND AIDING THEM—
3-12
AH-H!-A LIST OF ITS INHABITANTS--HM-HM--AH!!!
MISS HAZARD, I THINK I WILL TAKE MY FIRST VACATION!-I HAVE ALWAYS WANTED TO GO ON A-ER-HUNTING TRIP--AND-NOW-I WILL-
838

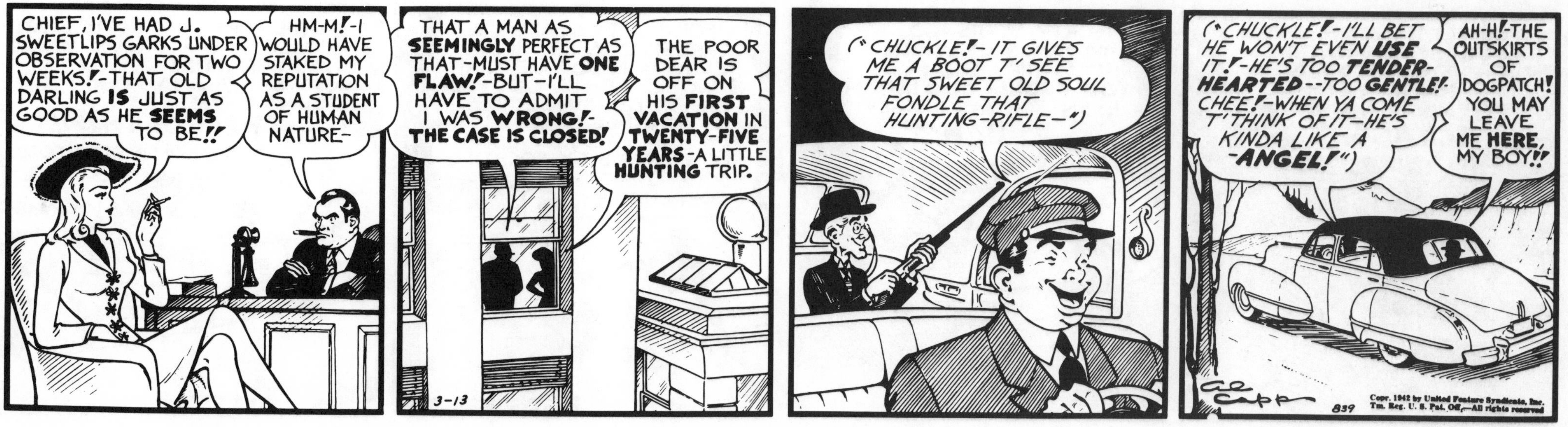
CHIEF, I'VE HAD J. SWEETLIPS GARKS UNDER OBSERVATION FOR TWO WEEKS!-THAT OLD DARLING IS JUST AS GOOD AS HE SEEMS TO BE!!
HM-M!-I WOULD HAVE STAKED MY REPUTATION AS A STUDENT OF HUMAN NATURE-
THAT A MAN AS SEEMINGLY PERFECT AS THAT-MUST HAVE ONE FLAW!-BUT-I'LL HAVE TO ADMIT I WAS WRONG!-THE CASE IS CLOSED!
THE POOR DEAR IS OFF ON HIS FIRST VACATION IN TWENTY-FIVE YEARS-A LITTLE HUNTING TRIP.
3-13
("CHUCKLE!-IT GIVES ME A BOOT T' SEE THAT SWEET OLD SOUL FONDLE THAT HUNTING-RIFLE-")
("CHUCKLE!-I'LL BET HE WON'T EVEN USE IT!-HE'S TOO TENDER-HEARTED--TOO GENTLE!-CHEE!-WHEN YA COME T'THINK OF IT-HE'S KINDA LIKE A -ANGEL!")
AH-H!-THE OUTSKIRTS OF DOGPATCH! YOU MAY LEAVE ME HERE, MY BOY!!
839
Copr. 1942 by United Feature Syndicate, Inc.
Tm. Reg. U. S. Pat. Off.—All rights reserved

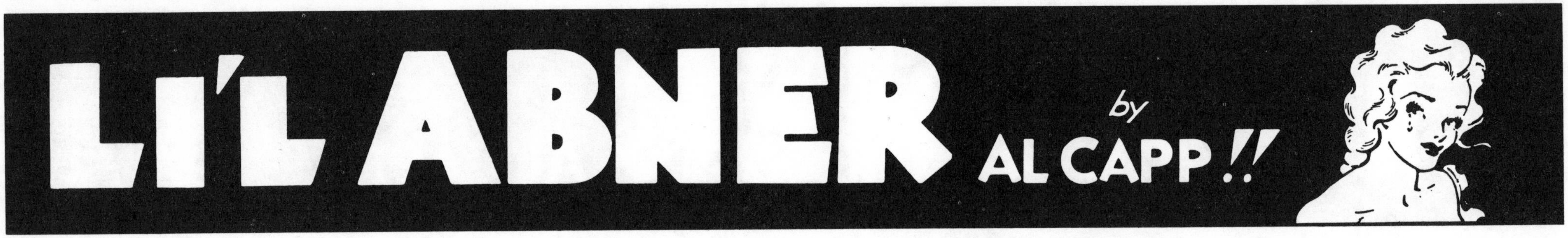
LI'L ABNER
by
AL CAPP!!

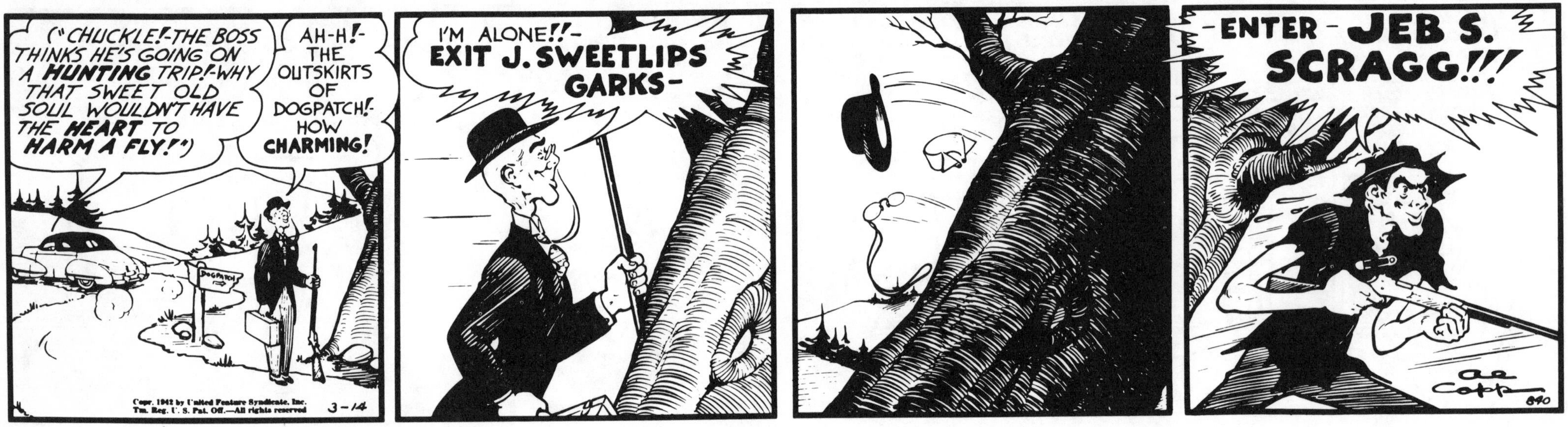
("CHUCKLE!-THE BOSS THINKS HE'S GOING ON A HUNTING TRIP!-WHY THAT SWEET OLD SOUL WOULDN'T HAVE THE HEART TO HARM A FLY!")
AH-H!-THE OUTSKIRTS OF DOGPATCH!-HOW CHARMING!
DOGPATCH
Copr. 1942 by United Feature Syndicate, Inc. Tm. Reg. U. S. Pat. Off.—All rights reserved
3-14
I'M ALONE!!- EXIT J. SWEETLIPS GARKS-
-ENTER- JEB S. SCRAGG!!!
840

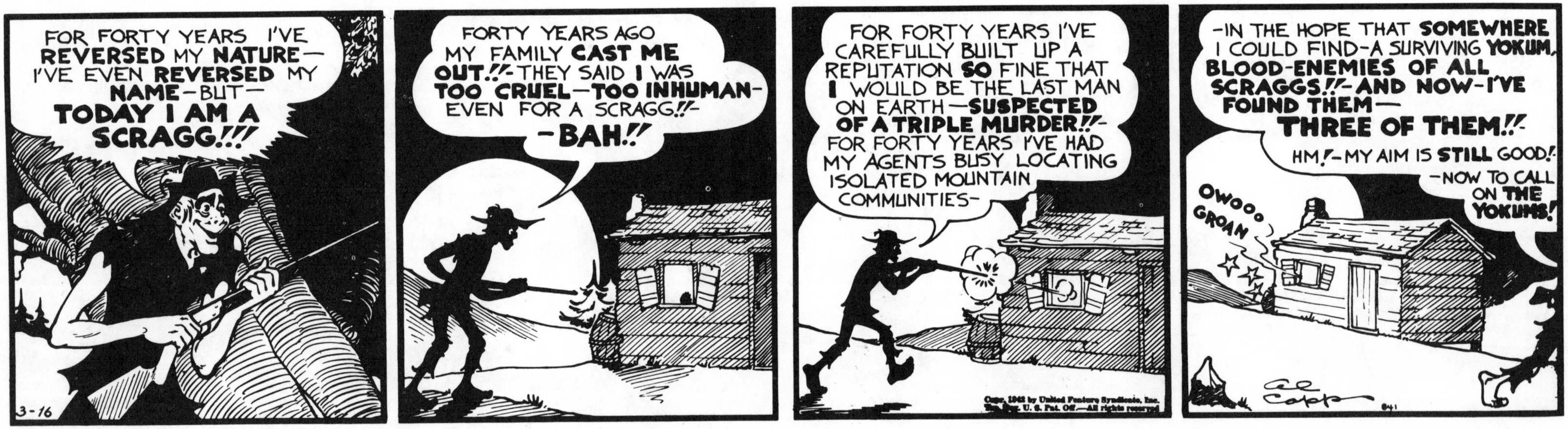
FOR FORTY YEARS I'VE REVERSED MY NATURE—I'VE EVEN REVERSED MY NAME-BUT-TODAY I AM A SCRAGG!!!
3-16
FORTY YEARS AGO MY FAMILY CAST ME OUT!!-THEY SAID I WAS TOO CRUEL-TOO INHUMAN-EVEN FOR A SCRAGG!!- -BAH!!
FOR FORTY YEARS I'VE CAREFULLY BUILT UP A REPUTATION SO FINE THAT I WOULD BE THE LAST MAN ON EARTH-SUSPECTED OF A TRIPLE MURDER!!-FOR FORTY YEARS I'VE HAD MY AGENTS BUSY LOCATING ISOLATED MOUNTAIN COMMUNITIES-
Copr. 1942 by United Feature Syndicate, Inc. Tm. Reg. U. S. Pat. Off.—All rights reserved
-IN THE HOPE THAT SOMEWHERE I COULD FIND-A SURVIVING YOKUM, BLOOD-ENEMIES OF ALL SCRAGGS!!-AND NOW-I'VE FOUND THEM-THREE OF THEM!!-
HM!-MY AIM IS STILL GOOD!-
-NOW TO CALL ON THE YOKUMS!
OWOOO GROAN
841

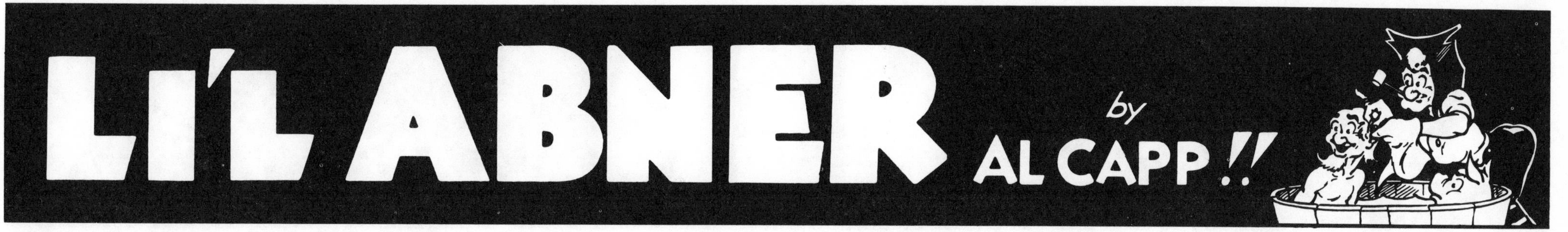
LI'L ABNER
by
AL CAPP!!

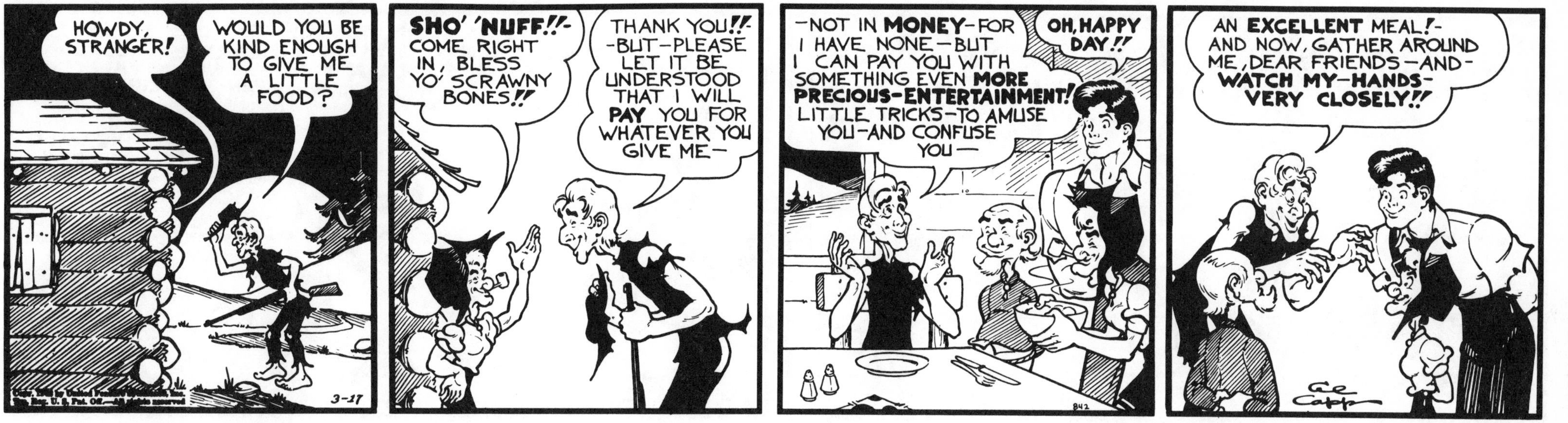
HOWDY, STRANGER!
WOULD YOU BE KIND ENOUGH TO GIVE ME A LITTLE FOOD?
Copr. 1942 by United Feature Syndicate, Inc. Tm. Reg. U. S. Pat. Off.—All rights reserved
3-17
SHO' 'NUFF!!- COME RIGHT IN, BLESS YO' SCRAWNY BONES!!
THANK YOU!!- -BUT-PLEASE LET IT BE UNDERSTOOD THAT I WILL PAY YOU FOR WHATEVER YOU GIVE ME-
-NOT IN MONEY-FOR I HAVE NONE-BUT I CAN PAY YOU WITH SOMETHING EVEN MORE PRECIOUS-ENTERTAINMENT! LITTLE TRICKS-TO AMUSE YOU-AND CONFUSE YOU-
OH, HAPPY DAY!!
842
AN EXCELLENT MEAL!- AND NOW, GATHER AROUND ME, DEAR FRIENDS-AND- WATCH MY-HANDS- VERY CLOSELY!!
Al Capp

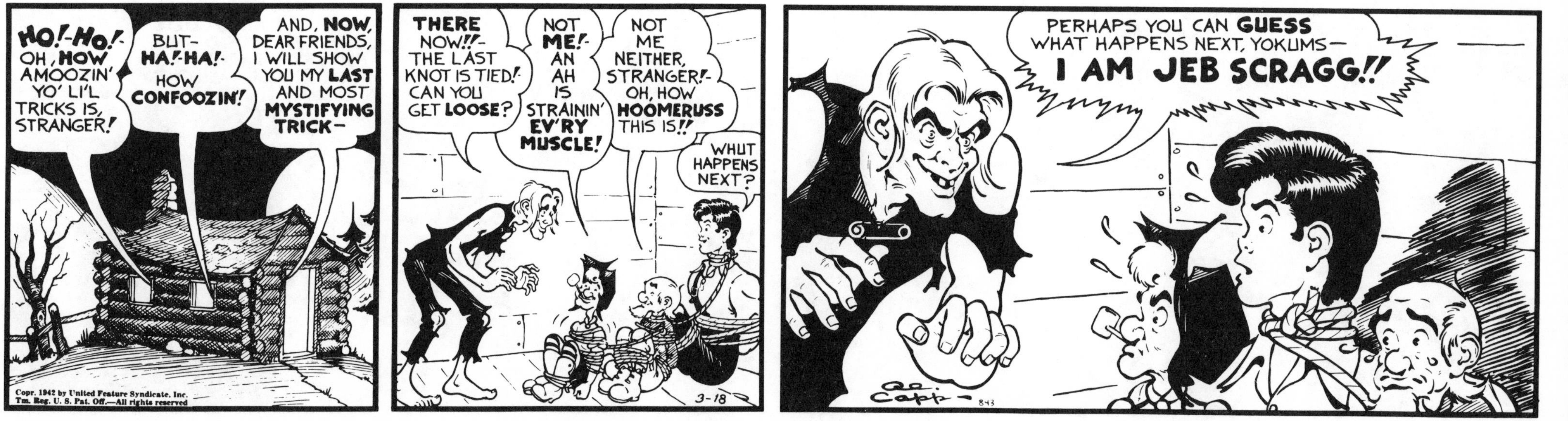
HO!-HO!- OH, HOW AMOOZIN' YO' LI'L TRICKS IS, STRANGER!
BUT- HA!-HA!- HOW CONFOOZIN'!
AND, NOW, DEAR FRIENDS, I WILL SHOW YOU MY LAST AND MOST MYSTIFYING TRICK-
Copr. 1942 by United Feature Syndicate, Inc. Tm. Reg. U. S. Pat. Off.—All rights reserved
THERE NOW!!- THE LAST KNOT IS TIED!- CAN YOU GET LOOSE?
NOT ME!- AN AH IS STRAININ' EV'RY MUSCLE!
NOT ME NEITHER, STRANGER!- OH, HOW HOOMERUSS THIS IS!!
WHUT HAPPENS NEXT?
3-18
PERHAPS YOU CAN GUESS WHAT HAPPENS NEXT, YOKUMS- I AM JEB SCRAGG!!
Al Capp
843

LI'L ABNER by AL CAPP!!

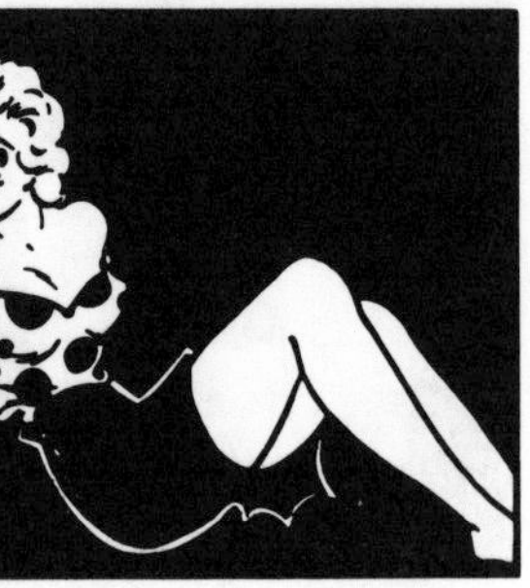

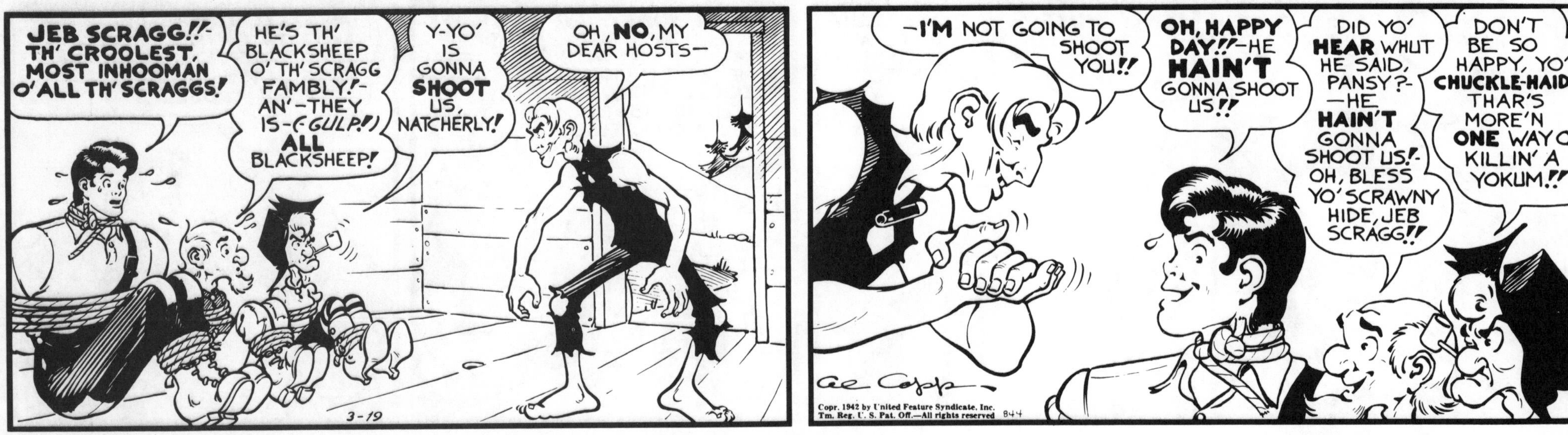

JEB SCRAGG!!-TH' CROOLEST, MOST INHOOMAN O'ALL TH' SCRAGGS!
HE'S TH' BLACKSHEEP O' TH' SCRAGG FAMBLY!-AN'-THEY IS-(-GULP!-) ALL BLACKSHEEP!
Y-YO' IS GONNA SHOOT US, NATCHERLY!
OH, NO, MY DEAR HOSTS—
3-19
-I'M NOT GOING TO SHOOT YOU!!
OH, HAPPY DAY!!-HE HAIN'T GONNA SHOOT US!!
DID YO' HEAR WHUT HE SAID, PANSY?-—HE HAIN'T GONNA SHOOT US!-OH, BLESS YO' SCRAWNY HIDE, JEB SCRAGG!!
DON'T BE SO HAPPY, YO' CHUCKLE-HAIDS! THAR'S MORE'N ONE WAY O' KILLIN' A YOKUM!!
Al Capp
Copr. 1942 by United Feature Syndicate, Inc. Tm. Reg. U. S. Pat. Off.—All rights reserved
844

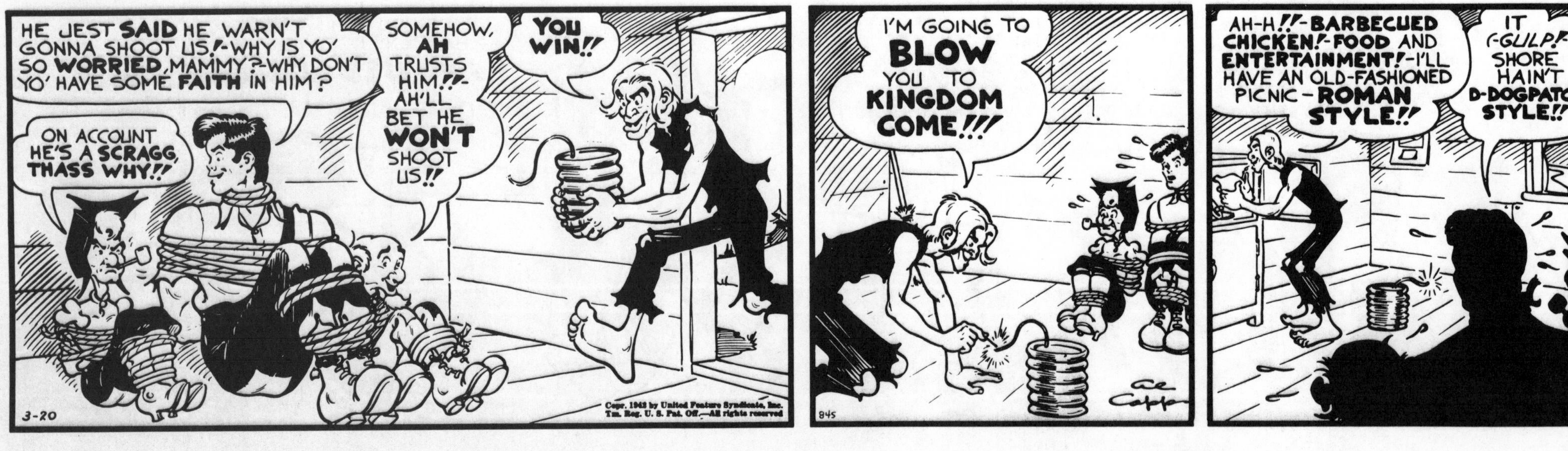

HE JEST SAID HE WARN'T GONNA SHOOT US!-WHY IS YO' SO WORRIED, MAMMY?-WHY DON'T YO' HAVE SOME FAITH IN HIM?
ON ACCOUNT HE'S A SCRAGG, THASS WHY!!
SOMEHOW, AH TRUSTS HIM!!-AH'LL BET HE WON'T SHOOT US!!
YOU WIN!!
3-20
Copr. 1942 by United Feature Syndicate, Inc. Tm. Reg. U. S. Pat. Off.—All rights reserved
I'M GOING TO BLOW YOU TO KINGDOM COME!!!
Al Capp
845
AH-H!!-BARBECUED CHICKEN!-FOOD AND ENTERTAINMENT!-I'LL HAVE AN OLD-FASHIONED PICNIC-ROMAN STYLE!!
IT (-GULP!-) SHORE HAIN'T D-DOGPATCH STYLE!!

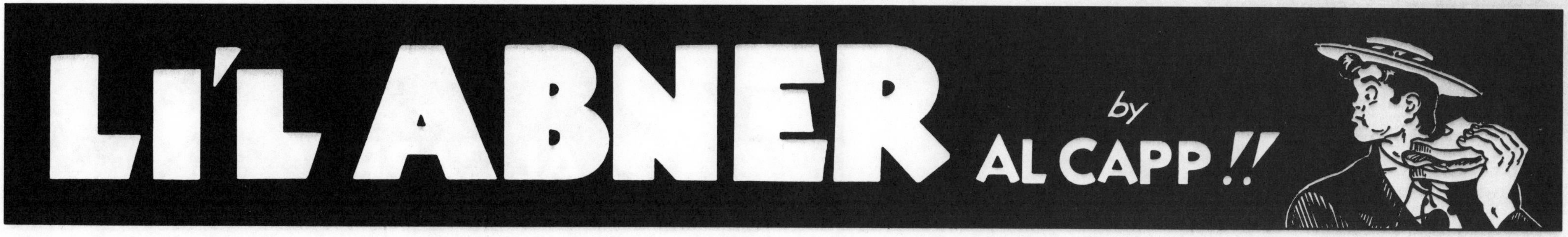
LI'L ABNER
by
AL CAPP!!

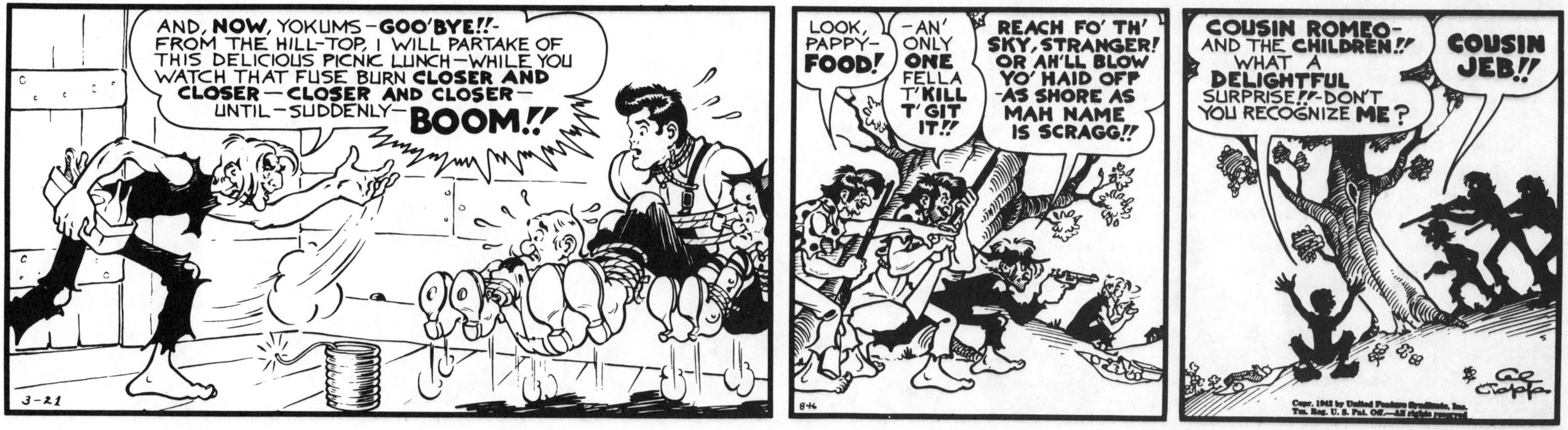
AND, NOW, YOKUMS–GOO'BYE!!- FROM THE HILL-TOP, I WILL PARTAKE OF THIS DELICIOUS PICNIC LUNCH–WHILE YOU WATCH THAT FUSE BURN CLOSER AND CLOSER–CLOSER AND CLOSER–UNTIL–SUDDENLY–BOOM!!
3-21
LOOK, PAPPY–FOOD!
–AN' ONLY ONE FELLA T'KILL T'GIT IT!!
REACH FO' TH' SKY, STRANGER! OR AH'LL BLOW YO' HAID OFF -AS SHORE AS MAH NAME IS SCRAGG!!
846
COUSIN ROMEO–AND THE CHILDREN!! WHAT A DELIGHTFUL SURPRISE!!-DON'T YOU RECOGNIZE ME?
COUSIN JEB!!
Al Capp
Copr. 1942 by United Feature Syndicate, Inc.
Tm. Reg. U. S. Pat. Off.—All rights reserved

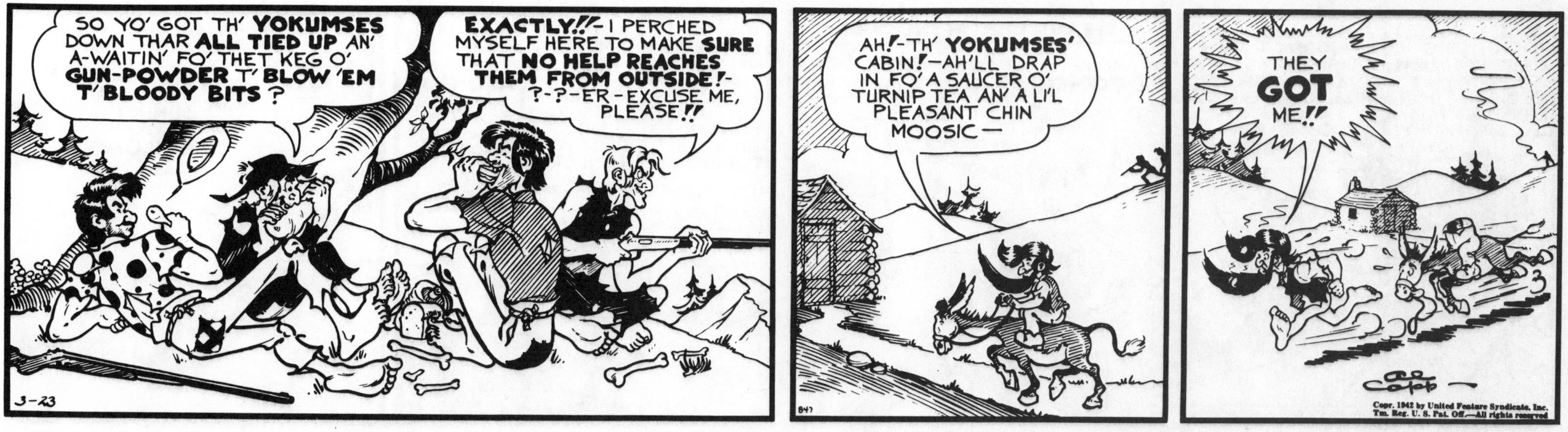
SO YO' GOT TH' YOKUMSES DOWN THAR ALL TIED UP AN' A-WAITIN' FO' THET KEG O' GUN-POWDER T' BLOW 'EM T' BLOODY BITS?
EXACTLY!!-I PERCHED MYSELF HERE TO MAKE SURE THAT NO HELP REACHES THEM FROM OUTSIDE!- ?-?-ER-EXCUSE ME, PLEASE!!
3-23
AH!-TH' YOKUMSES' CABIN!-AH'LL DRAP IN FO' A SAUCER O' TURNIP TEA AN' A LI'L PLEASANT CHIN MOOSIC–
847
THEY GOT ME!!
Al Capp
Copr. 1942 by United Feature Syndicate, Inc.
Tm. Reg. U. S. Pat. Off.—All rights reserved

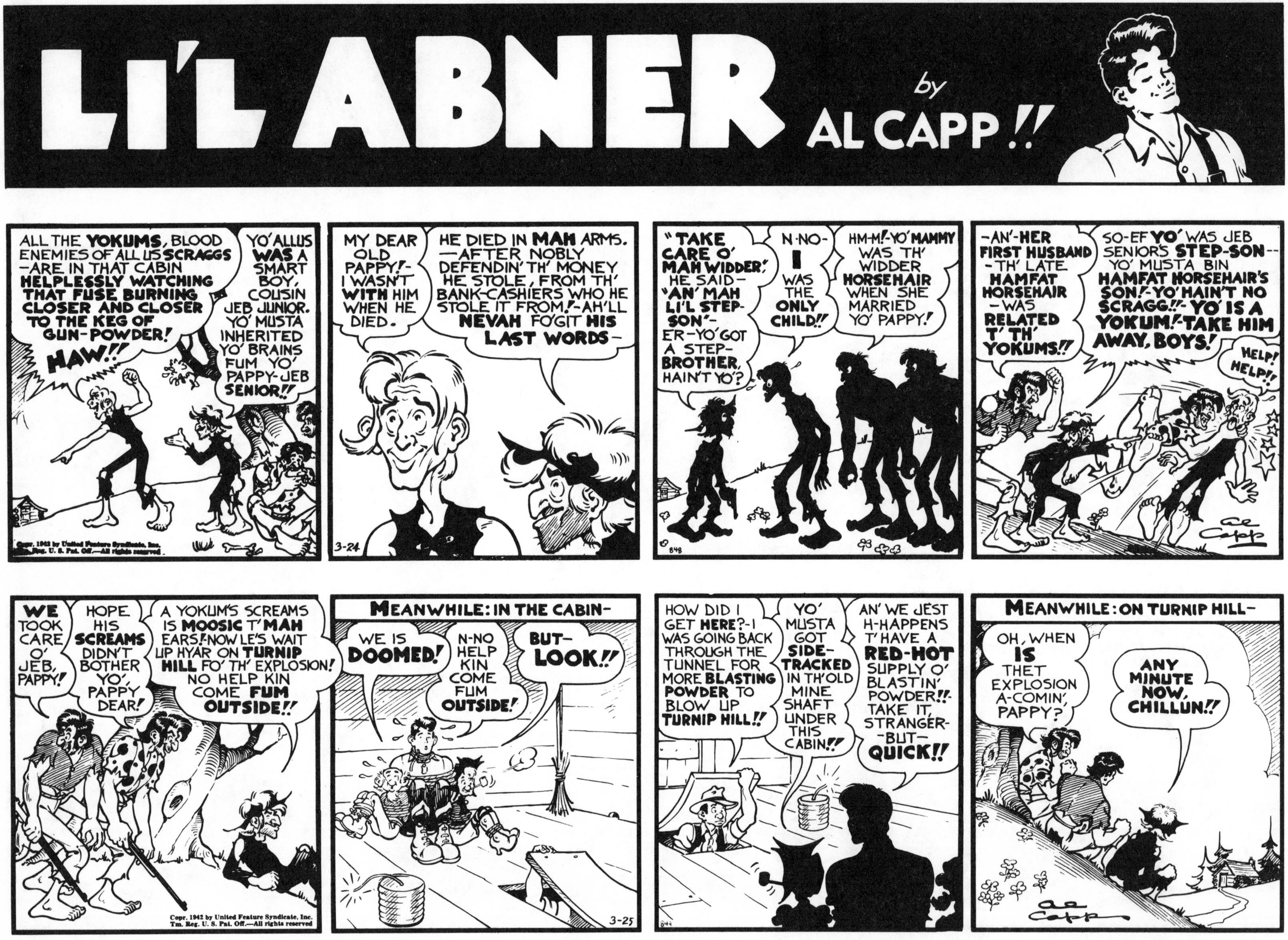
LI'L ABNER
by
AL CAPP!!
ALL THE YOKUMS, BLOOD ENEMIES OF ALL US SCRAGGS —ARE IN THAT CABIN HELPLESSLY WATCHING THAT FUSE BURNING CLOSER AND CLOSER TO THE KEG OF GUN-POWDER!
HAW!!
YO' ALLUS WAS A SMART BOY, COUSIN JEB JUNIOR. YO' MUSTA INHERITED YO' BRAINS FUM YO' PAPPY-JEB SENIOR!!
MY DEAR OLD PAPPY!-I WASN'T WITH HIM WHEN HE DIED.
HE DIED IN MAH ARMS. —AFTER NOBLY DEFENDIN' TH' MONEY HE STOLE, FROM TH' BANK-CASHIERS WHO HE STOLE IT FROM!-AH'LL NEVAH FO'GIT HIS LAST WORDS-
3-24
"TAKE CARE O' MAH WIDDER," HE SAID- "AN' MAH LI'L STEP-SON"- ER-YO' GOT A STEP-BROTHER, HAIN'T YO'?
N-NO- I WAS THE ONLY CHILD!!
HM-M!-YO' MAMMY WAS TH' WIDDER HORSEHAIR WHEN SHE MARRIED YO' PAPPY!
848
-AN'-HER FIRST HUSBAND -TH' LATE HAMFAT HORSEHAIR -WAS RELATED T' TH' YOKUMS!!
SO-EF YO' WAS JEB SENIOR'S STEP-SON-- YO' MUSTA BIN HAMFAT HORSEHAIR'S SON!-YO' HAIN'T NO SCRAGG!!-YO' IS A YOKUM!-TAKE HIM AWAY, BOYS!
HELP! HELP!!
AL CAPP
WE TOOK CARE O' JEB, PAPPY!
HOPE HIS SCREAMS DIDN'T BOTHER YO', PAPPY DEAR!
A YOKUM'S SCREAMS IS MOOSIC T' MAH EARS!-NOW LE'S WAIT UP HYAR ON TURNIP HILL FO' TH' EXPLOSION! NO HELP KIN COME FUM OUTSIDE!!
Copr. 1942 by United Feature Syndicate, Inc. Tm. Reg. U. S. Pat. Off.—All rights reserved
MEANWHILE: IN THE CABIN-
WE IS DOOMED!
N-NO HELP KIN COME FUM OUTSIDE!
BUT- LOOK!!
3-25
HOW DID I GET HERE?-I WAS GOING BACK THROUGH THE TUNNEL FOR MORE BLASTING POWDER TO BLOW UP TURNIP HILL!!
YO' MUSTA GOT SIDE-TRACKED IN TH'OLD MINE SHAFT UNDER THIS CABIN!!
AN' WE JEST H-HAPPENS T' HAVE A RED-HOT SUPPLY O' BLASTIN' POWDER!!-TAKE IT, STRANGER- -BUT- QUICK!!
849
MEANWHILE: ON TURNIP HILL-
OH, WHEN IS THET EXPLOSION A-COMIN', PAPPY?
ANY MINUTE NOW, CHILLUN!!
AL CAPP

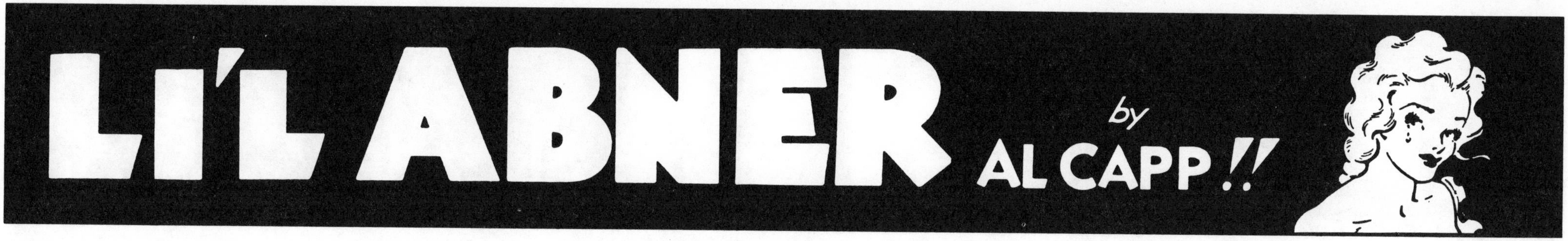
LI'L ABNER
by
AL CAPP!!

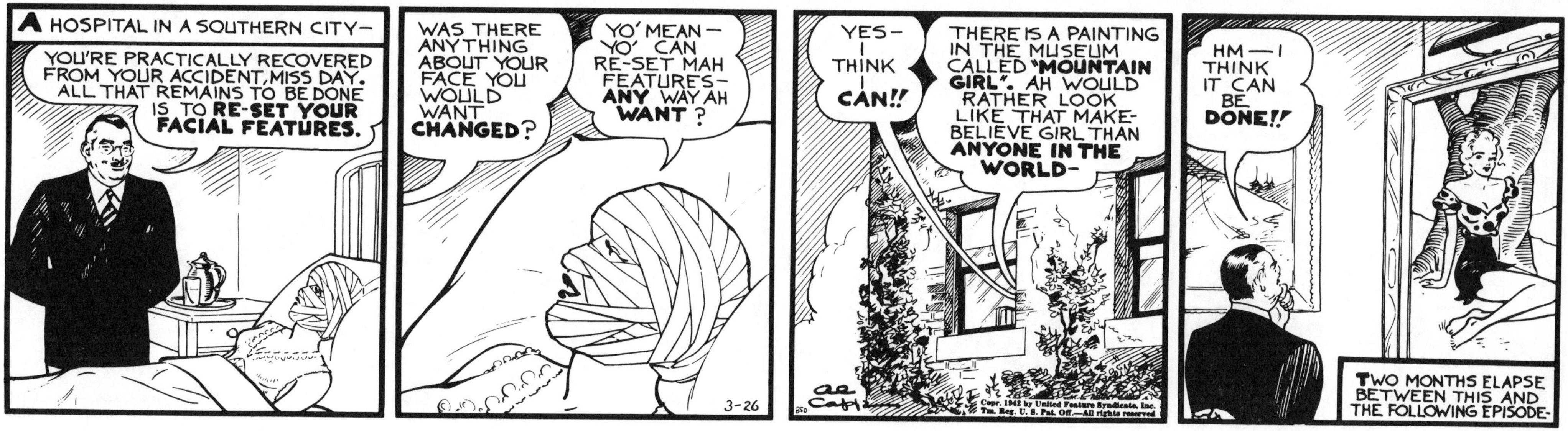
A HOSPITAL IN A SOUTHERN CITY—
YOU'RE PRACTICALLY RECOVERED FROM YOUR ACCIDENT, MISS DAY. ALL THAT REMAINS TO BE DONE IS TO RE-SET YOUR FACIAL FEATURES.
WAS THERE ANYTHING ABOUT YOUR FACE YOU WOULD WANT CHANGED?
YO' MEAN — YO' CAN RE-SET MAH FEATURES— ANY WAY AH WANT ?
3-26
YES— I THINK I CAN!!
THERE IS A PAINTING IN THE MUSEUM CALLED "MOUNTAIN GIRL". AH WOULD RATHER LOOK LIKE THAT MAKE-BELIEVE GIRL THAN ANYONE IN THE WORLD—
Copr. 1942 by United Feature Syndicate, Inc. Tm. Reg. U. S. Pat. Off.—All rights reserved
HM — I THINK IT CAN BE DONE!!
TWO MONTHS ELAPSE BETWEEN THIS AND THE FOLLOWING EPISODE—

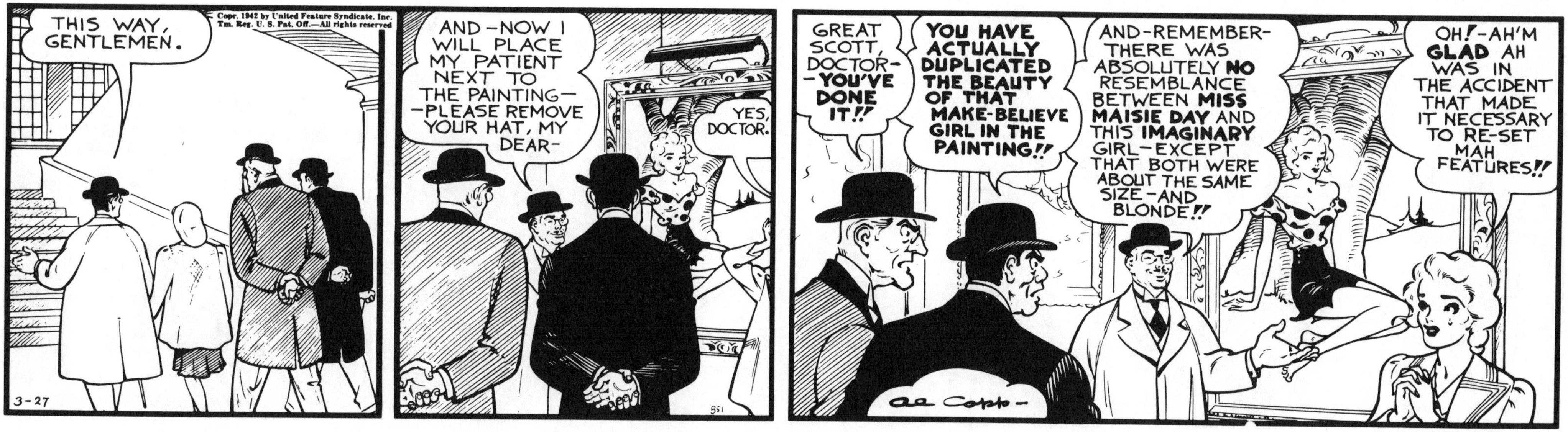
THIS WAY, GENTLEMEN.
Copr. 1942 by United Feature Syndicate, Inc. Tm. Reg. U. S. Pat. Off.—All rights reserved
3-27
AND—NOW I WILL PLACE MY PATIENT NEXT TO THE PAINTING— —PLEASE REMOVE YOUR HAT, MY DEAR—
YES, DOCTOR.
GREAT SCOTT, DOCTOR— —YOU'VE DONE IT!!
YOU HAVE ACTUALLY DUPLICATED THE BEAUTY OF THAT MAKE-BELIEVE GIRL IN THE PAINTING!!
AND—REMEMBER— THERE WAS ABSOLUTELY NO RESEMBLANCE BETWEEN MISS MAISIE DAY AND THIS IMAGINARY GIRL—EXCEPT THAT BOTH WERE ABOUT THE SAME SIZE—AND BLONDE!!
OH!—AH'M GLAD AH WAS IN THE ACCIDENT THAT MADE IT NECESSARY TO RE-SET MAH FEATURES!!

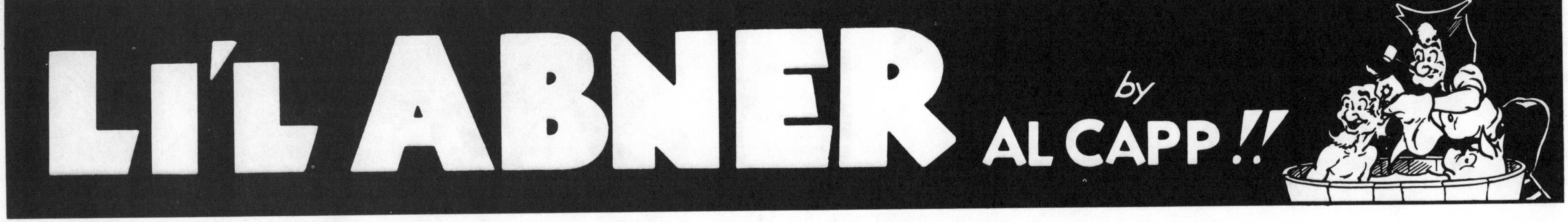
LI'L ABNER
by
AL CAPP!!

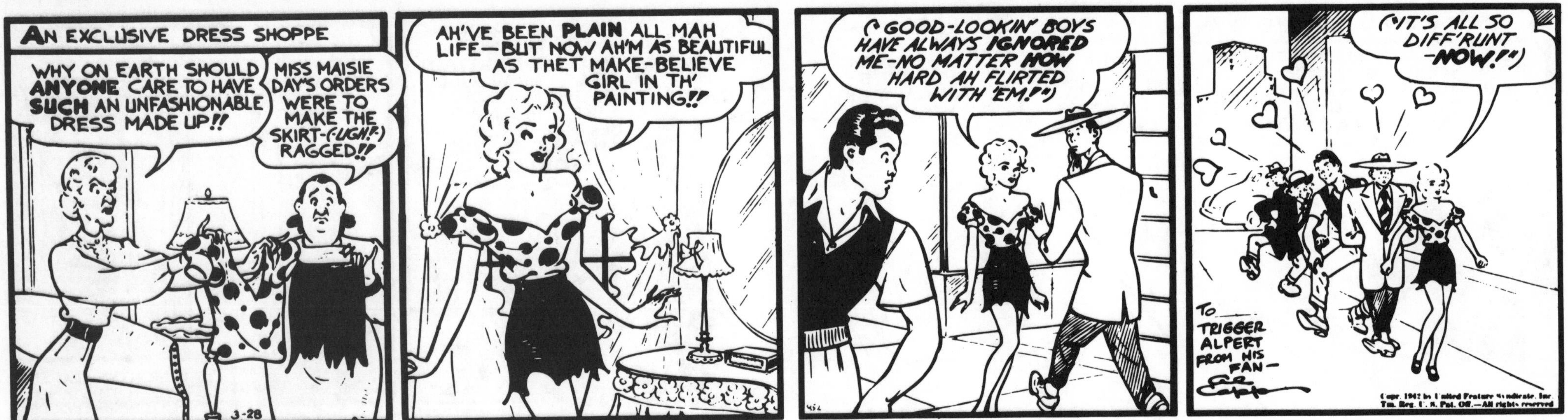
AN EXCLUSIVE DRESS SHOPPE
WHY ON EARTH SHOULD ANYONE CARE TO HAVE SUCH AN UNFASHIONABLE DRESS MADE UP!!
MISS MAISIE DAY'S ORDERS WERE TO MAKE THE SKIRT-(-UGH!-) RAGGED!!
3-28
AH'VE BEEN PLAIN ALL MAH LIFE—BUT NOW AH'M AS BEAUTIFUL AS THET MAKE-BELIEVE GIRL IN TH' PAINTING!!
("GOOD-LOOKIN' BOYS HAVE ALWAYS IGNORED ME-NO MATTER HOW HARD AH FLIRTED WITH 'EM!")
("IT'S ALL SO DIFF'RUNT -NOW!")
TO TRIGGER ALPERT FROM HIS FAN—
Copr. 1942 by United Feature Syndicate, Inc.
Tm. Reg. U. S. Pat. Off.—All rights reserved

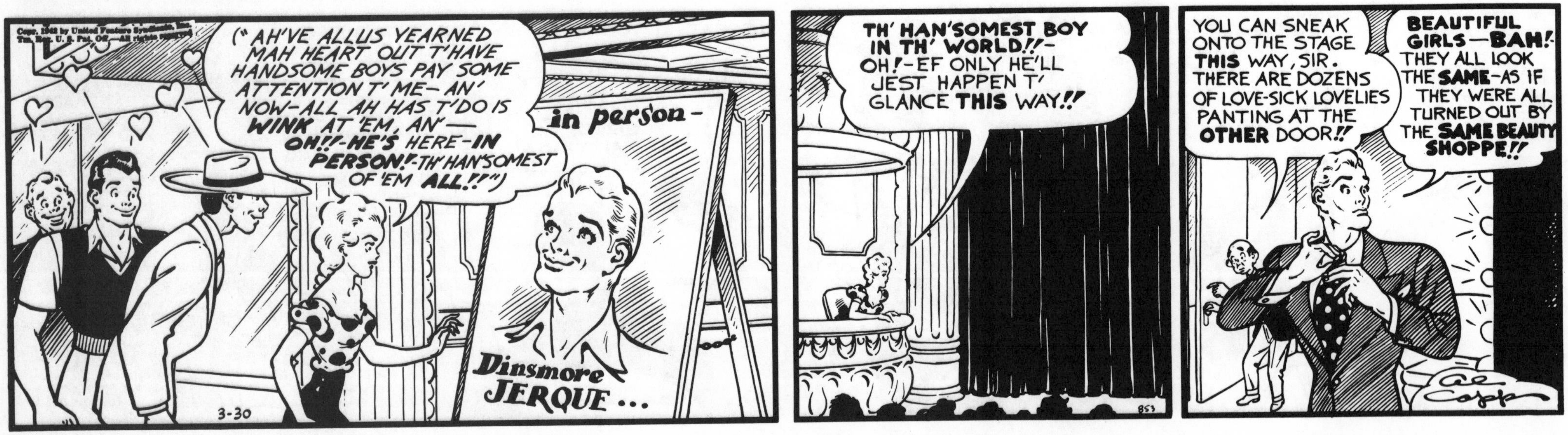
Copr. 1942 by United Feature Syndicate, Inc.
Tm. Reg. U. S. Pat. Off.—All rights reserved
("AH'VE ALLUS YEARNED MAH HEART OUT T'HAVE HANDSOME BOYS PAY SOME ATTENTION T' ME—AN' NOW-ALL AH HAS T'DO IS WINK AT 'EM, AN'— OH!!-HE'S HERE-IN PERSON!-TH' HAN'SOMEST OF 'EM ALL!!")
in person-
Dinsmore JERQUE...
3-30
TH' HAN'SOMEST BOY IN TH' WORLD!!- OH!-EF ONLY HE'LL JEST HAPPEN T' GLANCE THIS WAY!!
YOU CAN SNEAK ONTO THE STAGE THIS WAY, SIR. THERE ARE DOZENS OF LOVE-SICK LOVELIES PANTING AT THE OTHER DOOR!!
BEAUTIFUL GIRLS—BAH!- THEY ALL LOOK THE SAME—AS IF THEY WERE ALL TURNED OUT BY THE SAME BEAUTY SHOPPE!!

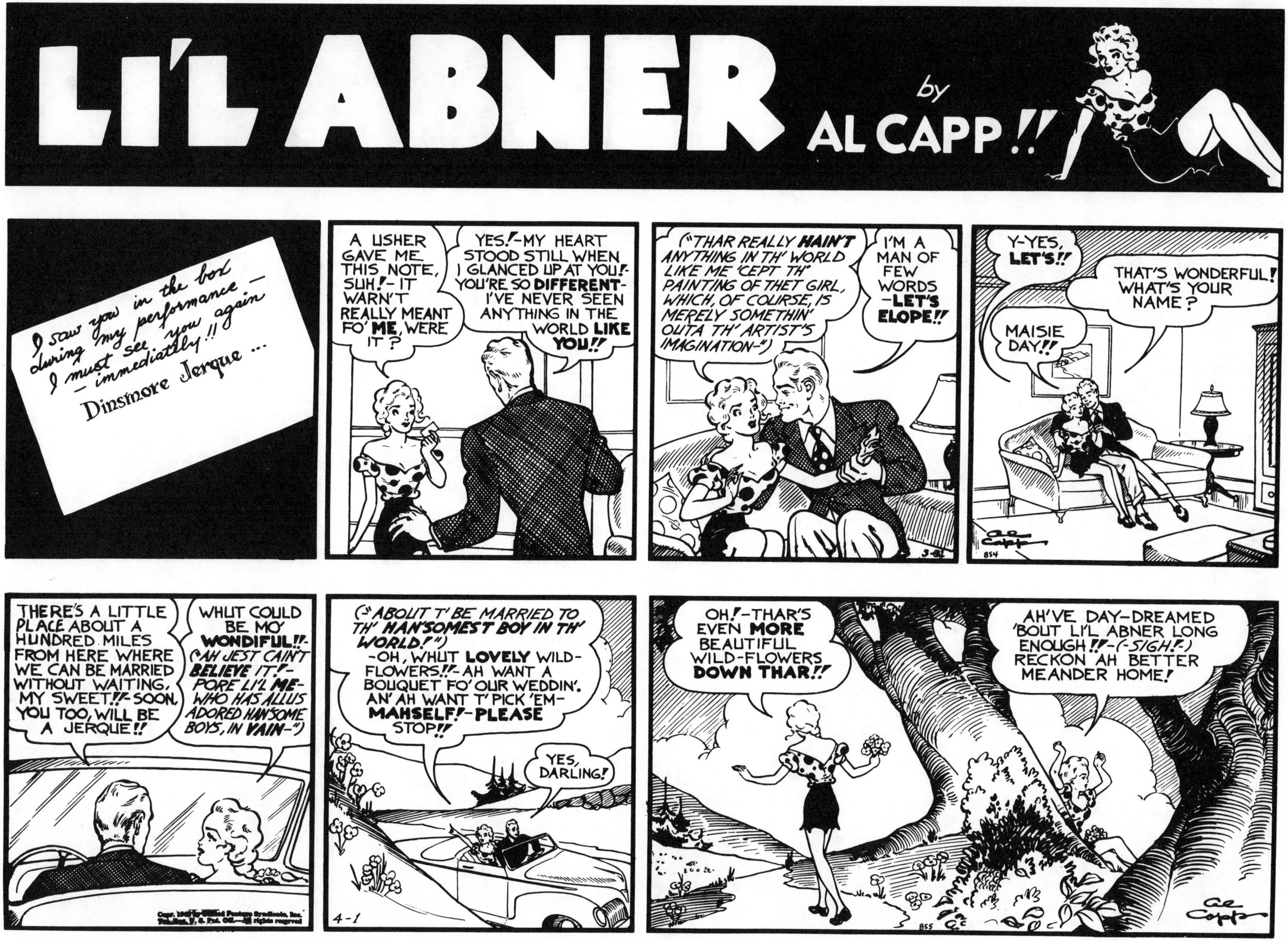

LI'L ABNER
by AL CAPP!!
I saw you in the box during my performance — I must see you again — immediately!!
Dinsmore Jerque ...
A USHER GAVE ME THIS NOTE, SUH!- IT WARN'T REALLY MEANT FO' ME, WERE IT?
YES!-MY HEART STOOD STILL WHEN I GLANCED UP AT YOU!- YOU'RE SO DIFFERENT- I'VE NEVER SEEN ANYTHING IN THE WORLD LIKE YOU!!
("THAR REALLY HAIN'T ANYTHING IN TH' WORLD LIKE ME 'CEPT TH' PAINTING OF THET GIRL, WHICH, OF COURSE, IS MERELY SOMETHIN' OUTA TH' ARTIST'S IMAGINATION-")
I'M A MAN OF FEW WORDS -LET'S ELOPE!!
3-31
Y-YES, LET'S!!
THAT'S WONDERFUL! WHAT'S YOUR NAME?
MAISIE DAY!!
AL CAPP
854
THERE'S A LITTLE PLACE ABOUT A HUNDRED MILES FROM HERE WHERE WE CAN BE MARRIED WITHOUT WAITING, MY SWEET!!- SOON, YOU TOO, WILL BE A JERQUE!!
WHUT COULD BE MO' WONDIFUL!!- ("AH JEST CAIN'T BELIEVE IT!- PORE LI'L ME- WHO HAS ALLUS ADORED HAN'SOME BOYS, IN VAIN-")
(-"ABOUT T' BE MARRIED TO TH' HAN'SOMEST BOY IN TH' WORLD!")
-OH, WHUT LOVELY WILD-FLOWERS!!-AH WANT A BOUQUET FO' OUR WEDDIN'. AN' AH WANT T' PICK 'EM MAHSELF!-PLEASE STOP!!
YES, DARLING!
4-1
OH!-THAR'S EVEN MORE BEAUTIFUL WILD-FLOWERS DOWN THAR!!
AH'VE DAY-DREAMED 'BOUT LI'L ABNER LONG ENOUGH!!-(-SIGH!-) RECKON AH BETTER MEANDER HOME!
AL CAPP
855

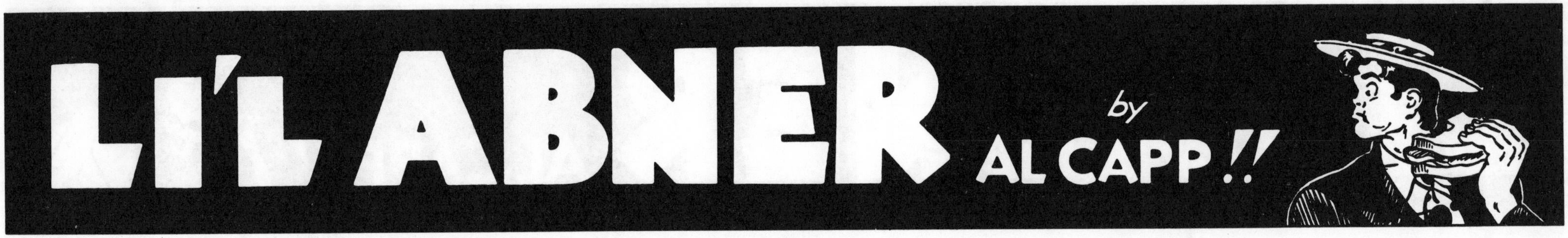
LI'L ABNER
by
AL CAPP!!

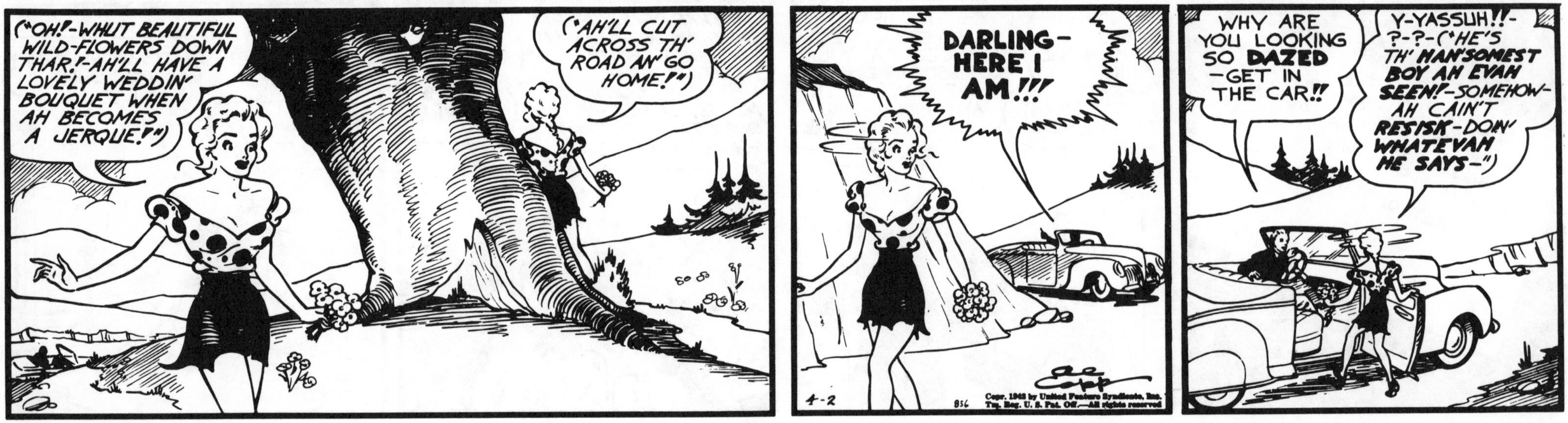
("OH!-WHUT BEAUTIFUL WILD-FLOWERS DOWN THAR!-AH'LL HAVE A LOVELY WEDDIN' BOUQUET WHEN AH BECOMES A JERQUE!")
("AH'LL CUT ACROSS TH' ROAD AN' GO HOME!")
DARLING-HERE I AM!!!
4-2
856
Copr. 1942 by United Feature Syndicate, Inc. Tm. Reg. U. S. Pat. Off.—All rights reserved
WHY ARE YOU LOOKING SO DAZED -GET IN THE CAR!!
Y-YASSUH!!-?-?-("HE'S TH' HAN'SOMEST BOY AH EVAH SEEN!-SOMEHOW-AH CAIN'T RESISK-DOIN' WHATEVAH HE SAYS-")

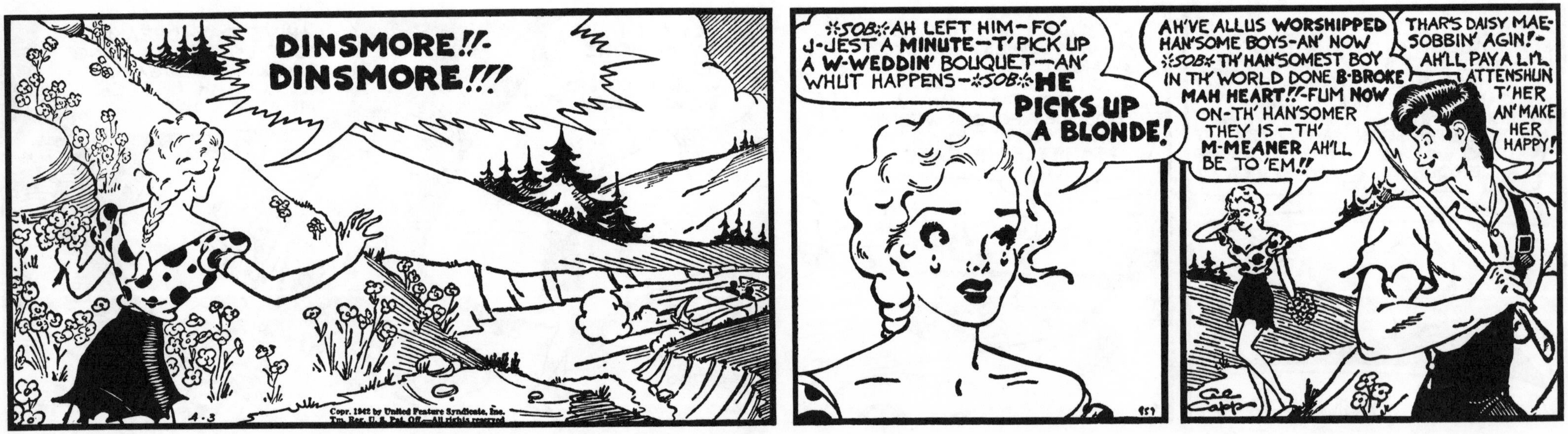
DINSMORE!!-DINSMORE!!!
4-3
Copr. 1942 by United Feature Syndicate, Inc. Tm. Reg. U. S. Pat. Off.—All rights reserved
SOB AH LEFT HIM-FO' J-JEST A MINUTE-T' PICK UP A W-WEDDIN' BOUQUET-AN' WHUT HAPPENS-*SOB* HE PICKS UP A BLONDE!
857
AH'VE ALLUS WORSHIPPED HAN'SOME BOYS-AN' NOW *SOB* TH' HAN'SOMEST BOY IN TH' WORLD DONE B-BROKE MAH HEART!!-FUM NOW ON-TH' HAN'SOMER THEY IS-TH' M-MEANER AH'LL BE TO 'EM!!
THAR'S DAISY MAE-SOBBIN' AGIN!-AH'LL PAY A LI'L ATTENSHUN T'HER AN' MAKE HER HAPPY!

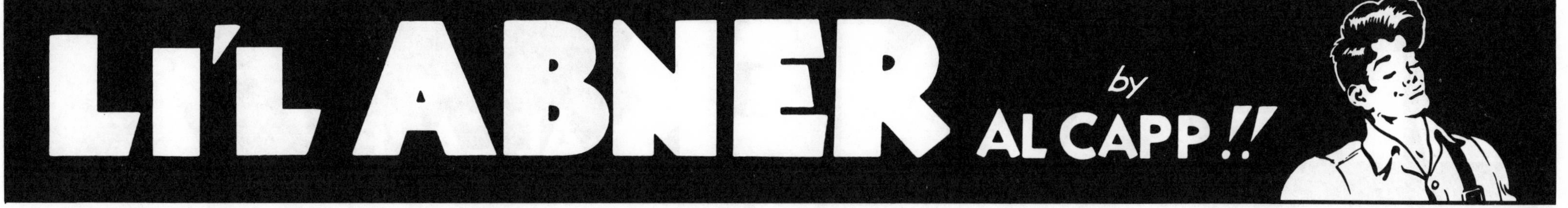
LI'L ABNER
by
AL CAPP!!

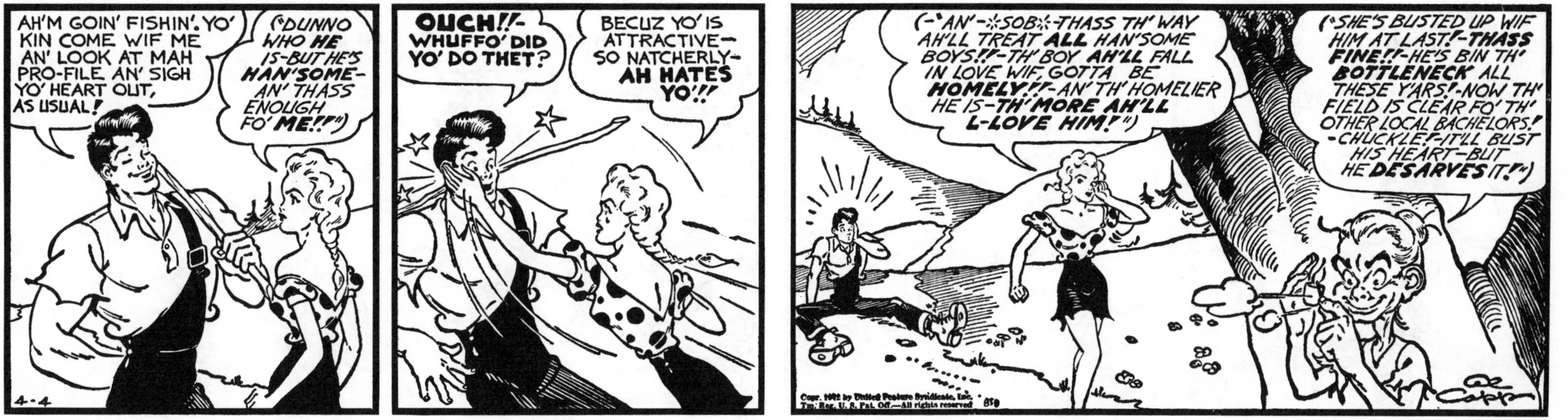
AH'M GOIN' FISHIN'. YO' KIN COME WIF ME AN' LOOK AT MAH PRO-FILE AN' SIGH YO' HEART OUT, AS USUAL!
("DUNNO WHO HE IS-BUT HE'S HAN'SOME-AN' THASS ENOUGH FO' ME!!")
4-4
OUCH!!-WHUFFO' DID YO' DO THET?
BECUZ YO' IS ATTRACTIVE-SO NATCHERLY-AH HATES YO'!!
(-"AN'-*SOB*-THASS TH' WAY AH'LL TREAT ALL HAN'SOME BOYS!!-TH' BOY AH'LL FALL IN LOVE WIF, GOTTA BE HOMELY!!-AN' TH' HOMELIER HE IS-TH' MORE AH'LL L-LOVE HIM!")
("SHE'S BUSTED UP WIF HIM AT LAST!-THASS FINE!!-HE'S BIN TH' BOTTLENECK ALL THESE Y'ARS!-NOW TH' FIELD IS CLEAR FO' TH' OTHER LOCAL BACHELORS!-CHUCKLE!-IT'LL BUST HIS HEART-BUT HE DESARVES IT!")
Copr. 1942 by United Feature Syndicate, Inc. Tm. Reg. U. S. Pat. Off.—All rights reserved
AL CAPP

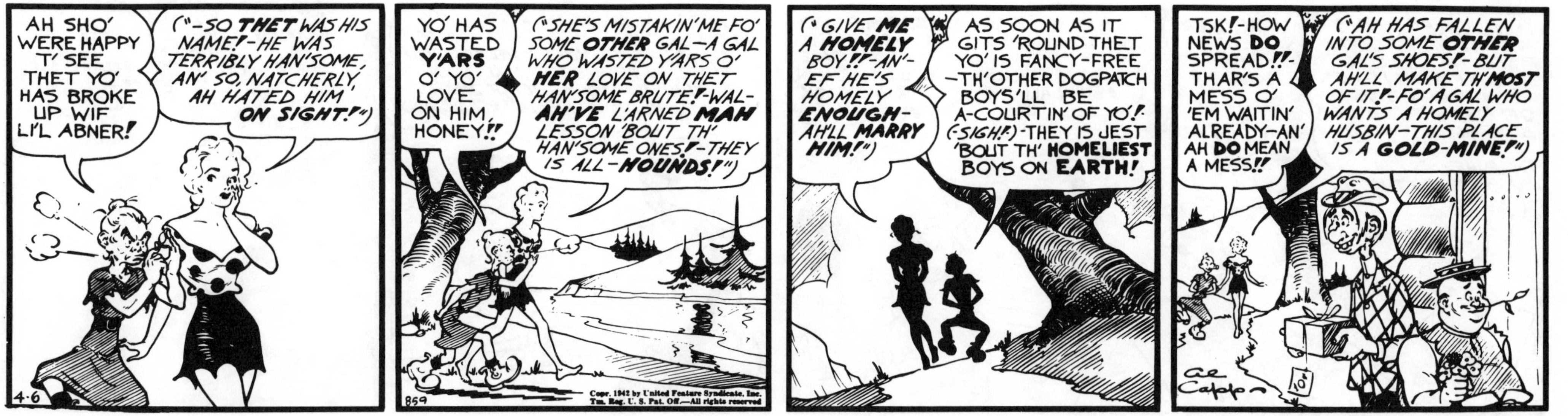
AH SHO' WERE HAPPY T' SEE THET YO' HAS BROKE UP WIF LI'L ABNER!
("-SO THET WAS HIS NAME!-HE WAS TERRIBLY HAN'SOME, AN' SO, NATCHERLY, AH HATED HIM ON SIGHT!")
4-6
YO' HAS WASTED Y'ARS O' YO' LOVE ON HIM, HONEY!!
("SHE'S MISTAKIN' ME FO' SOME OTHER GAL-A GAL WHO WASTED Y'ARS O' HER LOVE ON THET HAN'SOME BRUTE!-WAL-AH'VE L'ARNED MAH LESSON 'BOUT TH' HAN'SOME ONES!-THEY IS ALL-HOUNDS!")
Copr. 1942 by United Feature Syndicate, Inc. Tm. Reg. U. S. Pat. Off.—All rights reserved
("GIVE ME A HOMELY BOY!!-AN'-EF HE'S HOMELY ENOUGH-AH'LL MARRY HIM!")
AS SOON AS IT GITS 'ROUND THET YO' IS FANCY-FREE-TH' OTHER DOGPATCH BOYS'LL BE A-COURTIN' OF YO'!-(-SIGH!-)-THEY IS JEST 'BOUT TH' HOMELIEST BOYS ON EARTH!
TSK!-HOW NEWS DO SPREAD!!-THAR'S A MESS O' 'EM WAITIN' ALREADY-AN' AH DO MEAN A MESS!!
("AH HAS FALLEN INTO SOME OTHER GAL'S SHOES!-BUT AH'LL MAKE TH' MOST OF IT!-FO' A GAL WHO WANTS A HOMELY HUSBIN-THIS PLACE IS A GOLD-MINE!")
AL CAPP

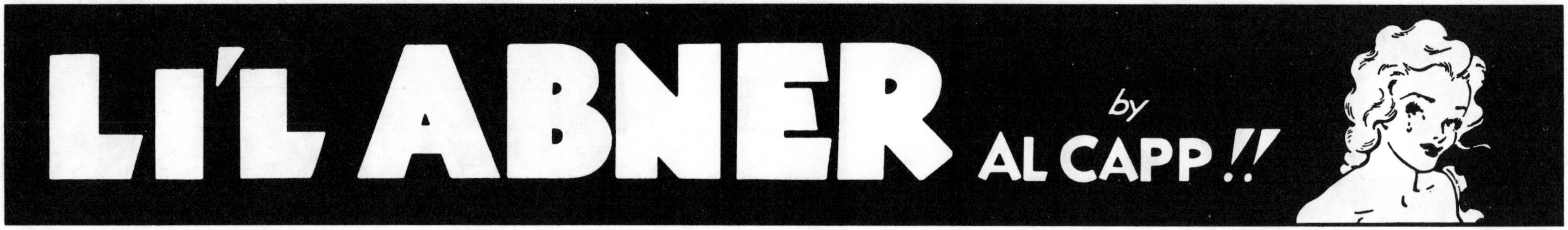
LI'L ABNER
by AL CAPP!!

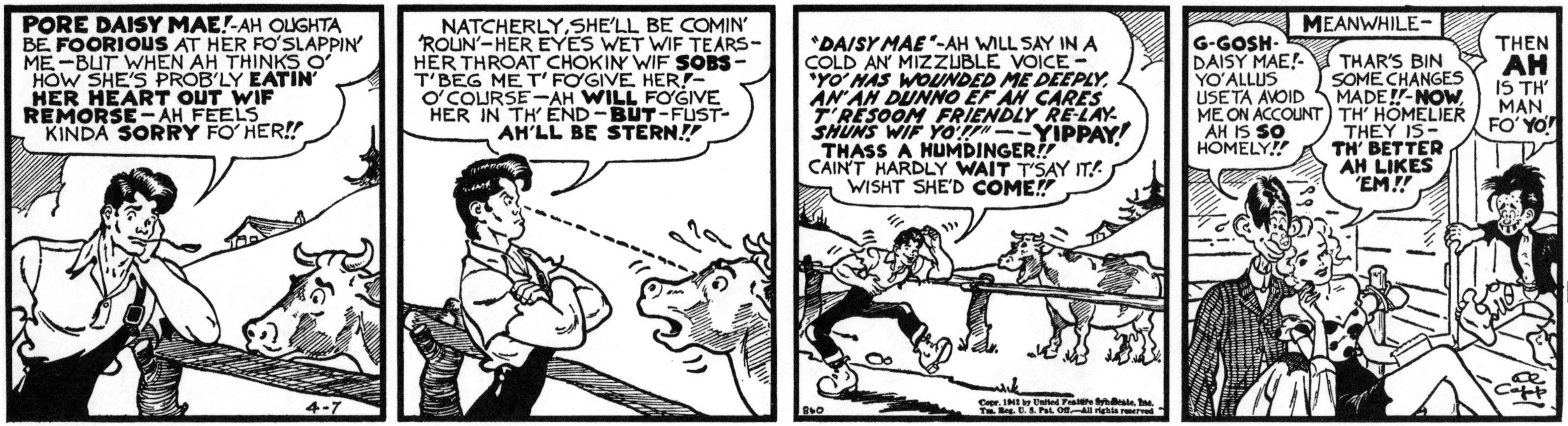
PORE DAISY MAE!-AH OUGHTA BE FOORIOUS AT HER FO'SLAPPIN' ME—BUT WHEN AH THINKS O' HOW SHE'S PROB'LY EATIN' HER HEART OUT WIF REMORSE—AH FEELS KINDA SORRY FO' HER!!
4-7
NATCHERLY, SHE'LL BE COMIN' 'ROUN'—HER EYES WET WIF TEARS-HER THROAT CHOKIN' WIF SOBS-T'BEG ME T' FO'GIVE HER!-O'COURSE—AH WILL FO'GIVE HER IN TH' END—BUT-FUST-AH'LL BE STERN!!
"DAISY MAE"-AH WILL SAY IN A COLD AN' MIZZUBLE VOICE-"YO' HAS WOUNDED ME DEEPLY, AN' AH DUNNO EF AH CARES T' RESOOM FRIENDLY RE-LAY-SHUNS WIF YO'!!!"—YIPPAY! THASS A HUMDINGER!! CAIN'T HARDLY WAIT T'SAY IT!-WISHT SHE'D COME!!
860
Copr. 1942 by United Feature Syndicate, Inc. Tm. Reg. U. S. Pat. Off.—All rights reserved
MEANWHILE-
G-GOSH-DAISY MAE!-YO' ALLUS USETA AVOID ME ON ACCOUNT AH IS SO HOMELY!!
THAR'S BIN SOME CHANGES MADE!!-NOW, TH' HOMELIER THEY IS-TH' BETTER AH LIKES 'EM!!
THEN AH IS TH' MAN FO' YO'!
Al Capp

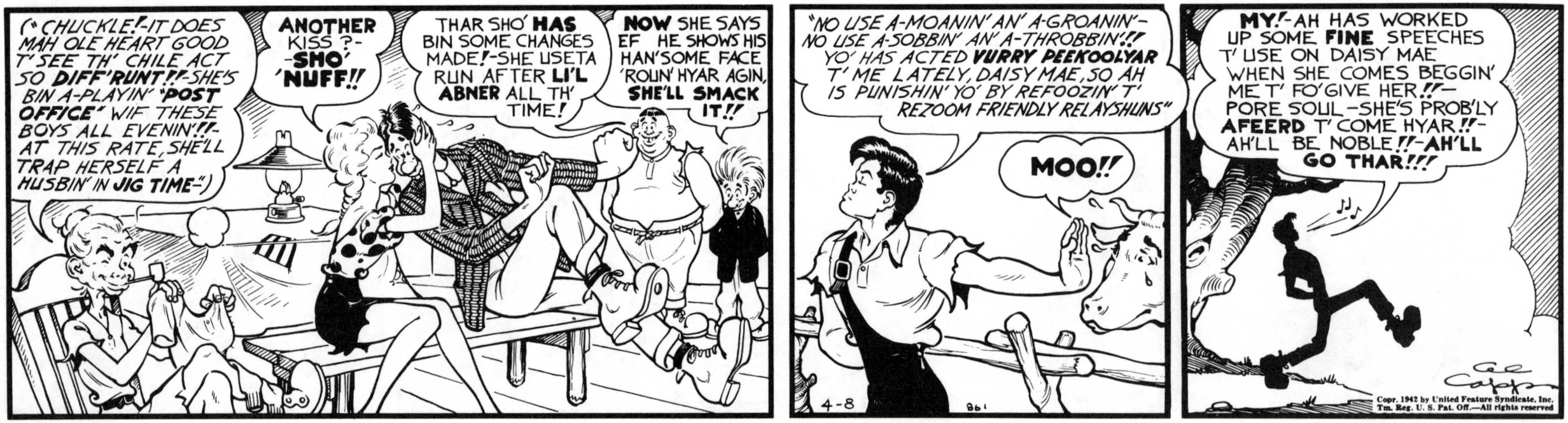
("CHUCKLE!-IT DOES MAH OLE HEART GOOD T' SEE TH' CHILE ACT SO DIFF'RUNT!!-SHE'S BIN A-PLAYIN' "POST OFFICE" WIF THESE BOYS ALL EVENIN'!!-AT THIS RATE, SHE'LL TRAP HERSELF A HUSBIN' IN JIG TIME-")
ANOTHER KISS?-SHO' 'NUFF!!
THAR SHO' HAS BIN SOME CHANGES MADE!-SHE USETA RUN AFTER LI'L ABNER ALL TH' TIME!
NOW SHE SAYS EF HE SHOWS HIS HAN'SOME FACE 'ROUN' HYAR AGIN, SHE'LL SMACK IT!!
"NO USE A-MOANIN' AN' A-GROANIN'-NO USE A-SOBBIN' AN' A-THROBBIN'!!-YO' HAS ACTED VURRY PEEKOOLYAR T' ME LATELY, DAISY MAE, SO AH IS PUNISHIN' YO' BY REFOOZIN' T' REZOOM FRIENDLY RELAYSHUNS"
MOO!!
4-8
861
MY!-AH HAS WORKED UP SOME FINE SPEECHES T' USE ON DAISY MAE WHEN SHE COMES BEGGIN' ME T' FO'GIVE HER!!-PORE SOUL-SHE'S PROB'LY AFEERD T' COME HYAR!!-AH'LL BE NOBLE!!-AH'LL GO THAR!!!
Al Capp
Copr. 1942 by United Feature Syndicate, Inc. Tm. Reg. U. S. Pat. Off.—All rights reserved

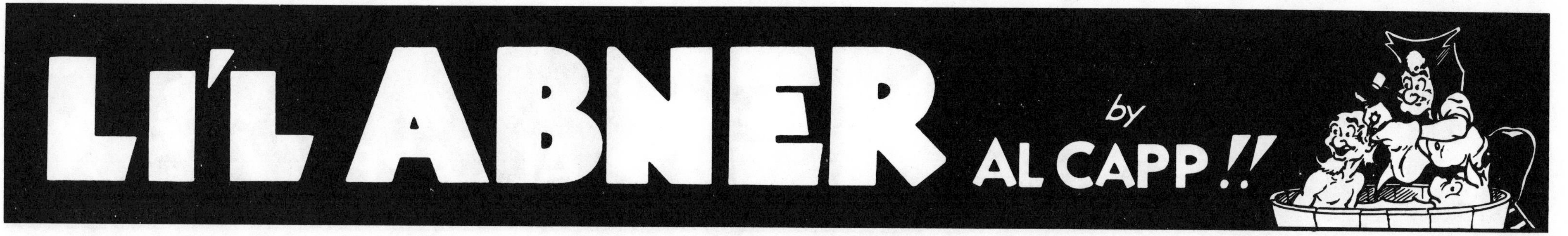
LI'L ABNER
by
AL CAPP!!

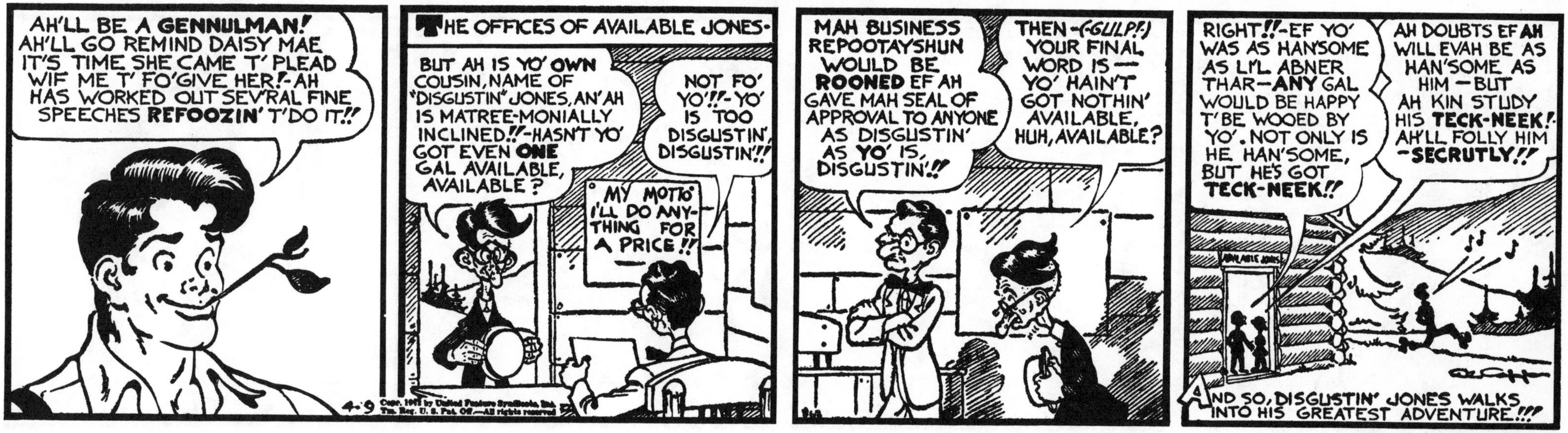
AH'LL BE A **GENNULMAN!** AH'LL GO REMIND DAISY MAE IT'S TIME SHE CAME T' PLEAD WIF ME T' FO'GIVE HER!-AH HAS WORKED OUT SEV'RAL FINE SPEECHES **REFOOZIN'** T'DO IT!!
4-9
THE OFFICES OF AVAILABLE JONES-
BUT AH IS YO' **OWN** COUSIN, NAME OF "DISGUSTIN" JONES, AN' AH IS MATREE-MONIALLY INCLINED!!-HASN'T YO' GOT EVEN **ONE** GAL AVAILABLE, AVAILABLE?
NOT FO' YO'!!-YO' IS TOO DISGUSTIN', DISGUSTIN'!!
MY MOTTO I'LL DO ANYTHING FOR A PRICE!!
MAH BUSINESS REPOOTAYSHUN WOULD BE **ROONED** EF AH GAVE MAH SEAL OF APPROVAL TO ANYONE AS DISGUSTIN' AS **YO'** IS, DISGUSTIN'!!
THEN-(GULP!) YOUR FINAL WORD IS— YO' HAIN'T GOT NOTHIN' AVAILABLE, HUH, AVAILABLE?
RIGHT!!-EF YO' WAS AS HAN'SOME AS LI'L ABNER THAR-**ANY** GAL WOULD BE HAPPY T'BE WOOED BY YO'. NOT ONLY IS HE HAN'SOME, BUT HE'S GOT **TECK-NEEK!!**
AH DOUBTS EF **AH** WILL EVAH BE AS HAN'SOME AS HIM-BUT AH KIN STUDY HIS **TECK-NEEK!** AH'LL FOLLY HIM **-SECRUTLY!!**
AND SO, DISGUSTIN' JONES WALKS INTO HIS GREATEST ADVENTURE!!!

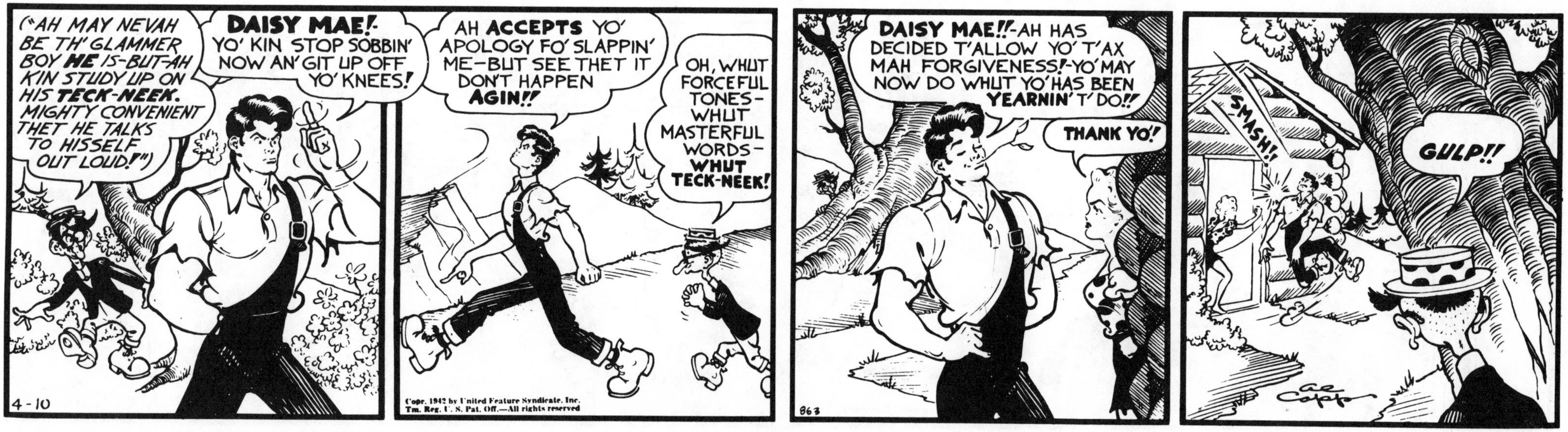
("AH MAY NEVAH BE TH' GLAMMER BOY **HE** IS-BUT-AH KIN STUDY UP ON HIS **TECK-NEEK.** MIGHTY CONVENIENT THET HE TALKS TO HISSELF OUT LOUD!")
DAISY MAE!- YO' KIN STOP SOBBIN' NOW AN' GIT UP OFF YO' KNEES!
4-10
AH **ACCEPTS** YO' APOLOGY FO' SLAPPIN' ME-BUT SEE THET IT DON'T HAPPEN **AGIN!!**
OH, WHUT FORCEFUL TONES- WHUT MASTERFUL WORDS- **WHUT TECK-NEEK!**
Copr. 1942 by United Feature Syndicate, Inc. Tm. Reg. U. S. Pat. Off.—All rights reserved
DAISY MAE!!-AH HAS DECIDED T'ALLOW YO' T'AX MAH FORGIVENESS!-YO' MAY NOW DO WHUT YO' HAS BEEN **YEARNIN'** T'DO!!
THANK YO'!
SMASH!
GULP!!

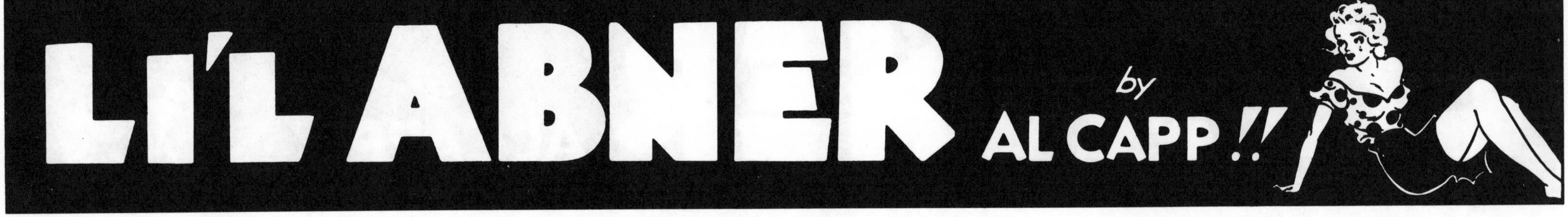
LI'L ABNER
by
AL CAPP!!

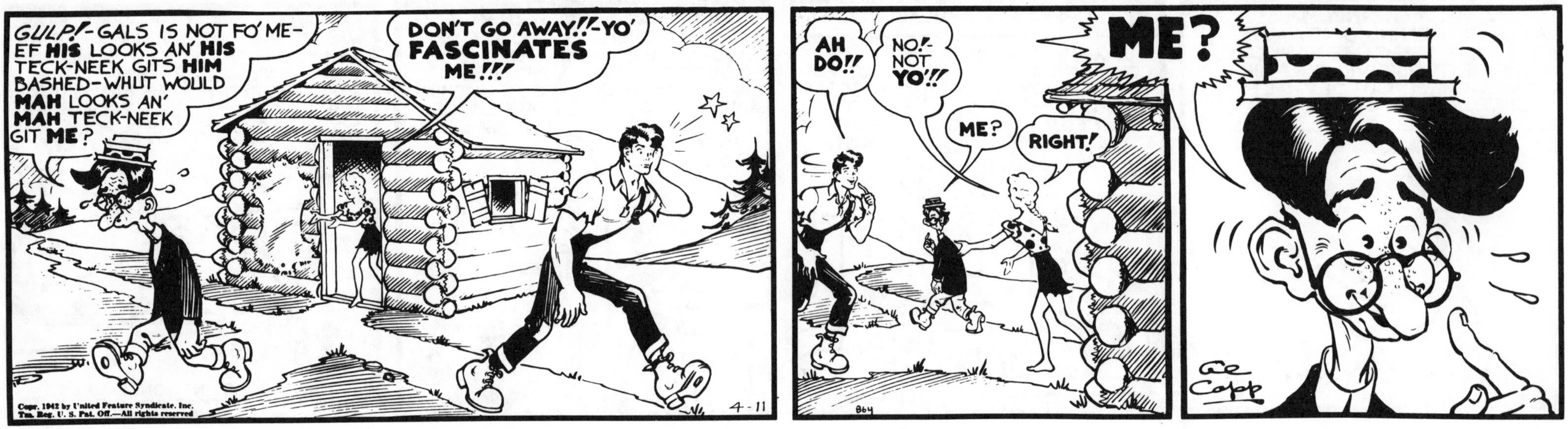
GULP!-GALS IS NOT FO' ME-EF HIS LOOKS AN' HIS TECK-NEEK GITS HIM BASHED-WHUT WOULD MAH LOOKS AN' MAH TECK-NEEK GIT ME?
DON'T GO AWAY!!-YO' FASCINATES ME!!!
Copr. 1942 by United Feature Syndicate, Inc.
Tm. Reg. U. S. Pat. Off.—All rights reserved
4-11
AH DO!!
NO!-NOT YO'!!
ME?
RIGHT!
864
ME?

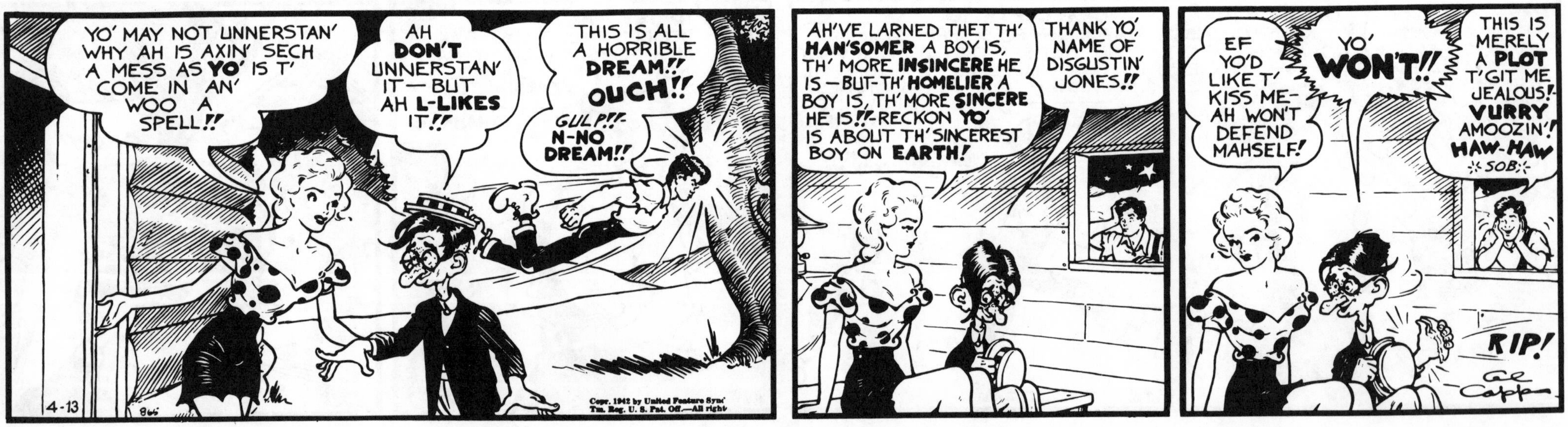
YO' MAY NOT UNNERSTAN' WHY AH IS AXIN' SECH A MESS AS YO' IS T' COME IN AN' WOO A SPELL!!
AH DON'T UNNERSTAN' IT—BUT AH L-LIKES IT!!
THIS IS ALL A HORRIBLE DREAM!! OUCH!!
GULP!!-N-NO DREAM!!
4-13
Copr. 1942 by United Feature Sync
Tm. Reg. U. S. Pat. Off.—All right
AH'VE LARNED THET TH' HAN'SOMER A BOY IS, TH' MORE INSINCERE HE IS—BUT-TH' HOMELIER A BOY IS, TH' MORE SINCERE HE IS!!-RECKON YO' IS ABOUT TH' SINCEREST BOY ON EARTH!
THANK YO', NAME OF DISGUSTIN' JONES!!
EF YO'D LIKE T' KISS ME-AH WON'T DEFEND MAHSELF!
YO' WON'T!!
THIS IS MERELY A PLOT T'GIT ME JEALOUS!-VURRY AMOOZIN'! HAW-HAW
SOB
RIP!

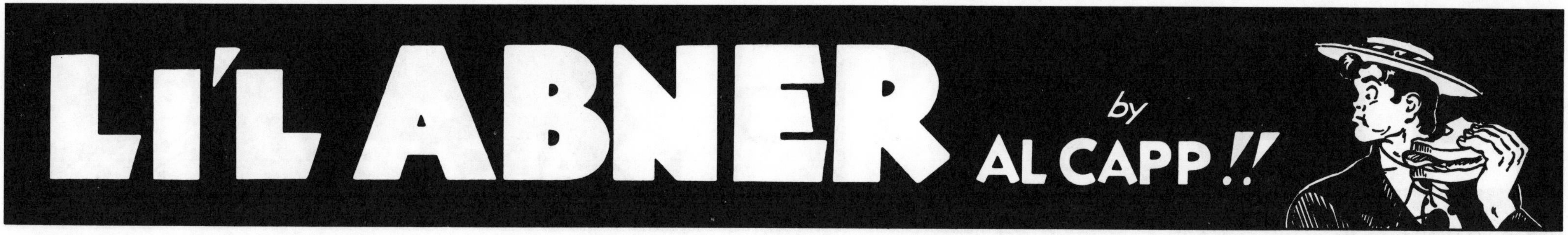
LI'L ABNER
by AL CAPP!!

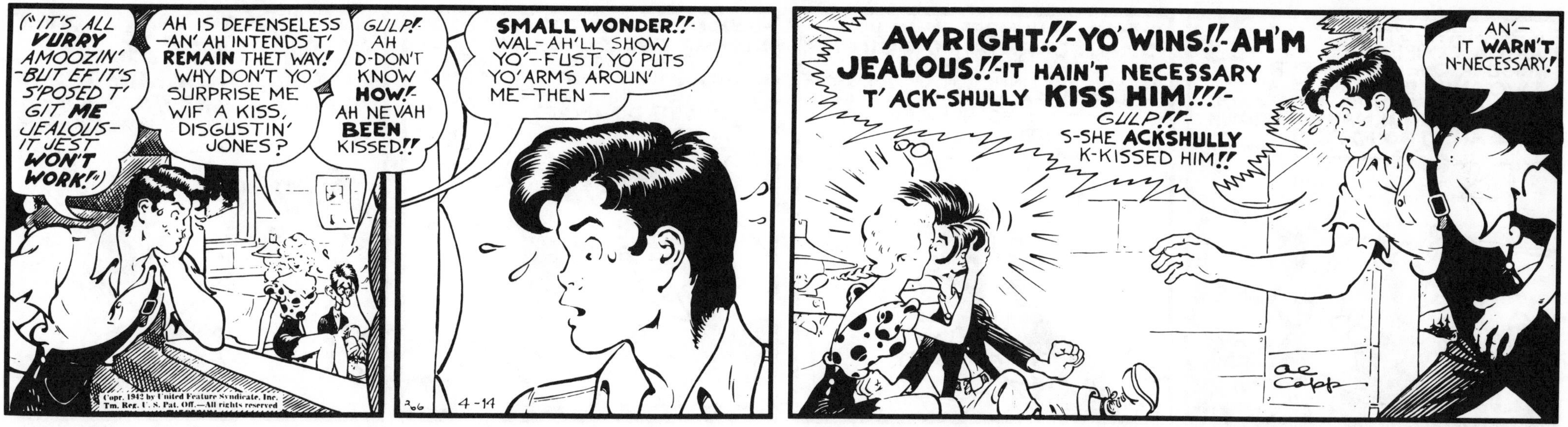
("IT'S ALL VURRY AMOOZIN' -BUT EF IT'S S'POSED T' GIT ME JEALOUS- IT JEST WON'T WORK!")
AH IS DEFENSELESS -AN' AH INTENDS T' REMAIN THET WAY! WHY DON'T YO' SURPRISE ME WIF A KISS, DISGUSTIN' JONES?
GULP!- AH D-DON'T KNOW HOW!- AH NEVAH BEEN KISSED!!
Copr. 1942 by United Feature Syndicate, Inc. Tm. Reg. U. S. Pat. Off.—All rights reserved
SMALL WONDER!!- WAL- AH'LL SHOW YO'--FUST, YO' PUTS YO' ARMS AROUN' ME—THEN—
4-14
AWRIGHT!!-YO' WINS!!-AH'M JEALOUS!!-IT HAIN'T NECESSARY T' ACK-SHULLY KISS HIM!!!-
GULP!!- S-SHE ACKSHULLY K-KISSED HIM!!
AN'- IT WARN'T N-NECESSARY!
Al Capp

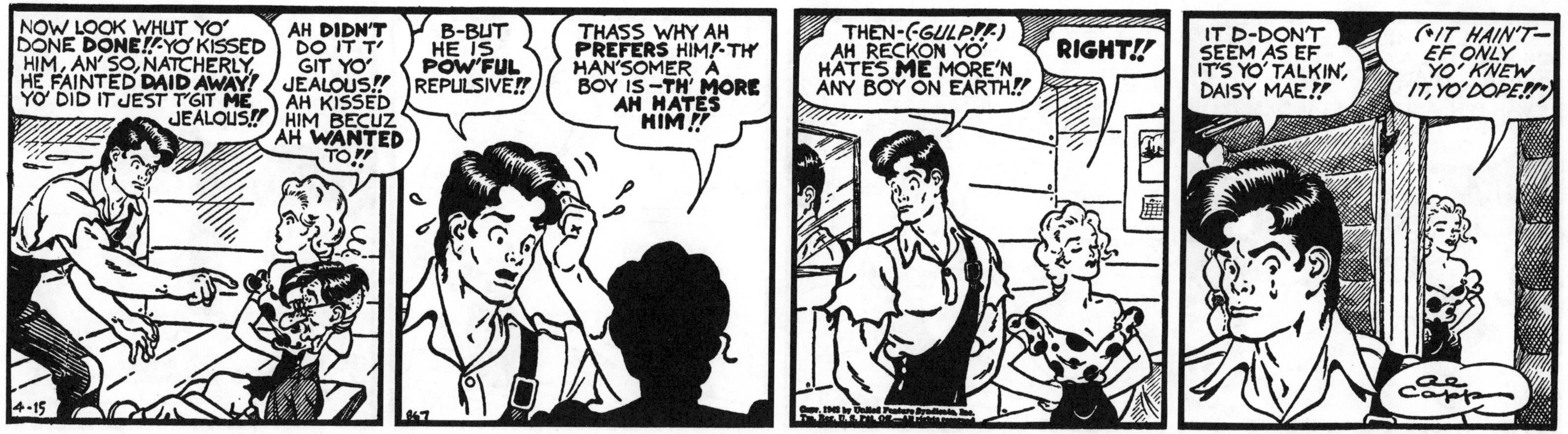
NOW LOOK WHUT YO' DONE DONE!!-YO' KISSED HIM, AN' SO, NATCHERLY, HE FAINTED DAID AWAY! YO' DID IT JEST T'GIT ME JEALOUS!!
AH DIDN'T DO IT T' GIT YO' JEALOUS!! AH KISSED HIM BECUZ AH WANTED TO!!
4-15
B-BUT HE IS POW'FUL REPULSIVE!!
THASS WHY AH PREFERS HIM!-TH' HAN'SOMER A BOY IS -TH' MORE AH HATES HIM!!
THEN-(-GULP!!-) AH RECKON YO' HATES ME MORE'N ANY BOY ON EARTH!!
RIGHT!!
IT D-DON'T SEEM AS EF IT'S YO' TALKIN', DAISY MAE!!
("IT HAIN'T- EF ONLY YO' KNEW IT, YO' DOPE!!")
Al Capp

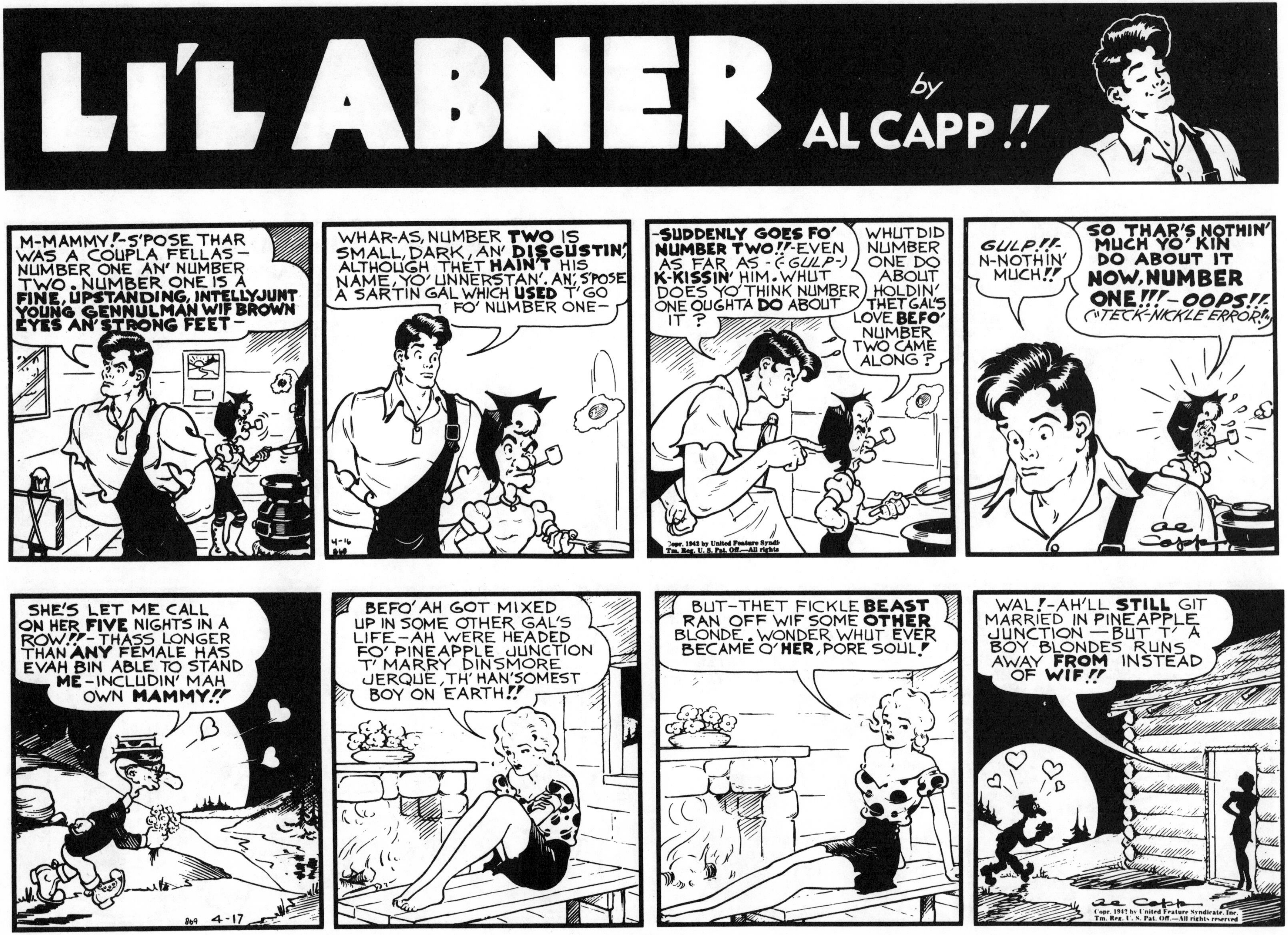
LI'L ABNER
by AL CAPP!!
M-MAMMY!-S'POSE THAR WAS A COUPLA FELLAS-NUMBER ONE AN' NUMBER TWO. NUMBER ONE IS A FINE, UPSTANDING, INTELLYJUNT YOUNG GENNULMAN WIF BROWN EYES AN' STRONG FEET-
WHAR-AS, NUMBER TWO IS SMALL, DARK, AN' DISGUSTIN', ALTHOUGH THET HAIN'T HIS NAME, YO' UNNERSTAN'. AN', S'POSE A SARTIN GAL WHICH USED T' GO FO' NUMBER ONE-
4-16
-SUDDENLY GOES FO' NUMBER TWO!!-EVEN AS FAR AS -(-GULP-) K-KISSIN' HIM. WHUT DOES YO' THINK NUMBER ONE OUGHTA DO ABOUT IT?
WHUT DID NUMBER ONE DO ABOUT HOLDIN' THET GAL'S LOVE BEFO' NUMBER TWO CAME ALONG?
Copr. 1942 by United Feature Syndi
Tm. Reg. U. S. Pat. Off.—All rights
GULP!!-N-NOTHIN' MUCH!!
SO THAR'S NOTHIN' MUCH YO' KIN DO ABOUT IT NOW, NUMBER ONE!!!-OOPS!!-("TECK-NICKLE ERROR!")
Al Capp
SHE'S LET ME CALL ON HER FIVE NIGHTS IN A ROW!!-THASS LONGER THAN ANY FEMALE HAS EVAH BIN ABLE TO STAND ME-INCLUDIN' MAH OWN MAMMY!!
869 4-17
BEFO' AH GOT MIXED UP IN SOME OTHER GAL'S LIFE-AH WERE HEADED FO' PINEAPPLE JUNCTION T' MARRY DINSMORE JERQUE, TH' HAN'SOMEST BOY ON EARTH!!
BUT-THET FICKLE BEAST RAN OFF WIF SOME OTHER BLONDE. WONDER WHUT EVER BECAME O' HER, PORE SOUL!
WAL!-AH'LL STILL GIT MARRIED IN PINEAPPLE JUNCTION-BUT T' A BOY BLONDES RUNS AWAY FROM INSTEAD OF WIF!!
Al Capp
Copr. 1942 by United Feature Syndicate, Inc.
Tm. Reg. U. S. Pat. Off.—All rights reserved

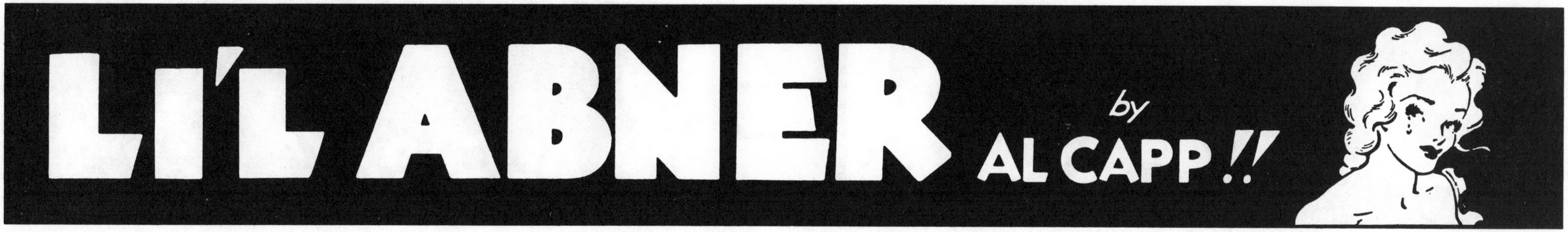

LI'L ABNER
by
AL CAPP!!

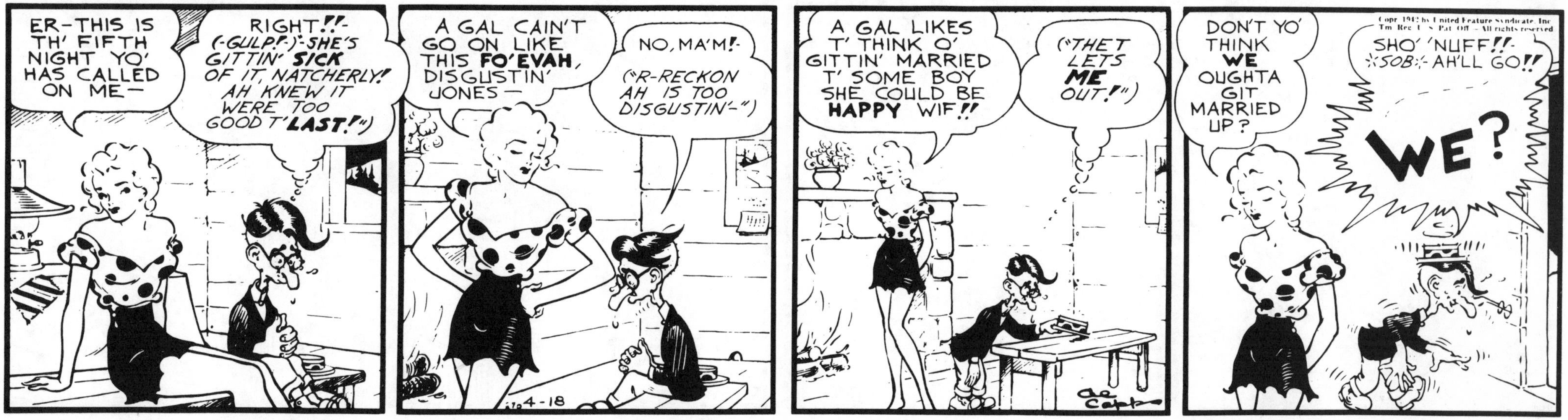

ER-THIS IS TH' FIFTH NIGHT YO' HAS CALLED ON ME-
RIGHT!!- (-GULP!-)-SHE'S GITTIN' SICK OF IT, NATCHERLY! AH KNEW IT WERE TOO GOOD T'LAST!")
A GAL CAIN'T GO ON LIKE THIS FO'EVAH, DISGUSTIN' JONES-
NO, MA'M!-
("R-RECKON AH IS TOO DISGUSTIN'-")
4-18
A GAL LIKES T' THINK O' GITTIN' MARRIED T' SOME BOY SHE COULD BE HAPPY WIF!!
("THET LETS ME OUT!")
Copr. 1942 by United Feature Syndicate, Inc. Tm. Reg. U. S. Pat. Off.—All rights reserved
DON'T YO' THINK WE OUGHTA GIT MARRIED UP?
SHO' 'NUFF!!- -SOB- AH'LL GO!!
WE?

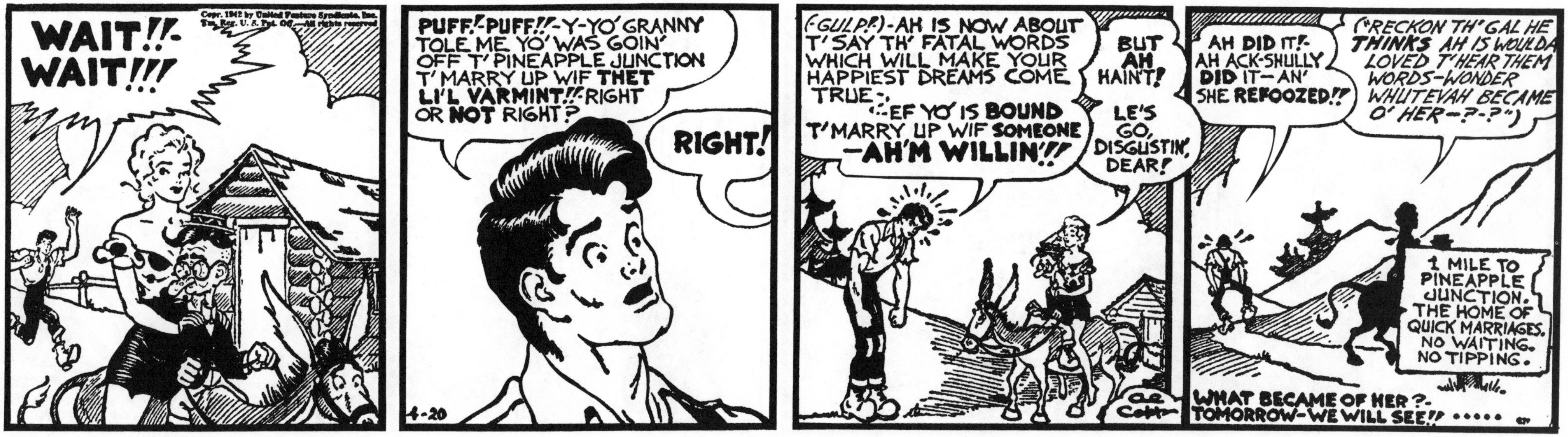

Copr. 1942 by United Feature Syndicate, Inc. Tm. Reg. U. S. Pat. Off.—All rights reserved
WAIT!!- WAIT!!!
PUFF!-PUFF!!-Y-YO' GRANNY TOLE ME YO' WAS GOIN' OFF T' PINEAPPLE JUNCTION T' MARRY UP WIF THET LI'L VARMINT!!-RIGHT OR NOT RIGHT?
RIGHT!
4-20
(-GULP!-)-AH IS NOW ABOUT T' SAY TH' FATAL WORDS WHICH WILL MAKE YOUR HAPPIEST DREAMS COME TRUE-. -EF YO' IS BOUND T'MARRY UP WIF SOMEONE -AH'M WILLIN'!!
BUT AH HAIN'T!
LE'S GO, DISGUSTIN', DEAR!
AH DID IT!- AH ACK-SHULLY DID IT-AN' SHE REFOOZED!!
("RECKON TH' GAL HE THINKS AH IS WOULDA LOVED T'HEAR THEM WORDS-WONDER WHUTEVAH BECAME O' HER-?-?")
1 MILE TO PINEAPPLE JUNCTION. THE HOME OF QUICK MARRIAGES. NO WAITING. NO TIPPING.
WHAT BECAME OF HER?- TOMORROW-WE WILL SEE!! .....

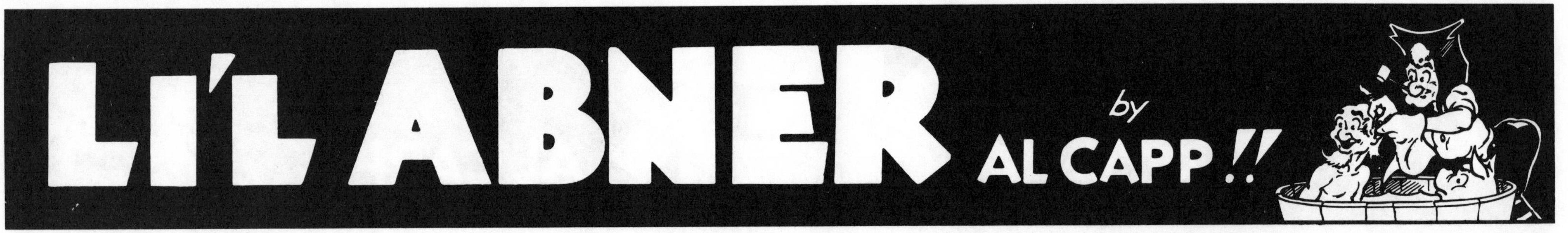
LI'L ABNER
by
AL CAPP!!

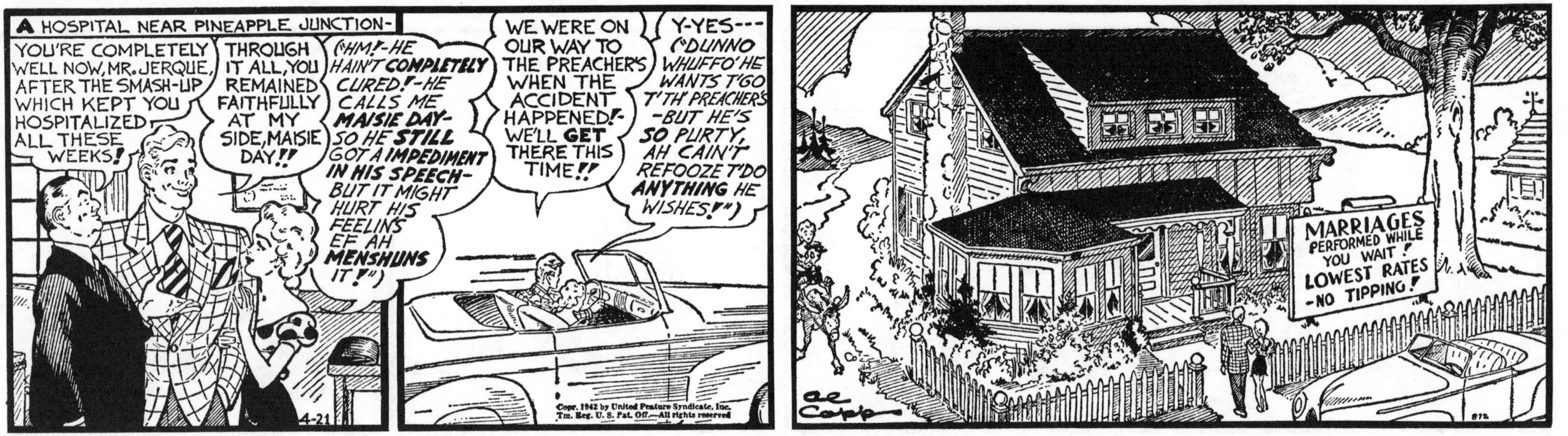
A HOSPITAL NEAR PINEAPPLE JUNCTION-
YOU'RE COMPLETELY WELL NOW, MR. JERQUE, AFTER THE SMASH-UP WHICH KEPT YOU HOSPITALIZED ALL THESE WEEKS!
THROUGH IT ALL, YOU REMAINED FAITHFULLY AT MY SIDE, MAISIE DAY!!
("HM!-HE HAIN'T COMPLETELY CURED!-HE CALLS ME MAISIE DAY-SO HE STILL GOT A IMPEDIMENT IN HIS SPEECH-BUT IT MIGHT HURT HIS FEELINS EF AH MENSHUNS IT!")
4-21
WE WERE ON OUR WAY TO THE PREACHER'S WHEN THE ACCIDENT HAPPENED!-WE'LL GET THERE THIS TIME!!
Y-YES---("DUNNO WHUFFO' HE WANTS T'GO T'TH' PREACHER'S-BUT HE'S SO PURTY, AH CAIN'T REFOOZE T'DO ANYTHING HE WISHES!")
Copr. 1942 by United Feature Syndicate, Inc. Tm. Reg. U. S. Pat. Off.—All rights reserved
MARRIAGES PERFORMED WHILE YOU WAIT! LOWEST RATES -NO TIPPING!
Al Capp

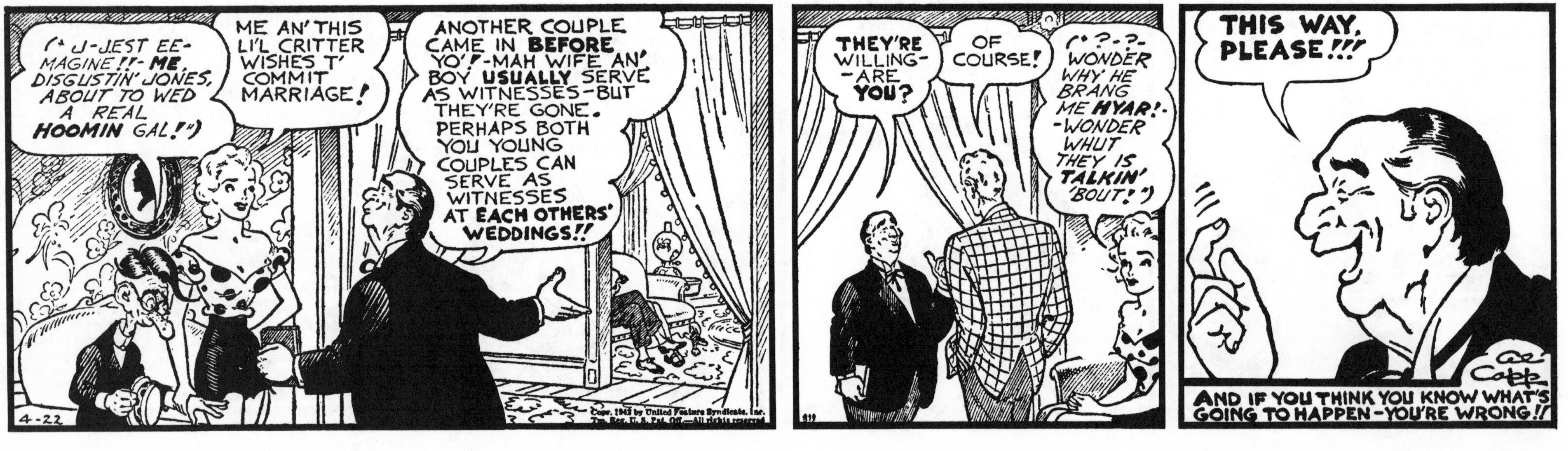
("J-JEST EE-MAGINE!!-ME, DISGUSTIN' JONES, ABOUT TO WED A REAL HOOMIN GAL!")
ME AN' THIS LI'L CRITTER WISHES T' COMMIT MARRIAGE!
ANOTHER COUPLE CAME IN BEFORE YO'!-MAH WIFE AN' BOY USUALLY SERVE AS WITNESSES-BUT THEY'RE GONE. PERHAPS BOTH YOU YOUNG COUPLES CAN SERVE AS WITNESSES AT EACH OTHERS' WEDDINGS!!
4-22
THEY'RE WILLING-ARE YOU?
OF COURSE!
("?-?-WONDER WHY HE BRANG ME HYAR!-WONDER WHUT THEY IS TALKIN' 'BOUT!")
THIS WAY, PLEASE!!!
Al Capp
AND IF YOU THINK YOU KNOW WHAT'S GOING TO HAPPEN-YOU'RE WRONG!!

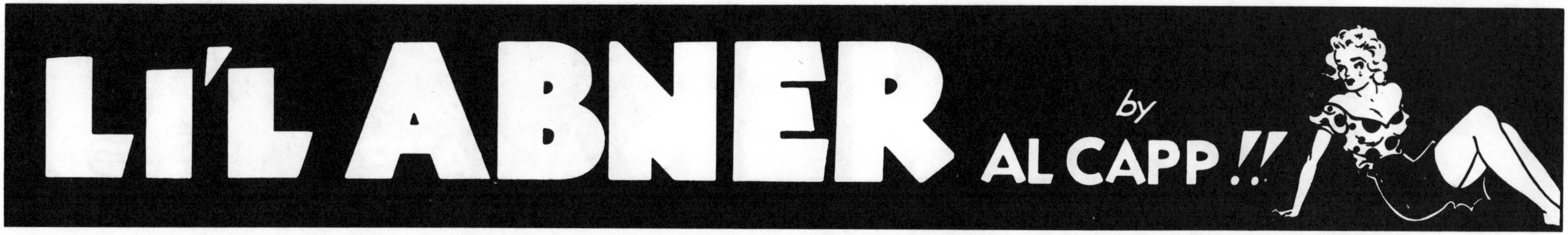
LI'L ABNER
by
AL CAPP!!

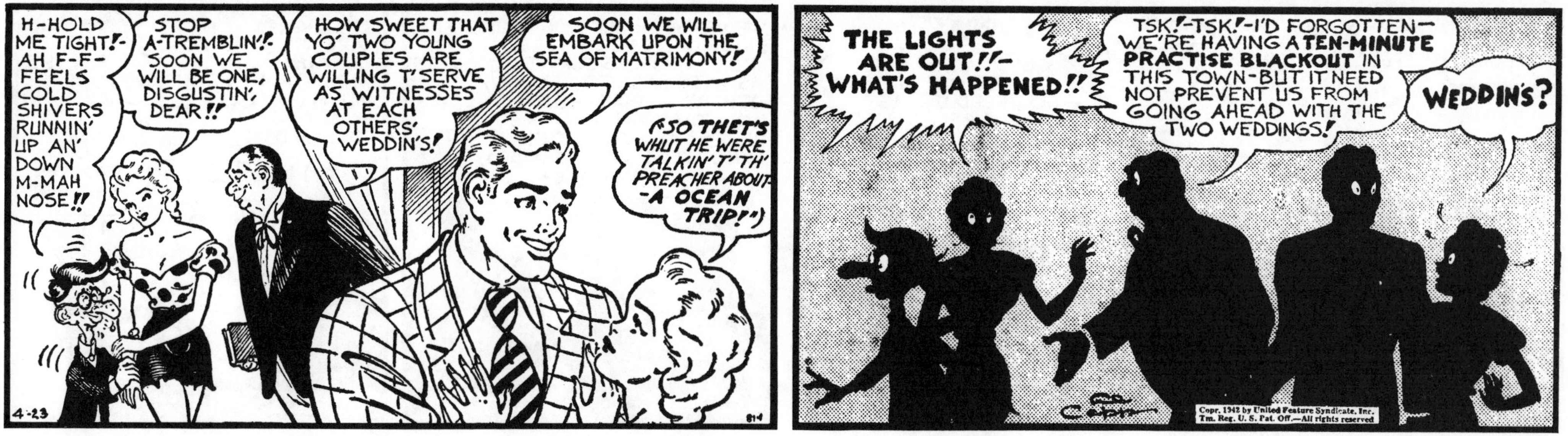
H-HOLD ME TIGHT!-AH F-F-FEELS COLD SHIVERS RUNNIN' UP AN' DOWN M-MAH NOSE!!
STOP A-TREMBLIN'!- SOON WE WILL BE ONE, DISGUSTIN', DEAR!!
HOW SWEET THAT YO' TWO YOUNG COUPLES ARE WILLING T' SERVE AS WITNESSES AT EACH OTHERS' WEDDIN'S!
SOON WE WILL EMBARK UPON THE SEA OF MATRIMONY!
("SO THET'S WHUT HE WERE TALKIN' T' TH' PREACHER ABOUT -A OCEAN TRIP!")
4-23
THE LIGHTS ARE OUT!!- WHAT'S HAPPENED!!
TSK!-TSK!-I'D FORGOTTEN- WE'RE HAVING A TEN-MINUTE PRACTISE BLACKOUT IN THIS TOWN-BUT IT NEED NOT PREVENT US FROM GOING AHEAD WITH THE TWO WEDDINGS!
WEDDIN'S?
Copr. 1942 by United Feature Syndicate, Inc. Tm. Reg. U. S. Pat. Off.—All rights reserved

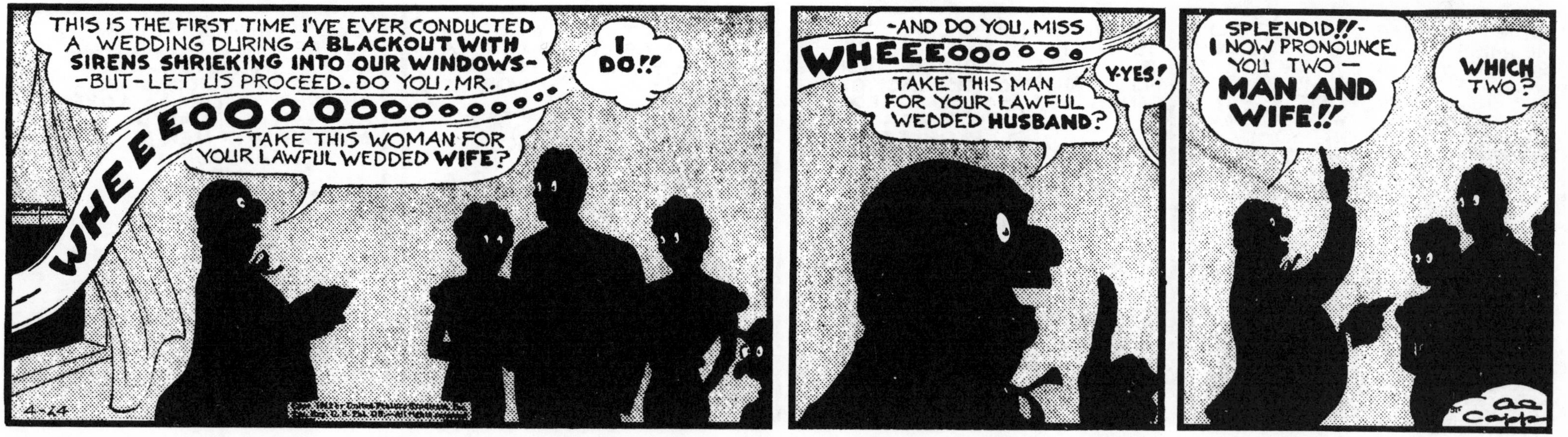
THIS IS THE FIRST TIME I'VE EVER CONDUCTED A WEDDING DURING A BLACKOUT WITH SIRENS SHRIEKING INTO OUR WINDOWS- -BUT-LET US PROCEED. DO YOU, MR.
WHEEEOOO OOOOOOOOOO
-TAKE THIS WOMAN FOR YOUR LAWFUL WEDDED WIFE?
I DO!!
4-24
-AND DO YOU, MISS
WHEEEOOOOOO
TAKE THIS MAN FOR YOUR LAWFUL WEDDED HUSBAND?
Y-YES!
SPLENDID!!- I NOW PRONOUNCE YOU TWO - MAN AND WIFE!!
WHICH TWO?

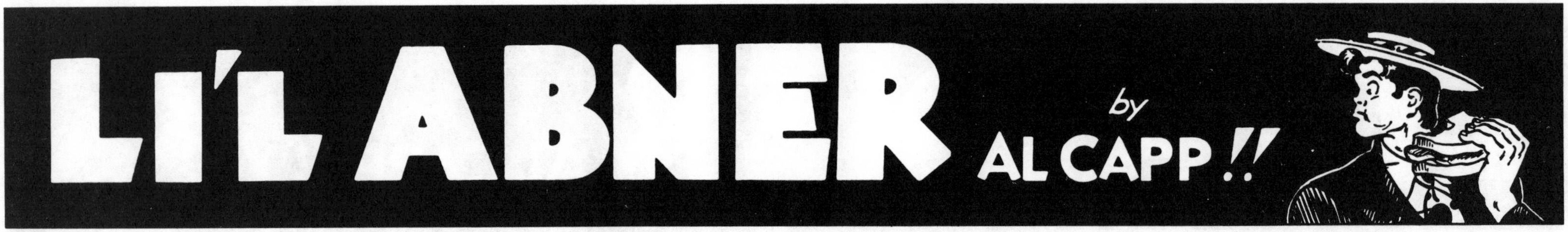
LI'L ABNER
by
AL CAPP!!

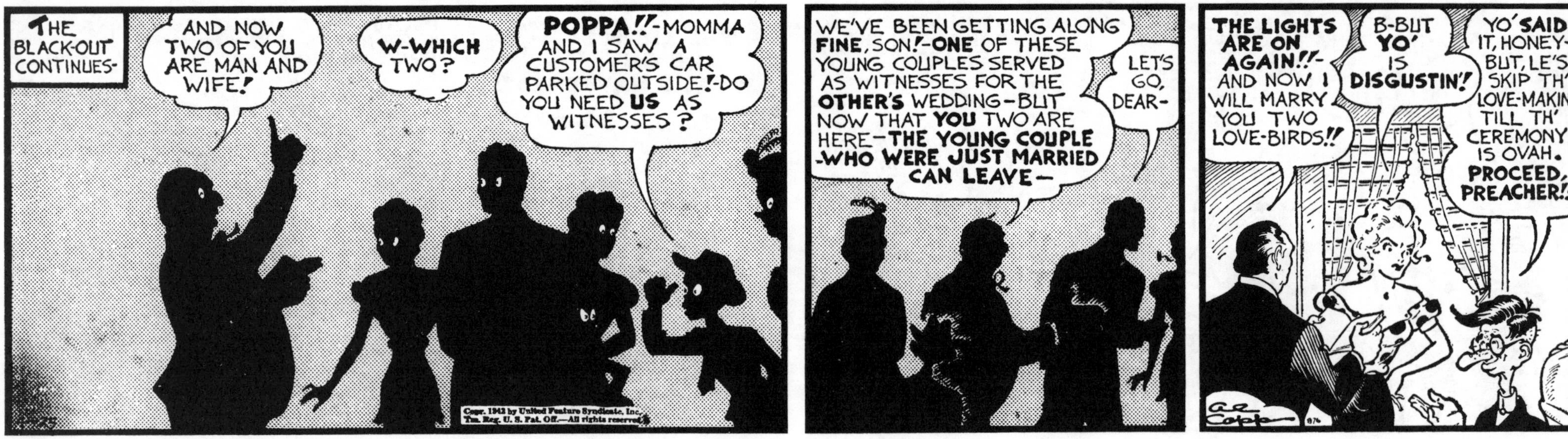
THE BLACK-OUT CONTINUES-
AND NOW TWO OF YOU ARE MAN AND WIFE!
W-WHICH TWO?
POPPA!!-MOMMA AND I SAW A CUSTOMER'S CAR PARKED OUTSIDE!-DO YOU NEED US AS WITNESSES?
Copr. 1942 by United Feature Syndicate, Inc. Tm. Reg. U. S. Pat. Off.—All rights reserved
WE'VE BEEN GETTING ALONG FINE, SON!-ONE OF THESE YOUNG COUPLES SERVED AS WITNESSES FOR THE OTHER'S WEDDING-BUT NOW THAT YOU TWO ARE HERE-THE YOUNG COUPLE -WHO WERE JUST MARRIED CAN LEAVE-
LET'S GO, DEAR-
THE LIGHTS ARE ON AGAIN!!- AND NOW I WILL MARRY YOU TWO LOVE-BIRDS!!
B-BUT YO' IS DISGUSTIN'!
YO' SAID IT, HONEY- BUT, LE'S SKIP TH' LOVE-MAKIN' TILL TH' CEREMONY IS OVAH. PROCEED, PREACHER!!

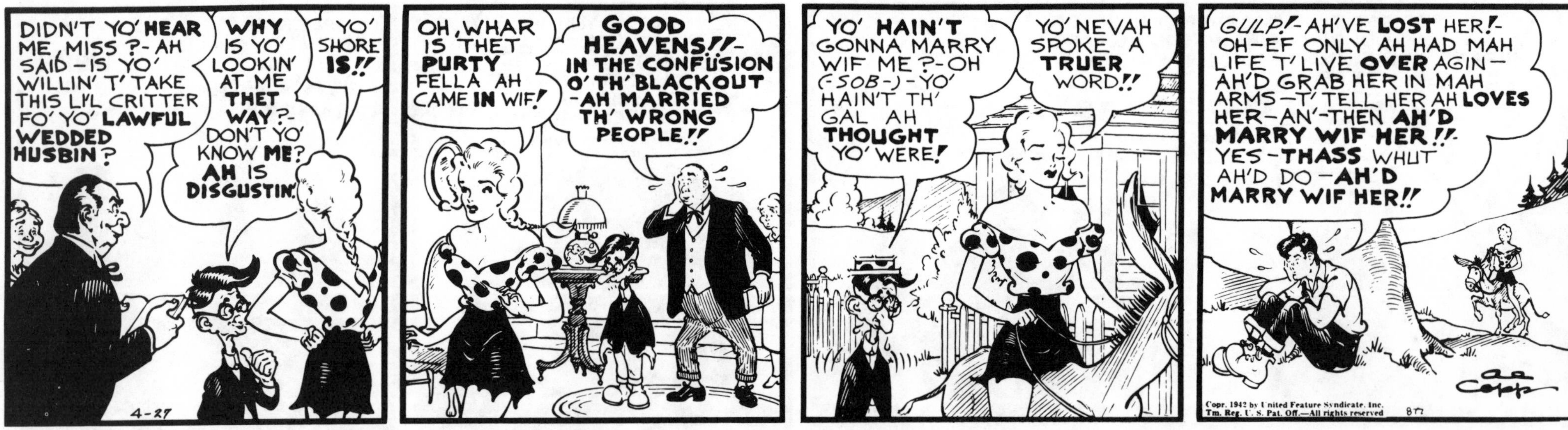
DIDN'T YO' HEAR ME, MISS?-AH SAID-IS YO' WILLIN' T' TAKE THIS LI'L CRITTER FO' YO' LAWFUL WEDDED HUSBIN?
WHY IS YO' LOOKIN' AT ME THET WAY?- DON'T YO' KNOW ME? AH IS DISGUSTIN'.
YO' SHORE IS!!
4-27
OH, WHAR IS THET PURTY FELLA AH CAME IN WIF!
GOOD HEAVENS!!- IN THE CONFUSION O' TH' BLACKOUT -AH MARRIED TH' WRONG PEOPLE!!
YO' HAIN'T GONNA MARRY WIF ME?-OH (-SOB-)-YO' HAIN'T TH' GAL AH THOUGHT YO' WERE!
YO' NEVAH SPOKE A TRUER WORD!!
GULP!-AH'VE LOST HER!- OH-EF ONLY AH HAD MAH LIFE T' LIVE OVER AGIN- AH'D GRAB HER IN MAH ARMS-T' TELL HER AH LOVES HER-AN'-THEN AH'D MARRY WIF HER!!- YES-THASS WHUT AH'D DO-AH'D MARRY WIF HER!!
Copr. 1942 by United Feature Syndicate, Inc. Tm. Reg. U. S. Pat. Off.—All rights reserved

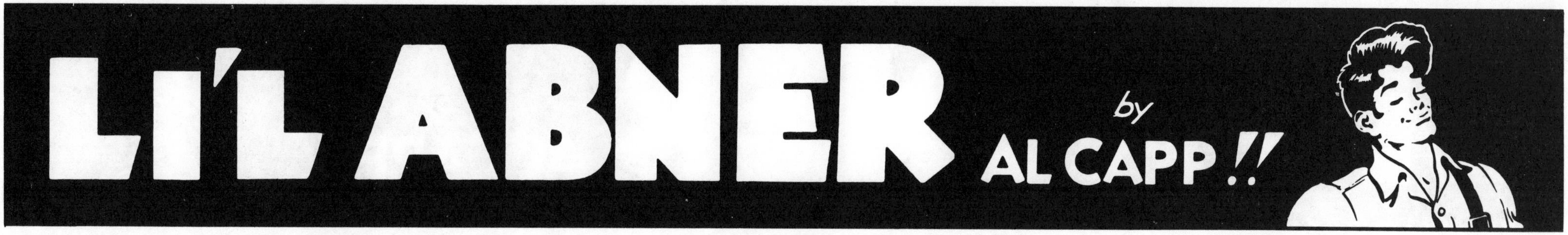
LI'L ABNER
by
AL CAPP!!

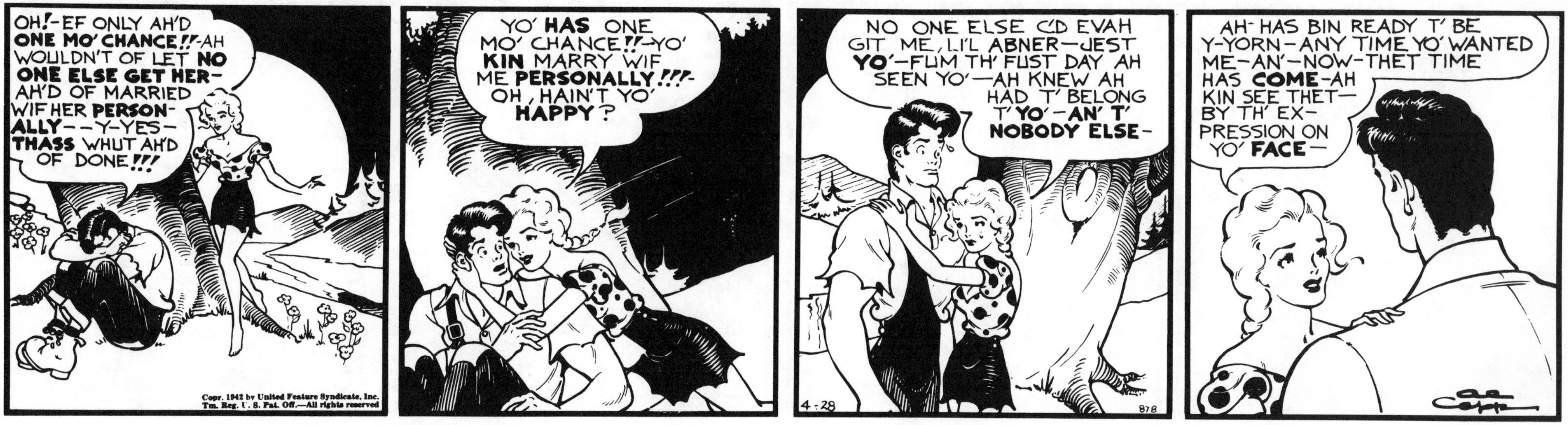
OH!-EF ONLY AH'D ONE MO' CHANCE!!-AH WOULDN'T OF LET NO ONE ELSE GET HER-AH'D OF MARRIED WIF HER PERSONALLY--Y-YES-THASS WHUT AH'D OF DONE!!!
Copr. 1942 by United Feature Syndicate, Inc. Tm. Reg. U. S. Pat. Off.—All rights reserved
YO' HAS ONE MO' CHANCE!!-YO' KIN MARRY WIF ME PERSONALLY!!!-OH, HAIN'T YO' HAPPY?
NO ONE ELSE C'D EVAH GIT ME, LI'L ABNER-JEST YO'-FUM TH' FUST DAY AH SEEN YO'-AH KNEW AH HAD T' BELONG T' YO'-AN' T' NOBODY ELSE-
4-28
878
AH- HAS BIN READY T' BE Y-YORN-ANY TIME YO' WANTED ME-AN'-NOW-THET TIME HAS COME-AH KIN SEE THET-BY TH' EX-PRESSION ON YO' FACE-

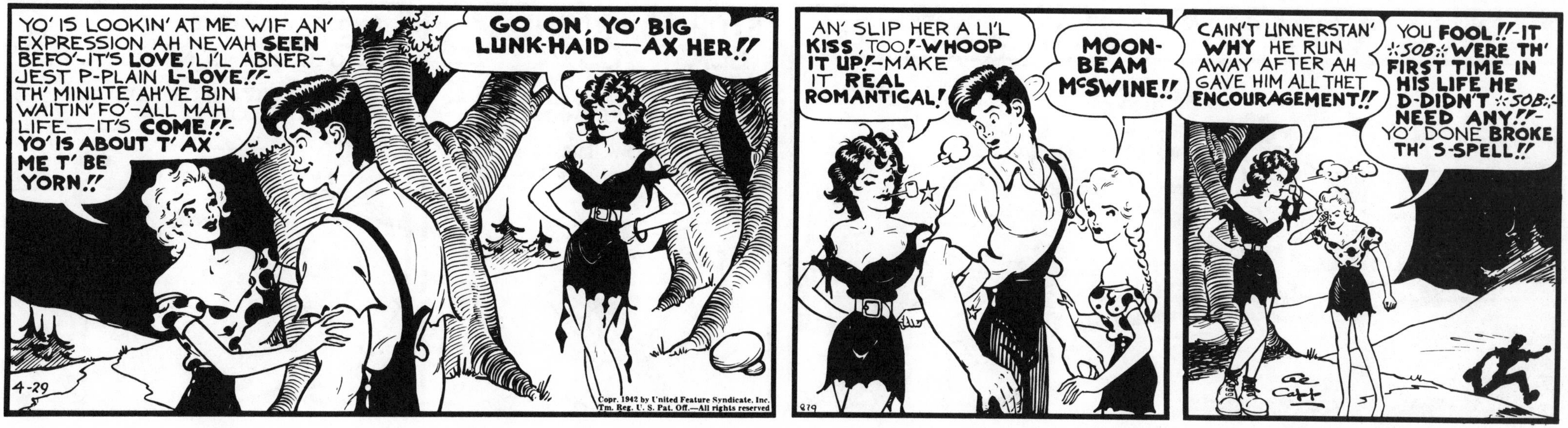
YO' IS LOOKIN' AT ME WIF AN' EXPRESSION AH NEVAH SEEN BEFO'-IT'S LOVE, LI'L ABNER-JEST P-PLAIN L-LOVE!!-TH' MINUTE AH'VE BIN WAITIN' FO'-ALL MAH LIFE-IT'S COME!!-YO' IS ABOUT T' AX ME T' BE YORN!!
GO ON, YO' BIG LUNK-HAID-AX HER!!
4-29
Copr. 1942 by United Feature Syndicate, Inc. Tm. Reg. U. S. Pat. Off.—All rights reserved
AN' SLIP HER A LI'L KISS, TOO!-WHOOP IT UP!-MAKE IT REAL ROMANTICAL!
MOON-BEAM McSWINE!!
879
CAIN'T UNNERSTAN' WHY HE RUN AWAY AFTER AH GAVE HIM ALL THET ENCOURAGEMENT!!
YOU FOOL!!-IT *SOB* WERE TH' FIRST TIME IN HIS LIFE HE D-DIDN'T *SOB* NEED ANY!!-YO' DONE BROKE TH' S-SPELL!!

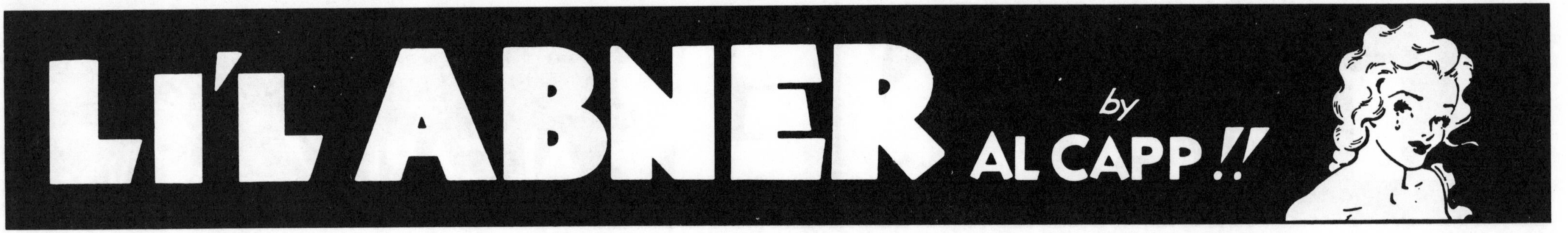
LI'L ABNER
by
AL CAPP!!

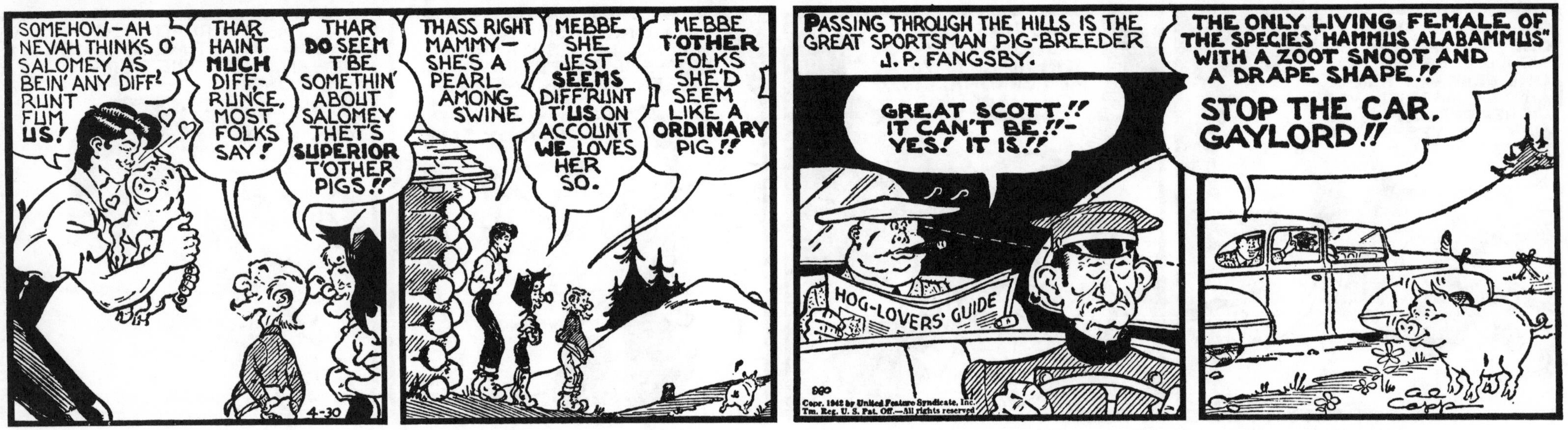
SOMEHOW–AH NEVAH THINKS O' SALOMEY AS BEIN' ANY DIFF'RUNT FUM **US**!
THAR HAINT **MUCH** DIFF-RUNCE, MOST FOLKS SAY!
THAR **DO** SEEM T'BE SOMETHIN' ABOUT SALOMEY THET'S **SUPERIOR** T'OTHER PIGS!!
4-30
THASS RIGHT MAMMY–SHE'S A PEARL AMONG SWINE
MEBBE SHE JEST **SEEMS** DIFF'RUNT T'**US** ON ACCOUNT **WE** LOVES HER SO.
MEBBE **T'OTHER** FOLKS SHE'D SEEM LIKE A **ORDINARY** PIG!!
PASSING THROUGH THE HILLS IS THE GREAT SPORTSMAN PIG-BREEDER J. P. FANGSBY.
GREAT SCOTT!! IT CAN'T BE!!–YES! IT IS!!
HOG-LOVERS' GUIDE
880
Copr. 1942 by United Feature Syndicate, Inc. Tm. Reg. U. S. Pat. Off.—All rights reserved
THE ONLY LIVING FEMALE OF THE SPECIES "HAMMUS ALABAMMUS" WITH A ZOOT SNOOT AND A DRAPE SHAPE!!
STOP THE CAR, GAYLORD!!

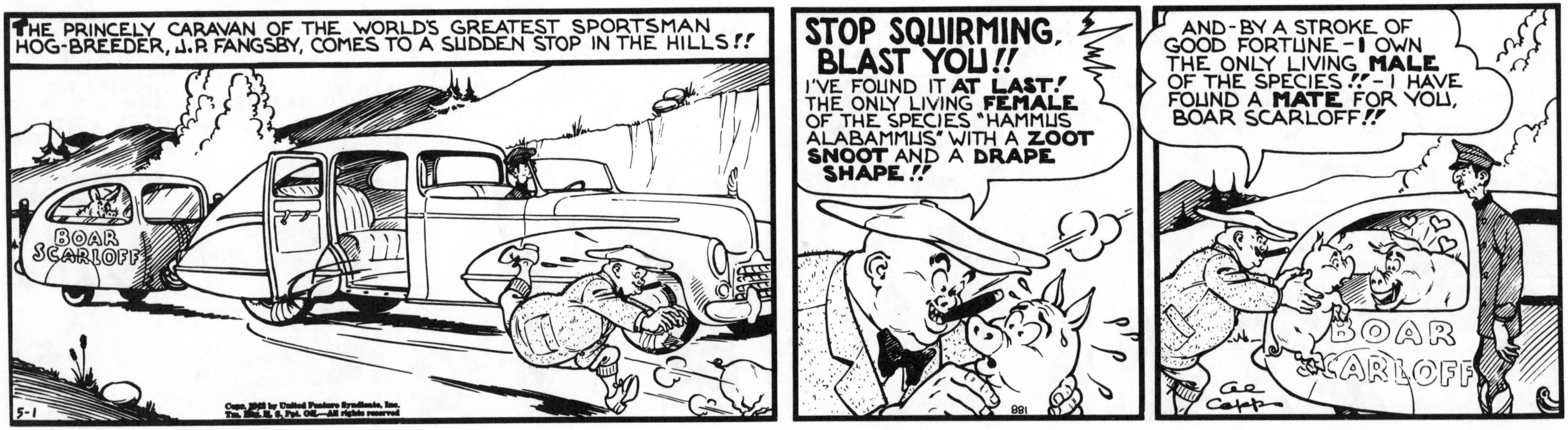
THE PRINCELY CARAVAN OF THE WORLD'S GREATEST SPORTSMAN HOG-BREEDER, J. P. FANGSBY, COMES TO A SUDDEN STOP IN THE HILLS!!
BOAR SCARLOFF
5-1
STOP SQUIRMING, BLAST YOU!!
I'VE FOUND IT **AT LAST**! THE ONLY LIVING **FEMALE** OF THE SPECIES "HAMMUS ALABAMMUS" WITH A **ZOOT SNOOT** AND A **DRAPE SHAPE**!!
881
AND–BY A STROKE OF GOOD FORTUNE–**I** OWN THE ONLY LIVING **MALE** OF THE SPECIES!!–I HAVE FOUND A **MATE** FOR YOU, BOAR SCARLOFF!!
BOAR SCARLOFF

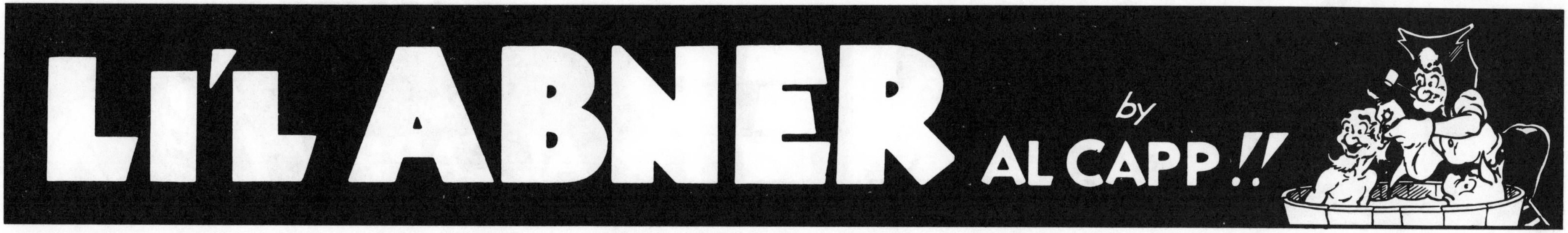
LI'L ABNER
by
AL CAPP !!

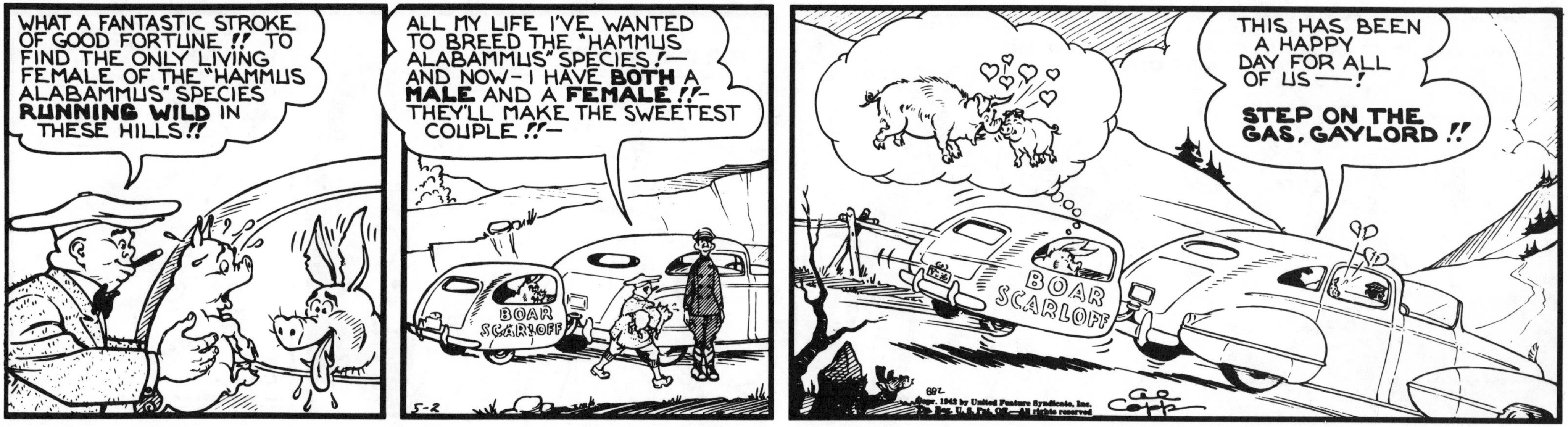
WHAT A FANTASTIC STROKE OF GOOD FORTUNE !! TO FIND THE ONLY LIVING FEMALE OF THE "HAMMUS ALABAMMUS" SPECIES **RUNNING WILD** IN THESE HILLS !!
ALL MY LIFE I'VE WANTED TO BREED THE "HAMMUS ALABAMMUS" SPECIES !— AND NOW – I HAVE **BOTH** A **MALE** AND A **FEMALE** !!– THEY'LL MAKE THE SWEETEST COUPLE !!—
BOAR SCARLOFF
5-2
THIS HAS BEEN A HAPPY DAY FOR ALL OF US —!
STEP ON THE GAS, GAYLORD !!
BOAR SCARLOFF
882
Copr. 1942 by United Feature Syndicate, Inc.
Tm Reg. U. S. Pat. Off.—All rights reserved
Al Capp

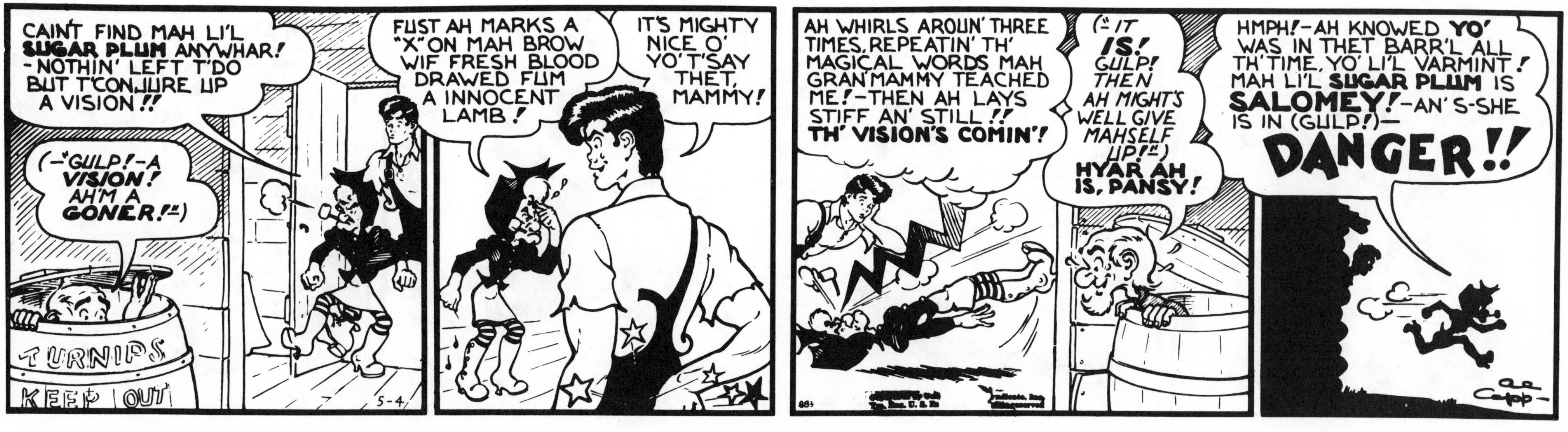
CAIN'T FIND MAH LI'L **SUGAR PLUM** ANYWHAR! – NOTHIN' LEFT T'DO BUT T'CONJURE UP A VISION !!
(–"GULP!–A **VISION!** AH'M A **GONER!**"–)
TURNIPS
KEEP OUT
FUST AH MARKS A "X" ON MAH BROW WIF FRESH BLOOD DRAWED FUM A INNOCENT LAMB !
IT'S MIGHTY NICE O' YO' T'SAY THET, MAMMY!
5-4
AH WHIRLS AROUN' THREE TIMES, REPEATIN' TH' MAGICAL WORDS MAH GRAN'MAMMY TEACHED ME !– THEN AH LAYS STIFF AN' STILL !! **TH' VISION'S COMIN'!**
("IT **IS!** GULP! THEN AH MIGHT'S WELL GIVE MAHSELF UP!!")
HYAR AH IS, PANSY!
HMPH!– AH KNOWED **YO'** WAS IN THET BARR'L ALL TH' TIME, YO' LI'L VARMINT ! MAH LI'L **SUGAR PLUM** IS **SALOMEY!** – AN' S-SHE IS IN (GULP!)—
DANGER !!
Al Capp

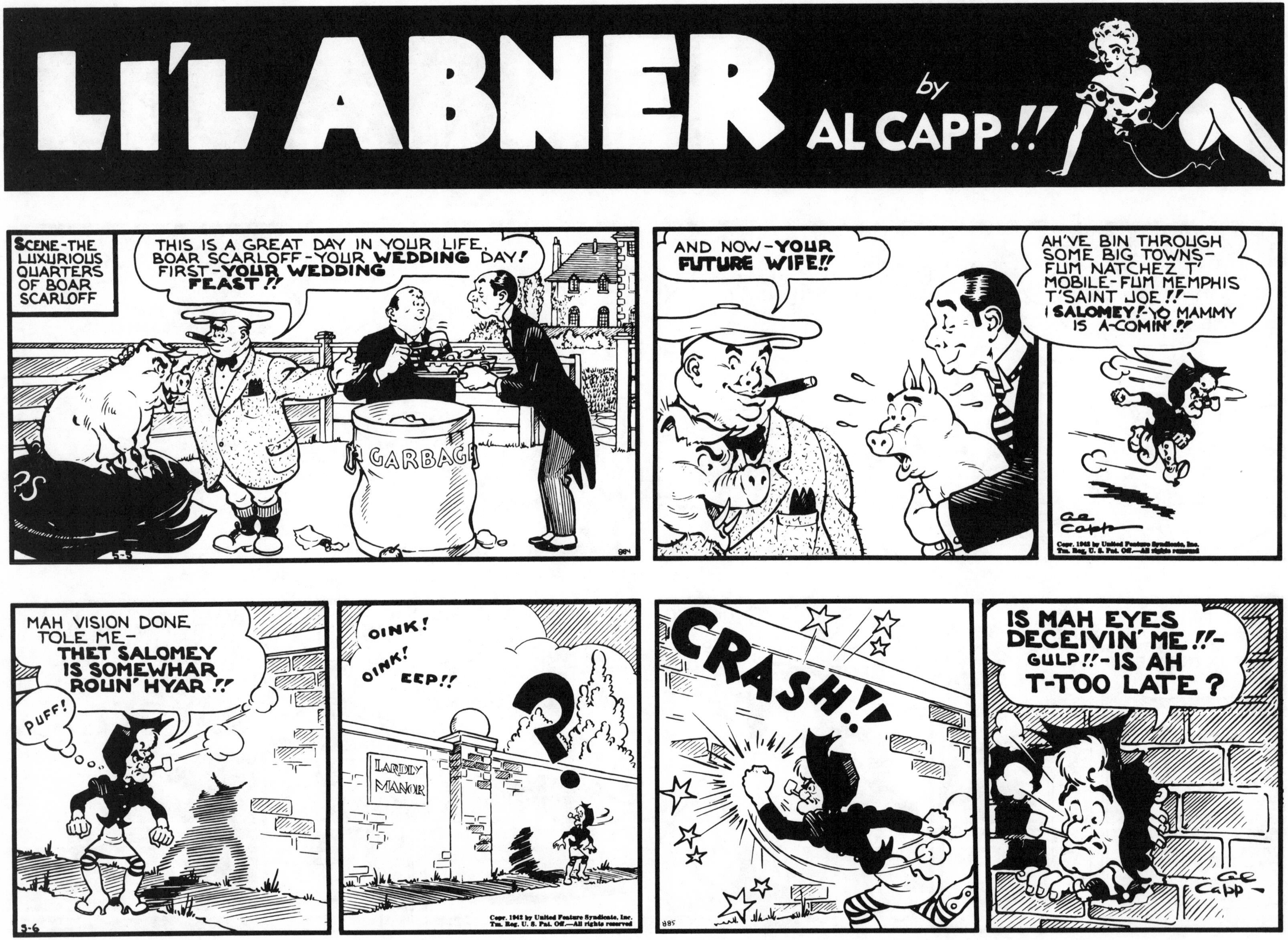

LI'L ABNER
by AL CAPP!!
SCENE-THE LUXURIOUS QUARTERS OF BOAR SCARLOFF
THIS IS A GREAT DAY IN YOUR LIFE, BOAR SCARLOFF-YOUR WEDDING DAY! FIRST-YOUR WEDDING FEAST!!
GARBAGE
AND NOW-YOUR FUTURE WIFE!!
AH'VE BIN THROUGH SOME BIG TOWNS-FUM NATCHEZ T' MOBILE-FUM MEMPHIS T'SAINT JOE!!- SALOMEY!-YO MAMMY IS A-COMIN'!!
Al Capp
Copr. 1942 by United Feature Syndicate, Inc. Tm. Reg. U. S. Pat. Off.—All rights reserved
MAH VISION DONE TOLE ME-THET SALOMEY IS SOMEWHAR ROUN' HYAR!!
PUFF!
OINK!
OINK!
EEP!!
?
LARDLY MANOR
Copr. 1942 by United Feature Syndicate, Inc. Tm. Reg. U. S. Pat. Off.—All rights reserved
CRASH!!
IS MAH EYES DECEIVIN' ME!!-GULP!!-IS AH T-TOO LATE?
Al Capp

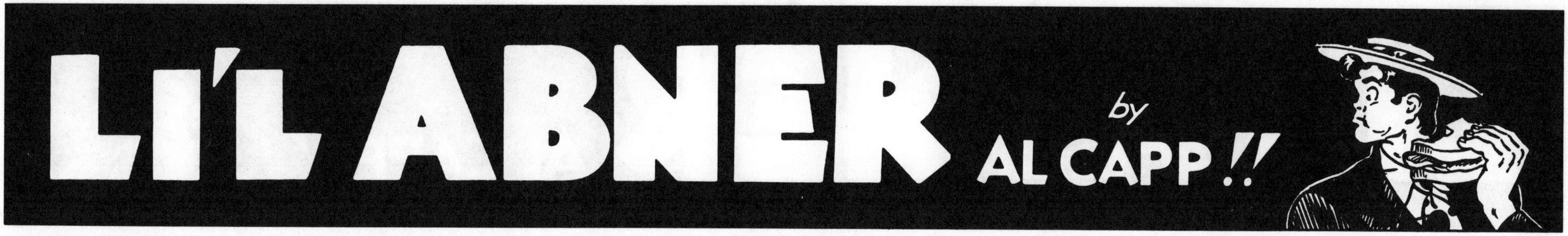
LI'L ABNER
by
AL CAPP!!

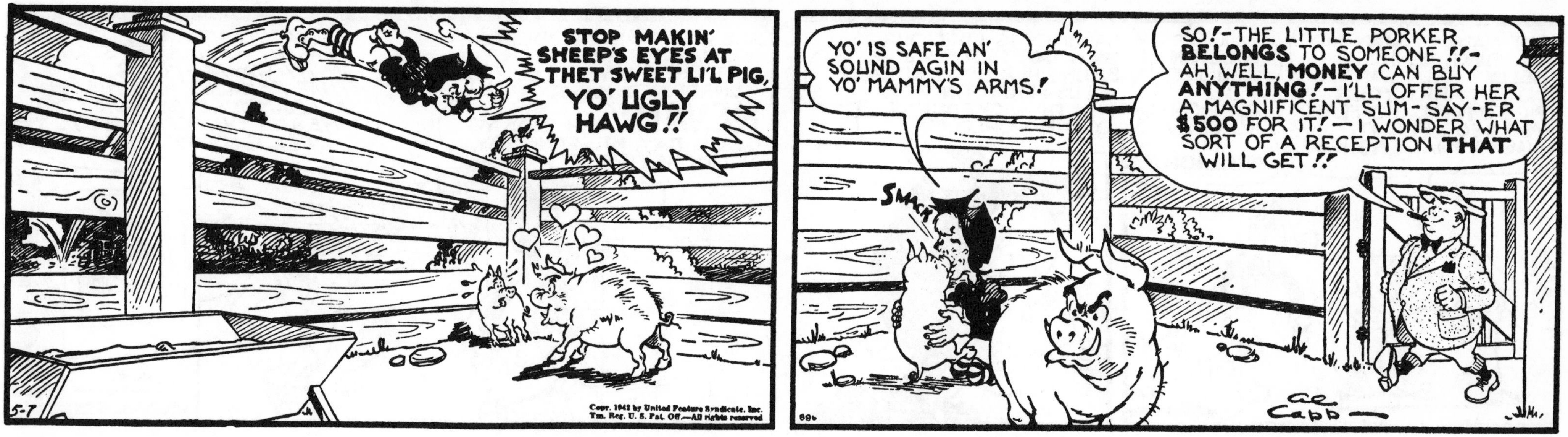
STOP MAKIN' SHEEP'S EYES AT THET SWEET LI'L PIG, YO' UGLY HAWG!!
5-7
Copr. 1942 by United Feature Syndicate, Inc. Tm. Reg. U. S. Pat. Off.—All rights reserved
YO' IS SAFE AN' SOUND AGIN IN YO' MAMMY'S ARMS!
SMACK
SO!—THE LITTLE PORKER BELONGS TO SOMEONE!!—AH, WELL, MONEY CAN BUY ANYTHING!—I'LL OFFER HER A MAGNIFICENT SUM—SAY—ER $500 FOR IT!—I WONDER WHAT SORT OF A RECEPTION THAT WILL GET!!
886
AL CAPP

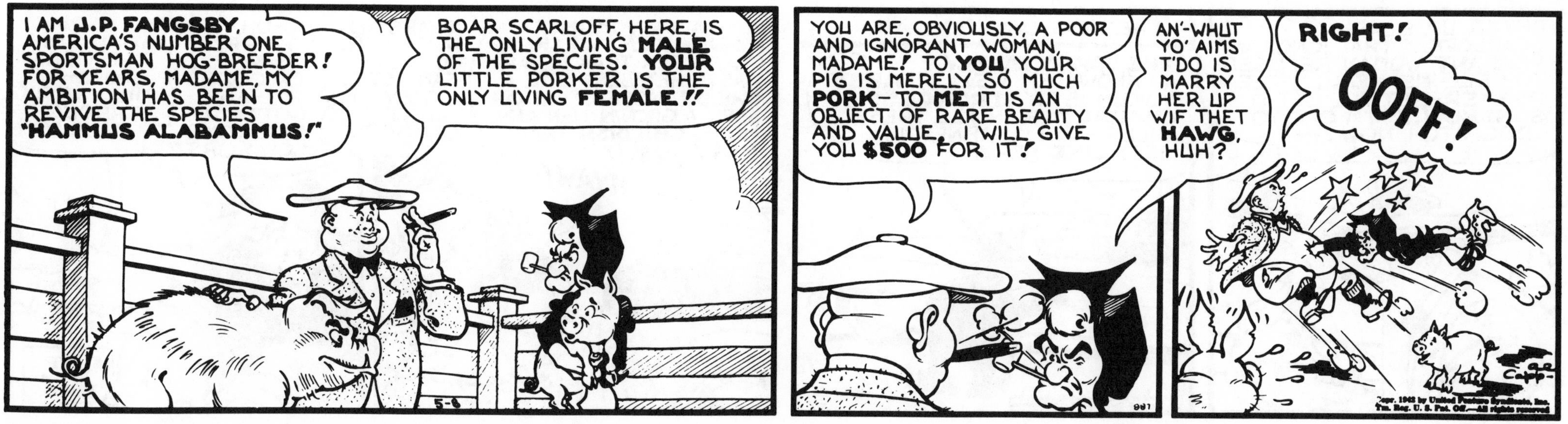
I AM J.P. FANGSBY, AMERICA'S NUMBER ONE SPORTSMAN HOG-BREEDER! FOR YEARS, MADAME, MY AMBITION HAS BEEN TO REVIVE THE SPECIES "HAMMUS ALABAMMUS!"
BOAR SCARLOFF, HERE, IS THE ONLY LIVING MALE OF THE SPECIES. YOUR LITTLE PORKER IS THE ONLY LIVING FEMALE!!
5-6
YOU ARE, OBVIOUSLY, A POOR AND IGNORANT WOMAN, MADAME! TO YOU, YOUR PIG IS MERELY SO MUCH PORK—TO ME IT IS AN OBJECT OF RARE BEAUTY AND VALUE. I WILL GIVE YOU $500 FOR IT!
AN'—WHUT YO' AIMS T'DO IS MARRY HER UP WIF THET HAWG, HUH?
887
RIGHT!
OOFF!
AL CAPP
Copr. 1942 by United Feature Syndicate, Inc. Tm. Reg. U. S. Pat. Off.—All rights reserved

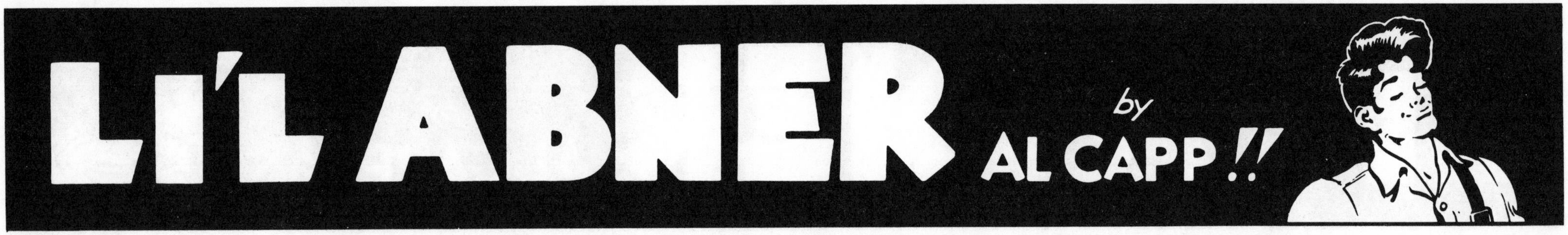
LI'L ABNER
by
AL CAPP!!

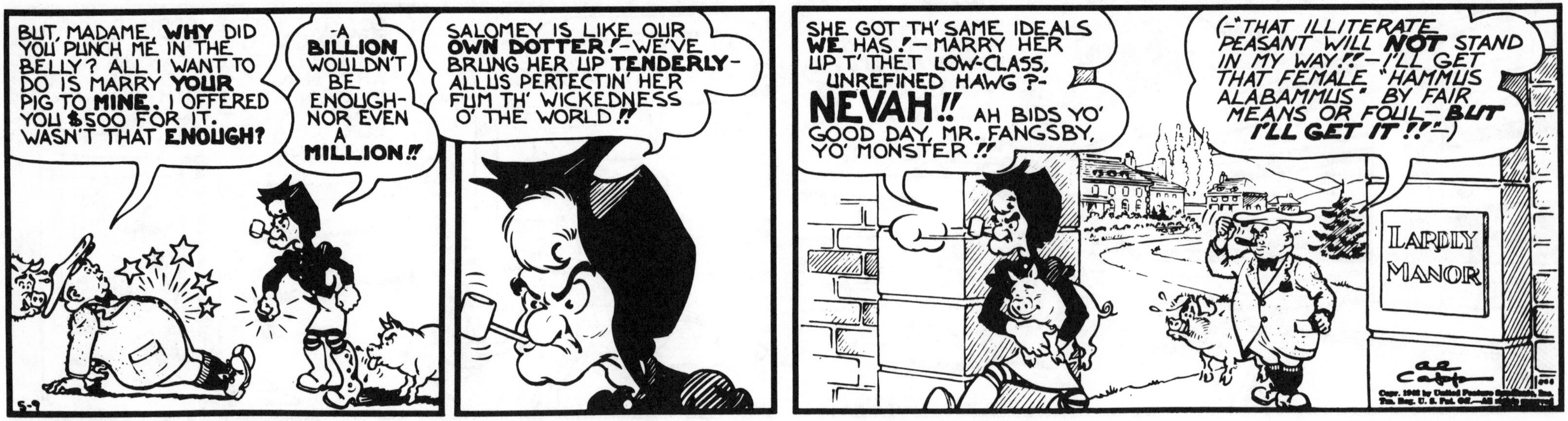
BUT, MADAME, WHY DID YOU PUNCH ME IN THE BELLY? ALL I WANT TO DO IS MARRY YOUR PIG TO MINE. I OFFERED YOU $500 FOR IT. WASN'T THAT ENOUGH?
-A BILLION WOULDN'T BE ENOUGH- NOR EVEN A MILLION!!
SALOMEY IS LIKE OUR OWN DOTTER!-WE'VE BRUNG HER UP TENDERLY- ALLUS PERTECTIN' HER FUM TH' WICKEDNESS O' THE WORLD!!
SHE GOT TH' SAME IDEALS WE HAS!-MARRY HER UP T' THET LOW-CLASS, UNREFINED HAWG?- NEVAH!! AH BIDS YO' GOOD DAY, MR. FANGSBY, YO' MONSTER!!
(-"THAT ILLITERATE PEASANT WILL NOT STAND IN MY WAY!!"-I'LL GET THAT FEMALE "HAMMUS ALABAMMUS" BY FAIR MEANS OR FOUL-BUT I'LL GET IT!!"-)
LARDLY MANOR
5-9

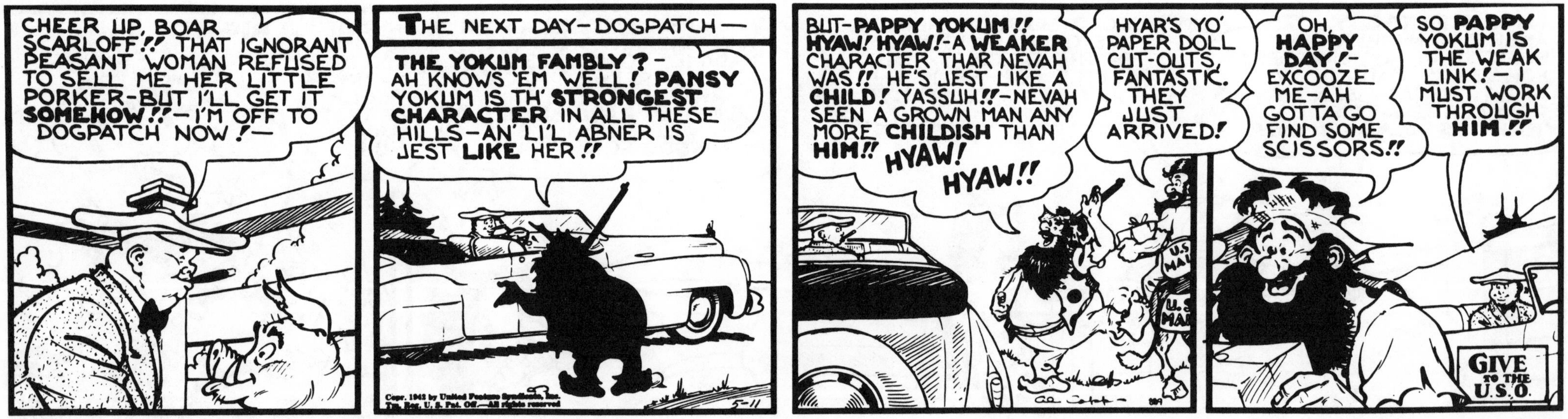
CHEER UP, BOAR SCARLOFF!! THAT IGNORANT PEASANT WOMAN REFUSED TO SELL ME HER LITTLE PORKER-BUT I'LL GET IT SOMEHOW!!-I'M OFF TO DOGPATCH NOW!-
THE NEXT DAY-DOGPATCH-
THE YOKUM FAMBLY?- AH KNOWS 'EM WELL! PANSY YOKUM IS TH' STRONGEST CHARACTER IN ALL THESE HILLS-AN' LI'L ABNER IS JEST LIKE HER!!
Copr. 1942 by United Feature Syndicate, Inc. Tm. Reg. U. S. Pat. Off.—All rights reserved
5-11
BUT-PAPPY YOKUM!! HYAW! HYAW!-A WEAKER CHARACTER THAR NEVAH WAS!! HE'S JEST LIKE A CHILD! YASSUH!!-NEVAH SEEN A GROWN MAN ANY MORE CHILDISH THAN HIM!! HYAW! HYAW!!
HYAR'S YO' PAPER DOLL CUT-OUTS, FANTASTIC. THEY JUST ARRIVED!
U.S. MAIL
OH, HAPPY DAY!- EXCOOZE ME-AH GOTTA GO FIND SOME SCISSORS!!
SO PAPPY YOKUM IS THE WEAK LINK!-I MUST WORK THROUGH HIM!!
GIVE TO THE U.S.O.

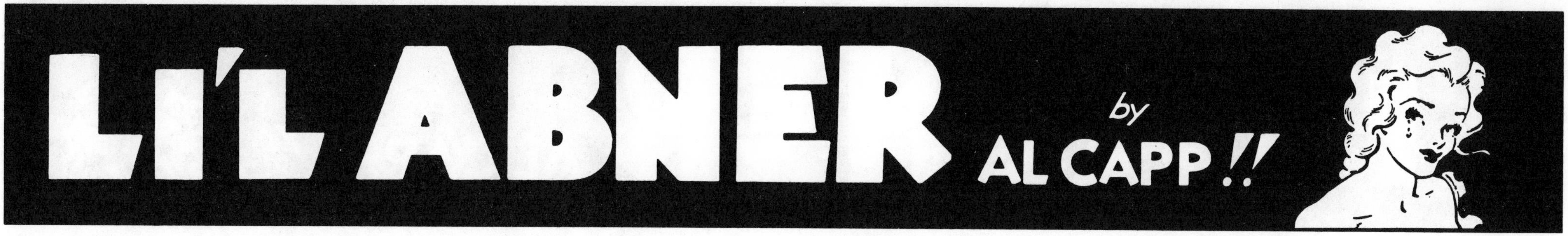
LI'L ABNER
by
AL CAPP!!

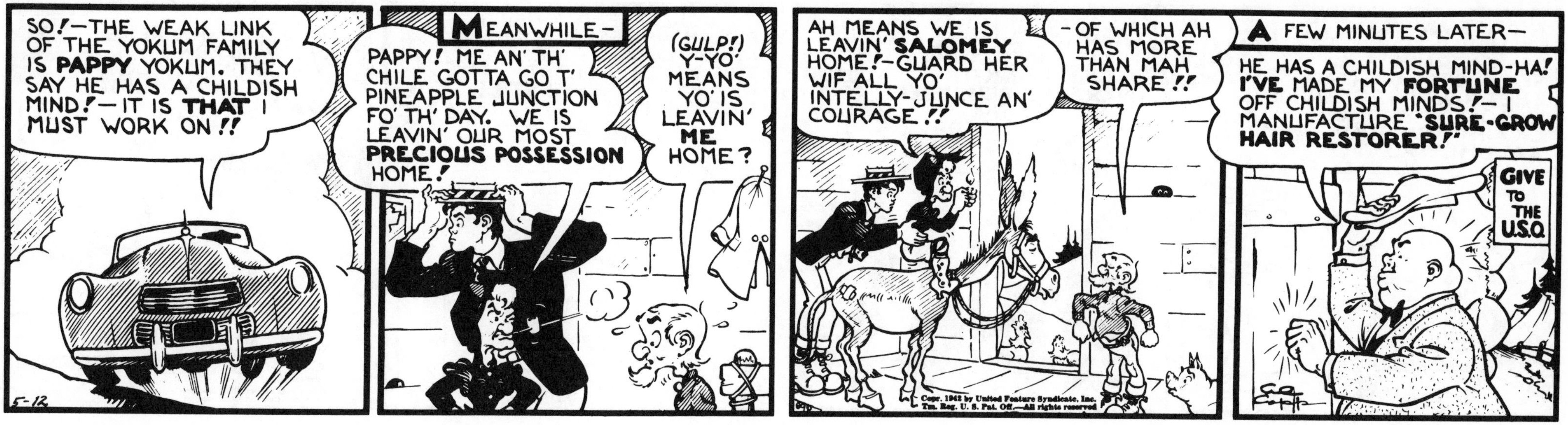
SO!—THE WEAK LINK OF THE YOKUM FAMILY IS PAPPY YOKUM. THEY SAY HE HAS A CHILDISH MIND!—IT IS THAT I MUST WORK ON!!
5-12
MEANWHILE—
PAPPY! ME AN' TH' CHILE GOTTA GO T' PINEAPPLE JUNCTION FO' TH' DAY. WE IS LEAVIN' OUR MOST PRECIOUS POSSESSION HOME!
(GULP!) Y-YO' MEANS YO' IS LEAVIN' ME HOME?
AH MEANS WE IS LEAVIN' SALOMEY HOME!—GUARD HER WIF ALL YO' INTELLY-JUNCE AN' COURAGE!!
-OF WHICH AH HAS MORE THAN MAH SHARE!!
Copr. 1942 by United Feature Syndicate, Inc. Tm. Reg. U. S. Pat. Off.—All rights reserved
A FEW MINUTES LATER—
HE HAS A CHILDISH MIND-HA! I'VE MADE MY FORTUNE OFF CHILDISH MINDS!—I MANUFACTURE "SURE-GROW HAIR RESTORER!"
GIVE TO THE U.S.O.

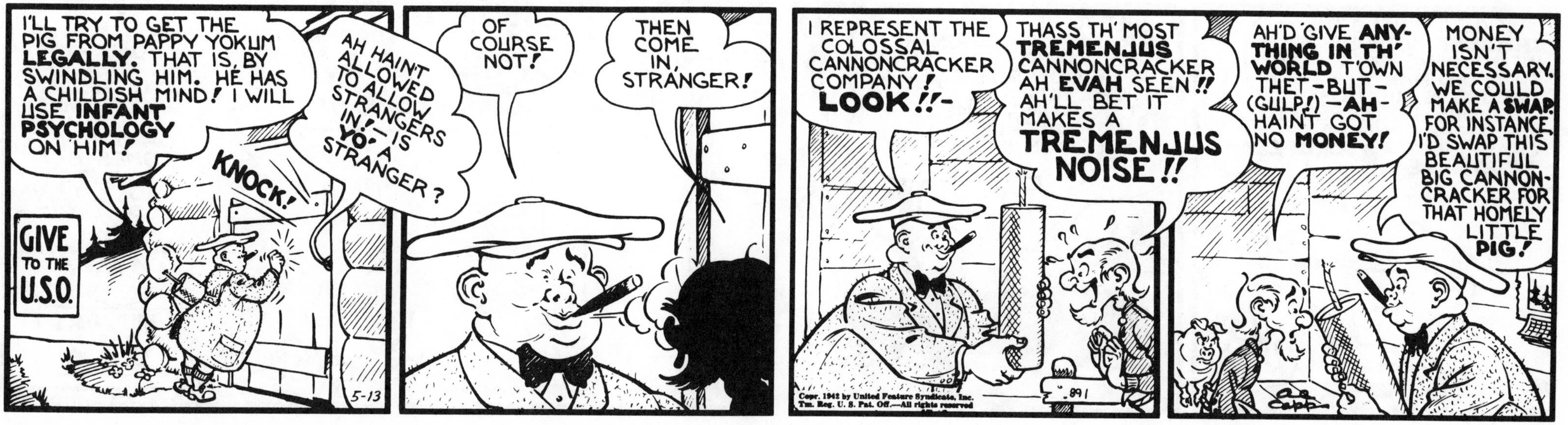
I'LL TRY TO GET THE PIG FROM PAPPY YOKUM LEGALLY. THAT IS, BY SWINDLING HIM. HE HAS A CHILDISH MIND! I WILL USE INFANT PSYCHOLOGY ON HIM!
KNOCK!
AH HAIN'T ALLOWED TO ALLOW STRANGERS IN!—IS YO' A STRANGER?
GIVE TO THE U.S.O.
OF COURSE NOT!
THEN COME IN, STRANGER!
5-13
I REPRESENT THE COLOSSAL CANNONCRACKER COMPANY! LOOK!!-
THASS TH' MOST TREMENJUS CANNONCRACKER AH EVAH SEEN!! AH'LL BET IT MAKES A TREMENJUS NOISE!!
Copr. 1942 by United Feature Syndicate, Inc. Tm. Reg. U. S. Pat. Off.—All rights reserved
AH'D GIVE ANY-THING IN TH' WORLD T'OWN THET—BUT—(GULP!)—AH HAIN'T GOT NO MONEY!
MONEY ISN'T NECESSARY. WE COULD MAKE A SWAP. FOR INSTANCE, I'D SWAP THIS BEAUTIFUL BIG CANNON-CRACKER FOR THAT HOMELY LITTLE PIG!

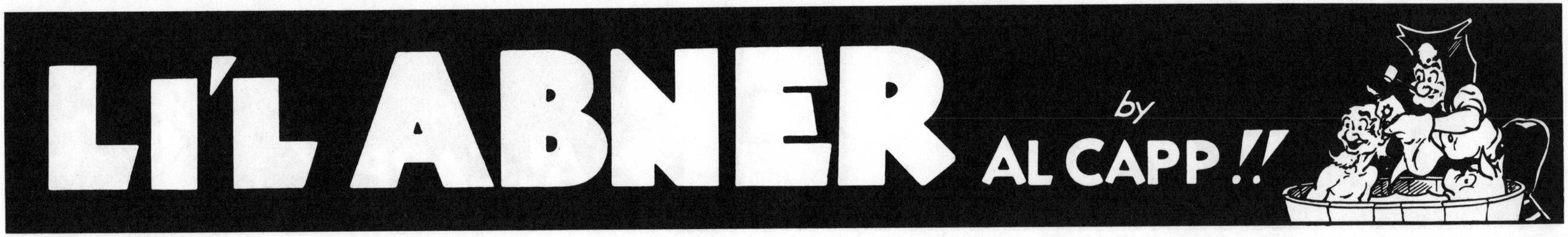
LI'L ABNER
by
AL CAPP !!

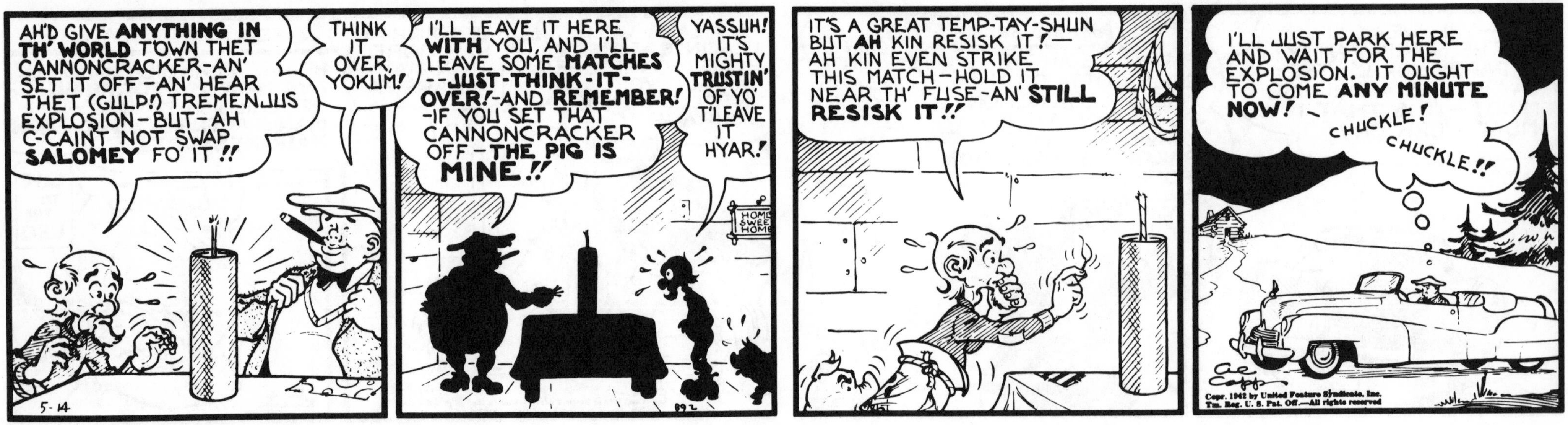
AH'D GIVE ANYTHING IN TH' WORLD T'OWN THET CANNONCRACKER-AN' SET IT OFF-AN' HEAR THET (GULP!) TREMENJUS EXPLOSION-BUT-AH C-CAINT NOT SWAP SALOMEY FO' IT!!
THINK IT OVER, YOKUM!
5-14
I'LL LEAVE IT HERE WITH YOU, AND I'LL LEAVE SOME MATCHES --JUST-THINK-IT-OVER!-AND REMEMBER! -IF YOU SET THAT CANNONCRACKER OFF-THE PIG IS MINE!!
YASSUH! IT'S MIGHTY TRUSTIN' OF YO' T'LEAVE IT HYAR!
HOME SWEET HOME
892
IT'S A GREAT TEMP-TAY-SHUN BUT AH KIN RESISK IT!-AH KIN EVEN STRIKE THIS MATCH-HOLD IT NEAR TH' FUSE-AN' STILL RESISK IT!!
I'LL JUST PARK HERE AND WAIT FOR THE EXPLOSION. IT OUGHT TO COME ANY MINUTE NOW!-
CHUCKLE!
CHUCKLE!!
Al Capp
Copr. 1942 by United Feature Syndicate, Inc. Tm. Reg. U. S. Pat. Off.—All rights reserved

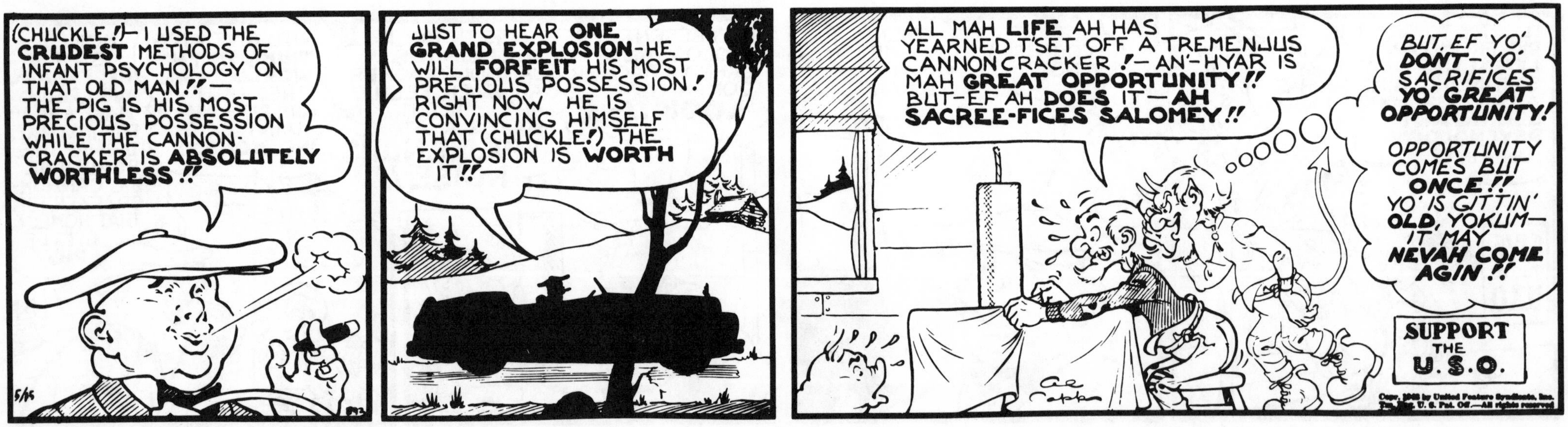
(CHUCKLE!)-I USED THE CRUDEST METHODS OF INFANT PSYCHOLOGY ON THAT OLD MAN!!-THE PIG IS HIS MOST PRECIOUS POSSESSION WHILE THE CANNON-CRACKER IS ABSOLUTELY WORTHLESS!!
5/15
JUST TO HEAR ONE GRAND EXPLOSION-HE WILL FORFEIT HIS MOST PRECIOUS POSSESSION! RIGHT NOW HE IS CONVINCING HIMSELF THAT (CHUCKLE!) THE EXPLOSION IS WORTH IT!!-
893
ALL MAH LIFE AH HAS YEARNED T'SET OFF A TREMENJUS CANNONCRACKER!-AN'-HYAR IS MAH GREAT OPPORTUNITY!! BUT-EF AH DOES IT-AH SACREE-FICES SALOMEY!!
BUT, EF YO' DONT-YO' SACRIFICES YO' GREAT OPPORTUNITY!
OPPORTUNITY COMES BUT ONCE!! YO' IS GITTIN' OLD, YOKUM-IT MAY NEVAH COME AGIN!!
SUPPORT THE U.S.O.
Al Capp
Tm. Reg. U. S. Pat. Off.—All rights reserved

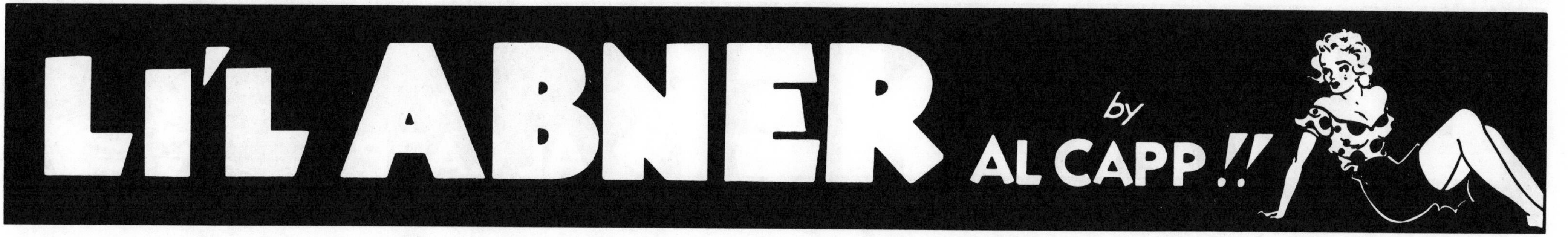
LI'L ABNER
by
AL CAPP!!

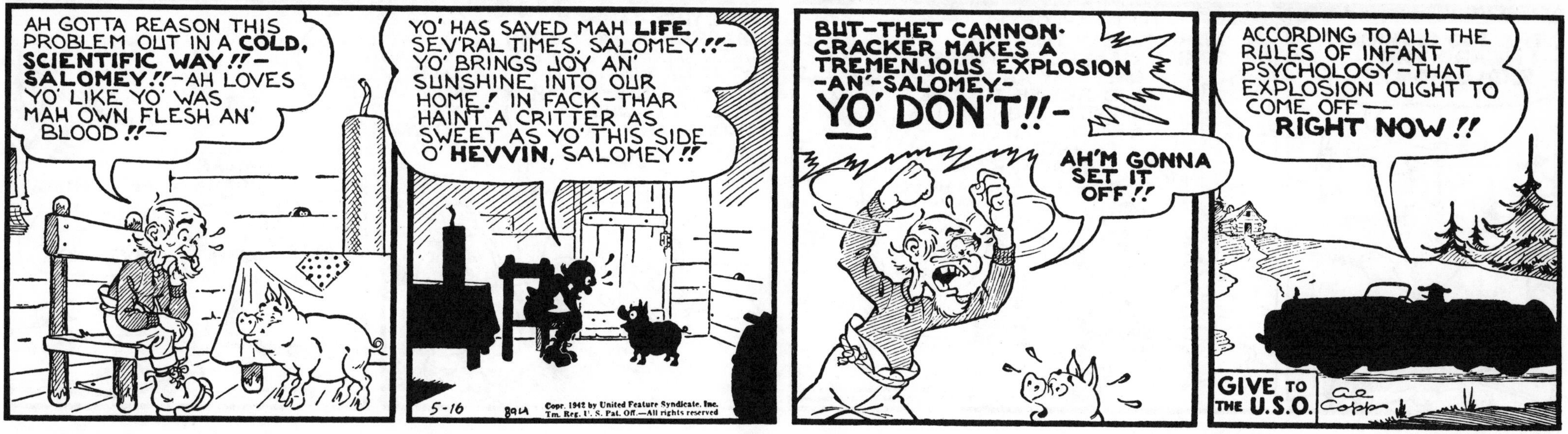
AH GOTTA REASON THIS PROBLEM OUT IN A COLD, SCIENTIFIC WAY!!–SALOMEY!!–AH LOVES YO' LIKE YO' WAS MAH OWN FLESH AN' BLOOD!!–
YO' HAS SAVED MAH LIFE SEV'RAL TIMES, SALOMEY!!–YO' BRINGS JOY AN' SUNSHINE INTO OUR HOME! IN FACK–THAR HAINT A CRITTER AS SWEET AS YO' THIS SIDE O' HEVVIN, SALOMEY!!
5-16
Copr. 1942 by United Feature Syndicate, Inc. Tm. Reg. U. S. Pat. Off.—All rights reserved
BUT–THET CANNON-CRACKER MAKES A TREMENJOUS EXPLOSION -AN'-SALOMEY- YO' DON'T!!–
AH'M GONNA SET IT OFF!!
ACCORDING TO ALL THE RULES OF INFANT PSYCHOLOGY–THAT EXPLOSION OUGHT TO COME OFF– RIGHT NOW!!
GIVE TO THE U.S.O.

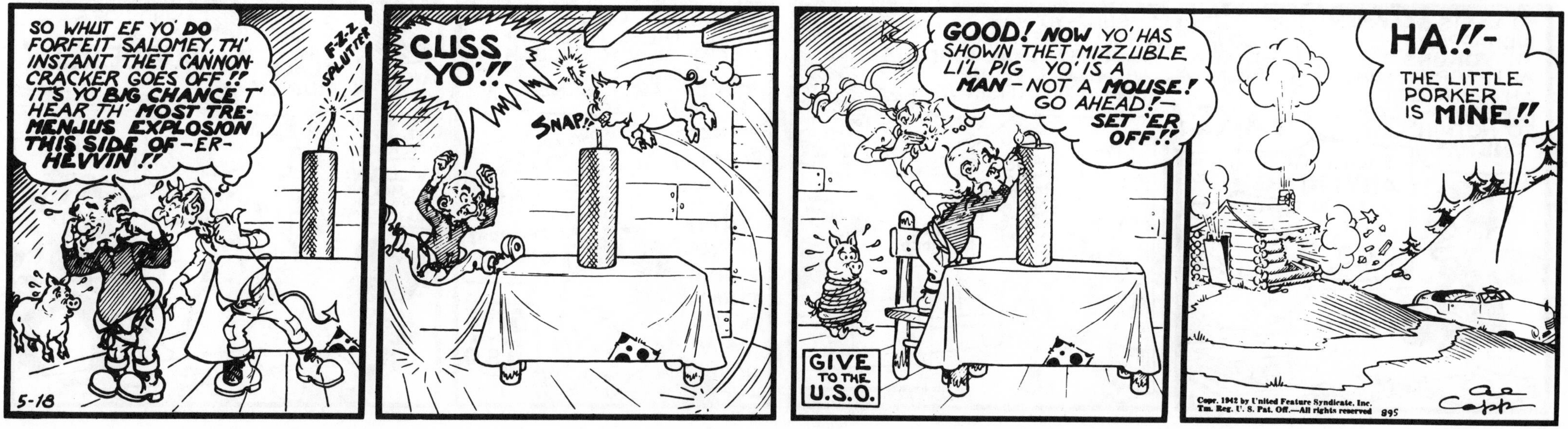
SO WHUT EF YO' DO FORFEIT SALOMEY, TH' INSTANT THET CANNON-CRACKER GOES OFF!! IT'S YO' BIG CHANCE T' HEAR TH' MOST TREMENJUS EXPLOSION THIS SIDE OF–ER–HEVVIN!!
F-Z-Z SPLUTTER
5-18
CUSS YO'!!
SNAP!!
GOOD! NOW YO' HAS SHOWN THET MIZZUBLE LI'L PIG YO' IS A MAN–NOT A MOUSE! GO AHEAD!–SET 'ER OFF!!
GIVE TO THE U.S.O.
HA!!– THE LITTLE PORKER IS MINE!!
Copr. 1942 by United Feature Syndicate, Inc. Tm. Reg. U. S. Pat. Off.—All rights reserved

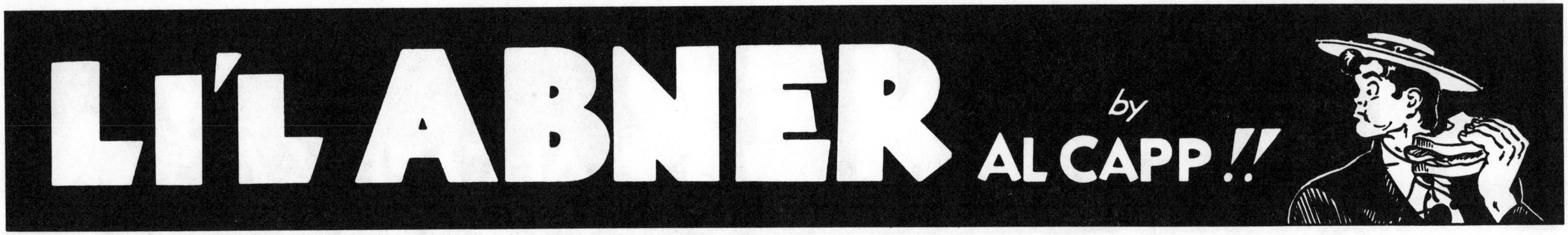
LI'L ABNER
by
AL CAPP!!

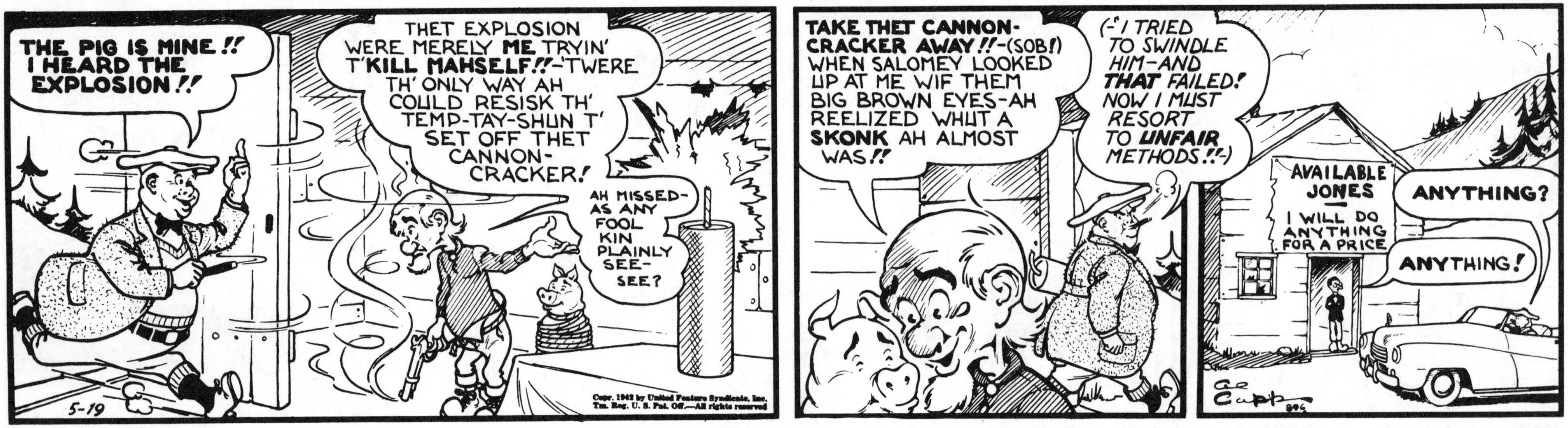
THE PIG IS MINE!! I HEARD THE EXPLOSION!!
THET EXPLOSION WERE MERELY ME TRYIN' T'KILL MAHSELF!!-'TWERE TH' ONLY WAY AH COULD RESISK TH' TEMP-TAY-SHUN T' SET OFF THET CANNON-CRACKER!
AH MISSED-AS ANY FOOL KIN PLAINLY SEE-SEE?
5-19
Copr. 1942 by United Feature Syndicate, Inc.
Tm. Reg. U. S. Pat. Off.—All rights reserved
TAKE THET CANNON-CRACKER AWAY!!-(SOB!) WHEN SALOMEY LOOKED UP AT ME WIF THEM BIG BROWN EYES-AH REELIZED WHUT A SKONK AH ALMOST WAS!!
(-"I TRIED TO SWINDLE HIM-AND THAT FAILED! NOW I MUST RESORT TO UNFAIR METHODS!!"-)
AVAILABLE JONES
I WILL DO ANYTHING FOR A PRICE
ANYTHING?
ANYTHING!
AL CAPP

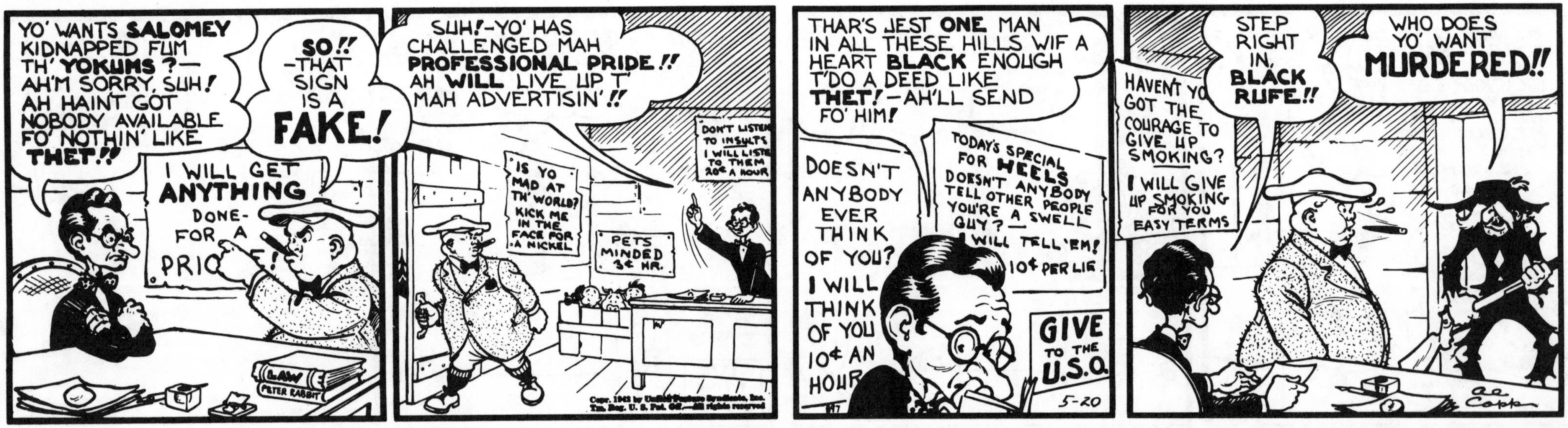
YO' WANTS SALOMEY KIDNAPPED FUM TH' YOKUMS?—AH'M SORRY, SUH! AH HAIN'T GOT NOBODY AVAILABLE FO' NOTHIN' LIKE THET!!
SO!! -THAT SIGN IS A FAKE!
I WILL GET ANYTHING DONE-FOR A PRIC
LAW
PETER RABBIT
SUH!-YO' HAS CHALLENGED MAH PROFESSIONAL PRIDE!! AH WILL LIVE UP T' MAH ADVERTISIN'!!
IS YO MAD AT TH' WORLD? KICK ME IN THE FACE FOR A NICKEL
PETS MINDED 3¢ HR.
DON'T LISTEN TO INSULTS I WILL LISTEN TO THEM 20¢ A HOUR
THAR'S JEST ONE MAN IN ALL THESE HILLS WIF A HEART BLACK ENOUGH T'DO A DEED LIKE THET!-AH'LL SEND FO' HIM!
DOESN'T ANYBODY EVER THINK OF YOU? I WILL THINK OF YOU 10¢ AN HOUR
TODAY'S SPECIAL FOR HEELS DOESN'T ANYBODY TELL OTHER PEOPLE YOU'RE A SWELL GUY? I WILL TELL 'EM! 10¢ PER LIE
GIVE TO THE U.S.O.
5-20
HAVEN'T YOU GOT THE COURAGE TO GIVE UP SMOKING? I WILL GIVE UP SMOKING FOR YOU EASY TERMS
STEP RIGHT IN, BLACK RUFE!!
WHO DOES YO' WANT MURDERED!!
AL CAPP

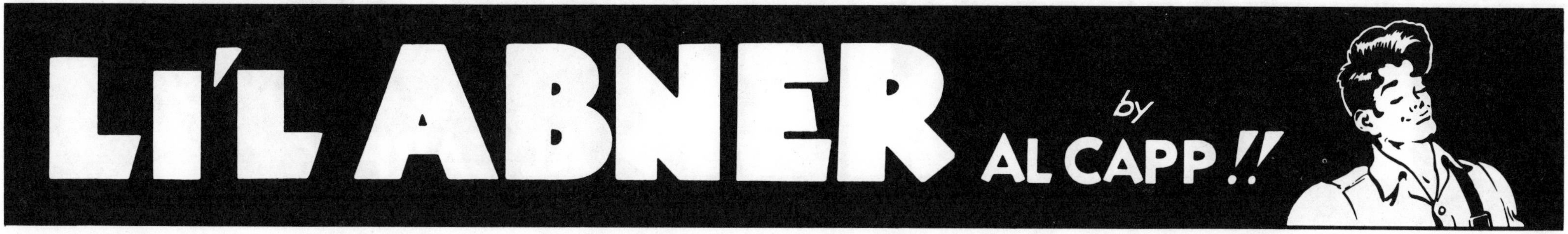
LI'L ABNER
by
AL CAPP!!

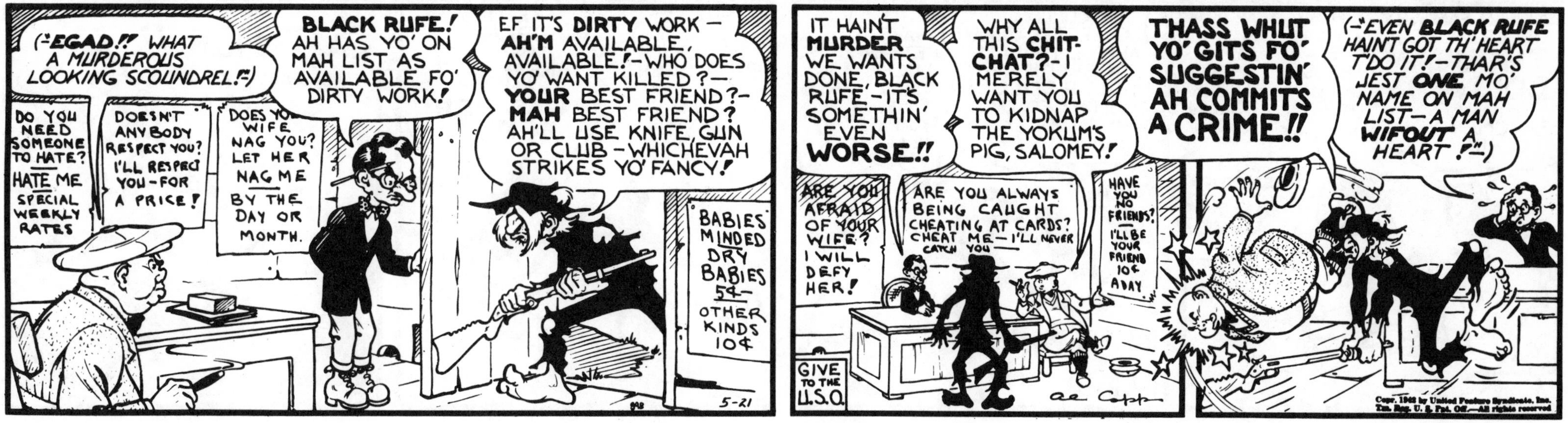
(-"EGAD!!" WHAT A MURDEROUS LOOKING SCOUNDREL!"-)
DO YOU NEED SOMEONE TO HATE? HATE ME SPECIAL WEEKLY RATES
DOESN'T ANYBODY RESPECT YOU? I'LL RESPECT YOU-FOR A PRICE!
DOES YOU WIFE NAG YOU? LET HER NAG ME BY THE DAY OR MONTH.
BLACK RUFE! AH HAS YO' ON MAH LIST AS AVAILABLE FO' DIRTY WORK!
EF IT'S DIRTY WORK — AH'M AVAILABLE, AVAILABLE!-WHO DOES YO' WANT KILLED?-YOUR BEST FRIEND?-MAH BEST FRIEND? AH'LL USE KNIFE, GUN OR CLUB - WHICHEVAH STRIKES YO' FANCY!
BABIES MINDED DRY BABIES 5¢- OTHER KINDS 10¢
5-21
IT HAIN'T MURDER WE WANTS DONE, BLACK RUFE-IT'S SOMETHIN' EVEN WORSE!!
WHY ALL THIS CHIT-CHAT?-I MERELY WANT YOU TO KIDNAP THE YOKUM'S PIG, SALOMEY!
ARE YOU AFRAID OF YOUR WIFE? I WILL DEFY HER!
ARE YOU ALWAYS BEING CAUGHT CHEATING AT CARDS? CHEAT ME—I'LL NEVER CATCH YOU
HAVE YOU NO FRIENDS? I'LL BE YOUR FRIEND 10¢ A DAY.
GIVE TO THE U.S.O.
al capp
THASS WHUT YO' GITS FO' SUGGESTIN' AH COMMITS A CRIME!!
(-"EVEN BLACK RUFE HAINT GOT TH' HEART T'DO IT!-THAR'S JEST ONE MO' NAME ON MAH LIST-A MAN WIFOUT A HEART!"-)
Copr. 1942 by United Feature Syndicate, Inc. Tm. Reg. U. S. Pat. Off.—All rights reserved

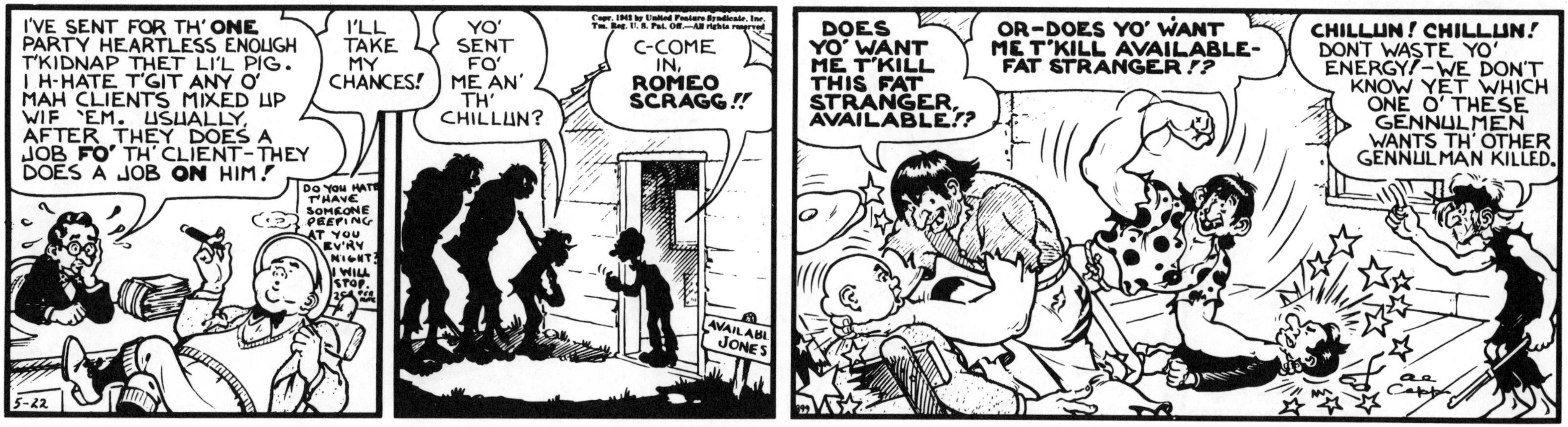
I'VE SENT FOR TH' ONE PARTY HEARTLESS ENOUGH T'KIDNAP THET LI'L PIG. I H-HATE T'GIT ANY O' MAH CLIENTS MIXED UP WIF 'EM. USUALLY, AFTER THEY DOES A JOB FO' TH' CLIENT-THEY DOES A JOB ON HIM!
I'LL TAKE MY CHANCES!
DO YOU HATE T'HAVE SOMEONE PEEPING AT YOU EV'RY NIGHT? I WILL STOP.
5-22
YO' SENT FO' ME AN' TH' CHILLUN?
C-COME IN, ROMEO SCRAGG!!
AVAILABL JONES
DOES YO' WANT ME T'KILL THIS FAT STRANGER, AVAILABLE!?
OR-DOES YO' WANT ME T'KILL AVAILABLE-FAT STRANGER!?
CHILLUN! CHILLUN! DONT WASTE YO' ENERGY!-WE DON'T KNOW YET WHICH ONE O' THESE GENNULMEN WANTS TH' OTHER GENNULMAN KILLED.
al capp

LI'L ABNER by AL CAPP!!

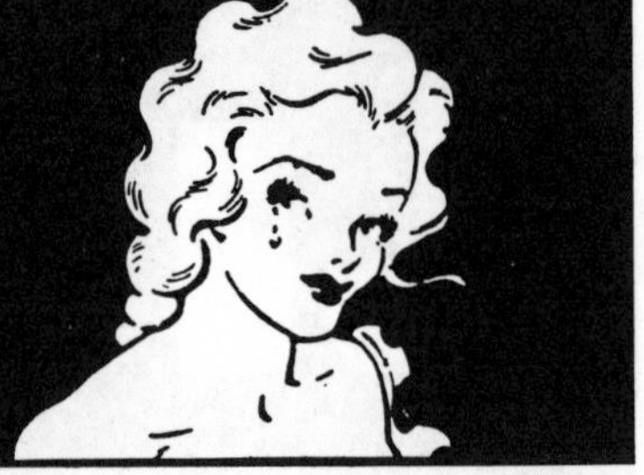

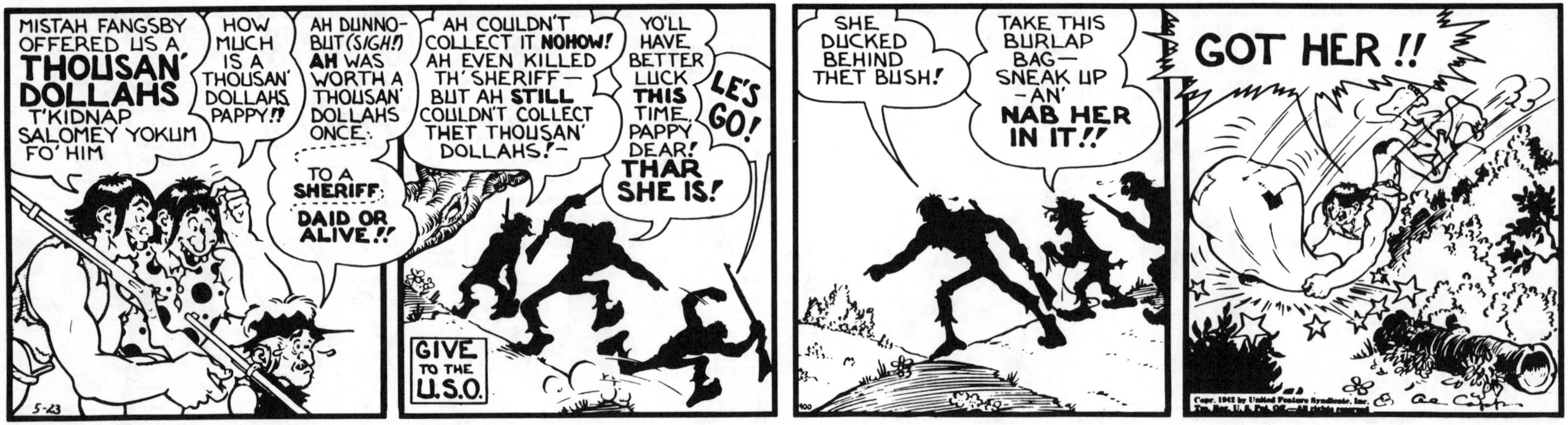

MISTAH FANGSBY OFFERED US A **THOUSAN' DOLLAHS** T'KIDNAP SALOMEY YOKUM FO' HIM
HOW MUCH IS A THOUSAN' DOLLAHS, PAPPY?!
AH DUNNO- BUT (SIGH!) **AH** WAS WORTH A THOUSAN' DOLLAHS ONCE-
TO A **SHERIFF**-
DAID OR ALIVE!!
5-23
AH COULDN'T COLLECT IT **NOHOW!** AH EVEN KILLED TH' SHERIFF— BUT AH **STILL** COULDN'T COLLECT THET THOUSAN' DOLLAHS!-
YO'LL HAVE BETTER LUCK **THIS** TIME, PAPPY DEAR! **THAR SHE IS!**
LE'S GO!
GIVE TO THE U.S.O.
SHE DUCKED BEHIND THET BUSH!
TAKE THIS BURLAP BAG— SNEAK UP -AN' **NAB HER IN IT!!**
GOT HER!!
Copr. 1942 by United Feature Syndicate, Inc. Tm. Reg. U. S. Pat. Off.—All rights reserved

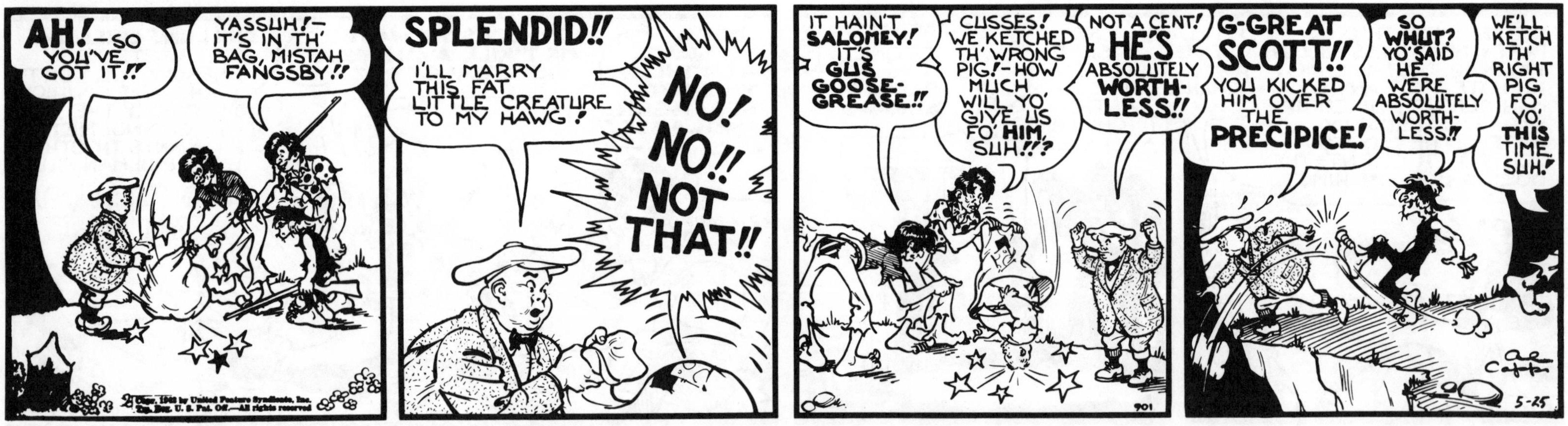

AH!—SO YOU'VE GOT IT!?
YASSUH!— IT'S IN TH' BAG, MISTAH FANGSBY!!
Copr. 1942 by United Feature Syndicate, Inc. Tm. Reg. U. S. Pat. Off.—All rights reserved
SPLENDID!!
I'LL MARRY THIS FAT LITTLE CREATURE TO MY HAWG!
NO! NO!! NOT THAT!!
IT HAIN'T **SALOMEY!** IT'S **GUS GOOSE-GREASE!!**
CUSSES! WE KETCHED TH' WRONG PIG!—HOW MUCH WILL YO' GIVE US FO' **HIM**, SUH!!?
NOT A CENT! **HE'S** ABSOLUTELY **WORTHLESS!!**
G-GREAT SCOTT!! YOU KICKED HIM OVER THE **PRECIPICE!**
SO **WHUT?** YO' SAID HE WERE ABSOLUTELY WORTH-LESS!!
WE'LL KETCH TH' RIGHT PIG FO' YO', **THIS** TIME, SUH!
5-25

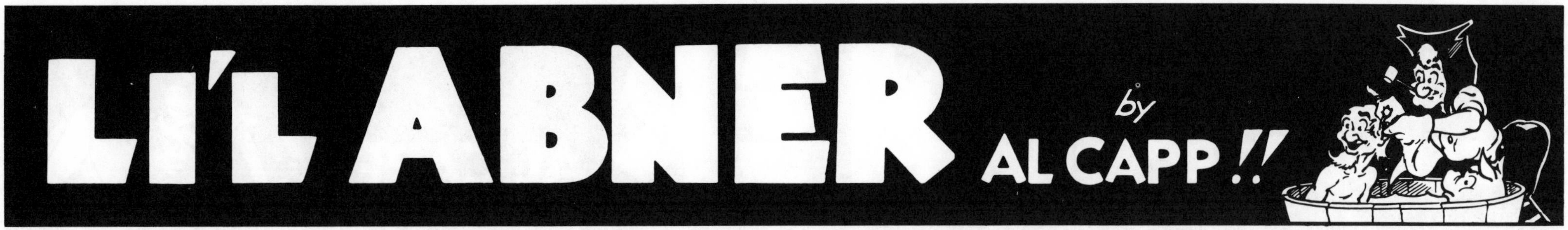
LI'L ABNER
by
AL CAPP!!

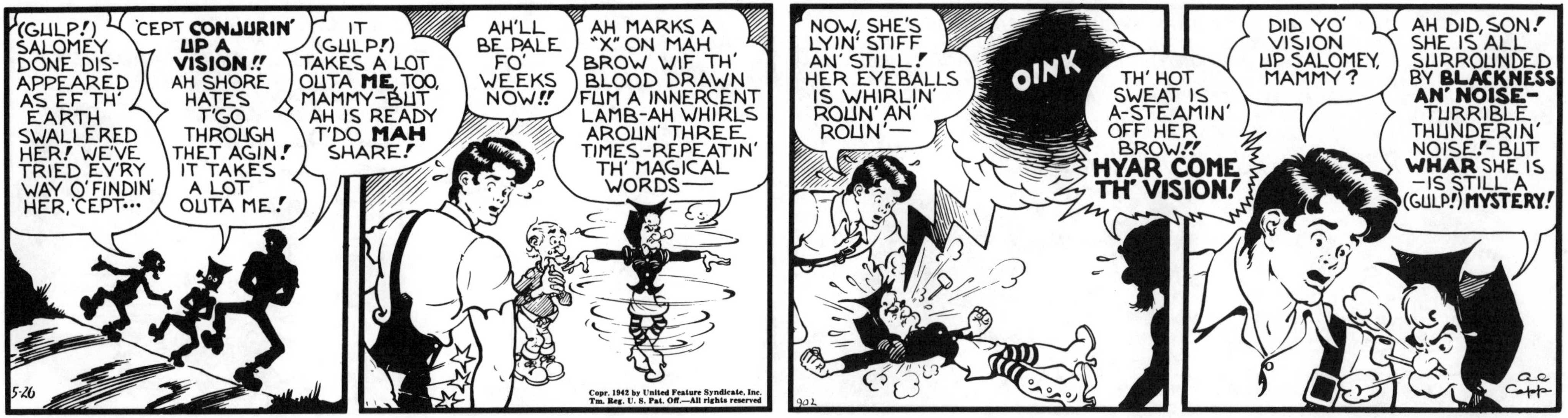
(GULP!) SALOMEY DONE DIS-APPEARED AS EF TH' EARTH SWALLERED HER! WE'VE TRIED EV'RY WAY O'FINDIN' HER, 'CEPT...
'CEPT CONJURIN' UP A VISION!! AH SHORE HATES T'GO THROUGH THET AGIN! IT TAKES A LOT OUTA ME!
5-26
IT (GULP!) TAKES A LOT OUTA ME, TOO, MAMMY-BUT AH IS READY T'DO MAH SHARE!
AH'LL BE PALE FO' WEEKS NOW!!
AH MARKS A "X" ON MAH BROW WIF TH' BLOOD DRAWN FUM A INNERCENT LAMB-AH WHIRLS AROUN' THREE TIMES-REPEATIN' TH' MAGICAL WORDS—
Copr. 1942 by United Feature Syndicate, Inc. Tm. Reg. U. S. Pat. Off.—All rights reserved
NOW, SHE'S LYIN' STIFF AN' STILL! HER EYEBALLS IS WHIRLIN' ROUN' AN' ROUN'—
OINK
TH' HOT SWEAT IS A-STEAMIN' OFF HER BROW!! HYAR COME TH' VISION!
902
DID YO' VISION UP SALOMEY, MAMMY?
AH DID, SON! SHE IS ALL SURROUNDED BY BLACKNESS AN' NOISE-TURRIBLE THUNDERIN' NOISE!-BUT WHAR SHE IS -IS STILL A (GULP!) MYSTERY!
AL CAPP

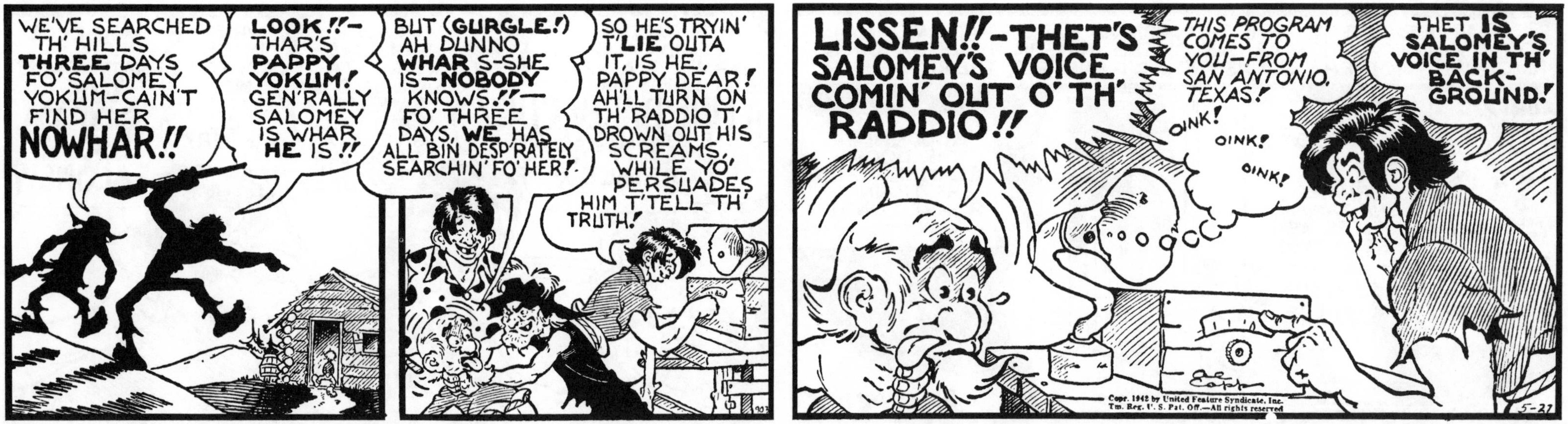
WE'VE SEARCHED TH' HILLS THREE DAYS FO' SALOMEY YOKUM-CAIN'T FIND HER NOWHAR!!
LOOK!!-THAR'S PAPPY YOKUM! GEN'RALLY SALOMEY IS WHAR HE IS!!
BUT (GURGLE!) AH DUNNO WHAR S-SHE IS—NOBODY KNOWS!!—FO' THREE DAYS, WE HAS ALL BIN DESP'RATELY SEARCHIN' FO' HER!
SO HE'S TRYIN' T'LIE OUTA IT, IS HE, PAPPY DEAR! AH'LL TURN ON TH' RADDIO T' DROWN OUT HIS SCREAMS, WHILE YO' PERSUADES HIM T'TELL TH' TRUTH!
LISSEN!!-THET'S SALOMEY'S VOICE COMIN' OUT O' TH' RADDIO!!
THIS PROGRAM COMES TO YOU-FROM SAN ANTONIO, TEXAS!
OINK!
OINK!
OINK!
THET IS SALOMEY'S VOICE IN TH' BACK-GROUND!
AL CAPP
Copr. 1942 by United Feature Syndicate, Inc. Tm. Reg. U. S. Pat. Off.—All rights reserved
5-27

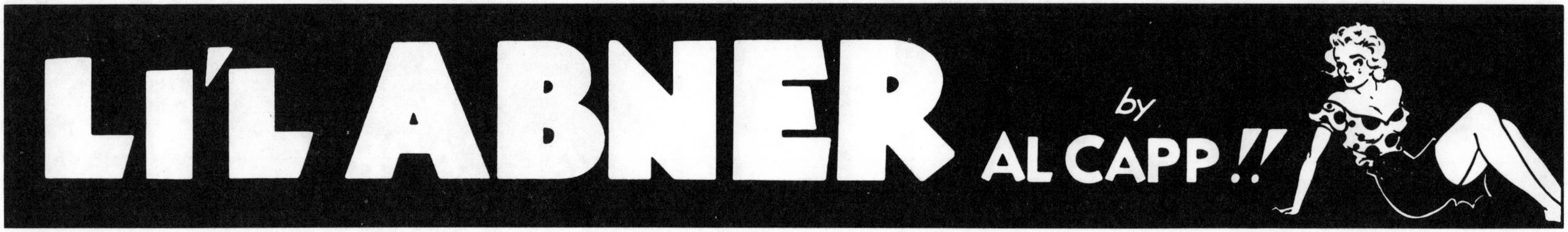

LI'L ABNER
by
AL CAPP!!

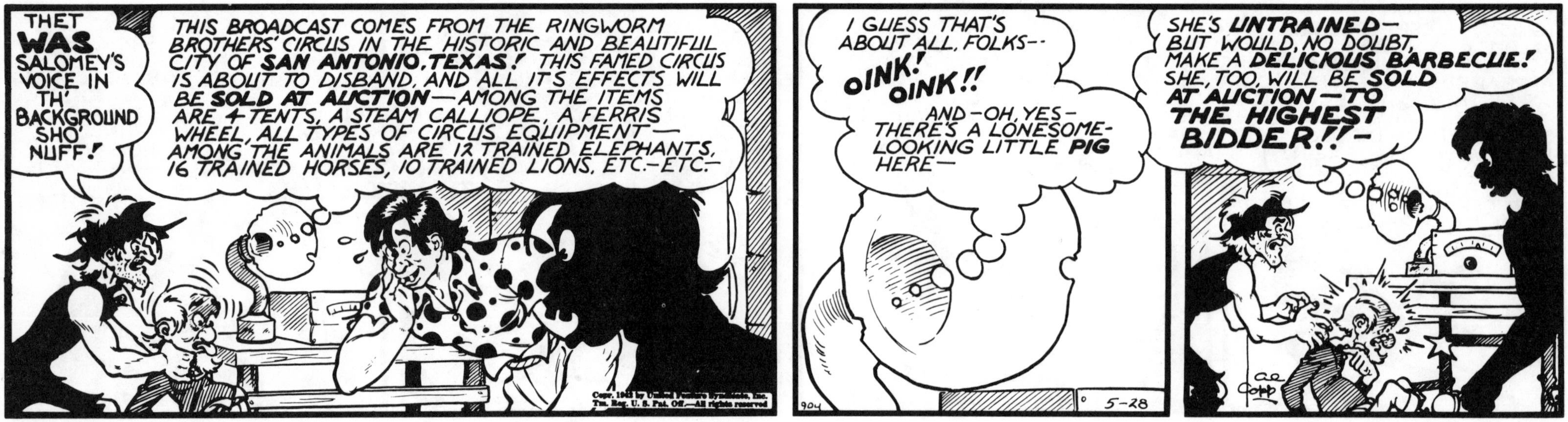

THET WAS SALOMEY'S VOICE IN TH' BACKGROUND SHO' NUFF!
THIS BROADCAST COMES FROM THE RINGWORM BROTHERS' CIRCUS IN THE HISTORIC AND BEAUTIFUL CITY OF SAN ANTONIO, TEXAS! THIS FAMED CIRCUS IS ABOUT TO DISBAND, AND ALL IT'S EFFECTS WILL BE SOLD AT AUCTION—AMONG THE ITEMS ARE 4 TENTS, A STEAM CALLIOPE, A FERRIS WHEEL, ALL TYPES OF CIRCUS EQUIPMENT— AMONG THE ANIMALS ARE 12 TRAINED ELEPHANTS, 16 TRAINED HORSES, 10 TRAINED LIONS, ETC.-ETC.-
I GUESS THAT'S ABOUT ALL, FOLKS--
OINK! OINK!!
AND-OH, YES- THERE'S A LONESOME-LOOKING LITTLE PIG HERE—
SHE'S UNTRAINED— BUT WOULD, NO DOUBT, MAKE A DELICIOUS BARBECUE! SHE, TOO, WILL BE SOLD AT AUCTION—TO THE HIGHEST BIDDER!!-
904
5-28
AL CAPP

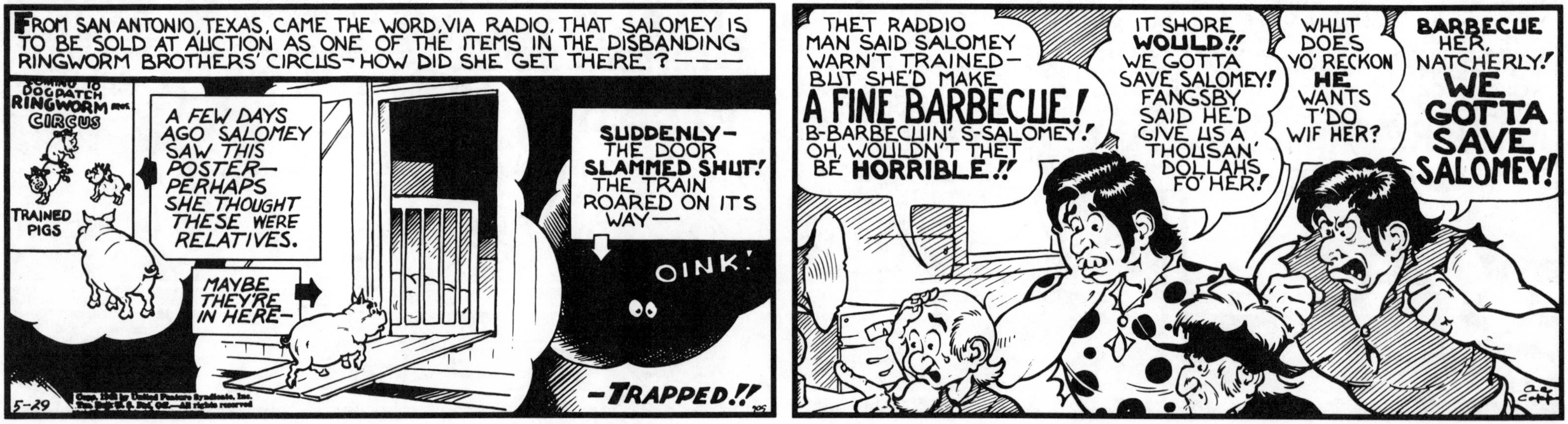

FROM SAN ANTONIO, TEXAS, CAME THE WORD, VIA RADIO, THAT SALOMEY IS TO BE SOLD AT AUCTION AS ONE OF THE ITEMS IN THE DISBANDING RINGWORM BROTHERS' CIRCUS- HOW DID SHE GET THERE ?———
DOGPATCH
RINGWORM
CIRCUS
TRAINED PIGS
A FEW DAYS AGO SALOMEY SAW THIS POSTER— PERHAPS SHE THOUGHT THESE WERE RELATIVES.
MAYBE THEY'RE IN HERE-
SUDDENLY- THE DOOR SLAMMED SHUT! THE TRAIN ROARED ON ITS WAY—
OINK!
-TRAPPED!!
5-29
905
THET RADDIO MAN SAID SALOMEY WARN'T TRAINED- BUT SHE'D MAKE A FINE BARBECUE! B-BARBECUIN' S-SALOMEY! OH, WOULDN'T THET BE HORRIBLE!!
IT SHORE WOULD!! WE GOTTA SAVE SALOMEY! FANGSBY SAID HE'D GIVE US A THOUSAN' DOLLAHS FO' HER!
WHUT DOES YO' RECKON HE WANTS T'DO WIF HER?
BARBECUE HER, NATCHERLY! WE GOTTA SAVE SALOMEY!
AL CAPP

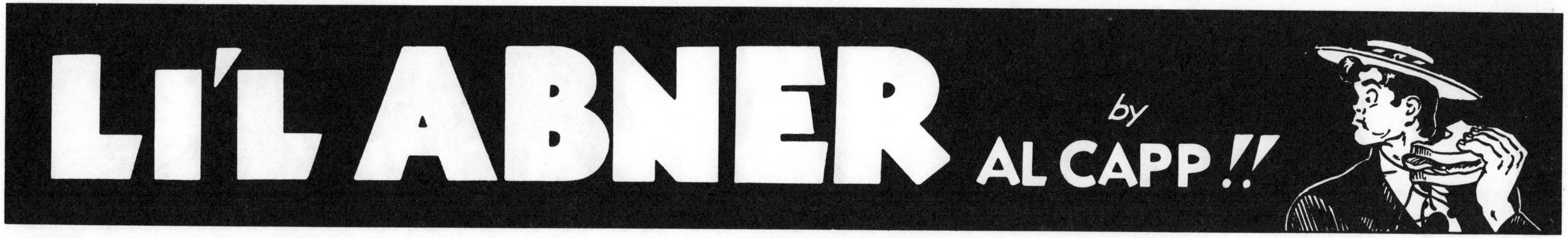
LI'L ABNER
by
AL CAPP!!

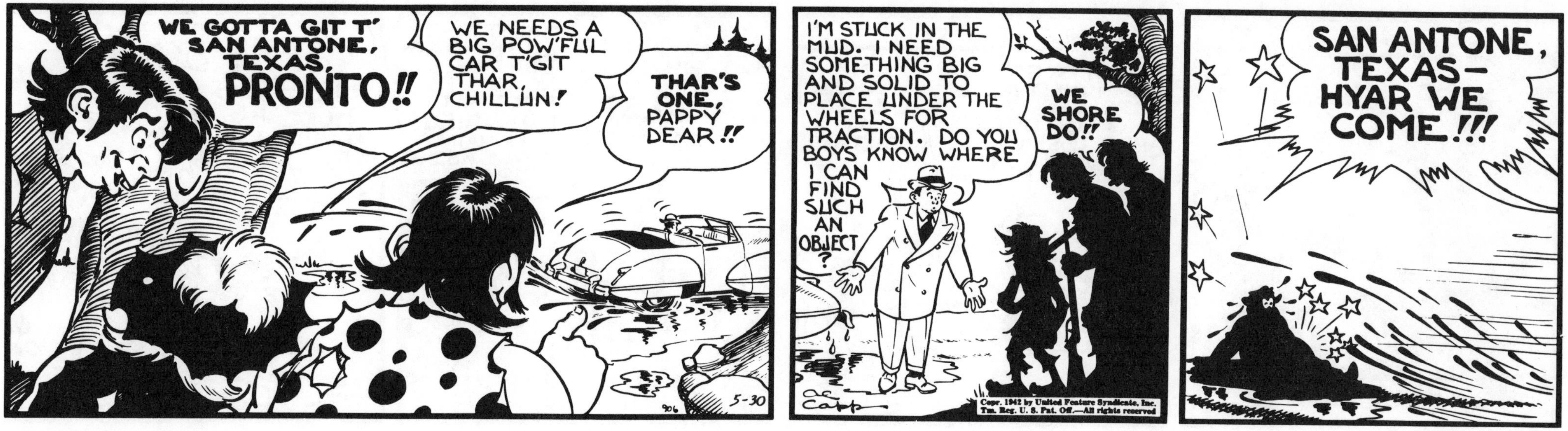
WE GOTTA GIT T' SAN ANTONE, TEXAS, PRONTO!!
WE NEEDS A BIG POW'FUL CAR T'GIT THAR, CHILLUN!
THAR'S ONE, PAPPY DEAR!!
906
5-30
I'M STUCK IN THE MUD. I NEED SOMETHING BIG AND SOLID TO PLACE UNDER THE WHEELS FOR TRACTION. DO YOU BOYS KNOW WHERE I CAN FIND SUCH AN OBJECT?
WE SHORE DO!!
Al Capp
Copr. 1942 by United Feature Syndicate, Inc. Tm. Reg. U. S. Pat. Off.—All rights reserved
SAN ANTONE, TEXAS— HYAR WE COME!!!

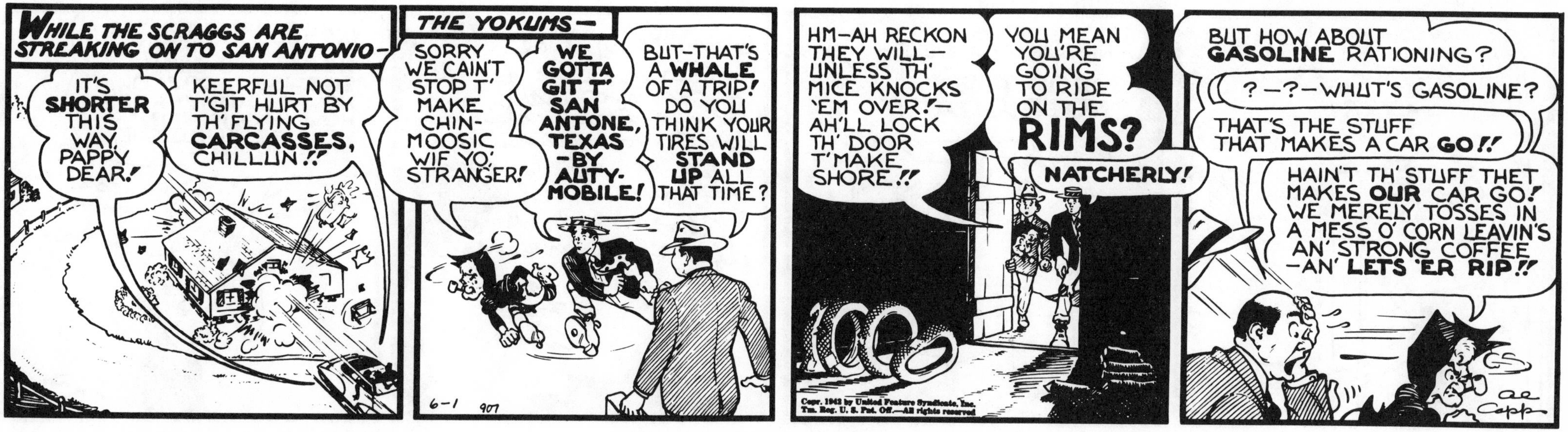
WHILE THE SCRAGGS ARE STREAKING ON TO SAN ANTONIO—
IT'S SHORTER THIS WAY, PAPPY DEAR!
KEERFUL NOT T'GIT HURT BY TH' FLYING CARCASSES, CHILLUN!!
THE YOKUMS—
SORRY WE CAIN'T STOP T' MAKE CHIN-MOOSIC WIF YO' STRANGER!
WE GOTTA GIT T' SAN ANTONE, TEXAS —BY AUTY-MOBILE!
BUT—THAT'S A WHALE OF A TRIP! DO YOU THINK YOUR TIRES WILL STAND UP ALL THAT TIME?
6-1
907
HM—AH RECKON THEY WILL— UNLESS TH' MICE KNOCKS 'EM OVER!— AH'LL LOCK TH' DOOR T'MAKE SHORE!!
YOU MEAN YOU'RE GOING TO RIDE ON THE RIMS?
NATCHERLY!
Copr. 1942 by United Feature Syndicate, Inc. Tm. Reg. U. S. Pat. Off.—All rights reserved
BUT HOW ABOUT GASOLINE RATIONING?
?—?—WHUT'S GASOLINE?
THAT'S THE STUFF THAT MAKES A CAR GO!!
HAIN'T TH' STUFF THET MAKES OUR CAR GO! WE MERELY TOSSES IN A MESS O' CORN LEAVIN'S AN' STRONG COFFEE —AN' LETS 'ER RIP!!
Al Capp

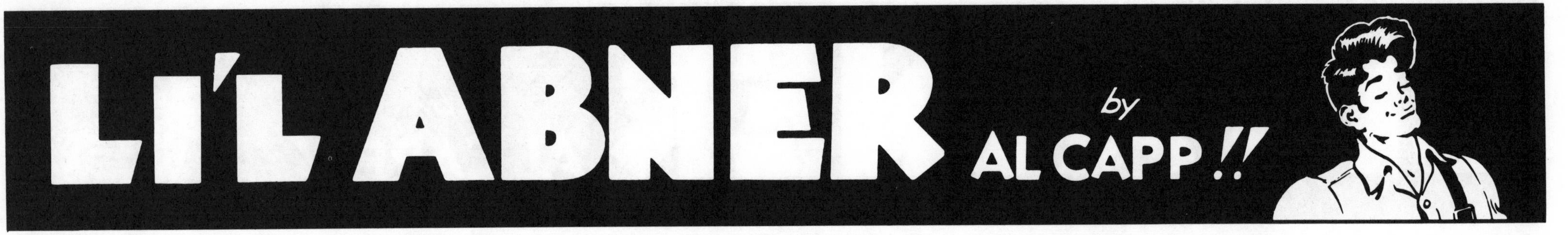
LI'L ABNER
by
AL CAPP!!

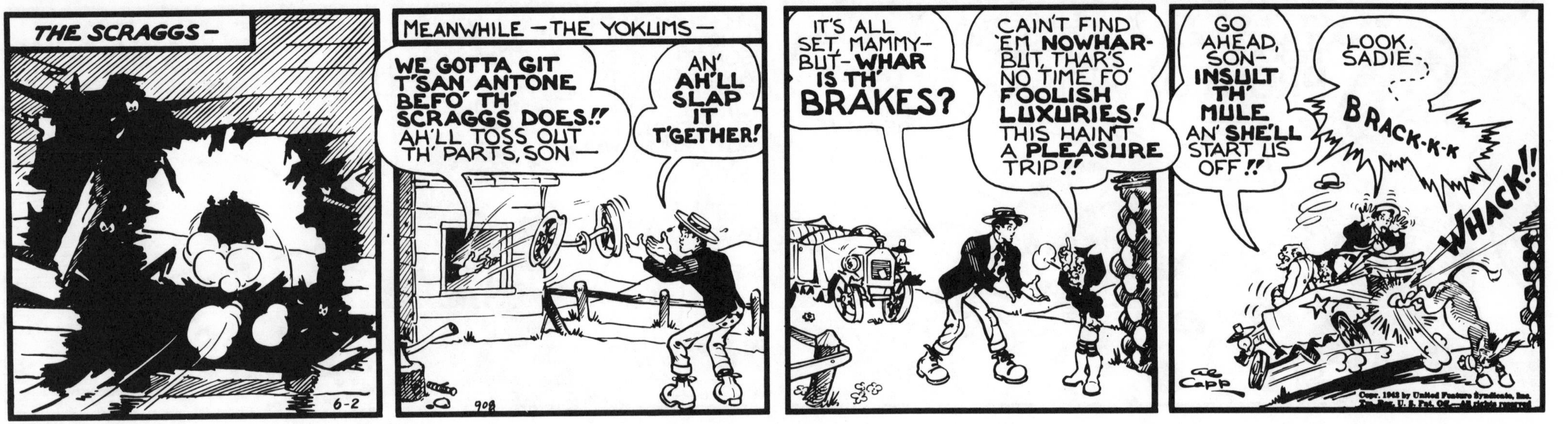
THE SCRAGGS—
6-2
MEANWHILE—THE YOKUMS—
WE GOTTA GIT T'SAN ANTONE BEFO' TH' SCRAGGS DOES!! AH'LL TOSS OUT TH' PARTS, SON—
AN' AH'LL SLAP IT T'GETHER!
IT'S ALL SET, MAMMY—BUT—WHAR IS TH' BRAKES?
CAIN'T FIND 'EM NOWHAR—BUT, THAR'S NO TIME FO' FOOLISH LUXURIES! THIS HAIN'T A PLEASURE TRIP!!
GO AHEAD, SON—INSULT TH' MULE AN' SHE'LL START US OFF!!
LOOK, SADIE
BRACK-K-K
WHACK!!
AL CAPP

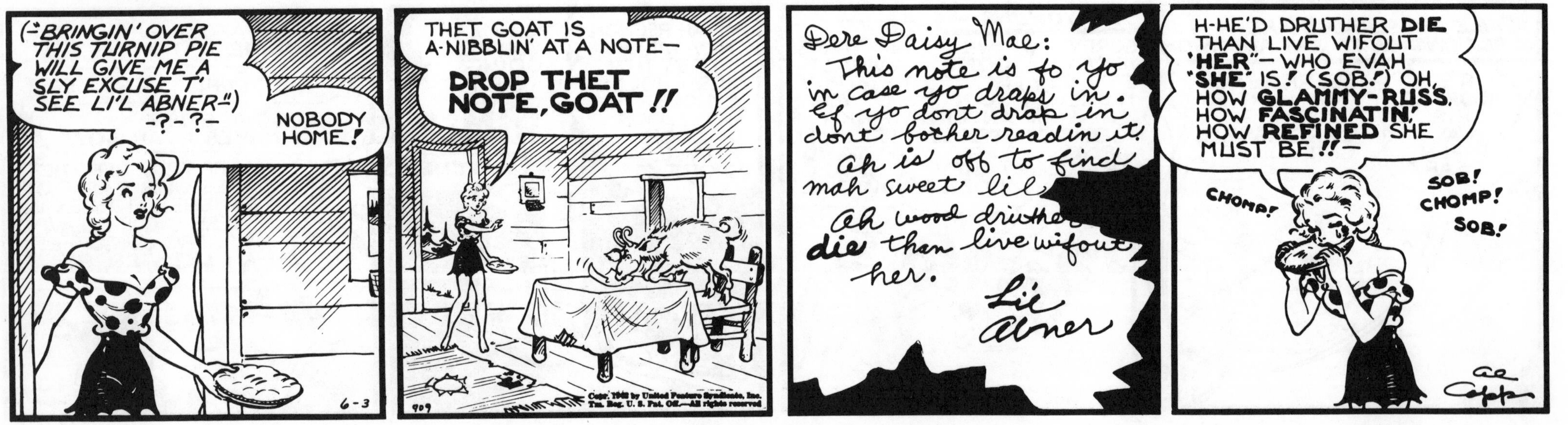
("BRINGIN' OVER THIS TURNIP PIE WILL GIVE ME A SLY EXCUSE T' SEE LI'L ABNER!") -?-?-
NOBODY HOME!
6-3
THET GOAT IS A-NIBBLIN' AT A NOTE—
DROP THET NOTE, GOAT!!
Copr. 1942 by United Feature Syndicate, Inc. Tm. Reg. U. S. Pat. Off.—All rights reserved
Dere Daisy Mae:
This note is fo yo in case yo draps in. Ef yo dont drap in dont bother readin it.
Ah is off to find mah sweet lil
Ah wood druther die than live wifout her.
Li'l Abner
H-HE'D DRUTHER DIE THAN LIVE WIFOUT "HER"—WHO EVAH "SHE" IS! (SOB!) OH, HOW GLAMMY-RUSS, HOW FASCINATIN', HOW REFINED SHE MUST BE!!—
CHOMP!
SOB! CHOMP! SOB!
AL CAPP

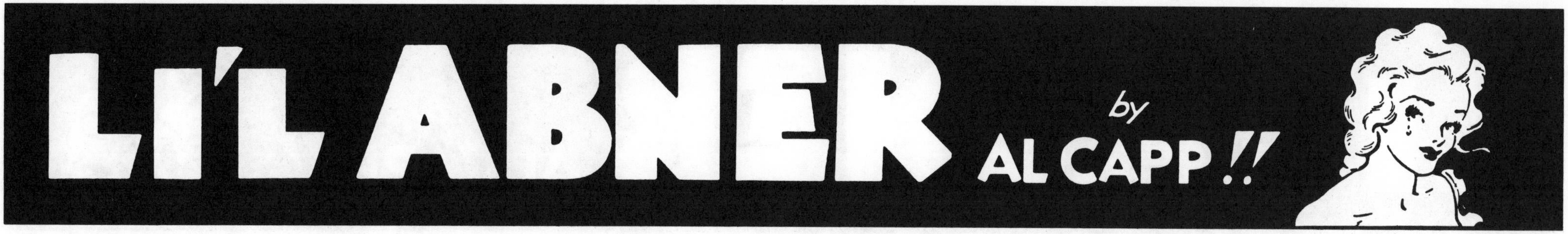
LI'L ABNER
by
AL CAPP!!

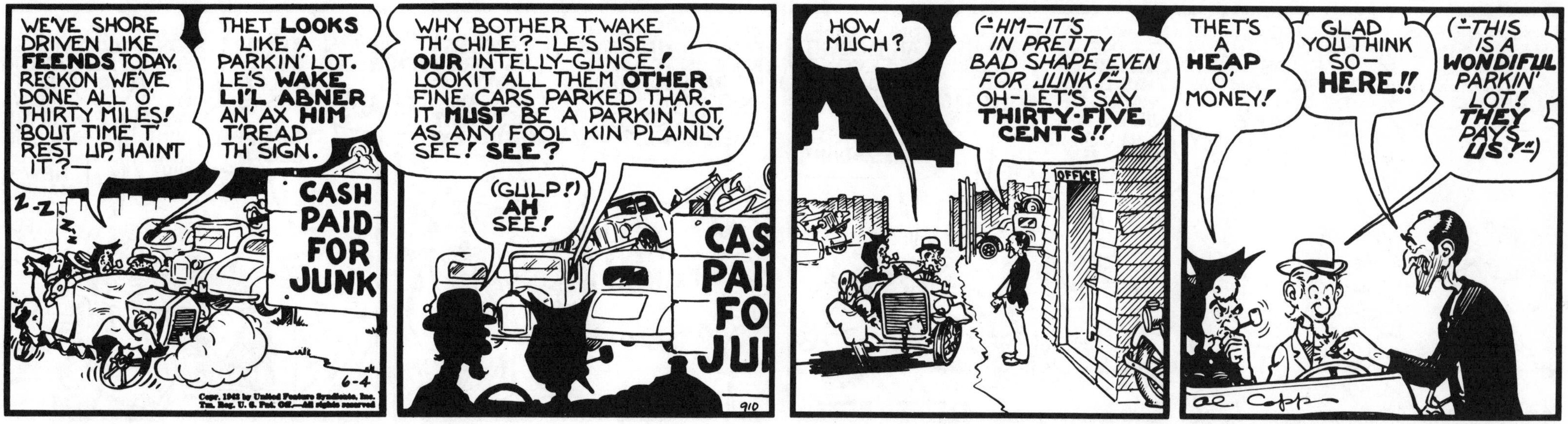
WE'VE SHORE DRIVEN LIKE FEENDS TODAY. RECKON WE'VE DONE ALL O' THIRTY MILES! 'BOUT TIME T' REST UP, HAIN'T IT?—
THET LOOKS LIKE A PARKIN' LOT. LE'S WAKE LI'L ABNER AN' AX HIM T'READ TH' SIGN.
Z-Z Z Z
CASH PAID FOR JUNK
6-4
Copr. 1942 by United Feature Syndicate, Inc. Tm. Reg. U. S. Pat. Off.—All rights reserved
WHY BOTHER T'WAKE TH' CHILE?—LE'S USE OUR INTELLY-GUNCE! LOOKIT ALL THEM OTHER FINE CARS PARKED THAR. IT MUST BE A PARKIN' LOT, AS ANY FOOL KIN PLAINLY SEE! SEE?
(GULP!) AH SEE!
CAS PAI FO JU
910
HOW MUCH?
("HM—IT'S IN PRETTY BAD SHAPE EVEN FOR JUNK!"—) OH—LET'S SAY THIRTY-FIVE CENTS!!
OFFICE
THET'S A HEAP O' MONEY!
GLAD YOU THINK SO— HERE!!
("THIS IS A WONDIFUL PARKIN' LOT! THEY PAYS US!"—)
Al Capp

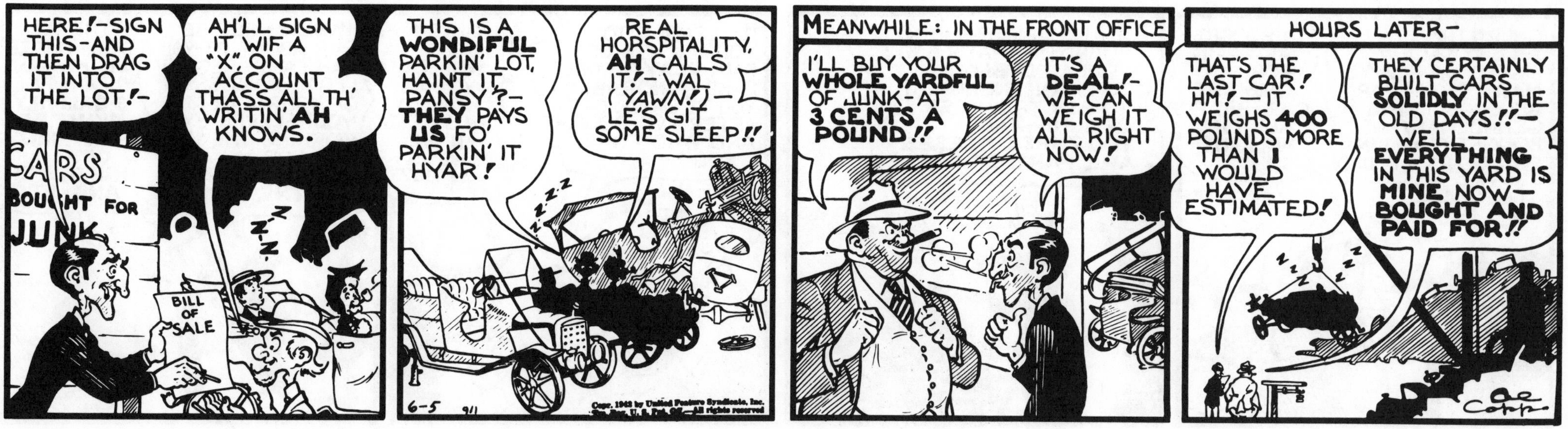
HERE!—SIGN THIS—AND THEN DRAG IT INTO THE LOT!—
AH'LL SIGN IT WIF A "X", ON ACCOUNT THASS ALL TH' WRITIN' AH KNOWS.
CARS BOUGHT FOR JUNK
Z Z Z
BILL OF SALE
THIS IS A WONDIFUL PARKIN' LOT, HAIN'T IT, PANSY?— THEY PAYS US FO' PARKIN' IT HYAR!
REAL HORSPITALITY, AH CALLS IT!—WAL (YAWN!)— LE'S GIT SOME SLEEP!!
Z-Z-Z
6-5 911
Copr. 1942 by United Feature Syndicate, Inc. Tm. Reg. U. S. Pat. Off.—All rights reserved
MEANWHILE: IN THE FRONT OFFICE
I'LL BUY YOUR WHOLE YARDFUL OF JUNK—AT 3 CENTS A POUND!!
IT'S A DEAL!— WE CAN WEIGH IT ALL, RIGHT NOW!
HOURS LATER—
THAT'S THE LAST CAR! HM!—IT WEIGHS 400 POUNDS MORE THAN I WOULD HAVE ESTIMATED!
THEY CERTAINLY BUILT CARS SOLIDLY IN THE OLD DAYS!!— WELL— EVERYTHING IN THIS YARD IS MINE NOW— BOUGHT AND PAID FOR!!
Z Z Z Z
Al Capp

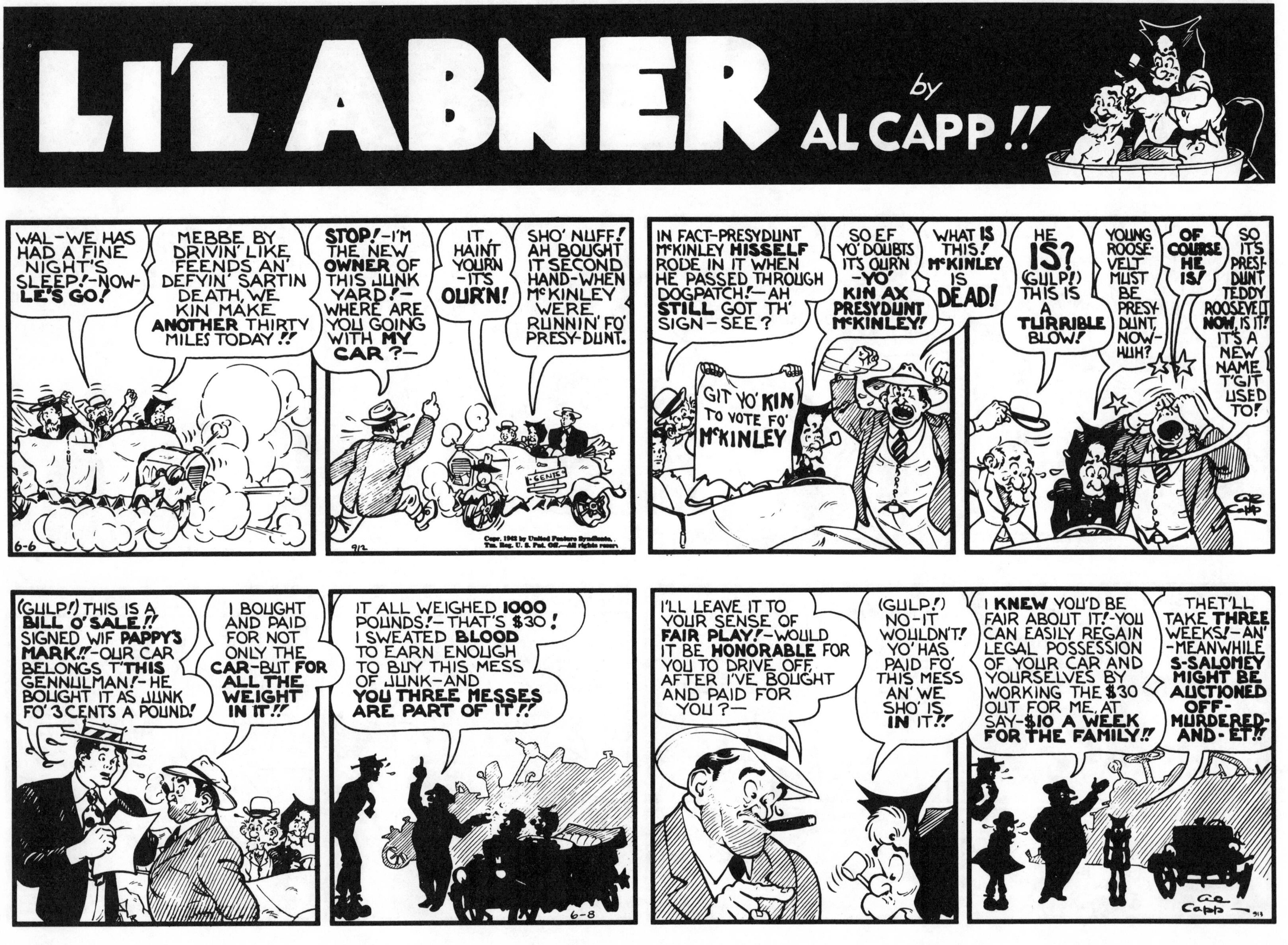
LI'L ABNER
by AL CAPP!!
WAL-WE HAS HAD A FINE NIGHT'S SLEEP!-NOW-LE'S GO!
MEBBE BY DRIVIN' LIKE FEENDS AN' DEFYIN' SARTIN DEATH, WE KIN MAKE ANOTHER THIRTY MILES TODAY!!
6-6
STOP!-I'M THE NEW OWNER OF THIS JUNK YARD!-WHERE ARE YOU GOING WITH MY CAR?-
IT HAIN'T YOURN-IT'S OUR'N!
SHO' NUFF! AH BOUGHT IT SECOND HAND-WHEN McKINLEY WERE RUNNIN' FO' PRESY-DUNT.
CENTS
9/2
Copr. 1942 by United Feature Syndicate, Tm. Reg. U. S. Pat. Off.—All rights reserv
IN FACT-PRESYDUNT McKINLEY HISSELF RODE IN IT WHEN HE PASSED THROUGH DOGPATCH!-AH STILL GOT TH' SIGN-SEE?
GIT YO' KIN TO VOTE FO' McKINLEY
SO EF YO' DOUBTS IT'S OUR'N-YO' KIN AX PRESYDUNT McKINLEY!
WHAT IS THIS! McKINLEY IS DEAD!
HE IS? (GULP!) THIS IS A TURRIBLE BLOW!
YOUNG ROOSEVELT MUST BE PRESYDUNT, NOW-HUH?
OF COURSE HE IS!
SO IT'S PRESYDUNT TEDDY ROOSEVELT NOW, IS IT!! IT'S A NEW NAME T'GIT USED TO!
AL CAPP
(GULP!) THIS IS A BILL O' SALE!! SIGNED WIF PAPPY'S MARK!!-OUR CAR BELONGS T'THIS GENNULMAN!-HE BOUGHT IT AS JUNK FO' 3 CENTS A POUND!
I BOUGHT AND PAID FOR NOT ONLY THE CAR-BUT FOR ALL THE WEIGHT IN IT!!
IT ALL WEIGHED 1000 POUNDS!-THAT'S $30! I SWEATED BLOOD TO EARN ENOUGH TO BUY THIS MESS OF JUNK-AND YOU THREE MESSES ARE PART OF IT!!
6-8
I'LL LEAVE IT TO YOUR SENSE OF FAIR PLAY!-WOULD IT BE HONORABLE FOR YOU TO DRIVE OFF, AFTER I'VE BOUGHT AND PAID FOR YOU?-
(GULP!) NO-IT WOULDN'T! YO' HAS PAID FO' THIS MESS AN' WE SHO' IS IN IT!!
I KNEW YOU'D BE FAIR ABOUT IT!-YOU CAN EASILY REGAIN LEGAL POSSESSION OF YOUR CAR AND YOURSELVES BY WORKING THE $30 OUT FOR ME, AT SAY-$10 A WEEK FOR THE FAMILY!!
THET'LL TAKE THREE WEEKS!-AN'-MEANWHILE S-SALOMEY MIGHT BE AUCTIONED OFF-MURDERED-AND-ET!!
AL CAPP
9/3

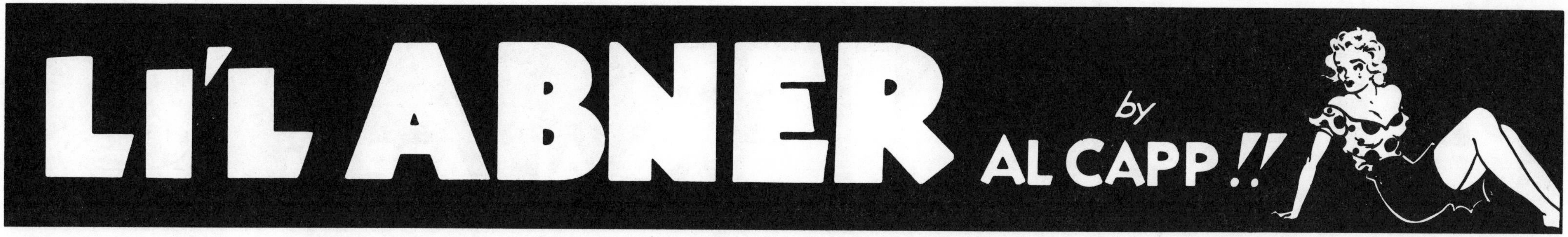
LI'L ABNER
by AL CAPP!!

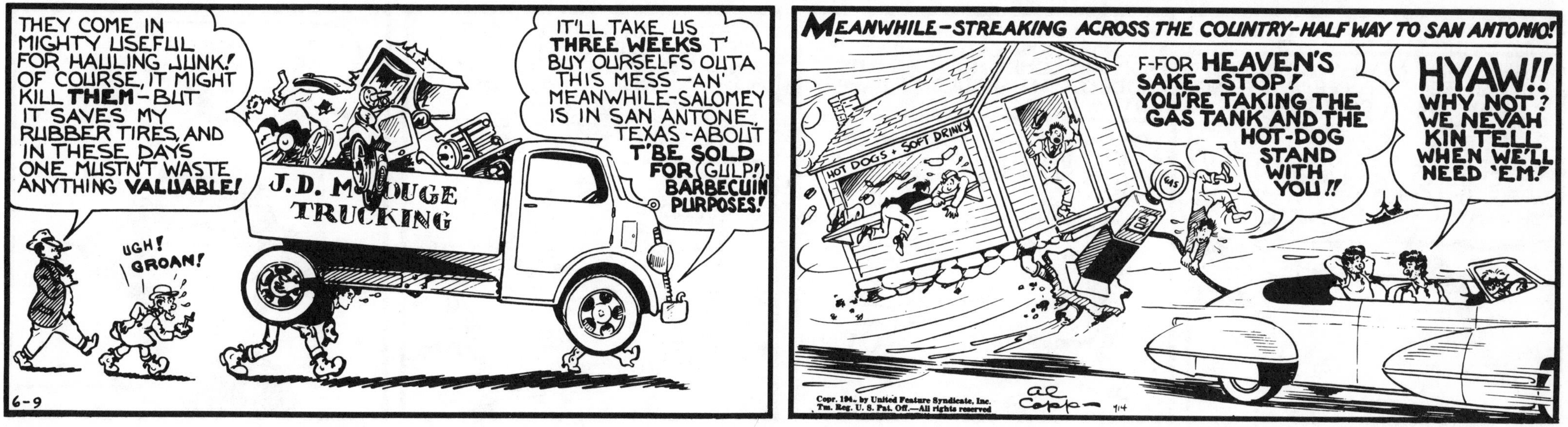
THEY COME IN MIGHTY USEFUL FOR HAULING JUNK! OF COURSE, IT MIGHT KILL THEM – BUT IT SAVES MY RUBBER TIRES, AND IN THESE DAYS ONE MUSTN'T WASTE ANYTHING VALUABLE!
UGH! GROAN!
J. D. McGOUGE TRUCKING
IT'LL TAKE US THREE WEEKS T' BUY OURSELFS OUTA THIS MESS – AN' MEANWHILE – SALOMEY IS IN SAN ANTONE, TEXAS – ABOUT T'BE SOLD FOR (GULP!) BARBECUIN' PURPOSES!
6-9
MEANWHILE – STREAKING ACROSS THE COUNTRY – HALF WAY TO SAN ANTONIO!
HOT DOGS + SOFT DRINKS
GAS
F-FOR HEAVEN'S SAKE – STOP! YOU'RE TAKING THE GAS TANK AND THE HOT-DOG STAND WITH YOU!!
HYAW!! WHY NOT? WE NEVAH KIN TELL WHEN WE'LL NEED 'EM!
Copr. 194_ by United Feature Syndicate, Inc.
Tm. Reg. U. S. Pat. Off.—All rights reserved
al capp

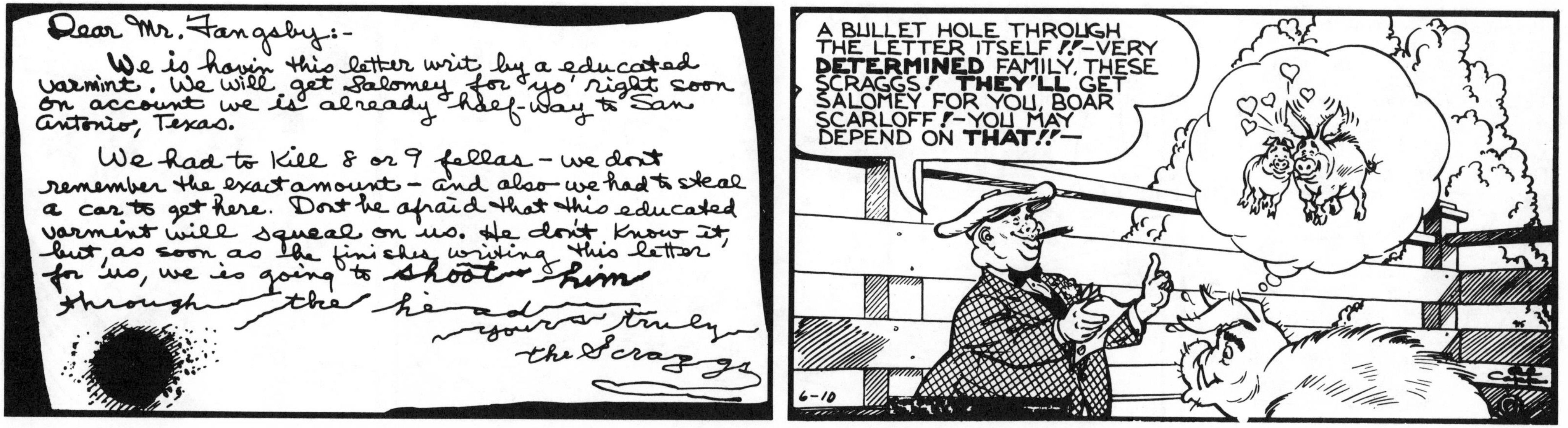
Dear Mr. Fangsby:-
We is havin this letter writ by a educated varmint. We will get Salomey for yo' right soon on account we is already half-way to San Antonio, Texas.
We had to kill 8 or 9 fellas – we dont remember the exact amount – and also we had to steal a car to get here. Dont be afraid that this educated varmint will squeal on us. He don't know it, but, as soon as he finishes writing this letter for us, we is going to shoot him through the head
yours truly
the Scraggs
A BULLET HOLE THROUGH THE LETTER ITSELF!! – VERY DETERMINED FAMILY, THESE SCRAGGS! THEY'LL GET SALOMEY FOR YOU, BOAR SCARLOFF! – YOU MAY DEPEND ON THAT!! –
6-10

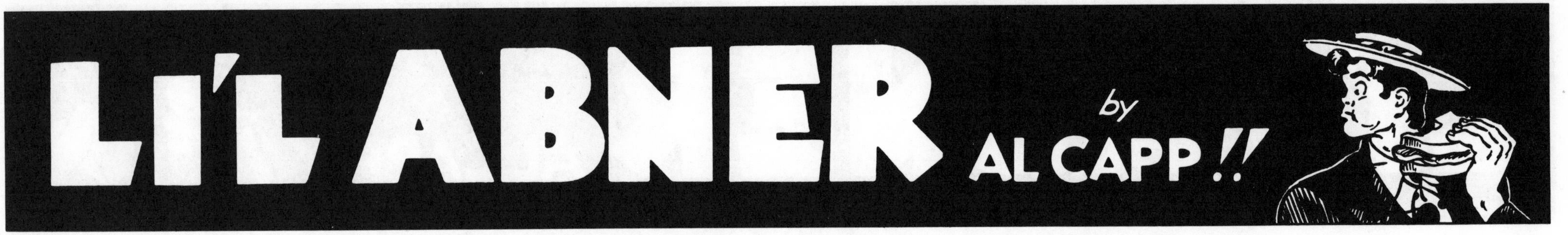
LI'L ABNER
by
AL CAPP!!

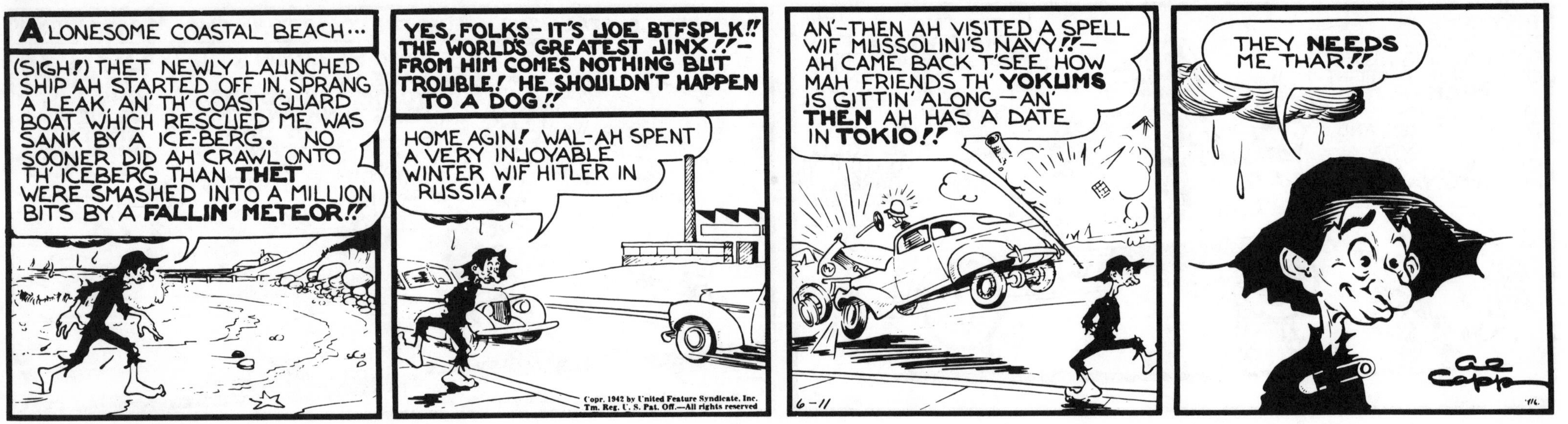
A LONESOME COASTAL BEACH…
(SIGH!) THET NEWLY LAUNCHED SHIP AH STARTED OFF IN, SPRANG A LEAK, AN' TH' COAST GUARD BOAT WHICH RESCUED ME WAS SANK BY A ICE-BERG. NO SOONER DID AH CRAWL ONTO TH' ICEBERG THAN THET WERE SMASHED INTO A MILLION BITS BY A FALLIN' METEOR!!
YES, FOLKS - IT'S JOE BTFSPLK!! THE WORLD'S GREATEST JINX!!— FROM HIM COMES NOTHING BUT TROUBLE! HE SHOULDN'T HAPPEN TO A DOG!!
HOME AGIN! WAL-AH SPENT A VERY INJOYABLE WINTER WIF HITLER IN RUSSIA!
Copr. 1942 by United Feature Syndicate, Inc.
Tm. Reg. U. S. Pat. Off.—All rights reserved
AN'-THEN AH VISITED A SPELL WIF MUSSOLINI'S NAVY!!— AH CAME BACK T'SEE HOW MAH FRIENDS TH' YOKUMS IS GITTIN' ALONG—AN' THEN AH HAS A DATE IN TOKIO!!
6-11
THEY NEEDS ME THAR!!
AL CAPP

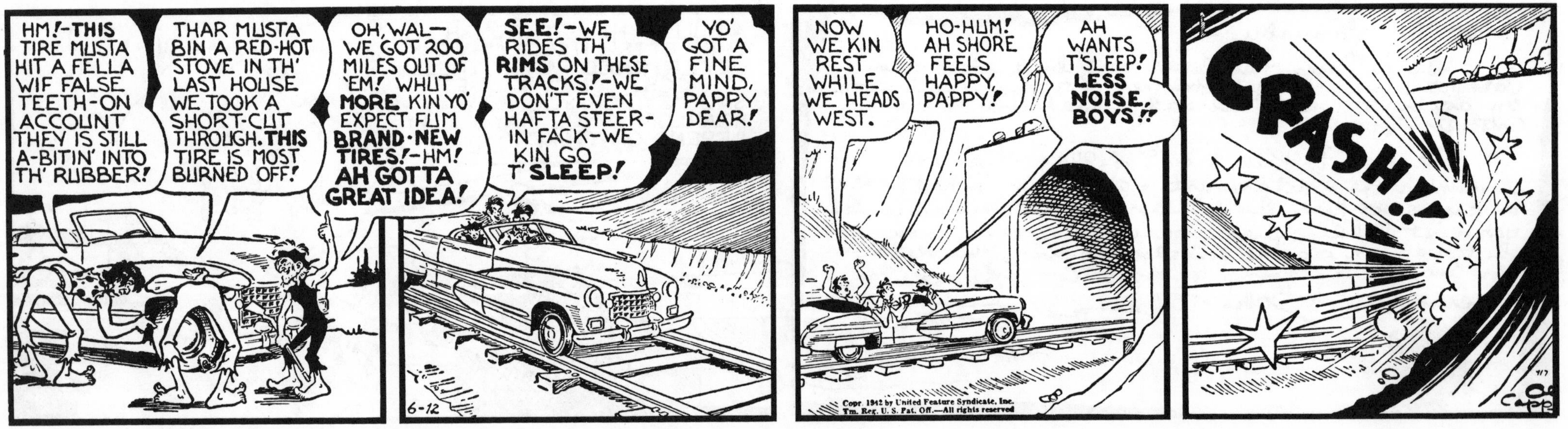
HM!-THIS TIRE MUSTA HIT A FELLA WIF FALSE TEETH-ON ACCOUNT THEY IS STILL A-BITIN' INTO TH' RUBBER!
THAR MUSTA BIN A RED-HOT STOVE IN TH' LAST HOUSE WE TOOK A SHORT-CUT THROUGH. THIS TIRE IS MOST BURNED OFF!
OH, WAL— WE GOT 200 MILES OUT OF 'EM! WHUT MORE KIN YO' EXPECT FUM BRAND-NEW TIRES!-HM! AH GOTTA GREAT IDEA!
SEE!-WE RIDES TH' RIMS ON THESE TRACKS!-WE DON'T EVEN HAFTA STEER-IN FACK-WE KIN GO T'SLEEP!
YO' GOT A FINE MIND, PAPPY DEAR!
6-12
NOW WE KIN REST WHILE WE HEADS WEST.
HO-HUM! AH SHORE FEELS HAPPY, PAPPY!
AH WANTS T'SLEEP! LESS NOISE, BOYS!!
Copr. 1942 by United Feature Syndicate, Inc.
Tm. Reg. U. S. Pat. Off.—All rights reserved
CRASH!!
AL CAPP

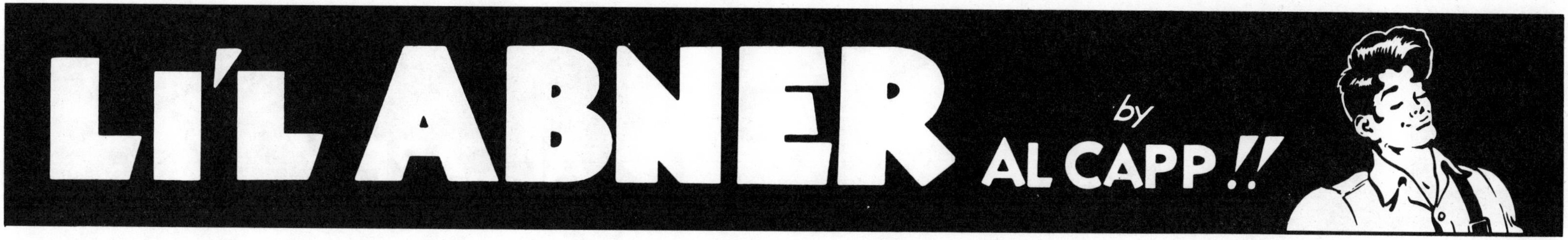
LI'L ABNER
by
AL CAPP!!

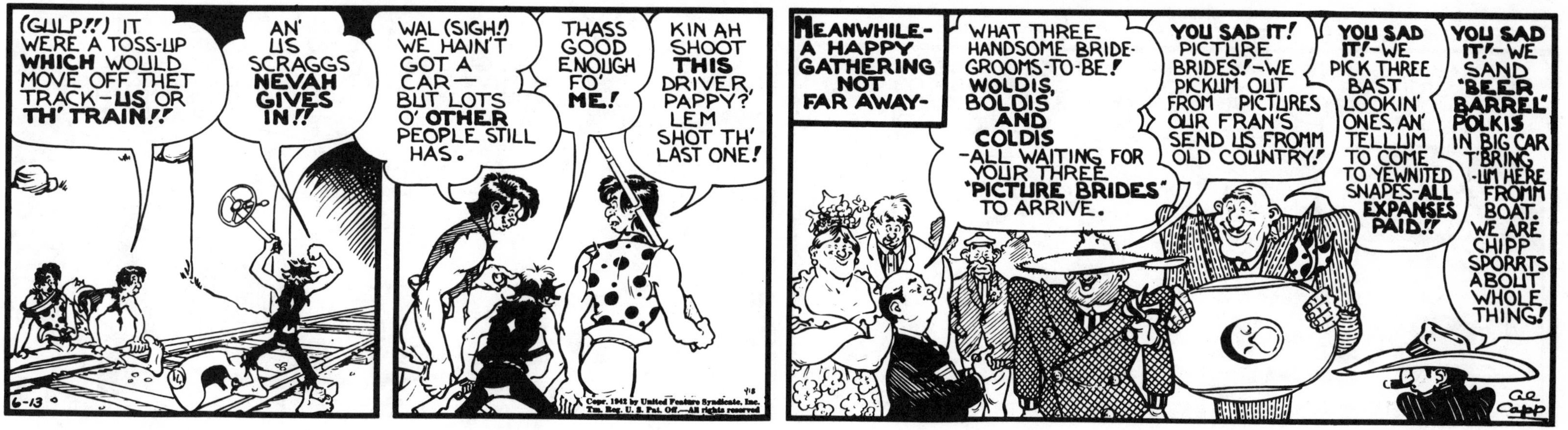
(GULP!!) IT WERE A TOSS-UP WHICH WOULD MOVE OFF THET TRACK—US OR TH' TRAIN!!
AN' US SCRAGGS NEVAH GIVES IN!!
6-13
WAL (SIGH!) WE HAIN'T GOT A CAR— BUT LOTS O' OTHER PEOPLE STILL HAS.
THASS GOOD ENOUGH FO' ME!
KIN AH SHOOT THIS DRIVER, PAPPY? LEM SHOT TH' LAST ONE!
Copr. 1942 by United Feature Syndicate, Inc. Tm. Reg. U. S. Pat. Off.—All rights reserved
MEANWHILE-A HAPPY GATHERING NOT FAR AWAY-
WHAT THREE HANDSOME BRIDE-GROOMS-TO-BE! WOLDIS, BOLDIS AND COLDIS -ALL WAITING FOR YOUR THREE "PICTURE BRIDES" TO ARRIVE.
YOU SAD IT! PICTURE BRIDES!-WE PICKUM OUT FROM PICTURES OUR FRAN'S SEND US FROMM OLD COUNTRY!
YOU SAD IT!-WE PICK THREE BAST LOOKIN' ONES, AN' TELLUM TO COME TO YEWNITED SNAPES-ALL EXPANSES PAID!!
YOU SAD IT!-WE SAND 'BEER BARREL' POLKIS IN BIG CAR T'BRING -UM HERE FROMM BOAT. WE ARE CHIPP SPORRTS ABOUT WHOLE THING!
AL CAPP

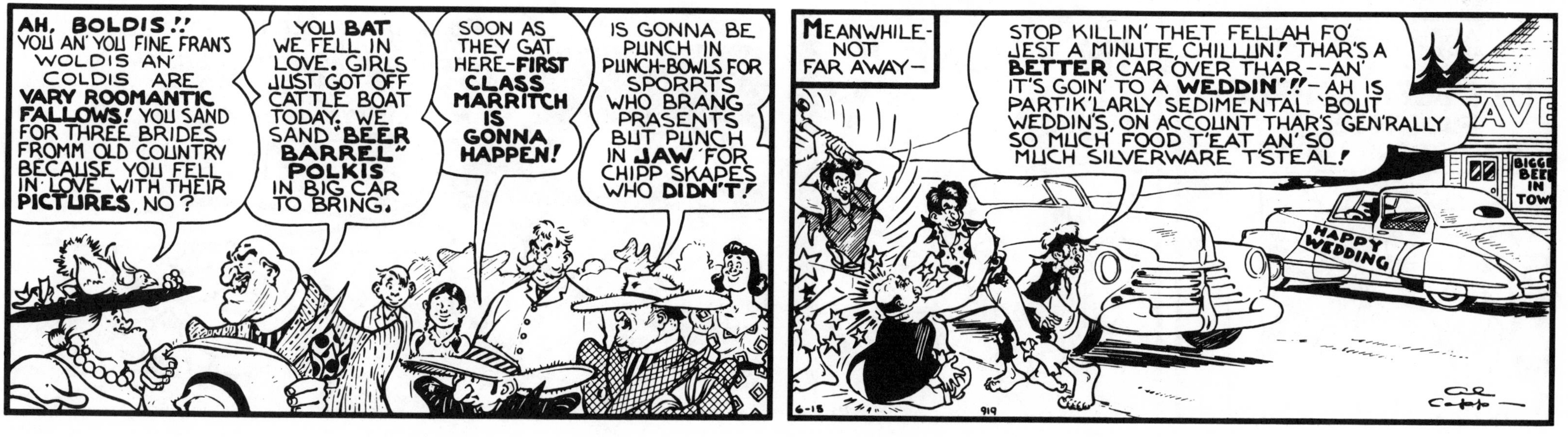
AH, BOLDIS!! YOU AN' YOU FINE FRAN'S WOLDIS AN' COLDIS ARE VARY ROOMANTIC FALLOWS! YOU SAND FOR THREE BRIDES FROMM OLD COUNTRY BECAUSE YOU FELL IN LOVE WITH THEIR PICTURES, NO?
YOU BAT WE FELL IN LOVE. GIRLS JUST GOT OFF CATTLE BOAT TODAY. WE SAND "BEER BARREL" POLKIS IN BIG CAR TO BRING.
SOON AS THEY GAT HERE-FIRST CLASS MARRITCH IS GONNA HAPPEN!
IS GONNA BE PUNCH IN PUNCH-BOWLS FOR SPORRTS WHO BRANG PRASENTS BUT PUNCH IN JAW FOR CHIPP SKAPES WHO DIDN'T!
MEANWHILE-NOT FAR AWAY—
STOP KILLIN' THET FELLAH FO' JEST A MINUTE, CHILLUN! THAR'S A BETTER CAR OVER THAR--AN' IT'S GOIN' TO A WEDDIN'!!-AH IS PARTIK'LARLY SEDIMENTAL 'BOUT WEDDIN'S, ON ACCOUNT THAR'S GEN'RALLY SO MUCH FOOD T'EAT AN' SO MUCH SILVERWARE T'STEAL!
HAPPY WEDDING
6-15
AL CAPP

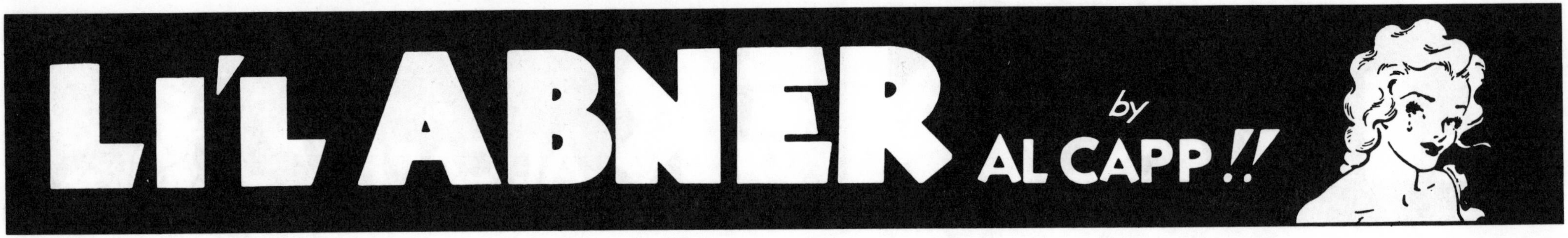
LI'L ABNER
by
AL CAPP!!

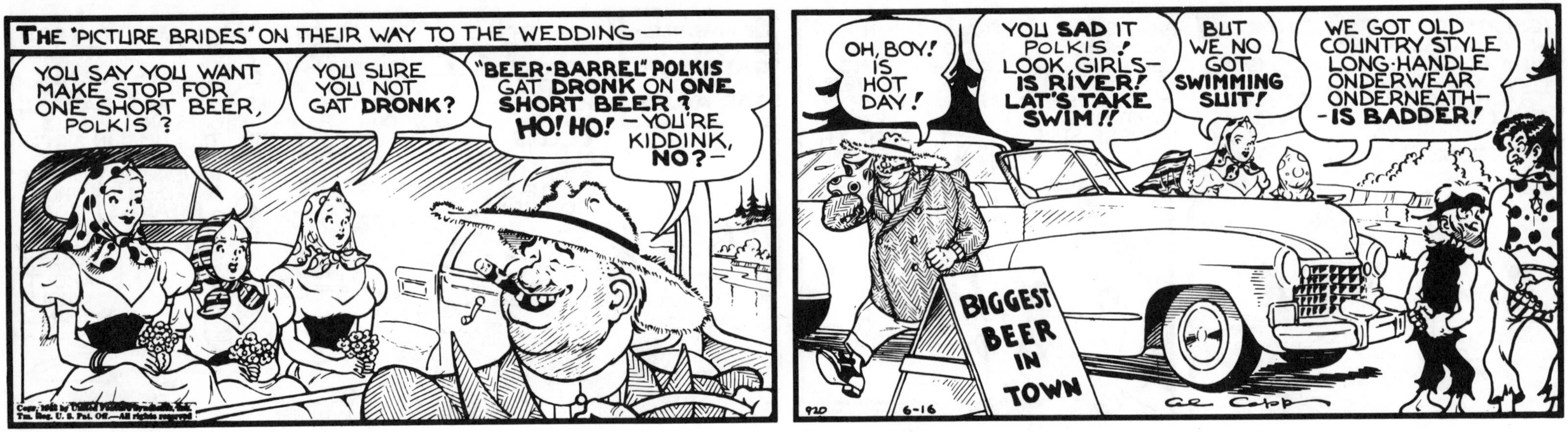
THE "PICTURE BRIDES" ON THEIR WAY TO THE WEDDING —
YOU SAY YOU WANT MAKE STOP FOR ONE SHORT BEER, POLKIS ?
YOU SURE YOU NOT GAT DRONK?
"BEER-BARREL" POLKIS GAT DRONK ON ONE SHORT BEER ? HO! HO! — YOU'RE KIDDINK, NO? —
OH, BOY! IS HOT DAY!
YOU SAD IT POLKIS! LOOK GIRLS — IS RIVER! LAT'S TAKE SWIM!!
BUT WE NO GOT SWIMMING SUIT!
WE GOT OLD COUNTRY STYLE LONG-HANDLE ONDERWEAR ONDERNEATH — IS BADDER!
BIGGEST BEER IN TOWN
920
6-16
Al Capp

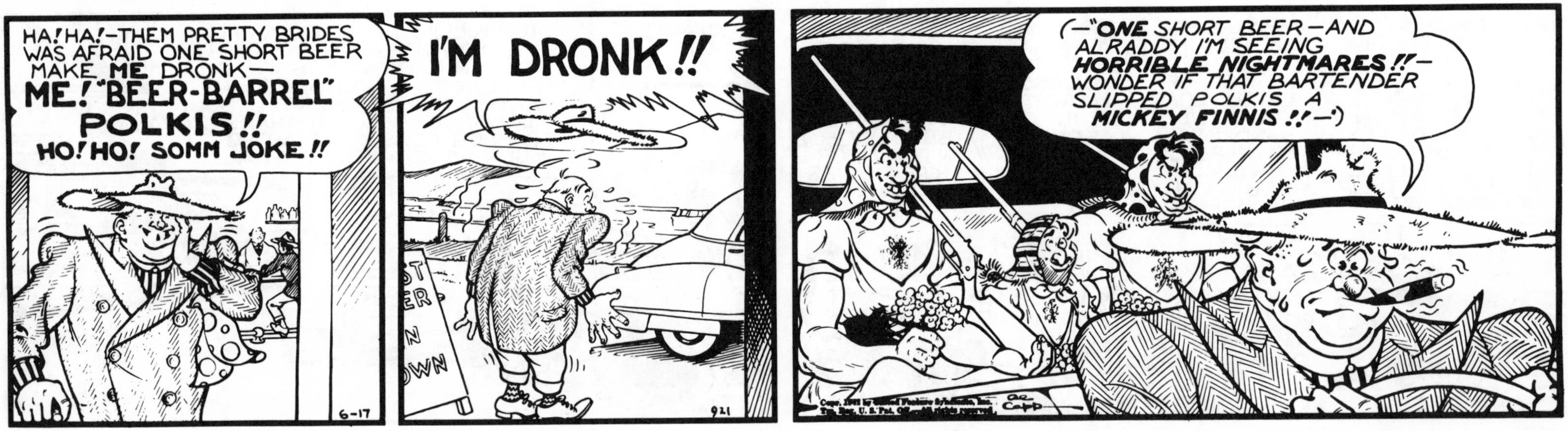
HA! HA! — THEM PRETTY BRIDES WAS AFRAID ONE SHORT BEER MAKE ME DRONK — ME! "BEER-BARREL" POLKIS!! HO! HO! SOMM JOKE!!
6-17
I'M DRONK!!
921
(— "ONE SHORT BEER — AND ALRADDY I'M SEEING HORRIBLE NIGHTMARES!! — WONDER IF THAT BARTENDER SLIPPED POLKIS A MICKEY FINNIS!! —")
Al Capp

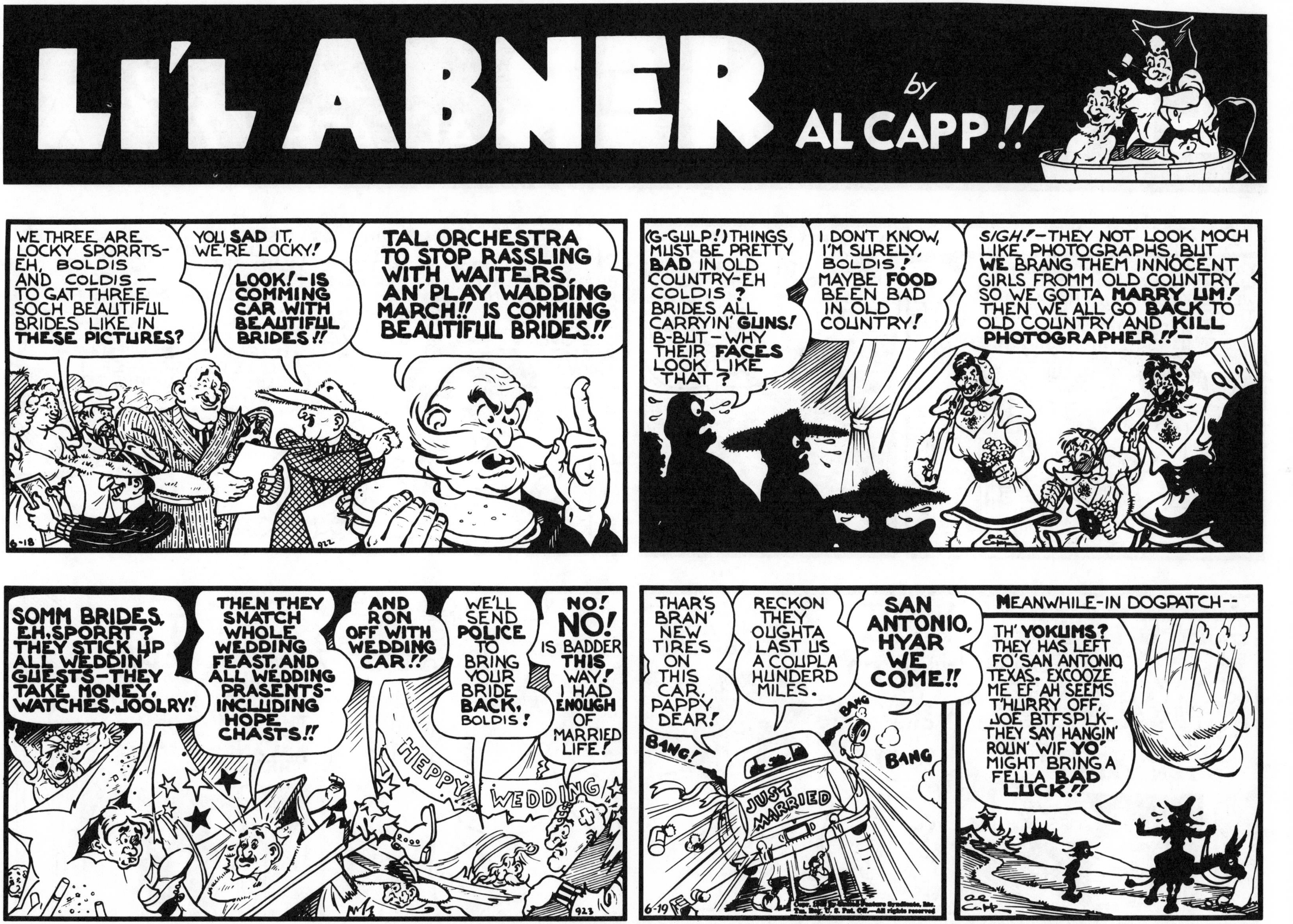

LI'L ABNER
by AL CAPP!!
WE THREE ARE LOCKY SPORRTS-EH, BOLDIS AND COLDIS — TO GAT THREE SOCH BEAUTIFUL BRIDES LIKE IN THESE PICTURES?
YOU SAD IT, WE'RE LOCKY!
LOOK!-IS COMMING CAR WITH BEAUTIFUL BRIDES!!
TAL ORCHESTRA TO STOP RASSLING WITH WAITERS, AN' PLAY WADDING MARCH!! IS COMMING BEAUTIFUL BRIDES!!
6-18
(G-GULP!) THINGS MUST BE PRETTY BAD IN OLD COUNTRY-EH COLDIS? BRIDES ALL CARRYIN' GUNS! B-BUT - WHY THEIR FACES LOOK LIKE THAT?
I DON'T KNOW, I'M SURELY, BOLDIS! MAYBE FOOD BEEN BAD IN OLD COUNTRY!
SIGH!—THEY NOT LOOK MOCH LIKE PHOTOGRAPHS, BUT WE BRANG THEM INNOCENT GIRLS FROMM OLD COUNTRY SO WE GOTTA MARRY UM! THEN WE ALL GO BACK TO OLD COUNTRY AND KILL PHOTOGRAPHER!!—
SOMM BRIDES, EH, SPORRT? THEY STICK UP ALL WEDDIN' GUESTS-THEY TAKE MONEY, WATCHES, JOOLRY!
THEN THEY SNATCH WHOLE WEDDING FEAST, AND ALL WEDDING PRASENTS-INCLUDING HOPE CHASTS!!
AND RON OFF WITH WEDDING CAR!!
WE'LL SEND POLICE TO BRING YOUR BRIDE BACK, BOLDIS!
NO! NO! IS BADDER THIS WAY! I HAD ENOUGH OF MARRIED LIFE!
HEPPY WEDDING!
THAR'S BRAN' NEW TIRES ON THIS CAR, PAPPY DEAR!
RECKON THEY OUGHTA LAST US A COUPLA HUNDERD MILES.
SAN ANTONIO, HYAR WE COME!!
BANG!
BANG
BANG
JUST MARRIED
6-19
MEANWHILE-IN DOGPATCH--
TH' YOKUMS? THEY HAS LEFT FO' SAN ANTONIO, TEXAS. EXCOOZE ME EF AH SEEMS T'HURRY OFF, JOE BTFSPLK-THEY SAY HANGIN' ROUN' WIF YO' MIGHT BRING A FELLA BAD LUCK!!

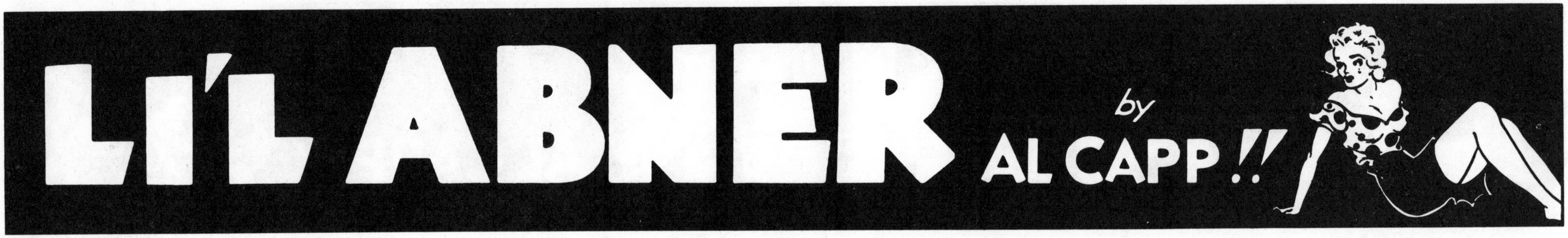
LI'L ABNER
by
AL CAPP!!

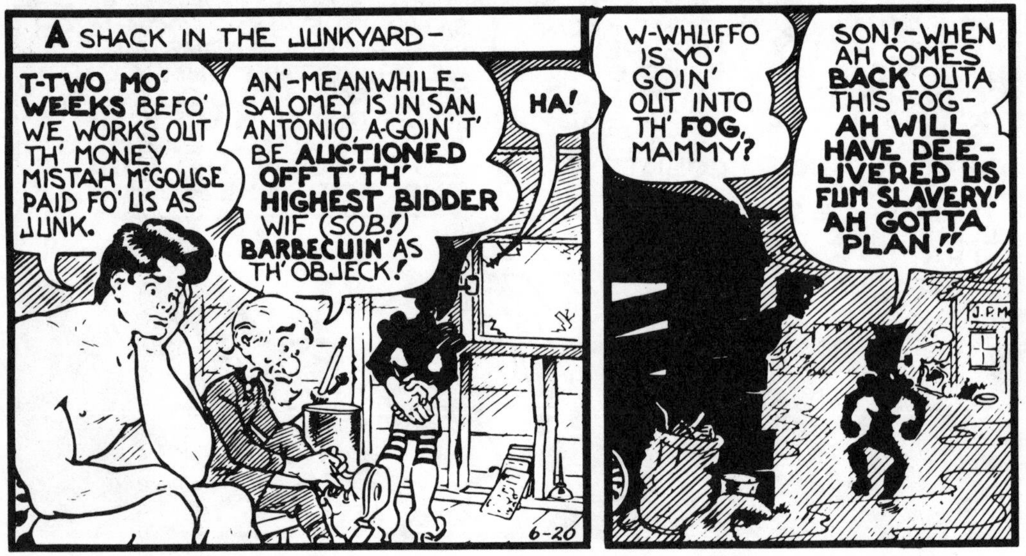
A SHACK IN THE JUNKYARD–
T-TWO MO' WEEKS BEFO' WE WORKS OUT TH' MONEY MISTAH MCGOUGE PAID FO' US AS JUNK.
AN'–MEANWHILE–SALOMEY IS IN SAN ANTONIO, A-GOIN' T' BE AUCTIONED OFF T' TH' HIGHEST BIDDER WIF (SOB!) BARBECUIN' AS TH' OBJECK!
HA!
6-20
W-WHUFFO IS YO' GOIN' OUT INTO TH' FOG, MAMMY?
SON!–WHEN AH COMES BACK OUTA THIS FOG–AH WILL HAVE DEE-LIVERED US FUM SLAVERY! AH GOTTA PLAN!!
J.P.M

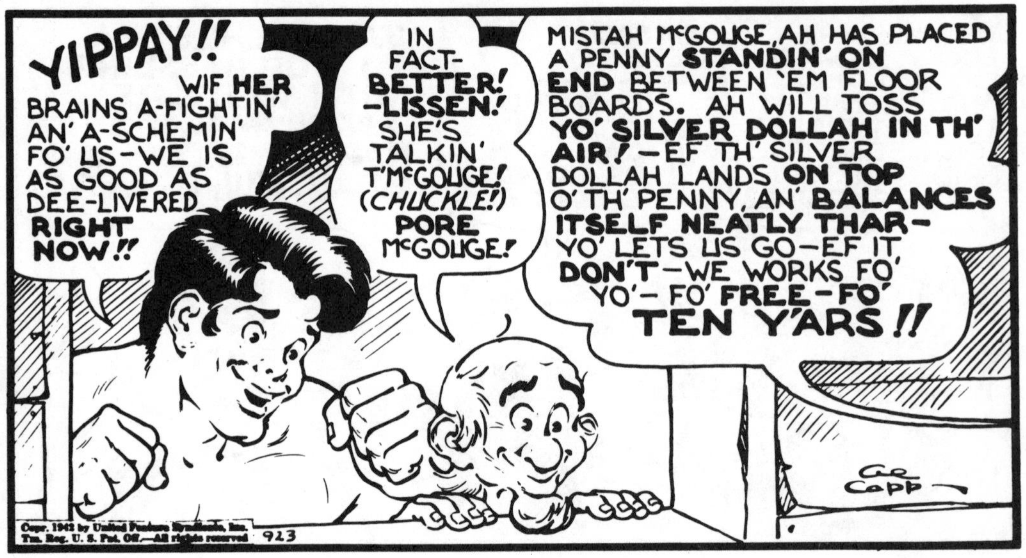
YIPPAY!! WIF HER BRAINS A-FIGHTIN' AN' A-SCHEMIN' FO' US–WE IS AS GOOD AS DEE-LIVERED RIGHT NOW!!
IN FACT–BETTER! –LISSEN! SHE'S TALKIN' T'MCGOUGE! (CHUCKLE!) PORE MCGOUGE!
MISTAH MCGOUGE, AH HAS PLACED A PENNY STANDIN' ON END BETWEEN 'EM FLOOR BOARDS. AH WILL TOSS YO' SILVER DOLLAH IN TH' AIR!–EF TH' SILVER DOLLAH LANDS ON TOP O' TH' PENNY, AN' BALANCES ITSELF NEATLY THAR–YO' LETS US GO–EF IT DON'T–WE WORKS FO' YO'–FO' FREE–FO' TEN Y'ARS!!
Al Capp
Copr. 1942 by United Feature Syndicate, Inc.
Tm. Reg. U. S. Pat. Off.—All rights reserved
9-23

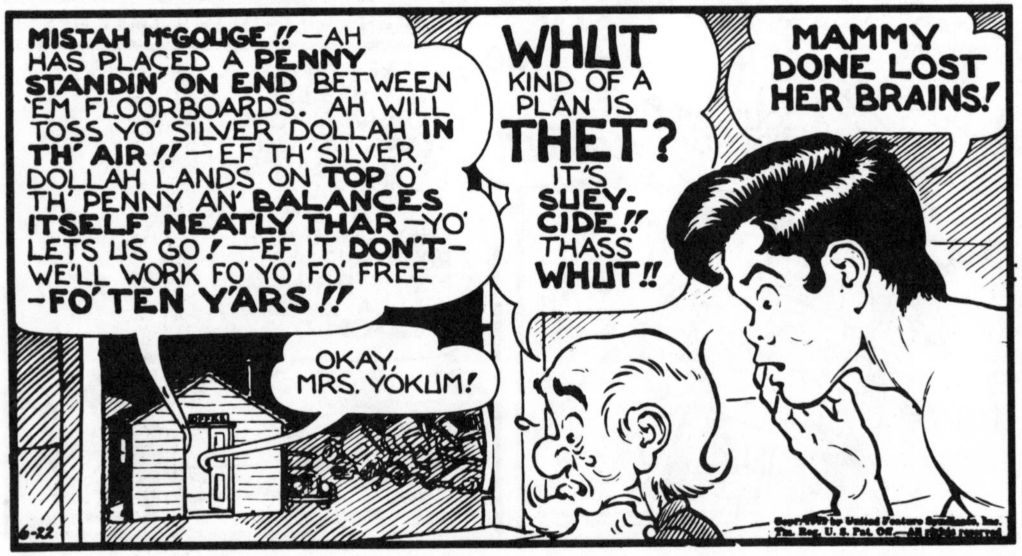
MISTAH MCGOUGE!!–AH HAS PLACED A PENNY STANDIN' ON END BETWEEN 'EM FLOORBOARDS. AH WILL TOSS YO' SILVER DOLLAH IN TH' AIR!!–EF TH' SILVER DOLLAH LANDS ON TOP O' TH' PENNY AN' BALANCES ITSELF NEATLY THAR–YO' LETS US GO!–EF IT DON'T–WE'LL WORK FO' YO' FO' FREE –FO' TEN Y'ARS!!
OKAY, MRS. YOKUM!
6-22
WHUT KIND OF A PLAN IS THET? IT'S SUEY-CIDE!! THASS WHUT!!
MAMMY DONE LOST HER BRAINS!

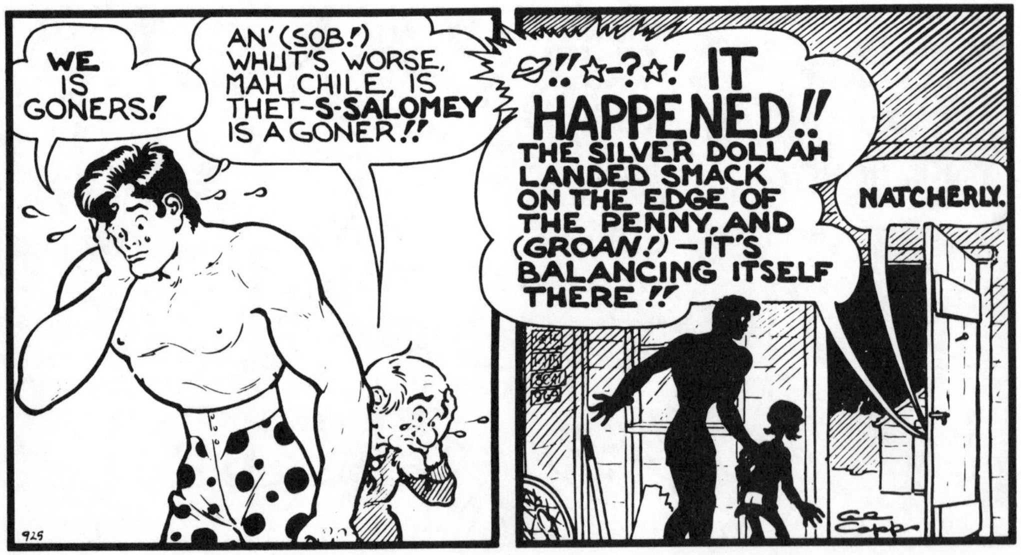
WE IS GONERS!
AN' (SOB!) WHUT'S WORSE, MAH CHILE, IS THET–S-SALOMEY IS A GONER!!
9-25
!!–?! IT HAPPENED!! THE SILVER DOLLAH LANDED SMACK ON THE EDGE OF THE PENNY, AND (GROAN!)–IT'S BALANCING ITSELF THERE!!
NATCHERLY.
Al Capp

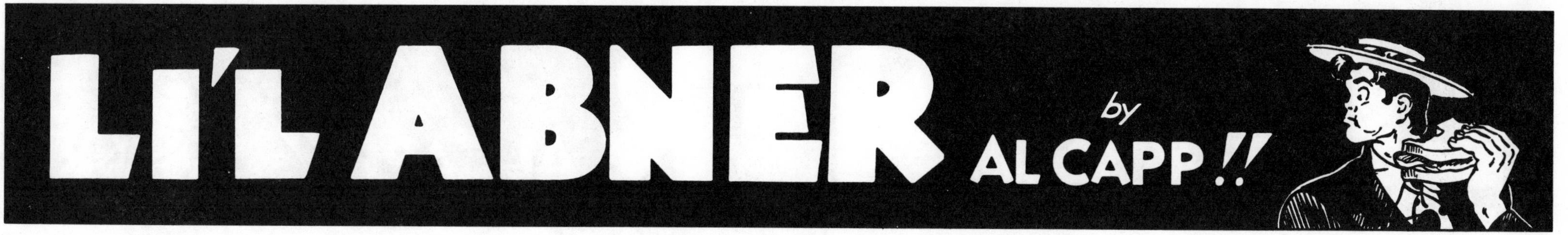
LI'L ABNER
by
AL CAPP!!

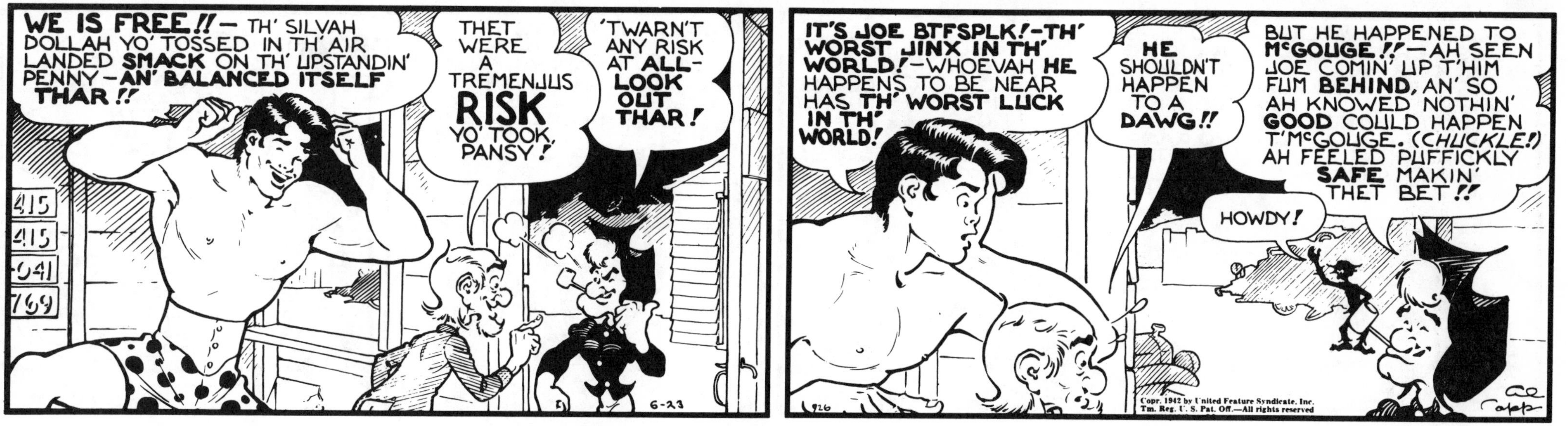
WE IS FREE!! — TH' SILVAH DOLLAH YO' TOSSED IN TH' AIR LANDED SMACK ON TH' UPSTANDIN' PENNY — AN' BALANCED ITSELF THAR!!
THET WERE A TREMENJUS RISK YO' TOOK, PANSY!
'TWARN'T ANY RISK AT ALL — LOOK OUT THAR!
415
415
041
769
6-23
IT'S JOE BTFSPLK! — TH' WORST JINX IN TH' WORLD! — WHOEVAH HE HAPPENS TO BE NEAR HAS TH' WORST LUCK IN TH' WORLD!
HE SHOULDN'T HAPPEN TO A DAWG!!
BUT HE HAPPENED TO McGOUGE!! — AH SEEN JOE COMIN' UP T'HIM FUM BEHIND, AN' SO AH KNOWED NOTHIN' GOOD COULD HAPPEN T'McGOUGE. (CHUCKLE!) AH FEELED PUFFICKLY SAFE MAKIN' THET BET!!
HOWDY!
926
Copr. 1942 by United Feature Syndicate, Inc.
Tm. Reg. U. S. Pat. Off.—All rights reserved
Al Capp

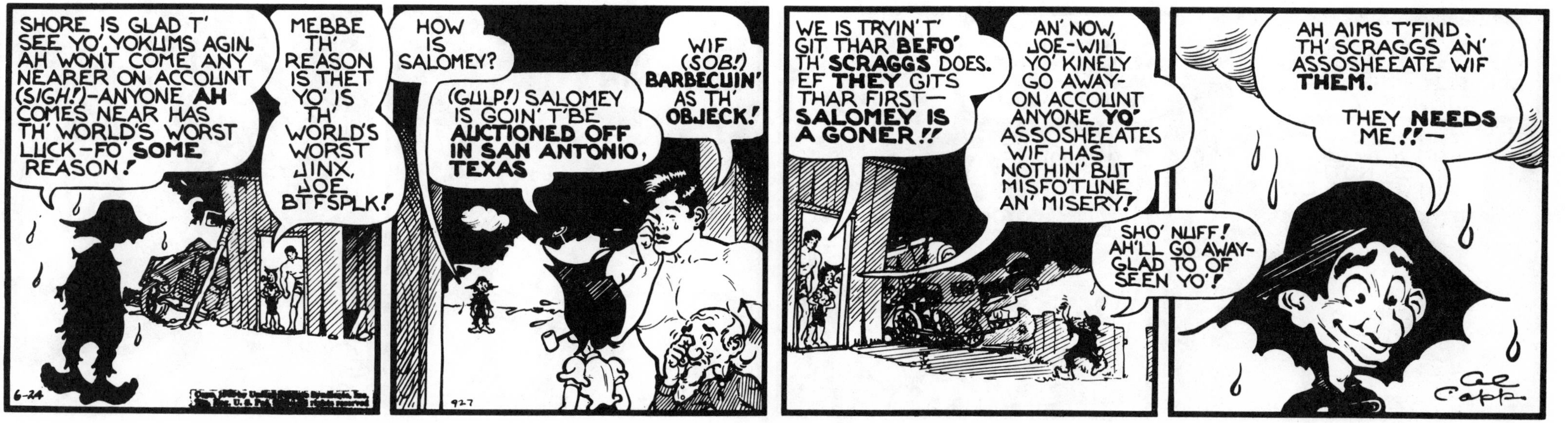
SHORE IS GLAD T' SEE YO', YOKUMS AGIN. AH WONT COME ANY NEARER ON ACCOUNT (SIGH!) — ANYONE AH COMES NEAR HAS TH' WORLD'S WORST LUCK — FO' SOME REASON!
MEBBE TH' REASON IS THET YO' IS TH' WORLD'S WORST JINX, JOE BTFSPLK!
6-24
HOW IS SALOMEY?
(GULP!) SALOMEY IS GOIN' T'BE AUCTIONED OFF IN SAN ANTONIO, TEXAS
WIF (SOB!) BARBECUIN' AS TH' OBJECK!
927
WE IS TRYIN' T' GIT THAR BEFO' TH' SCRAGGS DOES. EF THEY GITS THAR FIRST — SALOMEY IS A GONER!!
AN' NOW, JOE — WILL YO' KINELY GO AWAY — ON ACCOUNT ANYONE YO' ASSOSHEEATES WIF HAS NOTHIN' BUT MISFO'TUNE AN' MISERY!
SHO' NUFF! AH'LL GO AWAY — GLAD TO OF SEEN YO'!
AH AIMS T'FIND TH' SCRAGGS AN' ASSOSHEEATE WIF THEM.
THEY NEEDS ME!! —
Al Capp

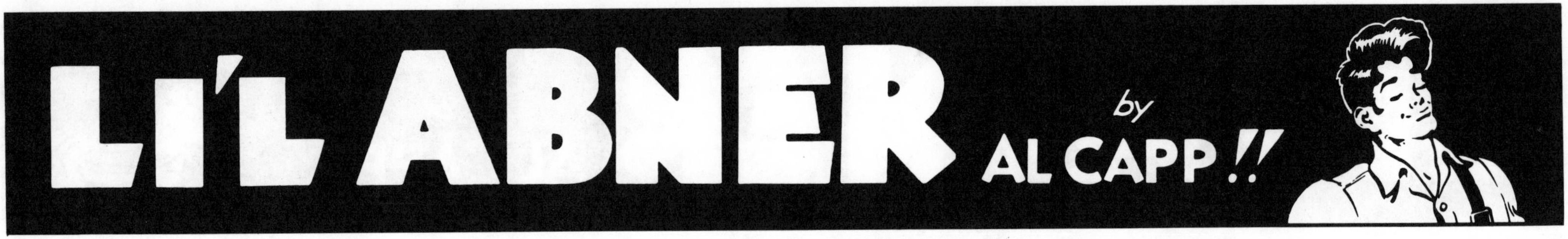
LI'L ABNER
by
AL CAPP!!

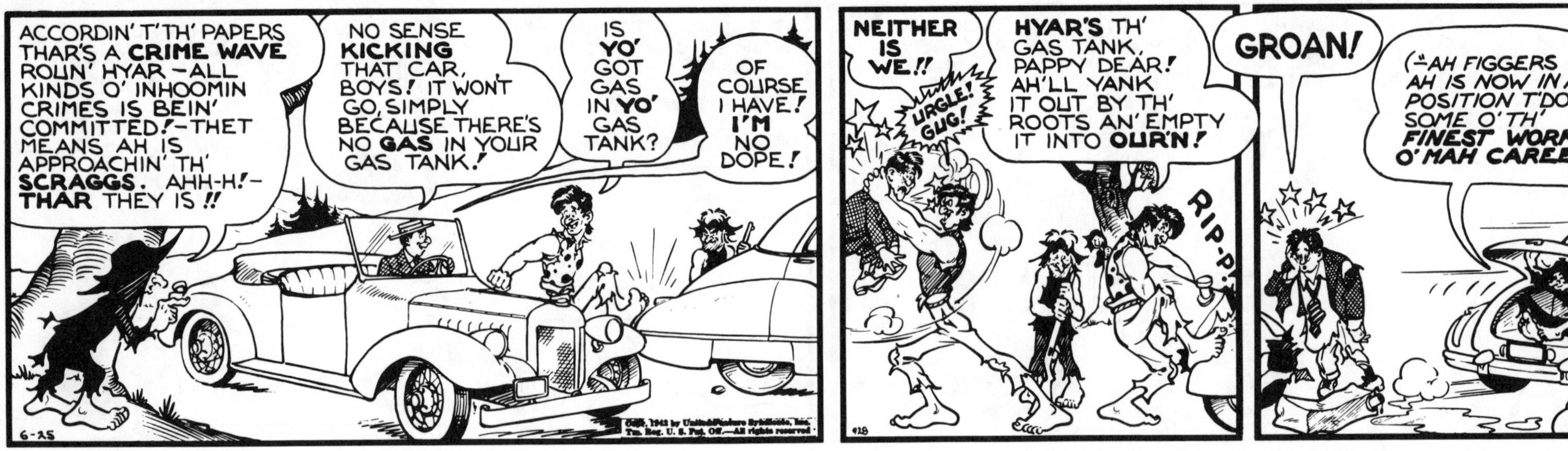
ACCORDIN' T'TH' PAPERS THAR'S A CRIME WAVE ROUN' HYAR—ALL KINDS O' INHOOMIN CRIMES IS BEIN' COMMITTED!—THET MEANS AH IS APPROACHIN' TH' SCRAGGS. AHH-H!—THAR THEY IS!!
NO SENSE KICKING THAT CAR, BOYS! IT WON'T GO, SIMPLY BECAUSE THERE'S NO GAS IN YOUR GAS TANK!
IS YO' GOT GAS IN YO' GAS TANK?
OF COURSE I HAVE! I'M NO DOPE!
6-25
Copr. 1942 by United Feature Syndicate, Inc. Tm. Reg. U. S. Pat. Off.—All rights reserved
NEITHER IS WE!!
URGLE! GUG!
HYAR'S TH' GAS TANK, PAPPY DEAR! AH'LL YANK IT OUT BY TH' ROOTS AN' EMPTY IT INTO OUR'N!
RIP-P!
GROAN!
(—AH FIGGERS AH IS NOW IN A POSITION T'DO SOME O'TH' FINEST WORK O'MAH CAREER!—)

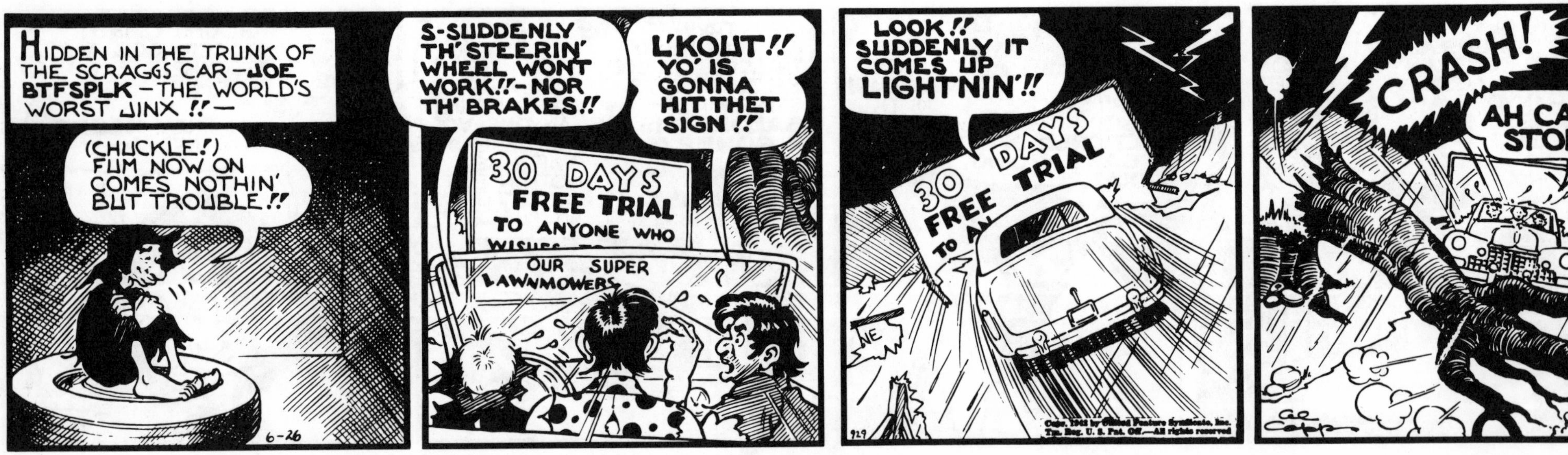
HIDDEN IN THE TRUNK OF THE SCRAGGS CAR—JOE BTFSPLK—THE WORLD'S WORST JINX!!—
(CHUCKLE!) FUM NOW ON COMES NOTHIN' BUT TROUBLE!!
6-26
S-SUDDENLY TH' STEERIN' WHEEL WON'T WORK!!—NOR TH' BRAKES!!
L'KOUT!! YO' IS GONNA HIT THET SIGN!!
30 DAYS FREE TRIAL TO ANYONE WHO
OUR SUPER LAWNMOWERS
LOOK!! SUDDENLY IT COMES UP LIGHTNIN'!!
30 DAYS FREE TRIAL TO AN
Copr. 1942 by United Feature Syndicate, Inc. Tm. Reg. U. S. Pat. Off.—All rights reserved
CRASH!
AH CAIN'T STOP!!

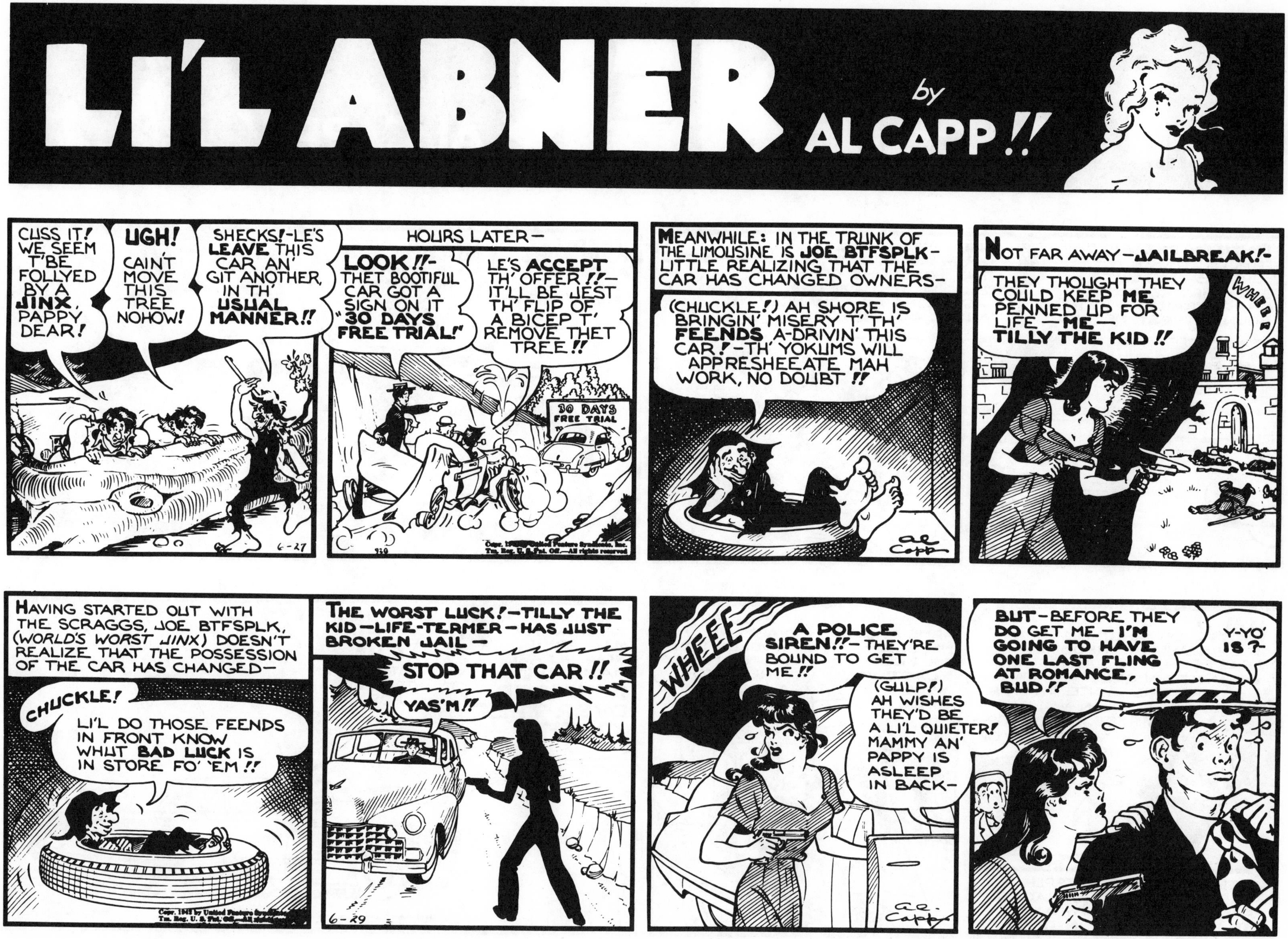
LI'L ABNER
by AL CAPP!!
CUSS IT! WE SEEM T'BE FOLLYED BY A JINX, PAPPY DEAR!
UGH! CAIN'T MOVE THIS TREE NOHOW!
SHECKS!-LE'S LEAVE THIS CAR AN' GIT ANOTHER, IN TH' USUAL MANNER!!
6-27
HOURS LATER–
LOOK!!- THET BOOTIFUL CAR GOT A SIGN ON IT "30 DAYS FREE TRIAL!"
LE'S ACCEPT TH' OFFER!!– IT'LL BE JEST TH' FLIP OF A BICEP T' REMOVE THET TREE!!
30 DAYS FREE TRIAL
MEANWHILE: IN THE TRUNK OF THE LIMOUSINE IS JOE BTFSPLK– LITTLE REALIZING THAT THE CAR HAS CHANGED OWNERS–
(CHUCKLE!) AH SHORE IS BRINGIN' MISERY T' TH' FEENDS A-DRIVIN' THIS CAR!–TH' YOKUMS WILL APPRESHEEATE MAH WORK, NO DOUBT!!
NOT FAR AWAY–JAILBREAK!–
THEY THOUGHT THEY COULD KEEP ME PENNED UP FOR LIFE–ME– TILLY THE KID!!
WHEE
HAVING STARTED OUT WITH THE SCRAGGS, JOE BTFSPLK, (WORLD'S WORST JINX) DOESN'T REALIZE THAT THE POSSESSION OF THE CAR HAS CHANGED–
CHUCKLE!
LI'L DO THOSE FEENDS IN FRONT KNOW WHUT BAD LUCK IS IN STORE FO' 'EM!!
THE WORST LUCK!–TILLY THE KID–LIFE-TERMER–HAS JUST BROKEN JAIL–
STOP THAT CAR!!
YAS'M!!
6-29
WHEEE
A POLICE SIREN!!– THEY'RE BOUND TO GET ME!!
(GULP!) AH WISHES THEY'D BE A LI'L QUIETER! MAMMY AN' PAPPY IS ASLEEP IN BACK–
BUT–BEFORE THEY DO GET ME–I'M GOING TO HAVE ONE LAST FLING AT ROMANCE, BUD!!
Y-YO' IS?–

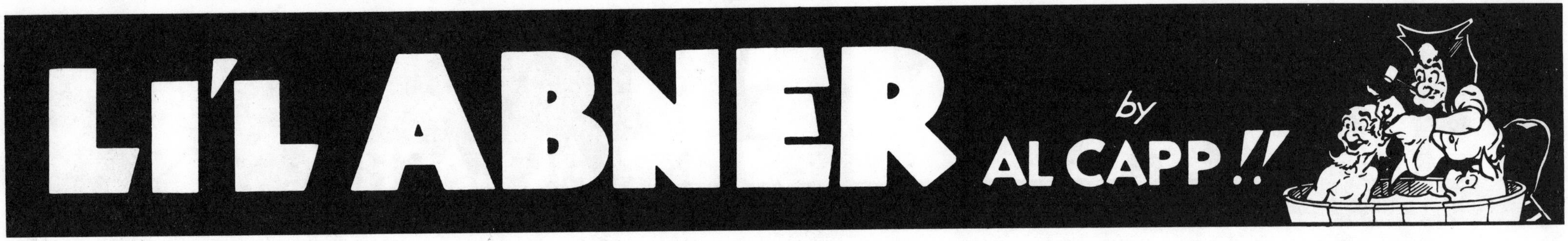
LI'L ABNER
by
AL CAPP!!

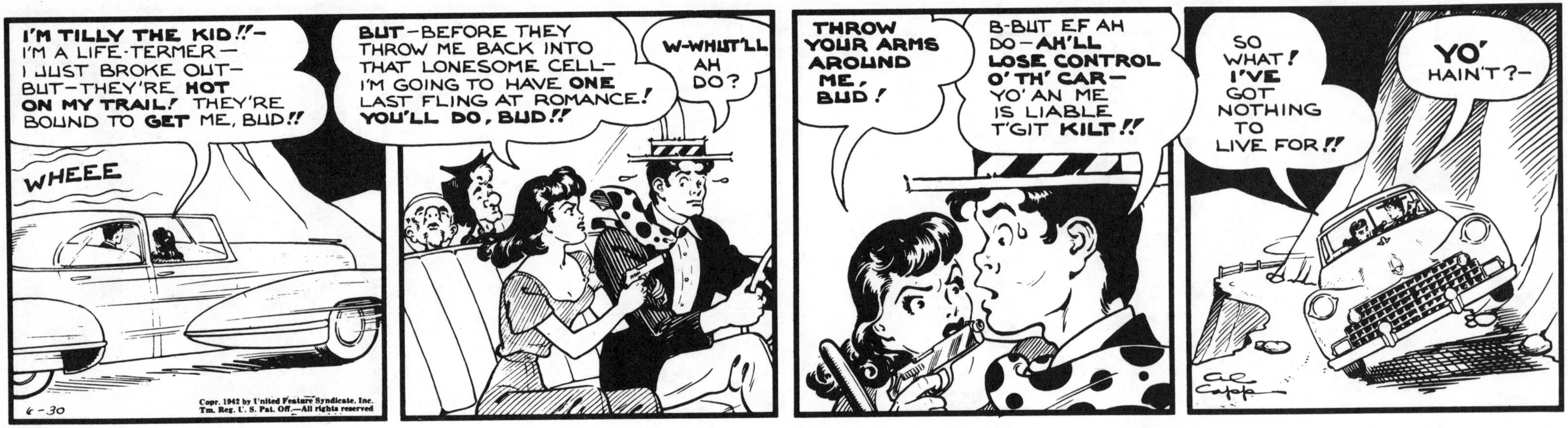
I'M TILLY THE KID!!– I'M A LIFE-TERMER– I JUST BROKE OUT– BUT–THEY'RE HOT ON MY TRAIL! THEY'RE BOUND TO GET ME, BUD!!
WHEEE
6-30
Copr. 1942 by United Feature Syndicate, Inc. Tm. Reg. U. S. Pat. Off.—All rights reserved
BUT–BEFORE THEY THROW ME BACK INTO THAT LONESOME CELL– I'M GOING TO HAVE ONE LAST FLING AT ROMANCE! YOU'LL DO, BUD!!
W-WHUT'LL AH DO?
THROW YOUR ARMS AROUND ME, BUD!
B-BUT EF AH DO–AH'LL LOSE CONTROL O' TH' CAR– YO' AN ME IS LIABLE T'GIT KILT!!
SO WHAT! I'VE GOT NOTHING TO LIVE FOR!!
YO' HAIN'T?–
AL CAPP

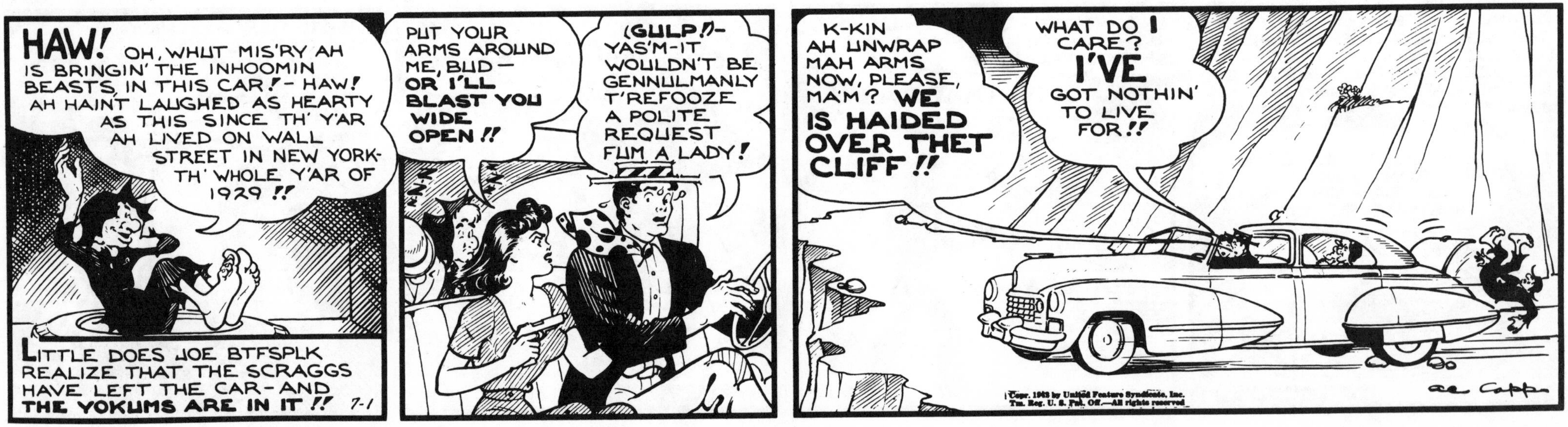
HAW! OH, WHUT MIS'RY AH IS BRINGIN' THE INHOOMIN BEASTS, IN THIS CAR!– HAW! AH HAINT LAUGHED AS HEARTY AS THIS SINCE TH' Y'AR AH LIVED ON WALL STREET IN NEW YORK– TH' WHOLE Y'AR OF 1929!!
LITTLE DOES JOE BTFSPLK REALIZE THAT THE SCRAGGS HAVE LEFT THE CAR–AND THE YOKUMS ARE IN IT!!
7-1
PUT YOUR ARMS AROUND ME, BUD– OR I'LL BLAST YOU WIDE OPEN!!
(GULP!)– YAS'M–IT WOULDN'T BE GENNULMANLY T'REFOOZE A POLITE REQUEST FUM A LADY!
K-KIN AH UNWRAP MAH ARMS NOW, PLEASE, MA'M? WE IS HAIDED OVER THET CLIFF!!
WHAT DO I CARE? I'VE GOT NOTHIN' TO LIVE FOR!!
Copr. 1942 by United Feature Syndicate, Inc. Tm. Reg. U. S. Pat. Off.—All rights reserved
AL CAPP

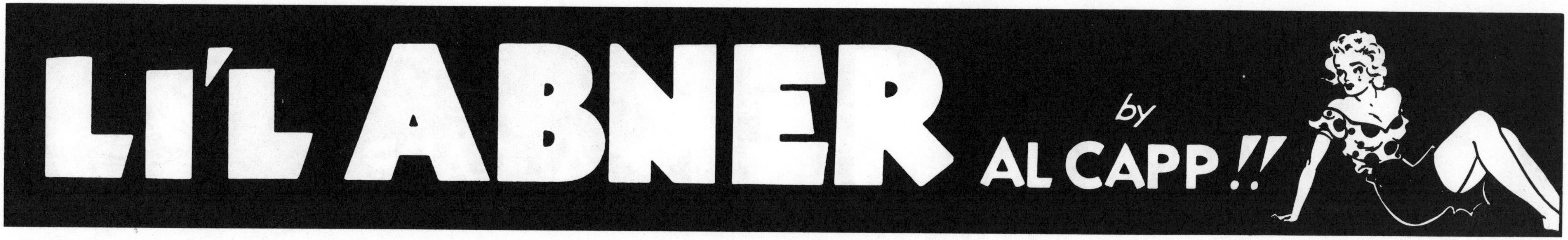
LI'L ABNER
by
AL CAPP!!

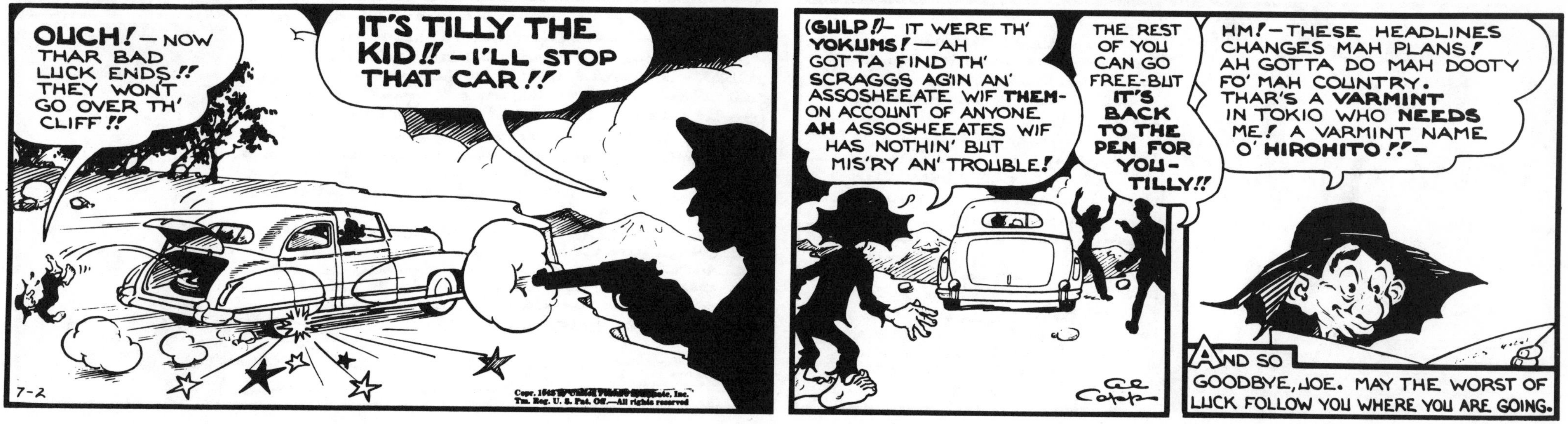
OUCH! — NOW THAR BAD LUCK ENDS!! THEY WON'T GO OVER TH' CLIFF!!
IT'S TILLY THE KID!! — I'LL STOP THAT CAR!!
7-2
(GULP!) — IT WERE TH' YOKUMS! — AH GOTTA FIND TH' SCRAGGS AGIN AN' ASSOSHEEATE WIF THEM — ON ACCOUNT OF ANYONE AH ASSOSHEEATES WIF HAS NOTHIN' BUT MIS'RY AN' TROUBLE!
THE REST OF YOU CAN GO FREE-BUT IT'S BACK TO THE PEN FOR YOU — TILLY!!
HM! — THESE HEADLINES CHANGES MAH PLANS! AH GOTTA DO MAH DOOTY FO' MAH COUNTRY. THAR'S A VARMINT IN TOKIO WHO NEEDS ME! A VARMINT NAME O' HIROHITO!! —
AND SO GOODBYE, JOE. MAY THE WORST OF LUCK FOLLOW YOU WHERE YOU ARE GOING.

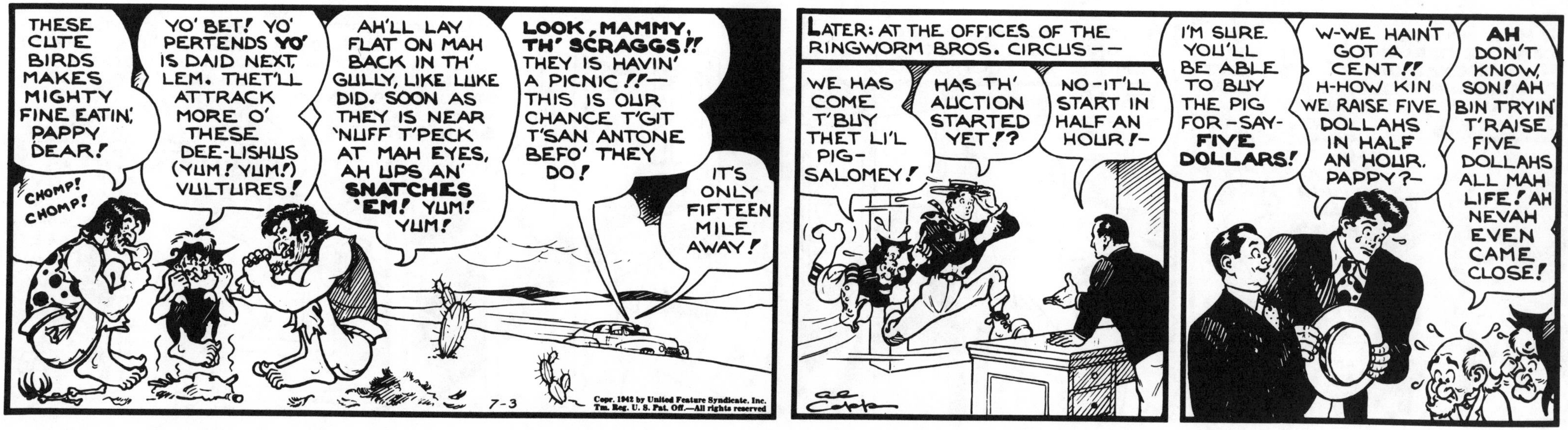
THESE CUTE BIRDS MAKES MIGHTY FINE EATIN', PAPPY DEAR!
CHOMP! CHOMP!
YO' BET! YO' PERTENDS YO' IS DAID NEXT, LEM. THET'LL ATTRACK MORE O' THESE DEE-LISHUS (YUM! YUM!) VULTURES!
AH'LL LAY FLAT ON MAH BACK IN TH' GULLY, LIKE LUKE DID. SOON AS THEY IS NEAR 'NUFF T'PECK AT MAH EYES, AH UPS AN' SNATCHES 'EM! YUM! YUM!
LOOK, MAMMY, TH' SCRAGGS!! THEY IS HAVIN' A PICNIC!! — THIS IS OUR CHANCE T'GIT T'SAN ANTONE BEFO' THEY DO!
IT'S ONLY FIFTEEN MILE AWAY!
7-3
Copr. 1942 by United Feature Syndicate, Inc. Tm. Reg. U. S. Pat. Off.—All rights reserved
LATER: AT THE OFFICES OF THE RINGWORM BROS. CIRCUS — —
WE HAS COME T'BUY THET LI'L PIG-SALOMEY!
HAS TH' AUCTION STARTED YET!?
NO-IT'LL START IN HALF AN HOUR! —
I'M SURE YOU'LL BE ABLE TO BUY THE PIG FOR — SAY — FIVE DOLLARS!
W-WE HAIN'T GOT A CENT!! H-HOW KIN WE RAISE FIVE DOLLAHS IN HALF AN HOUR, PAPPY? —
AH DON'T KNOW, SON! AH BIN TRYIN' T'RAISE FIVE DOLLAHS ALL MAH LIFE! AH NEVAH EVEN CAME CLOSE!

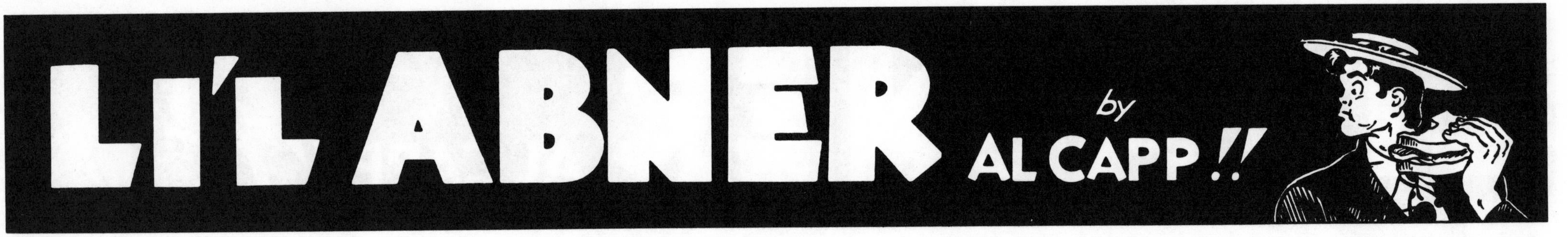
LI'L ABNER
by
AL CAPP!!

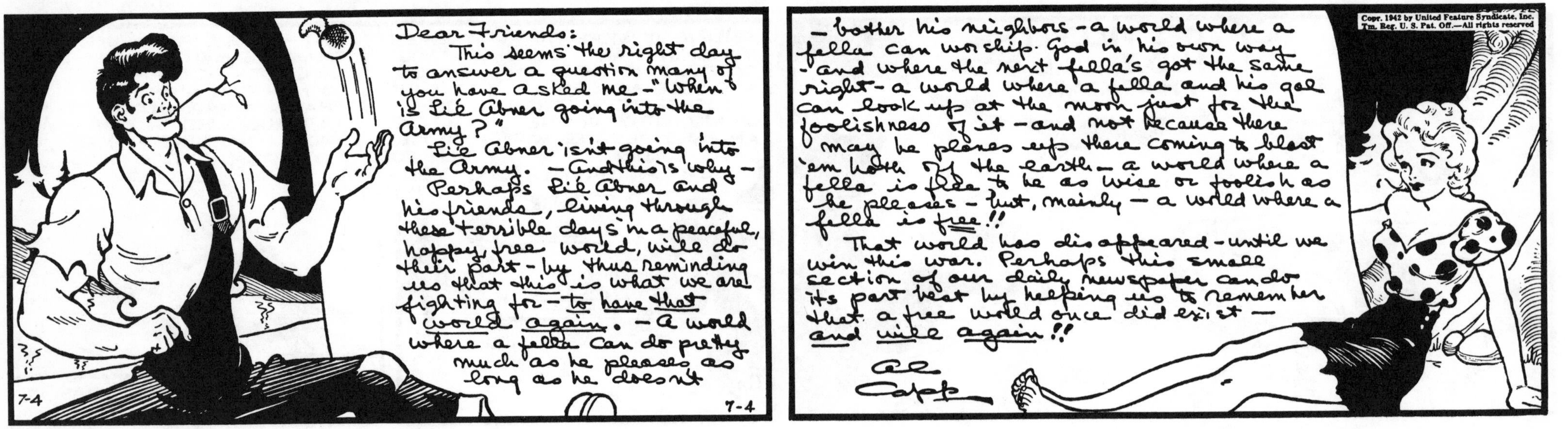
Dear Friends:
This seems the right day to answer a question many of you have asked me – "When is Li'l Abner going into the Army?"
Li'l Abner isn't going into the Army. – And this is why –
Perhaps Li'l Abner and his friends, living through these terrible days in a peaceful, happy, free world, will do their part – by thus reminding us that this is what we are fighting for – to have that world again. – A world where a fella can do pretty much as he pleases as long as he doesn't
7-4
7-4
– bother his neighbors – a world where a fella can worship God in his own way – and where the next fella's got the same right – a world where a fella and his gal can look up at the moon just for the foolishness of it – and not because there may be planes up there coming to blast 'em both off the earth – a world where a fella is free to be as wise or foolish as he pleases – but, mainly – a world where a fella is free!!
That world has disappeared – until we win this war. Perhaps this small section of our daily newspaper can do its part best by helping us to remember that a free world once did exist – and will again!!
Al Capp
Copr. 1942 by United Feature Syndicate, Inc.
Tm. Reg. U. S. Pat. Off.—All rights reserved

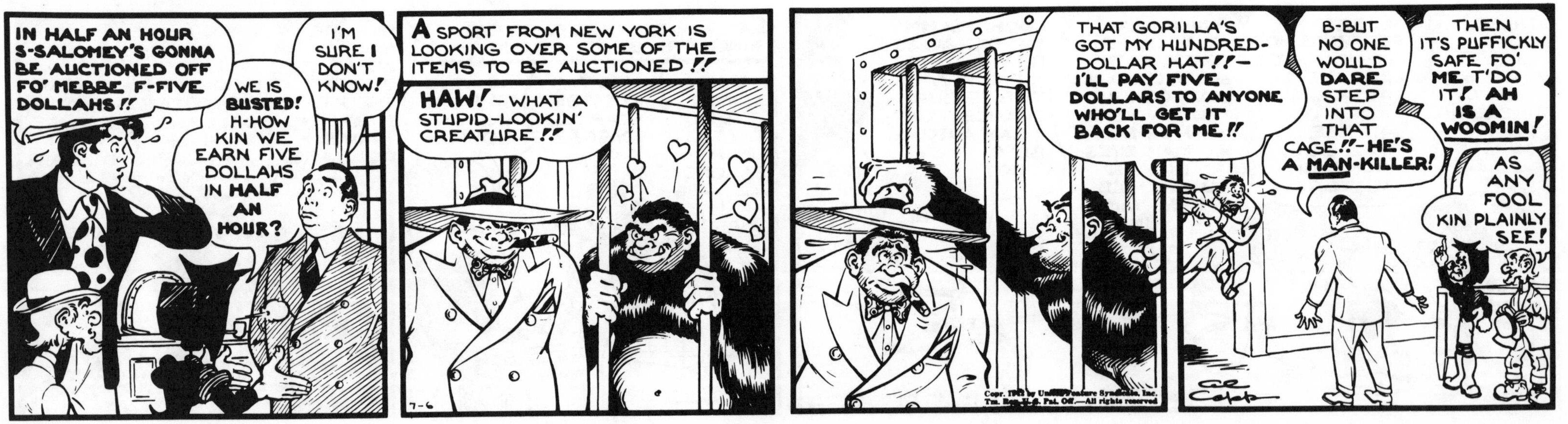
IN HALF AN HOUR S-SALOMEY'S GONNA BE AUCTIONED OFF FO' MEBBE F-FIVE DOLLAHS!!
WE IS BUSTED! H-HOW KIN WE EARN FIVE DOLLAHS IN HALF AN HOUR?
I'M SURE I DON'T KNOW!
A SPORT FROM NEW YORK IS LOOKING OVER SOME OF THE ITEMS TO BE AUCTIONED!!
HAW! – WHAT A STUPID-LOOKIN' CREATURE!!
7-6
THAT GORILLA'S GOT MY HUNDRED-DOLLAR HAT!! – I'LL PAY FIVE DOLLARS TO ANYONE WHO'LL GET IT BACK FOR ME!!
B-BUT NO ONE WOULD DARE STEP INTO THAT CAGE!! – HE'S A MAN-KILLER!
THEN IT'S PUFFICKLY SAFE FO' ME T'DO IT! AH IS A WOOMIN!
AS ANY FOOL KIN PLAINLY SEE!
Copr. 194? by United Feature Syndicate, Inc.
Tm. Reg. U. S. Pat. Off.—All rights reserved
Al Capp

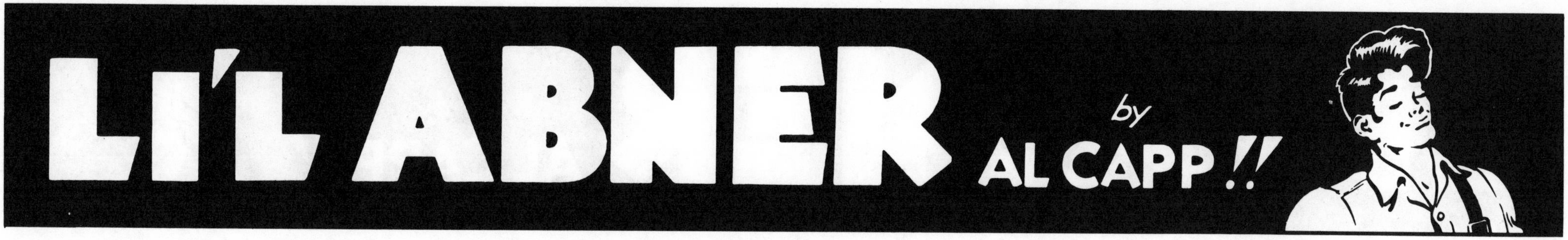
LI'L ABNER
by
AL CAPP !!

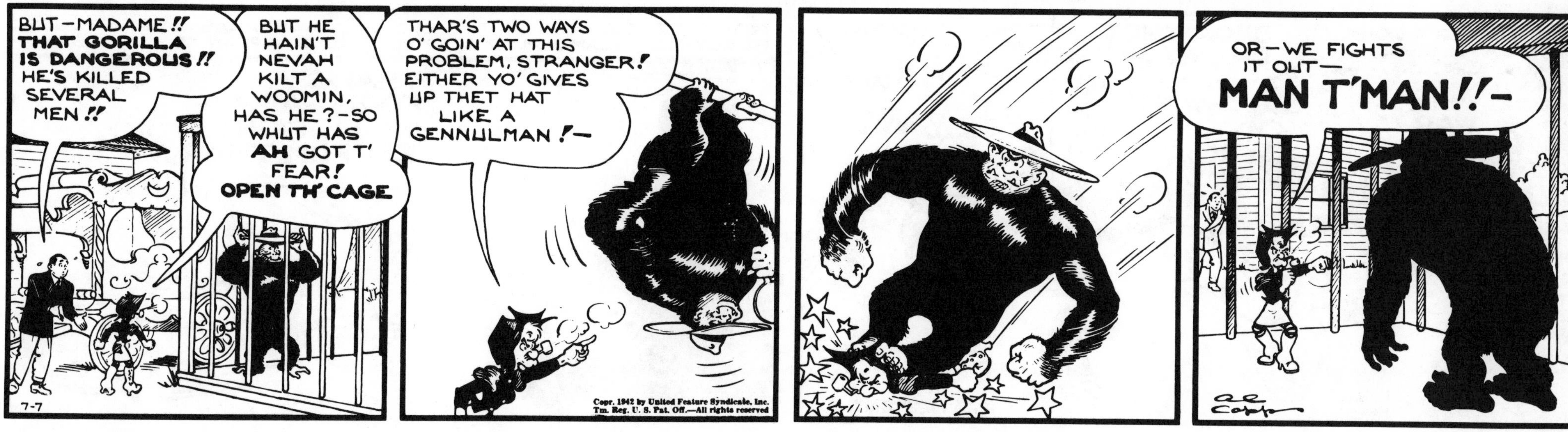
BUT—MADAME!! THAT GORILLA IS DANGEROUS!! HE'S KILLED SEVERAL MEN!!
BUT HE HAIN'T NEVAH KILT A WOOMIN, HAS HE?—SO WHUT HAS AH GOT T' FEAR! OPEN TH' CAGE
7-7
THAR'S TWO WAYS O' GOIN' AT THIS PROBLEM, STRANGER! EITHER YO' GIVES UP THET HAT LIKE A GENNULMAN!—
Copr. 1942 by United Feature Syndicate, Inc. Tm. Reg. U. S. Pat. Off.—All rights reserved
OR—WE FIGHTS IT OUT— MAN T'MAN!!—
Al Capp

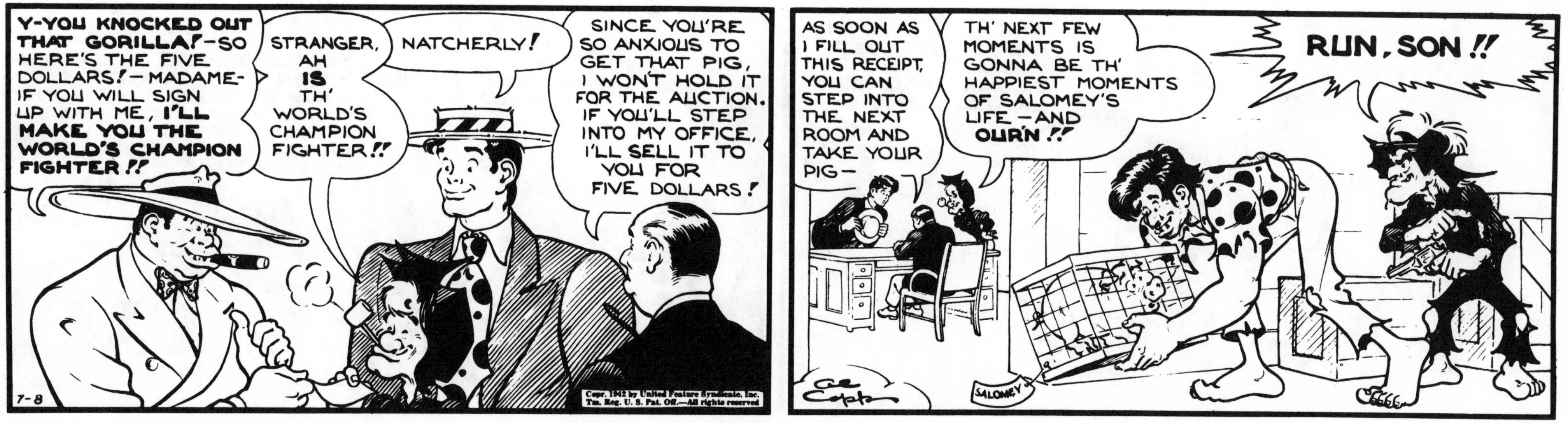
Y-YOU KNOCKED OUT THAT GORILLA!—SO HERE'S THE FIVE DOLLARS!—MADAME-IF YOU WILL SIGN UP WITH ME, I'LL MAKE YOU THE WORLD'S CHAMPION FIGHTER!!
STRANGER, AH IS TH' WORLD'S CHAMPION FIGHTER!!
NATCHERLY!
SINCE YOU'RE SO ANXIOUS TO GET THAT PIG, I WON'T HOLD IT FOR THE AUCTION. IF YOU'LL STEP INTO MY OFFICE, I'LL SELL IT TO YOU FOR FIVE DOLLARS!
7-8
Copr. 1942 by United Feature Syndicate, Inc. Tm. Reg. U. S. Pat. Off.—All rights reserved
AS SOON AS I FILL OUT THIS RECEIPT, YOU CAN STEP INTO THE NEXT ROOM AND TAKE YOUR PIG—
TH' NEXT FEW MOMENTS IS GONNA BE TH' HAPPIEST MOMENTS OF SALOMEY'S LIFE—AND OURN!!
RUN, SON!!
SALOMEY
Al Capp

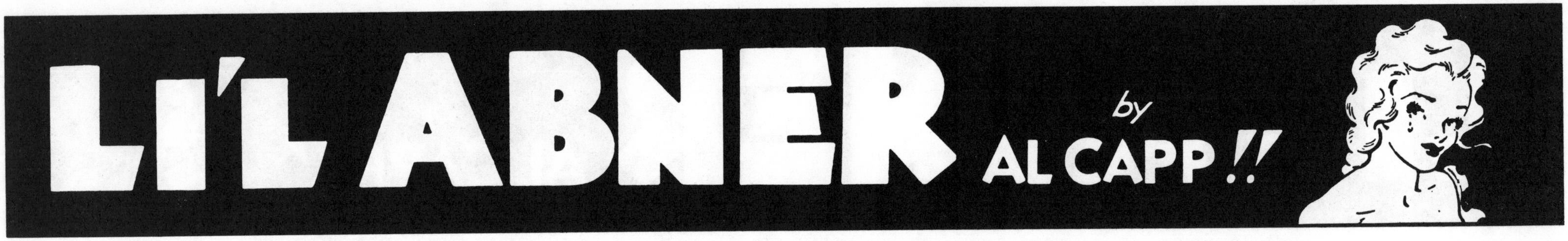
LI'L ABNER
by
AL CAPP!!

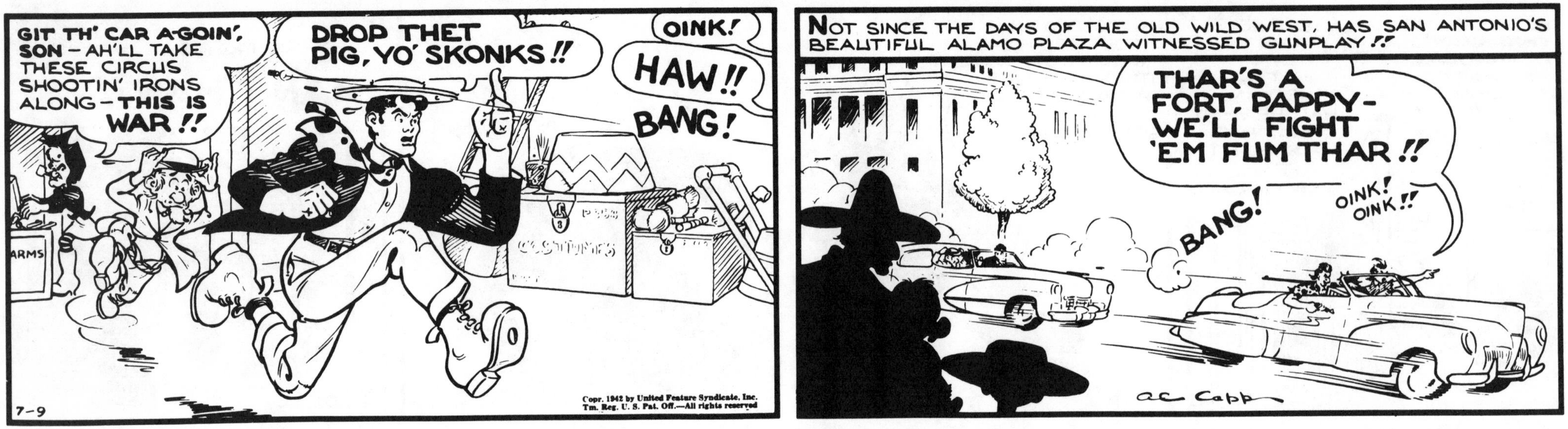
GIT TH' CAR A-GOIN', SON – AH'LL TAKE THESE CIRCUS SHOOTIN' IRONS ALONG – THIS IS WAR!!
DROP THET PIG, YO' SKONKS!!
OINK!
HAW!!
BANG!
ARMS
COSTUMES
7-9
Copr. 1942 by United Feature Syndicate, Inc. Tm. Reg. U. S. Pat. Off.—All rights reserved
NOT SINCE THE DAYS OF THE OLD WILD WEST, HAS SAN ANTONIO'S BEAUTIFUL ALAMO PLAZA WITNESSED GUNPLAY!!
THAR'S A FORT, PAPPY – WE'LL FIGHT 'EM FUM THAR!!
BANG!
OINK! OINK!!
Al Capp

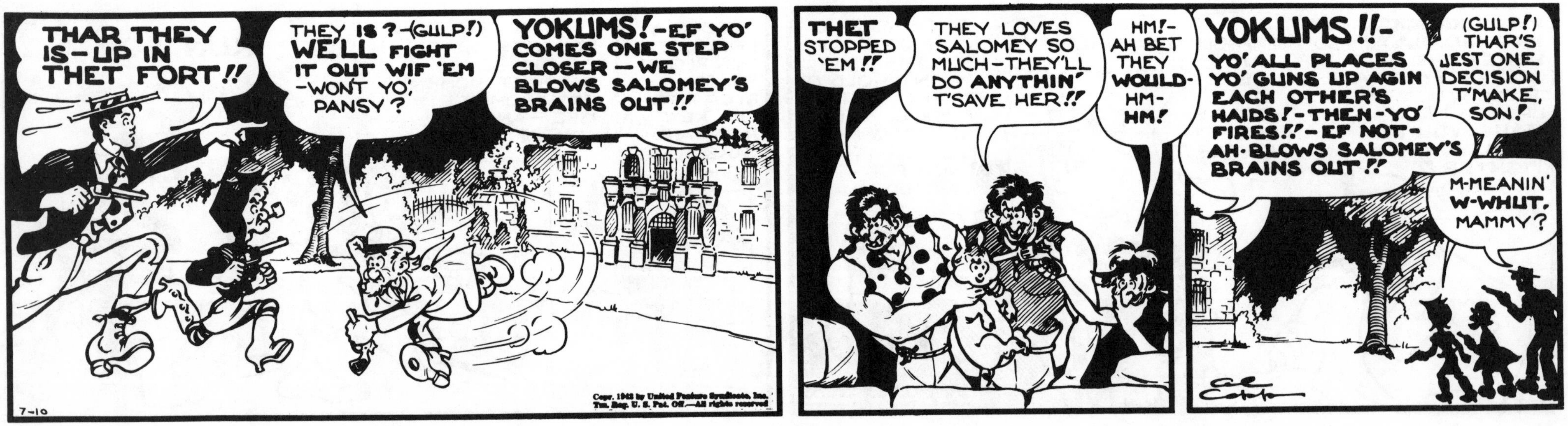
THAR THEY IS – UP IN THET FORT!!
THEY IS? – (GULP!) WE'LL FIGHT IT OUT WIF 'EM – WON'T YO', PANSY?
YOKUMS! – EF YO' COMES ONE STEP CLOSER – WE BLOWS SALOMEY'S BRAINS OUT!!
7-10
Copr. 1942 by United Feature Syndicate, Inc. Tm. Reg. U. S. Pat. Off.—All rights reserved
THET STOPPED 'EM!!
THEY LOVES SALOMEY SO MUCH – THEY'LL DO ANYTHIN' T'SAVE HER!!
HM! – AH BET THEY WOULD – HM-HM!
YOKUMS!! – YO' ALL PLACES YO' GUNS UP AGIN EACH OTHER'S HAIDS! – THEN – YO' FIRES!! – EF NOT – AH BLOWS SALOMEY'S BRAINS OUT!!
(GULP!) THAR'S JEST ONE DECISION T'MAKE, SON!
M-MEANIN' W-WHUT, MAMMY?
Al Capp

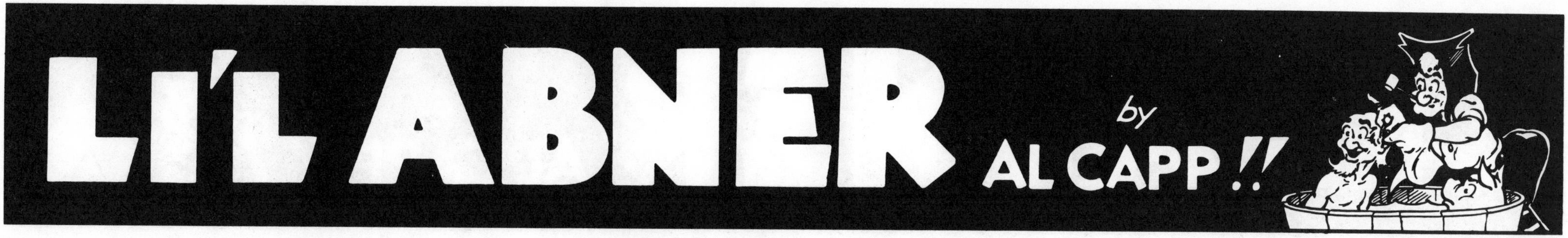
LI'L ABNER
by
AL CAPP!!

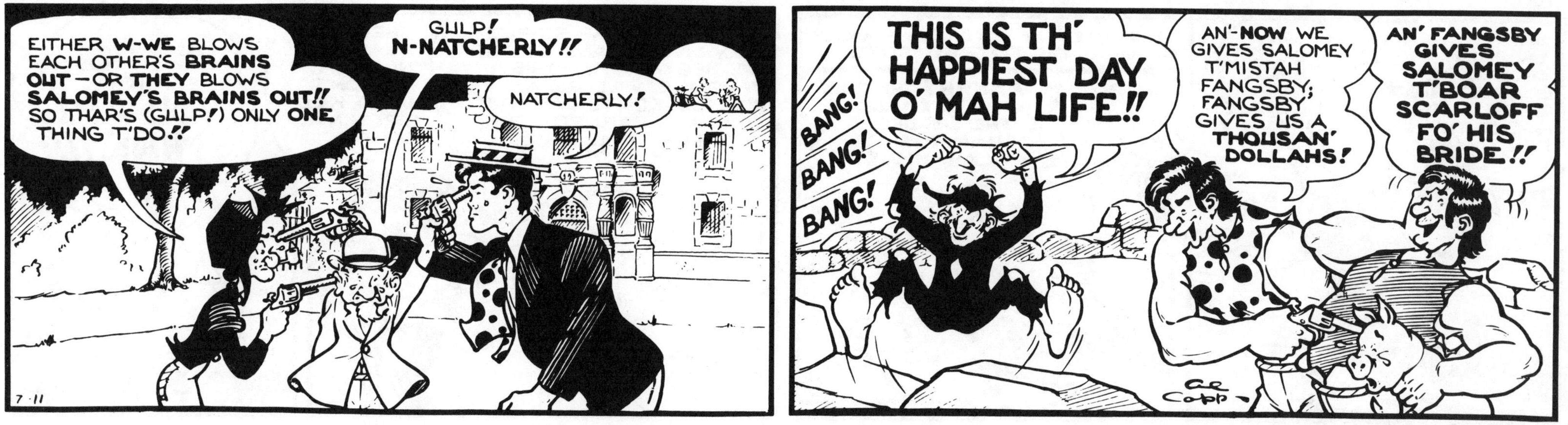
EITHER W-WE BLOWS EACH OTHER'S BRAINS OUT—OR THEY BLOWS SALOMEY'S BRAINS OUT!! SO THAR'S (GULP!) ONLY ONE THING T'DO!!
GULP! N-NATCHERLY!!
NATCHERLY!
7-11
THIS IS TH' HAPPIEST DAY O' MAH LIFE!!
BANG!
BANG!
BANG!
AN'-NOW WE GIVES SALOMEY T'MISTAH FANGSBY; FANGSBY GIVES US A THOUSAN' DOLLAHS!
AN' FANGSBY GIVES SALOMEY T'BOAR SCARLOFF FO' HIS BRIDE!!

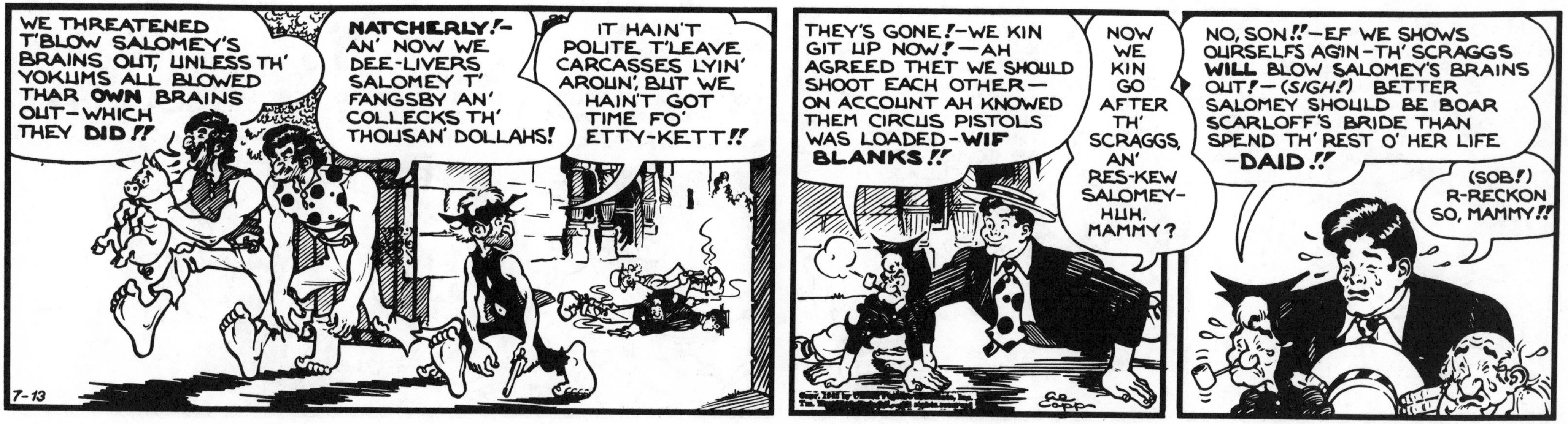
WE THREATENED T'BLOW SALOMEY'S BRAINS OUT, UNLESS TH' YOKUMS ALL BLOWED THAR OWN BRAINS OUT—WHICH THEY DID!!
NATCHERLY!—AN' NOW WE DEE-LIVERS SALOMEY T' FANGSBY AN' COLLECKS TH' THOUSAN' DOLLAHS!
IT HAIN'T POLITE T'LEAVE CARCASSES LYIN' AROUN', BUT WE HAIN'T GOT TIME FO' ETTY-KETT!!
7-13
THEY'S GONE!—WE KIN GIT UP NOW!—AH AGREED THET WE SHOULD SHOOT EACH OTHER—ON ACCOUNT AH KNOWED THEM CIRCUS PISTOLS WAS LOADED-WIF BLANKS!!
NOW WE KIN GO AFTER TH' SCRAGGS, AN' RES-KEW SALOMEY-HUH, MAMMY?
NO, SON!!—EF WE SHOWS OURSELFS AG'IN—TH' SCRAGGS WILL BLOW SALOMEY'S BRAINS OUT!—(SIGH!) BETTER SALOMEY SHOULD BE BOAR SCARLOFF'S BRIDE THAN SPEND TH' REST O' HER LIFE—DAID!!
(SOB!) R-RECKON SO, MAMMY!!

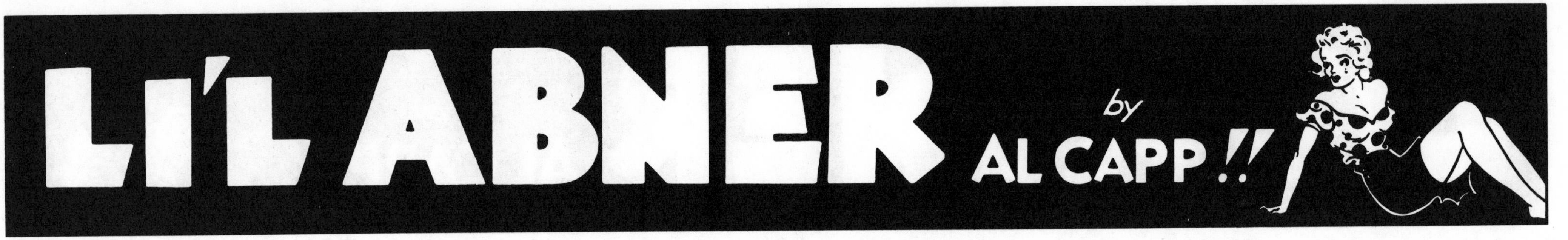
LI'L ABNER
by
AL CAPP!!

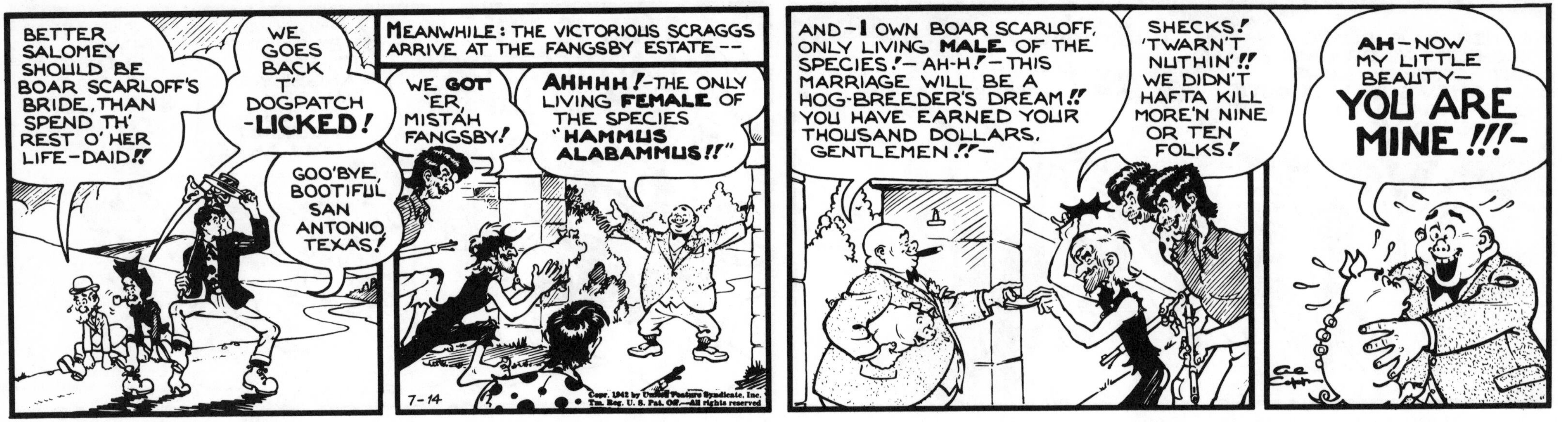
BETTER SALOMEY SHOULD BE BOAR SCARLOFF'S BRIDE, THAN SPEND TH' REST O' HER LIFE-DAID!!
WE GOES BACK T' DOGPATCH -LICKED!
GOO'BYE, BOOTIFUL SAN ANTONIO, TEXAS!
MEANWHILE: THE VICTORIOUS SCRAGGS ARRIVE AT THE FANGSBY ESTATE--
WE GOT 'ER, MISTAH FANGSBY!
AHHHH!-THE ONLY LIVING FEMALE OF THE SPECIES "HAMMUS ALABAMMUS!!"
7-14
Copr. 1942 by United Feature Syndicate, Inc. Tm. Reg. U. S. Pat. Off.—All rights reserved
AND-I OWN BOAR SCARLOFF, ONLY LIVING MALE OF THE SPECIES!-AH-H!-THIS MARRIAGE WILL BE A HOG-BREEDER'S DREAM!! YOU HAVE EARNED YOUR THOUSAND DOLLARS, GENTLEMEN!!-
SHECKS! 'TWARN'T NUTHIN'!! WE DIDN'T HAFTA KILL MORE'N NINE OR TEN FOLKS!
AH-NOW MY LITTLE BEAUTY- YOU ARE MINE!!!-

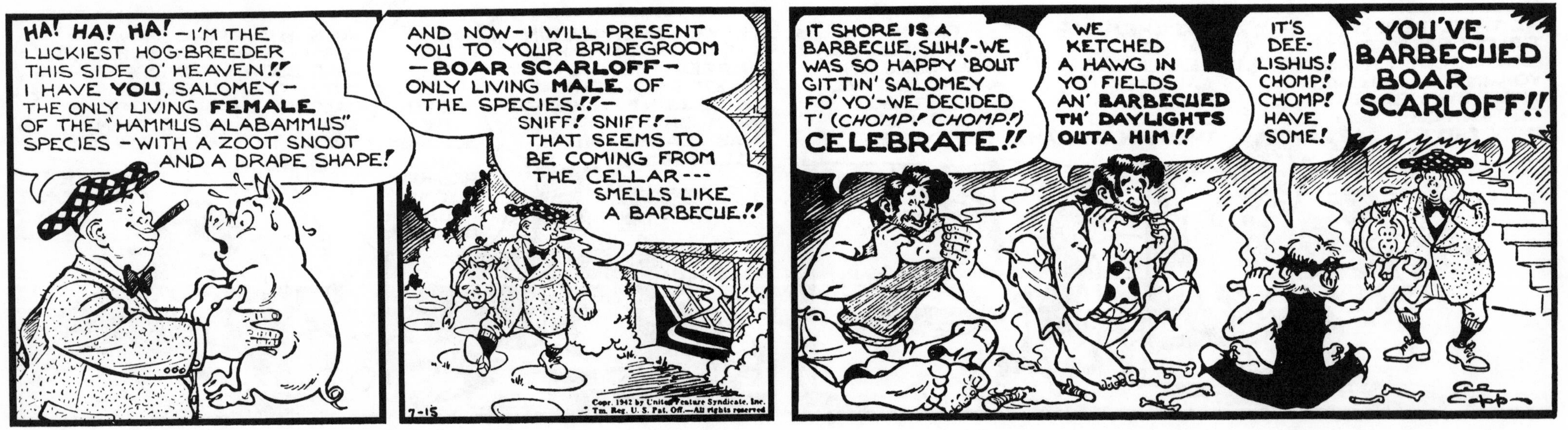
HA! HA! HA!-I'M THE LUCKIEST HOG-BREEDER THIS SIDE O' HEAVEN!! I HAVE YOU, SALOMEY-THE ONLY LIVING FEMALE OF THE "HAMMUS ALABAMMUS" SPECIES -WITH A ZOOT SNOOT AND A DRAPE SHAPE!
AND NOW-I WILL PRESENT YOU TO YOUR BRIDEGROOM -BOAR SCARLOFF- ONLY LIVING MALE OF THE SPECIES!!-
SNIFF! SNIFF!-THAT SEEMS TO BE COMING FROM THE CELLAR---SMELLS LIKE A BARBECUE!!
7-15
Copr. 1942 by United Feature Syndicate, Inc. Tm. Reg. U. S. Pat. Off.—All rights reserved
IT SHORE IS A BARBECUE, SUH!-WE WAS SO HAPPY 'BOUT GITTIN' SALOMEY FO' YO'-WE DECIDED T' (CHOMP! CHOMP!) CELEBRATE!!
WE KETCHED A HAWG IN YO' FIELDS AN' BARBECUED TH' DAYLIGHTS OUTA HIM!!
IT'S DEE-LISHUS! CHOMP! CHOMP! HAVE SOME!
YOU'VE BARBECUED BOAR SCARLOFF!!

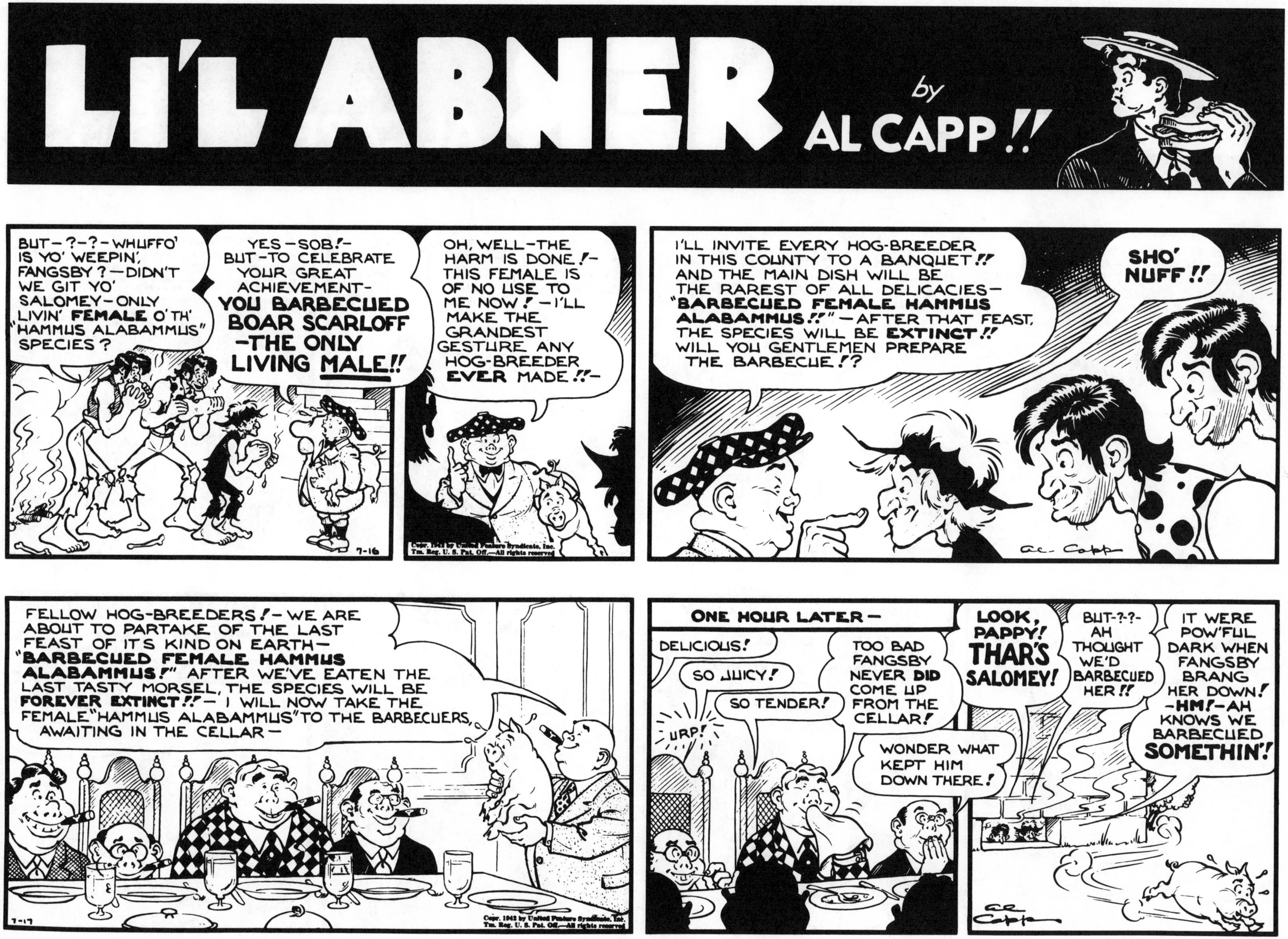

LI'L ABNER
by AL CAPP!!
BUT-?-?-WHUFFO' IS YO' WEEPIN', FANGSBY?-DIDN'T WE GIT YO' SALOMEY-ONLY LIVIN' FEMALE O'TH' "HAMMUS ALABAMMUS" SPECIES?
YES-SOB!-BUT-TO CELEBRATE YOUR GREAT ACHIEVEMENT- YOU BARBECUED BOAR SCARLOFF -THE ONLY LIVING MALE!!
OH, WELL-THE HARM IS DONE!-THIS FEMALE IS OF NO USE TO ME NOW!-I'LL MAKE THE GRANDEST GESTURE ANY HOG-BREEDER EVER MADE!!-
7-16
Copr. 1942 by United Feature Syndicate, Inc. Tm. Reg. U. S. Pat. Off.—All rights reserved
I'LL INVITE EVERY HOG-BREEDER IN THIS COUNTY TO A BANQUET!! AND THE MAIN DISH WILL BE THE RAREST OF ALL DELICACIES- "BARBECUED FEMALE HAMMUS ALABAMMUS!!"-AFTER THAT FEAST, THE SPECIES WILL BE EXTINCT!! WILL YOU GENTLEMEN PREPARE THE BARBECUE!?
SHO' NUFF!!
Al Capp
FELLOW HOG-BREEDERS!-WE ARE ABOUT TO PARTAKE OF THE LAST FEAST OF ITS KIND ON EARTH- "BARBECUED FEMALE HAMMUS ALABAMMUS!" AFTER WE'VE EATEN THE LAST TASTY MORSEL, THE SPECIES WILL BE FOREVER EXTINCT!!-I WILL NOW TAKE THE FEMALE "HAMMUS ALABAMMUS" TO THE BARBECUERS, AWAITING IN THE CELLAR-
7-17
Copr. 1942 by United Feature Syndicate, Inc. Tm. Reg. U. S. Pat. Off.—All rights reserved
ONE HOUR LATER-
DELICIOUS!
SO JUICY!
SO TENDER!
URP!
TOO BAD FANGSBY NEVER DID COME UP FROM THE CELLAR!
WONDER WHAT KEPT HIM DOWN THERE!
LOOK, PAPPY! THAR'S SALOMEY!
BUT-?-?-AH THOUGHT WE'D BARBECUED HER!!
IT WERE POW'FUL DARK WHEN FANGSBY BRANG HER DOWN!-HM!-AH KNOWS WE BARBECUED SOMETHIN'!
Al Capp

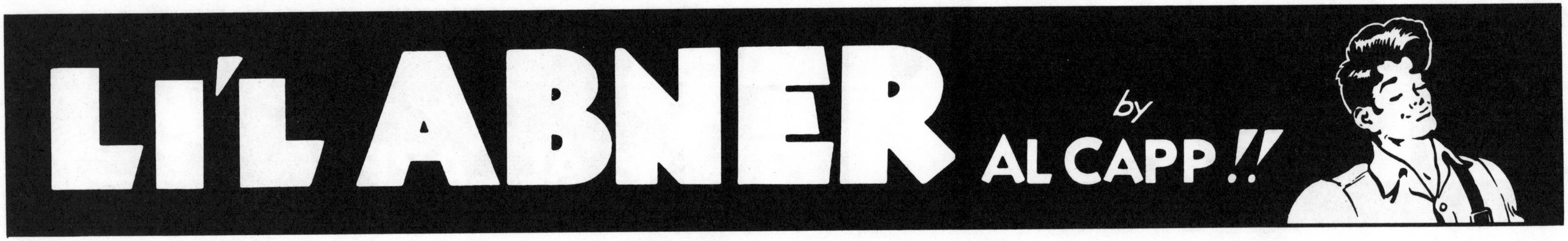
LI'L ABNER
by
AL CAPP!!

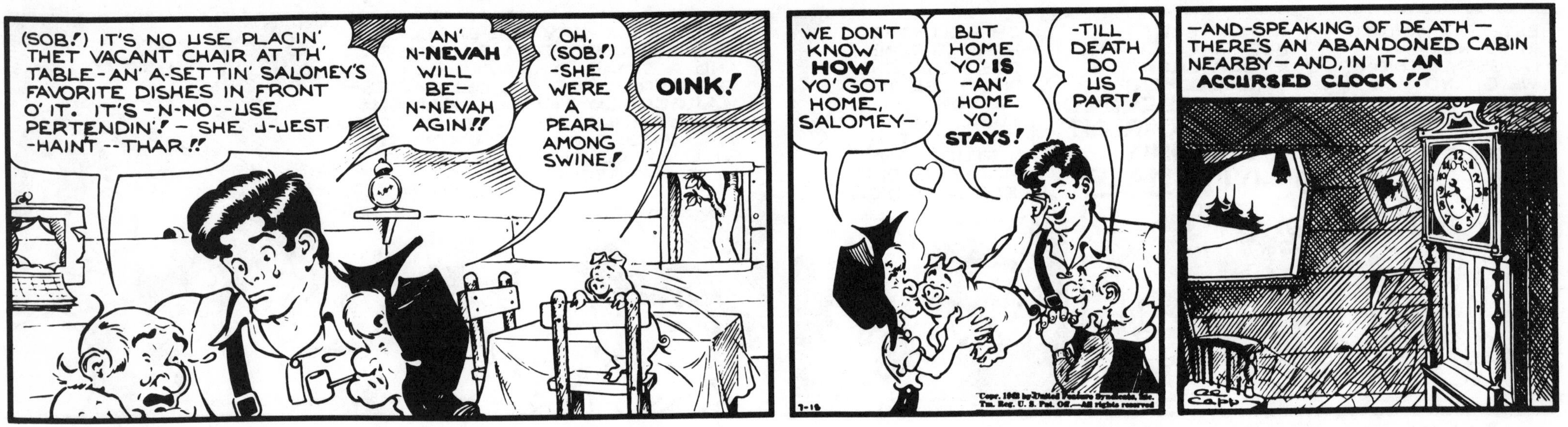
(SOB!) IT'S NO USE PLACIN' THET VACANT CHAIR AT TH' TABLE-AN' A-SETTIN' SALOMEY'S FAVORITE DISHES IN FRONT O' IT. IT'S-N-NO--USE PERTENDIN'!-SHE J-JEST -HAINT--THAR!!
AN' N-NEVAH WILL BE- N-NEVAH AGIN!!
OH, (SOB!) -SHE WERE A PEARL AMONG SWINE!
OINK!
WE DON'T KNOW HOW YO' GOT HOME, SALOMEY-
BUT HOME YO' IS -AN' HOME YO' STAYS!
-TILL DEATH DO US PART!
—AND-SPEAKING OF DEATH—THERE'S AN ABANDONED CABIN NEARBY—AND, IN IT—AN ACCURSED CLOCK!!

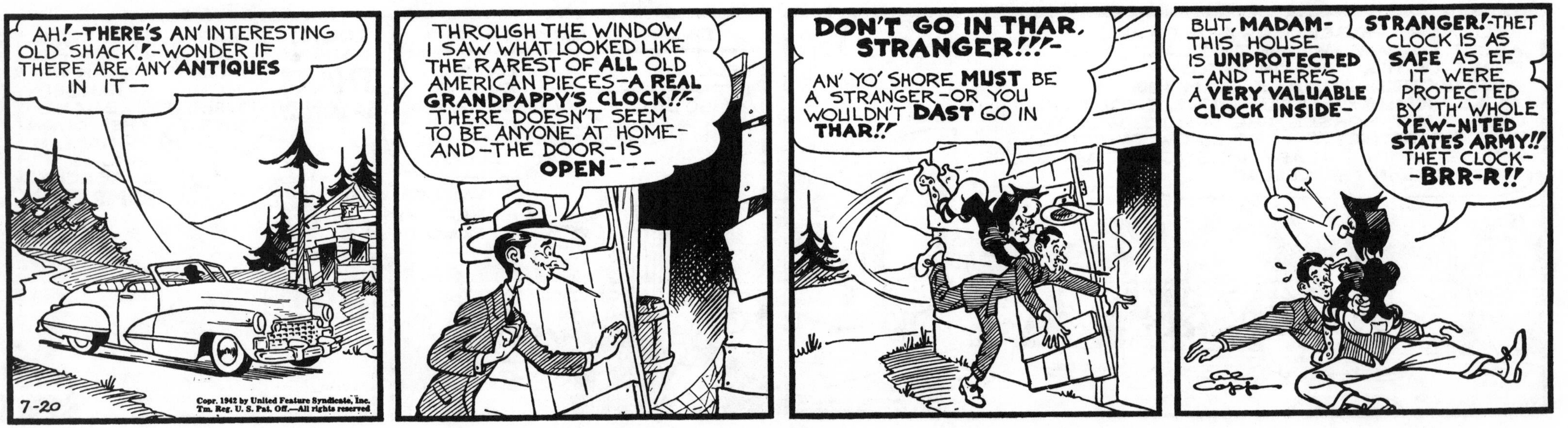
AH!-THERE'S AN' INTERESTING OLD SHACK!-WONDER IF THERE ARE ANY ANTIQUES IN IT—
7-20
Copr. 1942 by United Feature Syndicate, Inc. Tm. Reg. U. S. Pat. Off.—All rights reserved
THROUGH THE WINDOW I SAW WHAT LOOKED LIKE THE RAREST OF ALL OLD AMERICAN PIECES—A REAL GRANDPAPPY'S CLOCK!!-THERE DOESN'T SEEM TO BE ANYONE AT HOME-AND—THE DOOR—IS OPEN---
DON'T GO IN THAR, STRANGER!!!-
AN' YO' SHORE MUST BE A STRANGER—OR YOU WOULDN'T DAST GO IN THAR!!
BUT, MADAM-THIS HOUSE IS UNPROTECTED -AND THERE'S A VERY VALUABLE CLOCK INSIDE-
STRANGER!-THET CLOCK IS AS SAFE AS EF IT WERE PROTECTED BY TH' WHOLE YEW-NITED STATES ARMY!! THET CLOCK- -BRR-R!!

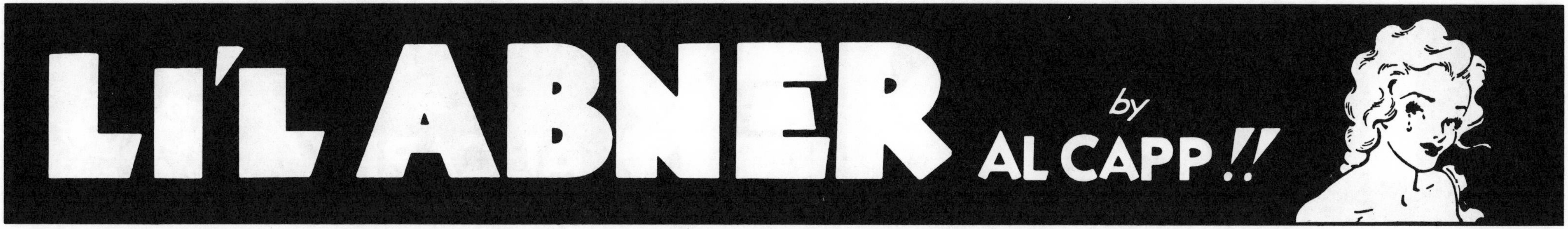
LI'L ABNER
by AL CAPP!!

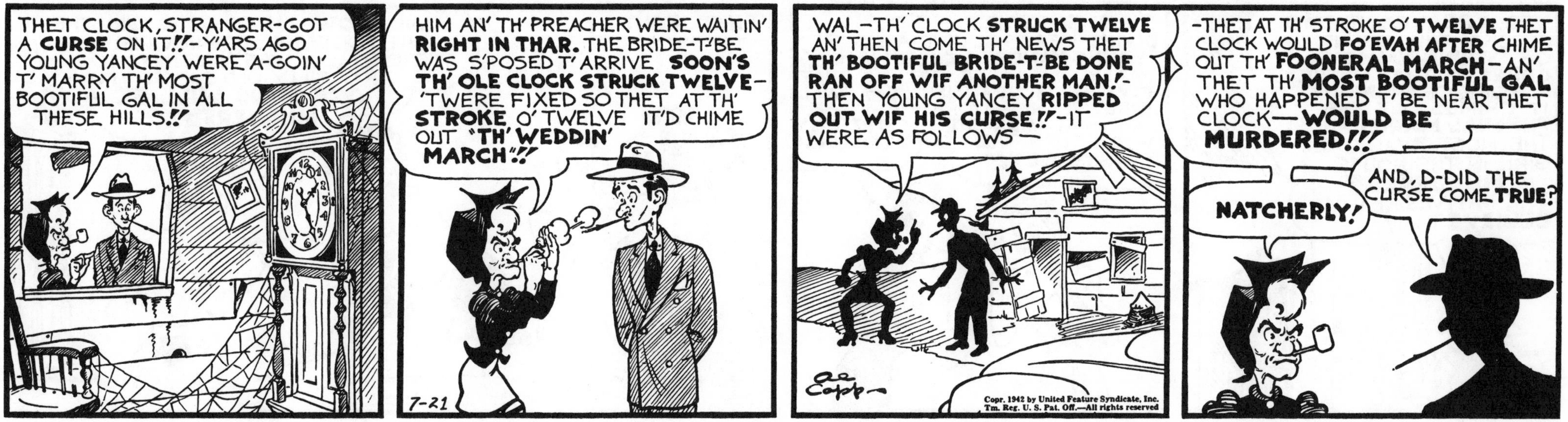
THET CLOCK, STRANGER-GOT A **CURSE** ON IT!!-Y'ARS AGO YOUNG YANCEY WERE A-GOIN' T' MARRY TH' MOST BOOTIFUL GAL IN ALL THESE HILLS!!
HIM AN' TH' PREACHER WERE WAITIN' **RIGHT IN THAR.** THE BRIDE-T'-BE WAS S'POSED T' ARRIVE **SOON'S TH' OLE CLOCK STRUCK TWELVE**-'TWERE FIXED SO THET AT TH' **STROKE** O' TWELVE IT'D CHIME OUT **"TH' WEDDIN' MARCH"!!**
7-21
WAL-TH' CLOCK **STRUCK TWELVE** AN' THEN COME TH' NEWS THET **TH' BOOTIFUL BRIDE-T'-BE DONE RAN OFF WIF ANOTHER MAN!**-THEN YOUNG YANCEY **RIPPED OUT WIF HIS CURSE!!**-IT WERE AS FOLLOWS—
Copr. 1942 by United Feature Syndicate, Inc. Tm. Reg. U. S. Pat. Off.—All rights reserved
-THET AT TH' STROKE O' **TWELVE** THET CLOCK WOULD **FO'EVAH AFTER** CHIME OUT TH' **FOONERAL MARCH**—AN' THET TH' **MOST BOOTIFUL GAL** WHO HAPPENED T' BE NEAR THET CLOCK—**WOULD BE MURDERED!!!**
AND, D-DID THE CURSE COME **TRUE**?
NATCHERLY!

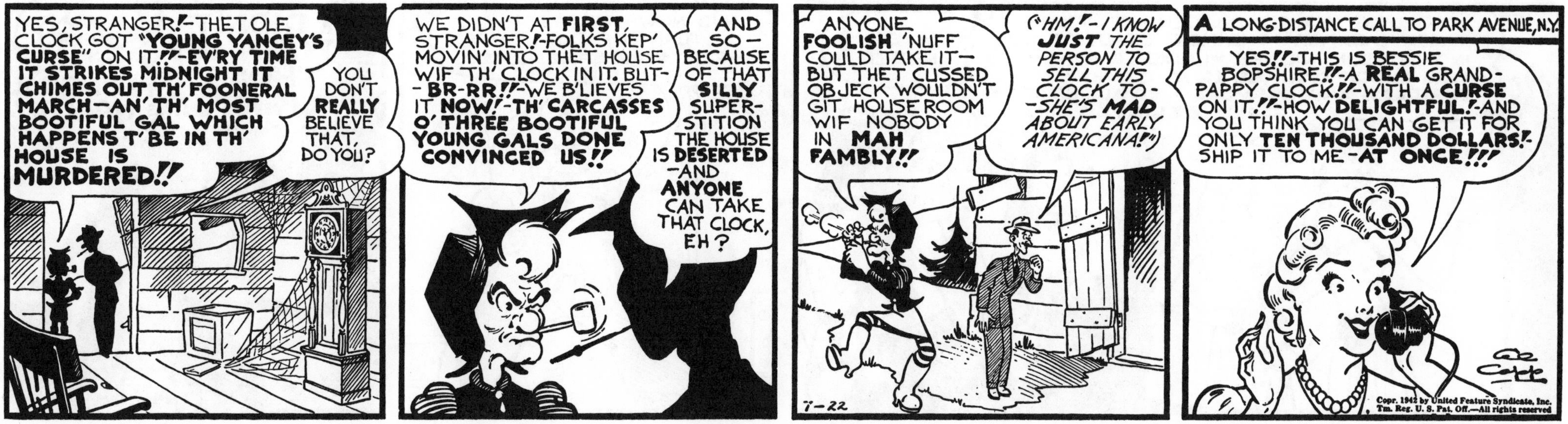
YES, STRANGER!-THET OLE CLOCK GOT **"YOUNG YANCEY'S CURSE"** ON IT!!-**EV'RY TIME IT STRIKES MIDNIGHT IT CHIMES OUT TH' FOONERAL MARCH—AN' TH' MOST BOOTIFUL GAL WHICH HAPPENS T' BE IN TH' HOUSE IS MURDERED!!**
YOU DON'T **REALLY** BELIEVE THAT, DO YOU?
WE DIDN'T AT **FIRST**, STRANGER!-FOLKS KEP' MOVIN' INTO THET HOUSE WIF TH' CLOCK IN IT. BUT-**BR-RR!!**-WE B'LIEVES IT **NOW!-TH' CARCASSES O' THREE BOOTIFUL YOUNG GALS DONE CONVINCED US!!**
AND SO-BECAUSE OF THAT **SILLY** SUPERSTITION THE HOUSE IS **DESERTED**-AND **ANYONE** CAN TAKE THAT CLOCK, EH?
ANYONE **FOOLISH** 'NUFF COULD TAKE IT—BUT THET CUSSED OBJECK WOULDN'T GIT HOUSE ROOM WIF NOBODY IN **MAH FAMBLY!!**
("HM!-I KNOW **JUST** THE PERSON TO SELL THIS CLOCK TO-SHE'S **MAD** ABOUT EARLY AMERICANA!")
7-22
A LONG-DISTANCE CALL TO PARK AVENUE, N.Y.
YES!!-THIS IS BESSIE BOPSHIRE!!-A **REAL** GRAND-PAPPY CLOCK!!-WITH A **CURSE** ON IT!!-HOW **DELIGHTFUL!**-AND YOU THINK YOU CAN GET IT FOR ONLY **TEN THOUSAND DOLLARS!**-SHIP IT TO ME-**AT ONCE!!!**
Copr. 1942 by United Feature Syndicate, Inc. Tm. Reg. U. S. Pat. Off.—All rights reserved

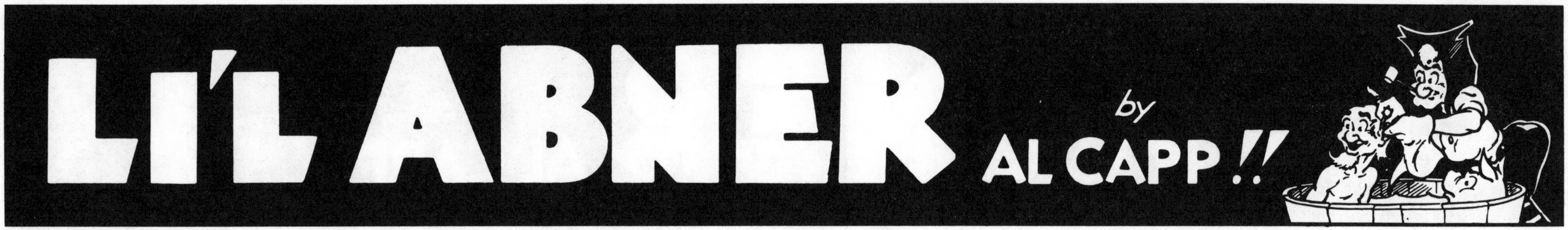
LI'L ABNER
by
AL CAPP!!

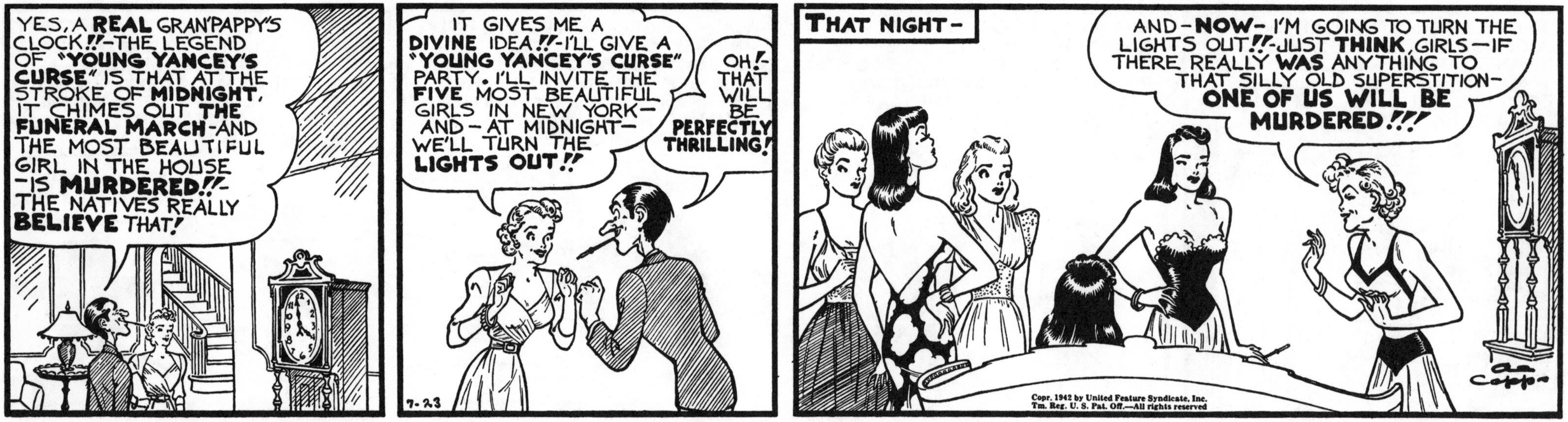
YES, A REAL GRAN'PAPPY'S CLOCK!!-THE LEGEND OF "YOUNG YANCEY'S CURSE" IS THAT AT THE STROKE OF MIDNIGHT, IT CHIMES OUT THE FUNERAL MARCH-AND THE MOST BEAUTIFUL GIRL IN THE HOUSE -IS MURDERED!!- THE NATIVES REALLY BELIEVE THAT!
IT GIVES ME A DIVINE IDEA!!-I'LL GIVE A "YOUNG YANCEY'S CURSE" PARTY. I'LL INVITE THE FIVE MOST BEAUTIFUL GIRLS IN NEW YORK— AND - AT MIDNIGHT— WE'LL TURN THE LIGHTS OUT!!
OH!- THAT WILL BE PERFECTLY THRILLING!
7-23
THAT NIGHT-
AND-NOW- I'M GOING TO TURN THE LIGHTS OUT!!-JUST THINK, GIRLS—IF THERE REALLY WAS ANYTHING TO THAT SILLY OLD SUPERSTITION- ONE OF US WILL BE MURDERED!!!
Copr. 1942 by United Feature Syndicate, Inc. Tm. Reg. U. S. Pat. Off.—All rights reserved
Al Capp

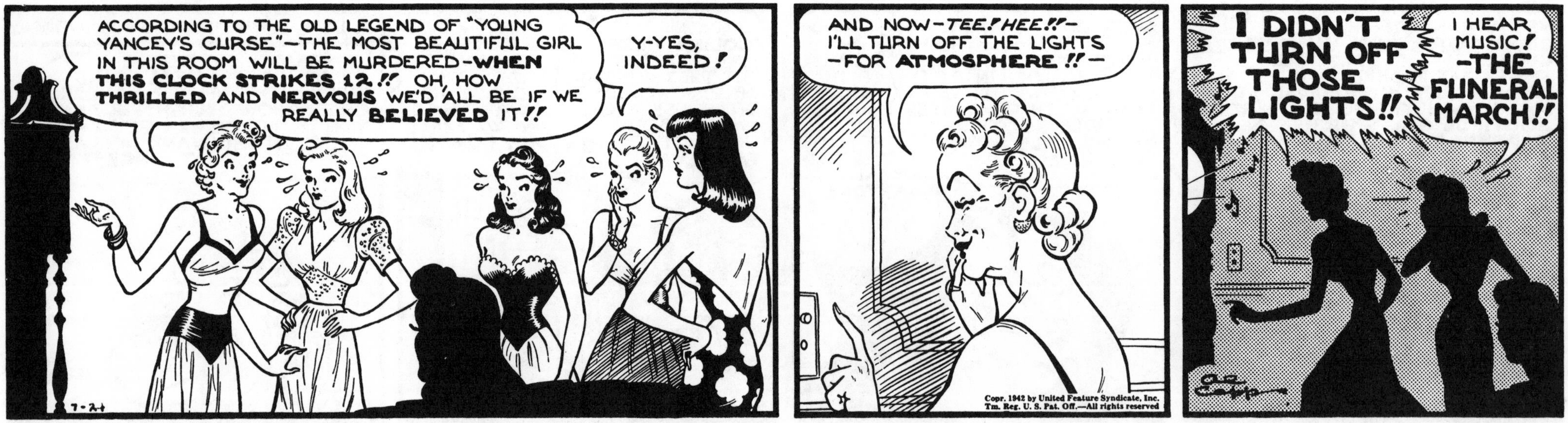
ACCORDING TO THE OLD LEGEND OF "YOUNG YANCEY'S CURSE"—THE MOST BEAUTIFUL GIRL IN THIS ROOM WILL BE MURDERED-WHEN THIS CLOCK STRIKES 12!! OH, HOW THRILLED AND NERVOUS WE'D ALL BE IF WE REALLY BELIEVED IT!!
Y-YES, INDEED!
7-24
AND NOW-TEE! HEE!!- I'LL TURN OFF THE LIGHTS -FOR ATMOSPHERE!!-
Copr. 1942 by United Feature Syndicate, Inc. Tm. Reg. U. S. Pat. Off.—All rights reserved
I DIDN'T TURN OFF THOSE LIGHTS!!
I HEAR MUSIC! -THE FUNERAL MARCH!!
Al Capp

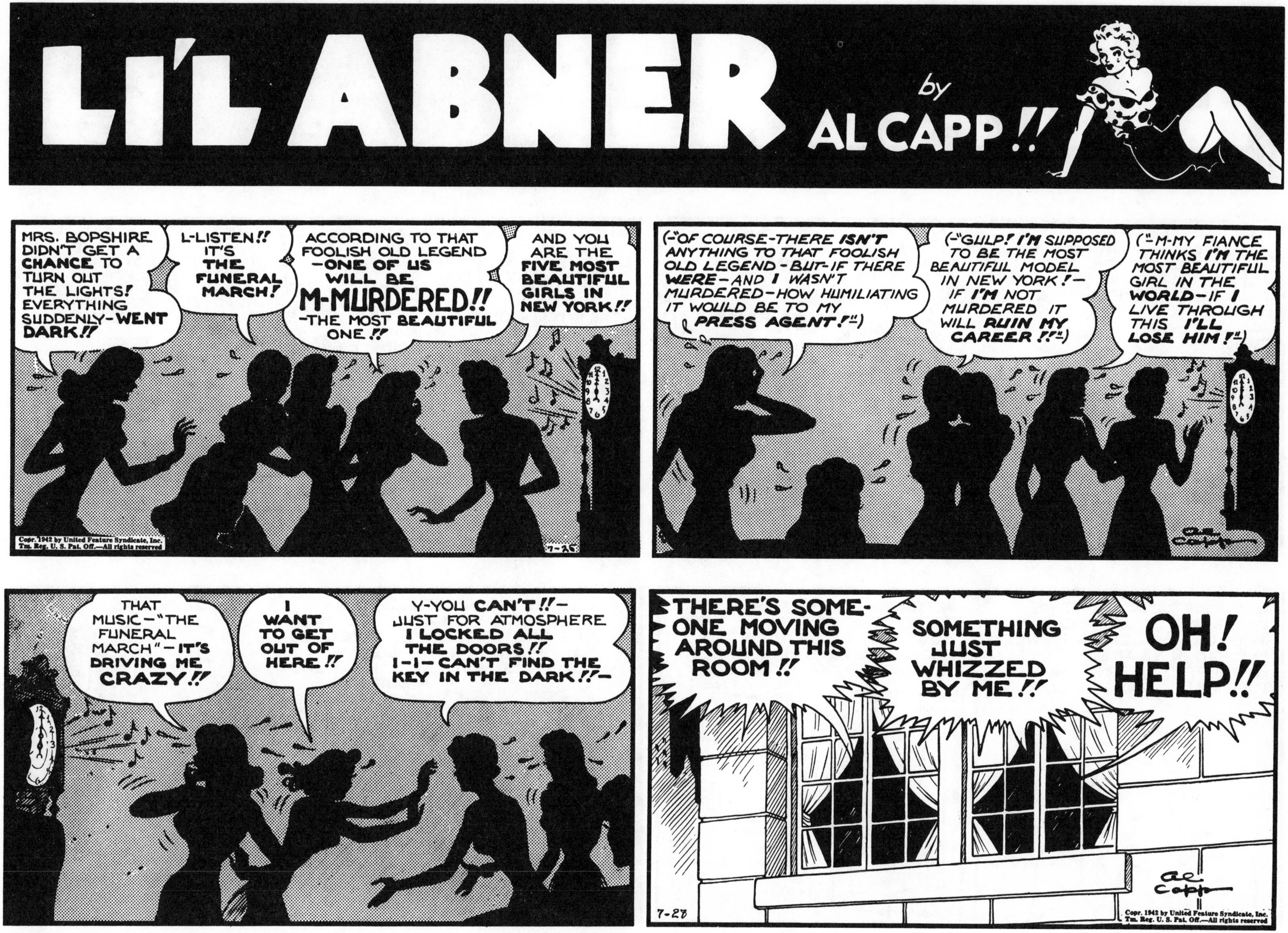
LI'L ABNER
by AL CAPP!!
MRS. BOPSHIRE DIDN'T GET A CHANCE TO TURN OUT THE LIGHTS! EVERYTHING SUDDENLY-WENT DARK!!
L-LISTEN!! IT'S THE FUNERAL MARCH!
ACCORDING TO THAT FOOLISH OLD LEGEND -ONE OF US WILL BE M-MURDERED!! -THE MOST BEAUTIFUL ONE!!
AND YOU ARE THE FIVE MOST BEAUTIFUL GIRLS IN NEW YORK!!
Copr. 1942 by United Feature Syndicate, Inc. Tm. Reg. U. S. Pat. Off.—All rights reserved
(-"OF COURSE-THERE ISN'T ANYTHING TO THAT FOOLISH OLD LEGEND-BUT-IF THERE WERE-AND I WASN'T MURDERED-HOW HUMILIATING IT WOULD BE TO MY PRESS AGENT!"-)
(-"GULP! I'M SUPPOSED TO BE THE MOST BEAUTIFUL MODEL IN NEW YORK!-IF I'M NOT MURDERED IT WILL RUIN MY CAREER!!"-)
("-M-MY FIANCE THINKS I'M THE MOST BEAUTIFUL GIRL IN THE WORLD-IF I LIVE THROUGH THIS I'LL LOSE HIM!"-)
THAT MUSIC-"THE FUNERAL MARCH"-IT'S DRIVING ME CRAZY!!
I WANT TO GET OUT OF HERE!!
Y-YOU CAN'T!!-JUST FOR ATMOSPHERE I LOCKED ALL THE DOORS!! I-I-CAN'T FIND THE KEY IN THE DARK!!-
THERE'S SOME-ONE MOVING AROUND THIS ROOM!!
SOMETHING JUST WHIZZED BY ME!!
OH! HELP!!
Copr. 1942 by United Feature Syndicate, Inc. Tm. Reg. U. S. Pat. Off.—All rights reserved

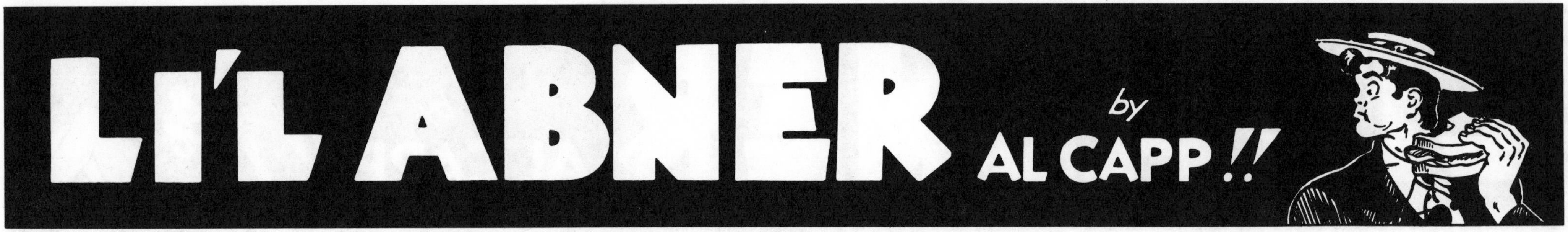
LI'L ABNER
by AL CAPP!!

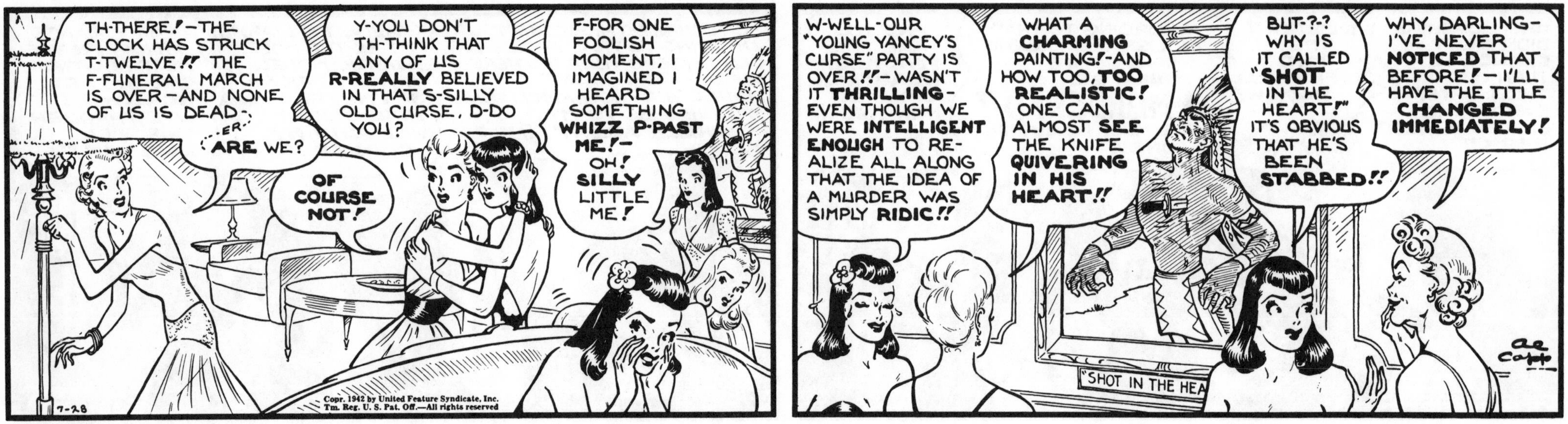
TH-THERE!-THE CLOCK HAS STRUCK T-TWELVE!! THE F-FUNERAL MARCH IS OVER-AND NONE OF US IS DEAD- -ER- ARE WE?
Y-YOU DON'T TH-THINK THAT ANY OF US R-REALLY BELIEVED IN THAT S-SILLY OLD CURSE, D-DO YOU?
OF COURSE NOT!
F-FOR ONE FOOLISH MOMENT, I IMAGINED I HEARD SOMETHING WHIZZ P-PAST ME!-OH! SILLY LITTLE ME!
7-28
Copr. 1942 by United Feature Syndicate, Inc. Tm. Reg. U. S. Pat. Off.—All rights reserved
W-WELL-OUR "YOUNG YANCEY'S CURSE" PARTY IS OVER!!-WASN'T IT THRILLING-EVEN THOUGH WE WERE INTELLIGENT ENOUGH TO RE-ALIZE ALL ALONG THAT THE IDEA OF A MURDER WAS SIMPLY RIDIC!!
WHAT A CHARMING PAINTING!-AND HOW TOO, TOO REALISTIC! ONE CAN ALMOST SEE THE KNIFE QUIVERING IN HIS HEART!!
BUT-?-? WHY IS IT CALLED "SHOT IN THE HEART!" IT'S OBVIOUS THAT HE'S BEEN STABBED!!
WHY, DARLING-I'VE NEVER NOTICED THAT BEFORE!-I'LL HAVE THE TITLE CHANGED IMMEDIATELY!
"SHOT IN THE HEA
AL CAPP

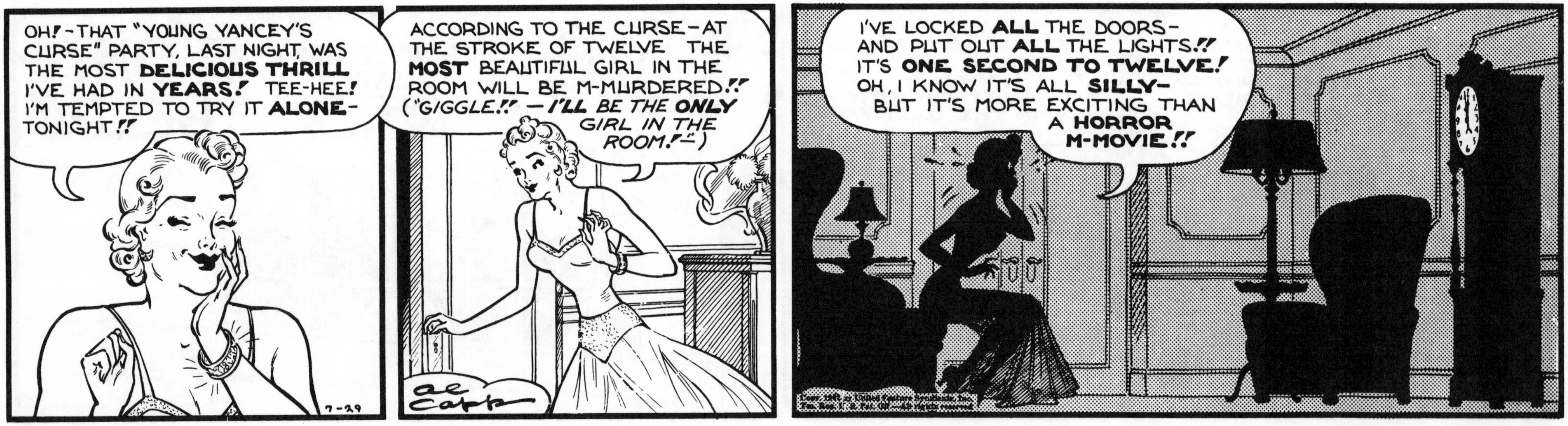
OH!-THAT "YOUNG YANCEY'S CURSE" PARTY, LAST NIGHT, WAS THE MOST DELICIOUS THRILL I'VE HAD IN YEARS! TEE-HEE! I'M TEMPTED TO TRY IT ALONE-TONIGHT!!
7-29
ACCORDING TO THE CURSE-AT THE STROKE OF TWELVE THE MOST BEAUTIFUL GIRL IN THE ROOM WILL BE M-MURDERED!! ("GIGGLE!!"-I'LL BE THE ONLY GIRL IN THE ROOM!-)
AL CAPP
I'VE LOCKED ALL THE DOORS-AND PUT OUT ALL THE LIGHTS!! IT'S ONE SECOND TO TWELVE! OH, I KNOW IT'S ALL SILLY-BUT IT'S MORE EXCITING THAN A HORROR M-MOVIE!!

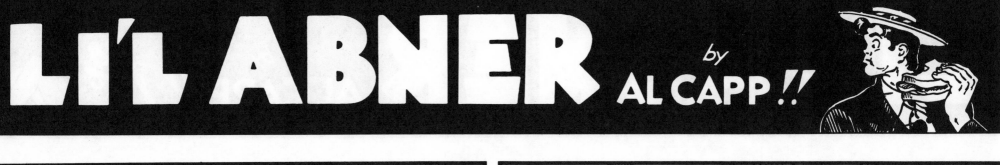

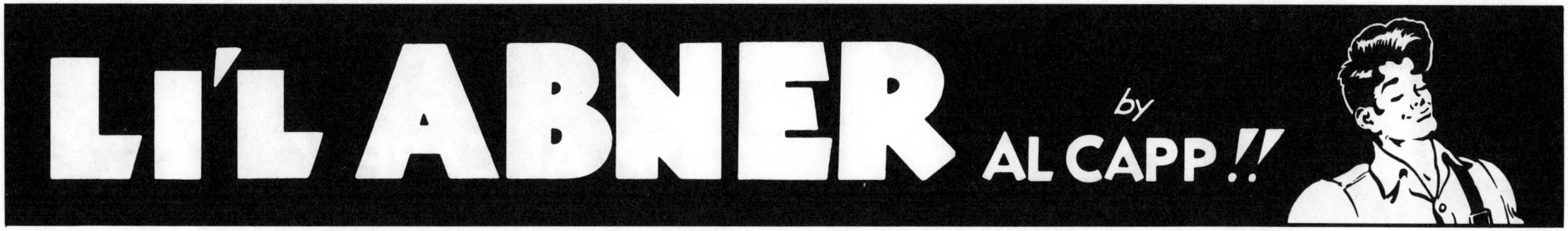
LI'L ABNER
by
AL CAPP!!

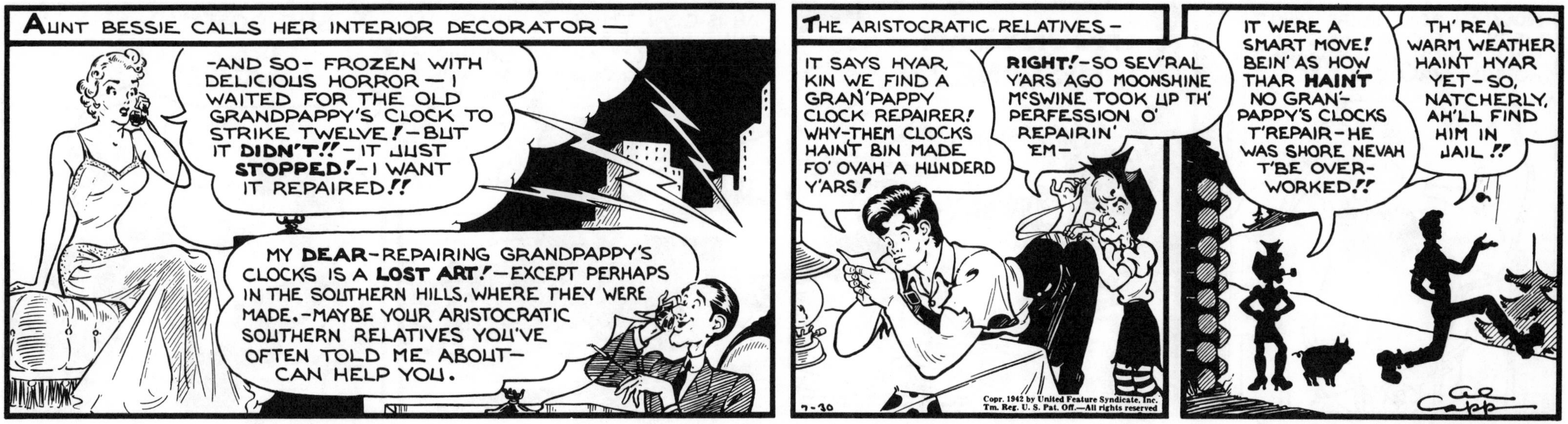
AUNT BESSIE CALLS HER INTERIOR DECORATOR—
-AND SO- FROZEN WITH DELICIOUS HORROR—I WAITED FOR THE OLD GRANDPAPPY'S CLOCK TO STRIKE TWELVE!-BUT IT DIDN'T!!-IT JUST STOPPED!-I WANT IT REPAIRED!!
MY DEAR-REPAIRING GRANDPAPPY'S CLOCKS IS A LOST ART!-EXCEPT PERHAPS IN THE SOUTHERN HILLS, WHERE THEY WERE MADE.-MAYBE YOUR ARISTOCRATIC SOUTHERN RELATIVES YOU'VE OFTEN TOLD ME ABOUT- CAN HELP YOU.
THE ARISTOCRATIC RELATIVES-
IT SAYS HYAR, KIN WE FIND A GRAN'PAPPY CLOCK REPAIRER! WHY-THEM CLOCKS HAIN'T BIN MADE FO' OVAH A HUNDERD Y'ARS!
RIGHT!-SO SEV'RAL Y'ARS AGO MOONSHINE McSWINE TOOK UP TH' PERFESSION O' REPAIRIN' 'EM-
7-30
Copr. 1942 by United Feature Syndicate, Inc. Tm. Reg. U. S. Pat. Off.—All rights reserved
IT WERE A SMART MOVE! BEIN' AS HOW THAR HAIN'T NO GRAN'-PAPPY'S CLOCKS T'REPAIR-HE WAS SHORE NEVAH T'BE OVER-WORKED!!
TH' REAL WARM WEATHER HAIN'T HYAR YET-SO, NATCHERLY, AH'LL FIND HIM IN JAIL!!
Al Capp

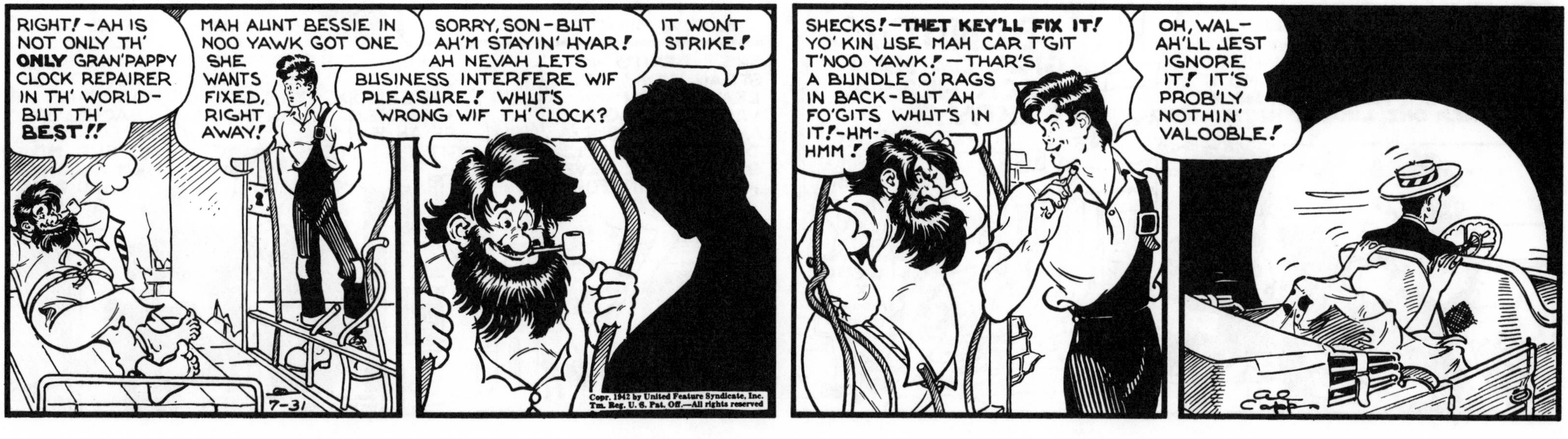
RIGHT!-AH IS NOT ONLY TH' ONLY GRAN'PAPPY CLOCK REPAIRER IN TH' WORLD-BUT TH' BEST!!
MAH AUNT BESSIE IN NOO YAWK GOT ONE SHE WANTS FIXED, RIGHT AWAY!
7-31
SORRY, SON-BUT AH'M STAYIN' HYAR! AH NEVAH LETS BUSINESS INTERFERE WIF PLEASURE! WHUT'S WRONG WIF TH' CLOCK?
IT WON'T STRIKE!
Copr. 1942 by United Feature Syndicate, Inc. Tm. Reg. U. S. Pat. Off.—All rights reserved
SHECKS!-THET KEY'LL FIX IT! YO' KIN USE MAH CAR T'GIT T'NOO YAWK!-THAR'S A BUNDLE O' RAGS IN BACK-BUT AH FO'GITS WHUT'S IN IT!-HM-HMM!
OH, WAL-AH'LL JEST IGNORE IT! IT'S PROB'LY NOTHIN' VALOOBLE!
Al Capp

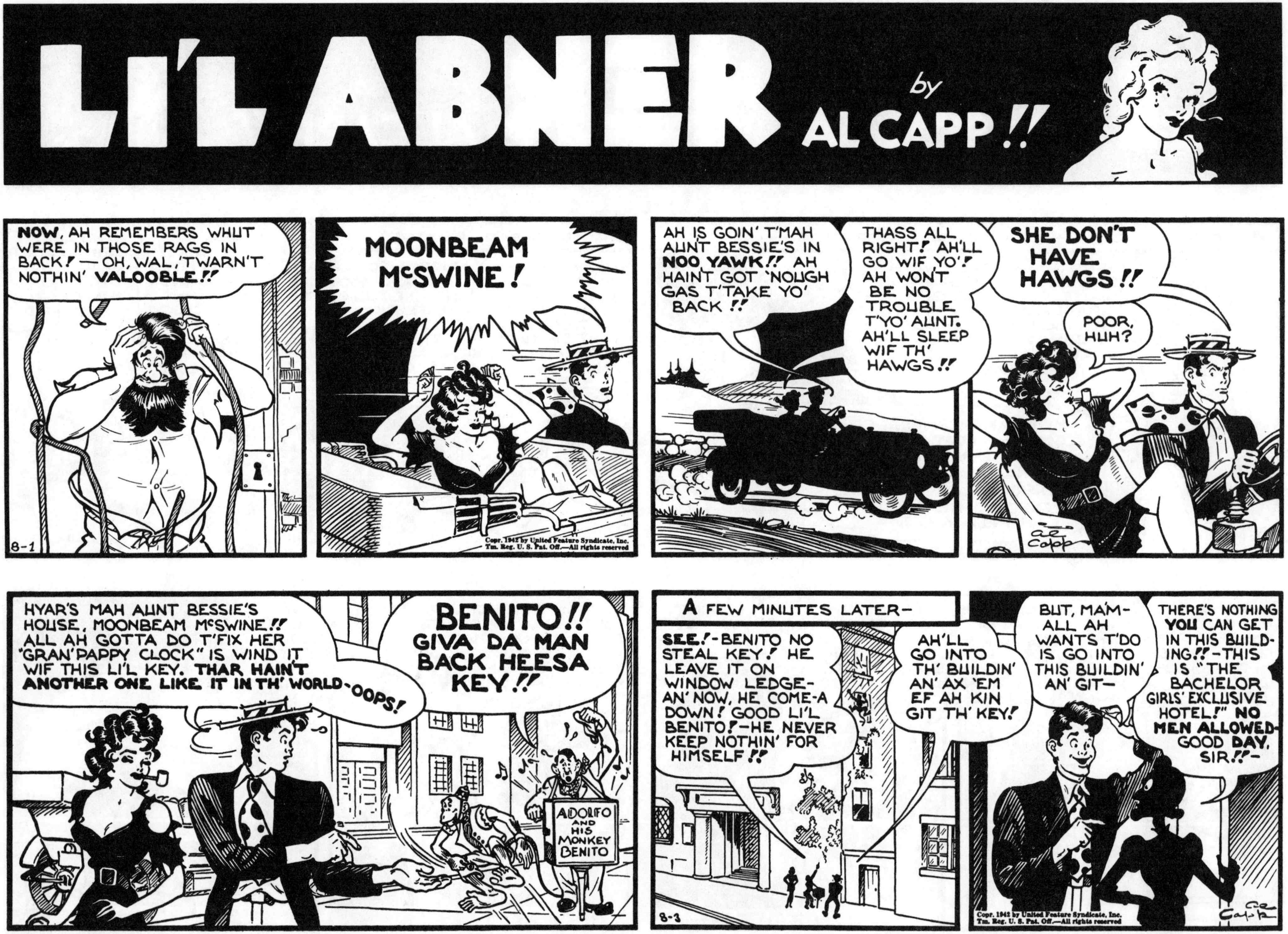
LI'L ABNER
by AL CAPP!!
8-1
NOW, AH REMEMBERS WHUT WERE IN THOSE RAGS IN BACK! —OH, WAL,'TWARN'T NOTHIN' VALOOBLE!!
MOONBEAM McSWINE!
Copr. 1942 by United Feature Syndicate, Inc. Tm. Reg. U. S. Pat. Off.—All rights reserved
AH IS GOIN' T'MAH AUNT BESSIE'S IN NOO YAWK!! AH HAIN'T GOT 'NOUGH GAS T'TAKE YO' BACK!!
THASS ALL RIGHT! AH'LL GO WIF YO'! AH WON'T BE NO TROUBLE T'YO' AUNT. AH'LL SLEEP WIF TH' HAWGS!!
SHE DON'T HAVE HAWGS!!
POOR, HUH?
HYAR'S MAH AUNT BESSIE'S HOUSE, MOONBEAM McSWINE!! ALL AH GOTTA DO T'FIX HER "GRAN'PAPPY CLOCK" IS WIND IT WIF THIS LI'L KEY. THAR HAIN'T ANOTHER ONE LIKE IT IN TH' WORLD-OOPS!
BENITO!! GIVA DA MAN BACK HEESA KEY!!
ADOLFO AND HIS MONKEY BENITO
8-3
A FEW MINUTES LATER—
SEE!-BENITO NO STEAL KEY! HE LEAVE IT ON WINDOW LEDGE-AN' NOW, HE COME-A DOWN! GOOD LI'L BENITO!-HE NEVER KEEP NOTHIN' FOR HIMSELF!!
AH'LL GO INTO TH' BUILDIN' AN' AX 'EM EF AH KIN GIT TH' KEY!
BUT, MA'M-ALL AH WANTS T'DO IS GO INTO THIS BUILDIN' AN' GIT—
THERE'S NOTHING YOU CAN GET IN THIS BUILDING!!-THIS IS "THE BACHELOR GIRLS' EXCLUSIVE HOTEL!" NO MEN ALLOWED-GOOD DAY, SIR!!-
Copr. 1942 by United Feature Syndicate, Inc. Tm. Reg. U. S. Pat. Off.—All rights reserved

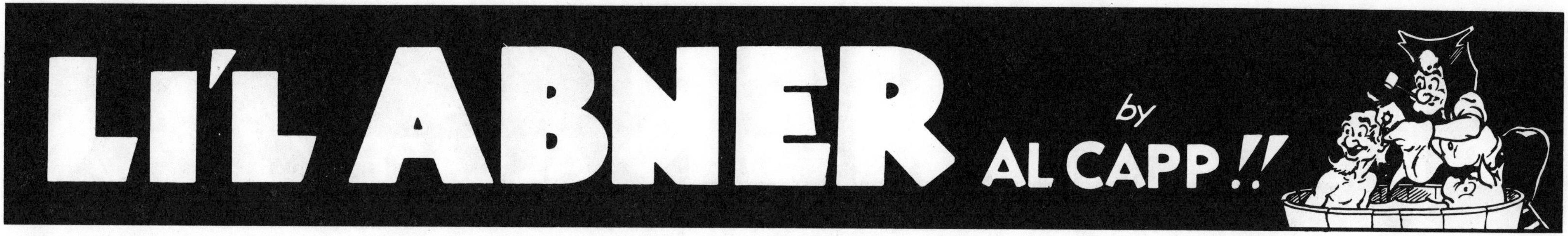
LI'L ABNER
by
AL CAPP!!

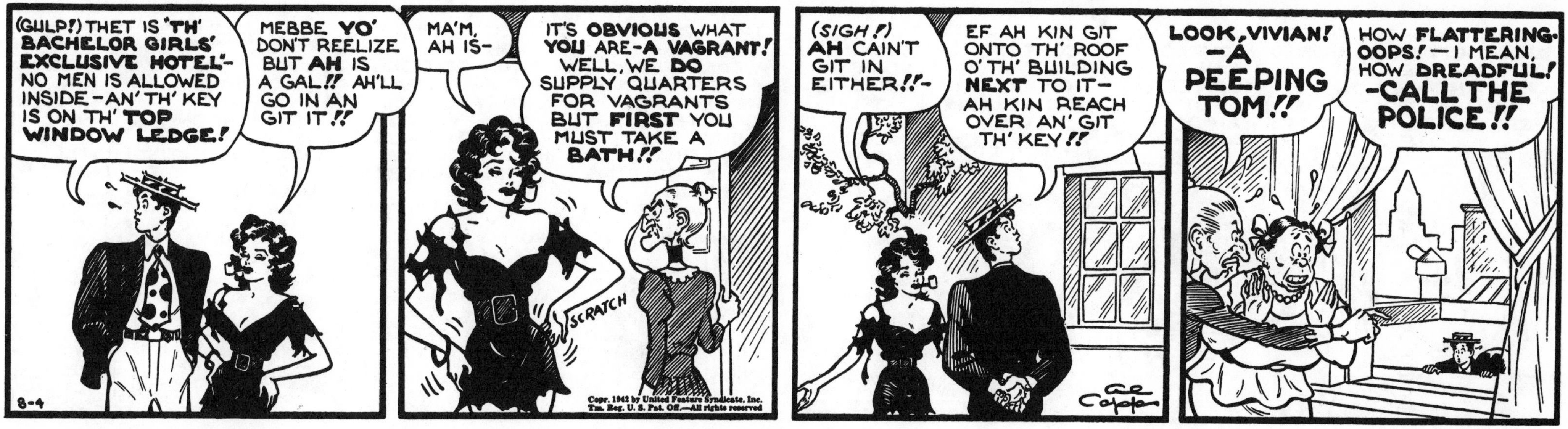
(GULP!) THET IS 'TH' BACHELOR GIRLS' EXCLUSIVE HOTEL'- NO MEN IS ALLOWED INSIDE-AN' TH' KEY IS ON TH' TOP WINDOW LEDGE!
MEBBE YO' DON'T REELIZE BUT AH IS A GAL!! AH'LL GO IN AN GIT IT!!
8-4
MA'M, AH IS-
IT'S OBVIOUS WHAT YOU ARE-A VAGRANT! WELL, WE DO SUPPLY QUARTERS FOR VAGRANTS BUT FIRST YOU MUST TAKE A BATH!!
SCRATCH
Copr. 1942 by United Feature Syndicate, Inc. Tm. Reg. U. S. Pat. Off.—All rights reserved
(SIGH!) AH CAIN'T GIT IN EITHER!!-
EF AH KIN GIT ONTO TH' ROOF O'TH' BUILDING NEXT TO IT- AH KIN REACH OVER AN' GIT TH' KEY!!
LOOK, VIVIAN! -A PEEPING TOM!!
HOW FLATTERING- OOPS!-I MEAN, HOW DREADFUL! -CALL THE POLICE!!

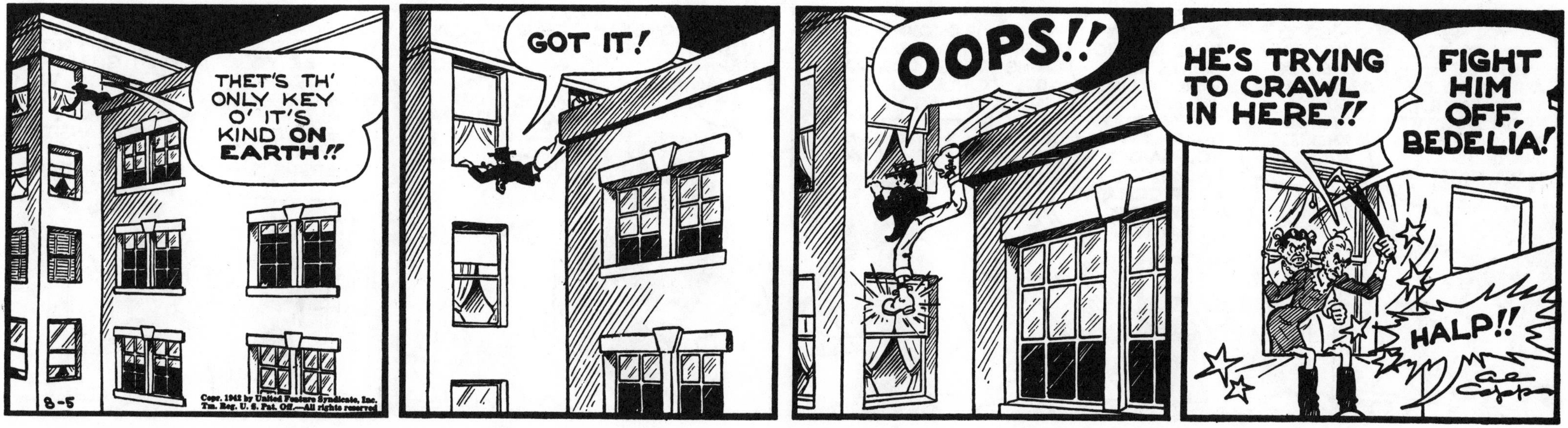
THET'S TH' ONLY KEY O' IT'S KIND ON EARTH!!
8-5
Copr. 1942 by United Feature Syndicate, Inc. Tm. Reg. U. S. Pat. Off.—All rights reserved
GOT IT!
OOPS!!
HE'S TRYING TO CRAWL IN HERE!!
FIGHT HIM OFF, BEDELIA!
HALP!!

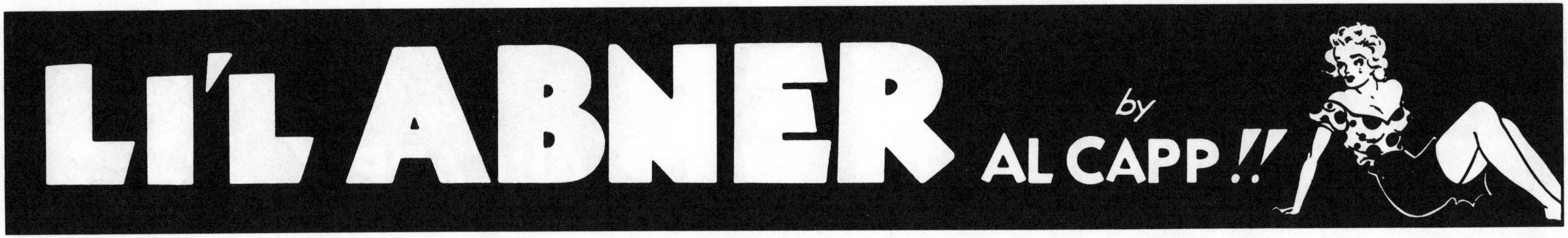
LI'L ABNER
by
AL CAPP!!

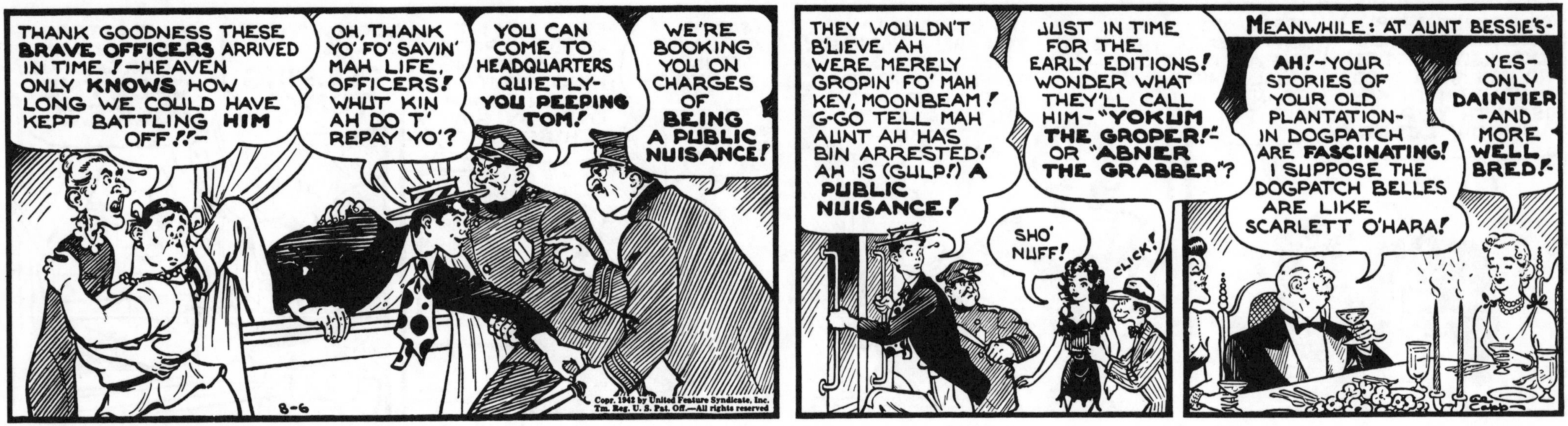
THANK GOODNESS THESE BRAVE OFFICERS ARRIVED IN TIME! —HEAVEN ONLY KNOWS HOW LONG WE COULD HAVE KEPT BATTLING HIM OFF!!—
OH, THANK YO' FO' SAVIN' MAH LIFE, OFFICERS! WHUT KIN AH DO T' REPAY YO'?
YOU CAN COME TO HEADQUARTERS QUIETLY- YOU PEEPING TOM!
WE'RE BOOKING YOU ON CHARGES OF BEING A PUBLIC NUISANCE!
8-6
Copr. 1942 by United Feature Syndicate, Inc. Tm. Reg. U. S. Pat. Off.—All rights reserved
THEY WOULDN'T B'LIEVE AH WERE MERELY GROPIN' FO' MAH KEY, MOONBEAM! G-GO TELL MAH AUNT AH HAS BIN ARRESTED! AH IS (GULP!) A PUBLIC NUISANCE!
JUST IN TIME FOR THE EARLY EDITIONS! WONDER WHAT THEY'LL CALL HIM—"YOKUM THE GROPER!"— OR "ABNER THE GRABBER"?
SHO' NUFF!
CLICK!
MEANWHILE: AT AUNT BESSIE'S-
AH!—YOUR STORIES OF YOUR OLD PLANTATION- IN DOGPATCH ARE FASCINATING! I SUPPOSE THE DOGPATCH BELLES ARE LIKE SCARLETT O'HARA!
YES- ONLY DAINTIER -AND MORE WELL BRED!-

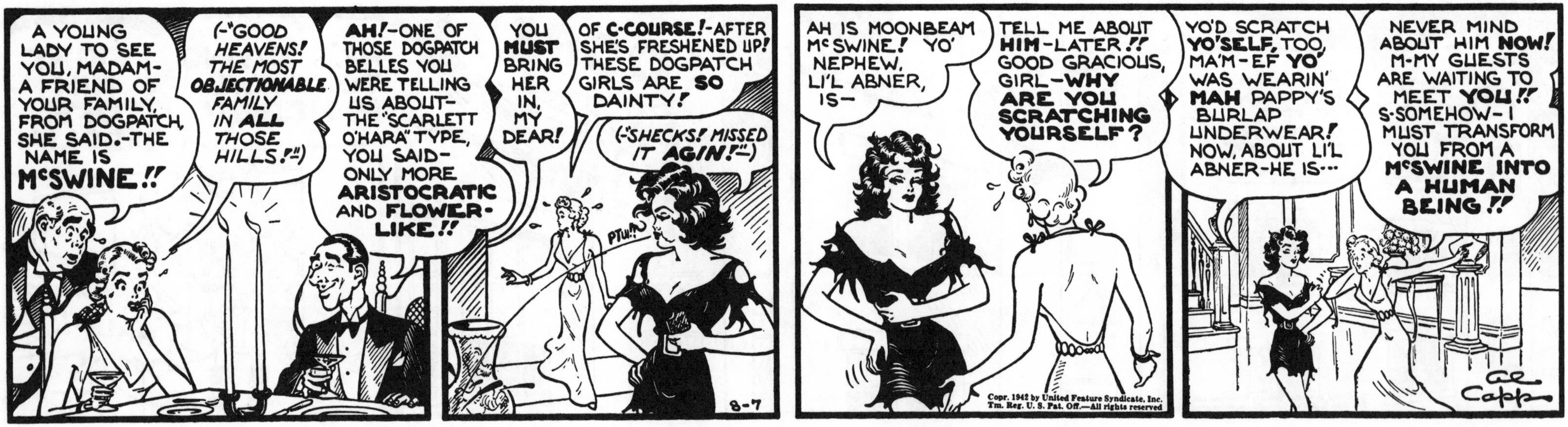
A YOUNG LADY TO SEE YOU, MADAM- A FRIEND OF YOUR FAMILY, FROM DOGPATCH, SHE SAID.-THE NAME IS McSWINE!!
(-"GOOD HEAVENS! THE MOST OBJECTIONABLE FAMILY IN ALL THOSE HILLS!"-)
AH!—ONE OF THOSE DOGPATCH BELLES YOU WERE TELLING US ABOUT— THE "SCARLETT O'HARA" TYPE, YOU SAID- ONLY MORE ARISTOCRATIC AND FLOWER-LIKE!!
YOU MUST BRING HER IN, MY DEAR!
OF C-COURSE!—AFTER SHE'S FRESHENED UP! THESE DOGPATCH GIRLS ARE SO DAINTY!
(-"SHECKS! MISSED IT AGIN!"-)
PTUI!!
8-7
AH IS MOONBEAM McSWINE! YO' NEPHEW, LI'L ABNER, IS—
TELL ME ABOUT HIM—LATER!! GOOD GRACIOUS, GIRL—WHY ARE YOU SCRATCHING YOURSELF?
Copr. 1942 by United Feature Syndicate, Inc. Tm. Reg. U. S. Pat. Off.—All rights reserved
YO'D SCRATCH YO'SELF, TOO, MA'M—EF YO' WAS WEARIN' MAH PAPPY'S BURLAP UNDERWEAR! NOW, ABOUT LI'L ABNER—HE IS···
NEVER MIND ABOUT HIM NOW! M-MY GUESTS ARE WAITING TO MEET YOU!! S-SOMEHOW—I MUST TRANSFORM YOU FROM A McSWINE INTO A HUMAN BEING!!
Al Capp

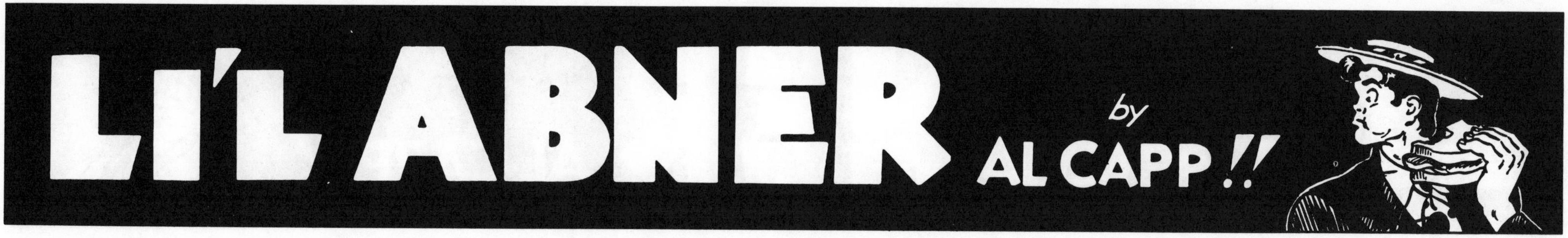
LI'L ABNER
by
AL CAPP!!

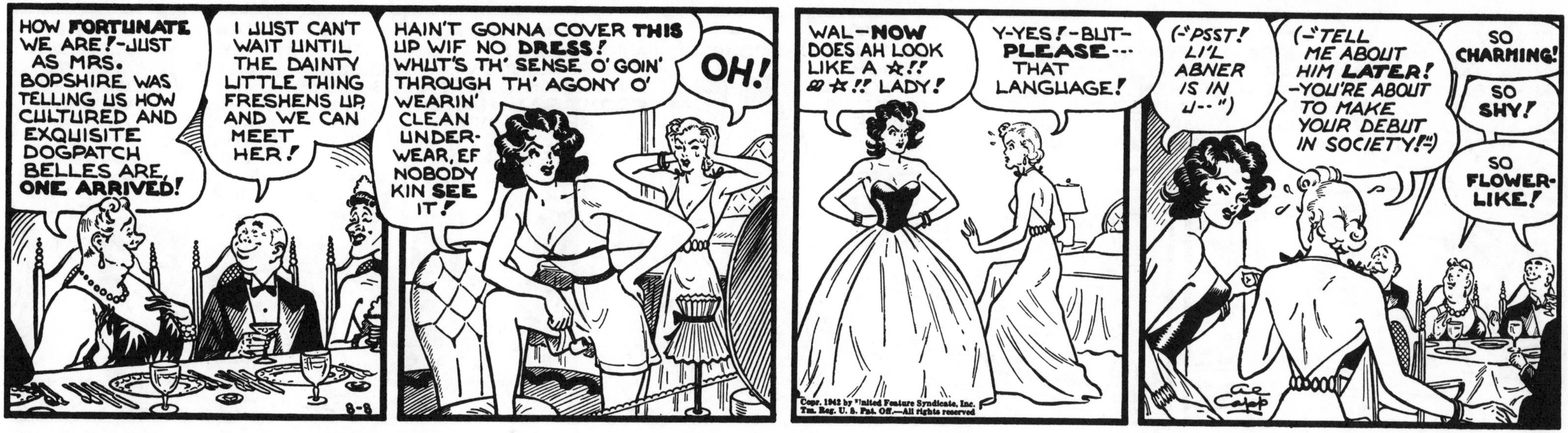
HOW FORTUNATE WE ARE!-JUST AS MRS. BOPSHIRE WAS TELLING US HOW CULTURED AND EXQUISITE DOGPATCH BELLES ARE, ONE ARRIVED!
I JUST CAN'T WAIT UNTIL THE DAINTY LITTLE THING FRESHENS UP, AND WE CAN MEET HER!
8-8
HAIN'T GONNA COVER THIS UP WIF NO DRESS! WHUT'S TH' SENSE O' GOIN' THROUGH TH' AGONY O' WEARIN' CLEAN UNDER-WEAR, EF NOBODY KIN SEE IT!
OH!
WAL—NOW DOES AH LOOK LIKE A ☆!! @☆!! LADY!
Y-YES!-BUT-PLEASE--- THAT LANGUAGE!
Copr. 1942 by United Feature Syndicate, Inc. Tm. Reg. U. S. Pat. Off.—All rights reserved
(-"PSST! LI'L ABNER IS IN J--")
(-"TELL ME ABOUT HIM LATER! -YOU'RE ABOUT TO MAKE YOUR DEBUT IN SOCIETY!"-)
SO CHARMING!
SO SHY!
SO FLOWER-LIKE!
AL CAPP

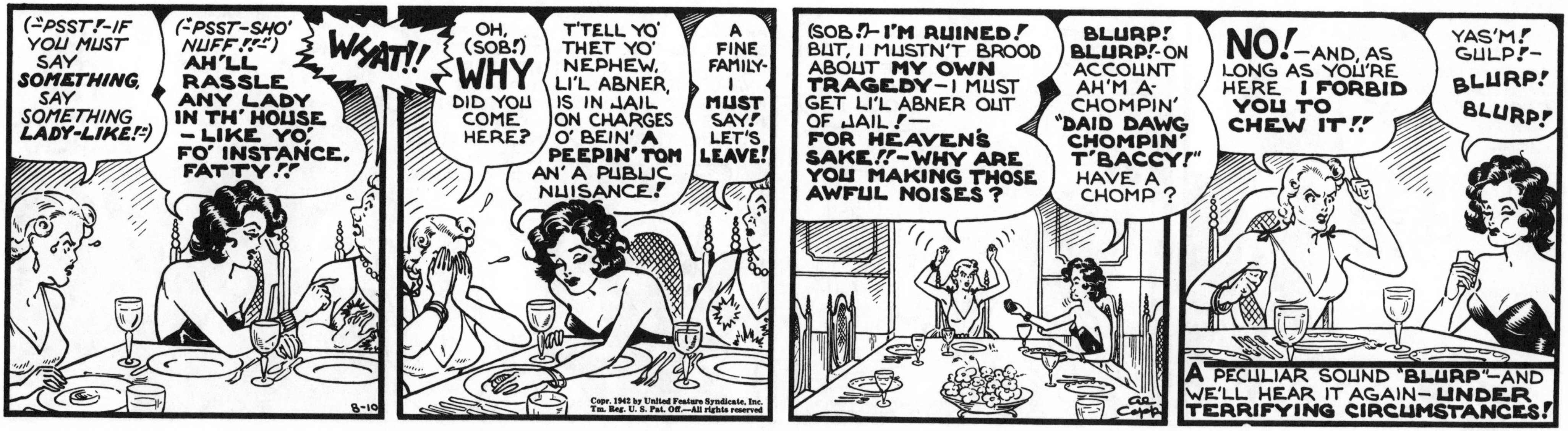
(-"PSST!-IF YOU MUST SAY SOMETHING, SAY SOMETHING LADY-LIKE!"-)
(-"PSST-SHO' NUFF!!"-) AH'LL RASSLE ANY LADY IN TH' HOUSE -LIKE YO', FO' INSTANCE, FATTY!!
WHAT!!
8-10
OH, (SOB!) WHY DID YOU COME HERE?
T'TELL YO' THET YO' NEPHEW, LI'L ABNER, IS IN JAIL ON CHARGES O' BEIN' A PEEPIN' TOM AN' A PUBLIC NUISANCE!
A FINE FAMILY-I MUST SAY! LET'S LEAVE!
Copr. 1942 by United Feature Syndicate, Inc. Tm. Reg. U. S. Pat. Off.—All rights reserved
(SOB!)-I'M RUINED! BUT, I MUSTN'T BROOD ABOUT MY OWN TRAGEDY-I MUST GET LI'L ABNER OUT OF JAIL!— FOR HEAVEN'S SAKE!!-WHY ARE YOU MAKING THOSE AWFUL NOISES?
BLURP! BLURP!-ON ACCOUNT AH'M A-CHOMPIN' "DAID DAWG CHOMPIN' T'BACCY!" HAVE A CHOMP?
AL CAPP
NO!—AND, AS LONG AS YOU'RE HERE I FORBID YOU TO CHEW IT!!
YAS'M! GULP!- BLURP! BLURP!
A PECULIAR SOUND "BLURP"—AND WE'LL HEAR IT AGAIN—UNDER TERRIFYING CIRCUMSTANCES!

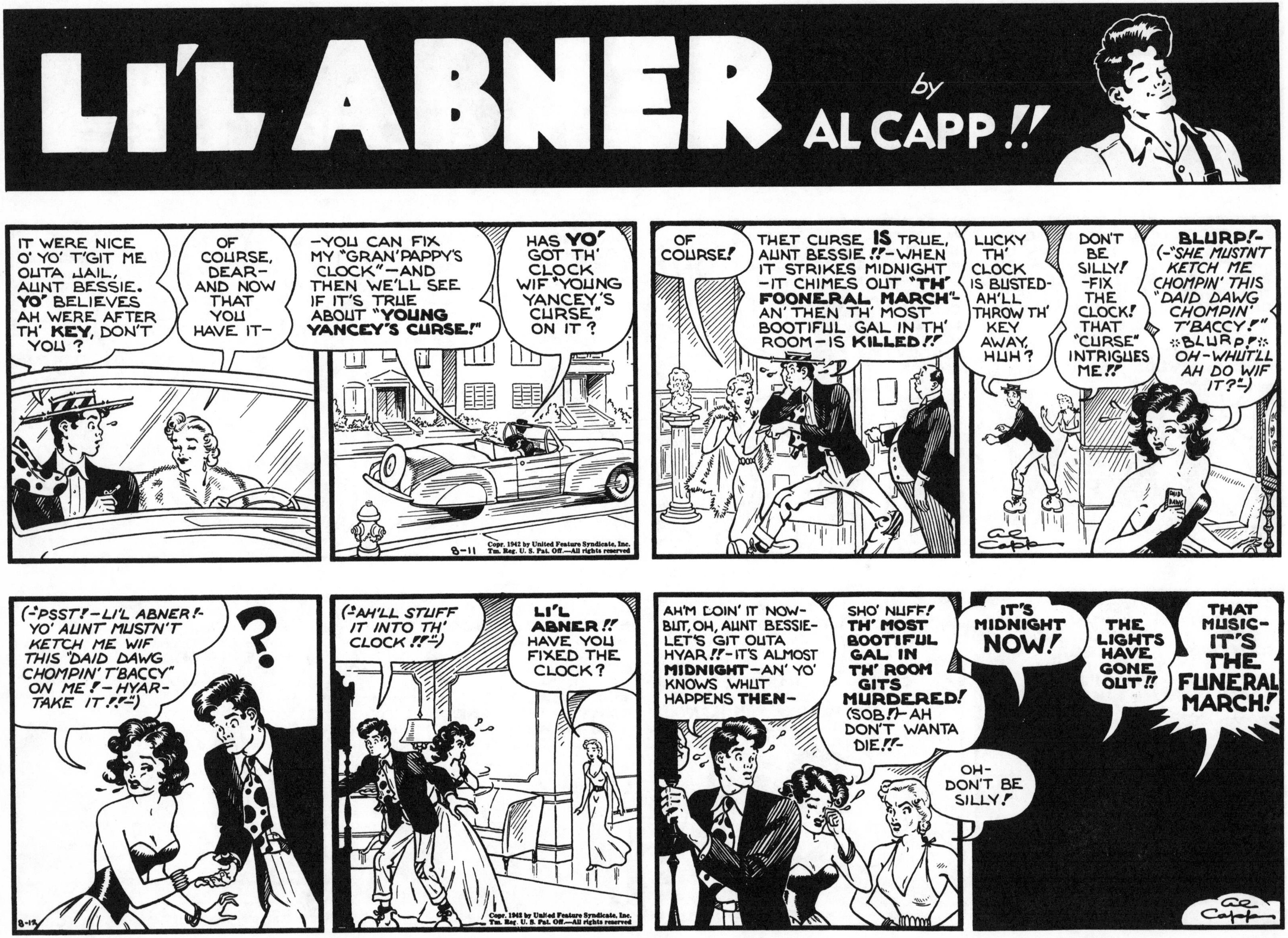
LI'L ABNER
by AL CAPP!!
IT WERE NICE O' YO' T'GIT ME OUTA JAIL, AUNT BESSIE. YO' BELIEVES AH WERE AFTER TH' KEY, DON'T YOU?
OF COURSE, DEAR- AND NOW THAT YOU HAVE IT-
-YOU CAN FIX MY "GRAN'PAPPY'S CLOCK"-AND THEN WE'LL SEE IF IT'S TRUE ABOUT "YOUNG YANCEY'S CURSE!"
HAS YO' GOT TH' CLOCK WIF "YOUNG YANCEY'S CURSE" ON IT?
8-11
Copr. 1942 by United Feature Syndicate, Inc. Tm. Reg. U. S. Pat. Off.—All rights reserved
OF COURSE!
THET CURSE IS TRUE, AUNT BESSIE!!-WHEN IT STRIKES MIDNIGHT-IT CHIMES OUT "TH' FOONERAL MARCH"-AN' THEN TH' MOST BOOTIFUL GAL IN TH' ROOM-IS KILLED!!
LUCKY TH' CLOCK IS BUSTED-AH'LL THROW TH' KEY AWAY, HUH?
DON'T BE SILLY! -FIX THE CLOCK! THAT "CURSE" INTRIGUES ME!!
BLURP!-(-"SHE MUSTN'T KETCH ME CHOMPIN' THIS "DAID DAWG CHOMPIN' T'BACCY!" *BLURP!* OH-WHUT'LL AH DO WIF IT?"-)
DAID DAWG
Al Capp
(-"PSST!-LI'L ABNER!-YO' AUNT MUSTN'T KETCH ME WIF THIS "DAID DAWG CHOMPIN' T'BACCY" ON ME!-HYAR-TAKE IT!!"-)
?
8-12
(-"AH'LL STUFF IT INTO TH' CLOCK!!"-)
LI'L ABNER!! HAVE YOU FIXED THE CLOCK?
Copr. 1942 by United Feature Syndicate, Inc. Tm. Reg. U. S. Pat. Off.—All rights reserved
AH'M DOIN' IT NOW-BUT, OH, AUNT BESSIE-LET'S GIT OUTA HYAR!!-IT'S ALMOST MIDNIGHT-AN' YO' KNOWS WHUT HAPPENS THEN-
SHO' NUFF! TH' MOST BOOTIFUL GAL IN TH' ROOM GITS MURDERED! (SOB!)-AH DON'T WANTA DIE!!-
OH-DON'T BE SILLY!
IT'S MIDNIGHT NOW!
THE LIGHTS HAVE GONE OUT!!
THAT MUSIC-IT'S THE FUNERAL MARCH!
Al Capp

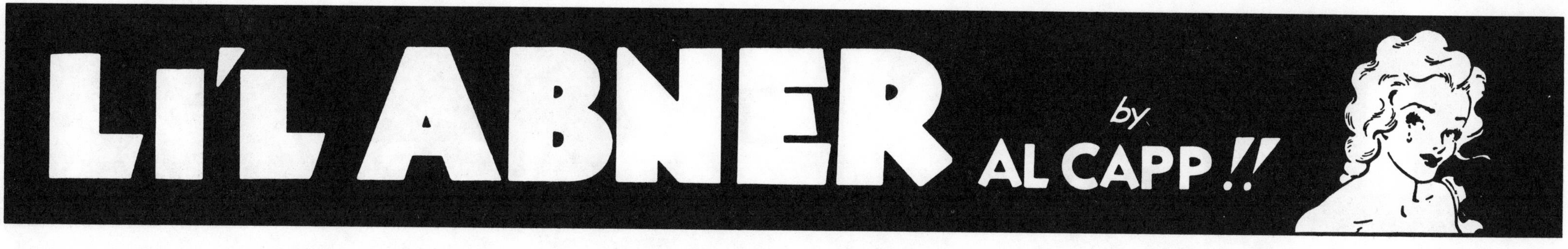
LI'L ABNER
by AL CAPP!!

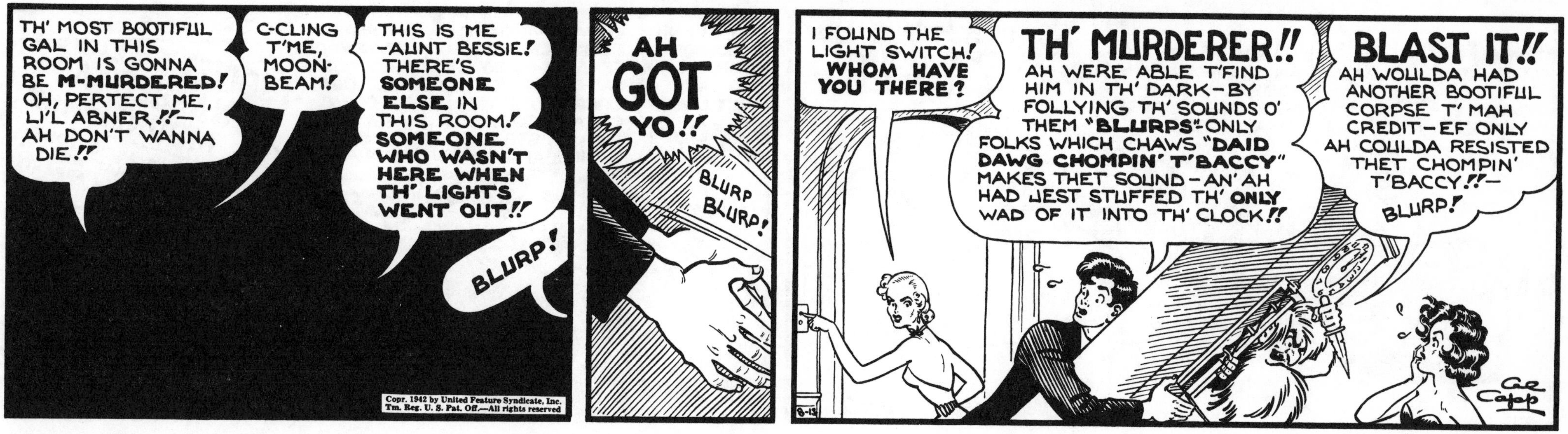
TH' MOST BOOTIFUL GAL IN THIS ROOM IS GONNA BE M-MURDERED! OH, PERFECT ME, LI'L ABNER!!— AH DON'T WANNA DIE!!
C-CLING T'ME, MOON-BEAM!
THIS IS ME -AUNT BESSIE! THERE'S SOMEONE ELSE IN THIS ROOM! SOMEONE WHO WASN'T HERE WHEN TH' LIGHTS WENT OUT!!
BLURP!
Copr. 1942 by United Feature Syndicate, Inc. Tm. Reg. U. S. Pat. Off.—All rights reserved
AH GOT YO!!
BLURP BLURP!
I FOUND THE LIGHT SWITCH! WHOM HAVE YOU THERE?
TH' MURDERER!! AH WERE ABLE T'FIND HIM IN TH' DARK—BY FOLLYING TH' SOUNDS O' THEM "BLURPS"-ONLY FOLKS WHICH CHAWS "DAID DAWG CHOMPIN' T'BACCY" MAKES THET SOUND—AN' AH HAD JEST STUFFED TH' ONLY WAD OF IT INTO TH' CLOCK!!
BLAST IT!! AH WOULDA HAD ANOTHER BOOTIFUL CORPSE T' MAH CREDIT—EF ONLY AH COULDA RESISTED THET CHOMPIN' T'BACCY!!— BLURP!
8-13
Al Capp

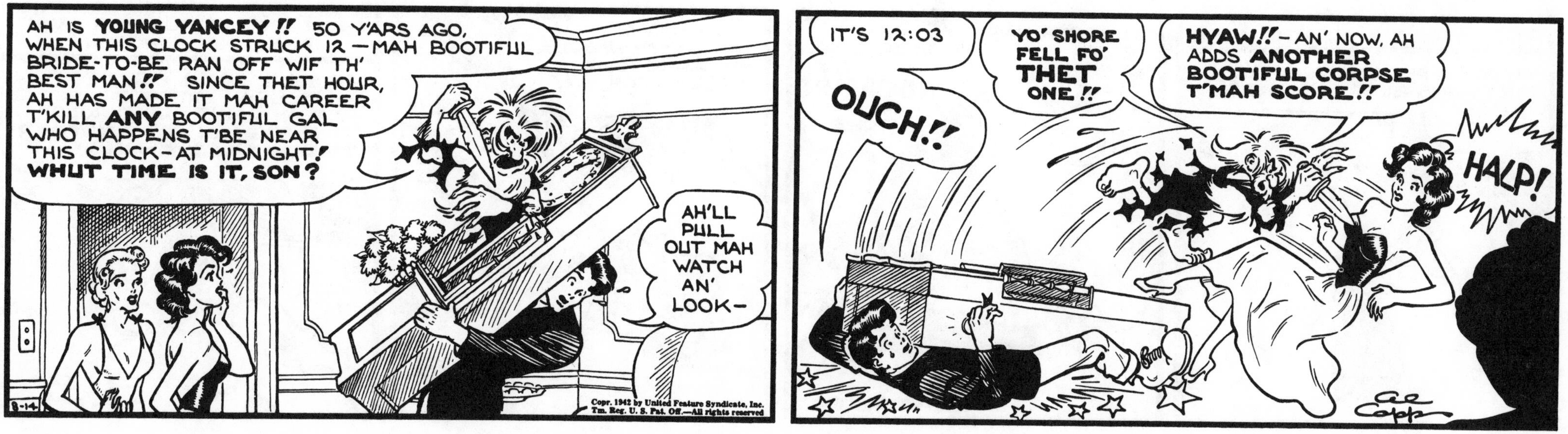
AH IS YOUNG YANCEY!! 50 Y'ARS AGO, WHEN THIS CLOCK STRUCK 12—MAH BOOTIFUL BRIDE-TO-BE RAN OFF WIF TH' BEST MAN!! SINCE THET HOUR, AH HAS MADE IT MAH CAREER T'KILL ANY BOOTIFUL GAL WHO HAPPENS T'BE NEAR THIS CLOCK-AT MIDNIGHT! WHUT TIME IS IT, SON?
AH'LL PULL OUT MAH WATCH AN' LOOK—
8-14
Copr. 1942 by United Feature Syndicate, Inc. Tm. Reg. U. S. Pat. Off.—All rights reserved
IT'S 12:03
OUCH!!
YO' SHORE FELL FO' THET ONE!!
HYAW!!—AN' NOW, AH ADDS ANOTHER BOOTIFUL CORPSE T'MAH SCORE!!
HALP!
Al Capp

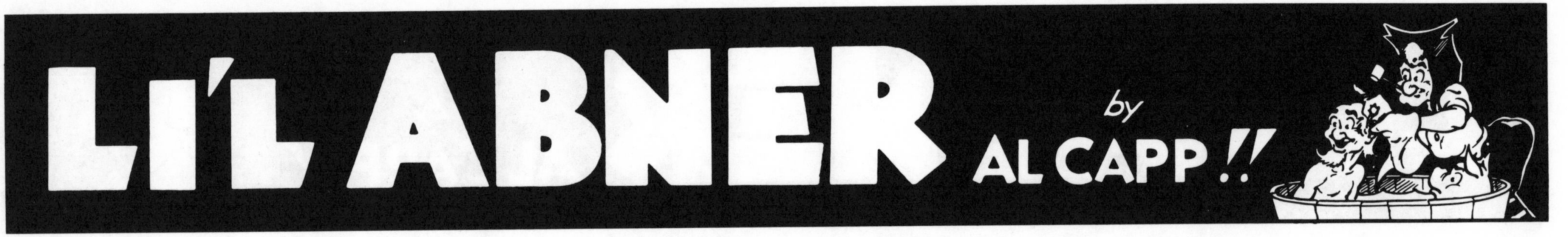
LI'L ABNER
by
AL CAPP!!

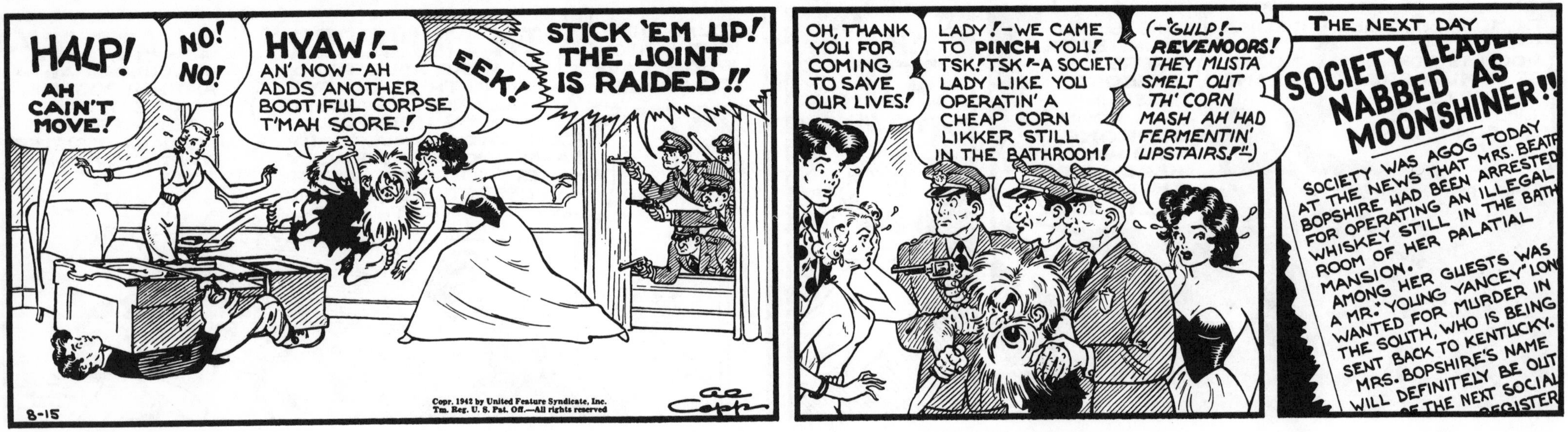
HALP!
AH CAIN'T MOVE!
NO! NO!
HYAW!— AN' NOW—AH ADDS ANOTHER BOOTIFUL CORPSE T'MAH SCORE!
EEK!
STICK 'EM UP! THE JOINT IS RAIDED!!
8-15
Copr. 1942 by United Feature Syndicate, Inc.
Tm. Reg. U. S. Pat. Off.—All rights reserved
OH, THANK YOU FOR COMING TO SAVE OUR LIVES!
LADY!—WE CAME TO PINCH YOU! TSK! TSK!—A SOCIETY LADY LIKE YOU OPERATIN' A CHEAP CORN LIKKER STILL IN THE BATHROOM!
(—"GULP!— REVENOORS! THEY MUSTA SMELT OUT TH' CORN MASH AH HAD FERMENTIN' UPSTAIRS!"—)
THE NEXT DAY
NABBED AS MOONSHINER!!
SOCIETY WAS AGOG TODAY AT THE NEWS THAT MRS. BEATR BOPSHIRE HAD BEEN ARRESTED FOR OPERATING AN ILLEGAL WHISKEY STILL IN THE BATH ROOM OF HER PALATIAL MANSION.
AMONG HER GUESTS WAS A MR. "YOUNG YANCEY" LON WANTED FOR MURDER IN THE SOUTH, WHO IS BEING SENT BACK TO KENTUCKY.
MRS. BOPSHIRE'S NAME WILL DEFINITELY BE OUT OF THE NEXT SOCIAL REGISTER

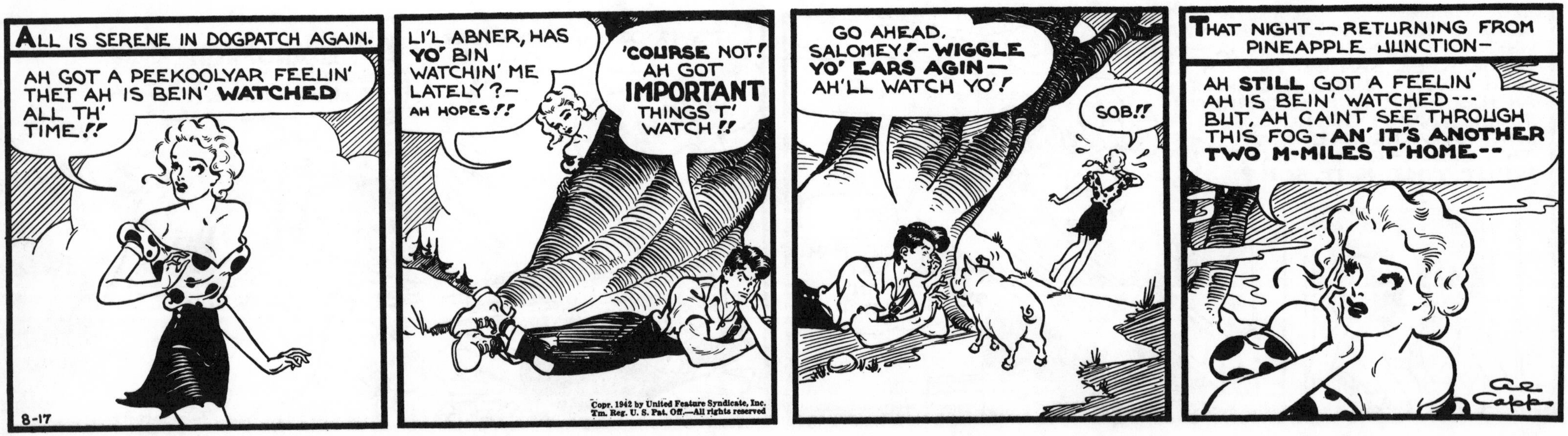
ALL IS SERENE IN DOGPATCH AGAIN.
AH GOT A PEEKOOLYAR FEELIN' THET AH IS BEIN' WATCHED ALL TH' TIME!!
8-17
LI'L ABNER, HAS YO' BIN WATCHIN' ME LATELY?— AH HOPES!!
'COURSE NOT! AH GOT IMPORTANT THINGS T' WATCH!!
Copr. 1942 by United Feature Syndicate, Inc.
Tm. Reg. U. S. Pat. Off.—All rights reserved
GO AHEAD, SALOMEY!—WIGGLE YO' EARS AGIN— AH'LL WATCH YO'!
SOB!!
THAT NIGHT—RETURNING FROM PINEAPPLE JUNCTION—
AH STILL GOT A FEELIN' AH IS BEIN' WATCHED--- BUT, AH CAINT SEE THROUGH THIS FOG—AN' IT'S ANOTHER TWO M-MILES T'HOME--

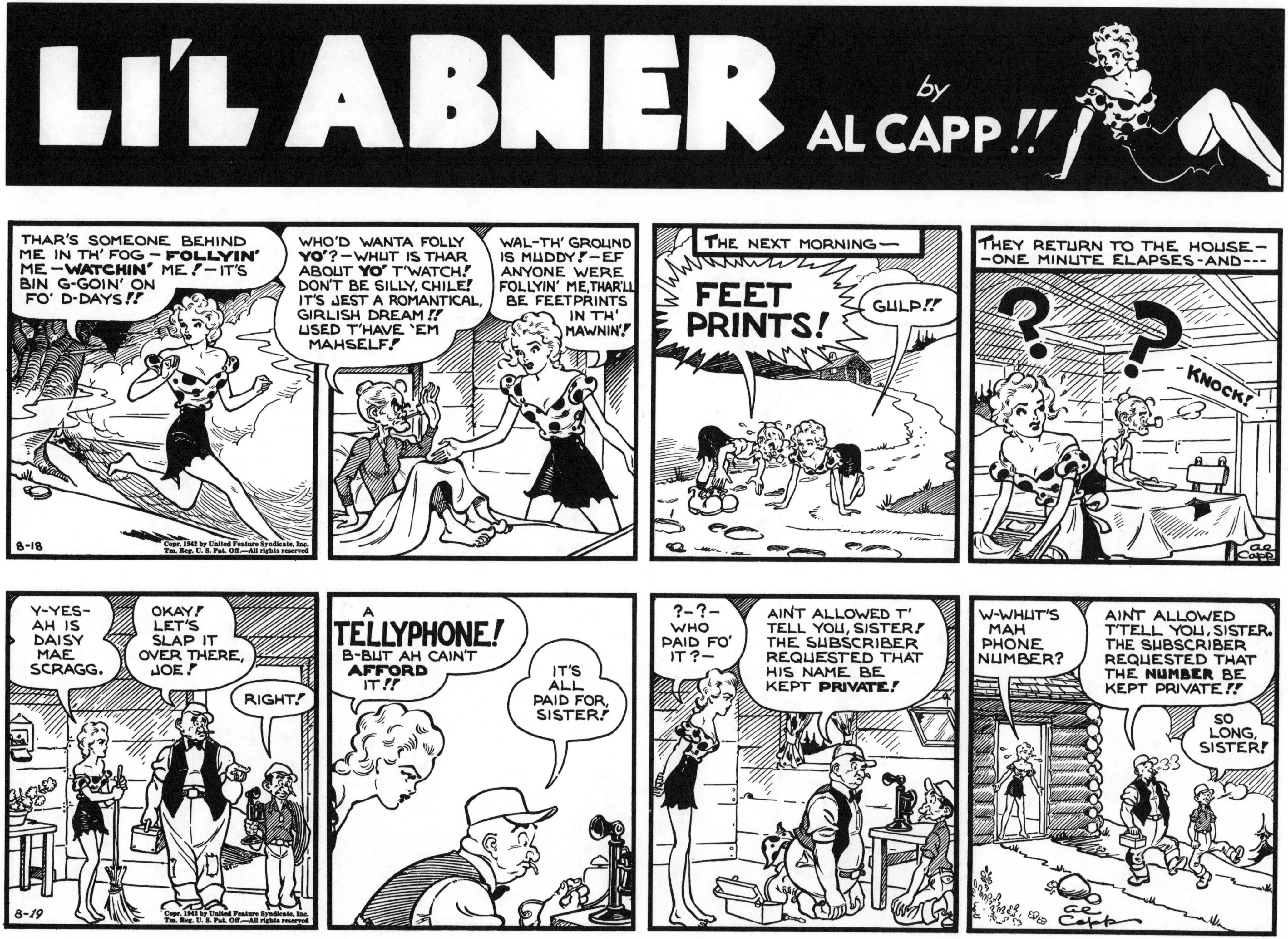
LI'L ABNER
by AL CAPP!!
THAR'S SOMEONE BEHIND ME IN TH' FOG — FOLLYIN' ME — WATCHIN' ME! — IT'S BIN G-GOIN' ON FO' D-DAYS!!
8-18
Copr. 1942 by United Feature Syndicate, Inc. Tm. Reg. U. S. Pat. Off.—All rights reserved
WHO'D WANTA FOLLY YO'? — WHUT IS THAR ABOUT YO' T'WATCH! DON'T BE SILLY, CHILE! IT'S JEST A ROMANTICAL, GIRLISH DREAM!! USED T'HAVE 'EM MAHSELF!
WAL-TH' GROUND IS MUDDY! — EF ANYONE WERE FOLLYIN' ME, THAR'LL BE FEETPRINTS IN TH' MAWNIN'!
THE NEXT MORNING —
FEET PRINTS!
GULP!!
THEY RETURN TO THE HOUSE — — ONE MINUTE ELAPSES — AND — — —
?
?
KNOCK!
Al Capp
Y-YES-AH IS DAISY MAE SCRAGG.
OKAY! LET'S SLAP IT OVER THERE, JOE!
RIGHT!
8-19
Copr. 1942 by United Feature Syndicate, Inc. Tm. Reg. U. S. Pat. Off.—All rights reserved
A TELLYPHONE! B-BUT AH CAIN'T AFFORD IT!!
IT'S ALL PAID FOR, SISTER!
?-?- WHO PAID FO' IT?—
AIN'T ALLOWED T' TELL YOU, SISTER! THE SUBSCRIBER REQUESTED THAT HIS NAME BE KEPT PRIVATE!
W-WHUT'S MAH PHONE NUMBER?
AIN'T ALLOWED T'TELL YOU, SISTER. THE SUBSCRIBER REQUESTED THAT THE NUMBER BE KEPT PRIVATE!!
SO LONG, SISTER!
Al Capp

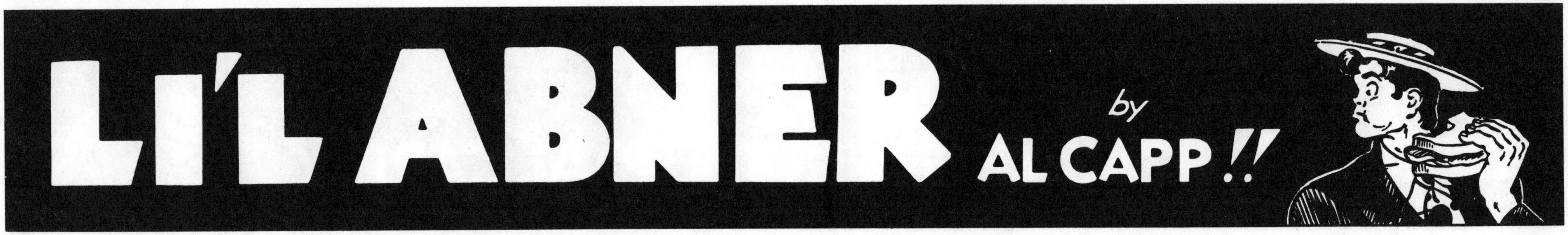

LI'L ABNER
by
AL CAPP!!

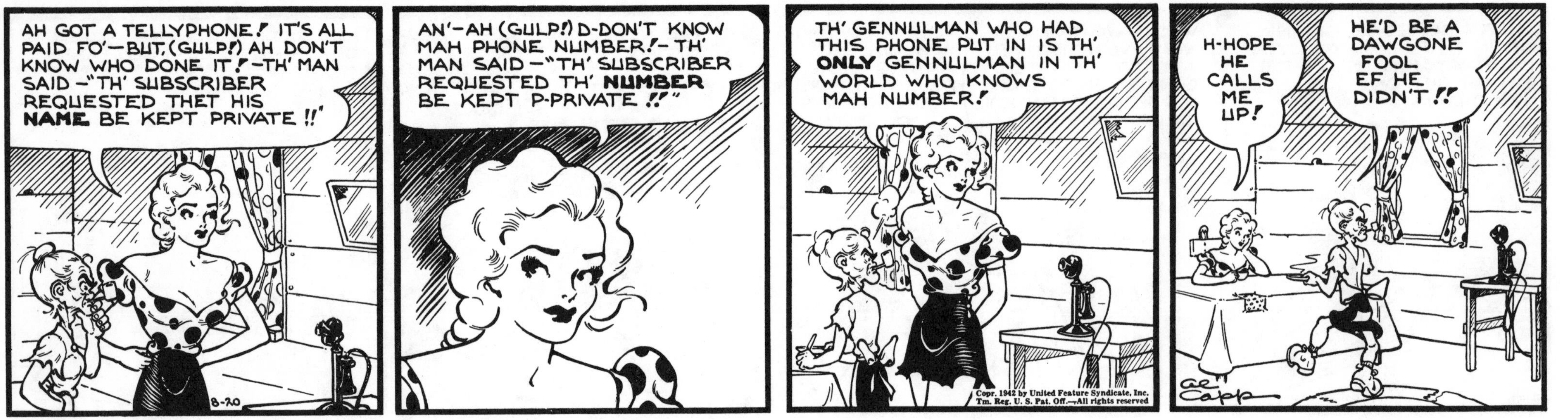

AH GOT A TELLYPHONE! IT'S ALL PAID FO'–BUT, (GULP!) AH DON'T KNOW WHO DONE IT!–TH' MAN SAID–"TH' SUBSCRIBER REQUESTED THET HIS **NAME** BE KEPT PRIVATE!!"
8-20
AN'–AH (GULP!) D-DON'T KNOW MAH PHONE NUMBER!–TH' MAN SAID–"TH' SUBSCRIBER REQUESTED TH' **NUMBER** BE KEPT P-PRIVATE!!"
TH' GENNULMAN WHO HAD THIS PHONE PUT IN IS TH' **ONLY** GENNULMAN IN TH' WORLD WHO KNOWS MAH NUMBER!
Copr. 1942 by United Feature Syndicate, Inc. Tm. Reg. U. S. Pat. Off.—All rights reserved
H-HOPE HE CALLS ME UP!
HE'D BE A DAWGONE FOOL EF HE DIDN'T!!
AL CAPP

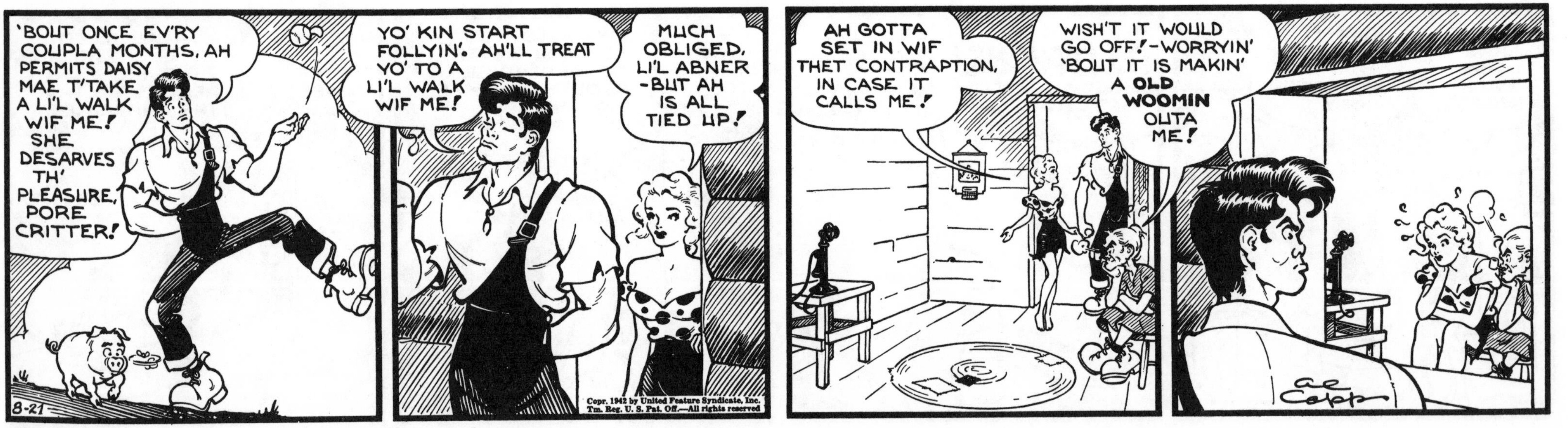

'BOUT ONCE EV'RY COUPLA MONTHS, AH PERMITS DAISY MAE T'TAKE A LI'L WALK WIF ME! SHE DESARVES TH' PLEASURE, PORE CRITTER!
8-21
YO' KIN START FOLLYIN'. AH'LL TREAT YO' TO A LI'L WALK WIF ME!
MUCH OBLIGED, LI'L ABNER–BUT AH IS ALL TIED UP!
Copr. 1942 by United Feature Syndicate, Inc. Tm. Reg. U. S. Pat. Off.—All rights reserved
AH GOTTA SET IN WIF THET CONTRAPTION, IN CASE IT CALLS ME!
WISH'T IT WOULD GO OFF!–WORRYIN' 'BOUT IT IS MAKIN' A **OLD WOOMIN** OUTA ME!
AL CAPP

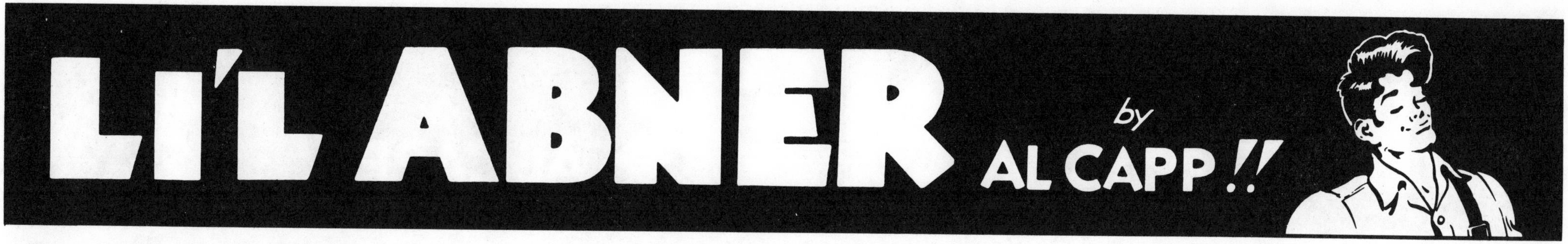
LI'L ABNER
by
AL CAPP!!

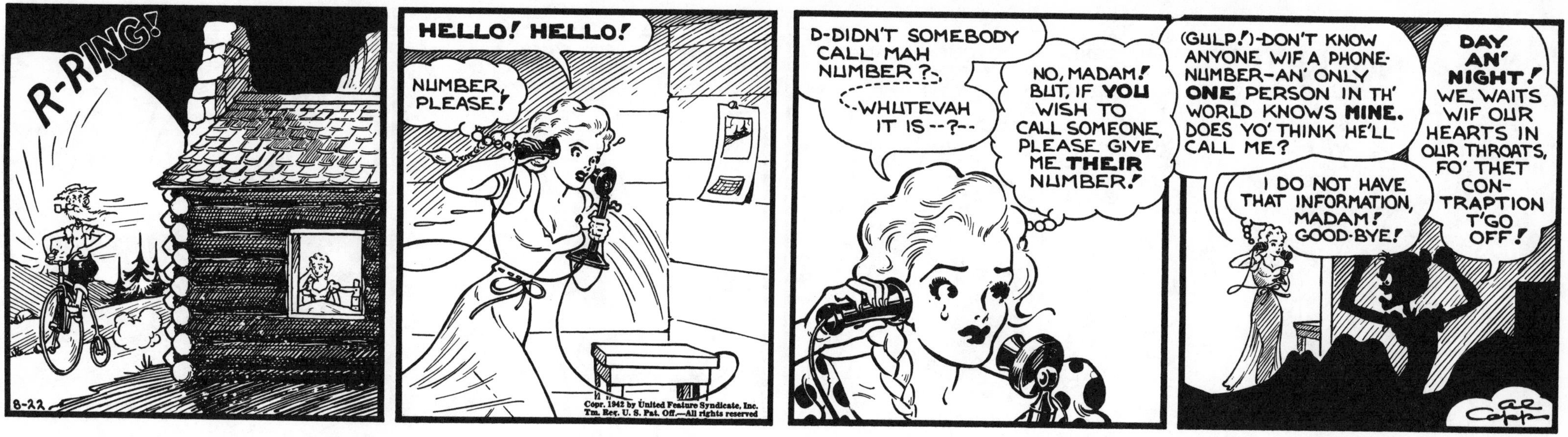
R-RING!
8-22
HELLO! HELLO!
NUMBER, PLEASE!
Copr. 1942 by United Feature Syndicate, Inc. Tm. Reg. U. S. Pat. Off.—All rights reserved
D-DIDN'T SOMEBODY CALL MAH NUMBER?
-WHUTEVAH IT IS--?--
NO, MADAM! BUT, IF YOU WISH TO CALL SOMEONE, PLEASE GIVE ME THEIR NUMBER!
(GULP!)-DON'T KNOW ANYONE WIF A PHONE-NUMBER-AN' ONLY ONE PERSON IN TH' WORLD KNOWS MINE. DOES YO' THINK HE'LL CALL ME?
I DO NOT HAVE THAT INFORMATION, MADAM! GOOD-BYE!
DAY AN' NIGHT! WE WAITS WIF OUR HEARTS IN OUR THROATS, FO' THET CON-TRAPTION T'GO OFF!
Al Capp

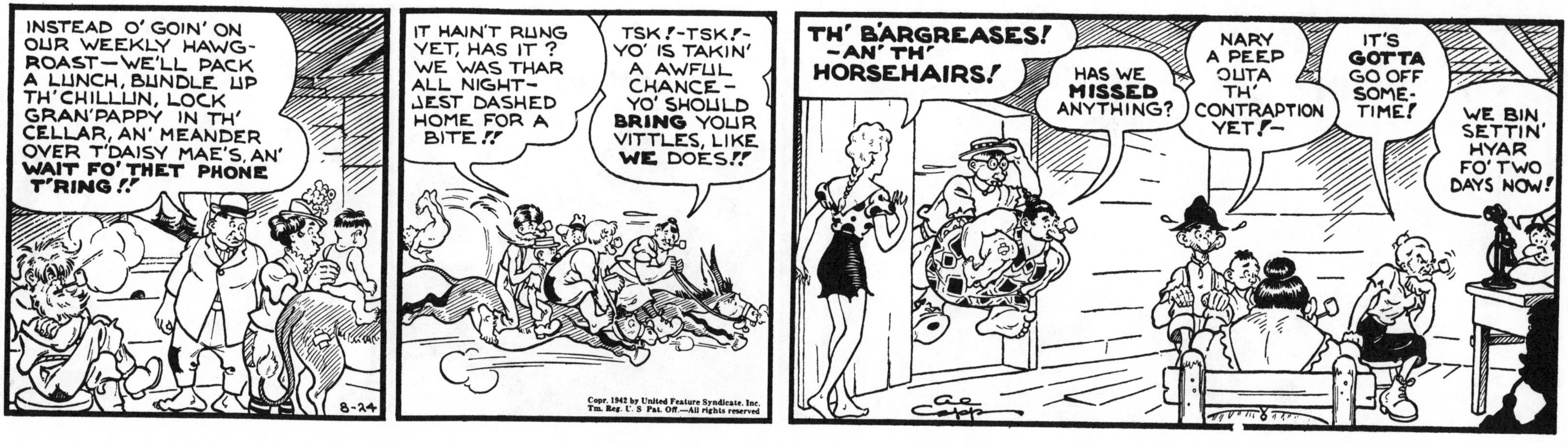
INSTEAD O' GOIN' ON OUR WEEKLY HAWG-ROAST—WE'LL PACK A LUNCH, BUNDLE UP TH' CHILLUN, LOCK GRAN'PAPPY IN TH' CELLAR, AN' MEANDER OVER T'DAISY MAE'S, AN' WAIT FO' THET PHONE T'RING!!
8-24
IT HAIN'T RUNG YET, HAS IT? WE WAS THAR ALL NIGHT-JEST DASHED HOME FOR A BITE!!
TSK!-TSK!-YO' IS TAKIN' A AWFUL CHANCE-YO' SHOULD BRING YOUR VITTLES, LIKE WE DOES!!
Copr. 1942 by United Feature Syndicate, Inc. Tm. Reg. U. S. Pat. Off.—All rights reserved
TH' B'ARGREASES! -AN' TH' HORSEHAIRS!
HAS WE MISSED ANYTHING?
NARY A PEEP OUTA TH' CONTRAPTION YET!—
IT'S GOTTA GO OFF SOME-TIME!
WE BIN SETTIN' HYAR FO' TWO DAYS NOW!
Al Capp

LI'L ABNER by AL CAPP!!

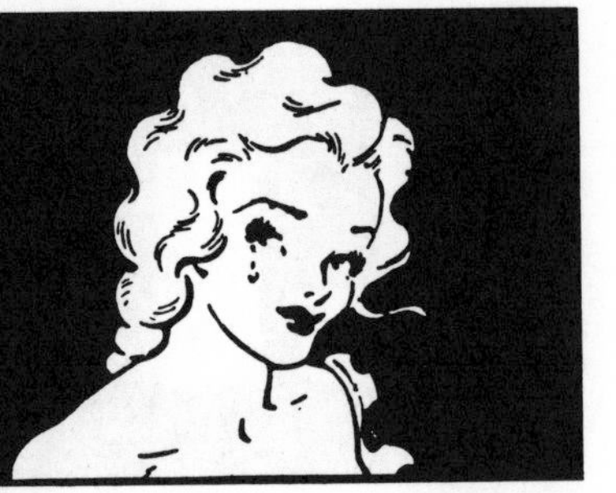

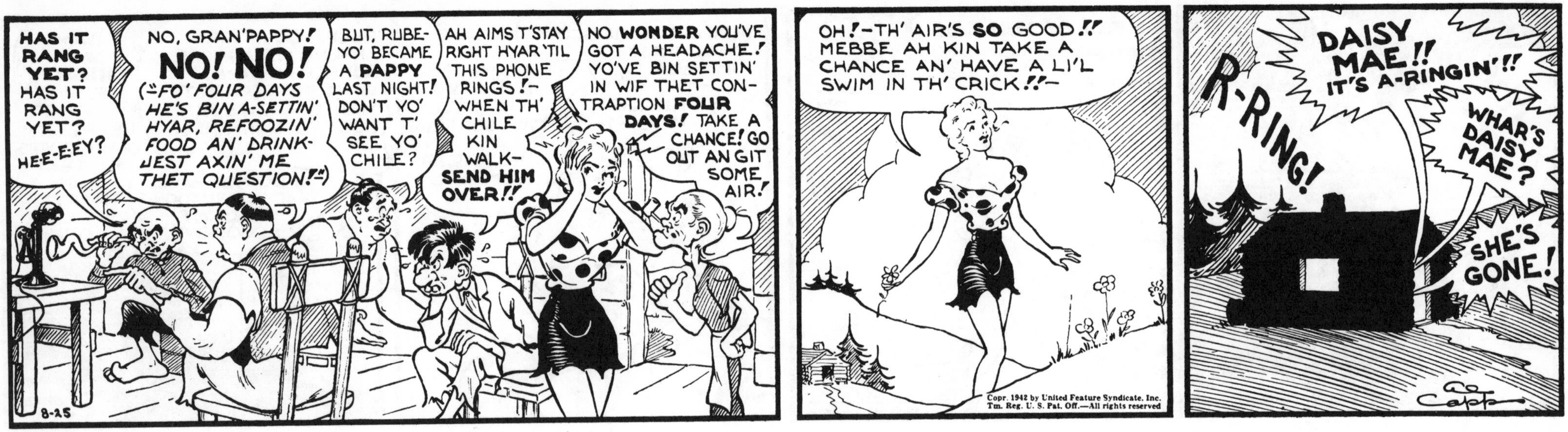
HAS IT RANG YET? HAS IT RANG YET? HE-E-E-EY?
NO, GRAN'PAPPY! NO! NO! (—FO' FOUR DAYS HE'S BIN A-SETTIN' HYAR, REFOOZIN' FOOD AN' DRINK-JEST AXIN' ME THET QUESTION!—)
BUT, RUBE-YO' BECAME A PAPPY LAST NIGHT! DON'T YO' WANT T' SEE YO' CHILE?
AH AIMS T'STAY RIGHT HYAR 'TIL THIS PHONE RINGS!—WHEN TH' CHILE KIN WALK-SEND HIM OVER!!
NO WONDER YOU'VE GOT A HEADACHE! YOU'VE BIN SETTIN' IN WIF THET CONTRAPTION FOUR DAYS! TAKE A CHANCE! GO OUT AN GIT SOME AIR!
8-25
OH!—TH' AIR'S SO GOOD!! MEBBE AH KIN TAKE A CHANCE AN' HAVE A LI'L SWIM IN TH' CRICK!!—
Copr. 1942 by United Feature Syndicate, Inc. Tm. Reg. U. S. Pat. Off.—All rights reserved
R-RING!
DAISY MAE!! IT'S A-RINGIN'!!
WHAR'S DAISY MAE?
SHE'S GONE!
Al Capp

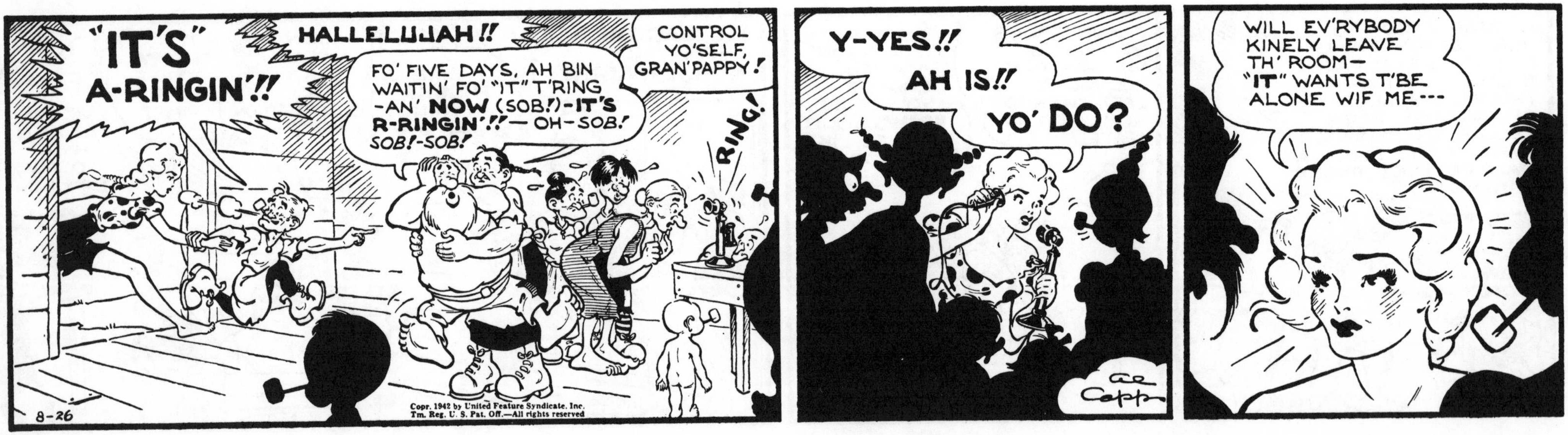
"IT'S" A-RINGIN'!!
HALLELUJAH!!
FO' FIVE DAYS, AH BIN WAITIN' FO' "IT" T'RING -AN' NOW (SOB!)-IT'S R-RINGIN'!!— OH-SOB! SOB!-SOB!
CONTROL YO'SELF, GRAN'PAPPY!
RING!
8-26
Copr. 1942 by United Feature Syndicate, Inc. Tm. Reg. U. S. Pat. Off.—All rights reserved
Y-YES!!
AH IS!!
YO' DO?
Al Capp
WILL EV'RYBODY KINELY LEAVE TH' ROOM— "IT" WANTS T'BE ALONE WIF ME---

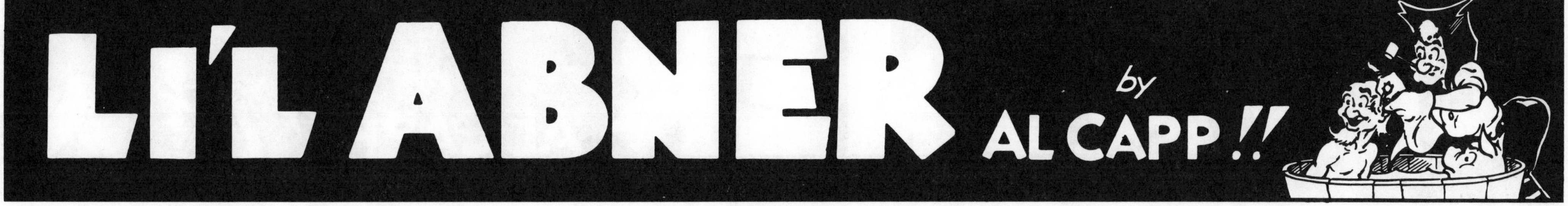
LI'L ABNER
by
AL CAPP !!

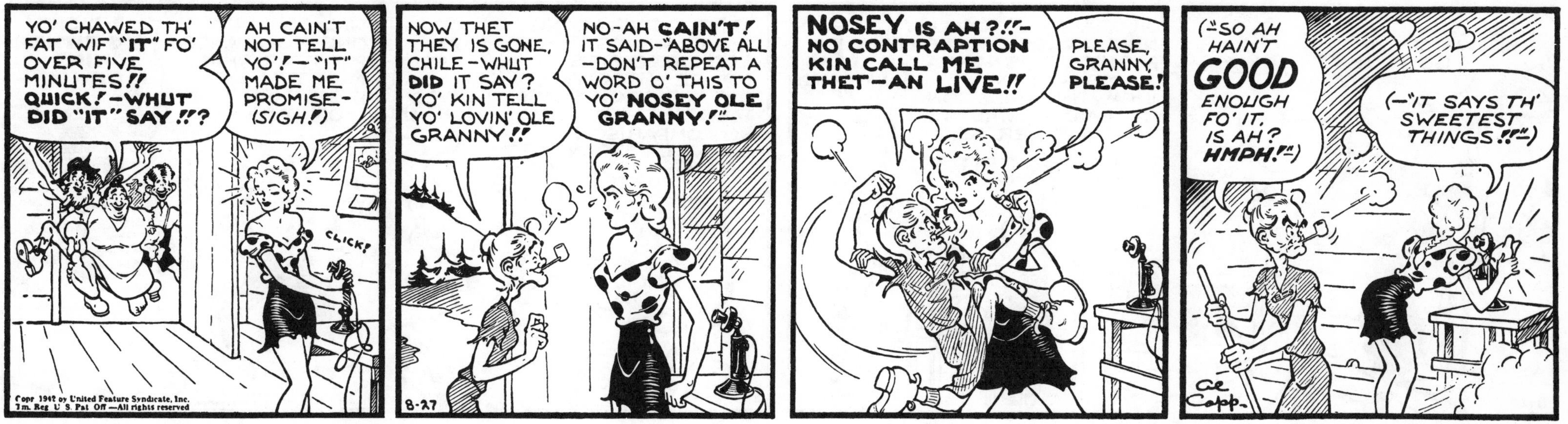
YO' CHAWED TH' FAT WIF "IT" FO' OVER FIVE MINUTES!! QUICK!—WHUT DID "IT" SAY!!?
AH CAIN'T NOT TELL YO'!—"IT" MADE ME PROMISE—(SIGH!)
CLICK!
Copr. 1942 by United Feature Syndicate, Inc. Tm. Reg. U.S. Pat. Off.—All rights reserved
NOW THET THEY IS GONE, CHILE—WHUT DID IT SAY? YO' KIN TELL YO' LOVIN' OLE GRANNY!!
NO—AH CAIN'T! IT SAID—"ABOVE ALL—DON'T REPEAT A WORD O' THIS TO YO' NOSEY OLE GRANNY!"—
8-27
NOSEY IS AH?!!—NO CONTRAPTION KIN CALL ME THET—AN LIVE!!
PLEASE, GRANNY, PLEASE!
(—"SO AH HAIN'T GOOD ENOUGH FO' IT, IS AH? HMPH!")
(—"IT SAYS TH' SWEETEST THINGS!!")
AL CAPP

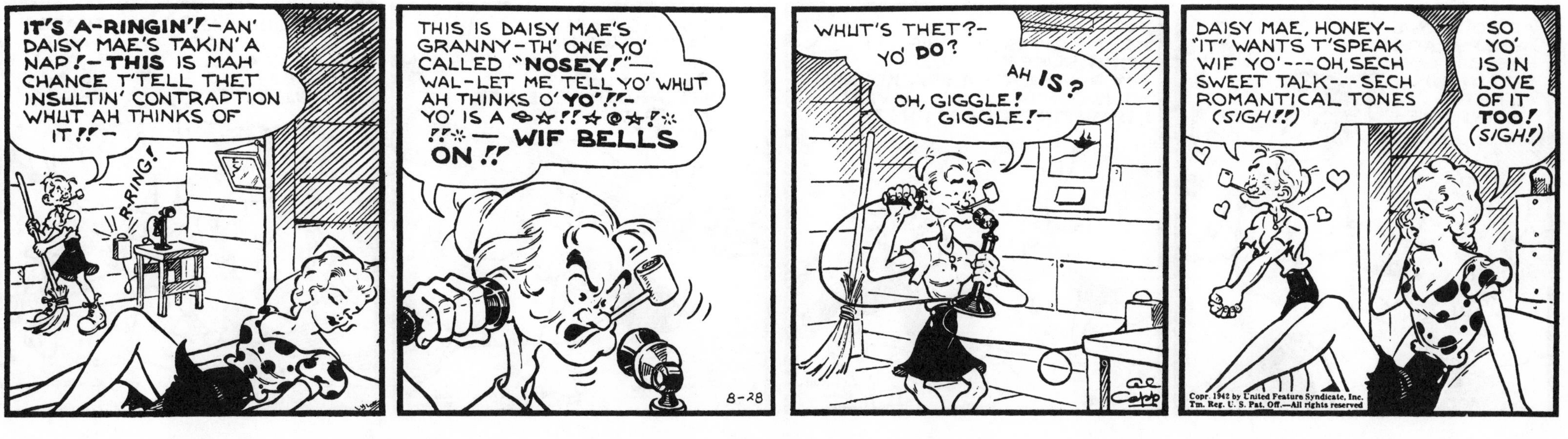
IT'S A-RINGIN'!—AN' DAISY MAE'S TAKIN' A NAP!—THIS IS MAH CHANCE T'TELL THET INSULTIN' CONTRAPTION WHUT AH THINKS OF IT!!—
R-RING!
THIS IS DAISY MAE'S GRANNY—TH' ONE YO' CALLED "NOSEY!"—WAL—LET ME TELL YO' WHUT AH THINKS O' YO'!!—YO' IS A ✫☆!!☆@☆!✲ !!✲—WIF BELLS ON!!
8-28
WHUT'S THET?—
YO' DO?
AH IS?
OH, GIGGLE! GIGGLE!—
AL CAPP
DAISY MAE, HONEY—"IT" WANTS T'SPEAK WIF YO'---OH, SECH SWEET TALK---SECH ROMANTICAL TONES (SIGH!!)
SO YO' IS IN LOVE OF IT TOO! (SIGH!)
Copr. 1942 by United Feature Syndicate, Inc. Tm. Reg. U.S. Pat. Off.—All rights reserved

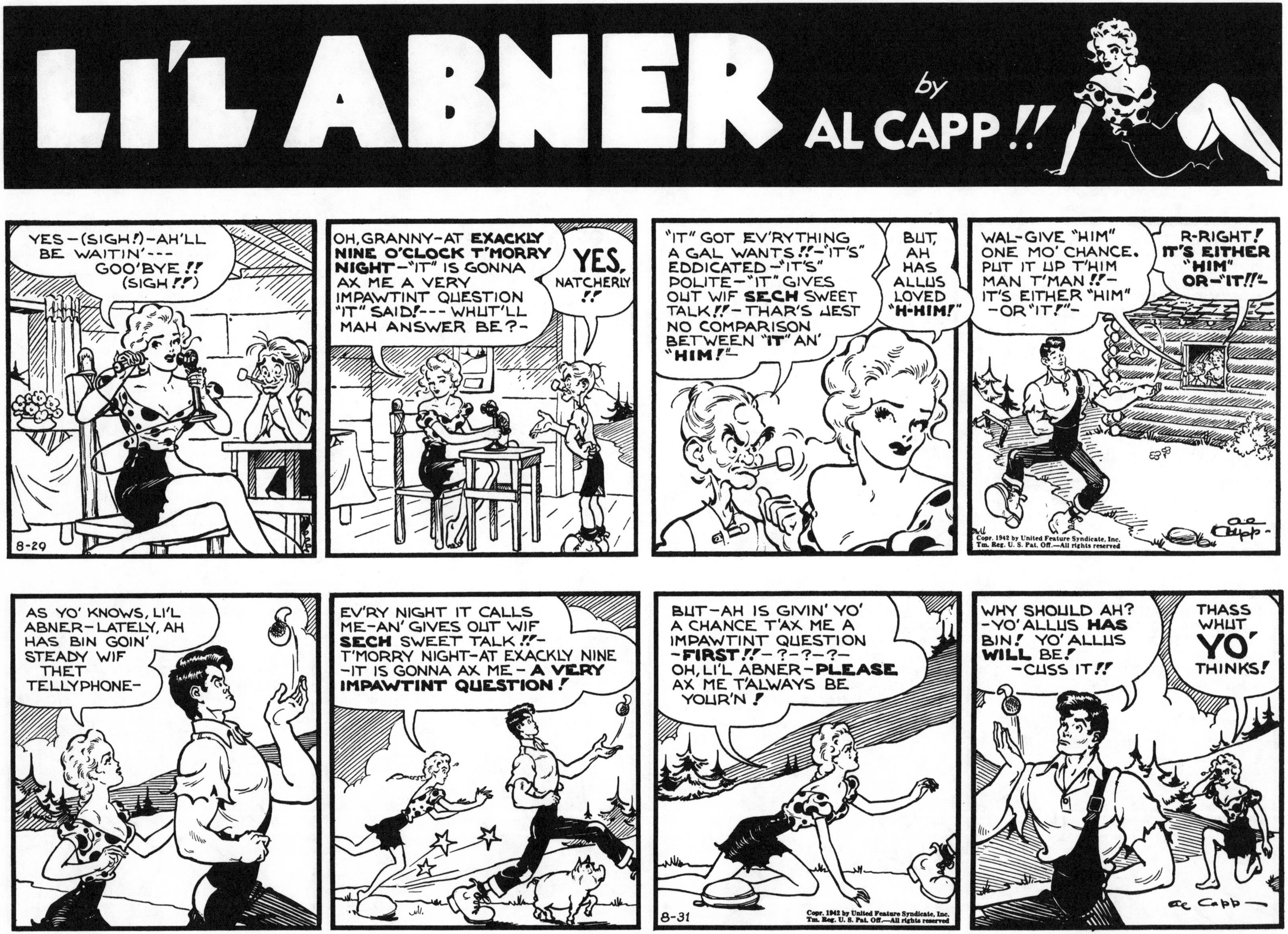

LI'L ABNER by AL CAPP!!
YES—(SIGH!)—AH'LL BE WAITIN'--- GOO'BYE!! (SIGH!!)
8-29
OH, GRANNY—AT EXACKLY NINE O'CLOCK T'MORRY NIGHT—"IT" IS GONNA AX ME A VERY IMPAWTINT QUESTION "IT" SAID!--- WHUT'LL MAH ANSWER BE?—
YES, NATCHERLY!!
"IT" GOT EV'RYTHING A GAL WANTS!!—"IT'S" EDDICATED—"IT'S" POLITE—"IT" GIVES OUT WIF SECH SWEET TALK!!—THAR'S JEST NO COMPARISON BETWEEN "IT" AN' "HIM!"—
BUT, AH HAS ALLUS LOVED "H-HIM!"
WAL—GIVE "HIM" ONE MO' CHANCE. PUT IT UP T'HIM MAN T'MAN!!— IT'S EITHER "HIM" —OR "IT!"—
R-RIGHT! IT'S EITHER "HIM" OR—"IT!!"—
Copr. 1942 by United Feature Syndicate, Inc. Tm. Reg. U. S. Pat. Off.—All rights reserved
AS YO' KNOWS, LI'L ABNER—LATELY, AH HAS BIN GOIN' STEADY WIF THET TELLYPHONE—
EV'RY NIGHT IT CALLS ME—AN' GIVES OUT WIF SECH SWEET TALK!!— T'MORRY NIGHT—AT EXACKLY NINE —IT IS GONNA AX ME—A VERY IMPAWTINT QUESTION!
BUT—AH IS GIVIN' YO' A CHANCE T'AX ME A IMPAWTINT QUESTION —FIRST!!—?—?—?— OH, LI'L ABNER—PLEASE AX ME T'ALWAYS BE YOUR'N!
8-31
Copr. 1942 by United Feature Syndicate, Inc. Tm. Reg. U. S. Pat. Off.—All rights reserved
WHY SHOULD AH? —YO' ALLUS HAS BIN! YO' ALLUS WILL BE! —CUSS IT!!
THASS WHUT YO' THINKS!
Al Capp

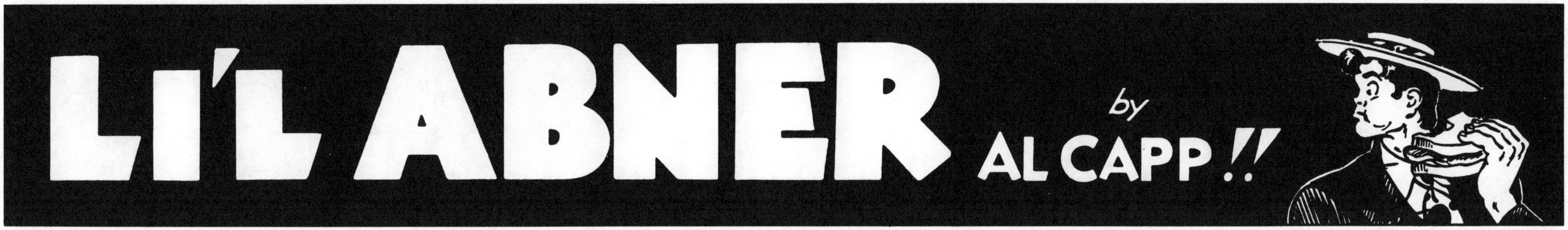
LI'L ABNER
by
AL CAPP!!

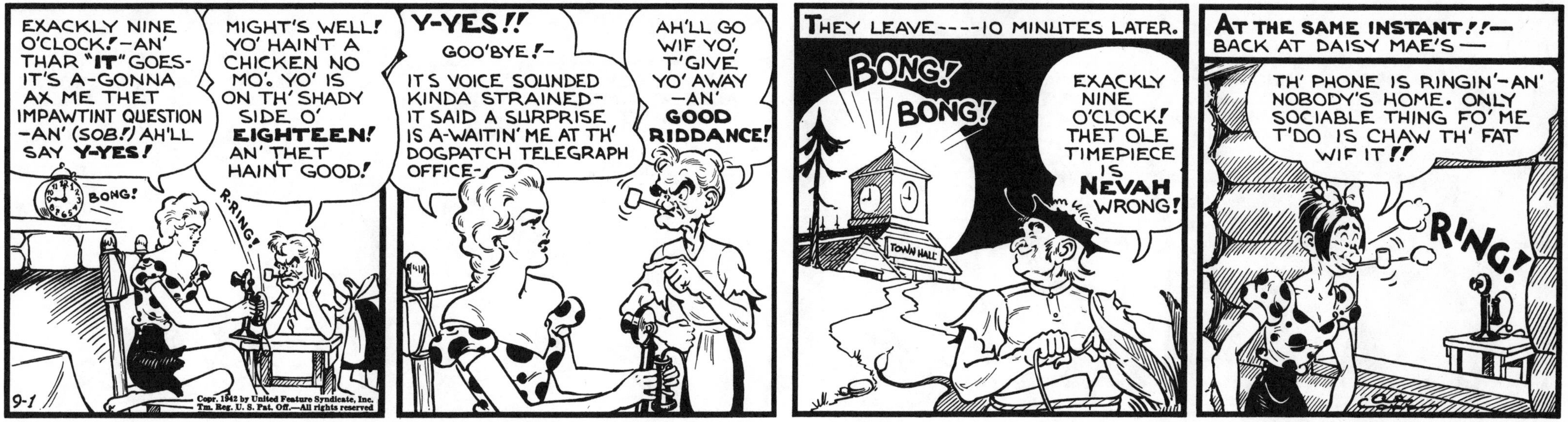
EXACKLY NINE O'CLOCK!—AN' THAR "IT" GOES- IT'S A-GONNA AX ME THET IMPAWTINT QUESTION -AN' (SOB!) AH'LL SAY Y-YES!
MIGHT'S WELL! YO' HAIN'T A CHICKEN NO MO'. YO' IS ON TH' SHADY SIDE O' EIGHTEEN! AN' THET HAIN'T GOOD!
BONG!
R-RING!
9-1
Copr. 1942 by United Feature Syndicate, Inc. Tm. Reg. U. S. Pat. Off.—All rights reserved
Y-YES!! GOO'BYE!- IT'S VOICE SOUNDED KINDA STRAINED- IT SAID A SURPRISE IS A-WAITIN' ME AT TH' DOGPATCH TELEGRAPH OFFICE-
AH'LL GO WIF YO', T'GIVE YO' AWAY -AN' GOOD RIDDANCE!
THEY LEAVE----10 MINUTES LATER.
BONG! BONG!
TOWN HALL
EXACKLY NINE O'CLOCK! THET OLE TIMEPIECE IS NEVAH WRONG!
AT THE SAME INSTANT!!— BACK AT DAISY MAE'S—
TH' PHONE IS RINGIN'-AN' NOBODY'S HOME. ONLY SOCIABLE THING FO' ME T'DO IS CHAW TH' FAT WIF IT!!
RING!

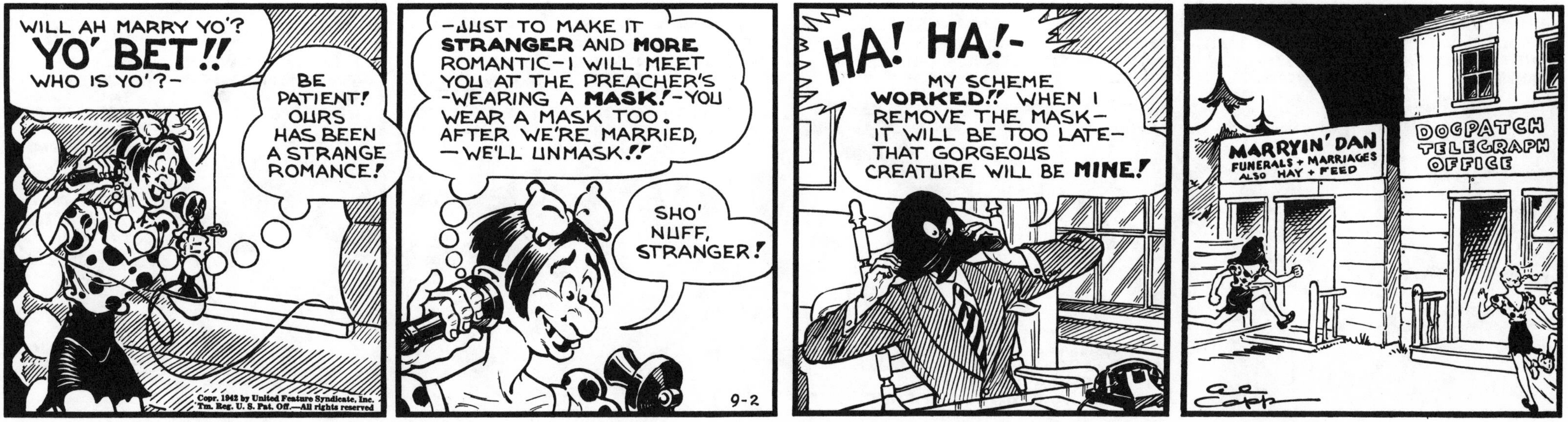
WILL AH MARRY YO'? YO' BET!! WHO IS YO'?-
BE PATIENT! OURS HAS BEEN A STRANGE ROMANCE!
Copr. 1942 by United Feature Syndicate, Inc. Tm. Reg. U. S. Pat. Off.—All rights reserved
-JUST TO MAKE IT STRANGER AND MORE ROMANTIC-I WILL MEET YOU AT THE PREACHER'S -WEARING A MASK!-YOU WEAR A MASK TOO. AFTER WE'RE MARRIED, —WE'LL UNMASK!!
SHO' NUFF, STRANGER!
9-2
HA! HA!- MY SCHEME WORKED!! WHEN I REMOVE THE MASK- IT WILL BE TOO LATE- THAT GORGEOUS CREATURE WILL BE MINE!
MARRYIN' DAN FUNERALS + MARRIAGES ALSO HAY + FEED
DOGPATCH TELEGRAPH OFFICE

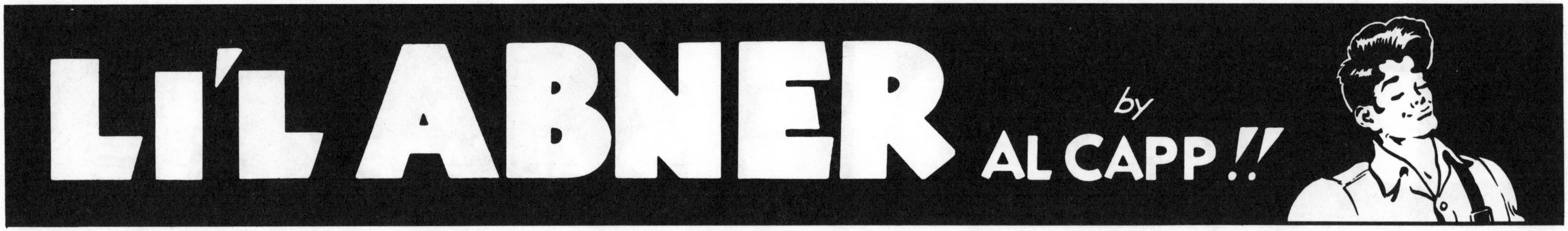
LI'L ABNER
by AL CAPP!!

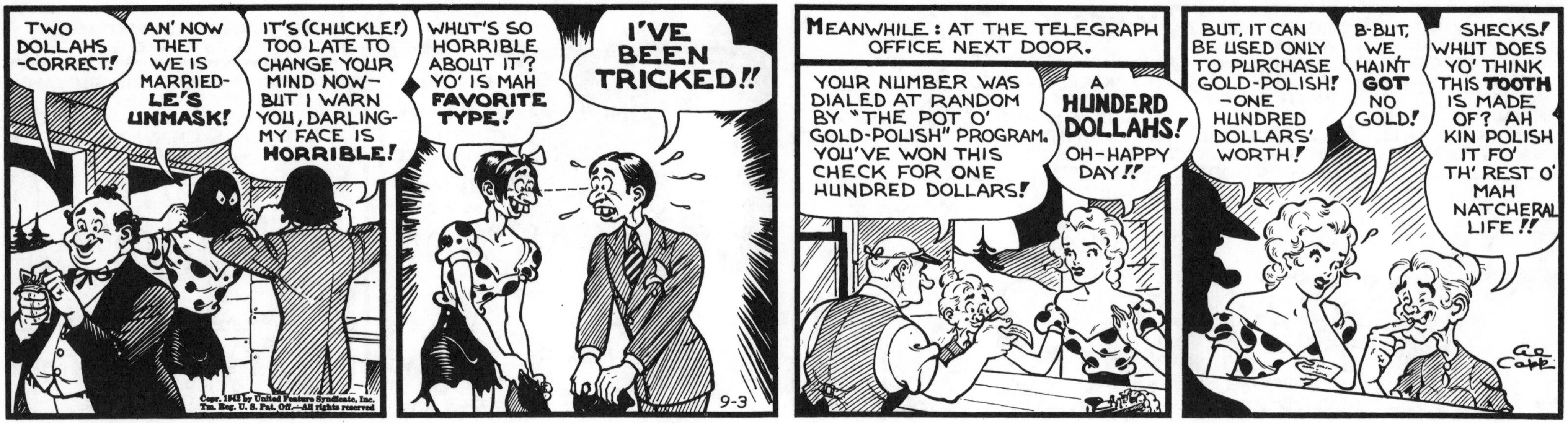
TWO DOLLAHS -CORRECT!
AN' NOW THET WE IS MARRIED- LE'S UNMASK!
IT'S (CHUCKLE!) TOO LATE TO CHANGE YOUR MIND NOW- BUT I WARN YOU, DARLING- MY FACE IS HORRIBLE!
Copr. 1942 by United Feature Syndicate, Inc. Tm. Reg. U. S. Pat. Off.—All rights reserved
WHUT'S SO HORRIBLE ABOUT IT? YO' IS MAH FAVORITE TYPE!
I'VE BEEN TRICKED!!
9-3
MEANWHILE: AT THE TELEGRAPH OFFICE NEXT DOOR.
YOUR NUMBER WAS DIALED AT RANDOM BY "THE POT O' GOLD-POLISH" PROGRAM. YOU'VE WON THIS CHECK FOR ONE HUNDRED DOLLARS!
A HUNDERD DOLLAHS! OH-HAPPY DAY!!
BUT, IT CAN BE USED ONLY TO PURCHASE GOLD-POLISH! -ONE HUNDRED DOLLARS' WORTH!
B-BUT, WE HAINT GOT NO GOLD!
SHECKS! WHUT DOES YO' THINK THIS TOOTH IS MADE OF? AH KIN POLISH IT FO' TH' REST O' MAH NATCHERAL LIFE!!
Al Capp

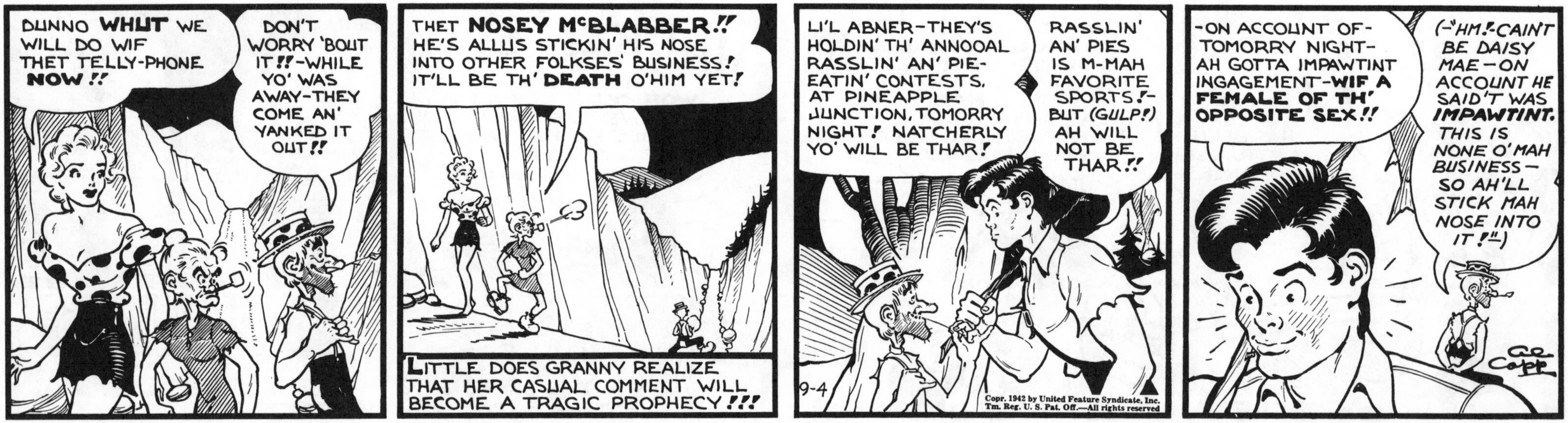
DUNNO WHUT WE WILL DO WIF THET TELLY-PHONE NOW!!
DON'T WORRY 'BOUT IT!!-WHILE YO' WAS AWAY-THEY COME AN' YANKED IT OUT!!
THET NOSEY McBLABBER!! HE'S ALLUS STICKIN' HIS NOSE INTO OTHER FOLKSES' BUSINESS! IT'LL BE TH' DEATH O'HIM YET!
LITTLE DOES GRANNY REALIZE THAT HER CASUAL COMMENT WILL BECOME A TRAGIC PROPHECY!!!
LI'L ABNER-THEY'S HOLDIN' TH' ANNOOAL RASSLIN' AN' PIE-EATIN' CONTESTS, AT PINEAPPLE JUNCTION, TOMORRY NIGHT! NATCHERLY YO' WILL BE THAR!
RASSLIN' AN' PIES IS M-MAH FAVORITE SPORTS!- BUT (GULP!) AH WILL NOT BE THAR!!
9-4
Copr. 1942 by United Feature Syndicate, Inc. Tm. Reg. U. S. Pat. Off.—All rights reserved
-ON ACCOUNT OF- TOMORRY NIGHT- AH GOTTA IMPAWTINT INGAGEMENT-WIF A FEMALE OF TH' OPPOSITE SEX!!
(-"HM!-CAIN'T BE DAISY MAE-ON ACCOUNT HE SAID'T WAS IMPAWTINT. THIS IS NONE O' MAH BUSINESS- SO AH'LL STICK MAH NOSE INTO IT!"-)
Al Capp

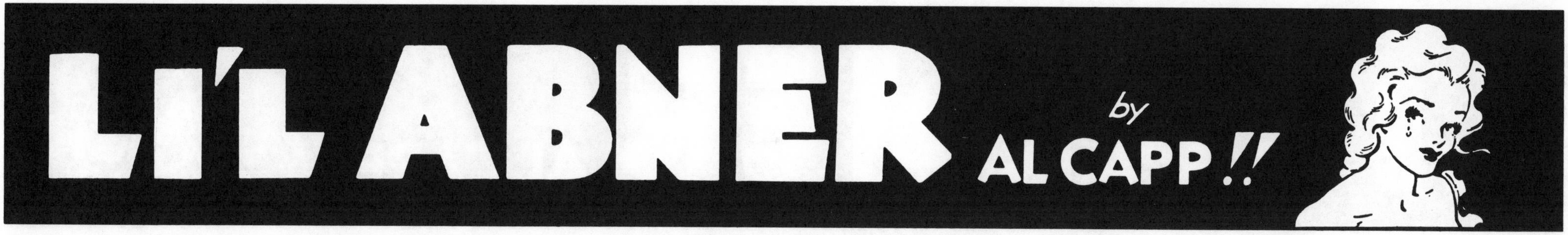
LI'L ABNER
by
AL CAPP!!

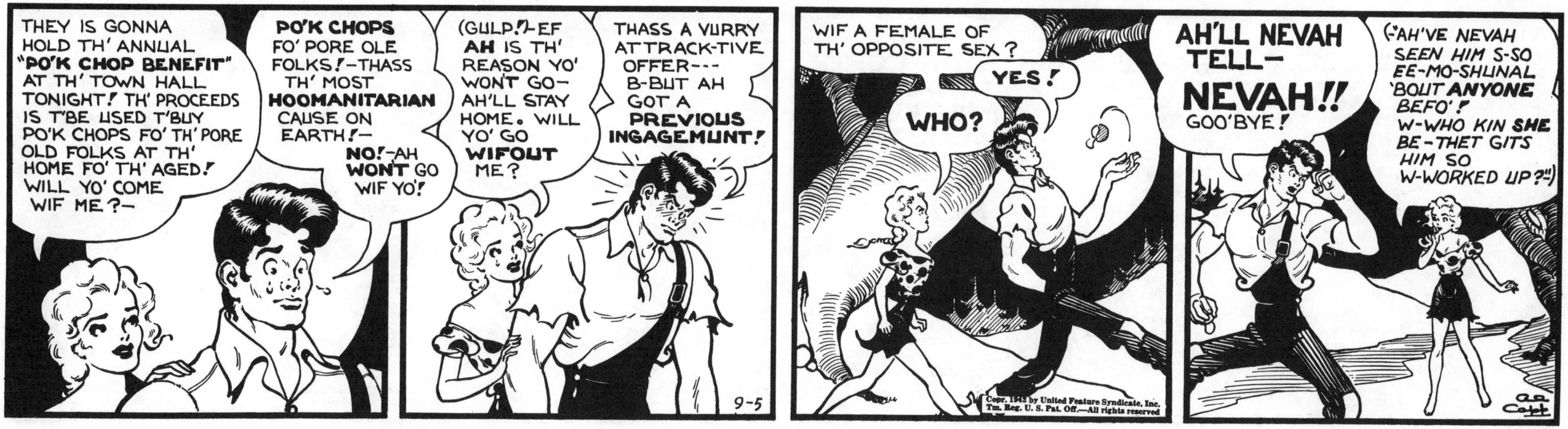
THEY IS GONNA HOLD TH' ANNUAL "PO'K CHOP BENEFIT" AT TH' TOWN HALL TONIGHT! TH' PROCEEDS IS T'BE USED T'BUY PO'K CHOPS FO' TH' PORE OLD FOLKS AT TH' HOME FO' TH' AGED! WILL YO' COME WIF ME?-
PO'K CHOPS FO' PORE OLE FOLKS!-THASS TH' MOST HOOMANITARIAN CAUSE ON EARTH!-
NO!-AH WON'T GO WIF YO'!
(GULP!)-EF AH IS TH' REASON YO' WON'T GO-AH'LL STAY HOME. WILL YO' GO WIFOUT ME?
THASS A VURRY ATTRACK-TIVE OFFER--- B-BUT AH GOT A PREVIOUS INGAGEMUNT!
9-5
WIF A FEMALE OF TH' OPPOSITE SEX?
YES!
WHO?
Copr. 1942 by United Feature Syndicate, Inc.
Tm. Reg. U. S. Pat. Off.—All rights reserved
AH'LL NEVAH TELL— NEVAH!! GOO'BYE!
(-"AH'VE NEVAH SEEN HIM S-SO EE-MO-SHUNAL 'BOUT ANYONE BEFO'! W-WHO KIN SHE BE-THET GITS HIM SO W-WORKED UP?"-)

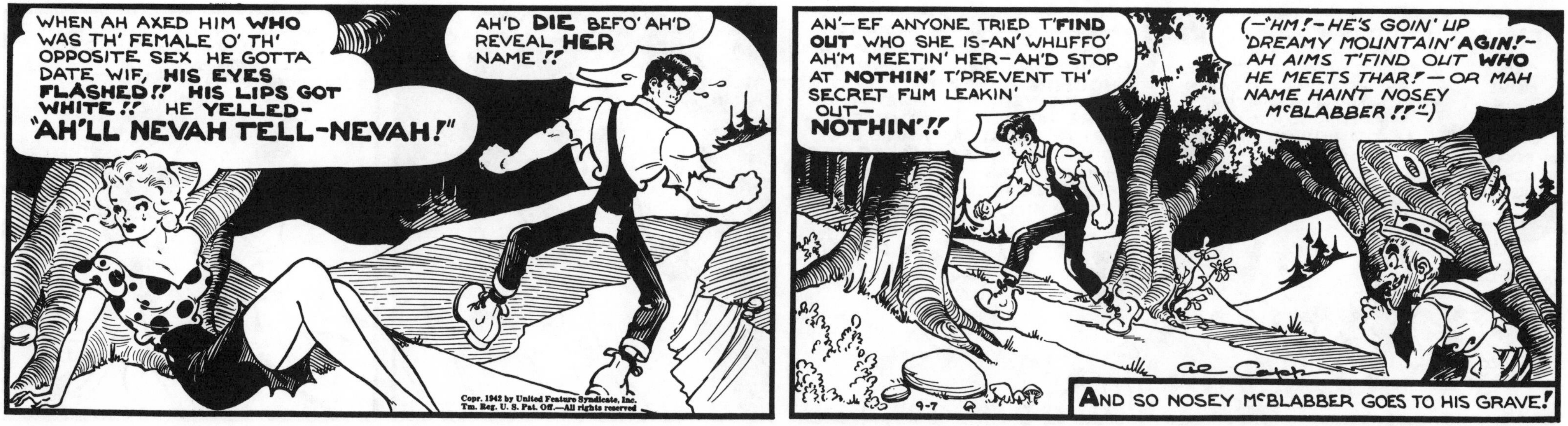
WHEN AH AXED HIM WHO WAS TH' FEMALE O' TH' OPPOSITE SEX HE GOTTA DATE WIF, HIS EYES FLASHED!! HIS LIPS GOT WHITE!! HE YELLED- "AH'LL NEVAH TELL-NEVAH!"
AH'D DIE BEFO' AH'D REVEAL HER NAME!!
Copr. 1942 by United Feature Syndicate, Inc.
Tm. Reg. U. S. Pat. Off.—All rights reserved
AN'-EF ANYONE TRIED T'FIND OUT WHO SHE IS-AN' WHUFFO' AH'M MEETIN' HER-AH'D STOP AT NOTHIN' T'PREVENT TH' SECRET FUM LEAKIN' OUT- NOTHIN'!!
(-"HM!-HE'S GOIN' UP 'DREAMY MOUNTAIN' AGIN!-AH AIMS T'FIND OUT WHO HE MEETS THAR!-OR MAH NAME HAIN'T NOSEY McBLABBER!!"-)
9-7
AND SO NOSEY McBLABBER GOES TO HIS GRAVE!

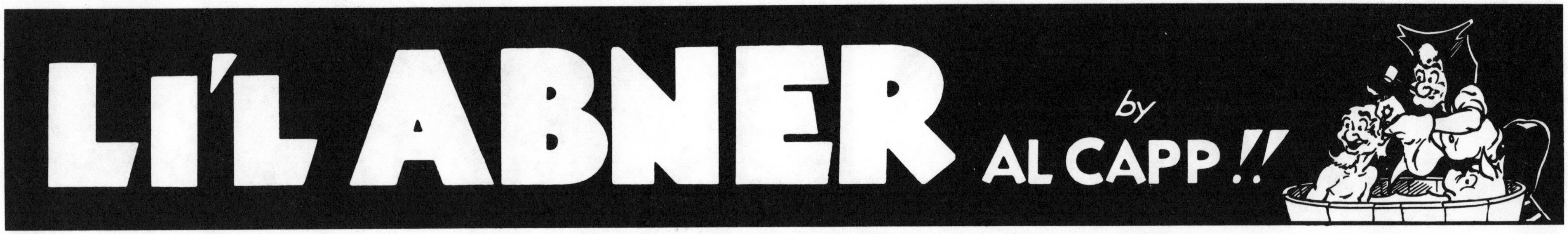
LI'L ABNER
by
AL CAPP!!

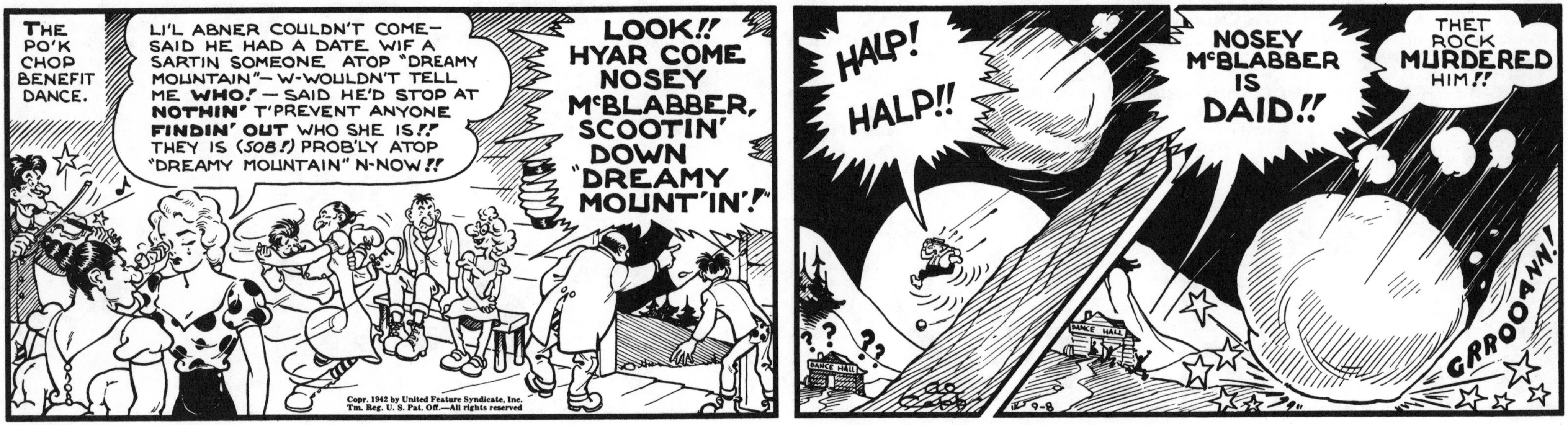
THE PO'K CHOP BENEFIT DANCE.
LI'L ABNER COULDN'T COME— SAID HE HAD A DATE WIF A SARTIN SOMEONE ATOP "DREAMY MOUNTAIN"— W-WOULDN'T TELL ME WHO!— SAID HE'D STOP AT NOTHIN' T'PREVENT ANYONE FINDIN' OUT WHO SHE IS!! THEY IS (SOB!) PROB'LY ATOP "DREAMY MOUNTAIN" N-NOW!!
LOOK!! HYAR COME NOSEY McBLABBER, SCOOTIN' DOWN "DREAMY MOUNT'IN'!"
Copr. 1942 by United Feature Syndicate, Inc. Tm. Reg. U. S. Pat. Off.—All rights reserved
HALP! HALP!!
NOSEY McBLABBER IS DAID!!
THET ROCK MURDERED HIM!!
DANCE HALL
GRROOANN!
9-8

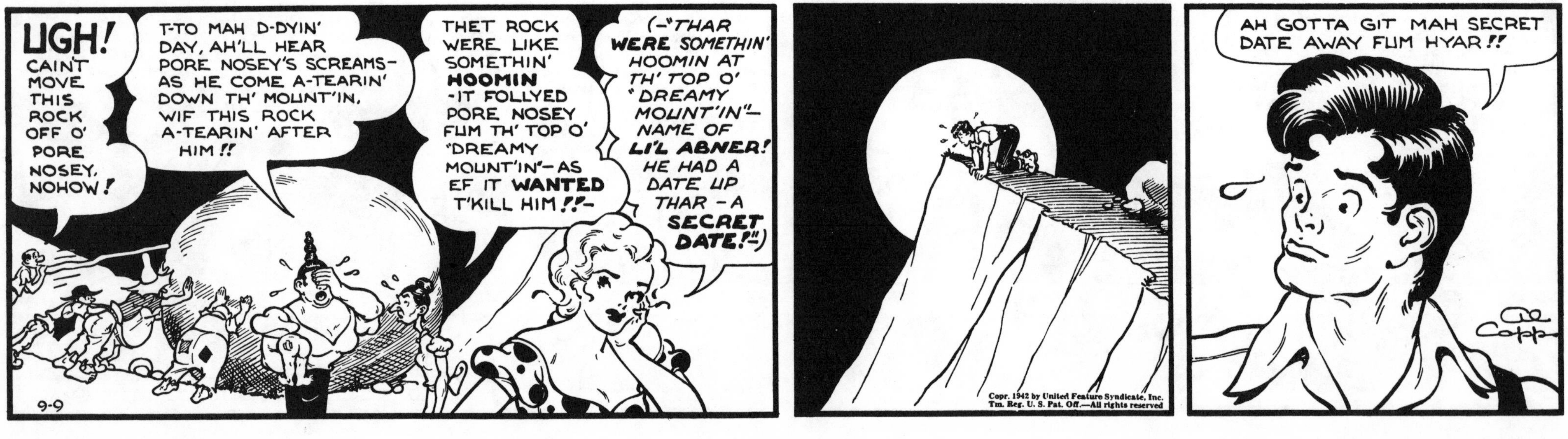
UGH! CAIN'T MOVE THIS ROCK OFF O' PORE NOSEY, NOHOW!
T-TO MAH D-DYIN' DAY, AH'LL HEAR PORE NOSEY'S SCREAMS— AS HE COME A-TEARIN' DOWN TH' MOUNT'IN, WIF THIS ROCK A-TEARIN' AFTER HIM!!
THET ROCK WERE LIKE SOMETHIN' HOOMIN —IT FOLLYED PORE NOSEY FUM TH' TOP O' "DREAMY MOUNT'IN"— AS EF IT WANTED T'KILL HIM!!—
(—"THAR WERE SOMETHIN' HOOMIN AT TH' TOP O' "DREAMY MOUNT'IN"— NAME OF LI'L ABNER! HE HAD A DATE UP THAR — A SECRET DATE!"—)
9-9
Copr. 1942 by United Feature Syndicate, Inc. Tm. Reg. U. S. Pat. Off.—All rights reserved
AH GOTTA GIT MAH SECRET DATE AWAY FUM HYAR!!

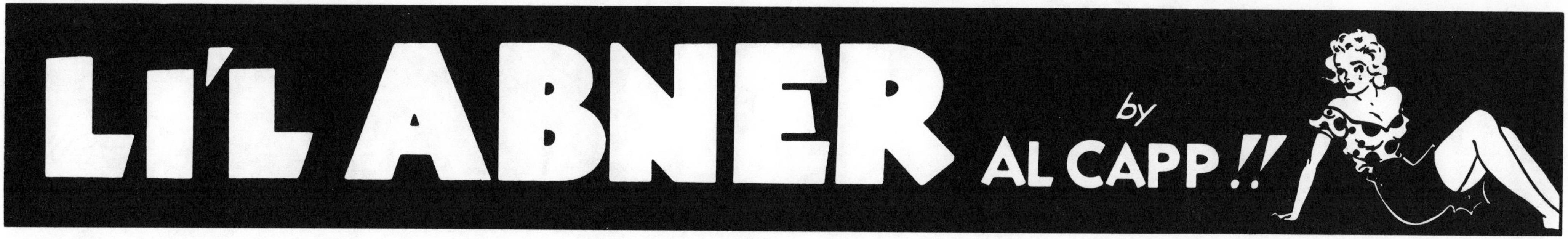
LI'L ABNER
by AL CAPP!!

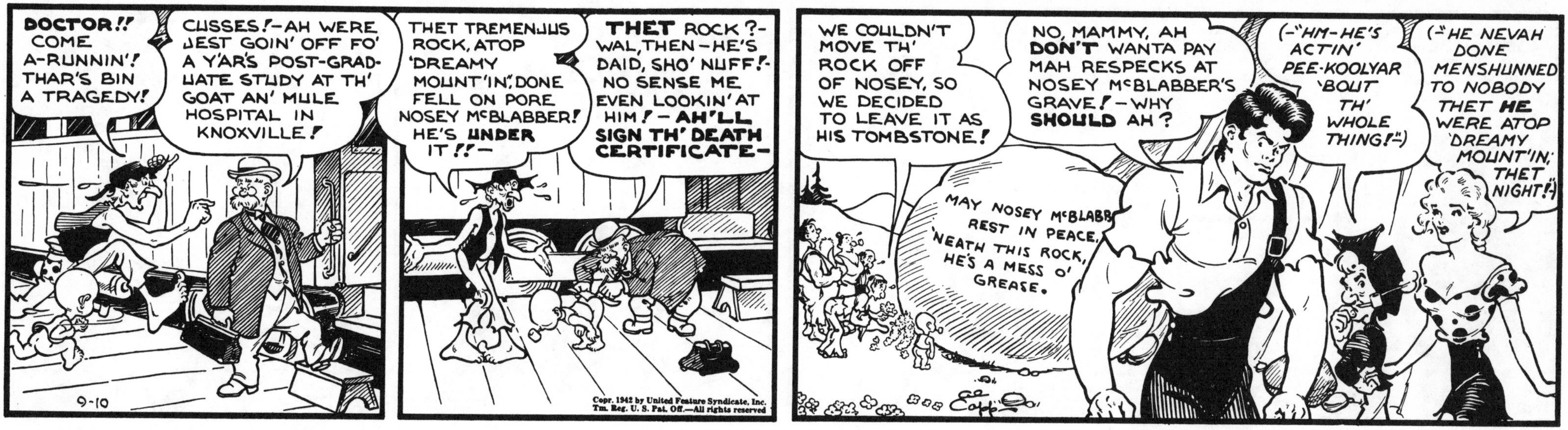
DOCTOR!! COME A-RUNNIN'! THAR'S BIN A TRAGEDY!
CUSSES!—AH WERE JEST GOIN' OFF FO' A Y'AR'S POST-GRADUATE STUDY AT TH' GOAT AN' MULE HOSPITAL IN KNOXVILLE!
9-10
THET TREMENJUS ROCK, ATOP 'DREAMY MOUNT'IN' DONE FELL ON PORE NOSEY McBLABBER! HE'S UNDER IT!!—
THET ROCK?—WAL, THEN—HE'S DAID, SHO' NUFF!—NO SENSE ME EVEN LOOKIN' AT HIM!—AH'LL SIGN TH' DEATH CERTIFICATE—
Copr. 1942 by United Feature Syndicate, Inc.
Tm. Reg. U. S. Pat. Off.—All rights reserved
WE COULDN'T MOVE TH' ROCK OFF OF NOSEY, SO WE DECIDED TO LEAVE IT AS HIS TOMBSTONE!
NO, MAMMY, AH DON'T WANTA PAY MAH RESPECKS AT NOSEY McBLABBER'S GRAVE!—WHY SHOULD AH?
(—"HM—HE'S ACTIN' PEE-KOOLYAR 'BOUT TH' WHOLE THING!"—)
(—"HE NEVAH DONE MENSHUNNED TO NOBODY THET HE WERE ATOP 'DREAMY MOUNT'IN,' THET NIGHT!"—)
MAY NOSEY McBLABB REST IN PEACE. 'NEATH THIS ROCK, HE'S A MESS O' GREASE.

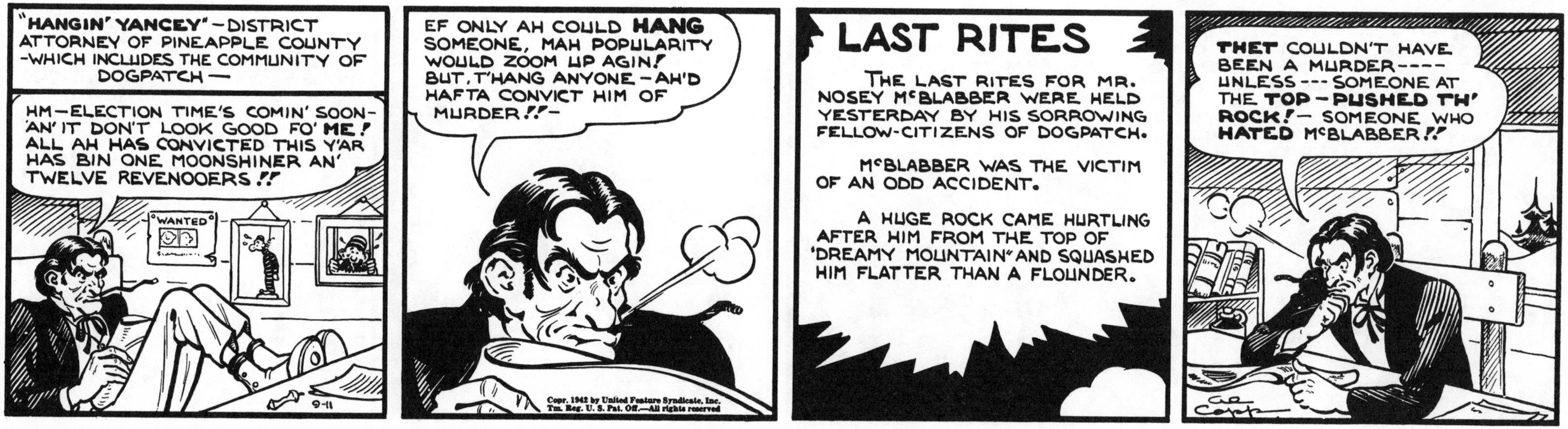
"HANGIN' YANCEY"—DISTRICT ATTORNEY OF PINEAPPLE COUNTY—WHICH INCLUDES THE COMMUNITY OF DOGPATCH—
HM—ELECTION TIME'S COMIN' SOON—AN' IT DON'T LOOK GOOD FO' ME! ALL AH HAS CONVICTED THIS Y'AR HAS BIN ONE MOONSHINER AN' TWELVE REVENOOERS!!
WANTED
9-11
EF ONLY AH COULD HANG SOMEONE, MAH POPULARITY WOULD ZOOM UP AGIN! BUT, T'HANG ANYONE—AH'D HAFTA CONVICT HIM OF MURDER!!—
Copr. 1942 by United Feature Syndicate, Inc.
Tm. Reg. U. S. Pat. Off.—All rights reserved
LAST RITES
THE LAST RITES FOR MR. NOSEY McBLABBER WERE HELD YESTERDAY BY HIS SORROWING FELLOW-CITIZENS OF DOGPATCH.
McBLABBER WAS THE VICTIM OF AN ODD ACCIDENT.
A HUGE ROCK CAME HURTLING AFTER HIM FROM THE TOP OF 'DREAMY MOUNTAIN' AND SQUASHED HIM FLATTER THAN A FLOUNDER.
THET COULDN'T HAVE BEEN A MURDER----UNLESS---SOMEONE AT THE TOP—PUSHED TH' ROCK!—SOMEONE WHO HATED McBLABBER!!

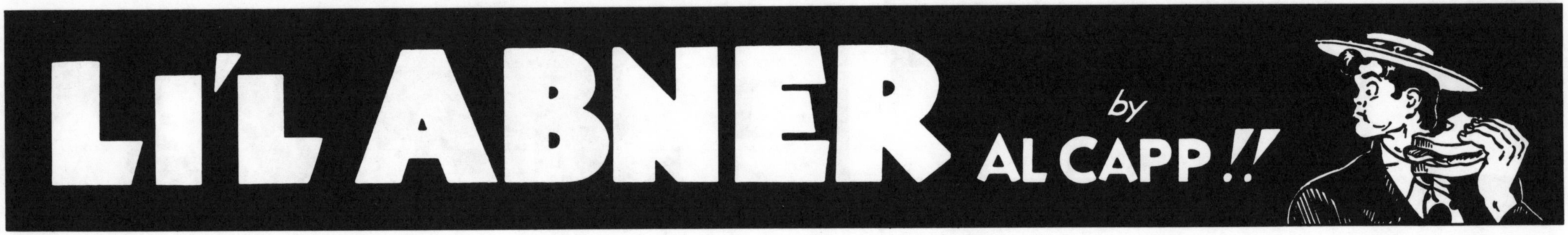
LI'L ABNER
by
AL CAPP!!

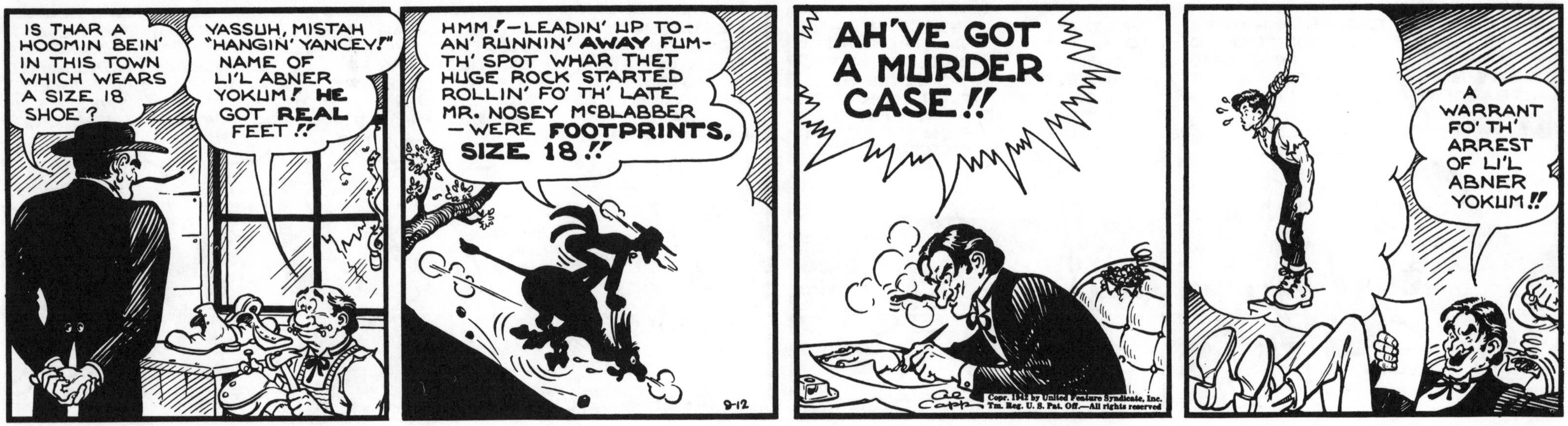
IS THAR A HOOMIN BEIN' IN THIS TOWN WHICH WEARS A SIZE 18 SHOE?
YASSUH, MISTAH "HANGIN' YANCEY!" NAME OF LI'L ABNER YOKUM! HE GOT REAL FEET!!
HMM!—LEADIN' UP TO—AN' RUNNIN' AWAY FUM—TH' SPOT WHAR THET HUGE ROCK STARTED ROLLIN' FO' TH' LATE MR. NOSEY McBLABBER—WERE FOOTPRINTS, SIZE 18!!
9-12
AH'VE GOT A MURDER CASE!!
Al Capp
Copr. 1942 by United Feature Syndicate, Inc.
Tm. Reg. U. S. Pat. Off.—All rights reserved
A WARRANT FO' TH' ARREST OF LI'L ABNER YOKUM!!

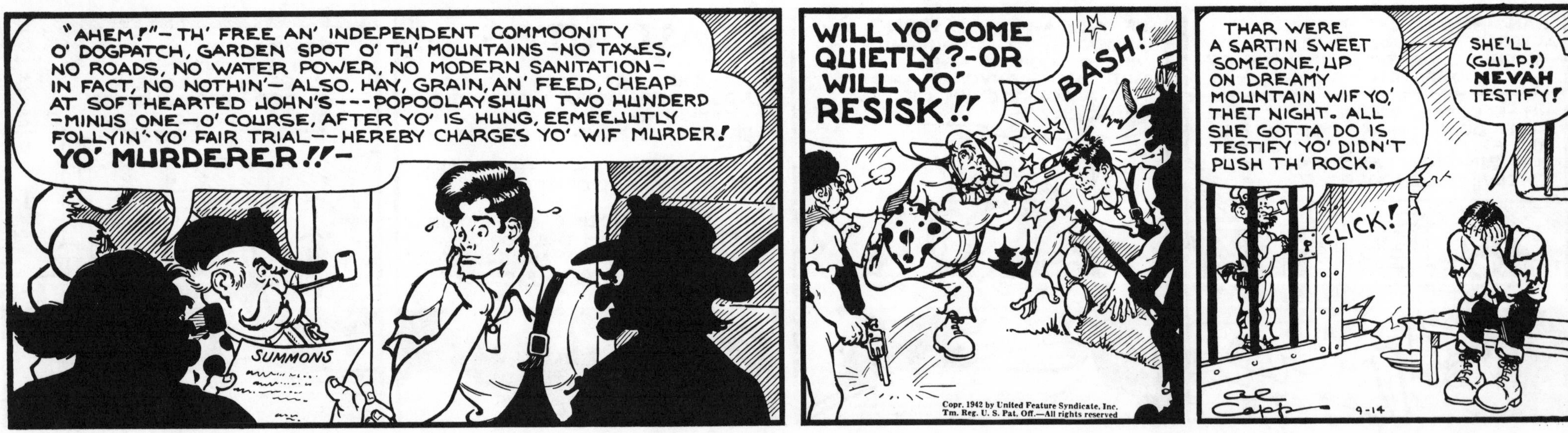
"AHEM!"—TH' FREE AN' INDEPENDENT COMMOONITY O' DOGPATCH, GARDEN SPOT O' TH' MOUNTAINS—NO TAXES, NO ROADS, NO WATER POWER, NO MODERN SANITATION—IN FACT, NO NOTHIN'—ALSO, HAY, GRAIN, AN' FEED, CHEAP AT SOFTHEARTED JOHN'S---POPOOLAYSHUN TWO HUNDERD—MINUS ONE—O' COURSE, AFTER YO' IS HUNG, EEMEEJUTLY FOLLYIN' YO' FAIR TRIAL--HEREBY CHARGES YO' WIF MURDER! YO' MURDERER!!—
SUMMONS
WILL YO' COME QUIETLY?—OR WILL YO' RESISK!!
BASH!
Copr. 1942 by United Feature Syndicate, Inc.
Tm. Reg. U. S. Pat. Off.—All rights reserved
THAR WERE A SARTIN SWEET SOMEONE, UP ON DREAMY MOUNTAIN WIF YO', THET NIGHT. ALL SHE GOTTA DO IS TESTIFY YO' DIDN'T PUSH TH' ROCK.
SHE'LL (GULP!) NEVAH TESTIFY!
CLICK!
Al Capp
9-14

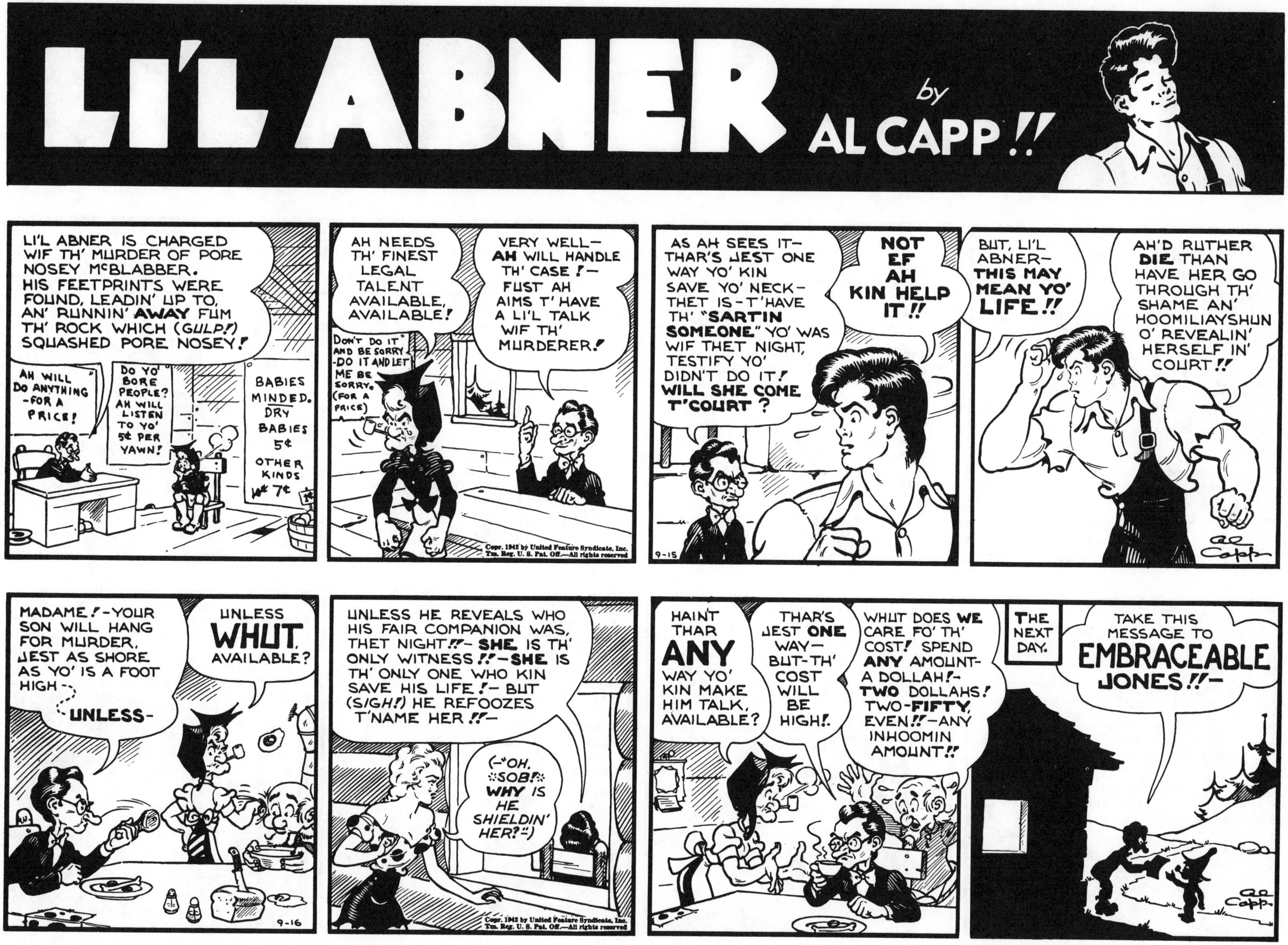

LI'L ABNER
by AL CAPP!!
LI'L ABNER IS CHARGED WIF TH' MURDER OF PORE NOSEY McBLABBER. HIS FEETPRINTS WERE FOUND, LEADIN' UP TO, AN' RUNNIN' AWAY FUM TH' ROCK WHICH (GULP!) SQUASHED PORE NOSEY!
AH WILL DO ANYTHING -FOR A PRICE!
DO YO' BORE PEOPLE? AH WILL LISTEN TO YO' 5¢ PER YAWN!
BABIES MINDED. DRY BABIES 5¢ OTHER KINDS 7¢
AH NEEDS TH' FINEST LEGAL TALENT AVAILABLE, AVAILABLE!
VERY WELL- AH WILL HANDLE TH' CASE!- FUST AH AIMS T' HAVE A LI'L TALK WIF TH' MURDERER!
DON'T DO IT AND BE SORRY -DO IT AND LET ME BE SORRY. (FOR A PRICE)
Copr. 1942 by United Feature Syndicate, Inc. Tm. Reg. U. S. Pat. Off.—All rights reserved
AS AH SEES IT- THAR'S JEST ONE WAY YO' KIN SAVE YO' NECK- THET IS-T'HAVE TH' "SARTIN SOMEONE" YO' WAS WIF THET NIGHT, TESTIFY YO' DIDN'T DO IT! WILL SHE COME T'COURT?
NOT EF AH KIN HELP IT!!
9-15
BUT, LI'L ABNER- THIS MAY MEAN YO' LIFE!!
AH'D RUTHER DIE THAN HAVE HER GO THROUGH TH' SHAME AN' HOOMILIAYSHUN O' REVEALIN' HERSELF IN' COURT!!
Al Capp
MADAME!-YOUR SON WILL HANG FOR MURDER, JEST AS SHORE AS YO' IS A FOOT HIGH- -UNLESS-
UNLESS WHUT, AVAILABLE?
9-16
UNLESS HE REVEALS WHO HIS FAIR COMPANION WAS, THET NIGHT!!-SHE IS TH' ONLY WITNESS!!-SHE IS TH' ONLY ONE WHO KIN SAVE HIS LIFE!- BUT (SIGH!) HE REFOOZES T'NAME HER!!-
(-"OH. SOB! WHY IS HE SHIELDIN' HER?"-)
Copr. 1942 by United Feature Syndicate, Inc. Tm. Reg. U. S. Pat. Off.—All rights reserved
HAIN'T THAR ANY WAY YO' KIN MAKE HIM TALK, AVAILABLE?
THAR'S JEST ONE WAY- BUT-TH' COST WILL BE HIGH!
WHUT DOES WE CARE FO' TH' COST! SPEND ANY AMOUNT- A DOLLAH!- TWO DOLLAHS! TWO-FIFTY, EVEN!!-ANY INHOOMIN AMOUNT!!
THE NEXT DAY.
TAKE THIS MESSAGE TO EMBRACEABLE JONES!!-
Al Capp

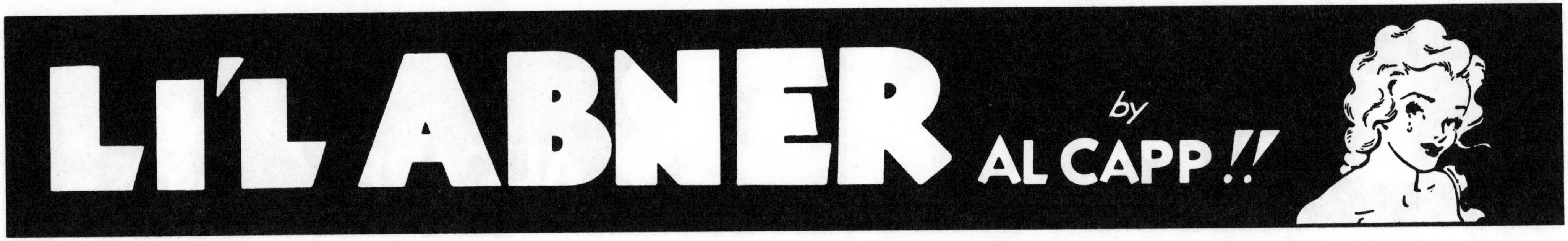

LI'L ABNER
by
AL CAPP!!

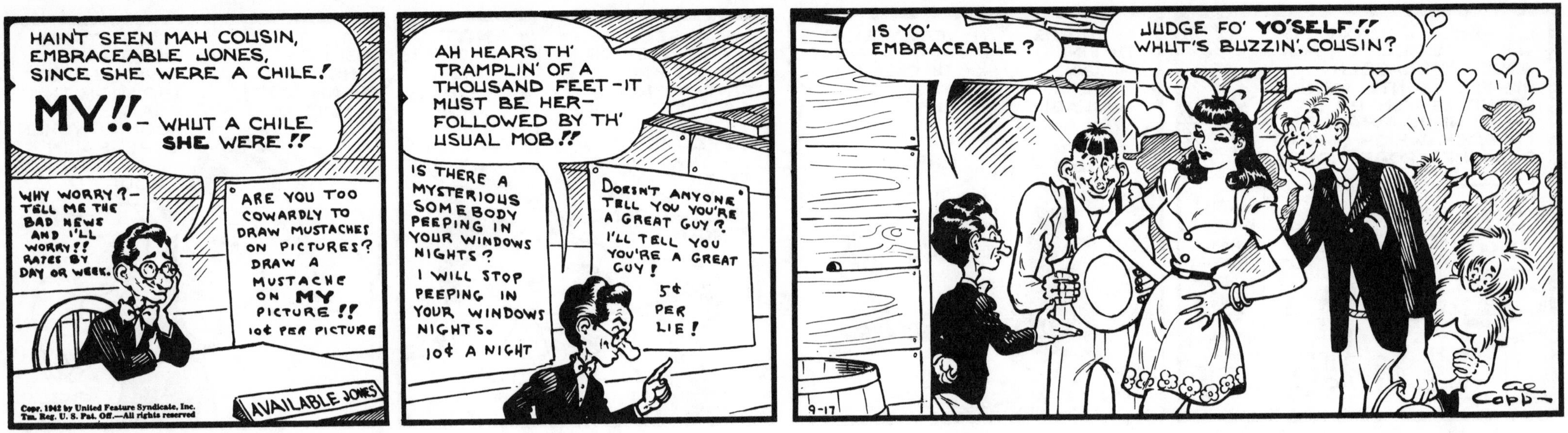

HAIN'T SEEN MAH COUSIN, EMBRACEABLE JONES, SINCE SHE WERE A CHILE! MY!!- WHUT A CHILE SHE WERE!!
WHY WORRY?- TELL ME THE BAD NEWS AND I'LL WORRY!! RATES BY DAY OR WEEK.
ARE YOU TOO COWARDLY TO DRAW MUSTACHES ON PICTURES? DRAW A MUSTACHE ON MY PICTURE!! 10¢ PER PICTURE
AVAILABLE JONES
Copr. 1942 by United Feature Syndicate, Inc. Tm. Reg. U. S. Pat. Off.—All rights reserved
AH HEARS TH' TRAMPLIN' OF A THOUSAND FEET-IT MUST BE HER- FOLLOWED BY TH' USUAL MOB!!
IS THERE A MYSTERIOUS SOMEBODY PEEPING IN YOUR WINDOWS NIGHTS? I WILL STOP PEEPING IN YOUR WINDOWS NIGHTS. 10¢ A NIGHT
DOESN'T ANYONE TELL YOU YOU'RE A GREAT GUY? I'LL TELL YOU YOU'RE A GREAT GUY! 5¢ PER LIE!
IS YO' EMBRACEABLE?
JUDGE FO' YO'SELF!! WHUT'S BUZZIN', COUSIN?
9-17
AL CAPP

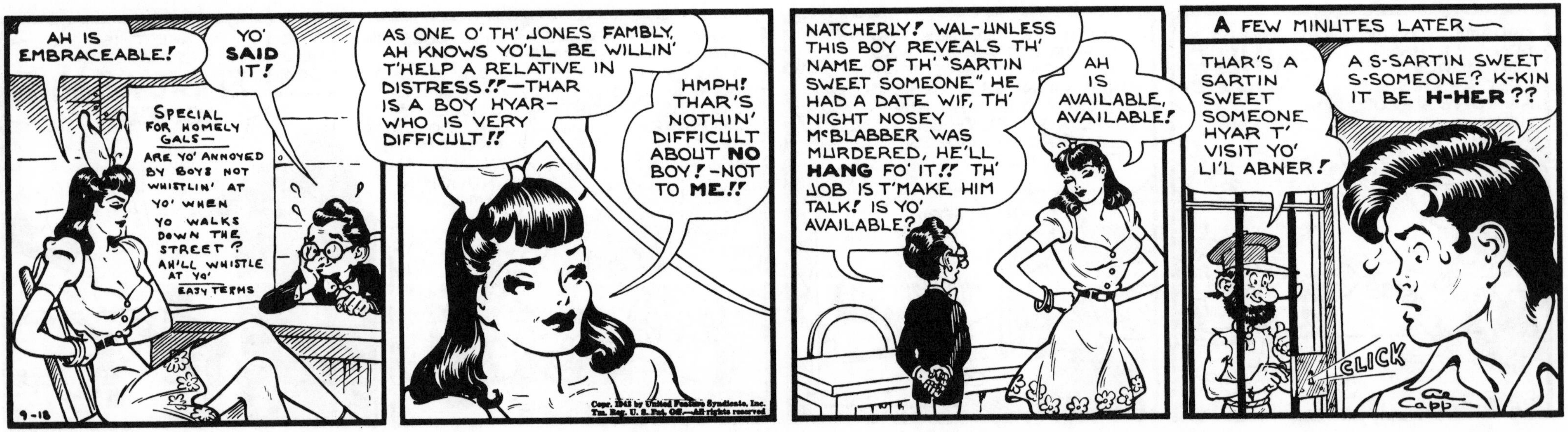

AH IS EMBRACEABLE!
YO' SAID IT!
SPECIAL FOR HOMELY GALS— ARE YO' ANNOYED BY BOYS NOT WHISTLIN' AT YO' WHEN YO WALKS DOWN THE STREET? AH'LL WHISTLE AT YO' EASY TERMS
9-18
AS ONE O' TH' JONES FAMBLY, AH KNOWS YO'LL BE WILLIN' T'HELP A RELATIVE IN DISTRESS!!-THAR IS A BOY HYAR- WHO IS VERY DIFFICULT!!
HMPH! THAR'S NOTHIN' DIFFICULT ABOUT NO BOY!-NOT TO ME!!
Copr. 1942 by United Feature Syndicate, Inc. Tm. Reg. U. S. Pat. Off.—All rights reserved
NATCHERLY! WAL-UNLESS THIS BOY REVEALS TH' NAME OF TH' "SARTIN SWEET SOMEONE" HE HAD A DATE WIF, TH' NIGHT NOSEY McBLABBER WAS MURDERED, HE'LL HANG FO' IT!! TH' JOB IS T'MAKE HIM TALK! IS YO' AVAILABLE?
AH IS AVAILABLE, AVAILABLE!
A FEW MINUTES LATER—
THAR'S A SARTIN SWEET SOMEONE HYAR T' VISIT YO' LI'L ABNER!
A S-SARTIN SWEET S-SOMEONE? K-KIN IT BE H-HER??
CLICK
AL CAPP

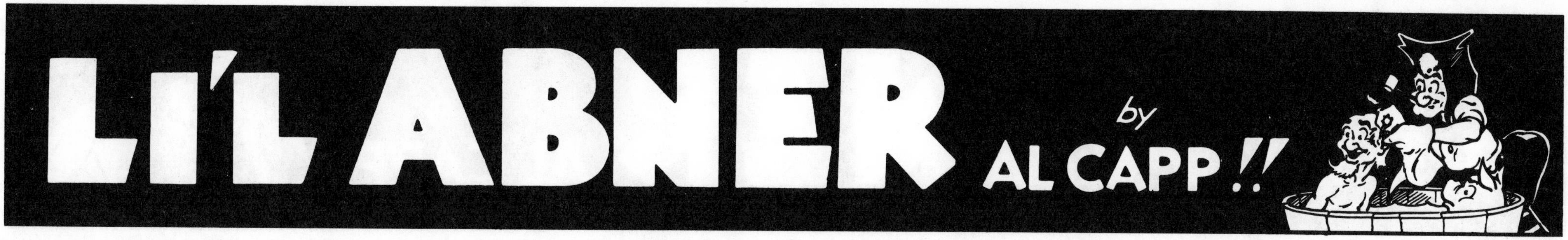

LI'L ABNER
by AL CAPP!!

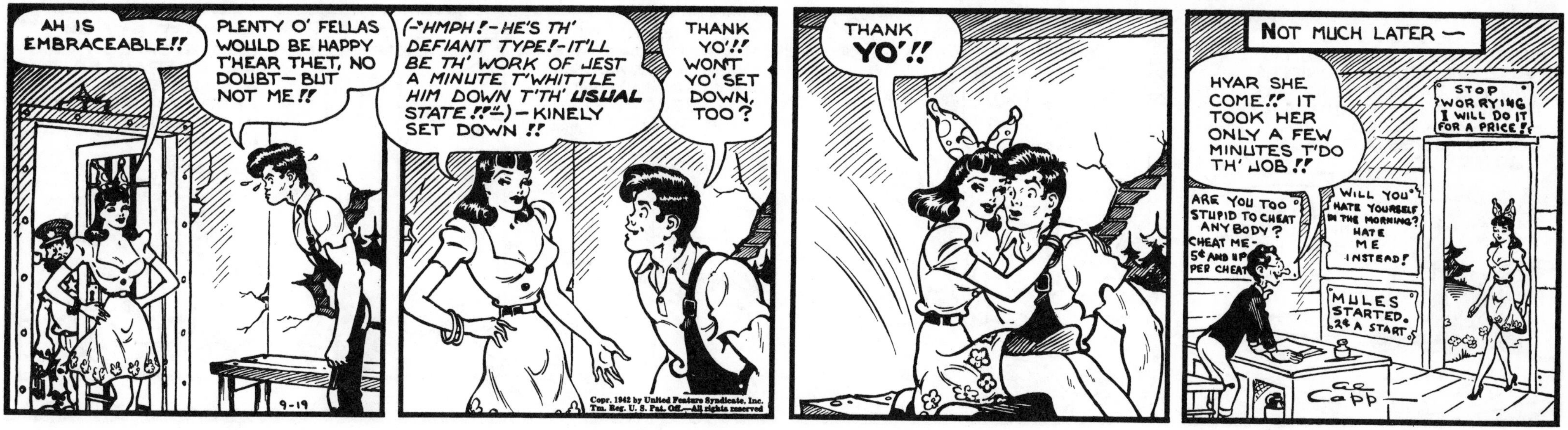

AH IS EMBRACEABLE!!
PLENTY O' FELLAS WOULD BE HAPPY T'HEAR THET, NO DOUBT—BUT NOT ME!!
9-19
(–"HMPH!–HE'S TH' DEFIANT TYPE!–IT'LL BE TH' WORK OF JEST A MINUTE T'WHITTLE HIM DOWN T'TH' USUAL STATE!!"–)–KINELY SET DOWN!!
THANK YO'!! WON'T YO' SET DOWN, TOO?
Copr. 1942 by United Feature Syndicate, Inc. Tm. Reg. U. S. Pat. Off.—All rights reserved
THANK YO'!!
NOT MUCH LATER—
HYAR SHE COME!! IT TOOK HER ONLY A FEW MINUTES T'DO TH' JOB!!
STOP WORRYING I WILL DO IT FOR A PRICE!
ARE YOU TOO STUPID TO CHEAT ANY BODY? CHEAT ME– 5¢ AND UP PER CHEAT
WILL YOU HATE YOURSELF IN THE MORNING? HATE ME INSTEAD!
MULES STARTED. 2¢ A START.
Al Capp

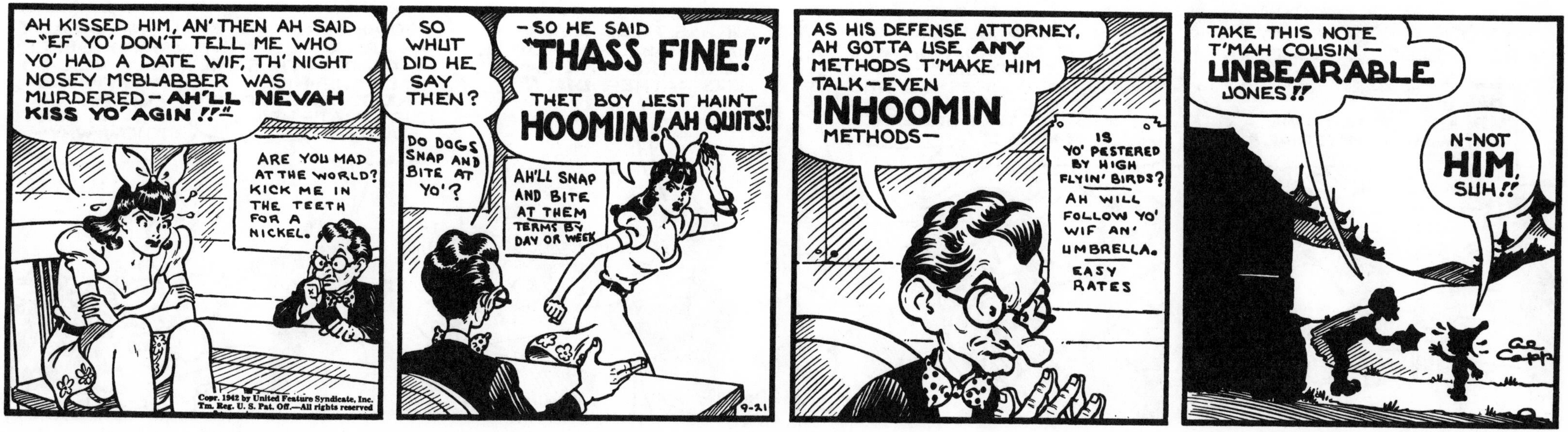

AH KISSED HIM, AN' THEN AH SAID –"EF YO' DON'T TELL ME WHO YO' HAD A DATE WIF, TH' NIGHT NOSEY McBLABBER WAS MURDERED–AH'LL NEVAH KISS YO' AGIN!!"
ARE YOU MAD AT THE WORLD? KICK ME IN THE TEETH FOR A NICKEL.
Copr. 1942 by United Feature Syndicate, Inc. Tm. Reg. U. S. Pat. Off.—All rights reserved
SO WHUT DID HE SAY THEN?
–SO HE SAID "THASS FINE!" THET BOY JEST HAIN'T HOOMIN! AH QUITS!
DO DOGS SNAP AND BITE AT YO'?
AH'LL SNAP AND BITE AT THEM TERMS BY DAY OR WEEK
9-21
AS HIS DEFENSE ATTORNEY, AH GOTTA USE ANY METHODS T'MAKE HIM TALK–EVEN INHOOMIN METHODS–
IS YO' PESTERED BY HIGH FLYIN' BIRDS? AH WILL FOLLOW YO' WIF AN' UMBRELLA. EASY RATES
TAKE THIS NOTE T'MAH COUSIN–UNBEARABLE JONES!!
N-NOT HIM, SUH!!
Al Capp

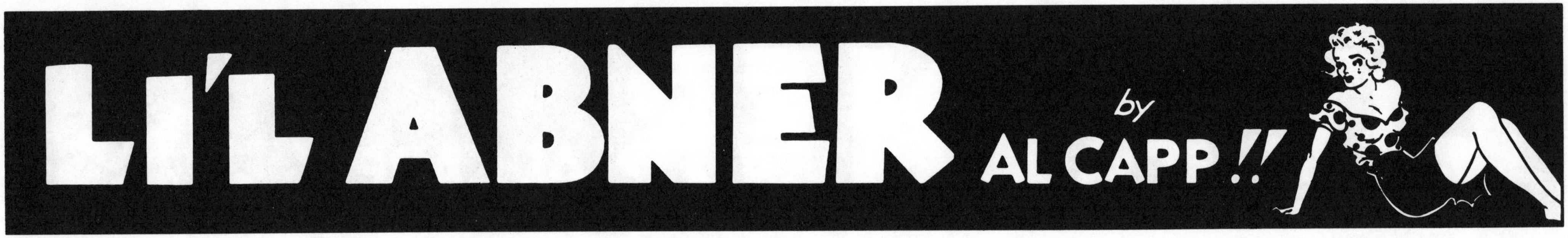
LI'L ABNER
by
AL CAPP!!

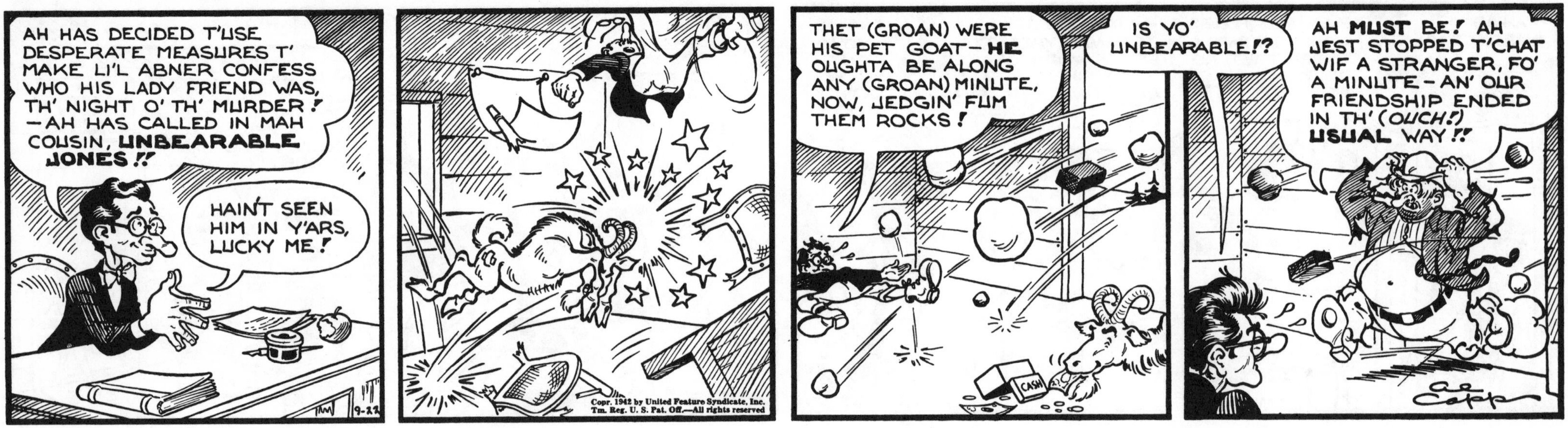
AH HAS DECIDED T'USE DESPERATE MEASURES T' MAKE LI'L ABNER CONFESS WHO HIS LADY FRIEND WAS, TH' NIGHT O' TH' MURDER! —AH HAS CALLED IN MAH COUSIN, **UNBEARABLE JONES!!**
HAIN'T SEEN HIM IN Y'ARS, LUCKY ME!
9-22
Copr. 1942 by United Feature Syndicate, Inc. Tm. Reg. U. S. Pat. Off.—All rights reserved
THET (GROAN) WERE HIS PET GOAT—**HE** OUGHTA BE ALONG ANY (GROAN) MINUTE, NOW, JEDGIN' FUM THEM ROCKS!
CASH
IS YO' UNBEARABLE!?
AH **MUST** BE! AH JEST STOPPED T'CHAT WIF A STRANGER, FO' A MINUTE—AN' OUR FRIENDSHIP ENDED IN TH' (*OUCH!*) **USUAL** WAY!!
al Capp

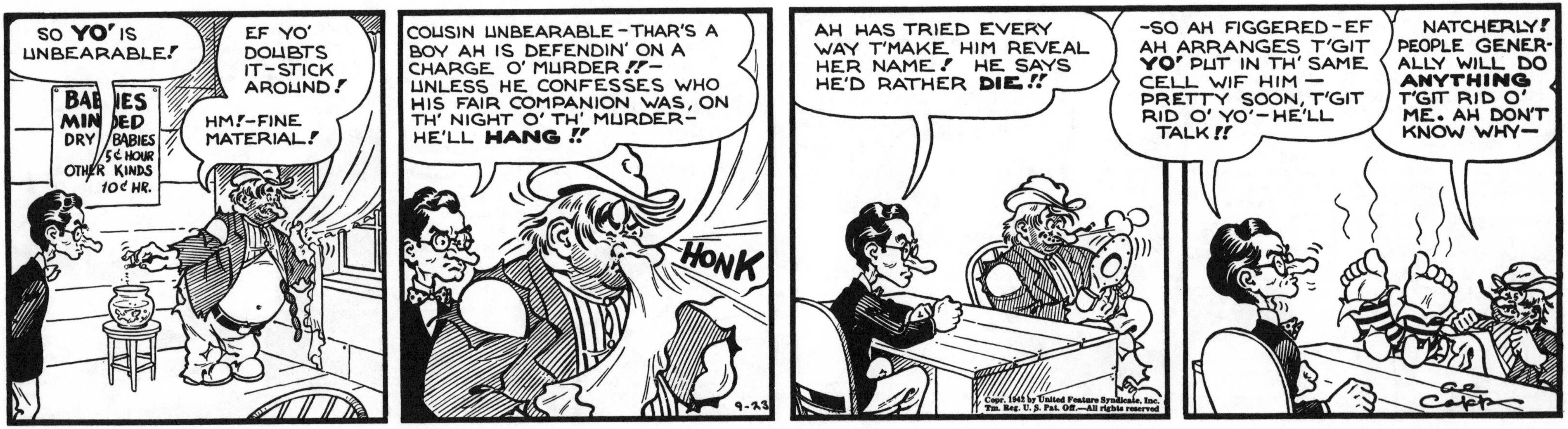
SO **YO'** IS UNBEARABLE!
EF YO' DOUBTS IT—STICK AROUND!
BABIES MINDED
DRY BABIES 5¢ HOUR
OTHER KINDS 10¢ HR.
HM!—FINE MATERIAL!
COUSIN UNBEARABLE—THAR'S A BOY AH IS DEFENDIN' ON A CHARGE O' MURDER!!—UNLESS HE CONFESSES WHO HIS FAIR COMPANION WAS, ON TH' NIGHT O' TH' MURDER—HE'LL **HANG!!**
HONK
9-23
AH HAS TRIED EVERY WAY T'MAKE HIM REVEAL HER NAME! HE SAYS HE'D RATHER **DIE!!**
Copr. 1942 by United Feature Syndicate, Inc. Tm. Reg. U. S. Pat. Off.—All rights reserved
—SO AH FIGGERED—EF AH ARRANGES T'GIT **YO'** PUT IN TH' SAME CELL WIF HIM—PRETTY SOON, T'GIT RID O' YO'—HE'LL TALK!!
NATCHERLY! PEOPLE GENERALLY WILL **DO ANYTHING** T'GIT RID O' ME. AH DON'T KNOW WHY—
al Capp

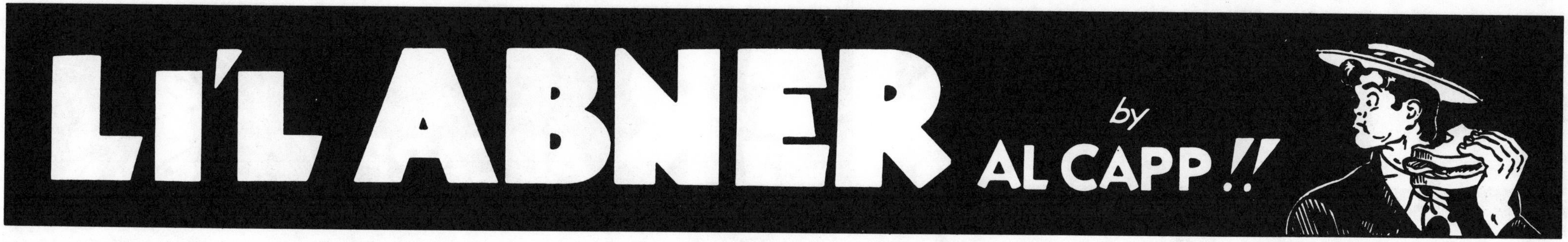
LI'L ABNER
by
AL CAPP!!

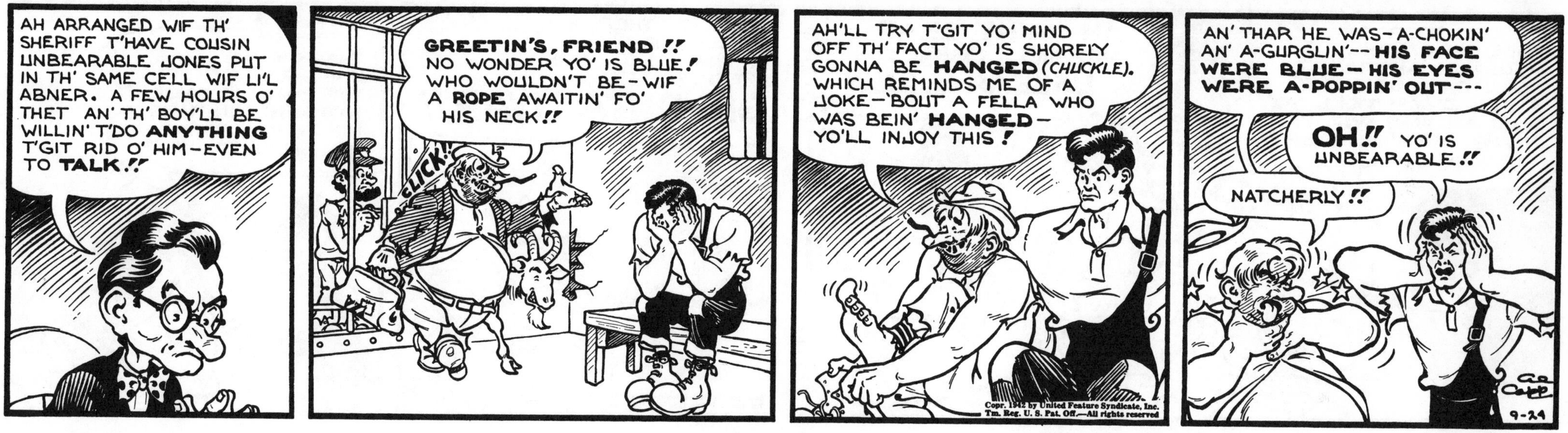
AH ARRANGED WIF TH' SHERIFF T'HAVE COUSIN UNBEARABLE JONES PUT IN TH' SAME CELL WIF LI'L ABNER. A FEW HOURS O' THET AN' TH' BOY'LL BE WILLIN' T'DO ANYTHING T'GIT RID O' HIM—EVEN TO TALK!!
GREETIN'S, FRIEND!! NO WONDER YO' IS BLUE! WHO WOULDN'T BE—WIF A ROPE AWAITIN' FO' HIS NECK!!
CLICK!
AH'LL TRY T'GIT YO' MIND OFF TH' FACT YO' IS SHORELY GONNA BE HANGED (CHUCKLE). WHICH REMINDS ME OF A JOKE—'BOUT A FELLA WHO WAS BEIN' HANGED—YO'LL INJOY THIS!
Copr. 1942 by United Feature Syndicate, Inc. Tm. Reg. U. S. Pat. Off.—All rights reserved
AN' THAR HE WAS—A-CHOKIN' AN' A-GURGLIN'—HIS FACE WERE BLUE—HIS EYES WERE A-POPPIN' OUT---
OH!! YO' IS UNBEARABLE!!
NATCHERLY!!
AL CAPP
9-24

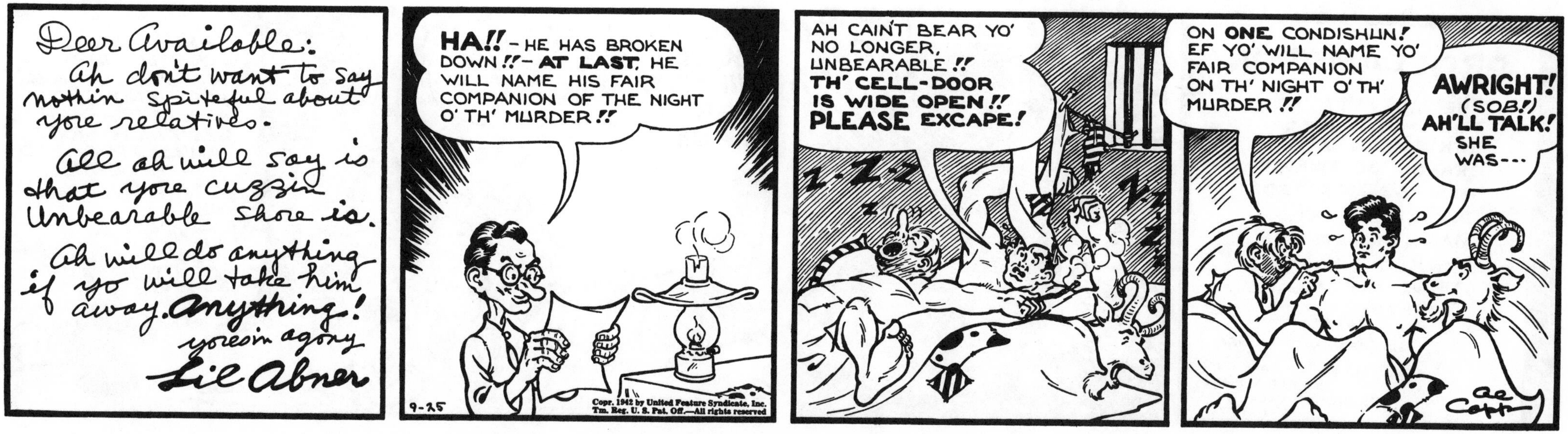
Deer Available:
Ah don't want to say nothin spiteful about yore relatives.
All ah will say is that yore cuzzin Unbearable shore is.
Ah will do anything if yo will take him away. Anything!
yores in agony
Lil Abner
HA!!—HE HAS BROKEN DOWN!!—AT LAST, HE WILL NAME HIS FAIR COMPANION OF THE NIGHT O' TH' MURDER!!
9-25
Copr. 1942 by United Feature Syndicate, Inc. Tm. Reg. U. S. Pat. Off.—All rights reserved
AH CAIN'T BEAR YO' NO LONGER, UNBEARABLE!! TH' CELL-DOOR IS WIDE OPEN!! PLEASE EXCAPE!
Z-Z-Z
ON ONE CONDISHUN! EF YO' WILL NAME YO' FAIR COMPANION ON TH' NIGHT O' TH' MURDER!!
AWRIGHT! (SOB!) AH'LL TALK! SHE WAS---
AL CAPP

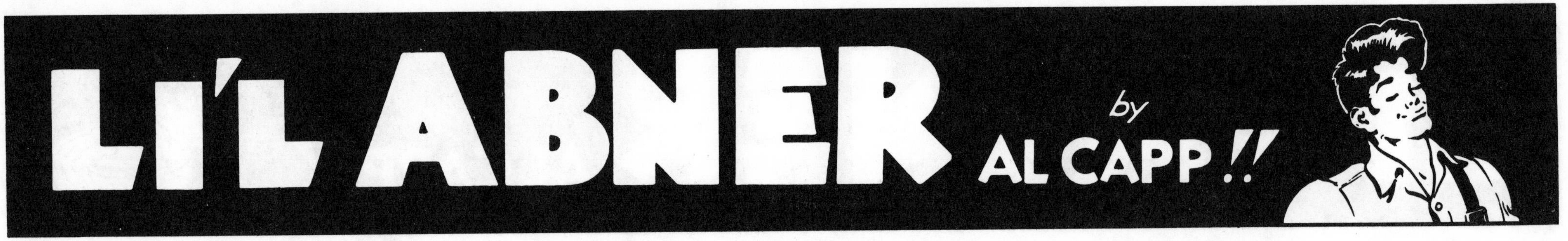

LI'L ABNER
by
AL CAPP !!

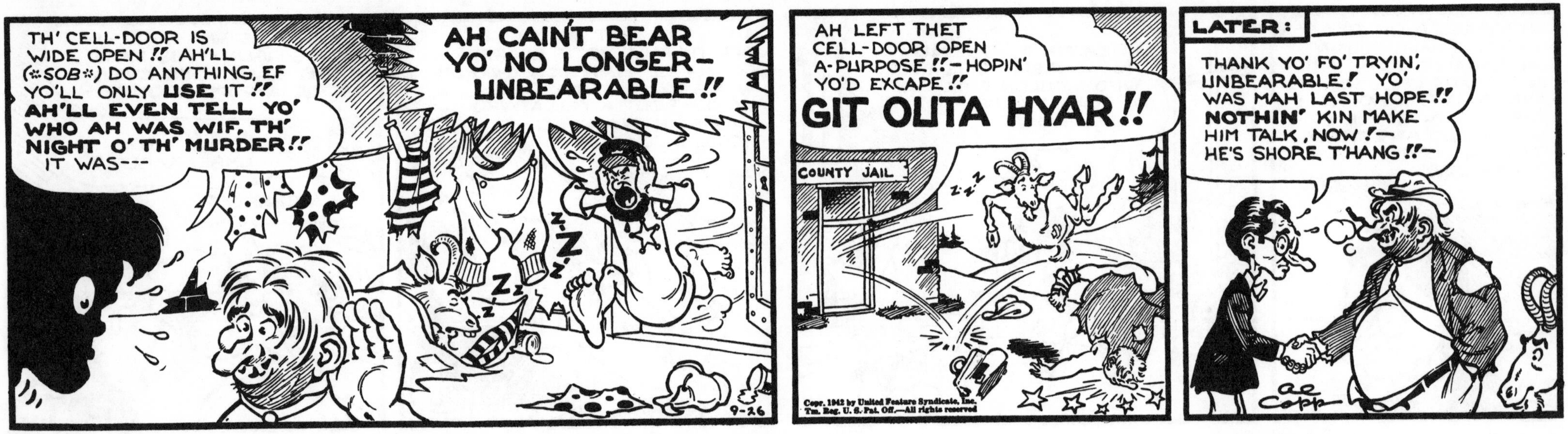

TH' CELL-DOOR IS WIDE OPEN !! AH'LL (*SOB*) DO ANYTHING, EF YO'LL ONLY USE IT !! AH'LL EVEN TELL YO' WHO AH WAS WIF, TH' NIGHT O' TH' MURDER !! IT WAS---
AH CAIN'T BEAR YO' NO LONGER- UNBEARABLE !!
9-26
AH LEFT THET CELL-DOOR OPEN A-PURPOSE !! - HOPIN' YO'D EXCAPE !!
GIT OUTA HYAR !!
COUNTY JAIL
Copr. 1942 by United Feature Syndicate, Inc. Tm. Reg. U. S. Pat. Off.—All rights reserved
LATER:
THANK YO' FO' TRYIN', UNBEARABLE ! YO' WAS MAH LAST HOPE !! NOTHIN' KIN MAKE HIM TALK, NOW !— HE'S SHORE T'HANG !!—
AL CAPP

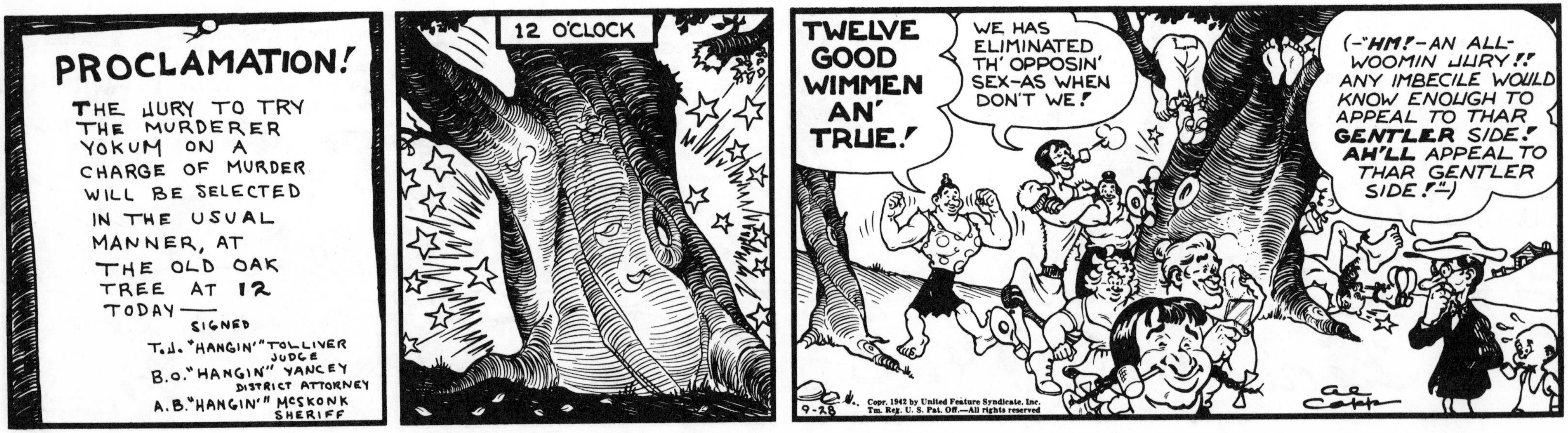

PROCLAMATION!
THE JURY TO TRY THE MURDERER YOKUM ON A CHARGE OF MURDER WILL BE SELECTED IN THE USUAL MANNER, AT THE OLD OAK TREE AT 12 TODAY —
SIGNED
T.J. "HANGIN'" TOLLIVER JUDGE
B.O. "HANGIN'" YANCEY DISTRICT ATTORNEY
A.B. "HANGIN'" McSKONK SHERIFF
12 O'CLOCK
TWELVE GOOD WIMMEN AN' TRUE !
WE HAS ELIMINATED TH' OPPOSIN' SEX—AS WHEN DON'T WE !
(—"HM! — AN ALL-WOOMIN JURY !! ANY IMBECILE WOULD KNOW ENOUGH TO APPEAL TO THAR GENTLER SIDE ! AH'LL APPEAL TO THAR GENTLER SIDE !"—)
9-28
Copr. 1942 by United Feature Syndicate, Inc. Tm. Reg. U. S. Pat. Off.—All rights reserved
AL CAPP

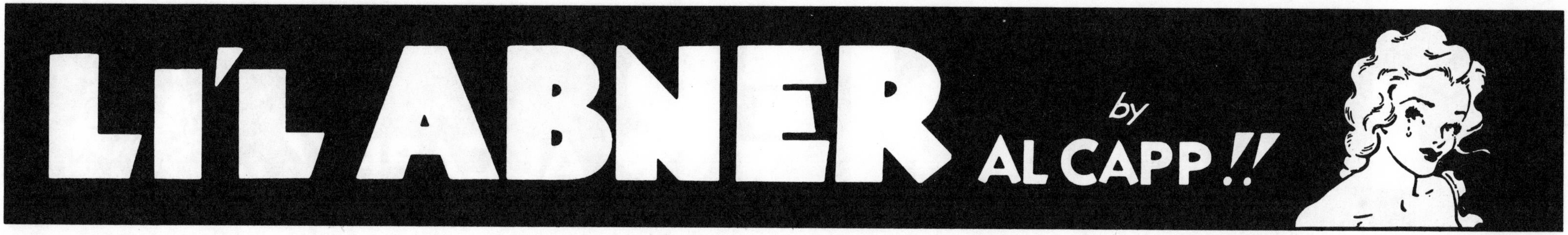
LI'L ABNER
by
AL CAPP!!

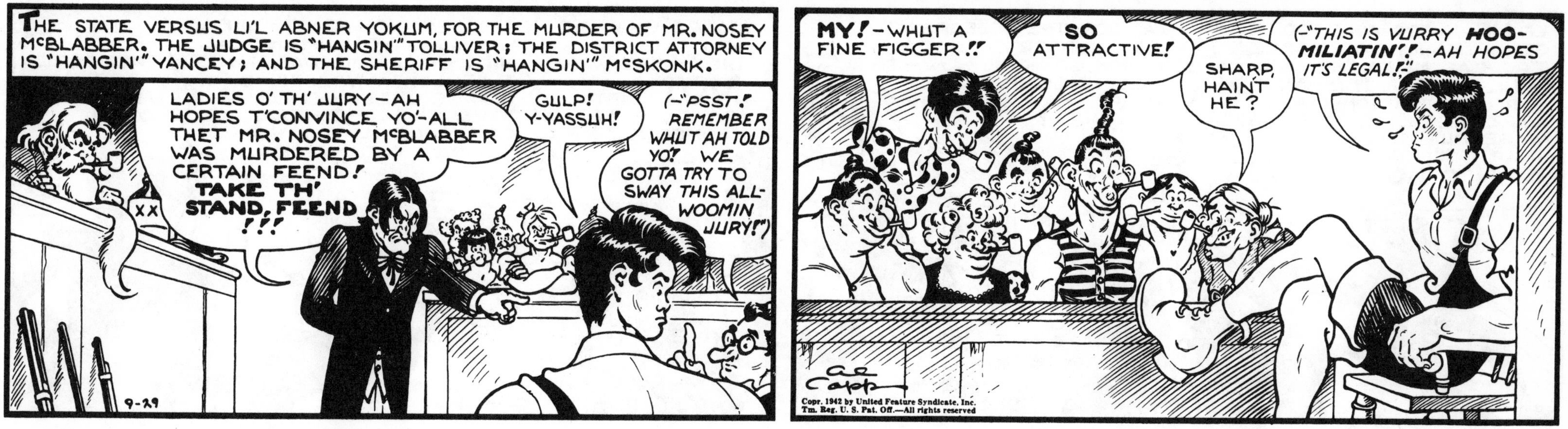
THE STATE VERSUS LI'L ABNER YOKUM, FOR THE MURDER OF MR. NOSEY McBLABBER. THE JUDGE IS "HANGIN'" TOLLIVER; THE DISTRICT ATTORNEY IS "HANGIN'" YANCEY; AND THE SHERIFF IS "HANGIN'" McSKONK.
LADIES O' TH' JURY—AH HOPES T'CONVINCE YO'-ALL THET MR. NOSEY McBLABBER WAS MURDERED BY A CERTAIN FEEND! TAKE TH' STAND, FEEND!!!
GULP! Y-YASSUH!
(—"PSST! REMEMBER WHUT AH TOLD YO! WE GOTTA TRY TO SWAY THIS ALL-WOOMIN JURY!")
XX
9-29
MY!—WHUT A FINE FIGGER!!
SO ATTRACTIVE!
SHARP, HAIN'T HE?
(—"THIS IS VURRY HOO-MILIATIN'!—AH HOPES IT'S LEGAL!—")
Al Capp
Copr. 1942 by United Feature Syndicate, Inc.
Tm. Reg. U. S. Pat. Off.—All rights reserved

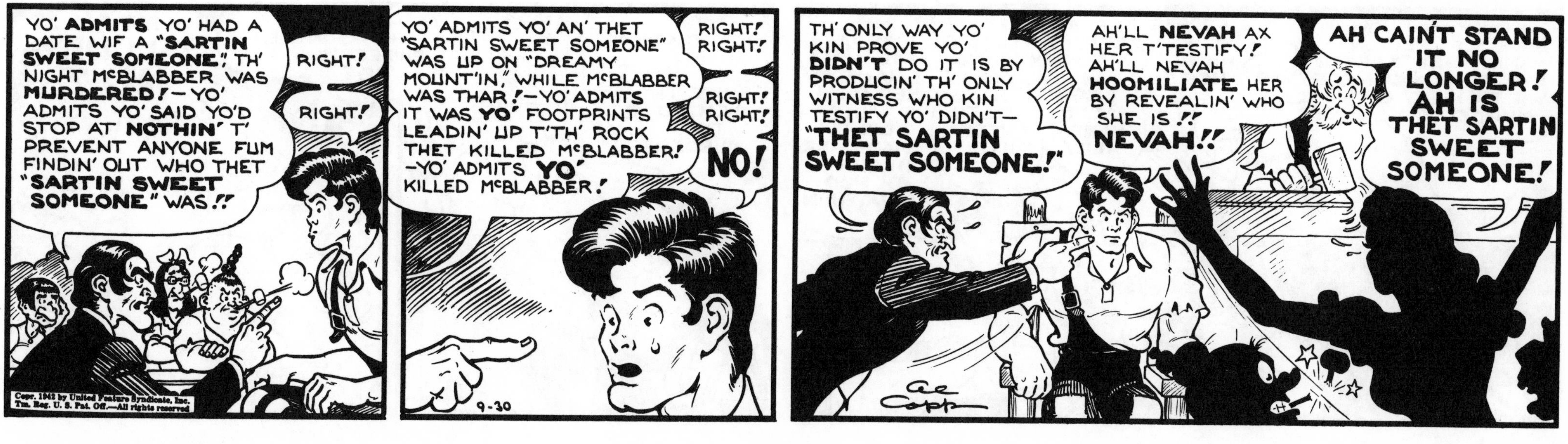
YO' ADMITS YO' HAD A DATE WIF A "SARTIN SWEET SOMEONE," TH' NIGHT McBLABBER WAS MURDERED!—YO' ADMITS YO' SAID YO'D STOP AT NOTHIN' T' PREVENT ANYONE FUM FINDIN' OUT WHO THET "SARTIN SWEET SOMEONE" WAS!!
RIGHT!
RIGHT!
Copr. 1942 by United Feature Syndicate, Inc.
Tm. Reg. U. S. Pat. Off.—All rights reserved
YO' ADMITS YO' AN' THET "SARTIN SWEET SOMEONE" WAS UP ON "DREAMY MOUNT'IN," WHILE McBLABBER WAS THAR!—YO' ADMITS IT WAS YO' FOOTPRINTS LEADIN' UP T'TH' ROCK THET KILLED McBLABBER!—YO' ADMITS YO' KILLED McBLABBER!
RIGHT! RIGHT!
RIGHT! RIGHT!
NO!
9-30
TH' ONLY WAY YO' KIN PROVE YO' DIDN'T DO IT IS BY PRODUCIN' TH' ONLY WITNESS WHO KIN TESTIFY YO' DIDN'T—"THET SARTIN SWEET SOMEONE!"
AH'LL NEVAH AX HER T'TESTIFY! AH'LL NEVAH HOOMILIATE HER BY REVEALIN' WHO SHE IS!! NEVAH!!
AH CAIN'T STAND IT NO LONGER! AH IS THET SARTIN SWEET SOMEONE!
Al Capp

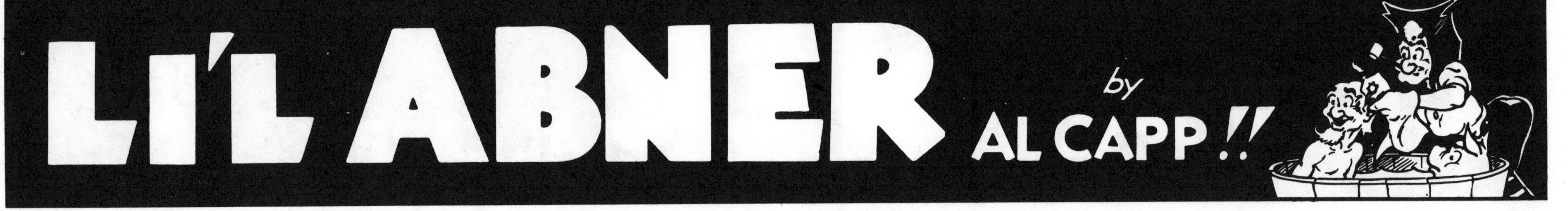
LI'L ABNER
by
AL CAPP!!

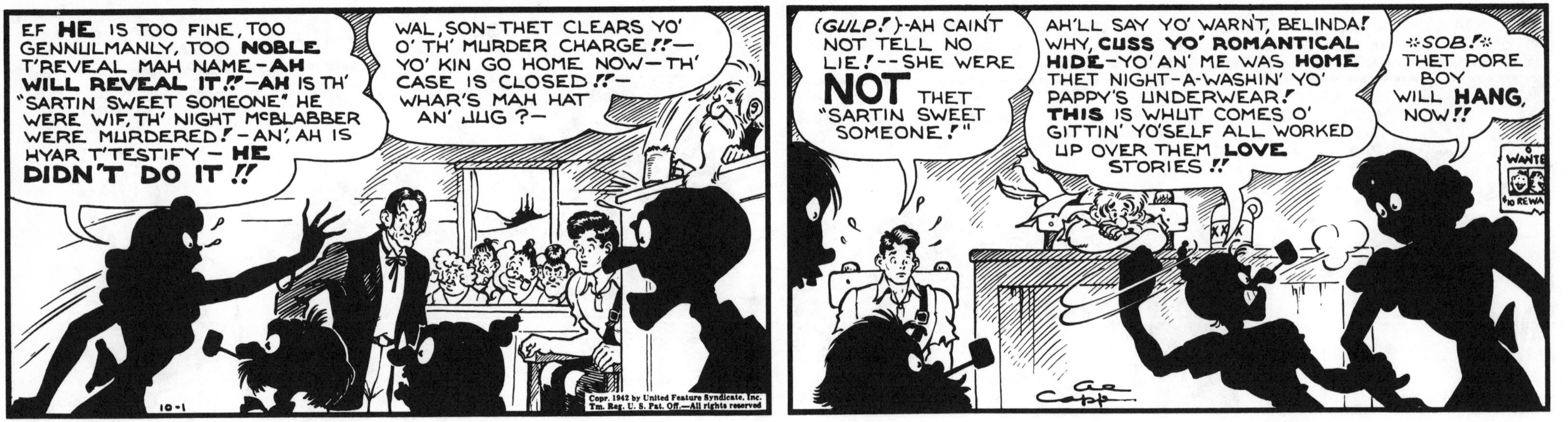
EF HE IS TOO FINE, TOO GENNULMANLY, TOO NOBLE T'REVEAL MAH NAME-AH WILL REVEAL IT!!-AH IS TH' "SARTIN SWEET SOMEONE" HE WERE WIF, TH' NIGHT McBLABBER WERE MURDERED!-AN', AH IS HYAR T'TESTIFY - HE DIDN'T DO IT!!
WAL, SON-THET CLEARS YO' O' TH' MURDER CHARGE!!- YO' KIN GO HOME NOW-TH' CASE IS CLOSED!!- WHAR'S MAH HAT AN' JUG?-
10-1
Copr. 1942 by United Feature Syndicate, Inc. Tm. Reg. U. S. Pat. Off.—All rights reserved
(GULP!)-AH CAIN'T NOT TELL NO LIE!--SHE WERE NOT THET "SARTIN SWEET SOMEONE!"
AH'LL SAY YO' WARN'T, BELINDA! WHY, CUSS YO' ROMANTICAL HIDE-YO' AN' ME WAS HOME THET NIGHT-A-WASHIN' YO' PAPPY'S UNDERWEAR! THIS IS WHUT COMES O' GITTIN' YO'SELF ALL WORKED UP OVER THEM LOVE STORIES!!
SOB! THET PORE BOY WILL HANG, NOW!!
WANTE
$10 REWA
Al Capp

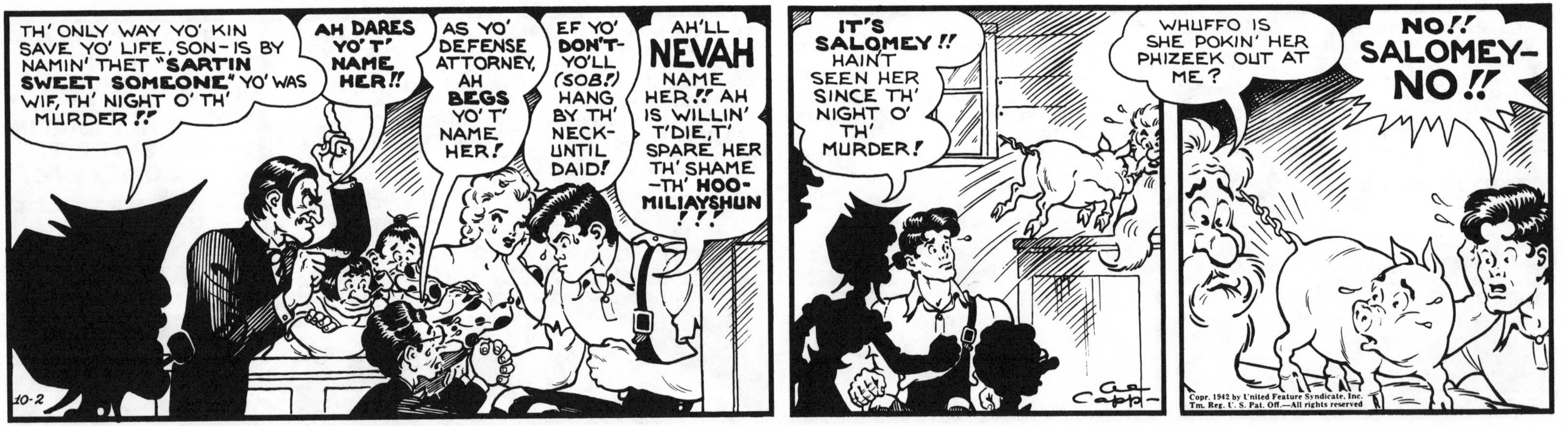
TH' ONLY WAY YO' KIN SAVE YO' LIFE, SON-IS BY NAMIN' THET "SARTIN SWEET SOMEONE" YO' WAS WIF, TH' NIGHT O' TH' MURDER!!
AH DARES YO' T' NAME HER!!
AS YO' DEFENSE ATTORNEY, AH BEGS YO' T' NAME HER!
EF YO' DON'T-YO'LL (SOB!) HANG BY TH' NECK-UNTIL DAID!
AH'LL NEVAH NAME HER!! AH IS WILLIN' T'DIE, T' SPARE HER TH' SHAME -TH' HOO-MILIAYSHUN!!!
10-2
IT'S SALOMEY!! HAIN'T SEEN HER SINCE TH' NIGHT O' TH' MURDER!
WHUFFO IS SHE POKIN' HER PHIZEEK OUT AT ME?
NO!! SALOMEY-NO!!
Al Capp
Copr. 1942 by United Feature Syndicate, Inc. Tm. Reg. U. S. Pat. Off.—All rights reserved

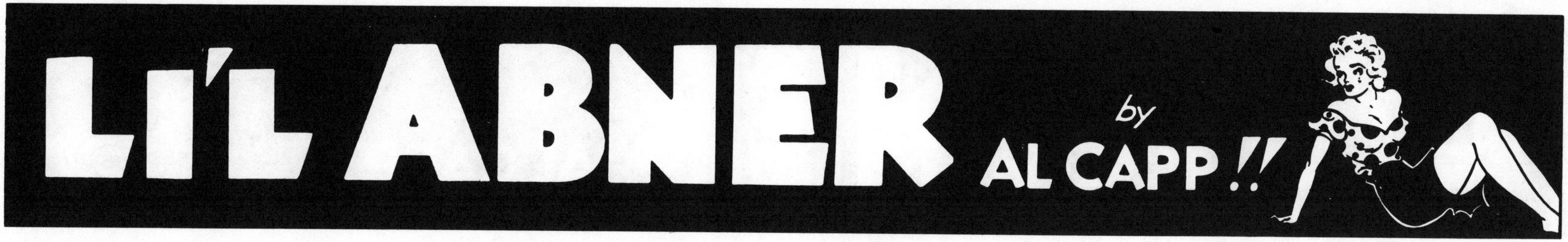
LI'L ABNER
by
AL CAPP!!

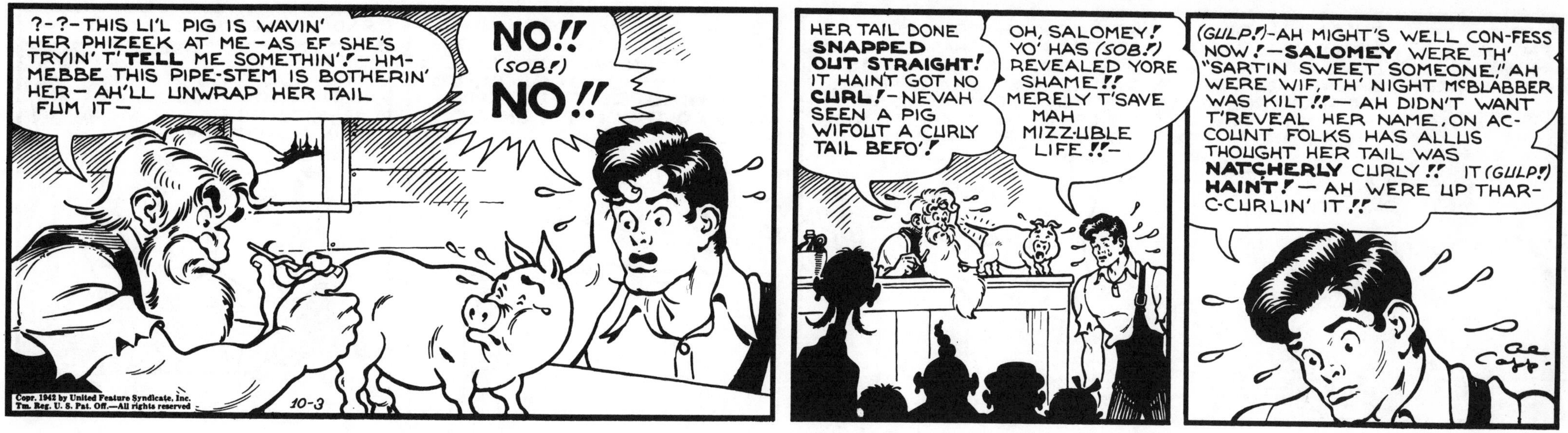
?-?-THIS LI'L PIG IS WAVIN' HER PHIZEEK AT ME-AS EF SHE'S TRYIN' T' TELL ME SOMETHIN'!-HM-MEBBE THIS PIPE-STEM IS BOTHERIN' HER-AH'LL UNWRAP HER TAIL FUM IT-
NO!! (SOB!) NO!!
Copr. 1942 by United Feature Syndicate, Inc. Tm. Reg. U. S. Pat. Off.—All rights reserved
10-3
HER TAIL DONE SNAPPED OUT STRAIGHT! IT HAIN'T GOT NO CURL!-NEVAH SEEN A PIG WIFOUT A CURLY TAIL BEFO'!
OH, SALOMEY! YO' HAS (SOB!) REVEALED YORE SHAME!! MERELY T'SAVE MAH MIZZ-UBLE LIFE!!-
(GULP!)-AH MIGHT'S WELL CON-FESS NOW!-SALOMEY WERE TH' "SARTIN SWEET SOMEONE," AH WERE WIF, TH' NIGHT McBLABBER WAS KILT!!-AH DIDN'T WANT T'REVEAL HER NAME, ON AC-COUNT FOLKS HAS ALLUS THOUGHT HER TAIL WAS NATCHERLY CURLY!! IT (GULP!) HAIN'T!-AH WERE UP THAR-C-CURLIN' IT!!-
Al Capp.

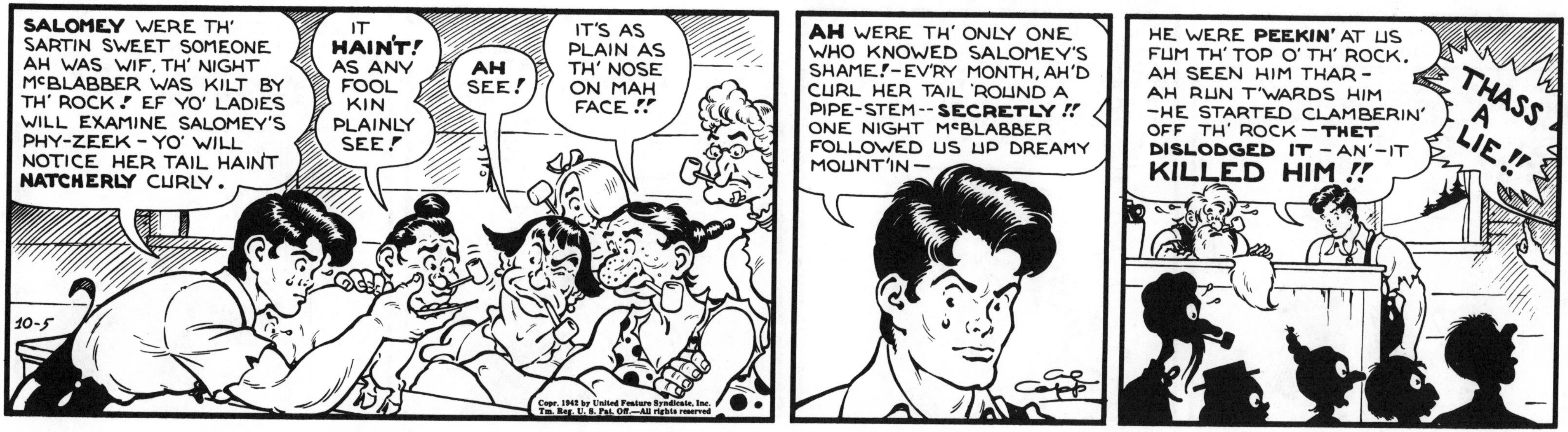
SALOMEY WERE TH' SARTIN SWEET SOMEONE AH WAS WIF, TH' NIGHT McBLABBER WAS KILT BY TH' ROCK! EF YO' LADIES WILL EXAMINE SALOMEY'S PHY-ZEEK-YO' WILL NOTICE HER TAIL HAINT NATCHERLY CURLY.
IT HAIN'T! AS ANY FOOL KIN PLAINLY SEE!
AH SEE!
IT'S AS PLAIN AS TH' NOSE ON MAH FACE!!
10-5
Copr. 1942 by United Feature Syndicate, Inc. Tm. Reg. U. S. Pat. Off.—All rights reserved
AH WERE TH' ONLY ONE WHO KNOWED SALOMEY'S SHAME!-EV'RY MONTH, AH'D CURL HER TAIL 'ROUND A PIPE-STEM--SECRETLY!! ONE NIGHT McBLABBER FOLLOWED US UP DREAMY MOUNT'IN-
Al Capp
HE WERE PEEKIN' AT US FUM TH' TOP O' TH' ROCK. AH SEEN HIM THAR-AH RUN T'WARDS HIM-HE STARTED CLAMBERIN' OFF TH' ROCK-THET DISLODGED IT-AN'-IT KILLED HIM!!
THASS A LIE!!

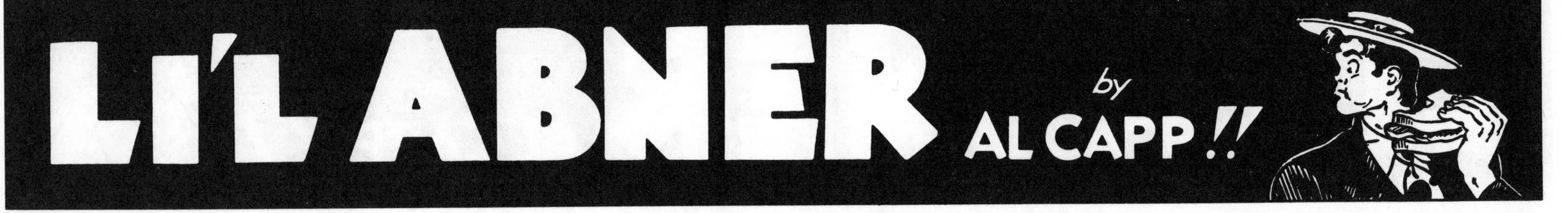
LI'L ABNER
by
AL CAPP!!

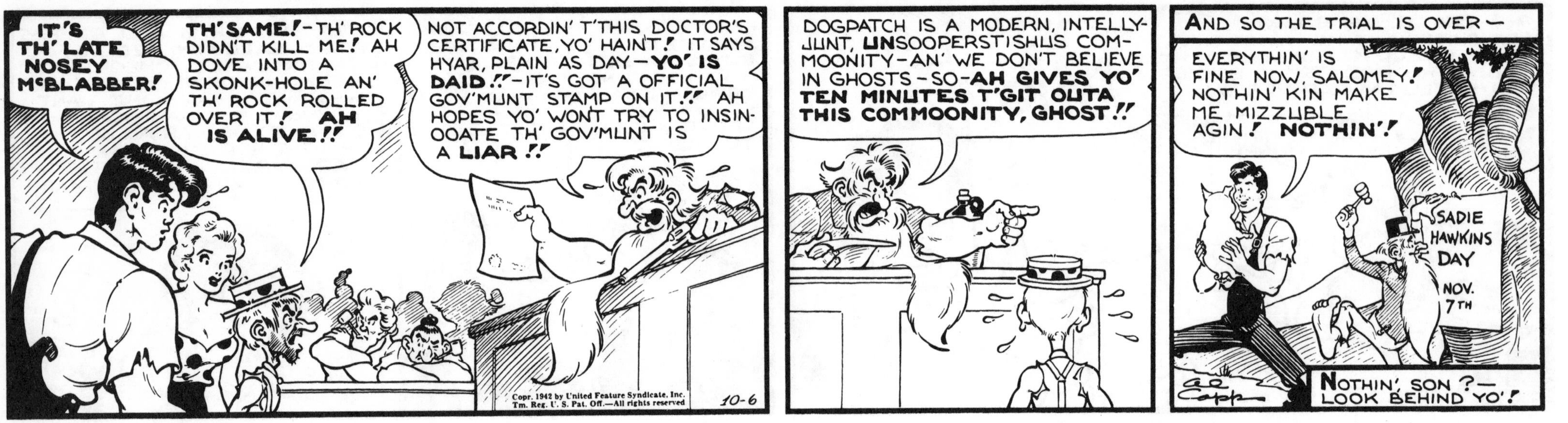
IT'S TH' LATE NOSEY McBLABBER!
TH' SAME!-TH' ROCK DIDN'T KILL ME! AH DOVE INTO A SKONK-HOLE AN' TH' ROCK ROLLED OVER IT! AH IS ALIVE!!
NOT ACCORDIN' T'THIS DOCTOR'S CERTIFICATE, YO' HAINT! IT SAYS HYAR, PLAIN AS DAY-YO' IS DAID!!-IT'S GOT A OFFICIAL GOV'MUNT STAMP ON IT!! AH HOPES YO' WON'T TRY TO INSIN-OOATE TH' GOV'MUNT IS A LIAR!!
Copr. 1942 by United Feature Syndicate, Inc. Tm. Reg. U. S. Pat. Off.—All rights reserved
10-6
DOGPATCH IS A MODERN, INTELLY-JUNT, UNSOOPERSTISHUS COM-MOONITY-AN' WE DON'T BELIEVE IN GHOSTS-SO-AH GIVES YO' TEN MINUTES T'GIT OUTA THIS COMMOONITY, GHOST!!
AND SO THE TRIAL IS OVER-
EVERYTHIN' IS FINE NOW, SALOMEY! NOTHIN' KIN MAKE ME MIZZUBLE AGIN! NOTHIN'!
SADIE HAWKINS DAY NOV. 7TH
NOTHIN', SON?- LOOK BEHIND YO'!

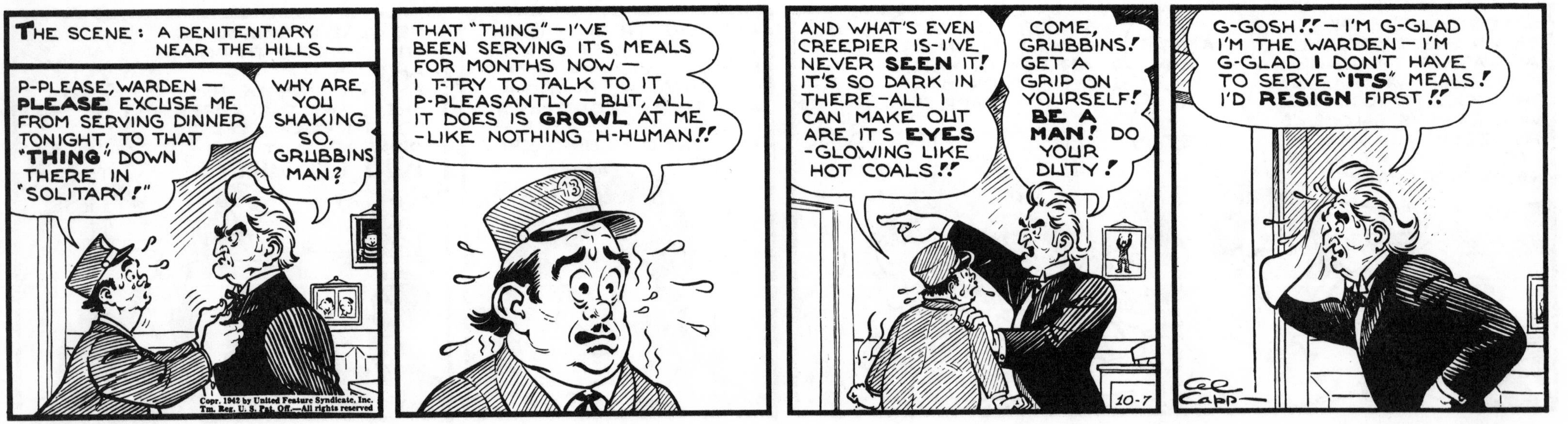
THE SCENE: A PENITENTIARY NEAR THE HILLS-
P-PLEASE, WARDEN-PLEASE EXCUSE ME FROM SERVING DINNER TONIGHT, TO THAT "THING" DOWN THERE IN "SOLITARY!"
WHY ARE YOU SHAKING SO, GRUBBINS MAN?
Copr. 1942 by United Feature Syndicate, Inc. Tm. Reg. U. S. Pat. Off.—All rights reserved
THAT "THING"-I'VE BEEN SERVING IT'S MEALS FOR MONTHS NOW-I T-TRY TO TALK TO IT P-PLEASANTLY-BUT, ALL IT DOES IS GROWL AT ME -LIKE NOTHING H-HUMAN!!
13
AND WHAT'S EVEN CREEPIER IS-I'VE NEVER SEEN IT! IT'S SO DARK IN THERE-ALL I CAN MAKE OUT ARE IT'S EYES -GLOWING LIKE HOT COALS!!
COME, GRUBBINS! GET A GRIP ON YOURSELF! BE A MAN! DO YOUR DUTY!
10-7
G-GOSH!!-I'M G-GLAD I'M THE WARDEN-I'M G-GLAD I DON'T HAVE TO SERVE "ITS" MEALS! I'D RESIGN FIRST!!

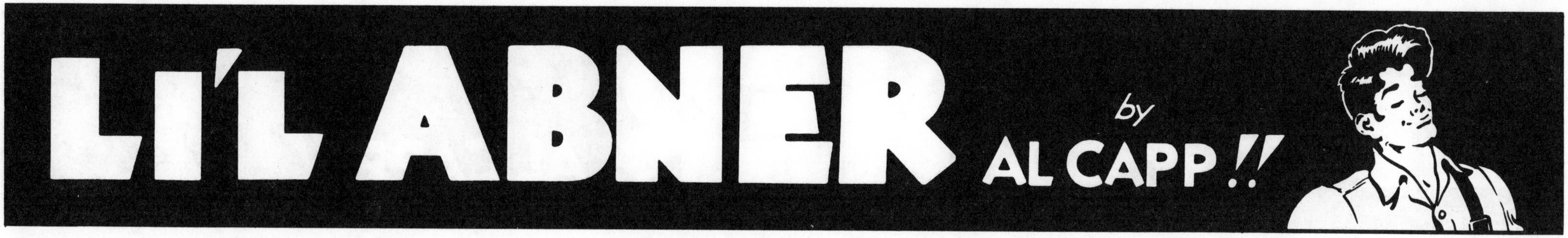
LI'L ABNER
by AL CAPP!!

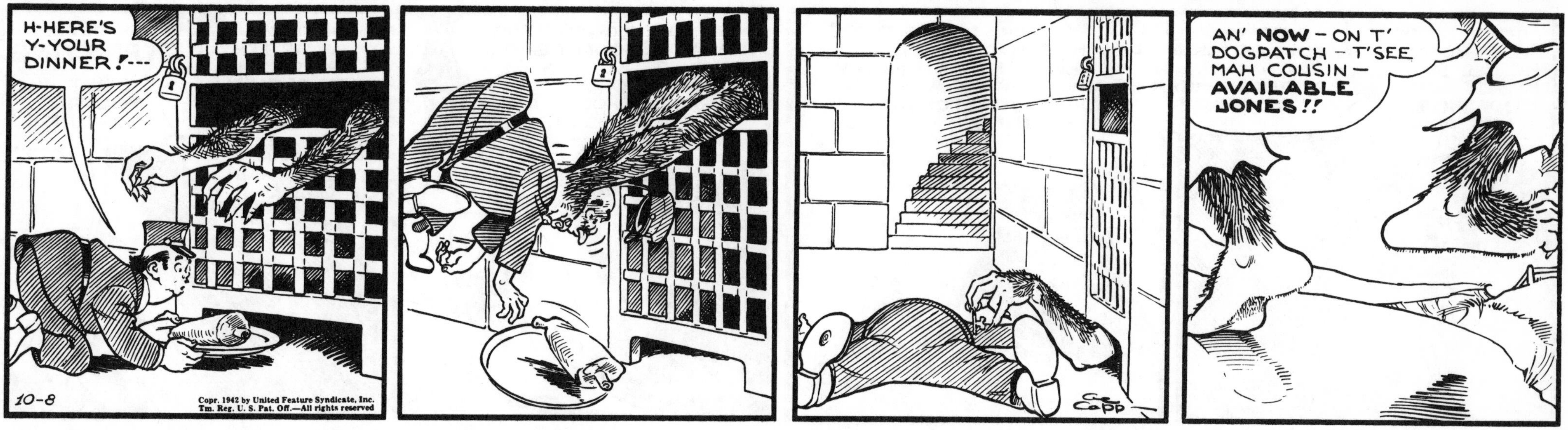
H-HERE'S Y-YOUR DINNER!---
AN' NOW - ON T' DOGPATCH - T'SEE MAH COUSIN - AVAILABLE JONES!!
10-8
Copr. 1942 by United Feature Syndicate, Inc. Tm. Reg. U. S. Pat. Off.—All rights reserved
AL CAPP

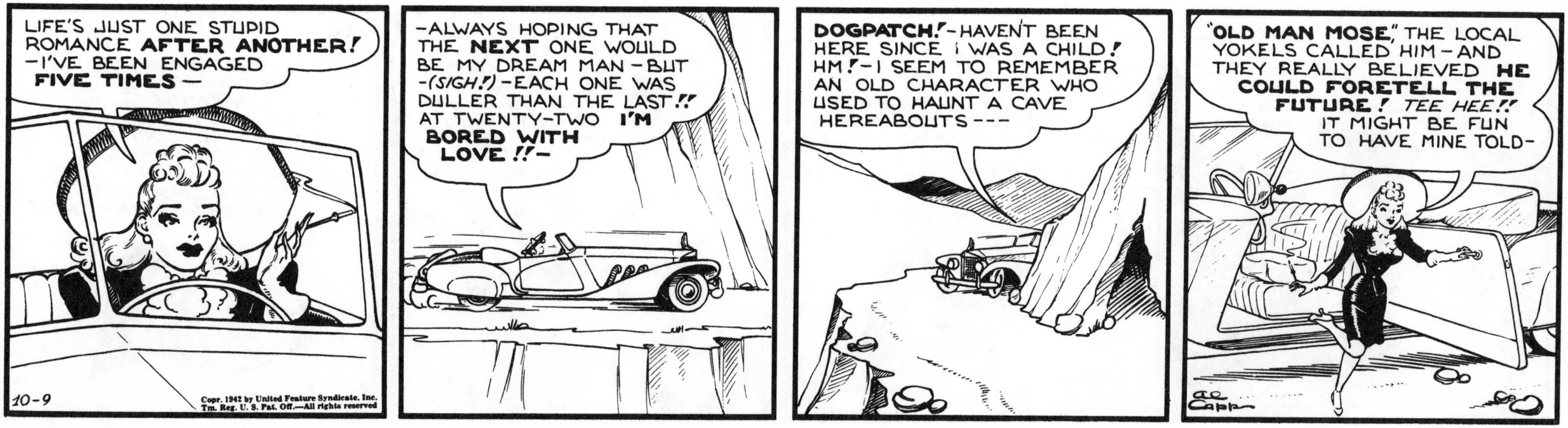
LIFE'S JUST ONE STUPID ROMANCE AFTER ANOTHER! -I'VE BEEN ENGAGED FIVE TIMES -
-ALWAYS HOPING THAT THE NEXT ONE WOULD BE MY DREAM MAN - BUT -(SIGH!) - EACH ONE WAS DULLER THAN THE LAST!! AT TWENTY-TWO I'M BORED WITH LOVE!!-
DOGPATCH! - HAVEN'T BEEN HERE SINCE I WAS A CHILD! HM! - I SEEM TO REMEMBER AN OLD CHARACTER WHO USED TO HAUNT A CAVE HEREABOUTS---
"OLD MAN MOSE," THE LOCAL YOKELS CALLED HIM - AND THEY REALLY BELIEVED HE COULD FORETELL THE FUTURE! TEE HEE!! IT MIGHT BE FUN TO HAVE MINE TOLD-
10-9
Copr. 1942 by United Feature Syndicate, Inc. Tm. Reg. U. S. Pat. Off.—All rights reserved
AL CAPP

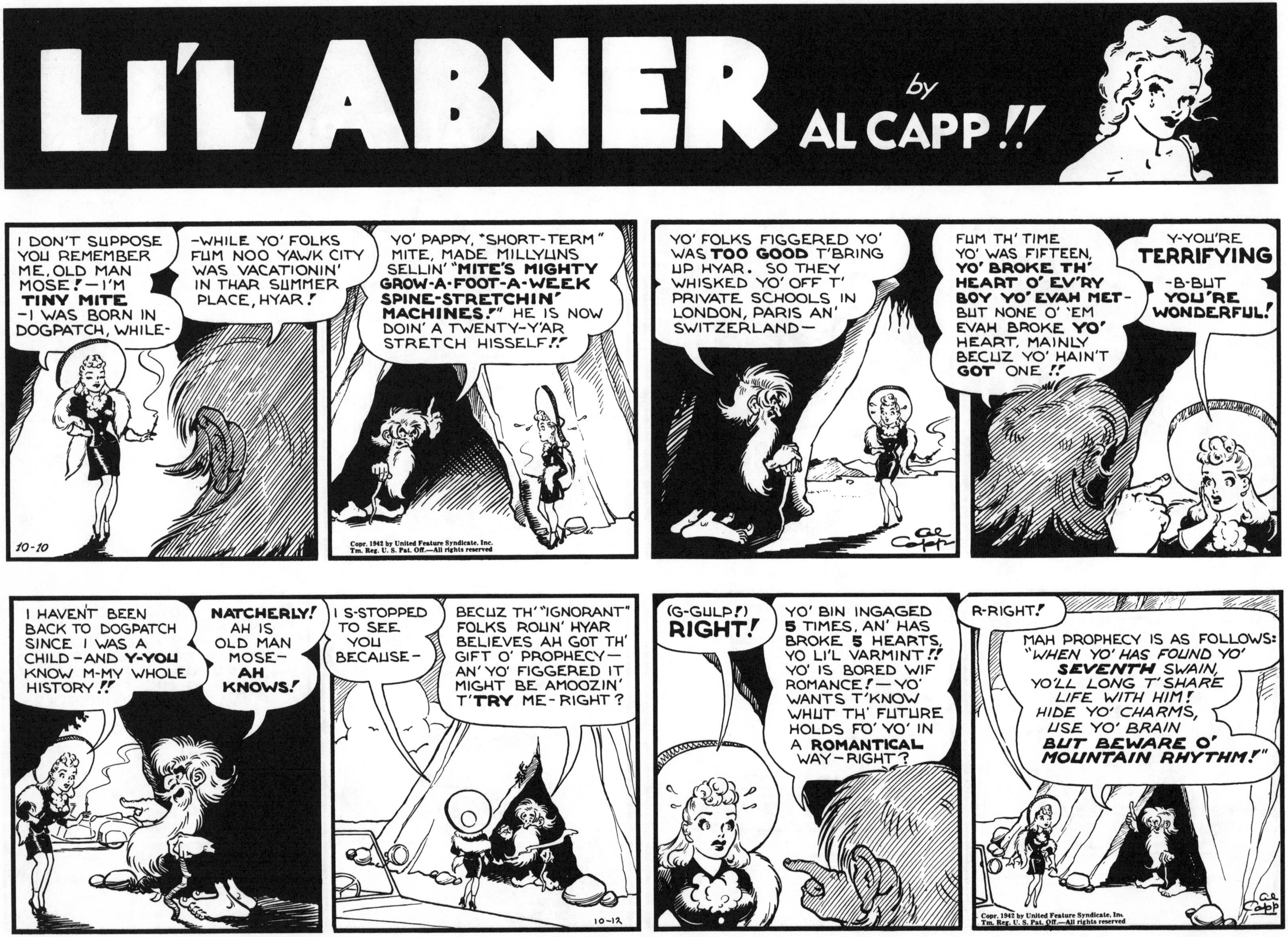

LI'L ABNER
by AL CAPP!!
I DON'T SUPPOSE YOU REMEMBER ME, OLD MAN MOSE!—I'M TINY MITE —I WAS BORN IN DOGPATCH, WHILE-
-WHILE YO' FOLKS FUM NOO YAWK CITY WAS VACATIONIN' IN THAR SUMMER PLACE, HYAR!
10-10
YO' PAPPY, "SHORT-TERM" MITE, MADE MILLYUNS SELLIN' "MITE'S MIGHTY GROW-A-FOOT-A-WEEK SPINE-STRETCHIN' MACHINES!" HE IS NOW DOIN' A TWENTY-Y'AR STRETCH HISSELF!!
Copr. 1942 by United Feature Syndicate, Inc. Tm. Reg. U. S. Pat. Off.—All rights reserved
YO' FOLKS FIGGERED YO' WAS TOO GOOD T'BRING UP HYAR. SO THEY WHISKED YO' OFF T' PRIVATE SCHOOLS IN LONDON, PARIS AN' SWITZERLAND—
FUM TH' TIME YO' WAS FIFTEEN, YO' BROKE TH' HEART O' EV'RY BOY YO' EVAH MET- BUT NONE O' 'EM EVAH BROKE YO' HEART, MAINLY BECUZ YO' HAIN'T GOT ONE!!
Y-YOU'RE TERRIFYING -B-BUT YOU'RE WONDERFUL!
I HAVEN'T BEEN BACK TO DOGPATCH SINCE I WAS A CHILD—AND Y-YOU KNOW M-MY WHOLE HISTORY!!
NATCHERLY! AH IS OLD MAN MOSE— AH KNOWS!
I S-STOPPED TO SEE YOU BECAUSE-
BECUZ TH' "IGNORANT" FOLKS ROUN' HYAR BELIEVES AH GOT TH' GIFT O' PROPHECY— AN' YO' FIGGERED IT MIGHT BE AMOOZIN' T'TRY ME-RIGHT?
10-12
(G-GULP!) RIGHT!
YO' BIN INGAGED 5 TIMES, AN' HAS BROKE 5 HEARTS, YO LI'L VARMINT!! YO' IS BORED WIF ROMANCE!—YO' WANTS T'KNOW WHUT TH' FUTURE HOLDS FO' YO' IN A ROMANTICAL WAY-RIGHT?
R-RIGHT!
MAH PROPHECY IS AS FOLLOWS: "WHEN YO' HAS FOUND YO' SEVENTH SWAIN, YO'LL LONG T'SHARE LIFE WITH HIM! HIDE YO' CHARMS, USE YO' BRAIN BUT BEWARE O' MOUNTAIN RHYTHM!"
Copr. 1942 by United Feature Syndicate, Inc Tm. Reg. U. S. Pat. Off.—All rights reserved

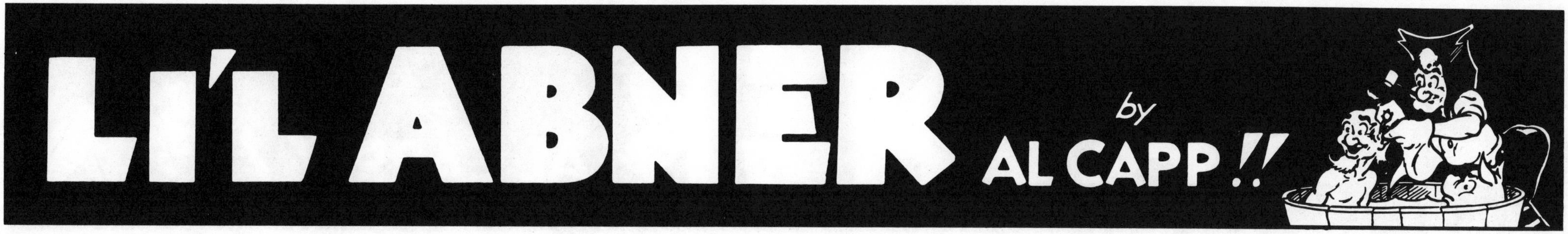
LI'L ABNER
by
AL CAPP!!

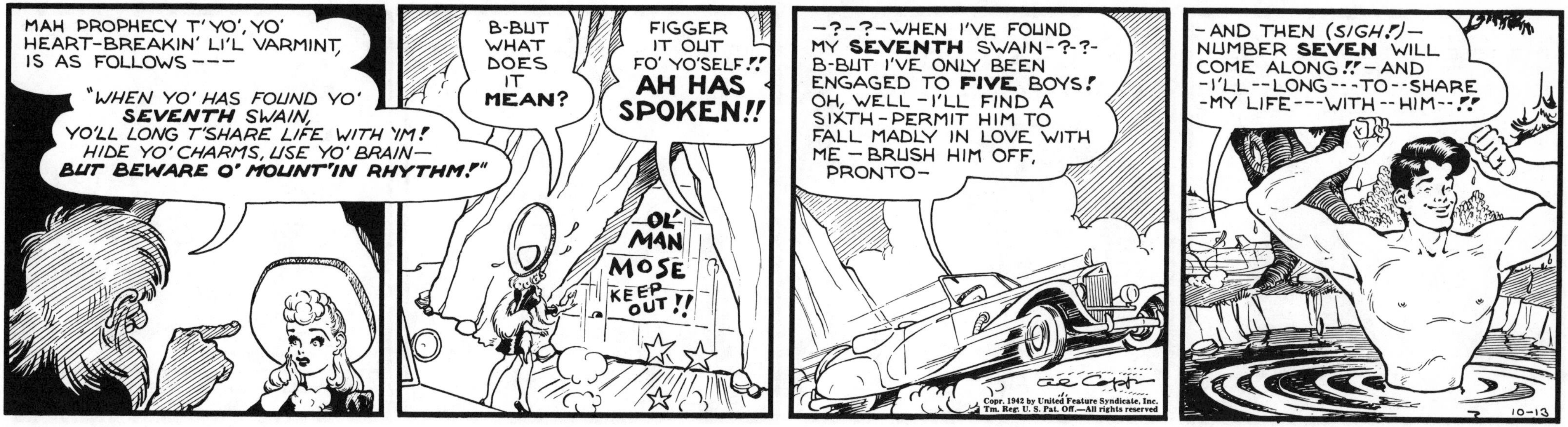
MAH PROPHECY T'YO', YO' HEART-BREAKIN' LI'L VARMINT, IS AS FOLLOWS---
"WHEN YO' HAS FOUND YO' SEVENTH SWAIN, YO'LL LONG T'SHARE LIFE WITH 'IM! HIDE YO' CHARMS, USE YO' BRAIN— BUT BEWARE O' MOUNT'IN RHYTHM!"
B-BUT WHAT DOES IT MEAN?
FIGGER IT OUT FO' YO'SELF!! AH HAS SPOKEN!!
OL' MAN MOSE KEEP OUT!!
–?–?–WHEN I'VE FOUND MY SEVENTH SWAIN–?–?– B-BUT I'VE ONLY BEEN ENGAGED TO FIVE BOYS! OH, WELL–I'LL FIND A SIXTH–PERMIT HIM TO FALL MADLY IN LOVE WITH ME–BRUSH HIM OFF, PRONTO–
Al Capp
Copr. 1942 by United Feature Syndicate, Inc. Tm. Reg. U. S. Pat. Off.—All rights reserved
–AND THEN (SIGH!)– NUMBER SEVEN WILL COME ALONG!!–AND –I'LL--LONG---TO--SHARE –MY LIFE---WITH--HIM--!!
10-13

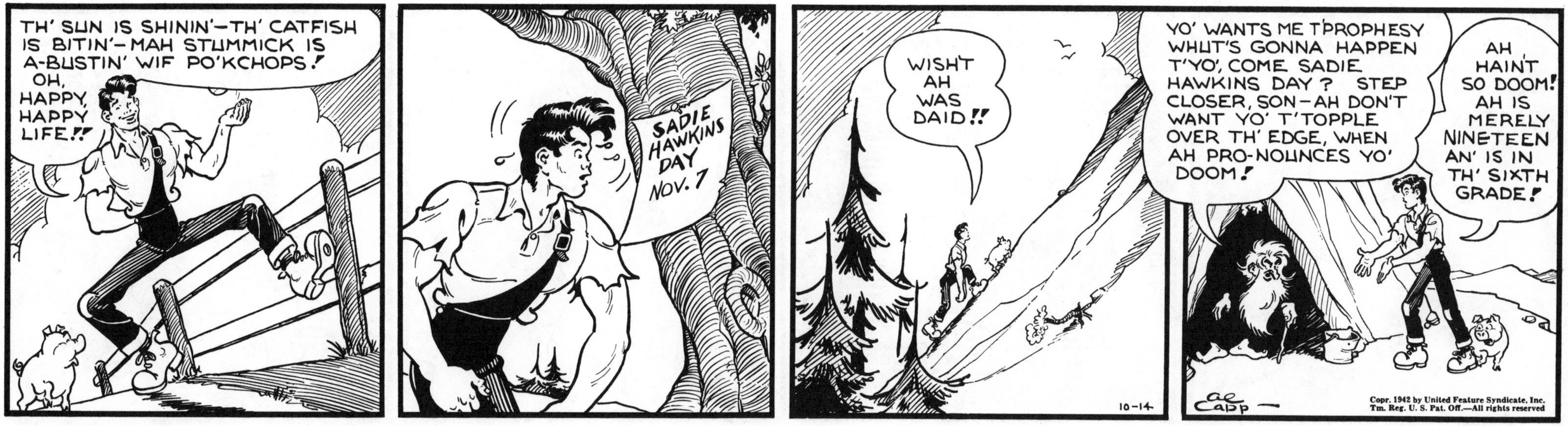
TH' SUN IS SHININ'–TH' CATFISH IS BITIN'–MAH STUMMICK IS A-BUSTIN' WIF PO'KCHOPS! OH, HAPPY, HAPPY LIFE!!
SADIE HAWKINS DAY NOV. 7
WISH'T AH WAS DAID!!
10-14
YO' WANTS ME T'PROPHESY WHUT'S GONNA HAPPEN T'YO', COME SADIE HAWKINS DAY? STEP CLOSER, SON–AH DON'T WANT YO' T'TOPPLE OVER TH' EDGE, WHEN AH PRO-NOUNCES YO' DOOM!
AH HAIN'T SO DOOM! AH IS MERELY NINETEEN AN' IS IN TH' SIXTH GRADE!
Al Capp
Copr. 1942 by United Feature Syndicate, Inc. Tm. Reg. U. S. Pat. Off.—All rights reserved

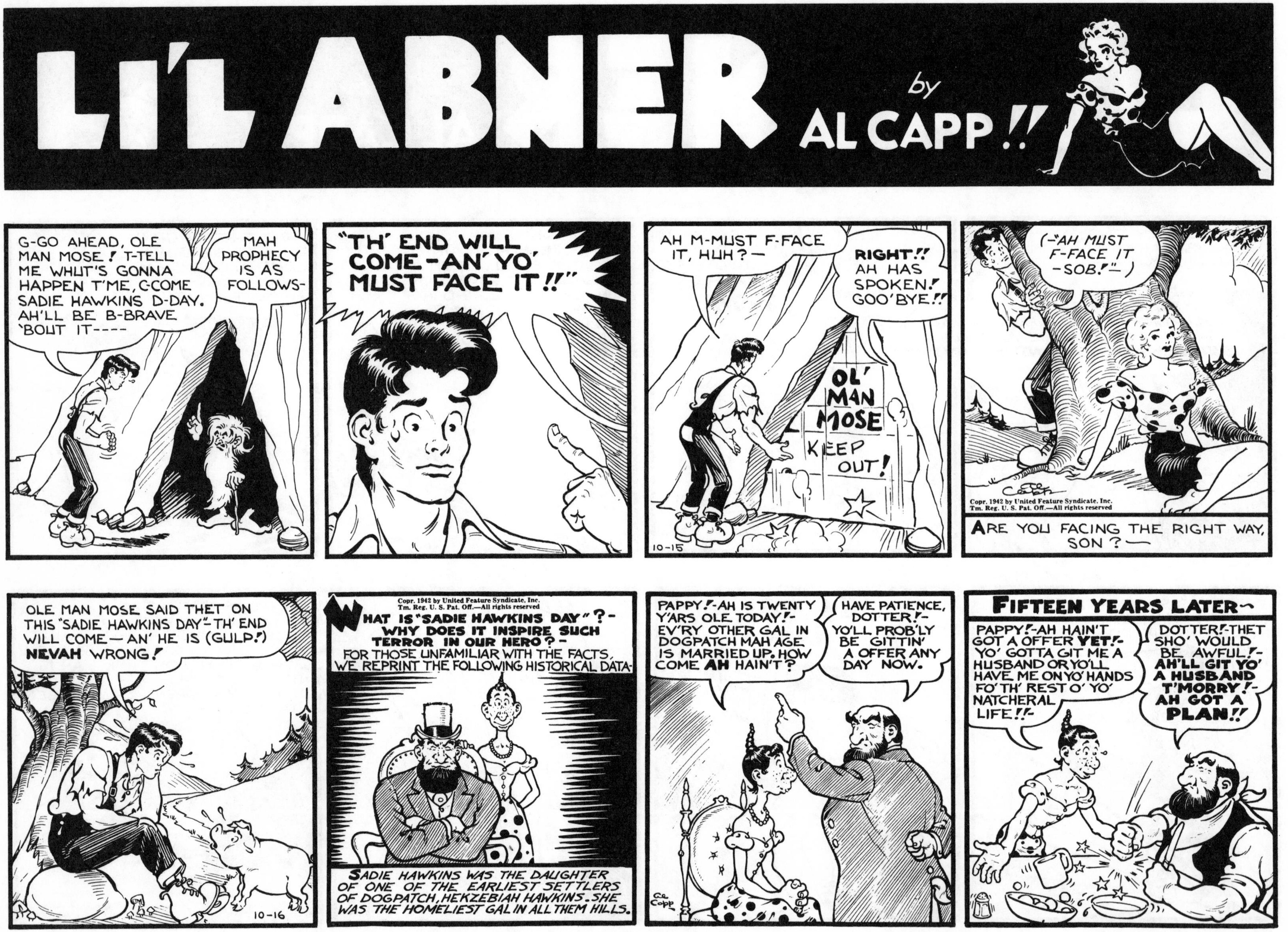
LI'L ABNER by AL CAPP!!
G-GO AHEAD, OLE MAN MOSE! T-TELL ME WHUT'S GONNA HAPPEN T'ME, G-COME SADIE HAWKINS D-DAY. AH'LL BE B-BRAVE 'BOUT IT----
MAH PROPHECY IS AS FOLLOWS-
"TH' END WILL COME-AN' YO' MUST FACE IT!!"
AH M-MUST F-FACE IT, HUH?—
RIGHT!! AH HAS SPOKEN! GOO'BYE!!
OL' MAN MOSE
KEEP OUT!
10-15
(-"AH MUST F-FACE IT -SOB!"-)
Copr. 1942 by United Feature Syndicate, Inc. Tm. Reg. U. S. Pat. Off.—All rights reserved
ARE YOU FACING THE RIGHT WAY, SON?—
OLE MAN MOSE SAID THET ON THIS "SADIE HAWKINS DAY"-TH' END WILL COME—AN' HE IS (GULP!) NEVAH WRONG!
10-16
Copr. 1942 by United Feature Syndicate, Inc. Tm. Reg. U. S. Pat. Off.—All rights reserved
WHAT IS "SADIE HAWKINS DAY"?- WHY DOES IT INSPIRE SUCH TERROR IN OUR HERO?-
FOR THOSE UNFAMILIAR WITH THE FACTS, WE REPRINT THE FOLLOWING HISTORICAL DATA-
SADIE HAWKINS WAS THE DAUGHTER OF ONE OF THE EARLIEST SETTLERS OF DOGPATCH, HEKZEBIAH HAWKINS. SHE WAS THE HOMELIEST GAL IN ALL THEM HILLS.
PAPPY!-AH IS TWENTY Y'ARS OLE TODAY!- EV'RY OTHER GAL IN DOGPATCH MAH AGE IS MARRIED UP. HOW COME AH HAIN'T?
HAVE PATIENCE, DOTTER!- YO'LL PROB'LY BE GITTIN' A OFFER ANY DAY NOW.
FIFTEEN YEARS LATER~
PAPPY!-AH HAIN'T GOT A OFFER YET!- YO' GOTTA GIT ME A HUSBAND OR YO'LL HAVE ME ON YO' HANDS FO'TH' REST O' YO' NATCHERAL LIFE!!-
DOTTER!-THET SHO' WOULD BE AWFUL!- AH'LL GIT YO' A HUSBAND T'MORRY!- AH GOT A PLAN!!

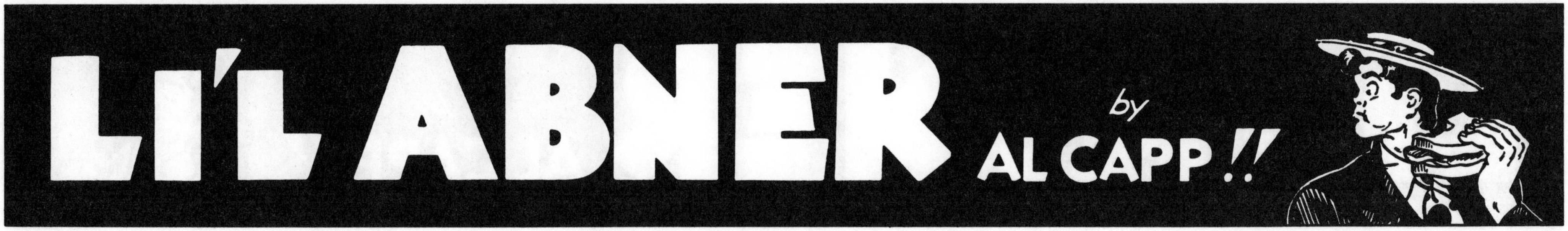
LI'L ABNER
by AL CAPP!!

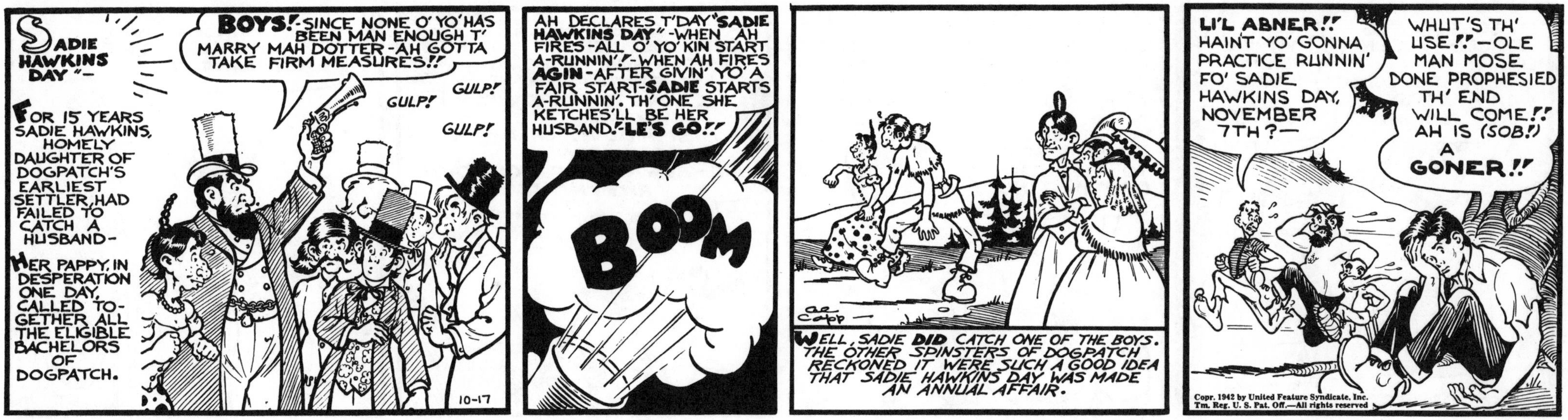
"SADIE HAWKINS DAY"-
FOR 15 YEARS SADIE HAWKINS, HOMELY DAUGHTER OF DOGPATCH'S EARLIEST SETTLER, HAD FAILED TO CATCH A HUSBAND-
HER PAPPY, IN DESPERATION ONE DAY, CALLED TOGETHER ALL THE ELIGIBLE BACHELORS OF DOGPATCH.
BOYS!-SINCE NONE O' YO' HAS BEEN MAN ENOUGH T' MARRY MAH DOTTER-AH GOTTA TAKE FIRM MEASURES!!
GULP!
GULP!
GULP!
10-17
AH DECLARES T'DAY "SADIE HAWKINS DAY"-WHEN AH FIRES-ALL O' YO' KIN START A-RUNNIN'!-WHEN AH FIRES AGIN-AFTER GIVIN' YO' A FAIR START-SADIE STARTS A-RUNNIN'. TH' ONE SHE KETCHES'LL BE HER HUSBAND!-LE'S GO!!
BOOM
WELL, SADIE DID CATCH ONE OF THE BOYS. THE OTHER SPINSTERS OF DOGPATCH RECKONED IT WERE SUCH A GOOD IDEA THAT SADIE HAWKINS DAY WAS MADE AN ANNUAL AFFAIR.
LI'L ABNER!! HAIN'T YO' GONNA PRACTICE RUNNIN' FO' SADIE HAWKINS DAY, NOVEMBER 7TH?-
WHUT'S TH' USE!!-OLE MAN MOSE DONE PROPHESIED TH' END WILL COME!! AH IS (SOB!) A GONER!!
Copr. 1942 by United Feature Syndicate, Inc. Tm. Reg. U. S. Pat. Off.—All rights reserved

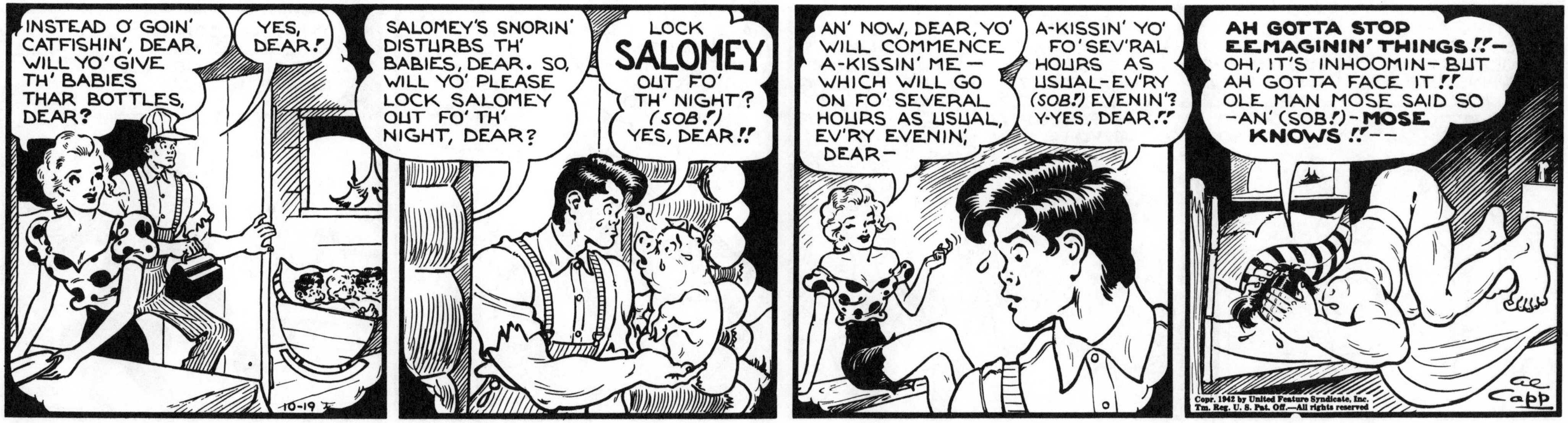
INSTEAD O' GOIN' CATFISHIN', DEAR, WILL YO' GIVE TH' BABIES THAR BOTTLES, DEAR?
YES, DEAR!
10-19
SALOMEY'S SNORIN' DISTURBS TH' BABIES, DEAR. SO, WILL YO' PLEASE LOCK SALOMEY OUT FO' TH' NIGHT, DEAR?
LOCK SALOMEY OUT FO' TH' NIGHT? (SOB!) YES, DEAR!!
AN' NOW, DEAR, YO' WILL COMMENCE A-KISSIN' ME- WHICH WILL GO ON FO' SEVERAL HOURS AS USUAL, EV'RY EVENIN', DEAR-
A-KISSIN' YO' FO' SEV'RAL HOURS AS USUAL-EV'RY (SOB!) EVENIN'? Y-YES, DEAR!!
AH GOTTA STOP EEMAGININ' THINGS!!- OH, IT'S INHOOMIN-BUT AH GOTTA FACE IT!! OLE MAN MOSE SAID SO -AN' (SOB!)-MOSE KNOWS!!--
Copr. 1942 by United Feature Syndicate, Inc. Tm. Reg. U. S. Pat. Off.—All rights reserved

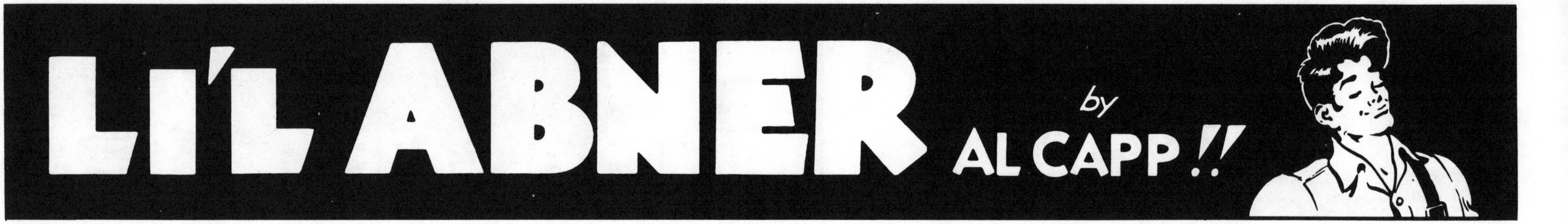
LI'L ABNER
by
AL CAPP!!

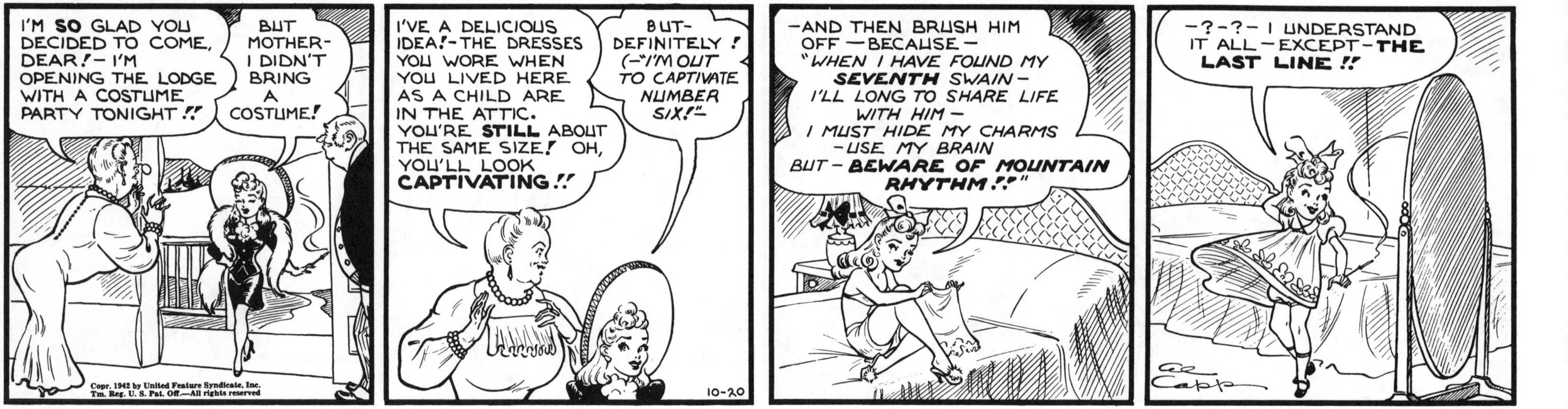
I'M **SO** GLAD YOU DECIDED TO COME, DEAR!—I'M OPENING THE LODGE WITH A COSTUME PARTY TONIGHT!!
BUT MOTHER—I DIDN'T BRING A COSTUME!
Copr. 1942 by United Feature Syndicate, Inc. Tm. Reg. U. S. Pat. Off.—All rights reserved
I'VE A DELICIOUS IDEA!—THE DRESSES YOU WORE WHEN YOU LIVED HERE AS A CHILD ARE IN THE ATTIC. YOU'RE **STILL** ABOUT THE SAME SIZE! OH, YOU'LL LOOK **CAPTIVATING!!**
BUT—DEFINITELY! (—"I'M OUT TO CAPTIVATE NUMBER SIX!"—
10-20
—AND THEN BRUSH HIM OFF—BECAUSE—"WHEN I HAVE FOUND MY **SEVENTH** SWAIN—I'LL LONG TO SHARE LIFE WITH HIM—I MUST HIDE MY CHARMS—USE MY BRAIN BUT—**BEWARE OF MOUNTAIN RHYTHM!!**"
—?—?—I UNDERSTAND IT ALL—EXCEPT—**THE LAST LINE!!**
AL CAPP

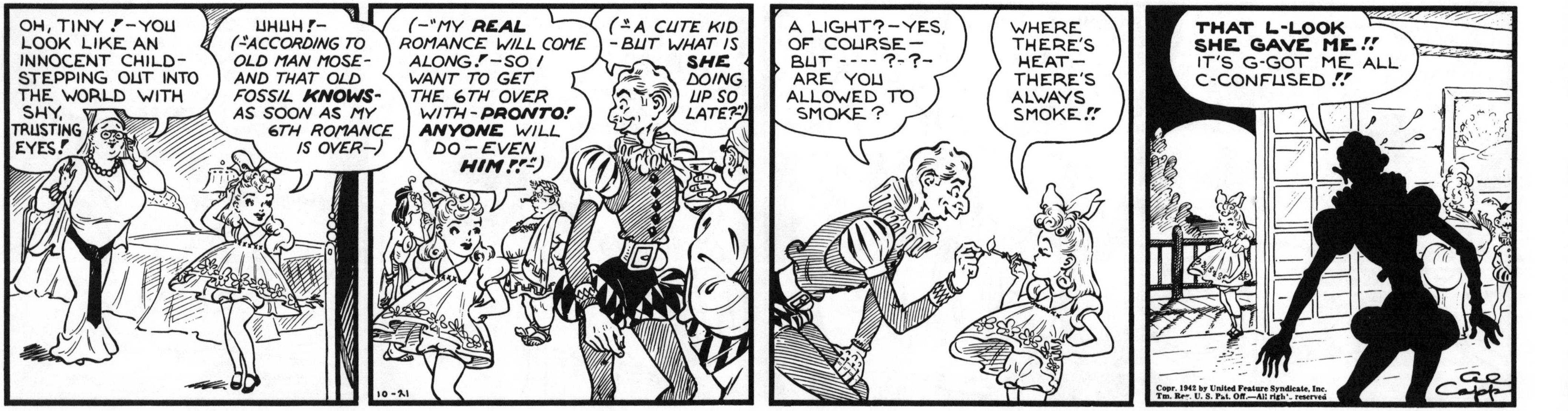
OH, TINY!—YOU LOOK LIKE AN INNOCENT CHILD—STEPPING OUT INTO THE WORLD WITH SHY, TRUSTING EYES!
UHUH!—(—"ACCORDING TO OLD MAN MOSE—AND THAT OLD FOSSIL **KNOWS**—AS SOON AS MY 6TH ROMANCE IS OVER—)
10-21
(—"MY **REAL** ROMANCE WILL COME ALONG!—SO I WANT TO GET THE 6TH OVER WITH—**PRONTO! ANYONE** WILL DO—EVEN **HIM!!**"—)
(—"A CUTE KID—BUT WHAT IS **SHE** DOING UP SO LATE?"—)
A LIGHT?—YES, OF COURSE—BUT ----?-?-ARE YOU ALLOWED TO SMOKE?
WHERE THERE'S HEAT—THERE'S ALWAYS SMOKE!!
THAT L-LOOK SHE GAVE ME!! IT'S G-GOT ME ALL C-CONFUSED!!
Copr. 1942 by United Feature Syndicate, Inc. Tm. Reg. U. S. Pat. Off.—All rights reserved
AL CAPP

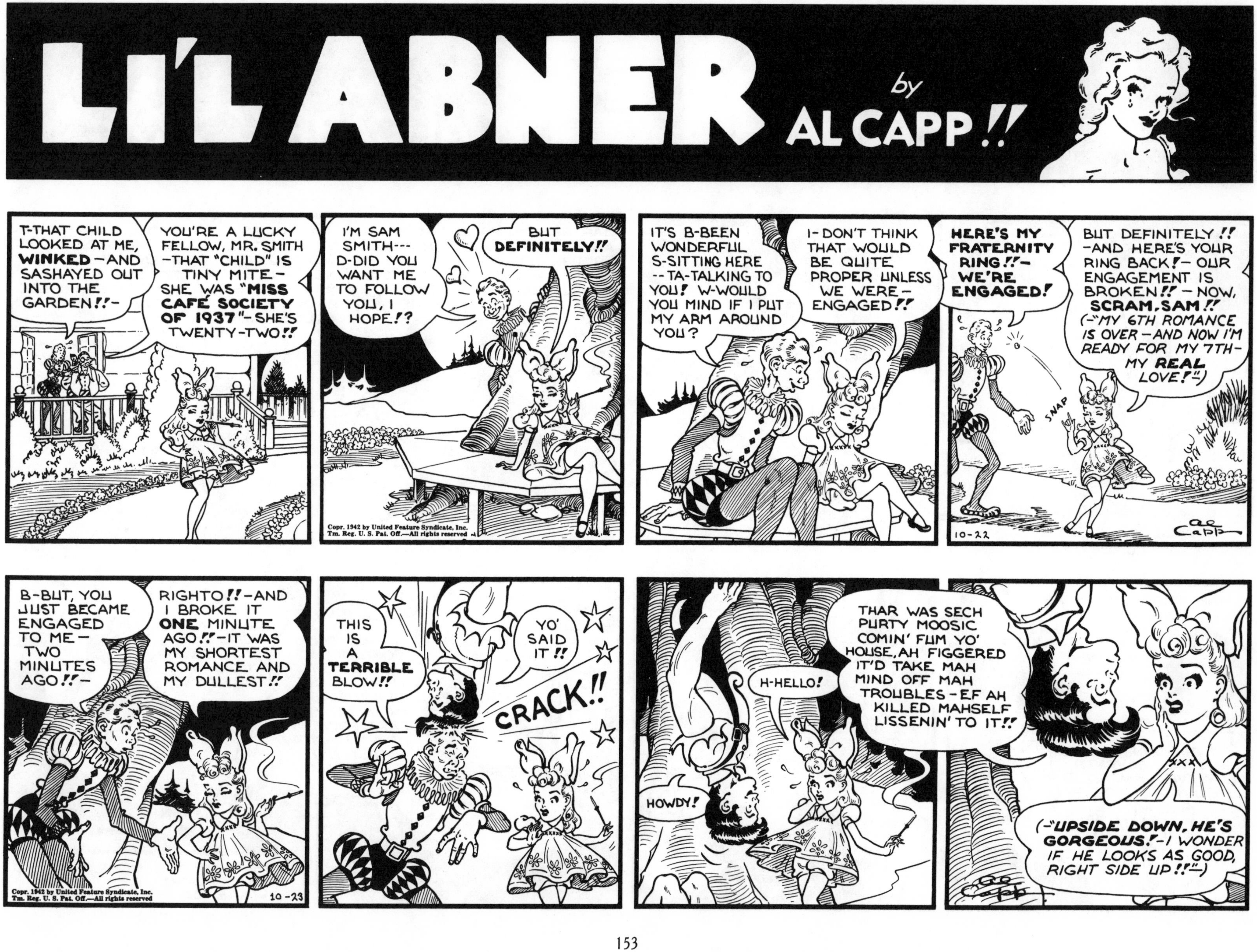
LI'L ABNER
by AL CAPP!!
T-THAT CHILD LOOKED AT ME, WINKED—AND SASHAYED OUT INTO THE GARDEN!!—
YOU'RE A LUCKY FELLOW, MR. SMITH—THAT "CHILD" IS TINY MITE—SHE WAS "MISS CAFÉ SOCIETY OF 1937"—SHE'S TWENTY-TWO!!
I'M SAM SMITH--- D-DID YOU WANT ME TO FOLLOW YOU, I HOPE!?
BUT DEFINITELY!!
Copr. 1942 by United Feature Syndicate, Inc. Tm. Reg. U. S. Pat. Off.—All rights reserved
IT'S B-BEEN WONDERFUL S-SITTING HERE --TA-TALKING TO YOU! W-WOULD YOU MIND IF I PUT MY ARM AROUND YOU?
I-DON'T THINK THAT WOULD BE QUITE PROPER UNLESS WE WERE—ENGAGED!!
HERE'S MY FRATERNITY RING!!—WE'RE ENGAGED!
BUT DEFINITELY!! —AND HERE'S YOUR RING BACK!—OUR ENGAGEMENT IS BROKEN!!—NOW, SCRAM, SAM!!
(—"MY 6TH ROMANCE IS OVER—AND NOW I'M READY FOR MY 7TH—MY REAL LOVE!"—)
SNAP
10-22
Al Capp
B-BUT, YOU JUST BECAME ENGAGED TO ME—TWO MINUTES AGO!!—
RIGHTO!!—AND I BROKE IT ONE MINUTE AGO!!—IT WAS MY SHORTEST ROMANCE AND MY DULLEST!!
Copr. 1942 by United Feature Syndicate, Inc. Tm. Reg. U. S. Pat. Off.—All rights reserved
10-23
THIS IS A TERRIBLE BLOW!!
YO' SAID IT!!
CRACK!!
H-HELLO!
HOWDY!
THAR WAS SECH PURTY MOOSIC COMIN' FUM YO' HOUSE, AH FIGGERED IT'D TAKE MAH MIND OFF MAH TROUBLES—EF AH KILLED MAHSELF LISSENIN' TO IT!!
(—"UPSIDE DOWN, HE'S GORGEOUS!—I WONDER IF HE LOOKS AS GOOD, RIGHT SIDE UP!!"—)
Al Capp

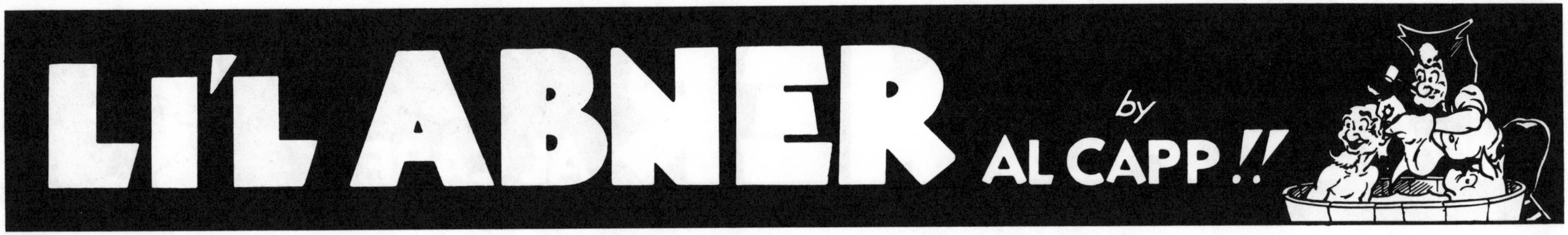
LI'L ABNER
by
AL CAPP!!

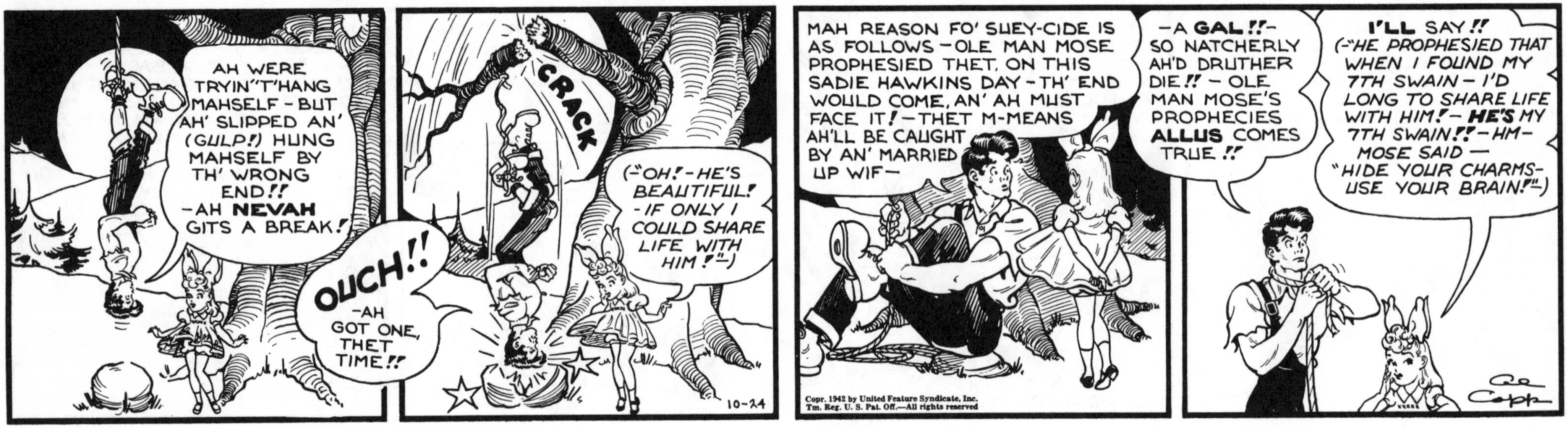
AH WERE TRYIN' T'HANG MAHSELF - BUT AH' SLIPPED AN' (GULP!) HUNG MAHSELF BY TH' WRONG END!! -AH NEVAH GITS A BREAK!
CRACK
OUCH!! -AH GOT ONE, THET TIME!!
(-"OH! - HE'S BEAUTIFUL! - IF ONLY I COULD SHARE LIFE WITH HIM!"-)
10-24
MAH REASON FO' SUEY-CIDE IS AS FOLLOWS - OLE MAN MOSE PROPHESIED THET, ON THIS SADIE HAWKINS DAY - TH' END WOULD COME, AN' AH MUST FACE IT! - THET M-MEANS AH'LL BE CAUGHT BY AN' MARRIED UP WIF -
-A GAL!! - SO NATCHERLY AH'D DRUTHER DIE!! - OLE MAN MOSE'S PROPHECIES ALLUS COMES TRUE!!
I'LL SAY!! (-"HE PROPHESIED THAT WHEN I FOUND MY 7TH SWAIN - I'D LONG TO SHARE LIFE WITH HIM! - HE'S MY 7TH SWAIN!! - HM - MOSE SAID - "HIDE YOUR CHARMS - USE YOUR BRAIN!"-)
Copr. 1942 by United Feature Syndicate, Inc. Tm. Reg. U. S. Pat. Off.—All rights reserved
Al Capp

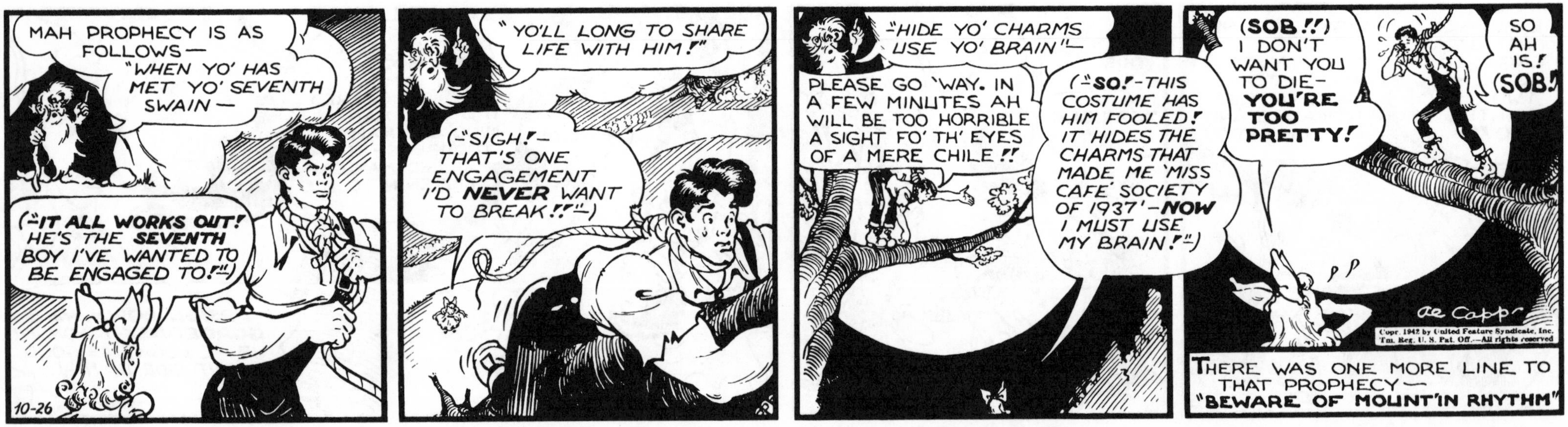
MAH PROPHECY IS AS FOLLOWS - "WHEN YO' HAS MET YO' SEVENTH SWAIN -
(-"IT ALL WORKS OUT! HE'S THE SEVENTH BOY I'VE WANTED TO BE ENGAGED TO!"-)
10-26
"YO'LL LONG TO SHARE LIFE WITH HIM!"
(-"SIGH! - THAT'S ONE ENGAGEMENT I'D NEVER WANT TO BREAK!!"-)
-"HIDE YO' CHARMS USE YO' BRAIN"-
PLEASE GO 'WAY. IN A FEW MINUTES AH WILL BE TOO HORRIBLE A SIGHT FO' TH' EYES OF A MERE CHILE!!
(-"SO! - THIS COSTUME HAS HIM FOOLED! IT HIDES THE CHARMS THAT MADE ME 'MISS CAFE' SOCIETY OF 1937' - NOW I MUST USE MY BRAIN!"-)
(SOB!!) I DON'T WANT YOU TO DIE - YOU'RE TOO PRETTY!
SO AH IS! (SOB!)
Al Capp
Copr. 1942 by United Feature Syndicate, Inc. Tm. Reg. U. S. Pat. Off.—All rights reserved
THERE WAS ONE MORE LINE TO THAT PROPHECY - "BEWARE OF MOUNT'IN RHYTHM"

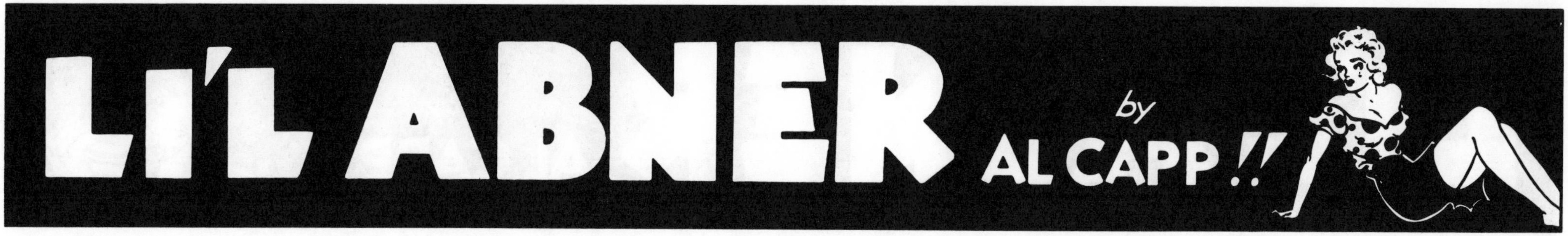
LI'L ABNER
by
AL CAPP!!

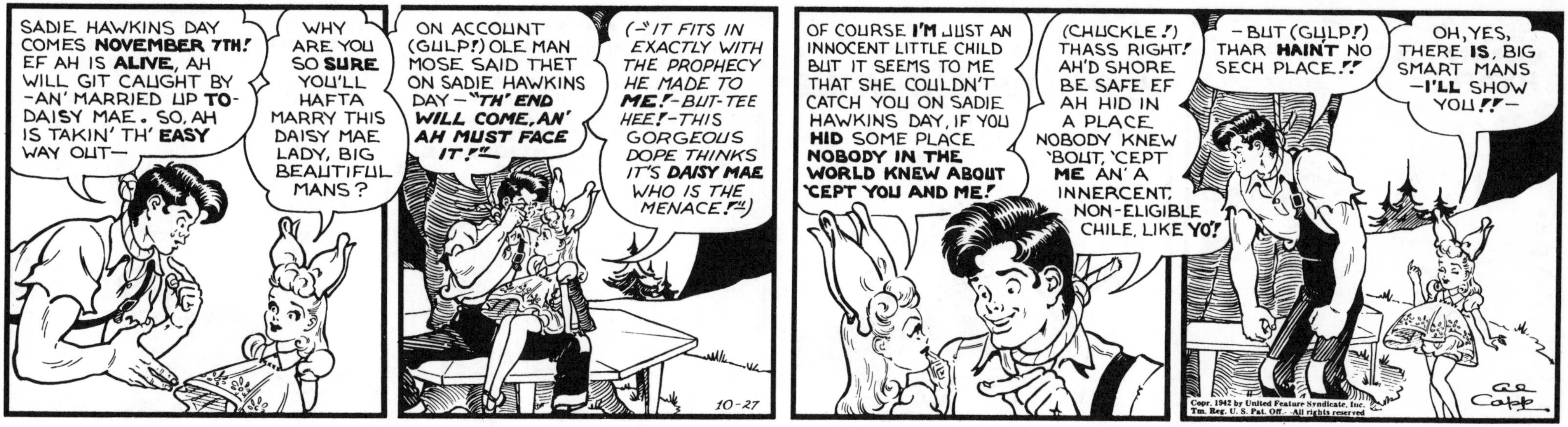
SADIE HAWKINS DAY COMES NOVEMBER 7TH! EF AH IS ALIVE, AH WILL GIT CAUGHT BY -AN' MARRIED UP TO- DAISY MAE. SO, AH IS TAKIN' TH' EASY WAY OUT—
WHY ARE YOU SO SURE YOU'LL HAFTA MARRY THIS DAISY MAE LADY, BIG BEAUTIFUL MANS?
ON ACCOUNT (GULP!) OLE MAN MOSE SAID THET ON SADIE HAWKINS DAY—"TH' END WILL COME, AN' AH MUST FACE IT!"
(—"IT FITS IN EXACTLY WITH THE PROPHECY HE MADE TO ME!—BUT-TEE HEE!—THIS GORGEOUS DOPE THINKS IT'S DAISY MAE WHO IS THE MENACE!")
10-27
OF COURSE I'M JUST AN INNOCENT LITTLE CHILD BUT IT SEEMS TO ME THAT SHE COULDN'T CATCH YOU ON SADIE HAWKINS DAY, IF YOU HID SOME PLACE NOBODY IN THE WORLD KNEW ABOUT 'CEPT YOU AND ME!
(CHUCKLE!) THASS RIGHT! AH'D SHORE BE SAFE EF AH HID IN A PLACE NOBODY KNEW 'BOUT, 'CEPT ME AN' A INNERCENT, NON-ELIGIBLE CHILE, LIKE YO'!
—BUT (GULP!) THAR HAIN'T NO SECH PLACE!!
OH, YES, THERE IS, BIG SMART MANS —I'LL SHOW YOU!!—
Copr. 1942 by United Feature Syndicate, Inc. Tm. Reg. U. S. Pat. Off.—All rights reserved

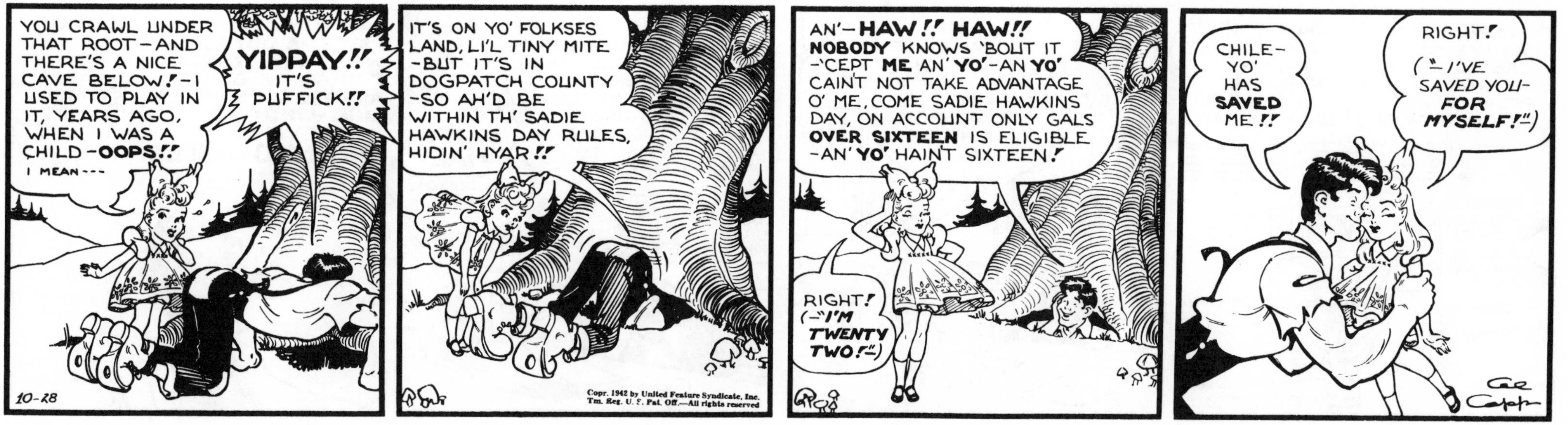
YOU CRAWL UNDER THAT ROOT—AND THERE'S A NICE CAVE BELOW!—I USED TO PLAY IN IT, YEARS AGO, WHEN I WAS A CHILD—OOPS!!
I MEAN---
YIPPAY!! IT'S PUFFICK!!
10-28
IT'S ON YO' FOLKSES LAND, LI'L TINY MITE —BUT IT'S IN DOGPATCH COUNTY —SO AH'D BE WITHIN TH' SADIE HAWKINS DAY RULES, HIDIN' HYAR!!
Copr. 1942 by United Feature Syndicate, Inc. Tm. Reg. U. S. Pat. Off.—All rights reserved
AN'—HAW!! HAW!! NOBODY KNOWS 'BOUT IT —'CEPT ME AN' YO'—AN YO' CAIN'T NOT TAKE ADVANTAGE O' ME, COME SADIE HAWKINS DAY, ON ACCOUNT ONLY GALS OVER SIXTEEN IS ELIGIBLE —AN' YO' HAIN'T SIXTEEN!
RIGHT! (—"I'M TWENTY TWO!")
CHILE— YO' HAS SAVED ME!!
RIGHT! (—"I'VE SAVED YOU— FOR MYSELF!")

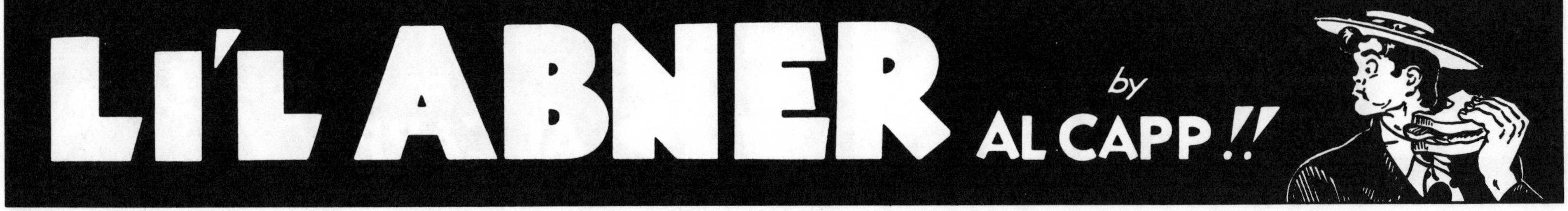
LI'L ABNER
by
AL CAPP!!

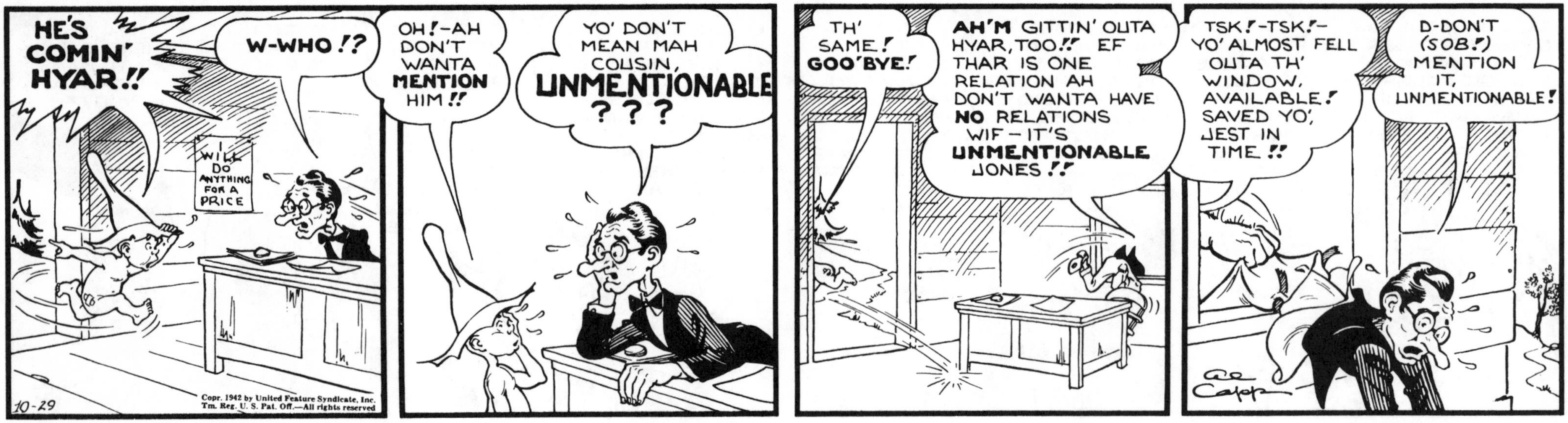
HE'S COMIN' HYAR!!
W-WHO!?
I WILL DO ANYTHING FOR A PRICE
10-29
Copr. 1942 by United Feature Syndicate, Inc. Tm. Reg. U. S. Pat. Off.—All rights reserved
OH!-AH DON'T WANTA MENTION HIM!!
YO' DON'T MEAN MAH COUSIN, UNMENTIONABLE???
TH' SAME! GOO'BYE!
AH'M GITTIN' OUTA HYAR, TOO!! EF THAR IS ONE RELATION AH DON'T WANTA HAVE NO RELATIONS WIF-IT'S UNMENTIONABLE JONES!!
TSK!-TSK!-YO' ALMOST FELL OUTA TH' WINDOW, AVAILABLE! SAVED YO', JEST IN TIME!!
D-DON'T (SOB!) MENTION IT, UNMENTIONABLE!
Al Capp

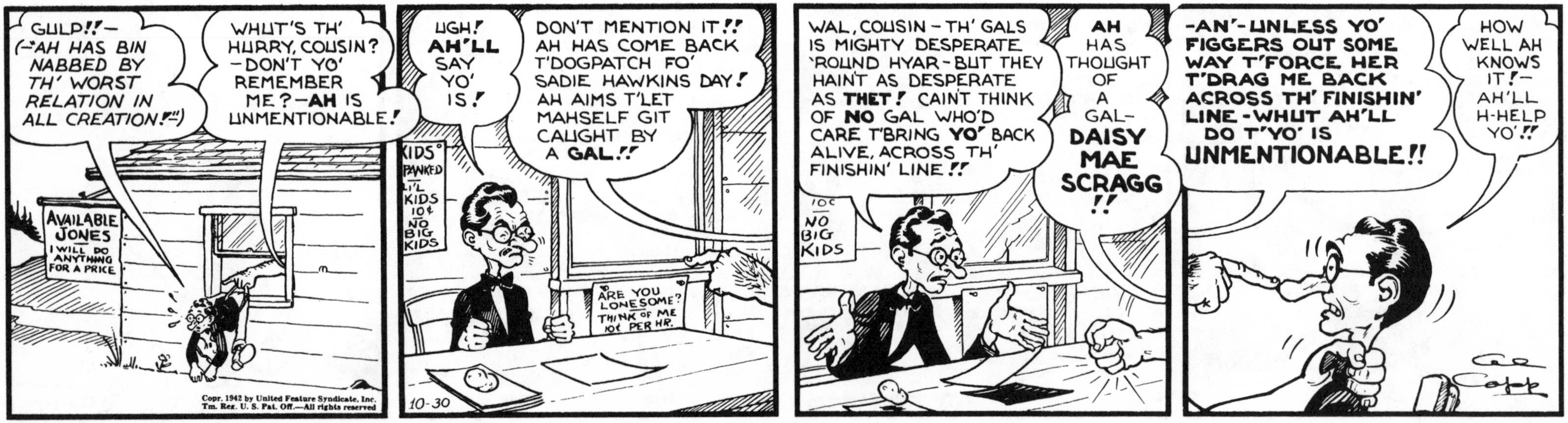
GULP!!-(-AH HAS BIN NABBED BY TH' WORST RELATION IN ALL CREATION!!-)
WHUT'S TH' HURRY, COUSIN? -DON'T YO' REMEMBER ME?-AH IS UNMENTIONABLE!
AVAILABLE JONES I WILL DO ANYTHING FOR A PRICE
Copr. 1942 by United Feature Syndicate, Inc. Tm. Reg. U. S. Pat. Off.—All rights reserved
UGH! AH'LL SAY YO' IS!
DON'T MENTION IT!! AH HAS COME BACK T'DOGPATCH FO' SADIE HAWKINS DAY! AH AIMS T'LET MAHSELF GIT CAUGHT BY A GAL!!
KIDS SPANKED LI'L KIDS 10¢ NO BIG KIDS
ARE YOU LONESOME? THINK OF ME 10¢ PER HR.
10-30
WAL, COUSIN-TH' GALS IS MIGHTY DESPERATE 'ROUND HYAR-BUT THEY HAIN'T AS DESPERATE AS THET! CAIN'T THINK OF NO GAL WHO'D CARE T'BRING YO' BACK ALIVE, ACROSS TH' FINISHIN' LINE!!
AH HAS THOUGHT OF A GAL-DAISY MAE SCRAGG!!
10¢ NO BIG KIDS
-AN'-UNLESS YO' FIGGERS OUT SOME WAY T'FORCE HER T'DRAG ME BACK ACROSS TH' FINISHIN' LINE-WHUT AH'LL DO T'YO' IS UNMENTIONABLE!!
HOW WELL AH KNOWS IT!-AH'LL H-HELP YO'!!
Al Capp

LI'L ABNER by AL CAPP!!

COUSIN AVAILABLE!! YO' GOTTA FIGGER OUT SOME SCHEME T'FORCE DAISY MAE T'COME BACK ACROSS TH' FINISHIN' LINE WIF **ME**, COME SADIE HAWKINS DAY!!

AH GOT IT ALL FIGGERED OUT, COUSIN UNMENTION-ABLE!—YOU RUNS AHEAD O' DAISY MAE, BY LONESOME POLECAT RIVER—

YO' PERTENDS T' FALL IN. YO' SCREAMS "*HALP! HALP!*"—NATCHERLY, SHE JUMPS IN T' SAVE YO'!

NATCHERLY!

10-31

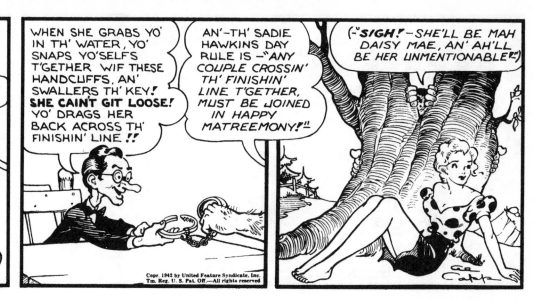

WHEN SHE GRABS YO' IN TH' WATER, YO' SNAPS YO'SELFS T'GETHER WIF THESE HANDCUFFS, AN' SWALLERS TH' KEY! **SHE CAINT GIT LOOSE!** YO' DRAGS HER BACK ACROSS TH' FINISHIN' LINE!!

AN'—TH' SADIE HAWKINS DAY RULE IS—"ANY COUPLE CROSSIN' TH' FINISHIN' LINE T'GETHER, MUST BE JOINED IN HAPPY MATREEMONY!"!!

(-"*SIGH!*—SHE'LL BE MAH DAISY MAE, AN' AH'LL BE HER UNMENTIONABLE*!")

Copr. 1942 by United Feature Syndicate, Inc.
Tm. Reg. U. S. Off.—All rights reserved

(-"THAR'S **KITTY HAWK**! SHE'S BIN AFTER ME EV'RY SADIE HAWKINS DAY FOR 9 Y'ARS, BUT, SO FAR, AH HAS ALLUS OUTRUN HER!"-)

YOO-HOO! AH WANTS T'SHOW YO' SOMETHIN' AH DREAMED UP, GUS GOOSEGREASE!

DON'T AX NO TECK-NICKLE QUESTIONS—JEST TURN ON TH' MOTOR!

Copr. 1942 by United Feature Syndicate, Inc.
Tm. Reg. U. S. Off.—All rights reserved

11-2

AH KIN MAKE 80 MILE A HOUR!!

AH CAIN'T EXCAPE **THET**! OH, UNHAPPY SADIE HAWKINS DAY!!

AH KIN JEST SEE MAHSELF, AFTER SADIE HAWKINS DAY—COOKIN' WITH GUS!!

ZOOM!!

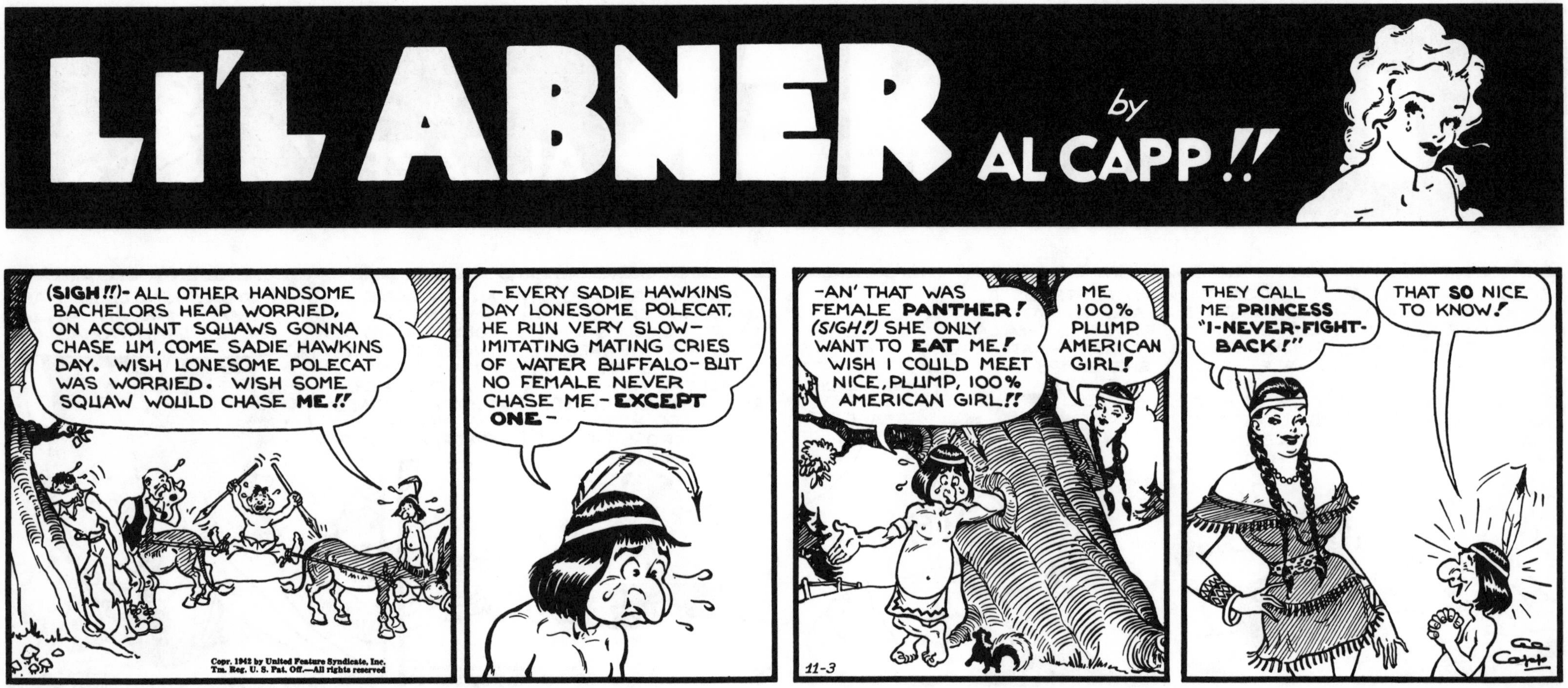
LI'L ABNER
by AL CAPP!!
(SIGH!!)-ALL OTHER HANDSOME BACHELORS HEAP WORRIED, ON ACCOUNT SQUAWS GONNA CHASE UM, COME SADIE HAWKINS DAY. WISH LONESOME POLECAT WAS WORRIED. WISH SOME SQUAW WOULD CHASE ME!!
Copr. 1942 by United Feature Syndicate, Inc. Tm. Reg. U. S. Pat. Off.—All rights reserved
-EVERY SADIE HAWKINS DAY LONESOME POLECAT, HE RUN VERY SLOW-IMITATING MATING CRIES OF WATER BUFFALO-BUT NO FEMALE NEVER CHASE ME-EXCEPT ONE-
-AN' THAT WAS FEMALE PANTHER! (SIGH!) SHE ONLY WANT TO EAT ME! WISH I COULD MEET NICE, PLUMP, 100% AMERICAN GIRL!!
ME 100% PLUMP AMERICAN GIRL!
11-3
THEY CALL ME PRINCESS "I-NEVER-FIGHT-BACK!"
THAT SO NICE TO KNOW!
Al Capp

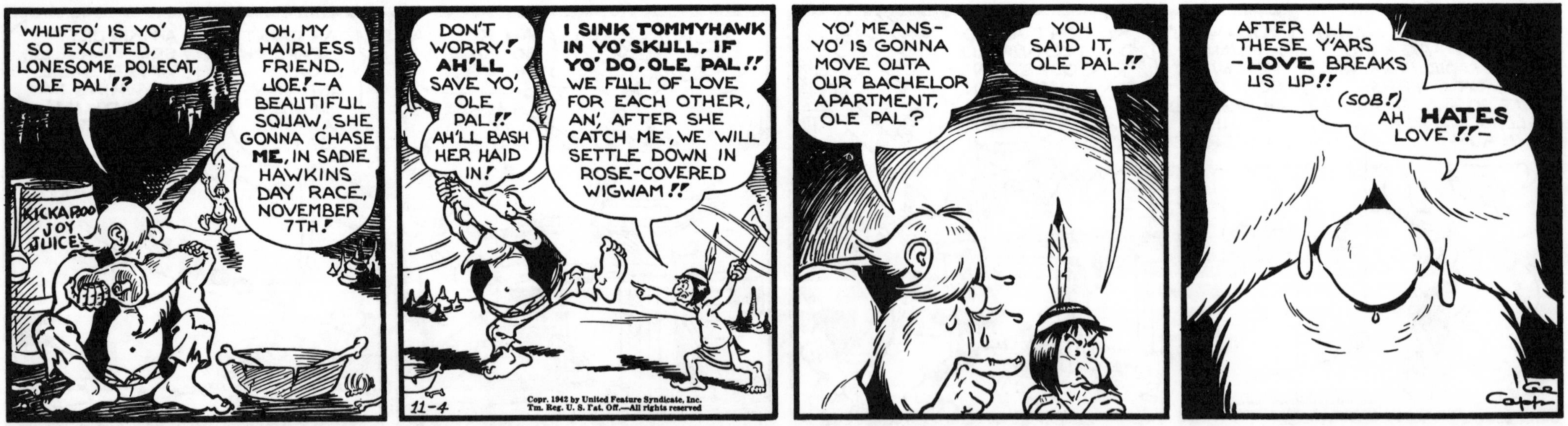
WHUFFO' IS YO' SO EXCITED, LONESOME POLECAT, OLE PAL!?
OH, MY HAIRLESS FRIEND, JOE!-A BEAUTIFUL SQUAW, SHE GONNA CHASE ME, IN SADIE HAWKINS DAY RACE, NOVEMBER 7TH!
KICKAPOO JOY JUICE
DON'T WORRY! AH'LL SAVE YO', OLE PAL!! AH'LL BASH HER HAID IN!
I SINK TOMMYHAWK IN YO' SKULL, IF YO' DO, OLE PAL!! WE FULL OF LOVE FOR EACH OTHER, AN', AFTER SHE CATCH ME, WE WILL SETTLE DOWN IN ROSE-COVERED WIGWAM!!
11-4
Copr. 1942 by United Feature Syndicate, Inc. Tm. Reg. U. S. Pat. Off.—All rights reserved
YO' MEANS-YO' IS GONNA MOVE OUTA OUR BACHELOR APARTMENT, OLE PAL?
YOU SAID IT, OLE PAL!!
AFTER ALL THESE Y'ARS -LOVE BREAKS US UP!!
(SOB!) AH HATES LOVE!!-
Al Capp

LI'L ABNER by AL CAPP!!

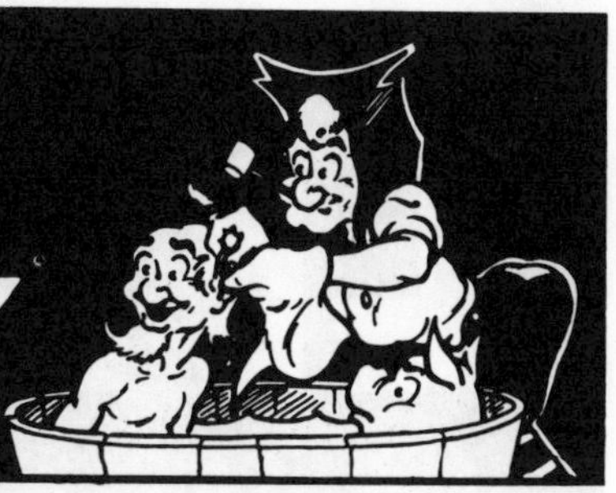

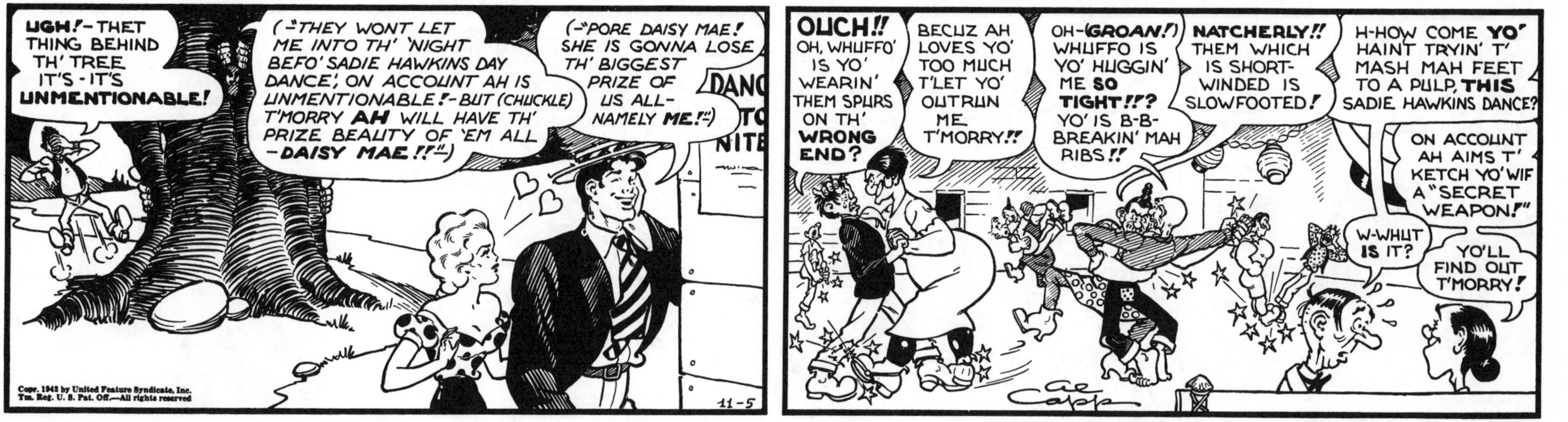

UGH!-THET THING BEHIND TH' TREE IT'S-IT'S UNMENTIONABLE!
(-"THEY WONT LET ME INTO TH' 'NIGHT BEFO' SADIE HAWKINS DAY DANCE', ON ACCOUNT AH IS UNMENTIONABLE!-BUT (CHUCKLE) T'MORRY AH WILL HAVE TH' PRIZE BEAUTY OF 'EM ALL -DAISY MAE!!"-)
(-"PORE DAISY MAE! SHE IS GONNA LOSE TH' BIGGEST PRIZE OF US ALL- NAMELY ME!"-)
DANC TO NITE
Copr. 1942 by United Feature Syndicate, Inc. Tm. Reg. U. S. Pat. Off.—All rights reserved
11-5
OUCH!! OH, WHUFFO' IS YO' WEARIN' THEM SPURS ON TH' WRONG END?
BECUZ AH LOVES YO' TOO MUCH T'LET YO' OUTRUN ME T'MORRY!!
OH-(GROAN!) WHUFFO IS YO' HUGGIN' ME SO TIGHT!!? YO' IS B-B-BREAKIN' MAH RIBS!!
NATCHERLY!! THEM WHICH IS SHORT-WINDED IS SLOWFOOTED!
H-HOW COME YO' HAINT TRYIN' T' MASH MAH FEET TO A PULP, THIS SADIE HAWKINS DANCE?
ON ACCOUNT AH AIMS T' KETCH YO' WIF A "SECRET WEAPON!"
W-WHUT IS IT?
YO'LL FIND OUT T'MORRY!
AL CAPP

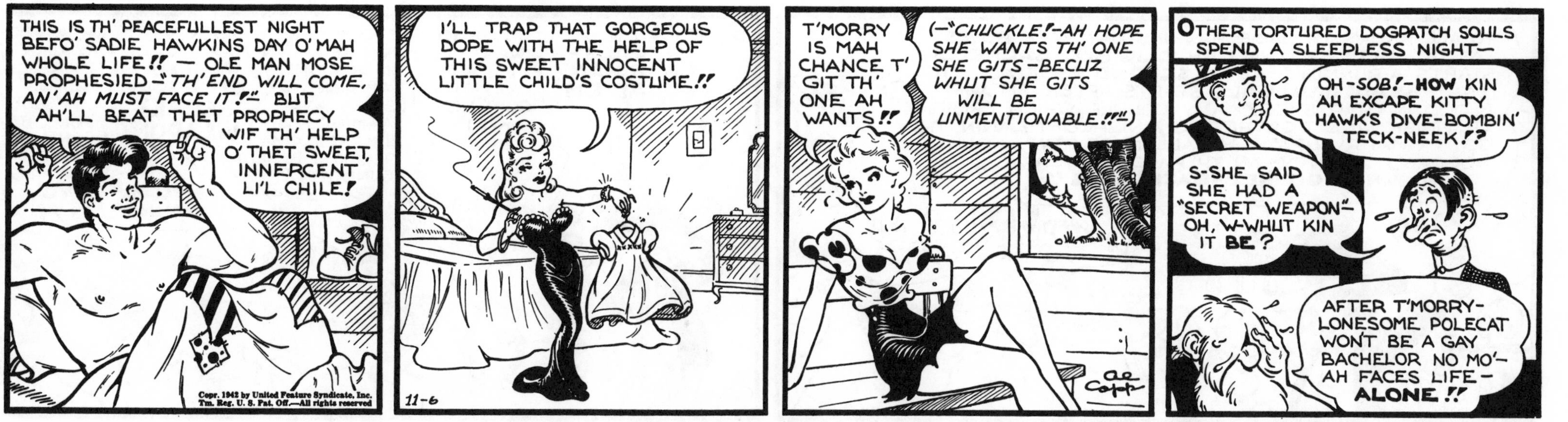

THIS IS TH' PEACEFULLEST NIGHT BEFO' SADIE HAWKINS DAY O'MAH WHOLE LIFE!! — OLE MAN MOSE PROPHESIED-"TH' END WILL COME, AN' AH MUST FACE IT!"- BUT AH'LL BEAT THET PROPHECY WIF TH' HELP O' THET SWEET, INNERCENT LI'L CHILE!
Copr. 1942 by United Feature Syndicate, Inc. Tm. Reg. U. S. Pat. Off.—All rights reserved
I'LL TRAP THAT GORGEOUS DOPE WITH THE HELP OF THIS SWEET INNOCENT LITTLE CHILD'S COSTUME.!!
11-6
T'MORRY IS MAH CHANCE T' GIT TH' ONE AH WANTS!!
(-"CHUCKLE!-AH HOPE SHE WANTS TH' ONE SHE GITS-BECUZ WHUT SHE GITS WILL BE UNMENTIONABLE.!!"-)
AL CAPP
OTHER TORTURED DOGPATCH SOULS SPEND A SLEEPLESS NIGHT—
OH-SOB!-HOW KIN AH EXCAPE KITTY HAWK'S DIVE-BOMBIN' TECK-NEEK!?
S-SHE SAID SHE HAD A "SECRET WEAPON"- OH, W-WHUT KIN IT BE?
AFTER T'MORRY- LONESOME POLECAT WON'T BE A GAY BACHELOR NO MO'- AH FACES LIFE- ALONE!!

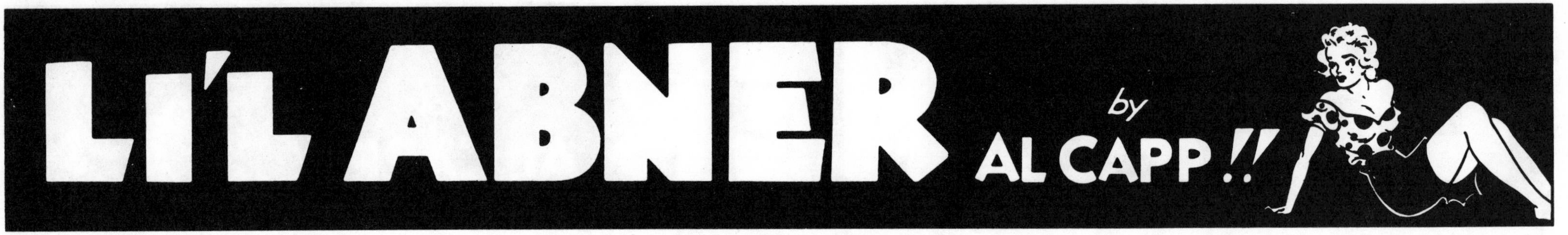
LI'L ABNER
by
AL CAPP!!

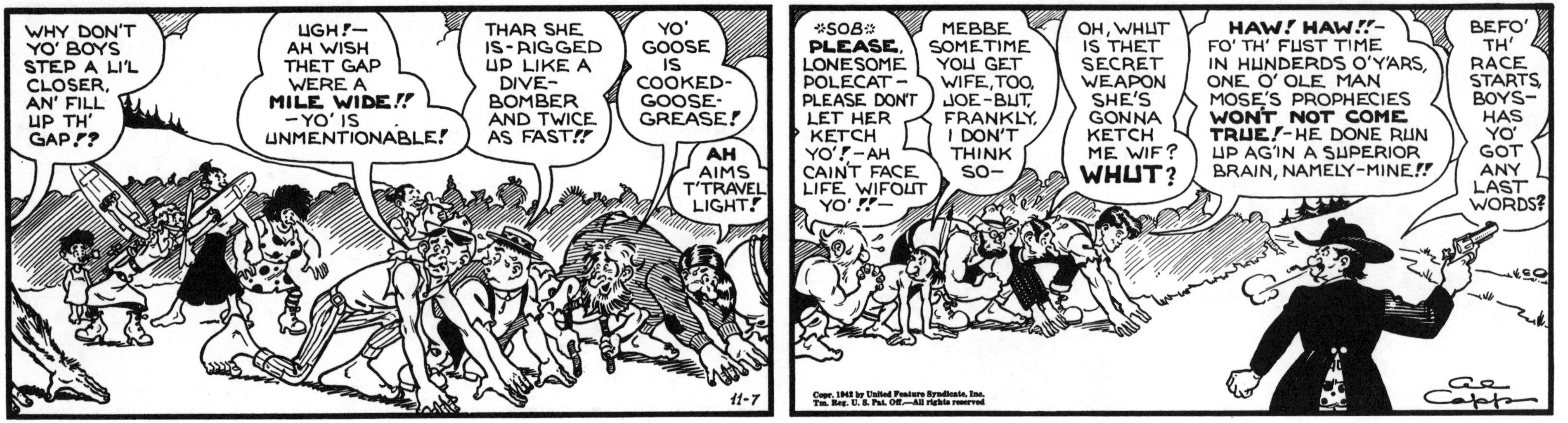
WHY DON'T YO' BOYS STEP A LI'L CLOSER, AN' FILL UP TH' GAP!?
UGH!— AH WISH THET GAP WERE A MILE WIDE!! —YO' IS UNMENTIONABLE!
THAR SHE IS-RIGGED UP LIKE A DIVE-BOMBER AND TWICE AS FAST!!
YO' GOOSE IS COOKED-GOOSE-GREASE!
AH AIMS T'TRAVEL LIGHT!
11-7
SOB PLEASE, LONESOME POLECAT-PLEASE DON'T LET HER KETCH YO'!-AH CAIN'T FACE LIFE WIFOUT YO'!!—
MEBBE SOMETIME YOU GET WIFE, TOO, JOE-BUT, FRANKLY, I DON'T THINK SO—
OH, WHUT IS THET SECRET WEAPON SHE'S GONNA KETCH ME WIF? WHUT?
HAW! HAW!!— FO' TH' FUST TIME IN HUNDERDS O'Y'ARS, ONE O' OLE MAN MOSE'S PROPHECIES WON'T NOT COME TRUE!-HE DONE RUN UP AG'IN A SUPERIOR BRAIN, NAMELY-MINE!!
BEFO' TH' RACE STARTS, BOYS-HAS YO' GOT ANY LAST WORDS?
Copr. 1942 by United Feature Syndicate, Inc.
Tm. Reg. U. S. Pat. Off.—All rights reserved
Al Capp

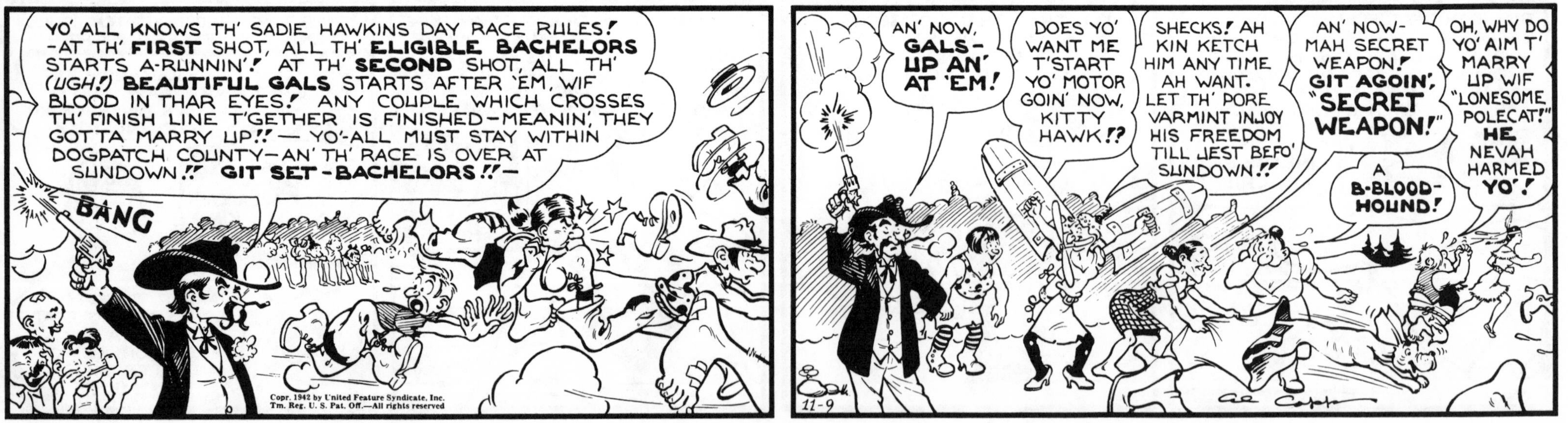
YO' ALL KNOWS TH' SADIE HAWKINS DAY RACE RULES! -AT TH' FIRST SHOT, ALL TH' ELIGIBLE BACHELORS STARTS A-RUNNIN'! AT TH' SECOND SHOT, ALL TH' (UGH!) BEAUTIFUL GALS STARTS AFTER 'EM, WIF BLOOD IN THAR EYES! ANY COUPLE WHICH CROSSES TH' FINISH LINE T'GETHER IS FINISHED-MEANIN', THEY GOTTA MARRY UP!!— YO'-ALL MUST STAY WITHIN DOGPATCH COUNTY-AN' TH' RACE IS OVER AT SUNDOWN!! GIT SET-BACHELORS!!—
BANG
Copr. 1942 by United Feature Syndicate, Inc.
Tm. Reg. U. S. Pat. Off.—All rights reserved
AN' NOW, GALS-UP AN' AT 'EM!
DOES YO' WANT ME T'START YO' MOTOR GOIN' NOW, KITTY HAWK!?
SHECKS! AH KIN KETCH HIM ANY TIME AH WANT. LET TH' PORE VARMINT INJOY HIS FREEDOM TILL JEST BEFO' SUNDOWN!!
AN' NOW-MAH SECRET WEAPON! GIT AGOIN', "SECRET WEAPON!"
A B-BLOOD-HOUND!
OH, WHY DO YO' AIM T' MARRY UP WIF "LONESOME POLECAT!" HE NEVAH HARMED YO'!
11-9
Al Capp

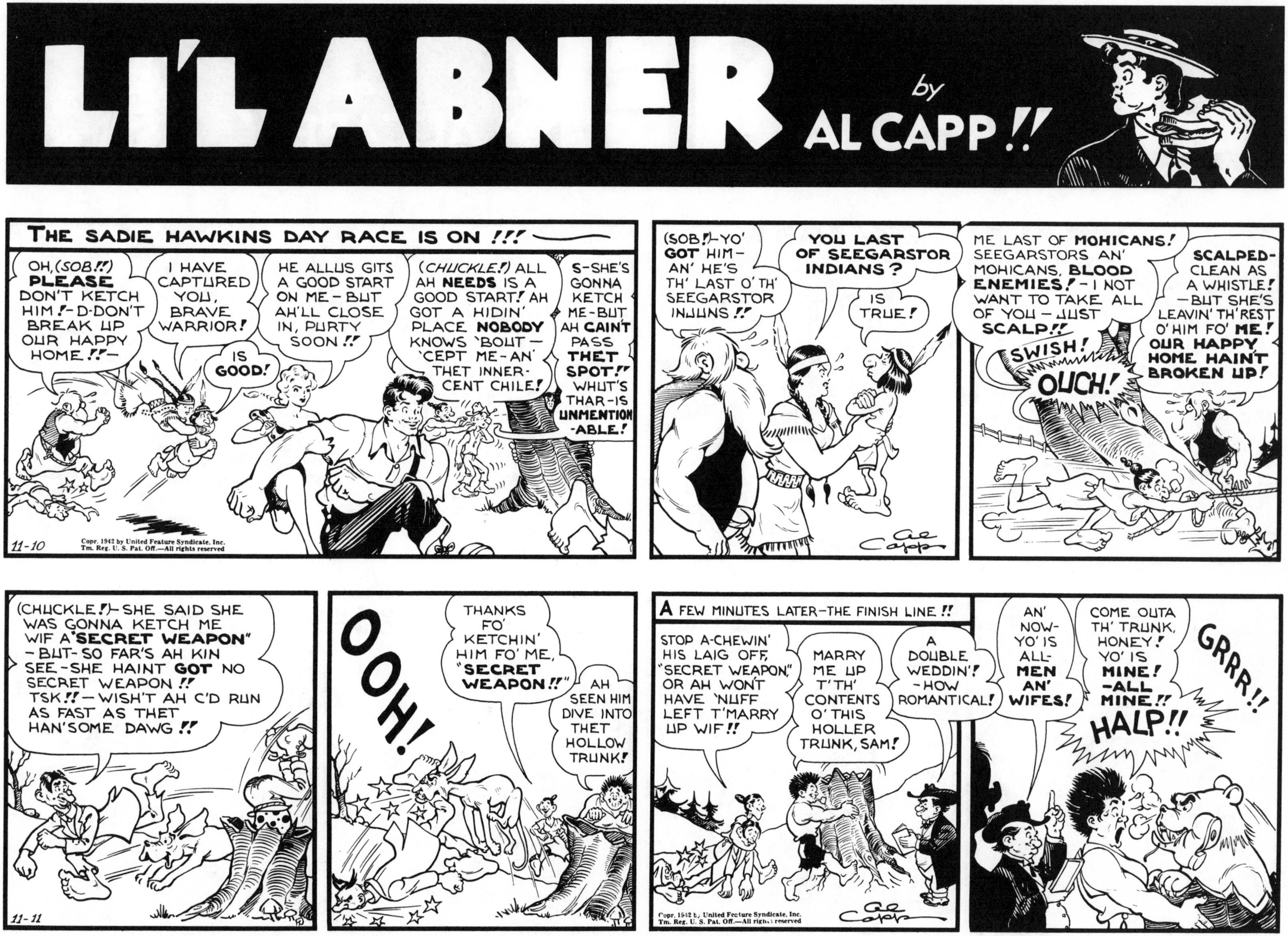

LI'L ABNER by AL CAPP!!
THE SADIE HAWKINS DAY RACE IS ON !!!
OH, (SOB!!) PLEASE DON'T KETCH HIM!-D-DON'T BREAK UP OUR HAPPY HOME!!-
I HAVE CAPTURED YOU, BRAVE WARRIOR!
IS GOOD!
HE ALLUS GITS A GOOD START ON ME-BUT AH'LL CLOSE IN, PURTY SOON!!
(CHUCKLE!) ALL AH NEEDS IS A GOOD START! AH GOT A HIDIN' PLACE NOBODY KNOWS 'BOUT-'CEPT ME-AN' THET INNER-CENT CHILE!
S-SHE'S GONNA KETCH ME-BUT AH CAIN'T PASS THET SPOT!" WHUT'S THAR-IS UNMENTION-ABLE!
11-10
Copr. 1942 by United Feature Syndicate, Inc. Tm. Reg. U. S. Pat. Off.—All rights reserved
(SOB!)-YO' GOT HIM-AN' HE'S TH' LAST O' TH' SEEGARSTOR INJUNS!!
YOU LAST OF SEEGARSTOR INDIANS?
IS TRUE!
Al Capp
ME LAST OF MOHICANS! SEEGARSTORS AN' MOHICANS, BLOOD ENEMIES!-I NOT WANT TO TAKE ALL OF YOU-JUST SCALP!!
SCALPED-CLEAN AS A WHISTLE! -BUT SHE'S LEAVIN' TH'REST O'HIM FO' ME! OUR HAPPY HOME HAIN'T BROKEN UP!
SWISH!
OUCH!
(CHUCKLE!)-SHE SAID SHE WAS GONNA KETCH ME WIF A "SECRET WEAPON" -BUT-SO FAR'S AH KIN SEE-SHE HAINT GOT NO SECRET WEAPON!! TSK!!-WISH'T AH C'D RUN AS FAST AS THET HAN'SOME DAWG!!
11-11
OOH!
THANKS FO' KETCHIN' HIM FO' ME, "SECRET WEAPON!!"
AH SEEN HIM DIVE INTO THET HOLLOW TRUNK!
A FEW MINUTES LATER-THE FINISH LINE!!
STOP A-CHEWIN' HIS LAIG OFF, "SECRET WEAPON," OR AH WON'T HAVE 'NUFF LEFT T'MARRY UP WIF!!
MARRY ME UP T'TH' CONTENTS O' THIS HOLLER TRUNK, SAM!
A DOUBLE WEDDIN'! -HOW ROMANTICAL!
Copr. 1942 by United Feature Syndicate, Inc. Tm. Reg. U. S. Pat. Off.—All rights reserved
Al Capp
AN' NOW-YO' IS ALL-MEN AN' WIFES!
COME OUTA TH' TRUNK, HONEY! YO' IS MINE! -ALL MINE!!
GRRRR!!
HALP!!

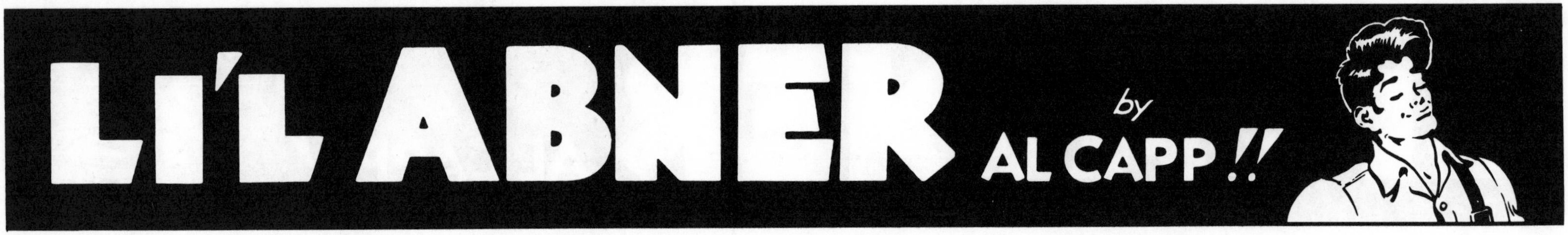
LI'L ABNER
by
AL CAPP!!

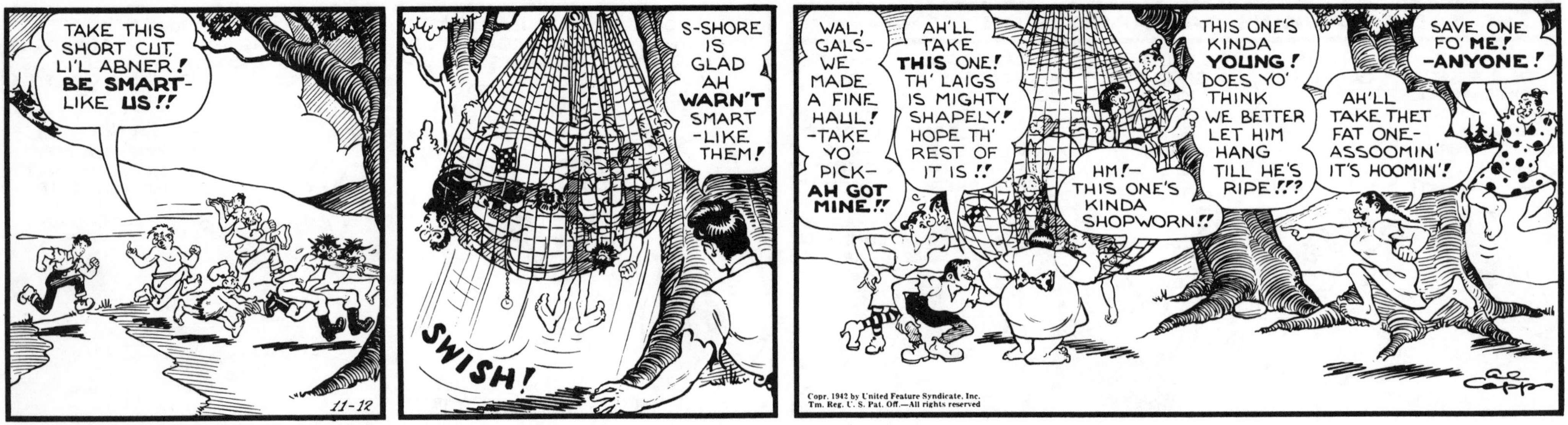
TAKE THIS SHORT CUT, LI'L ABNER! BE SMART- LIKE US!!
11-12
S-SHORE IS GLAD AH WARN'T SMART -LIKE THEM!
SWISH!
WAL, GALS- WE MADE A FINE HAUL! -TAKE YO' PICK- AH GOT MINE!!
AH'LL TAKE THIS ONE! TH' LAIGS IS MIGHTY SHAPELY! HOPE TH' REST OF IT IS!!
HM!- THIS ONE'S KINDA SHOPWORN!!
THIS ONE'S KINDA YOUNG! DOES YO' THINK WE BETTER LET HIM HANG TILL HE'S RIPE!!?
AH'LL TAKE THET FAT ONE- ASSOOMIN' IT'S HOOMIN'!
SAVE ONE FO' ME! -ANYONE!
Copr. 1942 by United Feature Syndicate, Inc. Tm. Reg. U. S. Pat. Off.—All rights reserved
Al Capp

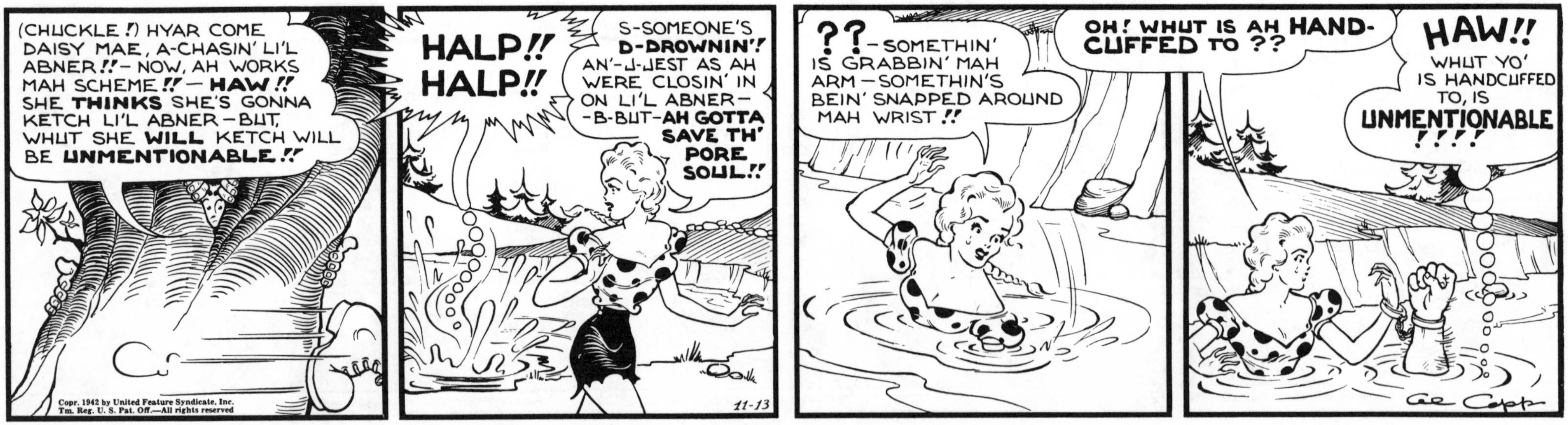
(CHUCKLE!) HYAR COME DAISY MAE, A-CHASIN' LI'L ABNER!!- NOW, AH WORKS MAH SCHEME!!- HAW!! SHE THINKS SHE'S GONNA KETCH LI'L ABNER-BUT, WHUT SHE WILL KETCH WILL BE UNMENTIONABLE!!
Copr. 1942 by United Feature Syndicate, Inc. Tm. Reg. U. S. Pat. Off.—All rights reserved
HALP!! HALP!!
S-SOMEONE'S D-DROWNIN'! AN'-J-JEST AS AH WERE CLOSIN' IN ON LI'L ABNER- -B-BUT-AH GOTTA SAVE TH' PORE SOUL!!
11-13
??-SOMETHIN' IS GRABBIN' MAH ARM-SOMETHIN'S BEIN' SNAPPED AROUND MAH WRIST!!
OH! WHUT IS AH HAND-CUFFED TO??
HAW!! WHUT YO' IS HANDCUFFED TO, IS UNMENTIONABLE!!!!
Al Capp

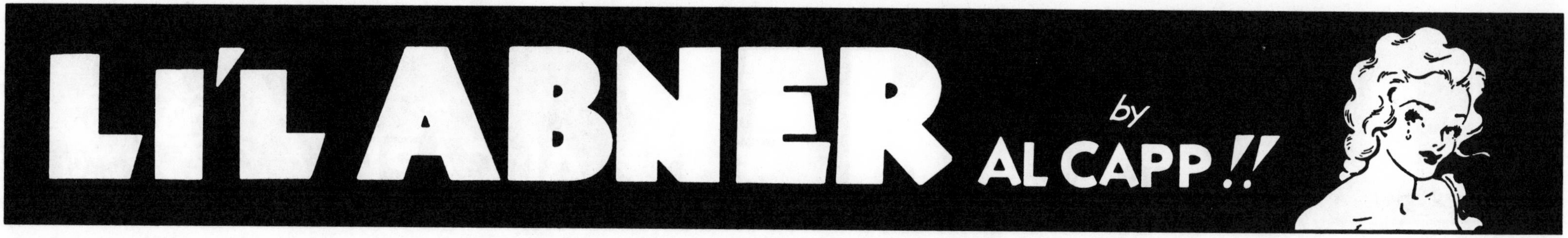
LI'L ABNER
by
AL CAPP!!

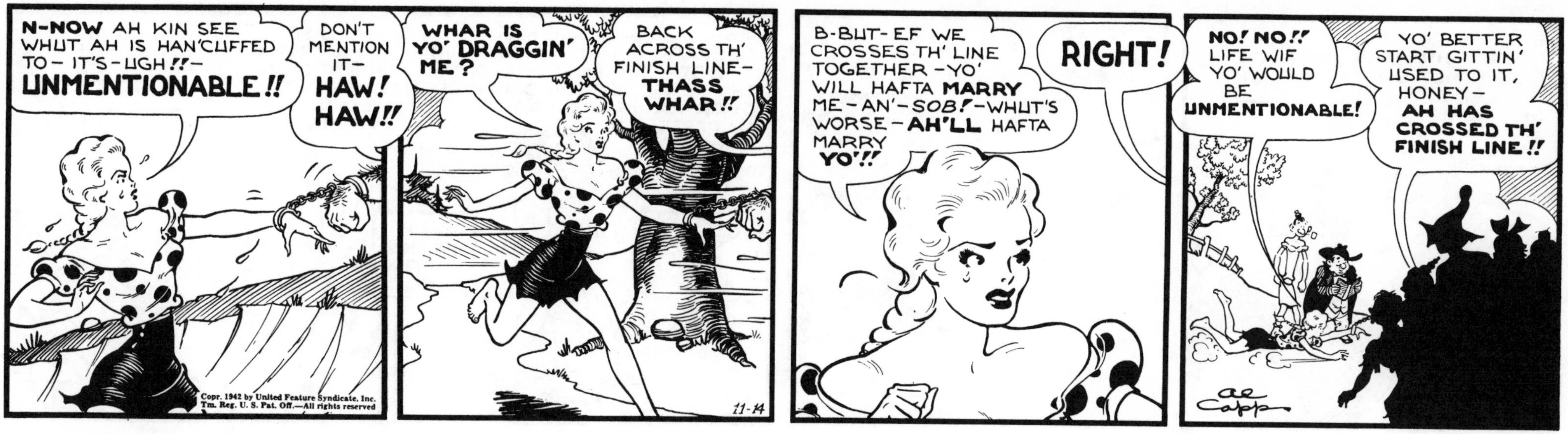
N-NOW AH KIN SEE WHUT AH IS HAN'CUFFED TO – IT'S – UGH!! – UNMENTIONABLE!!
DON'T MENTION IT – HAW! HAW!!
Copr. 1942 by United Feature Syndicate, Inc. Tm. Reg. U. S. Pat. Off.—All rights reserved
WHAR IS YO' DRAGGIN' ME?
BACK ACROSS TH' FINISH LINE – THASS WHAR!!
11-14
B-BUT – EF WE CROSSES TH' LINE TOGETHER – YO' WILL HAFTA MARRY ME – AN' – SOB! – WHUT'S WORSE – AH'LL HAFTA MARRY YO'!!
RIGHT!
NO! NO!! LIFE WIF YO' WOULD BE UNMENTIONABLE!
YO' BETTER START GITTIN' USED TO IT, HONEY – AH HAS CROSSED TH' FINISH LINE!!
Al Capp

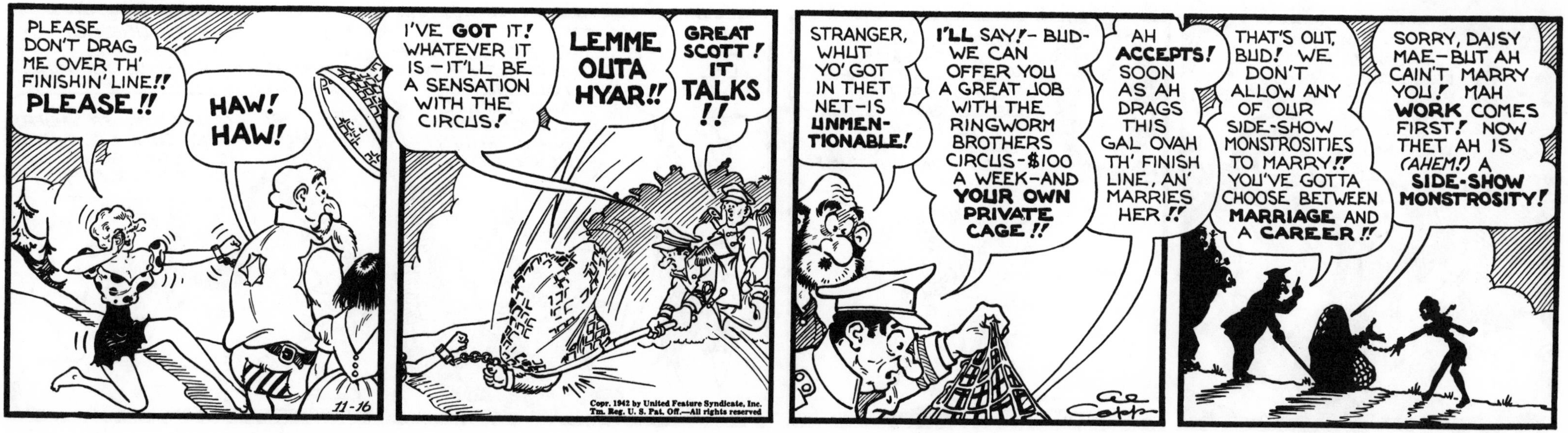
PLEASE DON'T DRAG ME OVER TH' FINISHIN' LINE!! PLEASE!!
HAW! HAW!
11-16
I'VE GOT IT! WHATEVER IT IS – IT'LL BE A SENSATION WITH THE CIRCUS!
LEMME OUTA HYAR!!
GREAT SCOTT! IT TALKS!!
Copr. 1942 by United Feature Syndicate, Inc. Tm. Reg. U. S. Pat. Off.—All rights reserved
STRANGER, WHUT YO' GOT IN THET NET – IS UNMENTIONABLE!
I'LL SAY! – BUD – WE CAN OFFER YOU A GREAT JOB WITH THE RINGWORM BROTHERS CIRCUS – $100 A WEEK – AND YOUR OWN PRIVATE CAGE!!
AH ACCEPTS! SOON AS AH DRAGS THIS GAL OVAH TH' FINISH LINE, AN' MARRIES HER!!
Al Capp
THAT'S OUT, BUD! WE DON'T ALLOW ANY OF OUR SIDE-SHOW MONSTROSITIES TO MARRY!! YOU'VE GOTTA CHOOSE BETWEEN MARRIAGE AND A CAREER!!
SORRY, DAISY MAE – BUT AH CAIN'T MARRY YOU! MAH WORK COMES FIRST! NOW THET AH IS (AHEM!) A SIDE-SHOW MONSTROSITY!

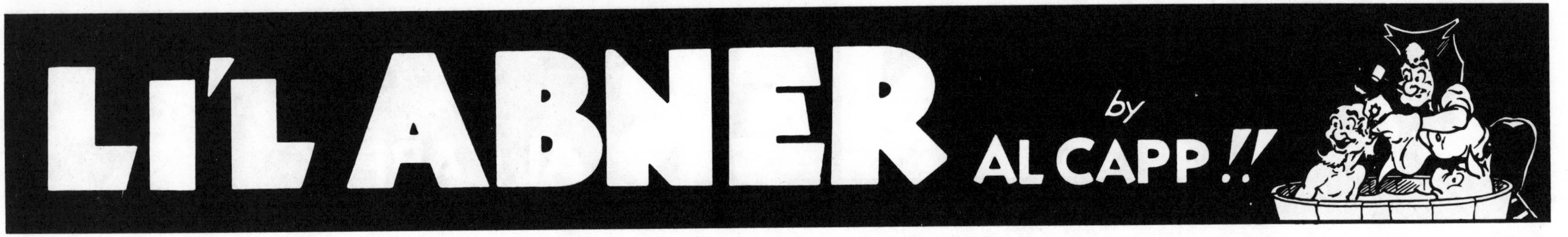

LI'L ABNER
by
AL CAPP!!

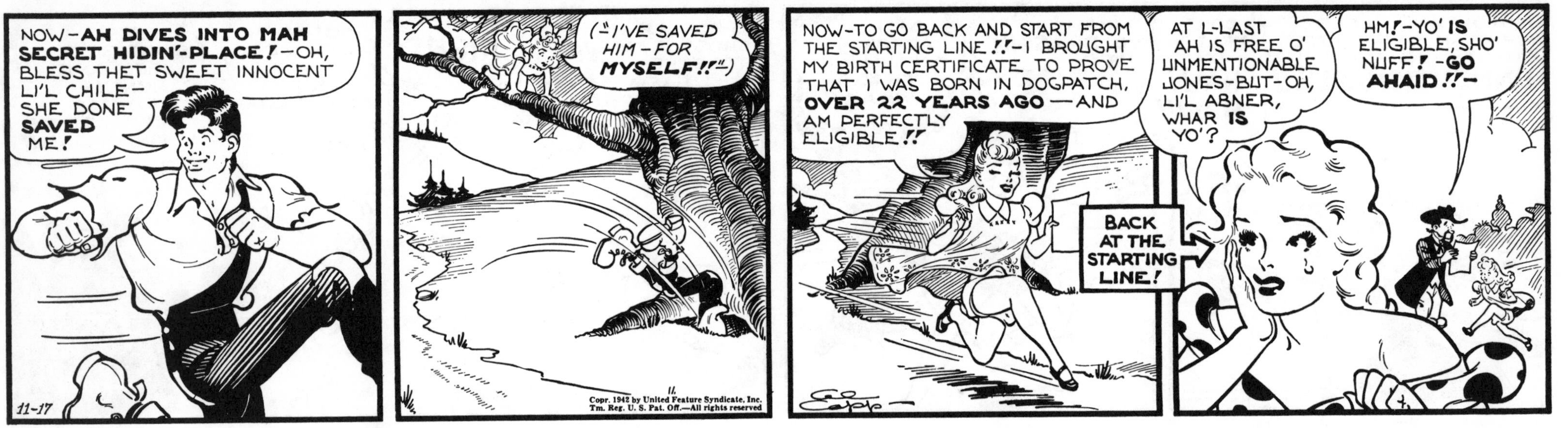

NOW-AH DIVES INTO MAH SECRET HIDIN'-PLACE!-OH, BLESS THET SWEET INNOCENT LI'L CHILE- SHE DONE SAVED ME!
11-17
(-"I'VE SAVED HIM-FOR MYSELF!!"-)
Copr. 1942 by United Feature Syndicate, Inc. Tm. Reg. U. S. Pat. Off.—All rights reserved
NOW-TO GO BACK AND START FROM THE STARTING LINE!!-I BROUGHT MY BIRTH CERTIFICATE TO PROVE THAT I WAS BORN IN DOGPATCH, OVER 22 YEARS AGO-AND AM PERFECTLY ELIGIBLE!!
BACK AT THE STARTING LINE!
AT L-LAST AH IS FREE O' UNMENTIONABLE JONES-BUT-OH, LI'L ABNER, WHAR IS YO'?
HM!-YO' IS ELIGIBLE, SHO' NUFF!-GO AHAID!!-

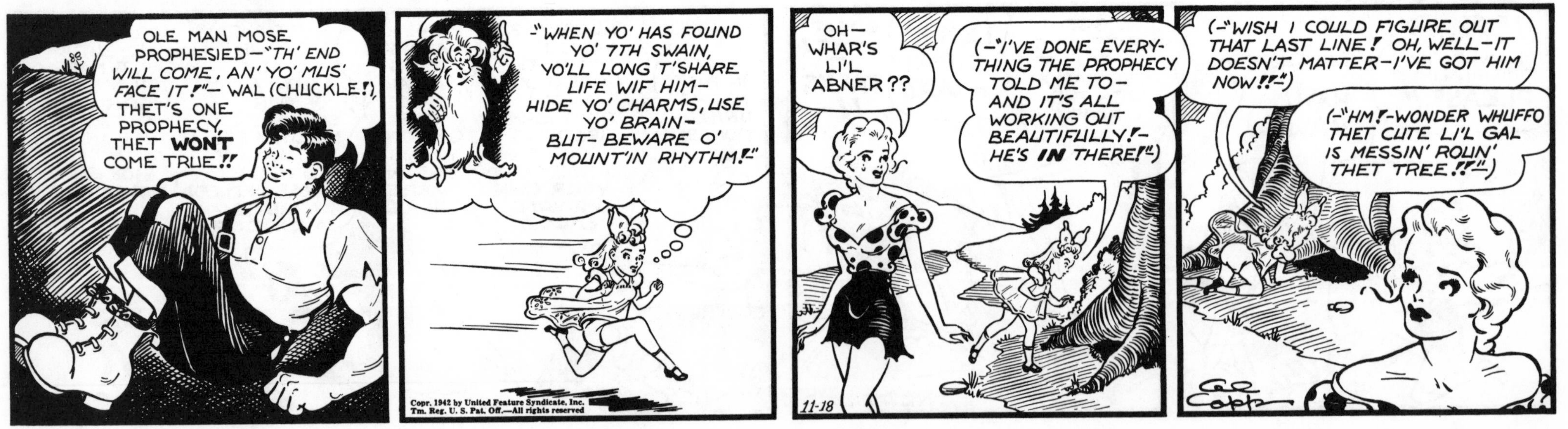

OLE MAN MOSE PROPHESIED-"TH' END WILL COME, AN' YO' MUS' FACE IT!"-WAL (CHUCKLE!), THET'S ONE PROPHECY, THET WON'T COME TRUE!!
-"WHEN YO' HAS FOUND YO' 7TH SWAIN, YO'LL LONG T'SHARE LIFE WIF HIM- HIDE YO' CHARMS, USE YO' BRAIN- BUT- BEWARE O' MOUNT'IN RHYTHM!"-
Copr. 1942 by United Feature Syndicate, Inc. Tm. Reg. U. S. Pat. Off.—All rights reserved
OH- WHAR'S LI'L ABNER??
(-"I'VE DONE EVERY-THING THE PROPHECY TOLD ME TO- AND IT'S ALL WORKING OUT BEAUTIFULLY!-HE'S IN THERE!"-)
11-18
(-"WISH I COULD FIGURE OUT THAT LAST LINE! OH, WELL-IT DOESN'T MATTER-I'VE GOT HIM NOW!!"-)
(-"HM!-WONDER WHUFFO THET CUTE LI'L GAL IS MESSIN' ROUN' THET TREE!!"-)

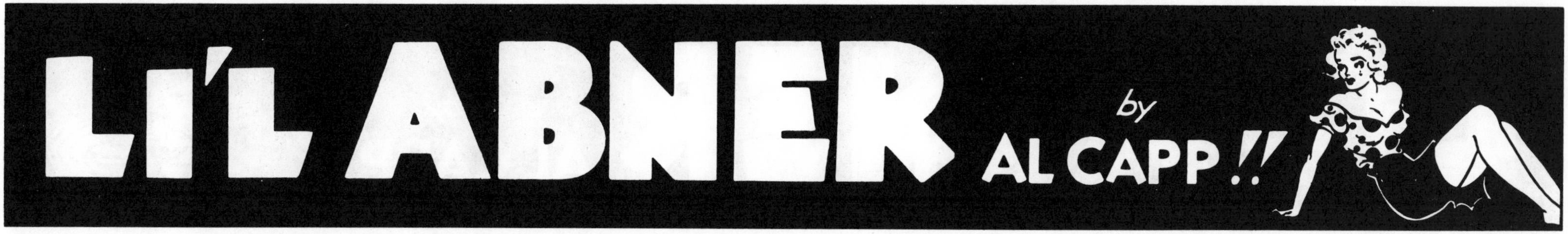
LI'L ABNER
by
AL CAPP!!

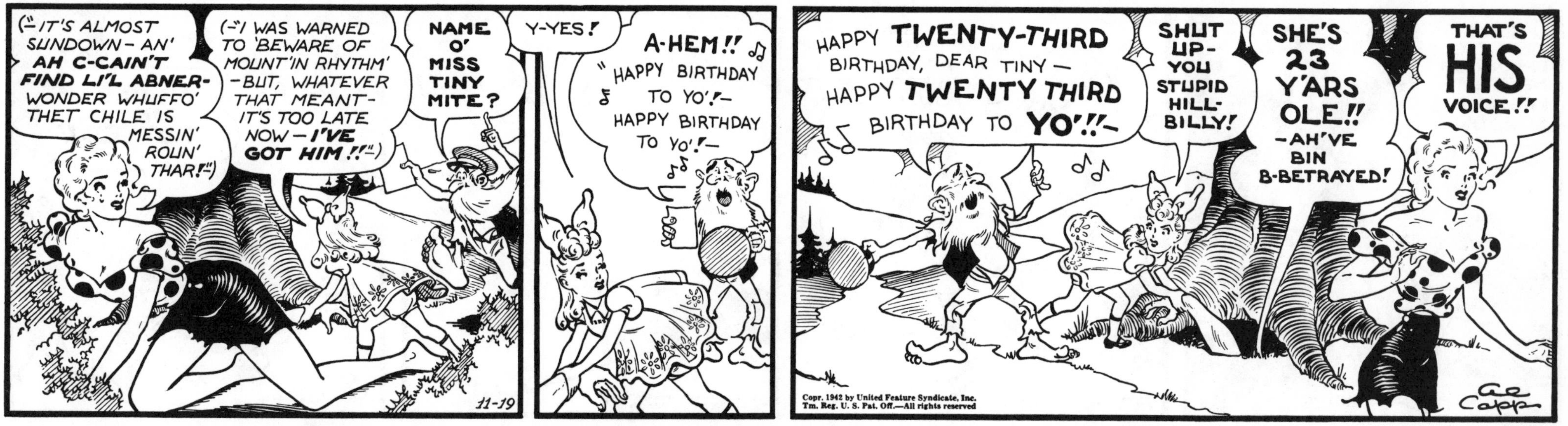
("–IT'S ALMOST SUNDOWN – AN' AH C-CAIN'T FIND LI'L ABNER – WONDER WHUFFO' THET CHILE IS MESSIN' ROUN' THAR!")
("–I WAS WARNED TO 'BEWARE OF MOUNT'IN RHYTHM' – BUT, WHATEVER THAT MEANT – IT'S TOO LATE NOW – I'VE GOT HIM!!")
NAME O' MISS TINY MITE?
Y-YES!
A-HEM!! "HAPPY BIRTHDAY TO YO'!– HAPPY BIRTHDAY TO YO'!–
11-19
HAPPY TWENTY-THIRD BIRTHDAY, DEAR TINY – HAPPY TWENTY THIRD BIRTHDAY TO YO'!!–
SHUT UP – YOU STUPID HILL-BILLY!
SHE'S 23 Y'ARS OLE!! – AH'VE BIN B-BETRAYED!
THAT'S HIS VOICE!!
Copr. 1942 by United Feature Syndicate, Inc.
Tm. Reg. U. S. Pat. Off.—All rights reserved
Al Capp

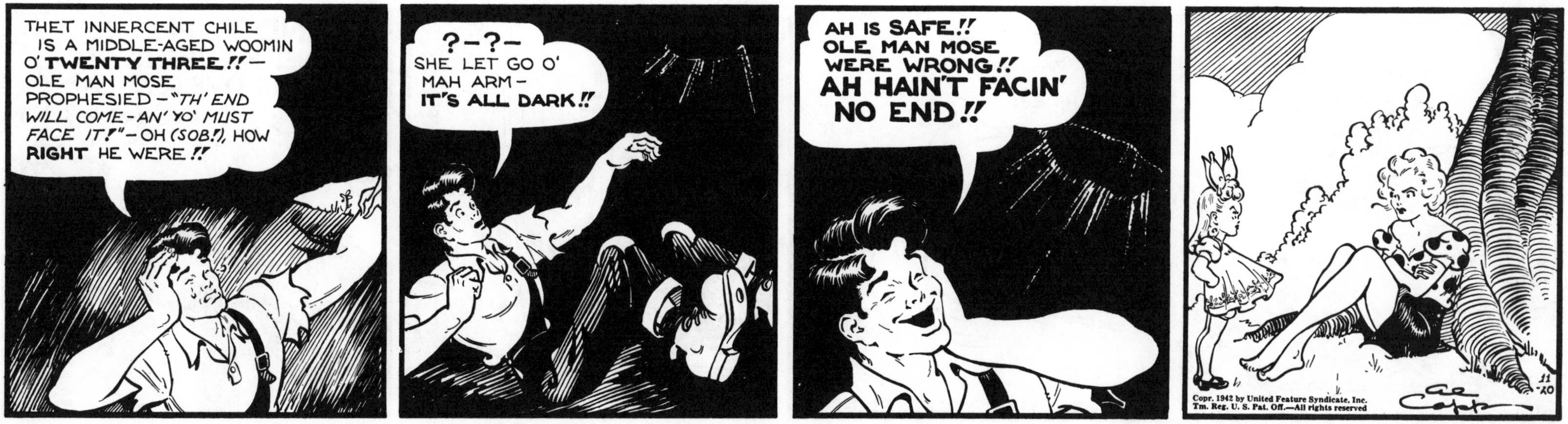
THET INNERCENT CHILE IS A MIDDLE-AGED WOOMIN O' TWENTY THREE!! – OLE MAN MOSE PROPHESIED – "TH' END WILL COME – AN' YO' MUST FACE IT!" – OH (SOB!), HOW RIGHT HE WERE!!
?–?– SHE LET GO O' MAH ARM – IT'S ALL DARK!!
AH IS SAFE!! OLE MAN MOSE WERE WRONG!! AH HAIN'T FACIN' NO END!!
11-20
Copr. 1942 by United Feature Syndicate, Inc.
Tm. Reg. U. S. Pat. Off.—All rights reserved
Al Capp

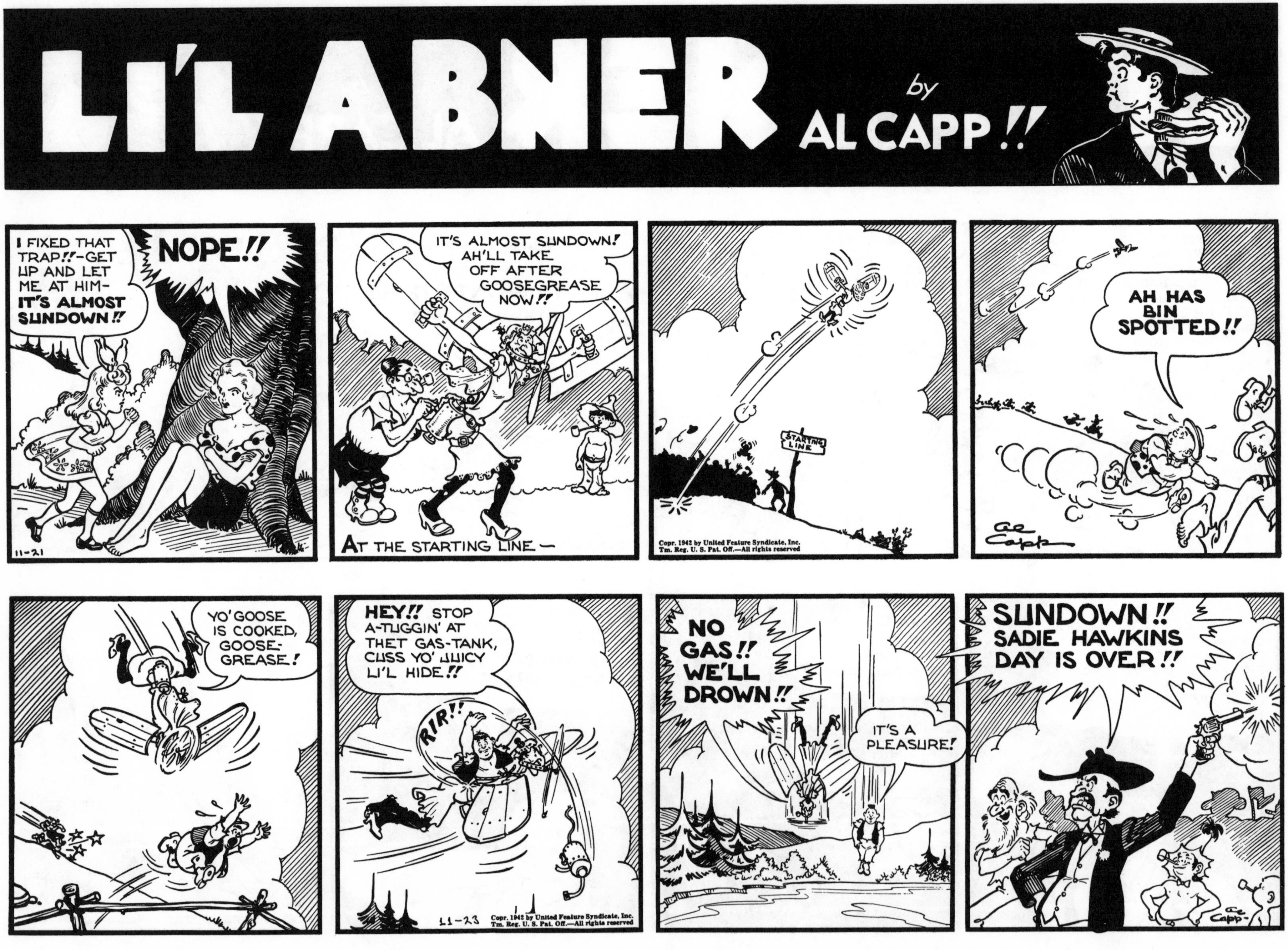

LI'L ABNER
by AL CAPP!!
I FIXED THAT TRAP!!–GET UP AND LET ME AT HIM– IT'S ALMOST SUNDOWN!!
NOPE!!
11-21
IT'S ALMOST SUNDOWN! AH'LL TAKE OFF AFTER GOOSEGREASE NOW!!
AT THE STARTING LINE–
STARTING LINE
Copr. 1942 by United Feature Syndicate, Inc. Tm. Reg. U. S. Pat. Off.—All rights reserved
AH HAS BIN SPOTTED!!
Al Capp
YO' GOOSE IS COOKED, GOOSE-GREASE!
HEY!! STOP A-TUGGIN' AT THET GAS-TANK, CUSS YO' JUICY LI'L HIDE!!
RIR!!
11-23
Copr. 1942 by United Feature Syndicate, Inc. Tm. Reg. U. S. Pat. Off.—All rights reserved
NO GAS!! WE'LL DROWN!!
IT'S A PLEASURE!
SUNDOWN!! SADIE HAWKINS DAY IS OVER!!
Al Capp

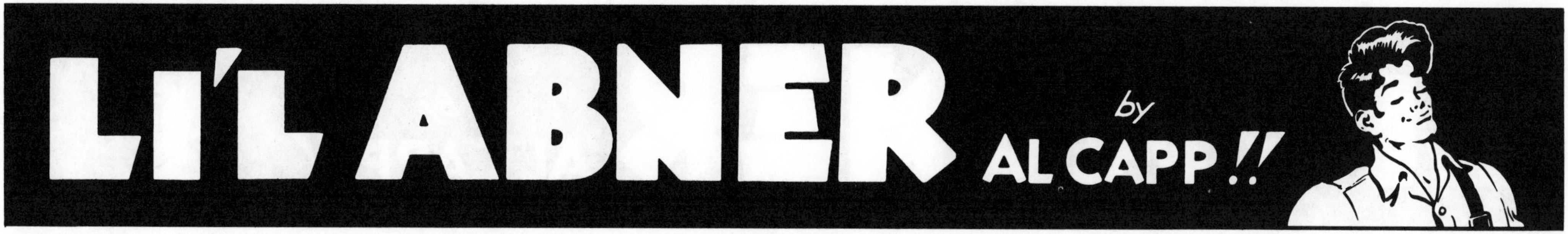
LI'L ABNER
by
AL CAPP!!

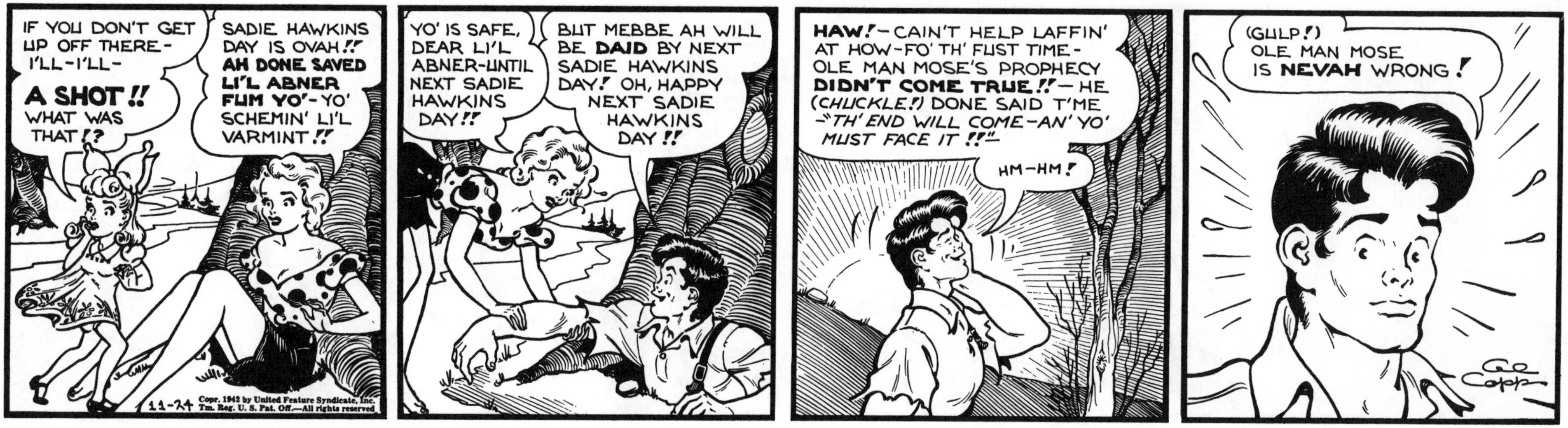
IF YOU DON'T GET UP OFF THERE- I'LL-I'LL-
A SHOT!! WHAT WAS THAT!?
SADIE HAWKINS DAY IS OVAH!! AH DONE SAVED LI'L ABNER FUM YO'-YO' SCHEMIN' LI'L VARMINT!!
11-24
Copr. 1942 by United Feature Syndicate, Inc. Tm. Reg. U. S. Pat. Off.—All rights reserved
YO' IS SAFE, DEAR LI'L ABNER-UNTIL NEXT SADIE HAWKINS DAY!!
BUT MEBBE AH WILL BE DAID BY NEXT SADIE HAWKINS DAY! OH, HAPPY NEXT SADIE HAWKINS DAY!!
HAW!-CAIN'T HELP LAFFIN' AT HOW-FO' TH' FUST TIME-OLE MAN MOSE'S PROPHECY DIDN'T COME TRUE!!-HE (CHUCKLE!) DONE SAID T'ME -"TH' END WILL COME-AN' YO' MUST FACE IT!!"
HM-HM!
(GULP!) OLE MAN MOSE IS NEVAH WRONG!
Al Capp

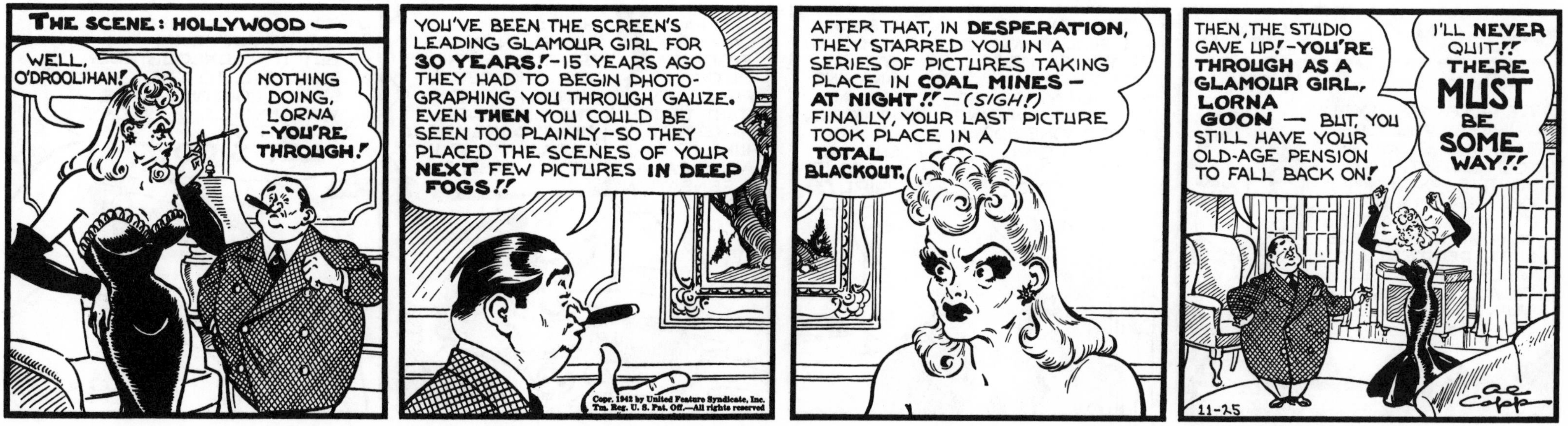
THE SCENE: HOLLYWOOD—
WELL, O'DROOLIHAN!
NOTHING DOING, LORNA -YOU'RE THROUGH!
YOU'VE BEEN THE SCREEN'S LEADING GLAMOUR GIRL FOR 30 YEARS!-15 YEARS AGO THEY HAD TO BEGIN PHOTOGRAPHING YOU THROUGH GAUZE. EVEN THEN YOU COULD BE SEEN TOO PLAINLY-SO THEY PLACED THE SCENES OF YOUR NEXT FEW PICTURES IN DEEP FOGS!!
Copr. 1942 by United Feature Syndicate, Inc. Tm. Reg. U. S. Pat. Off.—All rights reserved
AFTER THAT, IN DESPERATION, THEY STARRED YOU IN A SERIES OF PICTURES TAKING PLACE IN COAL MINES - AT NIGHT!!-(SIGH!) FINALLY, YOUR LAST PICTURE TOOK PLACE IN A TOTAL BLACKOUT.
THEN, THE STUDIO GAVE UP!-YOU'RE THROUGH AS A GLAMOUR GIRL, LORNA GOON — BUT, YOU STILL HAVE YOUR OLD-AGE PENSION TO FALL BACK ON!
I'LL NEVER QUIT!! THERE MUST BE SOME WAY!!
11-25
Al Capp

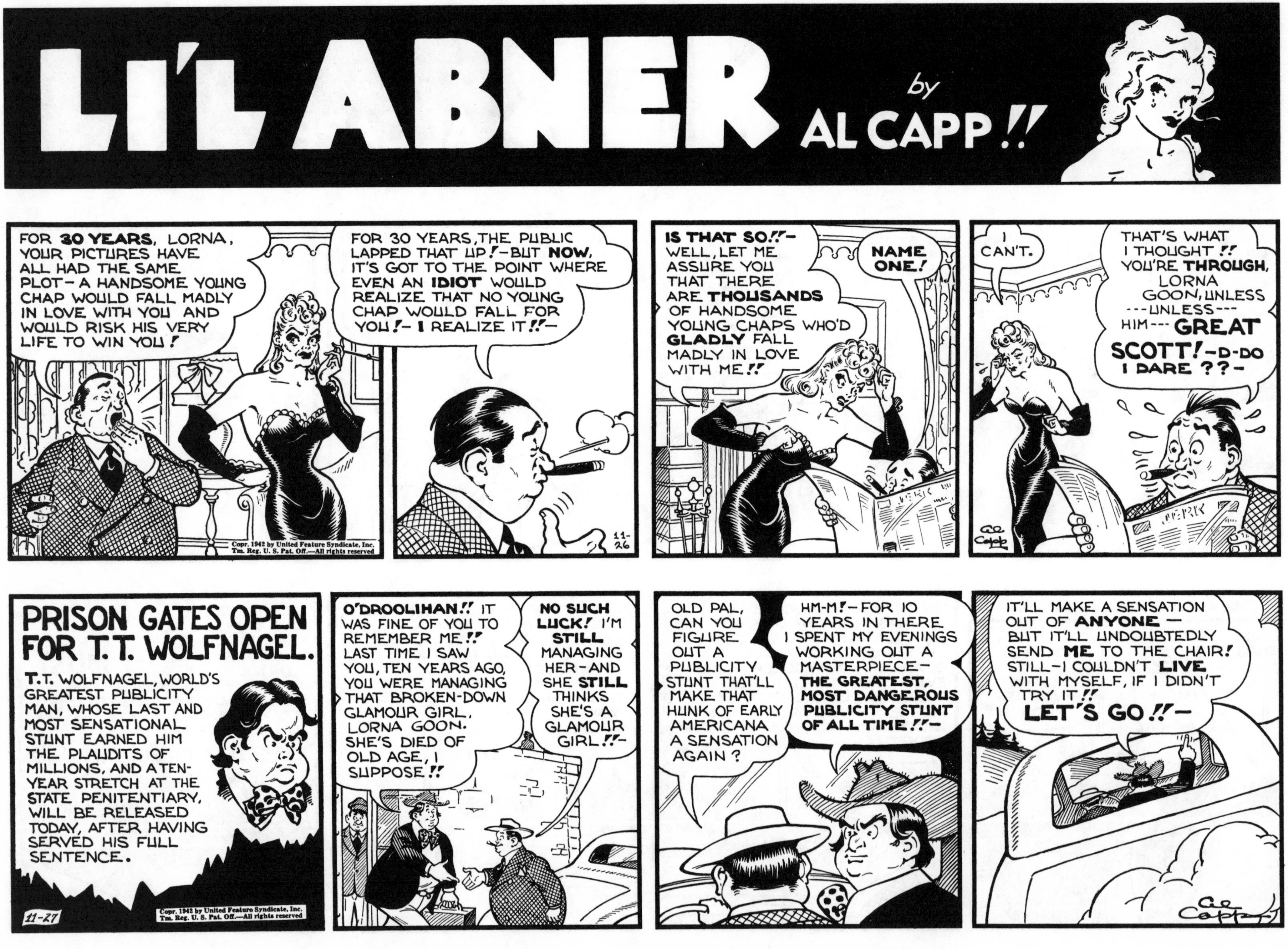

LI'L ABNER
by AL CAPP!!
FOR 30 YEARS, LORNA, YOUR PICTURES HAVE ALL HAD THE SAME PLOT – A HANDSOME YOUNG CHAP WOULD FALL MADLY IN LOVE WITH YOU AND WOULD RISK HIS VERY LIFE TO WIN YOU!
FOR 30 YEARS, THE PUBLIC LAPPED THAT UP!– BUT NOW, IT'S GOT TO THE POINT WHERE EVEN AN IDIOT WOULD REALIZE THAT NO YOUNG CHAP WOULD FALL FOR YOU!– I REALIZE IT!!–
Copr. 1942 by United Feature Syndicate, Inc. Tm. Reg. U. S. Pat. Off.—All rights reserved
11-26
IS THAT SO!!– WELL, LET ME ASSURE YOU THAT THERE ARE THOUSANDS OF HANDSOME YOUNG CHAPS WHO'D GLADLY FALL MADLY IN LOVE WITH ME!!
NAME ONE!
I CAN'T.
THAT'S WHAT I THOUGHT!! YOU'RE THROUGH, LORNA GOON, UNLESS ---UNLESS--- HIM--- GREAT SCOTT!–D-DO I DARE??–
PRISON GATES OPEN FOR T.T. WOLFNAGEL.
T.T. WOLFNAGEL, WORLD'S GREATEST PUBLICITY MAN, WHOSE LAST AND MOST SENSATIONAL STUNT EARNED HIM THE PLAUDITS OF MILLIONS, AND A TEN-YEAR STRETCH AT THE STATE PENITENTIARY, WILL BE RELEASED TODAY, AFTER HAVING SERVED HIS FULL SENTENCE.
11-27
Copr. 1942 by United Feature Syndicate, Inc. Tm. Reg. U. S. Pat. Off.—All rights reserved
O'DROOLIHAN!! IT WAS FINE OF YOU TO REMEMBER ME!! LAST TIME I SAW YOU, TEN YEARS AGO, YOU WERE MANAGING THAT BROKEN-DOWN GLAMOUR GIRL, LORNA GOON. SHE'S DIED OF OLD AGE, I SUPPOSE!!
NO SUCH LUCK! I'M STILL MANAGING HER – AND SHE STILL THINKS SHE'S A GLAMOUR GIRL!!–
OLD PAL, CAN YOU FIGURE OUT A PUBLICITY STUNT THAT'LL MAKE THAT HUNK OF EARLY AMERICANA A SENSATION AGAIN?
HM-M!– FOR 10 YEARS IN THERE I SPENT MY EVENINGS WORKING OUT A MASTERPIECE – THE GREATEST, MOST DANGEROUS PUBLICITY STUNT OF ALL TIME!!–
IT'LL MAKE A SENSATION OUT OF ANYONE – BUT IT'LL UNDOUBTEDLY SEND ME TO THE CHAIR! STILL – I COULDN'T LIVE WITH MYSELF, IF I DIDN'T TRY IT!!
LET'S GO!!–

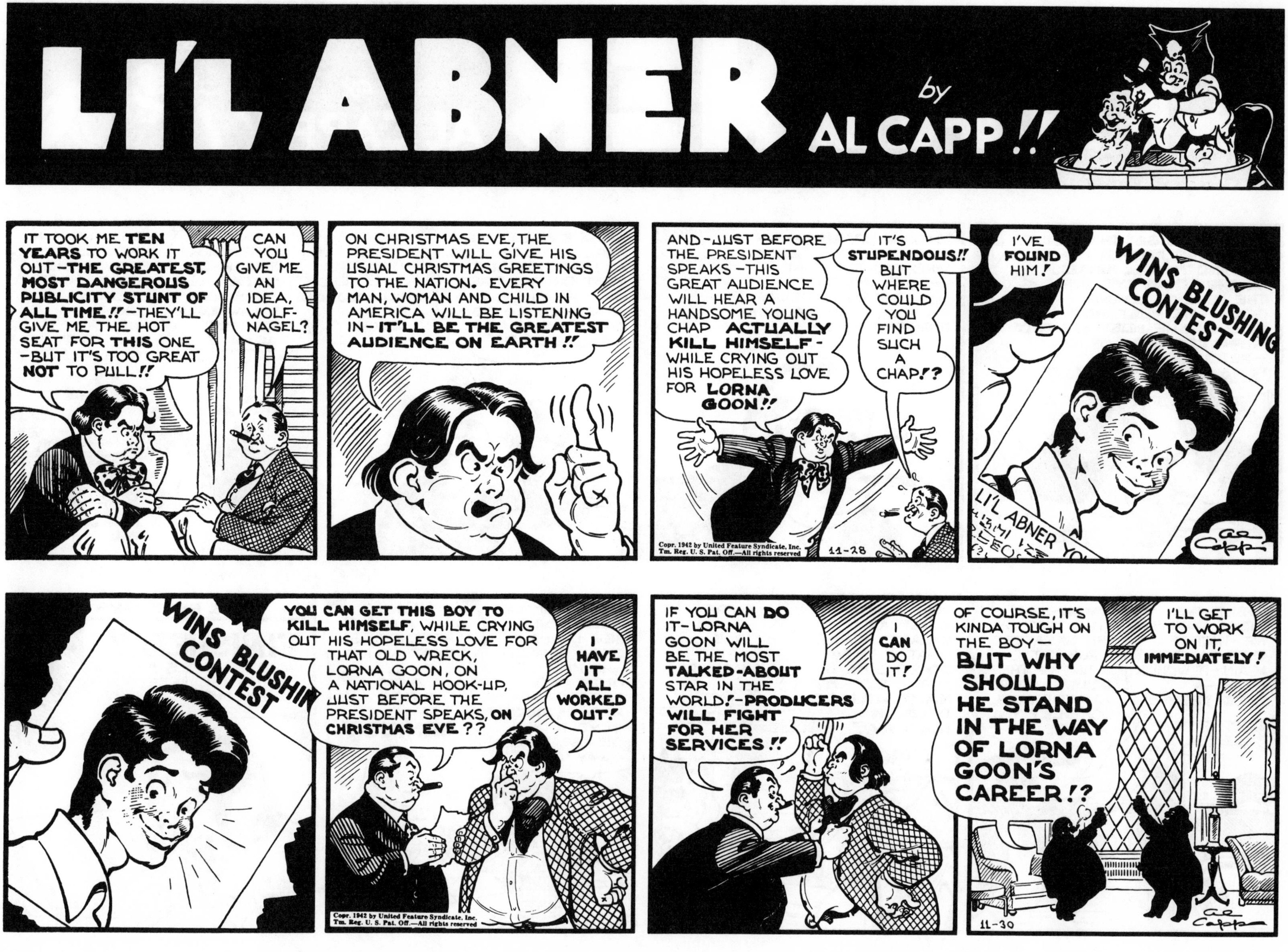
LI'L ABNER
by AL CAPP!!
IT TOOK ME TEN YEARS TO WORK IT OUT-THE GREATEST, MOST DANGEROUS PUBLICITY STUNT OF ALL TIME!!-THEY'LL GIVE ME THE HOT SEAT FOR THIS ONE -BUT IT'S TOO GREAT NOT TO PULL!!
CAN YOU GIVE ME AN IDEA, WOLF-NAGEL?
ON CHRISTMAS EVE, THE PRESIDENT WILL GIVE HIS USUAL CHRISTMAS GREETINGS TO THE NATION. EVERY MAN, WOMAN AND CHILD IN AMERICA WILL BE LISTENING IN-IT'LL BE THE GREATEST AUDIENCE ON EARTH!!
AND-JUST BEFORE THE PRESIDENT SPEAKS-THIS GREAT AUDIENCE WILL HEAR A HANDSOME YOUNG CHAP ACTUALLY KILL HIMSELF-WHILE CRYING OUT HIS HOPELESS LOVE FOR LORNA GOON!!
IT'S STUPENDOUS!! BUT WHERE COULD YOU FIND SUCH A CHAP!?
Copr. 1942 by United Feature Syndicate, Inc. Tm. Reg. U. S. Pat. Off.—All rights reserved
11-28
I'VE FOUND HIM!
WINS BLUSHING CONTEST
WINS BLUSHIN CONTEST
YOU CAN GET THIS BOY TO KILL HIMSELF, WHILE CRYING OUT HIS HOPELESS LOVE FOR THAT OLD WRECK, LORNA GOON, ON A NATIONAL HOOK-UP, JUST BEFORE THE PRESIDENT SPEAKS, ON CHRISTMAS EVE??
I HAVE IT ALL WORKED OUT!
Copr. 1942 by United Feature Syndicate, Inc. Tm. Reg. U. S. Pat. Off.—All rights reserved
IF YOU CAN DO IT-LORNA GOON WILL BE THE MOST TALKED-ABOUT STAR IN THE WORLD!-PRODUCERS WILL FIGHT FOR HER SERVICES!!
I CAN DO IT!
OF COURSE, IT'S KINDA TOUGH ON THE BOY-BUT WHY SHOULD HE STAND IN THE WAY OF LORNA GOON'S CAREER!?
I'LL GET TO WORK ON IT, IMMEDIATELY!
11-30

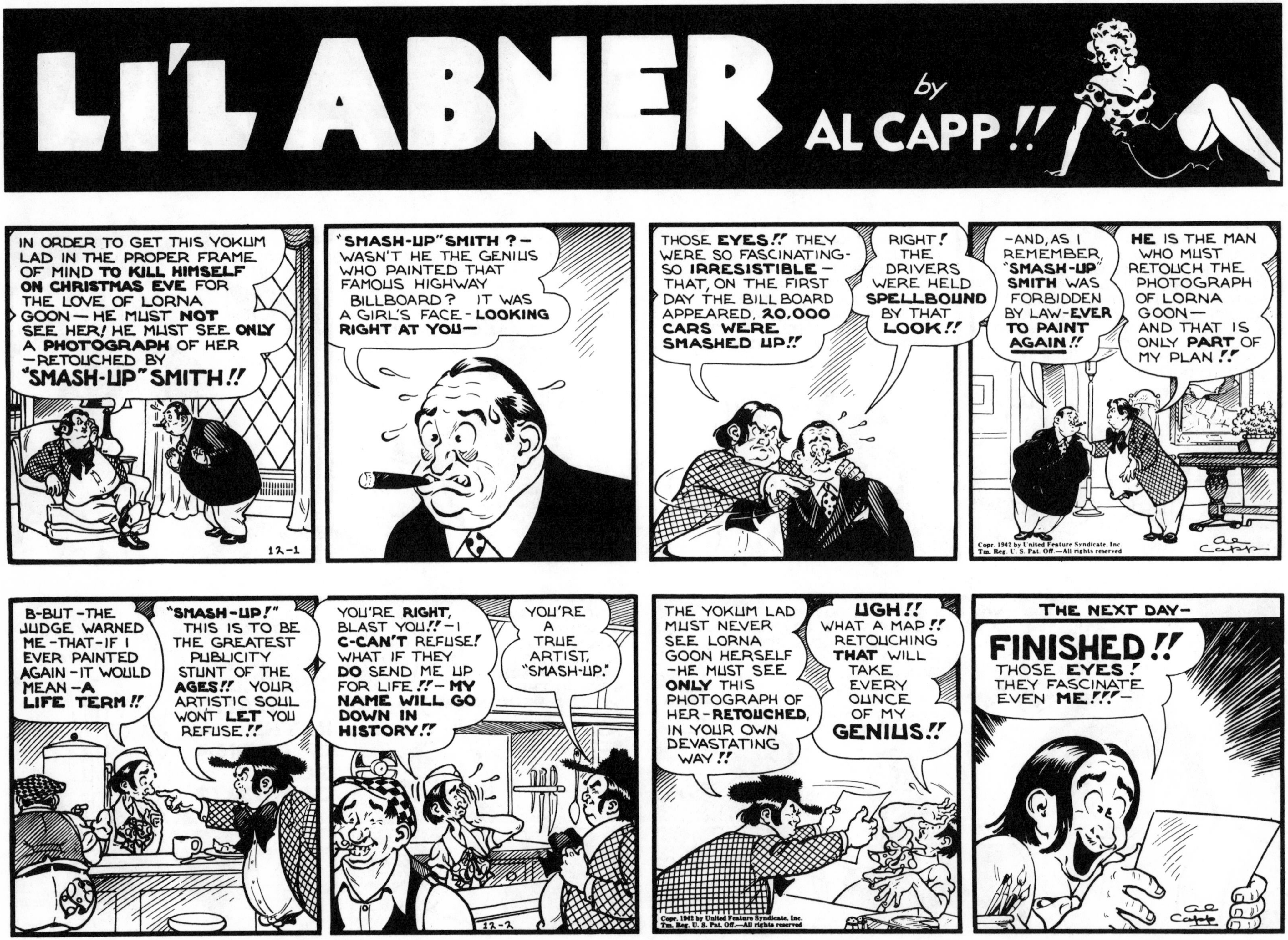
LI'L ABNER
by AL CAPP!!
IN ORDER TO GET THIS YOKUM LAD IN THE PROPER FRAME OF MIND TO KILL HIMSELF ON CHRISTMAS EVE FOR THE LOVE OF LORNA GOON — HE MUST NOT SEE HER! HE MUST SEE ONLY A PHOTOGRAPH OF HER — RETOUCHED BY "SMASH-UP" SMITH!!
12-1
"SMASH-UP" SMITH? — WASN'T HE THE GENIUS WHO PAINTED THAT FAMOUS HIGHWAY BILLBOARD? IT WAS A GIRL'S FACE - LOOKING RIGHT AT YOU —
THOSE EYES!! THEY WERE SO FASCINATING - SO IRRESISTIBLE — THAT, ON THE FIRST DAY THE BILLBOARD APPEARED, 20,000 CARS WERE SMASHED UP!!
RIGHT! THE DRIVERS WERE HELD SPELLBOUND BY THAT LOOK!!
— AND, AS I REMEMBER, "SMASH-UP" SMITH WAS FORBIDDEN BY LAW - EVER TO PAINT AGAIN!!
HE IS THE MAN WHO MUST RETOUCH THE PHOTOGRAPH OF LORNA GOON — AND THAT IS ONLY PART OF MY PLAN!!
Copr. 1942 by United Feature Syndicate, Inc. Tm. Reg. U. S. Pat. Off.—All rights reserved
Al Capp
B-BUT - THE JUDGE WARNED ME - THAT - IF I EVER PAINTED AGAIN - IT WOULD MEAN - A LIFE TERM!!
"SMASH-UP!" THIS IS TO BE THE GREATEST PUBLICITY STUNT OF THE AGES!! YOUR ARTISTIC SOUL WON'T LET YOU REFUSE!!
YOU'RE RIGHT, BLAST YOU!! — I C-CAN'T REFUSE! WHAT IF THEY DO SEND ME UP FOR LIFE!! — MY NAME WILL GO DOWN IN HISTORY!!
YOU'RE A TRUE ARTIST, "SMASH-UP."
12-2
THE YOKUM LAD MUST NEVER SEE LORNA GOON HERSELF — HE MUST SEE ONLY THIS PHOTOGRAPH OF HER - RETOUCHED, IN YOUR OWN DEVASTATING WAY!!
UGH!! WHAT A MAP!! RETOUCHING THAT WILL TAKE EVERY OUNCE OF MY GENIUS!!
Copr. 1942 by United Feature Syndicate, Inc. Tm. Reg. U. S. Pat. Off.—All rights reserved
THE NEXT DAY —
FINISHED!! THOSE EYES! THEY FASCINATE EVEN ME!!! —
Al Capp

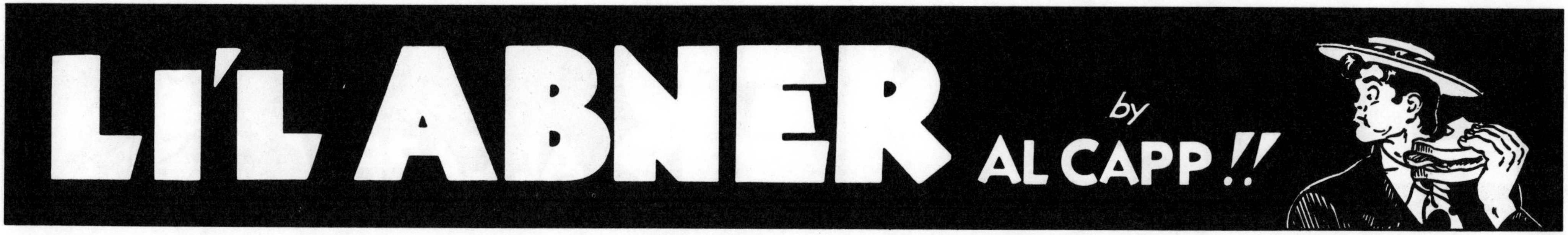
LI'L ABNER
by
AL CAPP!!

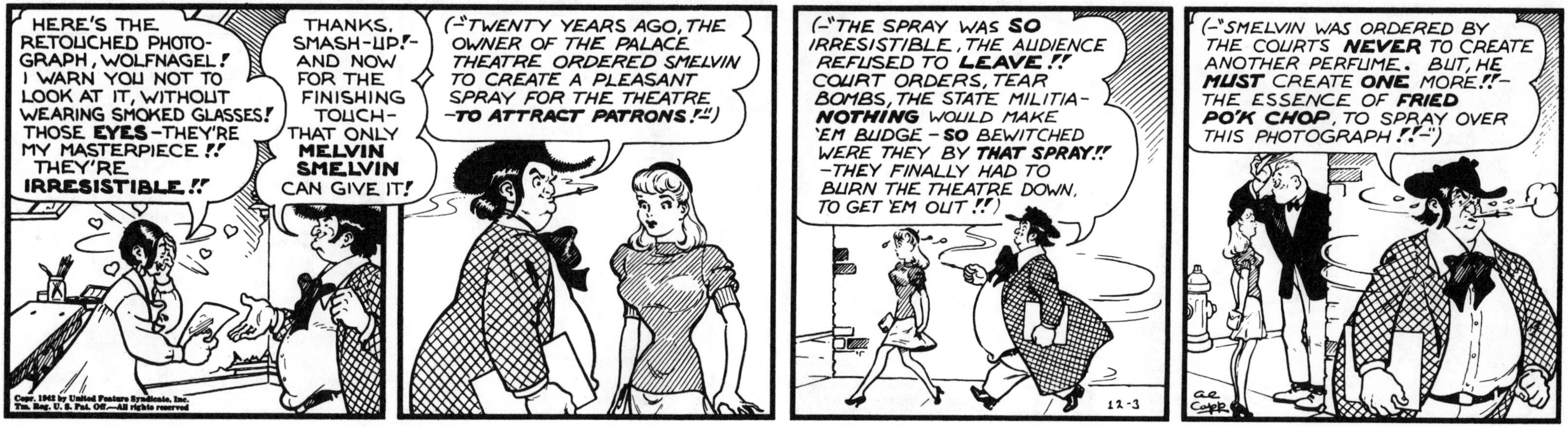
HERE'S THE RETOUCHED PHOTOGRAPH, WOLFNAGEL! I WARN YOU NOT TO LOOK AT IT, WITHOUT WEARING SMOKED GLASSES! THOSE EYES–THEY'RE MY MASTERPIECE!! THEY'RE IRRESISTIBLE!!
THANKS, SMASH-UP!–AND NOW FOR THE FINISHING TOUCH–THAT ONLY MELVIN SMELVIN CAN GIVE IT!
(–"TWENTY YEARS AGO, THE OWNER OF THE PALACE THEATRE ORDERED SMELVIN TO CREATE A PLEASANT SPRAY FOR THE THEATRE –TO ATTRACT PATRONS!"–)
(–"THE SPRAY WAS SO IRRESISTIBLE, THE AUDIENCE REFUSED TO LEAVE!! COURT ORDERS, TEAR BOMBS, THE STATE MILITIA–NOTHING WOULD MAKE 'EM BUDGE–SO BEWITCHED WERE THEY BY THAT SPRAY!! –THEY FINALLY HAD TO BURN THE THEATRE DOWN, TO GET 'EM OUT!!")
(–"SMELVIN WAS ORDERED BY THE COURTS NEVER TO CREATE ANOTHER PERFUME. BUT, HE MUST CREATE ONE MORE!!–THE ESSENCE OF FRIED PO'K CHOP, TO SPRAY OVER THIS PHOTOGRAPH!!"–)
Copr. 1942 by United Feature Syndicate, Inc. Tm. Reg. U. S. Pat. Off.—All rights reserved
12-3
Al Capp

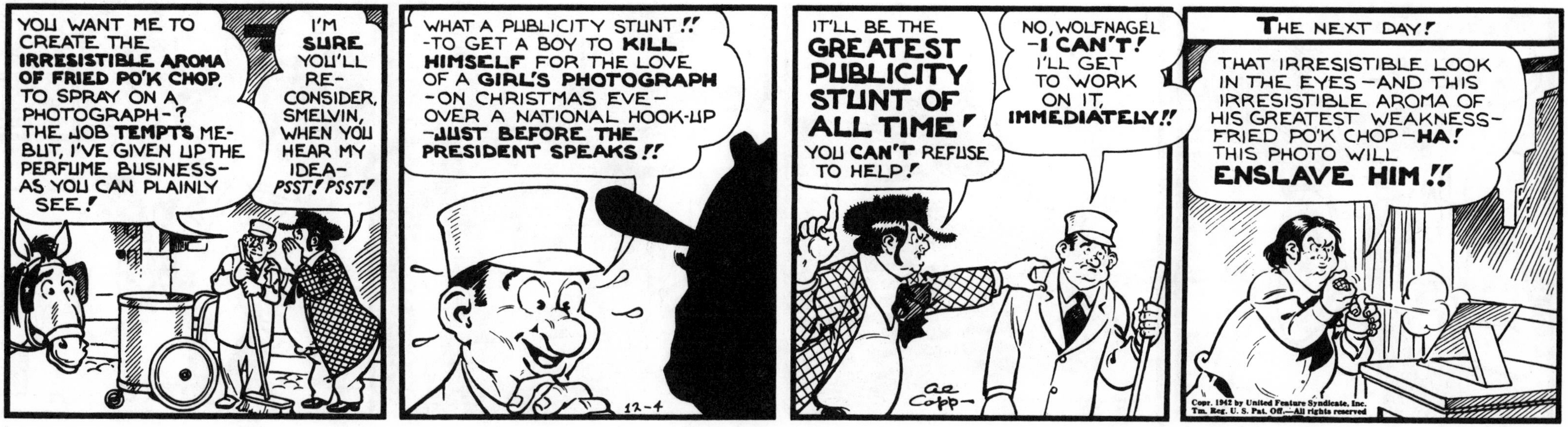
YOU WANT ME TO CREATE THE IRRESISTIBLE AROMA OF FRIED PO'K CHOP, TO SPRAY ON A PHOTOGRAPH–? THE JOB TEMPTS ME–BUT, I'VE GIVEN UP THE PERFUME BUSINESS–AS YOU CAN PLAINLY SEE!
I'M SURE YOU'LL RECONSIDER, SMELVIN, WHEN YOU HEAR MY IDEA–PSST! PSST!
WHAT A PUBLICITY STUNT!! –TO GET A BOY TO KILL HIMSELF FOR THE LOVE OF A GIRL'S PHOTOGRAPH –ON CHRISTMAS EVE–OVER A NATIONAL HOOK-UP –JUST BEFORE THE PRESIDENT SPEAKS!!
12-4
IT'LL BE THE GREATEST PUBLICITY STUNT OF ALL TIME! YOU CAN'T REFUSE TO HELP!
NO, WOLFNAGEL –I CAN'T! I'LL GET TO WORK ON IT, IMMEDIATELY!!
Al Capp
THE NEXT DAY!
THAT IRRESISTIBLE LOOK IN THE EYES–AND THIS IRRESISTIBLE AROMA OF HIS GREATEST WEAKNESS–FRIED PO'K CHOP–HA! THIS PHOTO WILL ENSLAVE HIM!!
Copr. 1942 by United Feature Syndicate, Inc. Tm. Reg. U. S. Pat. Off.—All rights reserved

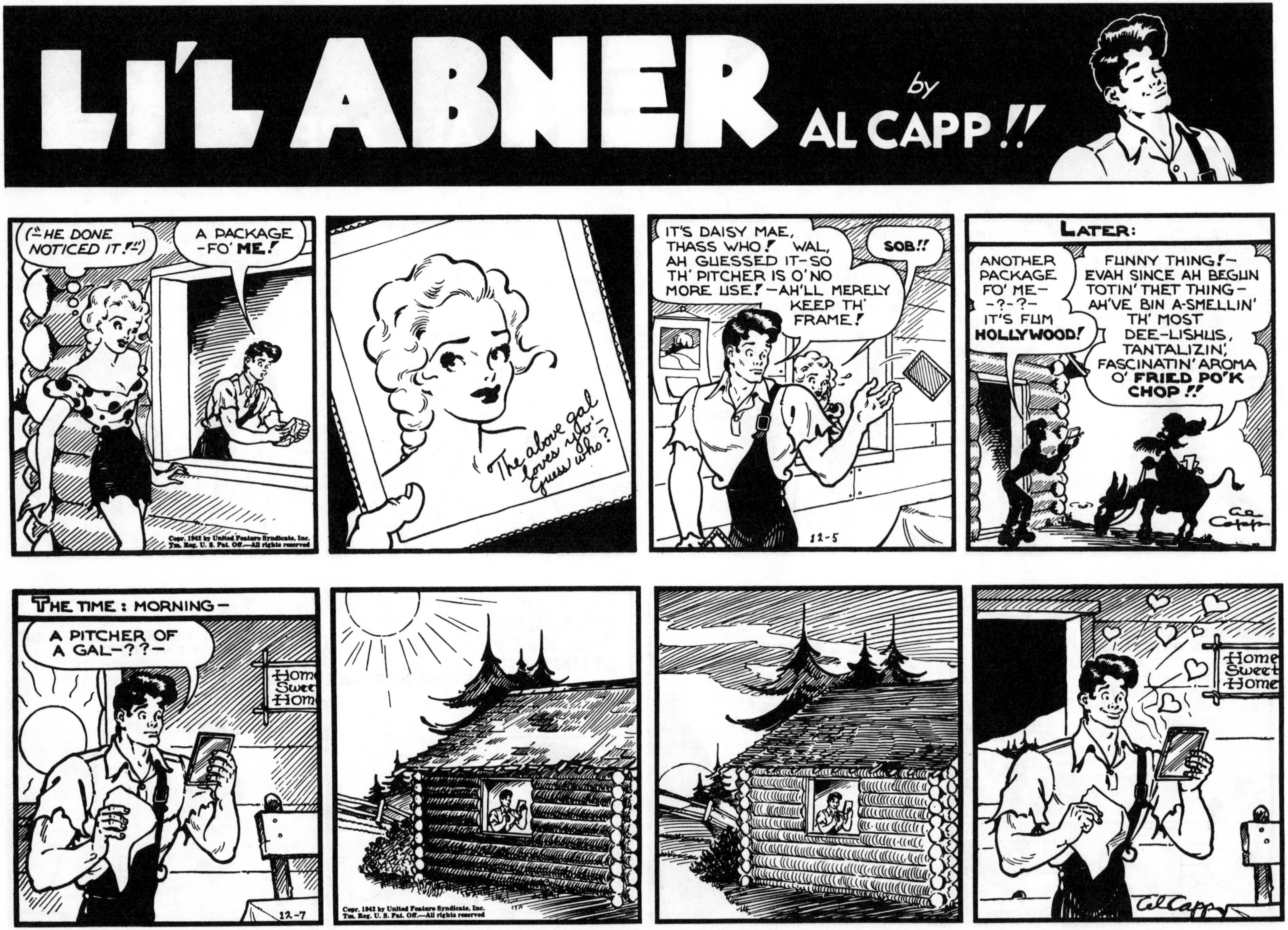
LI'L ABNER
by AL CAPP!!
("–HE DONE NOTICED IT!"–")
A PACKAGE –FO' ME!
Copr. 1942 by United Feature Syndicate, Inc. Tm. Reg. U. S. Pat. Off.—All rights reserved
The above gal loves yo'– Guess who?
IT'S DAISY MAE, THASS WHO! WAL, AH GUESSED IT–SO TH' PITCHER IS O'NO MORE USE!–AH'LL MERELY KEEP TH' FRAME!
SOB!!
12-5
LATER:
ANOTHER PACKAGE FO' ME– –?–?– IT'S FUM HOLLYWOOD!
FUNNY THING!– EVAH SINCE AH BEGUN TOTIN' THET THING– AH'VE BIN A-SMELLIN' TH' MOST DEE-LISHUS, TANTALIZIN', FASCINATIN' AROMA O' FRIED PO'K CHOP!!
Al Capp
THE TIME: MORNING–
A PITCHER OF A GAL–??–
12-7
Copr. 1942 by United Feature Syndicate, Inc. Tm. Reg. U. S. Pat. Off.—All rights reserved
Home Sweet Home
Al Capp

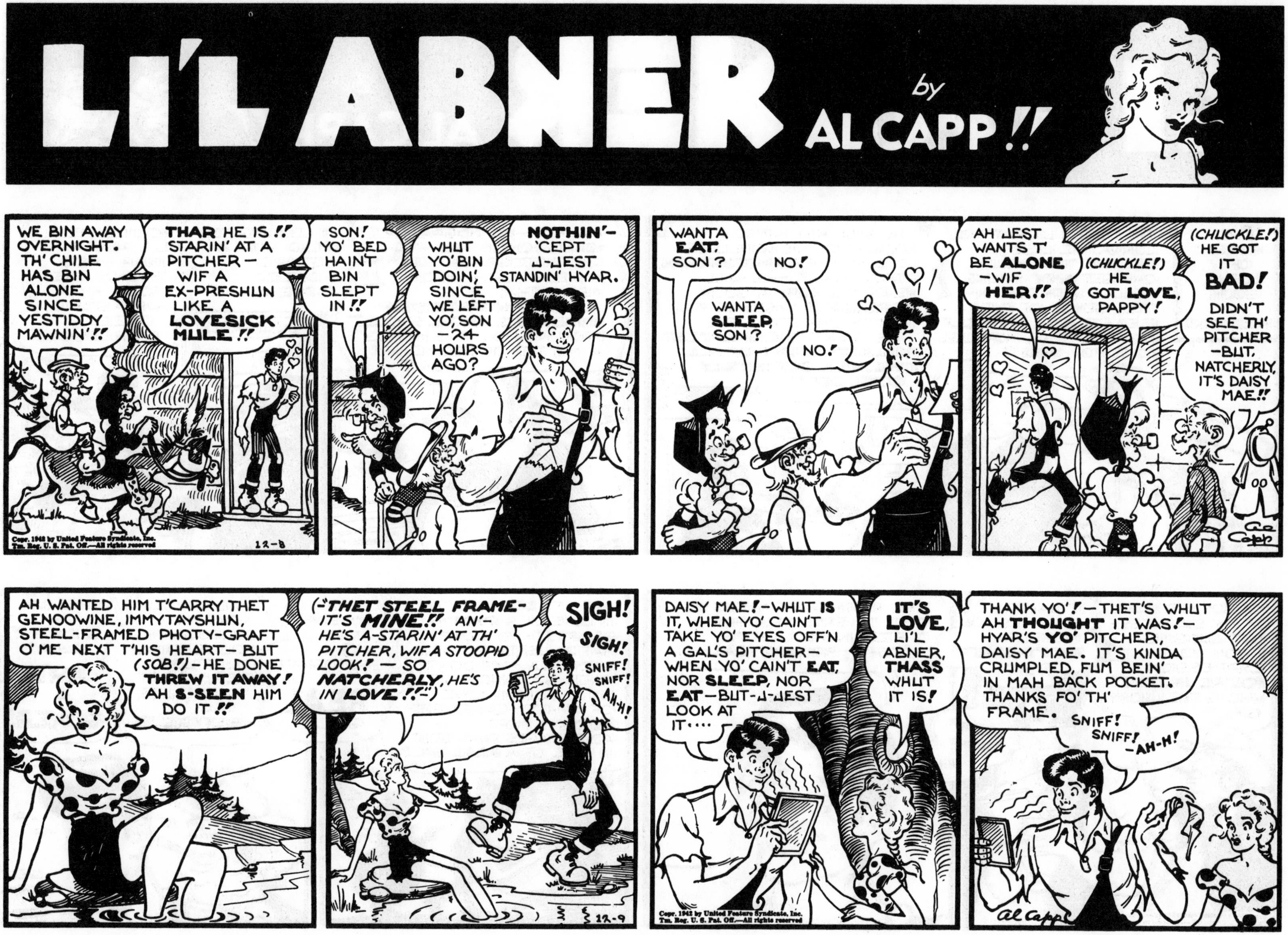
LI'L ABNER
by AL CAPP!!
WE BIN AWAY OVERNIGHT. TH' CHILE HAS BIN ALONE SINCE YESTIDDY MAWNIN'!!
THAR HE IS!! STARIN' AT A PITCHER – WIF A EX-PRESHUN LIKE A LOVESICK MULE!!
SON! YO' BED HAIN'T BIN SLEPT IN!!
WHUT YO' BIN DOIN', SINCE WE LEFT YO', SON – 24 HOURS AGO?
NOTHIN' – 'CEPT J-JEST STANDIN' HYAR.
WANTA EAT, SON?
NO!
WANTA SLEEP, SON?
NO!
AH JEST WANTS T' BE ALONE – WIF HER!!
(CHUCKLE!) HE GOT LOVE, PAPPY!
(CHUCKLE!) HE GOT IT BAD! DIDN'T SEE TH' PITCHER – BUT, NATCHERLY, IT'S DAISY MAE!!
Copr. 1942 by United Feature Syndicate, Inc. Tm. Reg. U. S. Pat. Off.—All rights reserved
12-8
AH WANTED HIM T'CARRY THET GENOOWINE, IMMYTAYSHUN, STEEL-FRAMED PHOTY-GRAFT O' ME NEXT T'HIS HEART – BUT (SOB!) – HE DONE THREW IT AWAY! AH S-SEEN HIM DO IT!!
(– THET STEEL FRAME – IT'S MINE!! AN' – HE'S A-STARIN' AT TH' PITCHER, WIF A STOOPID LOOK! – SO NATCHERLY, HE'S IN LOVE!! –)
SIGH! SIGH! SNIFF! SNIFF! AH-H!
12-9
DAISY MAE! – WHUT IS IT, WHEN YO' CAIN'T TAKE YO' EYES OFF'N A GAL'S PITCHER – WHEN YO' CAIN'T EAT, NOR SLEEP, NOR EAT – BUT – J-JEST LOOK AT IT....
IT'S LOVE, LI'L ABNER, THASS WHUT IT IS!
THANK YO'! – THET'S WHUT AH THOUGHT IT WAS! – HYAR'S YO' PITCHER, DAISY MAE. IT'S KINDA CRUMPLED, FUM BEIN' IN MAH BACK POCKET. THANKS FO' TH' FRAME.
SNIFF! SNIFF! – AH-H!
Copr. 1942 by United Feature Syndicate, Inc. Tm. Reg. U. S. Pat. Off.—All rights reserved
al capp

LI'L ABNER
by
AL CAPP!!
THE HOME OF LORNA GOON, IN HOLLYWOOD
THE MORE I LOOK AT YOU, LORNA, THE LESS I BELIEVE THAT YOU CAN GET ANY YOUNG FELLA – WITH THE INTELLIGENCE OF EVEN A FLEA – TO KILL HIMSELF BECAUSE OF HIS HOPELESS LOVE FOR YOU!!
HA!
HE WILL KILL HIMSELF BECAUSE OF HIS HOPELESS LOVE FOR HER PHOTOGRAPH, O'DROOLIHAN!! – HE WILL NEVER SEE LORNA GOON HERSELF!! I ASSURE YOU, THAT ON CHRISTMAS EVE THIS STUNT – THE GREATEST PUBLICITY STUNT OF ALL TIME, WILL DEFINITELY COME OFF!!
12-10
AND, NOW – TO DOGPATCH!! YOUNG YOKUM HAS HAD THE PHOTOGRAPH FOR A WEEK NOW – WHICH MEANS THAT HE IS ALREADY HOPELESSLY UNDER IT'S FATAL SPELL!! FROM NOW ON, IT IS MERELY A MATTER OF EGGING HIM ON!!
Copr. 1942 by United Feature Syndicate, Inc. Tm. Reg. U. S. Pat. Off.—All rights reserved
I'M LOOKING FOR A LAD WITH A STUPID, DAZED EXPRESSION!
YO' MUS' MEAN LI'L ABNER, THAR – HE'S TH' ONLY ONE ROUN' HYAR WIF A STUPID, DAZED EXPRESSION!
DOGPATCH
SNIFF! SNIFF! AHHH!
AL CAPP
MY BOY, IT'S NONE OF MY BUSINESS – BUT, JUDGING FROM YOUR EXPRESSION, YOU'RE IN LOVE! WHO IS THE LUCKY GIRL?
IT HAIN'T A GAL – IT'S MERELY A PHOTY-GRAFT! SIGH!
SNIFF! SNIFF! – AH-H!
Copr. 1942 by United Feature Syndicate, Inc. Tm. Reg. U. S. Pat. Off.—All rights reserved
THIS PHOTY-GRAFT MAKES ME FEEL TH' SAME AS A PAN O' SIZZLIN' PO'K CHOPS – (SIGH!) – ROMANTICAL –
12-11
OH! – IT'S SO NICE T'BE IN LOVE OF A PHOTY-GRAFT!! – YO' DON'T HAFTA LISSEN TO THEIR SILLY TALK – YO' DON'T HAFTA GO DANCIN' WIF 'EM! – BEIN' IN LOVE OF A PHOTY-GRAFT GOT SO MANY MORE ADVANTAGES THAN BEIN' IN LOVE OF A REAL GAL!
BUT, MY BOY – THAT IS A PHOTOGRAPH OF A REAL GIRL!!
AND – IF YOU LOVE HER PHOTOGRAPH YOU CERTAINLY MUST LOVE HER! – DIDN'T YOU REALIZE THAT, BEFORE!?
N-NO, SUH – AH DIDN'T!! (GULP!) AH'M A GONER!
AL CAPP

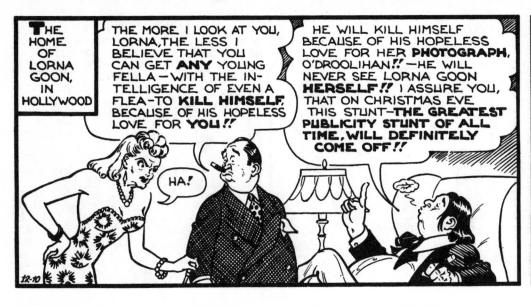

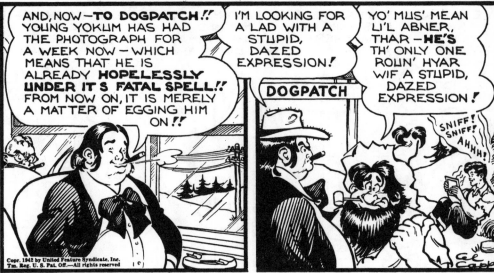

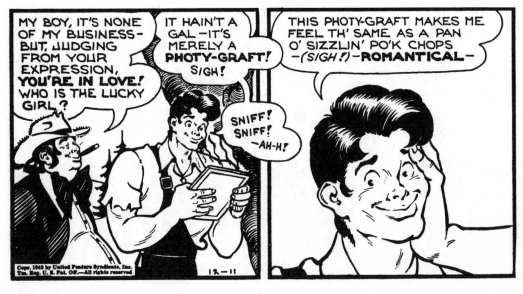

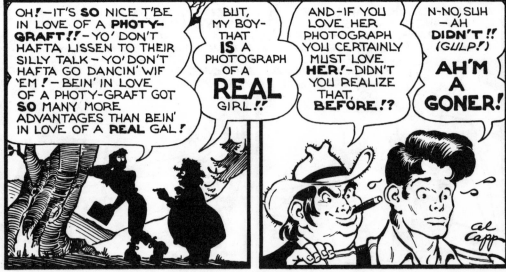

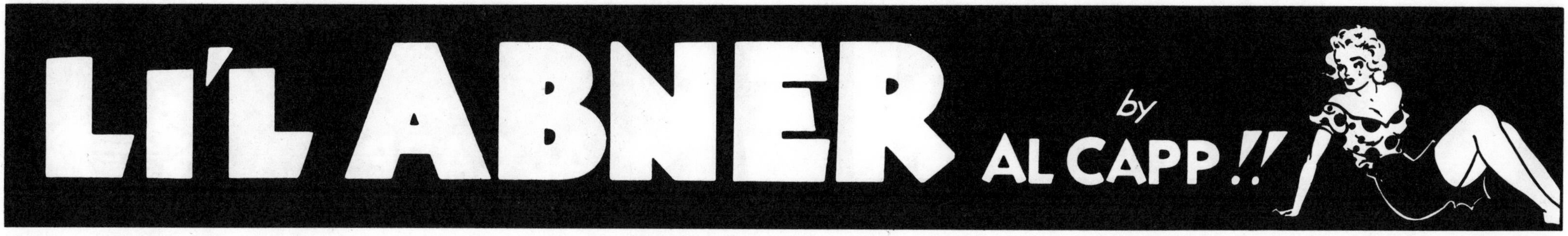
LI'L ABNER
by
AL CAPP!!

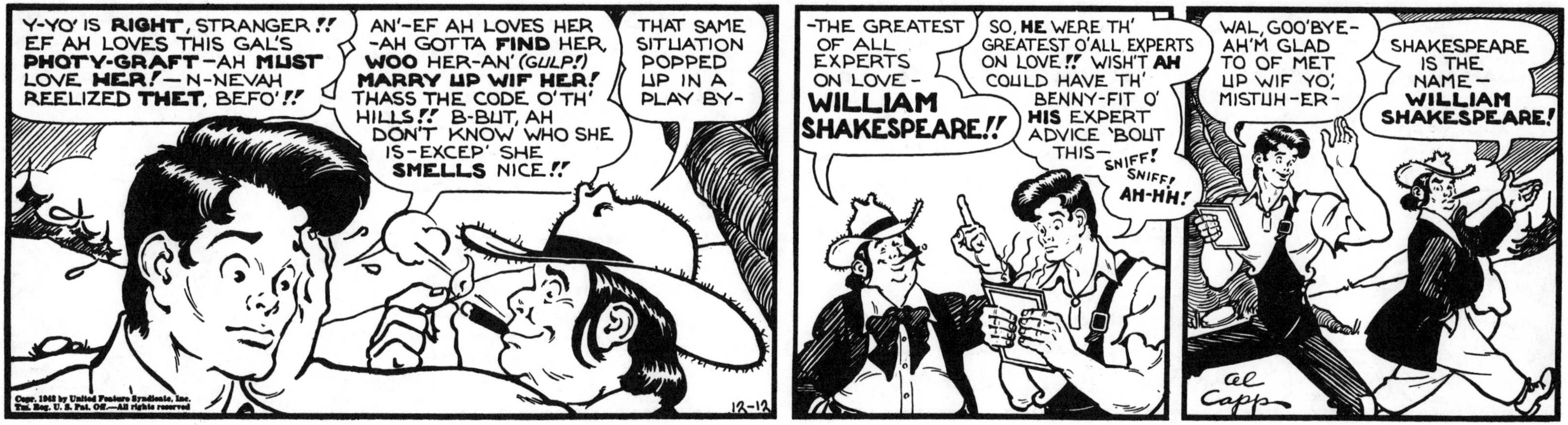
Y-YO' IS **RIGHT**, STRANGER!! EF AH LOVES THIS GAL'S **PHOTY-GRAFT**-AH **MUST** LOVE **HER!**—N-NEVAH REELIZED **THET**, BEFO'!!
AN'-EF AH LOVES HER -AH GOTTA **FIND** HER, **WOO** HER-AN' (GULP!) **MARRY UP WIF HER!** THASS THE CODE O'TH' HILLS!! B-BUT, AH DON'T KNOW WHO SHE IS-EXCEP' SHE **SMELLS** NICE!!
THAT SAME SITUATION POPPED UP IN A PLAY BY-
Copr. 1942 by United Feature Syndicate, Inc. Tm. Reg. U. S. Pat. Off.—All rights reserved
12-12
-THE GREATEST OF ALL EXPERTS ON LOVE- **WILLIAM SHAKESPEARE!!**
SO, **HE** WERE TH' GREATEST O'ALL EXPERTS ON LOVE!! WISH'T **AH** COULD HAVE TH' BENNY-FIT O' **HIS** EXPERT ADVICE 'BOUT THIS-
SNIFF! SNIFF! AH-HH!
WAL, GOO'BYE-AH'M GLAD TO OF MET UP WIF YO', MISTUH-ER-
SHAKESPEARE IS THE NAME- **WILLIAM SHAKESPEARE!**
al Capp

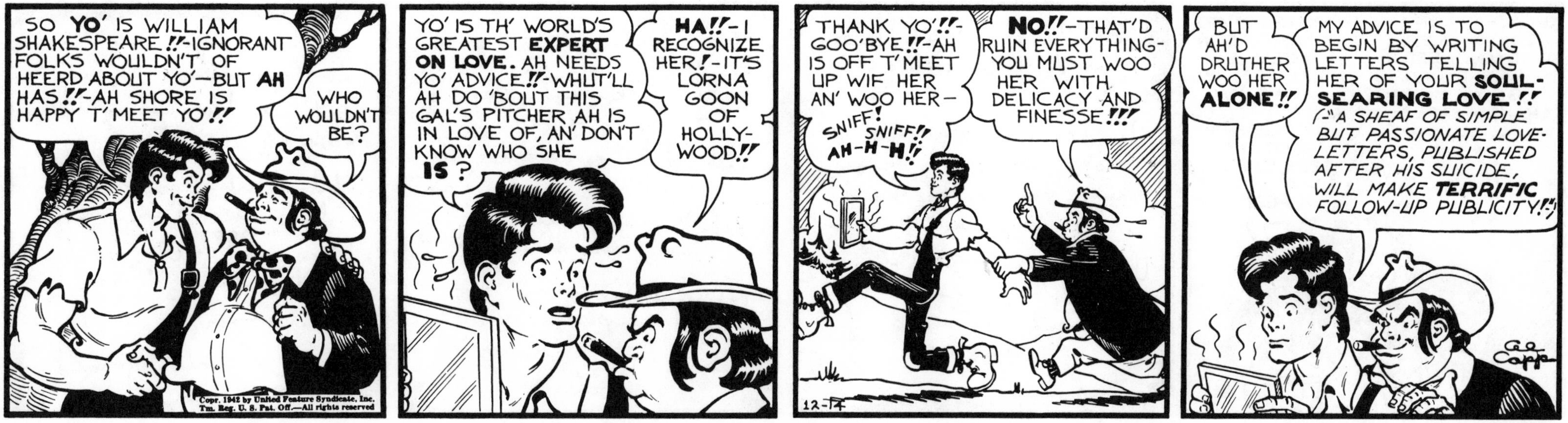
SO **YO'** IS WILLIAM SHAKESPEARE!!-IGNORANT FOLKS WOULDN'T OF HEERD ABOUT YO'—BUT **AH** HAS!!-AH SHORE IS HAPPY T'MEET YO'!!
WHO WOULDN'T BE?
Copr. 1942 by United Feature Syndicate, Inc. Tm. Reg. U. S. Pat. Off.—All rights reserved
YO' IS TH' WORLD'S GREATEST **EXPERT ON LOVE**. AH NEEDS YO' ADVICE!!-WHUT'LL AH DO 'BOUT THIS GAL'S PITCHER AH IS IN LOVE OF, AN' DON'T KNOW WHO SHE **IS**?
HA!!-I RECOGNIZE HER!-IT'S LORNA GOON OF HOLLY-WOOD!!
THANK YO'!!-GOO'BYE!!-AH IS OFF T'MEET UP WIF HER AN' WOO HER-
SNIFF! SNIFF!! AH-H-H!!
NO!!-THAT'D RUIN EVERYTHING-YOU MUST WOO HER WITH DELICACY AND FINESSE!!!
12-14
BUT AH'D DRUTHER WOO HER **ALONE!!**
MY ADVICE IS TO BEGIN BY WRITING LETTERS TELLING HER OF YOUR **SOUL-SEARING LOVE!!** (-"A SHEAF OF SIMPLE BUT PASSIONATE LOVE-LETTERS, PUBLISHED AFTER HIS SUICIDE, WILL MAKE **TERRIFIC** FOLLOW-UP PUBLICITY!!")
al Capp

LI'L ABNER
by AL CAPP!!
AH IS TH' LUCKIEST BOY ALIVE, T'GIT TH' LOVE-ADVICE OF YO', WILLIAM SHAKESPEARE!!
CALL ME BILL! GO AHEAD! POUR YOUR HEART OUT TO HER!!
Deer Lorna Goon:
All mah life, ah has preferred cat-fishin', skonk-huntin' an' rasslin' "Earth-Quake" McGoon to the company of wimmen of the opposite sex.
After seein' yore pitcher ah reelize what a fool ah has bin!
Ah prefers yore company to thet of cat-fishes, skonks and thet sloppy beast McGoon.
Ah jest sets an' smells yore pitcher all day. In other words, ah loves yo'.
Ah is a fine-lookin boy of 18 wif strong, clean feet and a fust-class edjoocayshun. Next year, ah'll be in the second class!
Ah is sendin' yo' mah pitcher, so yo' kin fall in love of me, same as ah has, wif yo'.
Please write to me eemeejutly, informin' me how soon yo' would like to marry up wif me.
Respeckfully yorn,
Abner Yokum, Age 18
writ by hand
← The one on the left is me.
Copr. 1942 by United Feature Syndicate, Inc. Tm. Reg. U. S. Pat. Off.—All rights reserved
12-15
GULP!-AH DIDN'T GIT NO ANSWER T' THET LOVE-LETTER AH WRIT T'LORNA GOON, MISTAH SHAKESPEARE!
(-MAYBE THAT'S BECAUSE I DIDN'T MAIL THE LETTER!-I'M SAVING 'EM ALL FOR FOLLOW-UP PUBLICITY, AFTER THE SUICIDE!-)-ER-WHY NOT TRY A POEM, SON?
12-16
Ef Ah Had Mah Druthers
by A. Yokum, Age 18
Ah druther hold yo' hand beneath the moon
Than bash in the haid of Earthquake McGoon
Ah druther gaze into yore eyes
than eat a mess of polecat pies
Copr. 1942 by United Feature Syndicate, Inc. Tm. Reg. U. S. Pat. Off.—All rights reserved
Ah druther see yore smile so sweet
Than see mah pappy wash his feet
Ah druther waste the whole day wif yo'
Than waste the same wif Hairless Joe
Ah druther win yo' fo' a prize
Than win a hawg of equal size
To have yo' an' to have no other
Thet is the thing Ah'd mostly druther?
Ah'd druther jump in the lake tomorror moon
Than not get no letter fum Lorna Goon
writ by hand.
Al Capp

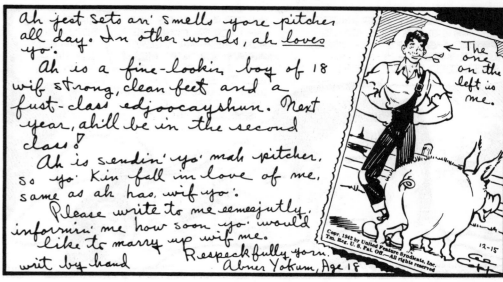

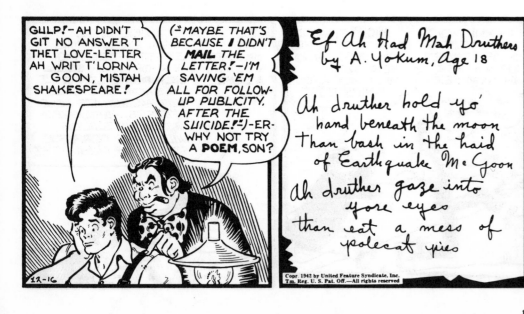

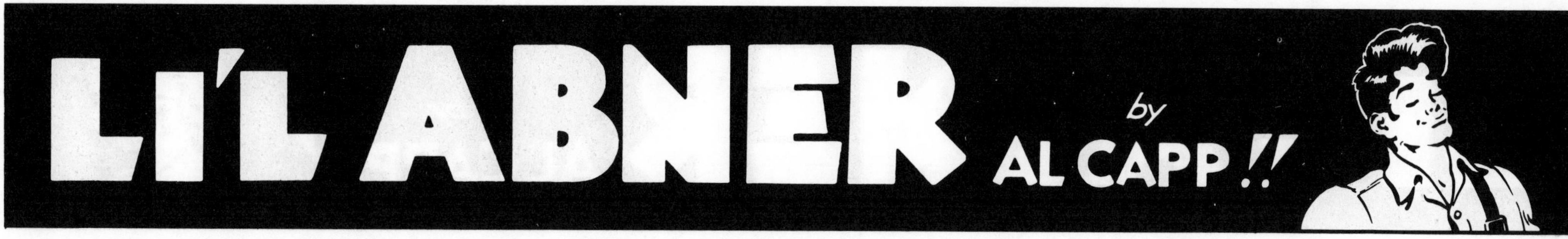

LI'L ABNER
by AL CAPP!!

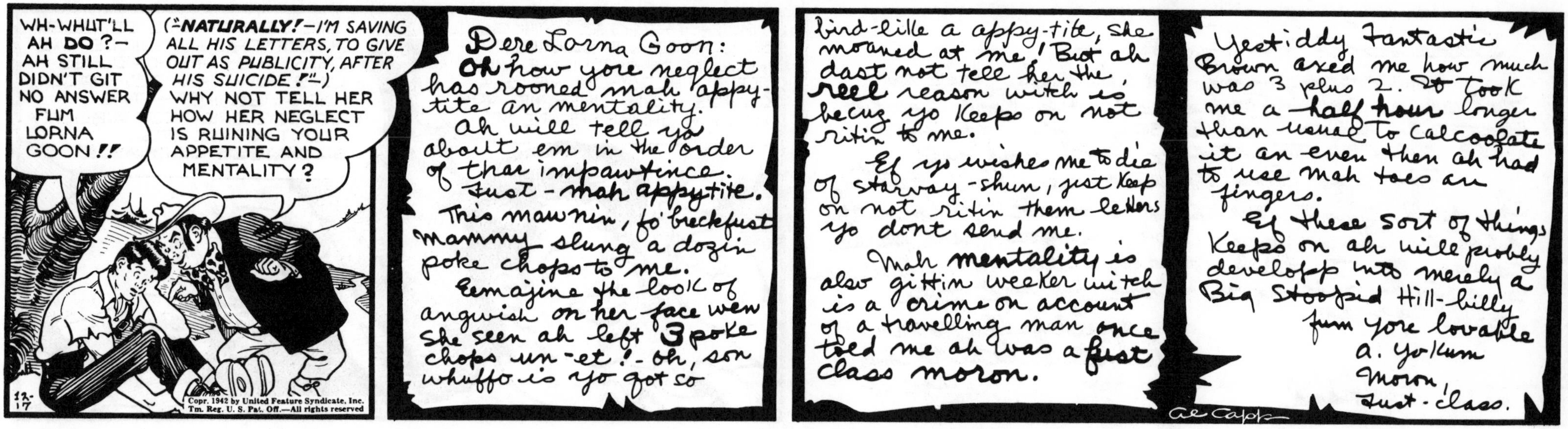

WH-WHUT'LL AH DO?- AH STILL DIDN'T GIT NO ANSWER FUM LORNA GOON!!
("NATURALLY!-I'M SAVING ALL HIS LETTERS, TO GIVE OUT AS PUBLICITY, AFTER HIS SUICIDE!") WHY NOT TELL HER HOW HER NEGLECT IS RUINING YOUR APPETITE AND MENTALITY?
12-17
Copr. 1942 by United Feature Syndicate, Inc. Tm. Reg. U. S. Pat. Off.—All rights reserved
Dere Lorna Goon:
Oh how yore neglect has rooned mah appy-tite an mentality.
Ah will tell yo about em in the order of thar impawtince.
Fust - mah appytite.
This mawnin, fo' breckfust mammy slung a dozin poke chops to me.
Eemajine the look of angwish on her face wen she seen ah left 3 poke chops un-et! - oh, son whuffo is yo got so
bird-like a appy-tite, she moaned at me! But ah dast not tell her the reel reason witch is becuz yo keeps on not ritin to me.
Ef yo wishes me to die of starvay-shun, just keep on not ritin them letters yo dont send me.
Mah mentality is also gittin weeker witch is a crime on account of a travelling man once toed me ah was a fust class moron.
Yestiddy Fantastic Brown axed me how much was 3 plus 2. It took me a half hour longer than usual to calcoolate it an even then ah had to use mah toes an fingers.
Ef these sort of things keeps on ah will probly developp into merely a Big Stoopid Hill-billy
fum yore lovable
A. Yokum
Moron,
Fust-class.
Al Capp

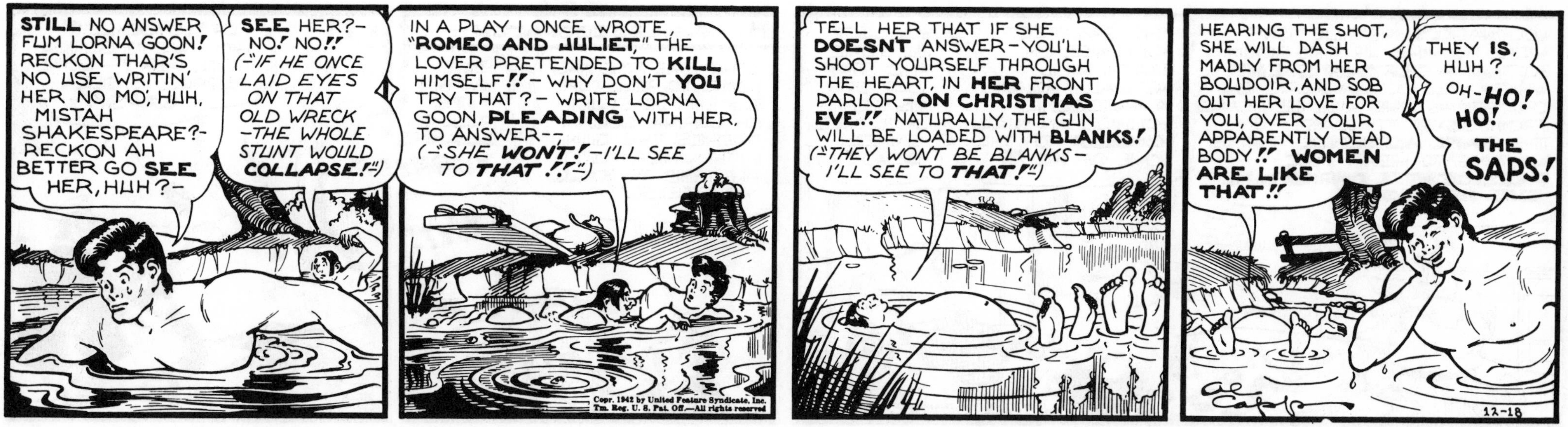

STILL NO ANSWER FUM LORNA GOON! RECKON THAR'S NO USE WRITIN' HER NO MO', HUH, MISTAH SHAKESPEARE?- RECKON AH BETTER GO SEE HER, HUH?-
SEE HER?- NO! NO!! ("IF HE ONCE LAID EYES ON THAT OLD WRECK - THE WHOLE STUNT WOULD COLLAPSE!")
IN A PLAY I ONCE WROTE, "ROMEO AND JULIET," THE LOVER PRETENDED TO KILL HIMSELF!!- WHY DON'T YOU TRY THAT?- WRITE LORNA GOON, PLEADING WITH HER, TO ANSWER-- ("SHE WON'T!-I'LL SEE TO THAT!!")
Copr. 1942 by United Feature Syndicate, Inc. Tm. Reg. U. S. Pat. Off.—All rights reserved
TELL HER THAT IF SHE DOESN'T ANSWER-YOU'LL SHOOT YOURSELF THROUGH THE HEART, IN HER FRONT PARLOR-ON CHRISTMAS EVE!! NATURALLY, THE GUN WILL BE LOADED WITH BLANKS! ("THEY WON'T BE BLANKS - I'LL SEE TO THAT!")
HEARING THE SHOT, SHE WILL DASH MADLY FROM HER BOUDOIR, AND SOB OUT HER LOVE FOR YOU, OVER YOUR APPARENTLY DEAD BODY!! WOMEN ARE LIKE THAT!!
THEY IS, HUH? OH-HO! HO! THE SAPS!
Al Capp
12-18

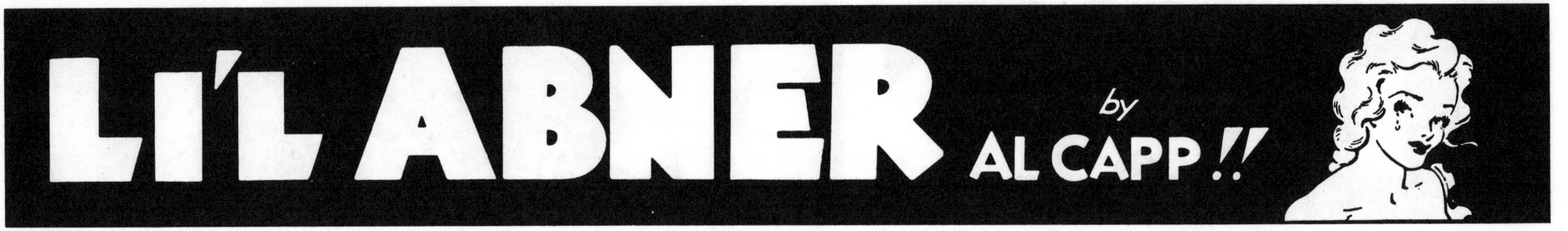

LI'L ABNER
by
AL CAPP!!

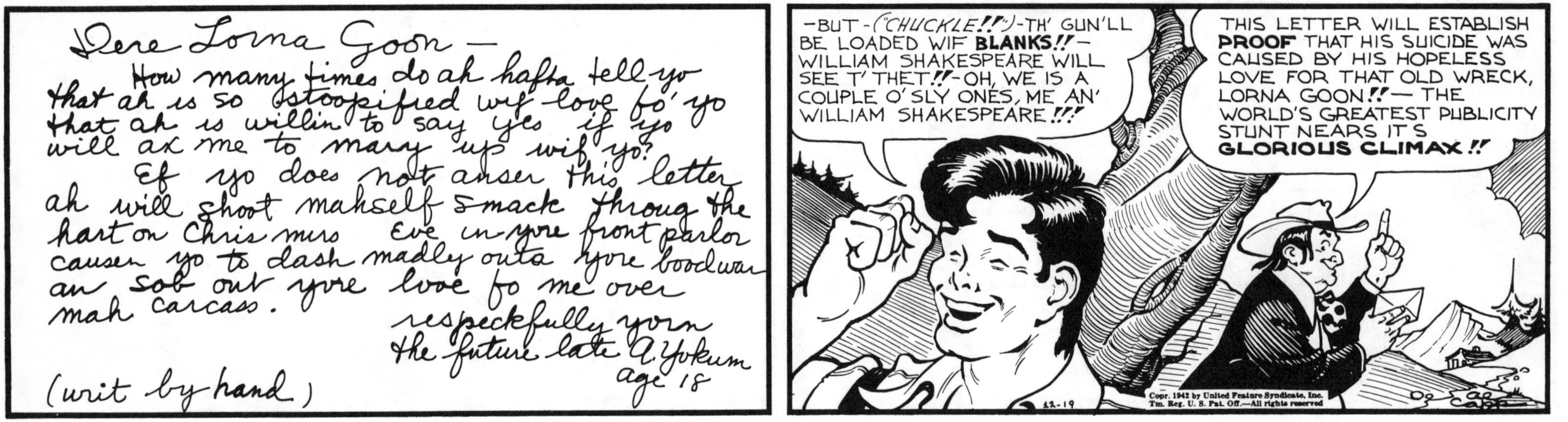

Dere Lorna Goon —
How many times do ah hafta tell yo that ah is so stoopified wif love fo' yo that ah is willin to say yes if yo will ax me to marry up wif yo?
Ef yo does not anser this letter ah will shoot mahself smack throug the hart on Chrismus Eve in yore front parlor causen yo to dash madly outa yore boodwar an sob out yore love fo me over mah carcass.
respeckfully yorn
the future late A. Yokum
age 18
(writ by hand)
—BUT-("CHUCKLE!!")-TH' GUN'LL BE LOADED WIF **BLANKS!!**— WILLIAM SHAKESPEARE WILL SEE T' THET!!-OH, WE IS A COUPLE O' SLY ONES, ME AN' WILLIAM SHAKESPEARE!!!
THIS LETTER WILL ESTABLISH **PROOF** THAT HIS SUICIDE WAS CAUSED BY HIS HOPELESS LOVE FOR THAT OLD WRECK, LORNA GOON!!— THE WORLD'S GREATEST PUBLICITY STUNT NEARS IT'S **GLORIOUS CLIMAX!!**
Copr. 1942 by United Feature Syndicate, Inc. Tm. Reg. U. S. Pat. Off.—All rights reserved
12-19
Al Capp

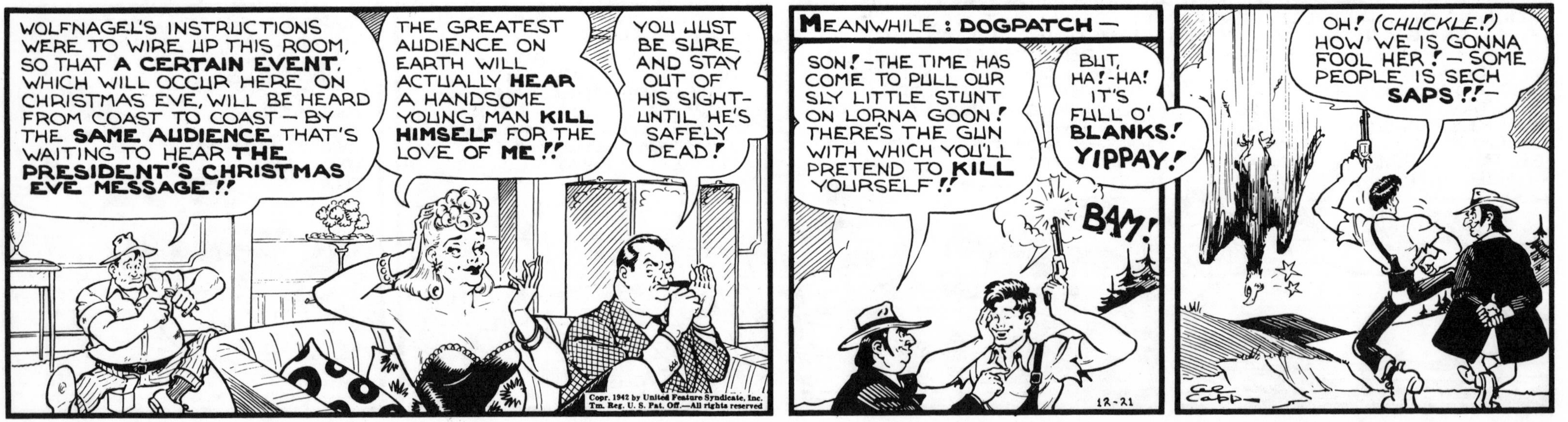

WOLFNAGEL'S INSTRUCTIONS WERE TO WIRE UP THIS ROOM, SO THAT **A CERTAIN EVENT**, WHICH WILL OCCUR HERE ON CHRISTMAS EVE, WILL BE HEARD FROM COAST TO COAST— BY THE **SAME AUDIENCE** THAT'S WAITING TO HEAR **THE PRESIDENT'S CHRISTMAS EVE MESSAGE!!**
THE GREATEST AUDIENCE ON EARTH WILL ACTUALLY **HEAR** A HANDSOME YOUNG MAN **KILL HIMSELF** FOR THE LOVE **OF ME!!**
YOU JUST BE SURE AND STAY OUT OF HIS SIGHT— UNTIL HE'S SAFELY DEAD!
Copr. 1942 by United Feature Syndicate, Inc. Tm. Reg. U. S. Pat. Off.—All rights reserved
MEANWHILE : **DOGPATCH**—
SON!—THE TIME HAS COME TO PULL OUR SLY LITTLE STUNT ON LORNA GOON! THERE'S THE GUN WITH WHICH YOU'LL PRETEND TO **KILL** YOURSELF!!
BUT, HA!-HA! IT'S FULL O' **BLANKS! YIPPAY!**
BAM!
12-21
OH! (CHUCKLE!) HOW WE IS GONNA FOOL HER!— SOME PEOPLE IS SECH **SAPS!!**—
Al Capp

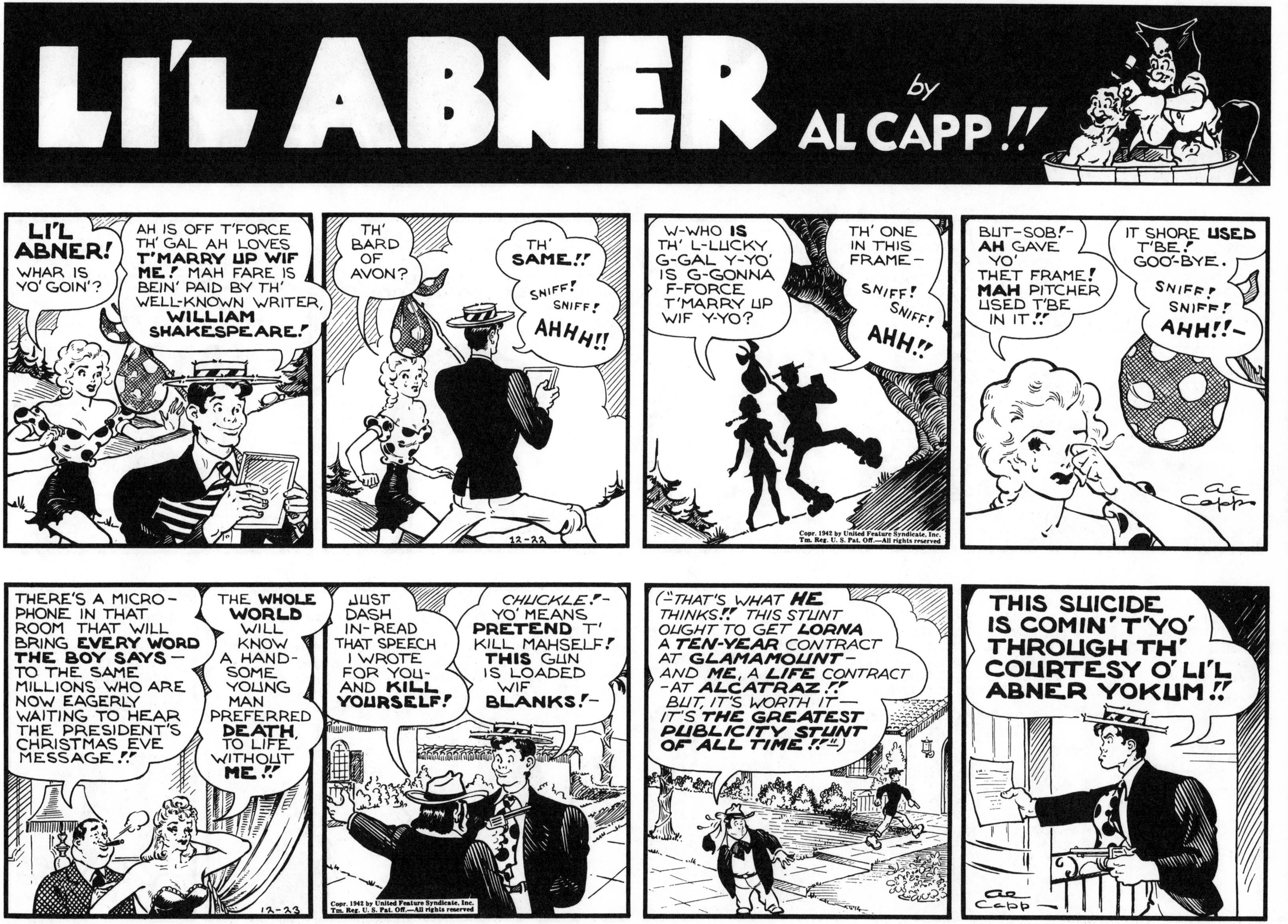

LI'L ABNER
by
AL CAPP!!
LI'L ABNER! WHAR IS YO' GOIN'?
AH IS OFF T'FORCE TH' GAL AH LOVES T'MARRY UP WIF ME! MAH FARE IS BEIN' PAID BY TH' WELL-KNOWN WRITER, WILLIAM SHAKESPEARE!
TH' BARD OF AVON?
TH' SAME!!
SNIFF! SNIFF! AHHH!!
12-22
W-WHO IS TH' L-LUCKY G-GAL Y-YO' IS G-GONNA F-FORCE T'MARRY UP WIF Y-YO?
TH' ONE IN THIS FRAME –
SNIFF! SNIFF! AHH!!
Copr. 1942 by United Feature Syndicate, Inc. Tm. Reg. U. S. Pat. Off.—All rights reserved
BUT–SOB!– AH GAVE YO' THET FRAME! MAH PITCHER USED T'BE IN IT!!
IT SHORE USED T'BE! GOO'-BYE.
SNIFF! SNIFF! AHH!!–
Al Capp
THERE'S A MICRO-PHONE IN THAT ROOM THAT WILL BRING EVERY WORD THE BOY SAYS – TO THE SAME MILLIONS WHO ARE NOW EAGERLY WAITING TO HEAR THE PRESIDENT'S CHRISTMAS EVE MESSAGE!!
THE WHOLE WORLD WILL KNOW A HAND-SOME YOUNG MAN PREFERRED DEATH, TO LIFE WITHOUT ME!!
12-23
JUST DASH IN-READ THAT SPEECH I WROTE FOR YOU-AND KILL YOURSELF!
CHUCKLE!– YO' MEANS PRETEND T' KILL MAHSELF! THIS GUN IS LOADED WIF BLANKS!–
Copr. 1942 by United Feature Syndicate, Inc. Tm. Reg. U. S. Pat. Off.—All rights reserved
("THAT'S WHAT HE THINKS!! THIS STUNT OUGHT TO GET LORNA A TEN-YEAR CONTRACT AT GLAMAMOUNT – AND ME, A LIFE CONTRACT – AT ALCATRAZ!! BUT, IT'S WORTH IT – IT'S THE GREATEST PUBLICITY STUNT OF ALL TIME!!")
THIS SUICIDE IS COMIN' T'YO' THROUGH TH' COURTESY O' LI'L ABNER YOKUM!!
Al Capp

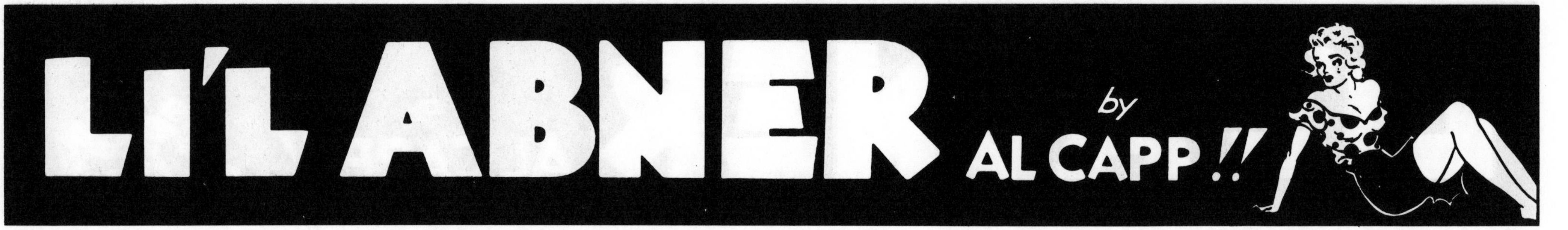
LI'L ABNER
by
AL CAPP!!

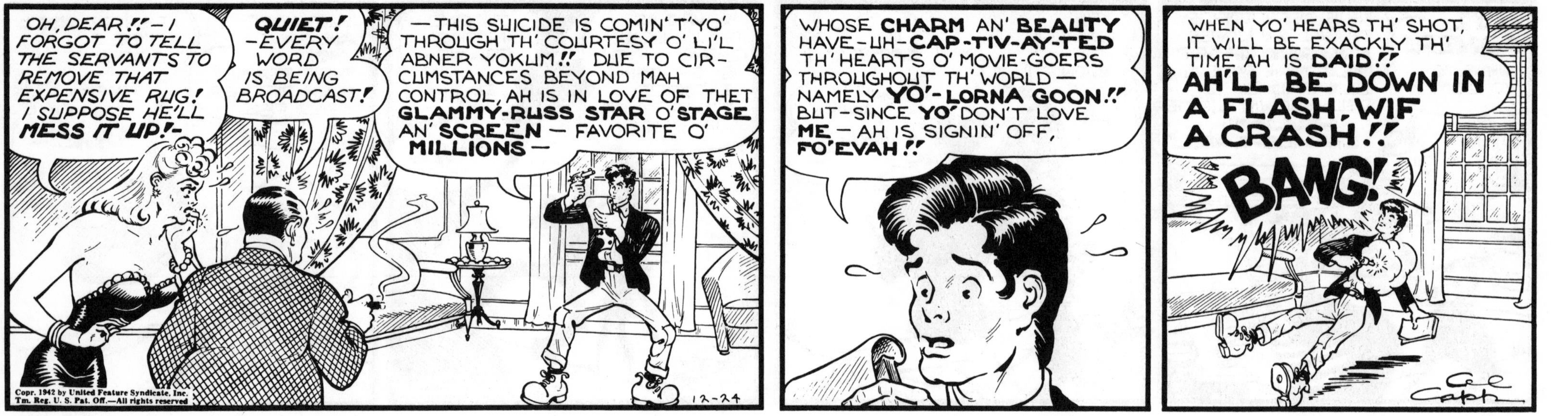
OH, DEAR!!–I FORGOT TO TELL THE SERVANTS TO REMOVE THAT EXPENSIVE RUG! I SUPPOSE HE'LL MESS IT UP!–
QUIET! –EVERY WORD IS BEING BROADCAST!
–THIS SUICIDE IS COMIN' T'YO' THROUGH TH' COURTESY O' LI'L ABNER YOKUM!! DUE TO CIR-CUMSTANCES BEYOND MAH CONTROL, AH IS IN LOVE OF THET GLAMMY-RUSS STAR O' STAGE AN' SCREEN – FAVORITE O' MILLIONS –
Copr. 1942 by United Feature Syndicate, Inc. Tm. Reg. U. S. Pat. Off.—All rights reserved
12-24
WHOSE CHARM AN' BEAUTY HAVE–UH–CAP-TIV-AY-TED TH' HEARTS O' MOVIE-GOERS THROUGHOUT TH' WORLD – NAMELY YO'–LORNA GOON!! BUT–SINCE YO' DON'T LOVE ME – AH IS SIGNIN' OFF, FO'EVAH!!
WHEN YO' HEARS TH' SHOT, IT WILL BE EXACKLY TH' TIME AH IS DAID!! AH'LL BE DOWN IN A FLASH, WIF A CRASH!!
BANG!
Al Capp

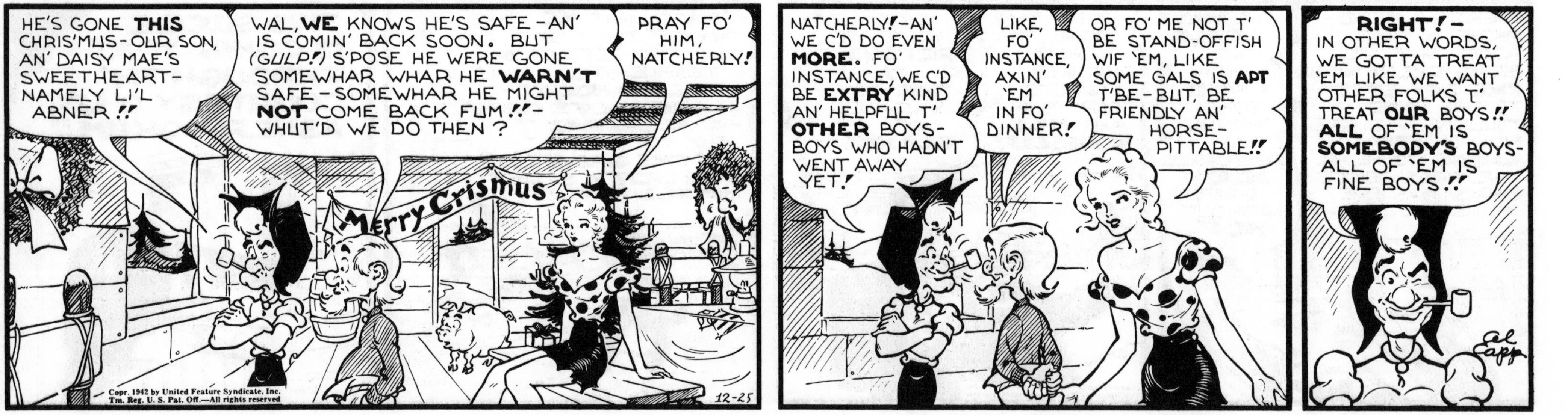
HE'S GONE THIS CHRIS'MUS–OUR SON, AN' DAISY MAE'S SWEETHEART– NAMELY LI'L ABNER!!
WAL, WE KNOWS HE'S SAFE–AN' IS COMIN' BACK SOON. BUT (GULP!) S'POSE HE WERE GONE SOMEWHAR WHAR HE WARN'T SAFE–SOMEWHAR HE MIGHT NOT COME BACK FUM!!– WHUT'D WE DO THEN?
PRAY FO' HIM, NATCHERLY!
Merry Crismus
Copr. 1942 by United Feature Syndicate, Inc. Tm. Reg. U. S. Pat. Off.—All rights reserved
12-25
NATCHERLY!–AN' WE C'D DO EVEN MORE. FO' INSTANCE, WE C'D BE EXTRY KIND AN' HELPFUL T' OTHER BOYS– BOYS WHO HADN'T WENT AWAY YET!
LIKE, FO' INSTANCE, AXIN' 'EM IN FO' DINNER!
OR FO' ME NOT T' BE STAND-OFFISH WIF 'EM, LIKE SOME GALS IS APT T'BE–BUT, BE FRIENDLY AN' HORSE-PITTABLE!!
RIGHT!– IN OTHER WORDS, WE GOTTA TREAT 'EM LIKE WE WANT OTHER FOLKS T' TREAT OUR BOYS!! ALL OF 'EM IS SOMEBODY'S BOYS– ALL OF 'EM IS FINE BOYS!!
Al Capp

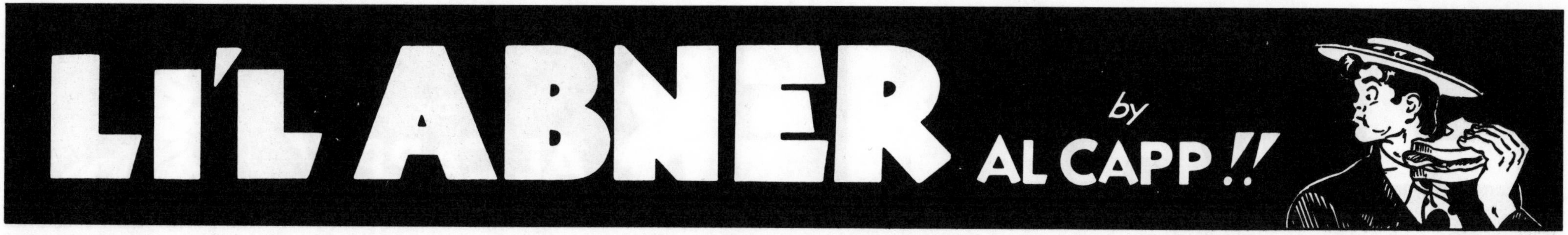
LI'L ABNER
by
AL CAPP!!

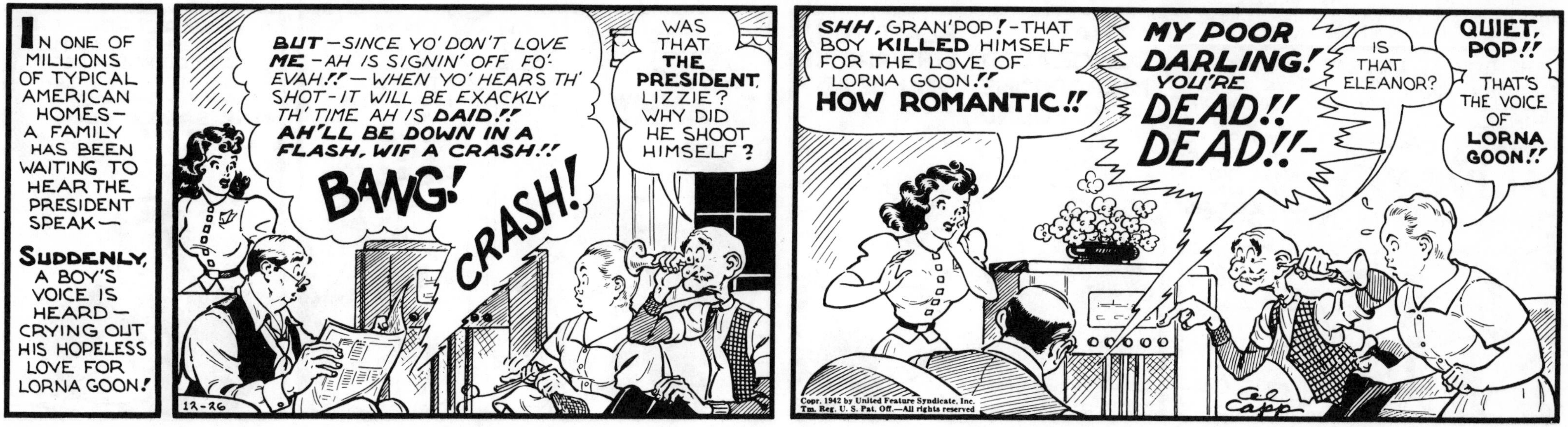
IN ONE OF MILLIONS OF TYPICAL AMERICAN HOMES— A FAMILY HAS BEEN WAITING TO HEAR THE PRESIDENT SPEAK—
SUDDENLY, A BOY'S VOICE IS HEARD— CRYING OUT HIS HOPELESS LOVE FOR LORNA GOON!
BUT—SINCE YO' DON'T LOVE ME—AH IS SIGNIN' OFF FO'EVAH!!—WHEN YO' HEARS TH' SHOT-IT WILL BE EXACKLY TH' TIME AH IS DAID!! AH'LL BE DOWN IN A FLASH, WIF A CRASH!!
BANG!
CRASH!
WAS THAT THE PRESIDENT, LIZZIE? WHY DID HE SHOOT HIMSELF?
12-26
SHH, GRAN'POP!-THAT BOY KILLED HIMSELF FOR THE LOVE OF LORNA GOON!! HOW ROMANTIC!!
MY POOR DARLING! YOU'RE DEAD!! DEAD!!-
IS THAT ELEANOR?
QUIET, POP!! THAT'S THE VOICE OF LORNA GOON!!
Copr. 1942 by United Feature Syndicate, Inc. Tm. Reg. U. S. Pat. Off.—All rights reserved
Al Capp

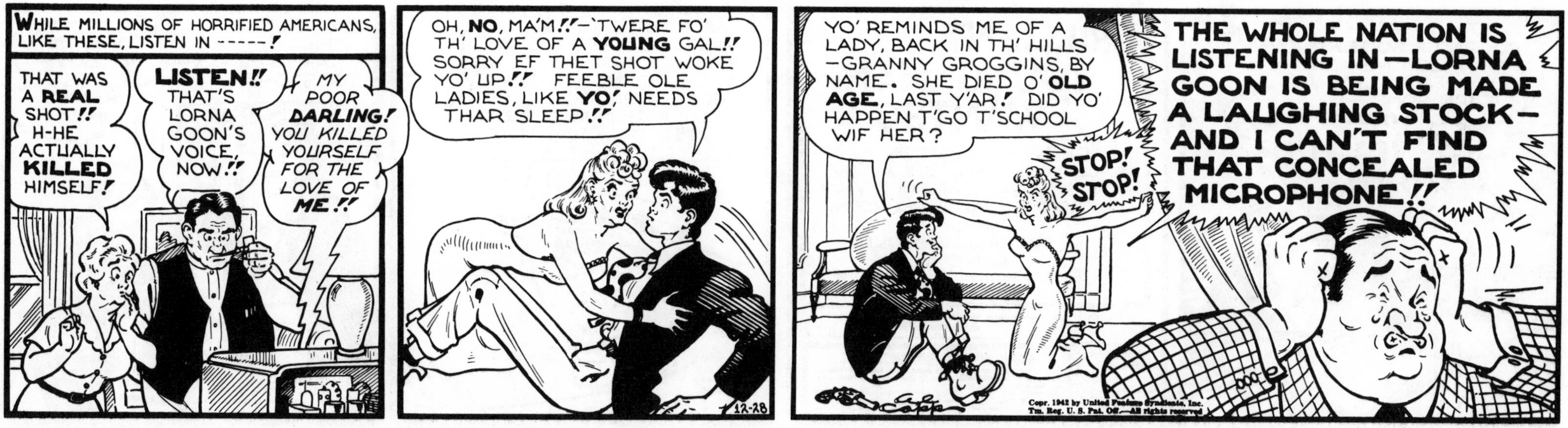
WHILE MILLIONS OF HORRIFIED AMERICANS, LIKE THESE, LISTEN IN -----!
THAT WAS A REAL SHOT!! H-HE ACTUALLY KILLED HIMSELF!
LISTEN!! THAT'S LORNA GOON'S VOICE, NOW!!
MY POOR DARLING! YOU KILLED YOURSELF FOR THE LOVE OF ME!!
OH, NO, MA'M!!-'TWERE FO' TH' LOVE OF A YOUNG GAL!! SORRY EF THET SHOT WOKE YO' UP!! FEEBLE OLE LADIES, LIKE YO', NEEDS THAR SLEEP!!
12-28
YO' REMINDS ME OF A LADY, BACK IN TH' HILLS —GRANNY GROGGINS, BY NAME. SHE DIED O' OLD AGE, LAST Y'AR! DID YO' HAPPEN T'GO T'SCHOOL WIF HER?
STOP! STOP!
THE WHOLE NATION IS LISTENING IN—LORNA GOON IS BEING MADE A LAUGHING STOCK— AND I CAN'T FIND THAT CONCEALED MICROPHONE!!
Al Capp
Copr. 1942 by United Feature Syndicate, Inc. Tm. Reg. U. S. Pat. Off.—All rights reserved

LI'L ABNER by AL CAPP!!

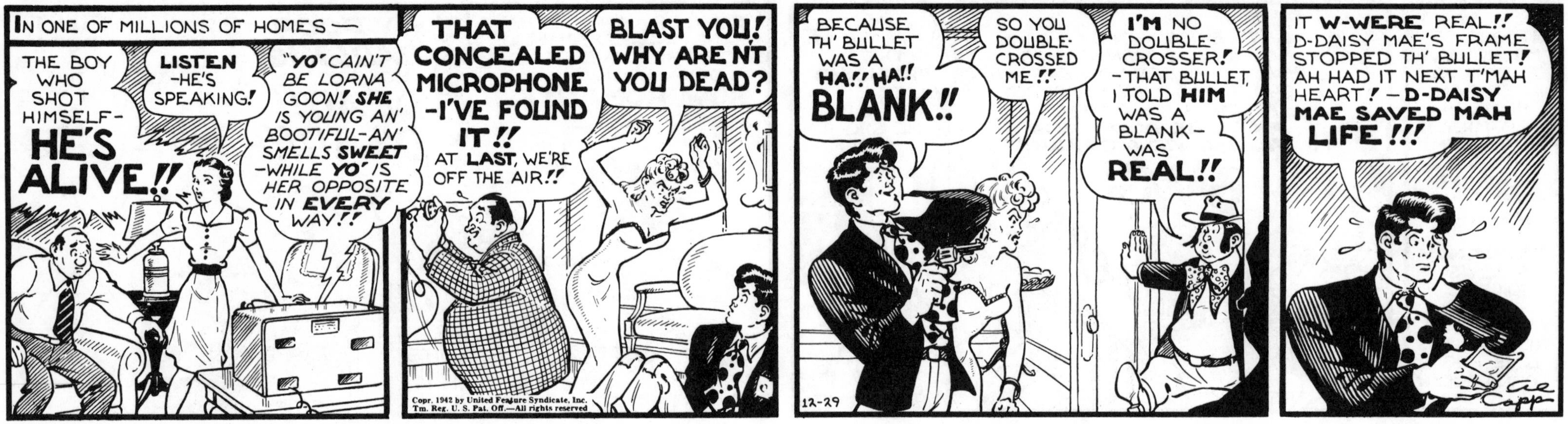

IN ONE OF MILLIONS OF HOMES —
THE BOY WHO SHOT HIMSELF- **HE'S ALIVE!!**
LISTEN -HE'S SPEAKING!
"**YO'** CAIN'T BE LORNA GOON! **SHE** IS YOUNG AN' BOOTIFUL-AN' SMELLS **SWEET** -WHILE **YO'** IS HER OPPOSITE IN **EVERY** WAY!!"
THAT CONCEALED MICROPHONE -I'VE FOUND IT!! AT **LAST**, WE'RE OFF THE AIR!!
BLAST YOU! WHY ARE N'T YOU DEAD?
Copr. 1942 by United Feature Syndicate, Inc. Tm. Reg. U. S. Pat. Off.—All rights reserved
BECAUSE TH' BULLET WAS A **HA!! HA!! BLANK!!**
SO YOU DOUBLE-CROSSED ME!!
I'M NO DOUBLE-CROSSER! -THAT BULLET, I TOLD **HIM** WAS A BLANK- WAS **REAL!!**
12-29
IT **W-WERE** REAL!! D-DAISY MAE'S FRAME STOPPED TH' BULLET! AH HAD IT NEXT T'MAH HEART! - **D-DAISY MAE SAVED MAH LIFE!!!**
Al Capp

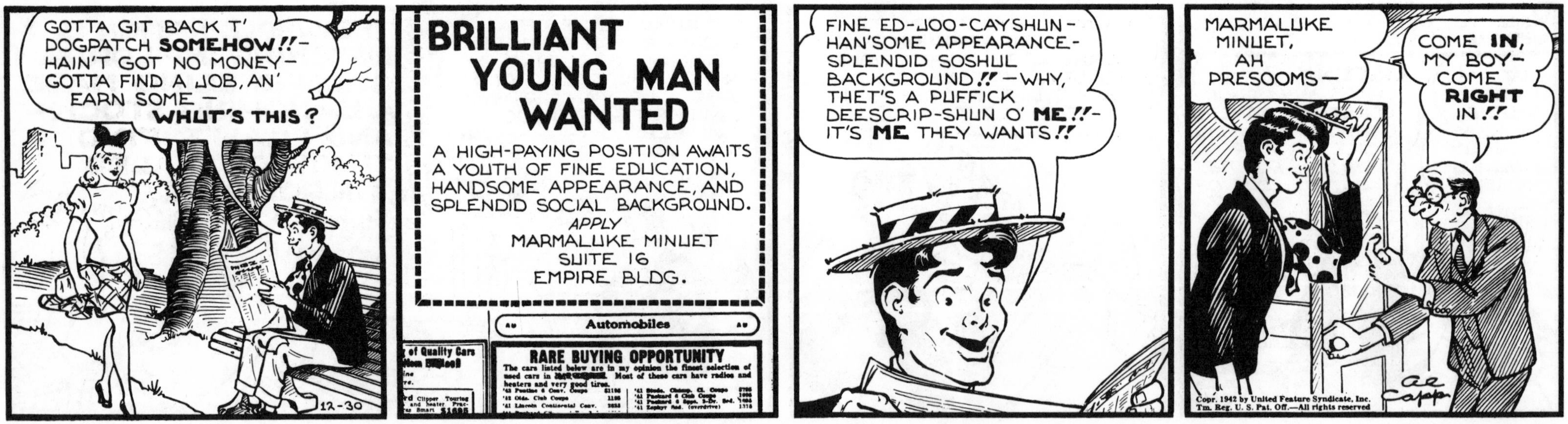

GOTTA GIT BACK T' DOGPATCH **SOMEHOW!!**- HAIN'T GOT NO MONEY- GOTTA FIND A JOB, AN' EARN SOME- **WHUT'S THIS?**
12-30
BRILLIANT YOUNG MAN WANTED
A HIGH-PAYING POSITION AWAITS A YOUTH OF FINE EDUCATION, HANDSOME APPEARANCE, AND SPLENDID SOCIAL BACKGROUND.
APPLY MARMALUKE MINUET SUITE 16 EMPIRE BLDG.
Automobiles
RARE BUYING OPPORTUNITY
FINE ED-JOO-CAYSHUN- HAN'SOME APPEARANCE- SPLENDID SOSHUL BACKGROUND!! -WHY, THET'S A PUFFICK DEESCRIP-SHUN O' **ME!!**- IT'S **ME** THEY WANTS!!
MARMALUKE MINUET, AH PRESOOMS—
COME **IN**, MY BOY- COME **RIGHT** IN!!
Copr. 1942 by United Feature Syndicate, Inc. Tm. Reg. U. S. Pat. Off.—All rights reserved
Al Capp

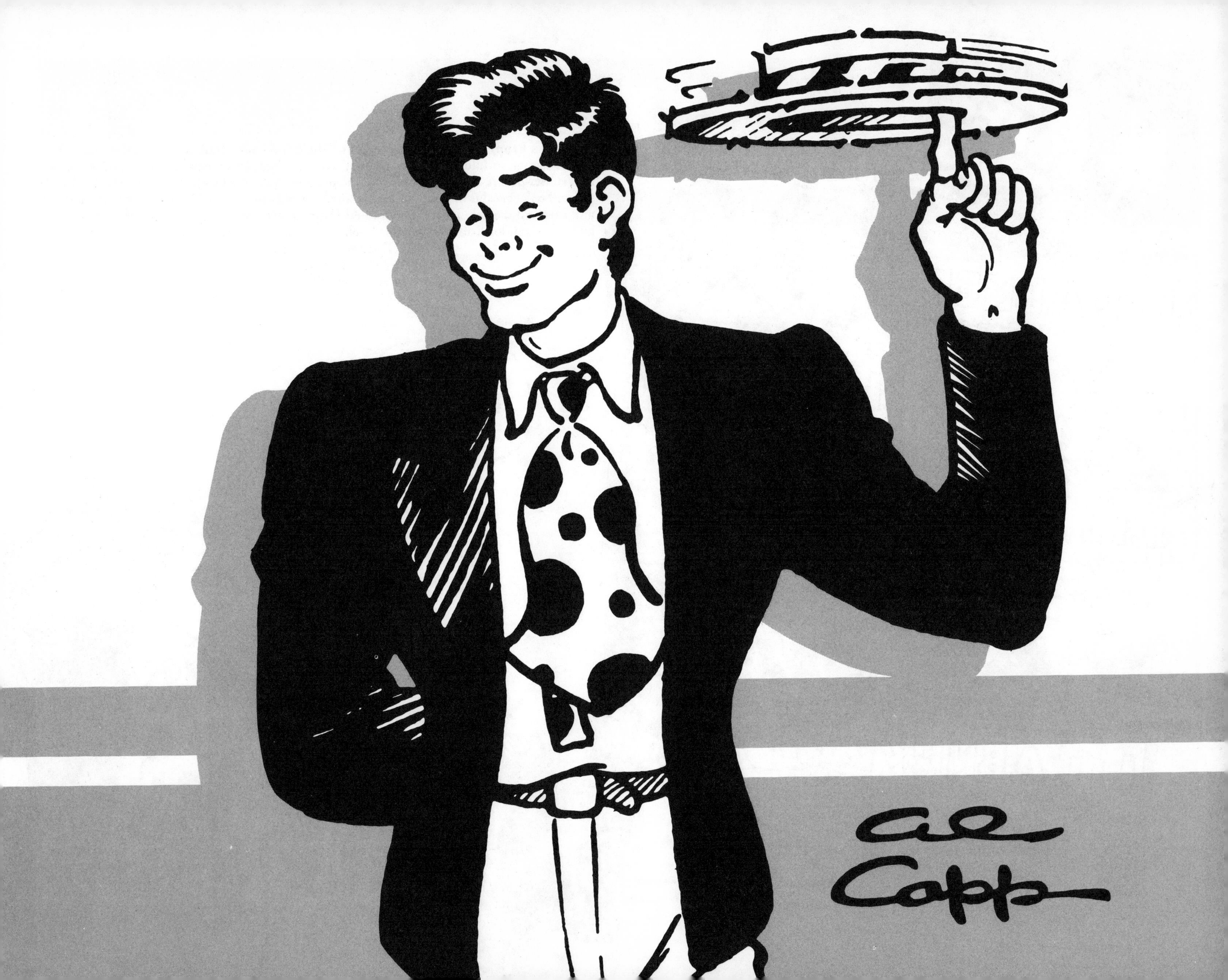
Al Capp

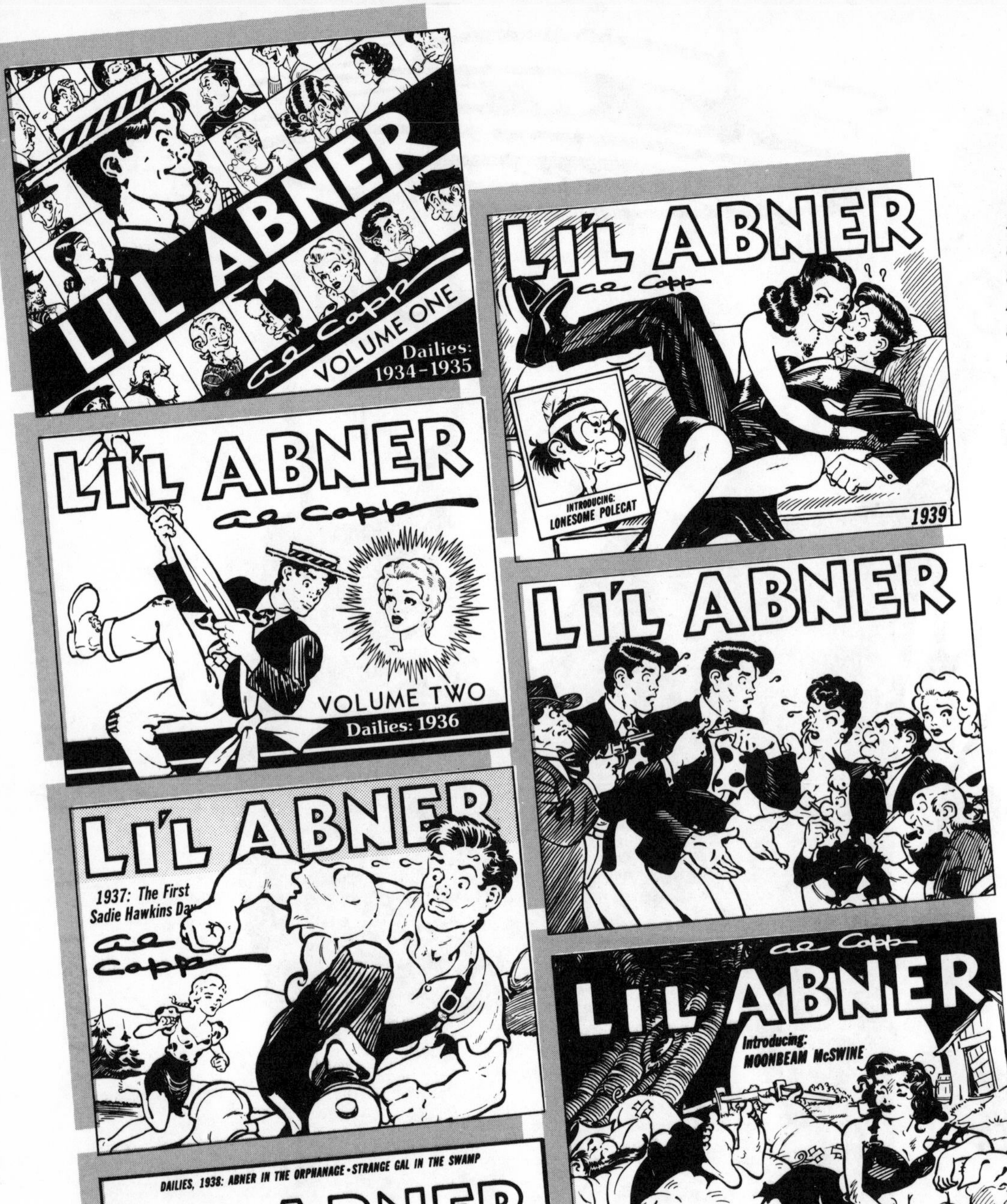
LI'L ABNER
VOLUME ONE
Dailies: 1934-1935
LI'L ABNER
VOLUME TWO
Dailies: 1936
LI'L ABNER
1937: The First Sadie Hawkins Day
DAILIES, 1938: ABNER IN THE ORPHANAGE • STRANGE GAL IN THE SWAMP
LI'L ABNER
LI'L ABNER
INTRODUCING: LONESOME POLECAT
1939
LI'L ABNER
LI'L ABNER
Introducing: MOONBEAM McSWINE
DAILIES: 1941

And it *is* a happy day when you can get *all* the *Li'l Abner* volumes published so far—and subscribe to future volumes to boot! Kitchen Sink Press has both back volumes and subscriptions available of the *complete* reprinting of Al Capp's *Li'l Abner*. Each *Abner* book contains at least one year's worth of daily strips. You'll get complete stories and meet all the fabulous characters Al Capp created. For subscription information and a free catalog listing all our fine books, magazines and comic books, drop a card to:

Kitchen Sink Press
No. 2 Swamp Rd.
Princeton WI 54968

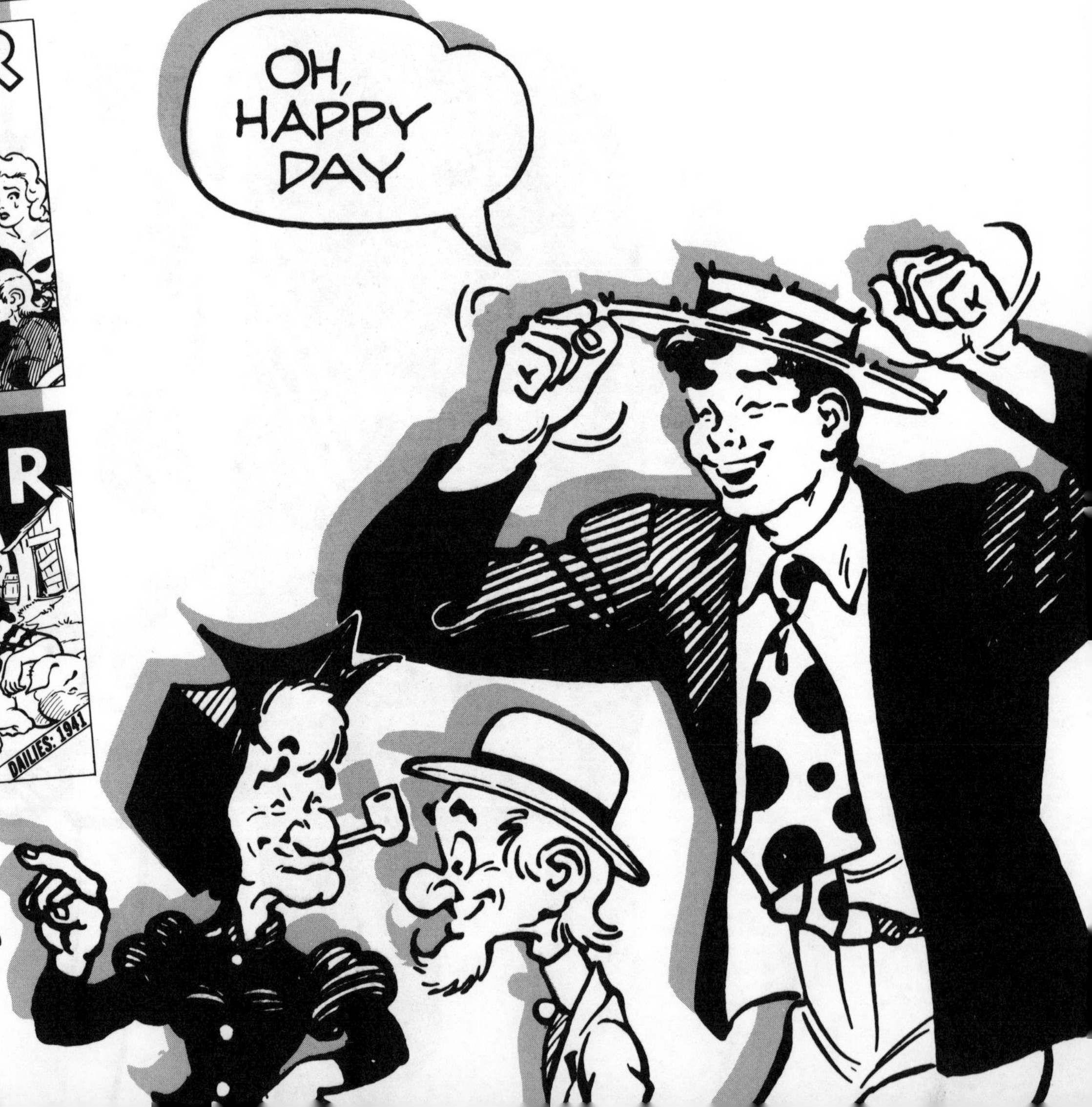
OH, HAPPY DAY